# SOVIET ECONOMY 1940 - 1965

VLADIMIR KATKOFF, Ph.D.

CHAIRMAN, DEPARTMENT OF ECONOMICS

UNIVERSITY OF BALTIMORE

GREENWOOD PRESS, PUBLISHERS
WESTPORT, CONNECTICUT

Library of Congress Cataloging in Publication Data

Katkoff, Vladimir.
    Soviet economy, 1940-1965

    Reprint of the ed. published by Dangary Pub. Co.,
Baltimore.
    Includes bibliographies.
    1.  Russia--Economic conditions--1945-1955.
2.  Russia--Economic policy--1959-1965.  I.  Title.
[HC336.K32  1973]        330.9'47'084        73-11750
ISBN 0-8371-7085-0

Originally published in 1961 by Dangary Publishing Co.,
Baltimore

Reprinted with the permission of Vladimir Katkoff.

Reprinted in 1973 by Greenwood Press,
A division of Congressional Information Service, Inc.
88 Post Road West, Westport, Connecticut 06881

Library of Congress catalog card number 73-11750
ISBN 0-8371-7085-0

Printed in the United States of America

10 9 8 7 6 5 4 3 2

# Preface

~~~~~~~~~

T HERE HAS been a long tradition of conviction that the economic
system of the Soviet Union is very inefficient and bureaucratic. It
has been fashionable to discredit Soviet announcements of their economic
achievements. We were skeptical of the plowing up of virgin lands in the
eastern parts of the USSR and were fond of comparing the purchasing
power of daily wages of American and Soviet workers, disregarding the
existing taxation and social systems in both countries. We did not believe
the scientific accomplishments claimed by the USSR. It was reported that
Harry S. Truman, during one of his early morning walks in New York,
said to accompanying reporters: "I don't believe it," when he was asked
to comment on the first sputnik launched by the Soviets a day earlier. In
any discussion of Soviet economics it is easy to slide, quite unwittingly,
into mere controversies and away from economic analysis. It is precisely
for this reason that I use economic analysis rather than the so-called
criticism which is loosely used in convincing the public that recent Soviet
economic growth simply "ain't so."

Today we no longer ridicule Soviet science, which has shown evidence
that it can perform striking feats of achievement; we have become quite
serious about the Russian challenge to our supremacy in underdeveloped
areas. But as some of our old preconceptions are disappearing, many of
us remain skeptical of Soviet economic progress. This is inconsistent. We
accept Soviet scientific claims because our own capability can out-match
Soviet achievements without basic adjustments in our existing institutions.
But we are reluctant to accept reports of Soviet industrial gains because they
suggest that the classical concepts of capitalism are being challenged and
we do not have new theoretical tools with which to meet competition from
the Soviets.

I use the official Soviet statistics not because of belief in their credibility
but as an experienced ring-fighter who gives more credit to his opponent's

i

ability in order to be better prepared for the contest. In any case, it would be dangerous to treat Soviet statistics as if they were metaphysical speculations in which anyone could adopt the method most advantageous to his own evaluation. In other words, evidence seems to be accumulating that the giant is awakening and flexing his muscles; the prospect for reevaluation of our attitude toward the USSR appears to be reasonably certain.

I am conscious of the guessing game in the magnitude and reliability of Soviet economic growth rates. But it is much easier to analyze the Soviet statistics than a host of independent sources, each different qualitatively and quantitatively. Thus, the credibility of Soviet statistics must be intelligently faced, and I believe it is just a question of time before the official Soviet statistics are accepted by all Western students as our military and scientific students have accepted them. On the basis of my own experience in research for the government I believe that Soviet statistics are basically unpadded and have more validity than some of the methods and assumptions which are used in the independent estimates.

There are many books dealing with the Soviet Union; most of them are specialized, limited to a discussion of specific economic sectors. A number of them are products of either attraction to or detestation of the Soviet Union. There is no single volume that covers all major component factors and all the changes that have taken place since Stalin's death, particularly since the reorganization of industrial management in 1958. This book attempts a synthesis of current material which until today had to be sought, without economic analysis by Western standards, in the Soviet press.

This volume has several major purposes. First, it describes the organizational and operational patterns of the Soviet economy prior to and since Stalin's death. This background is indispensible for comprehension of the development of the Russian economy since 1917. Second, it examines the Soviets' capability to produce industrial goods and foodstuffs. Third, it evaluates the socio-economic adjustments which have taken place under Khrushchev. Fourth, it probes the recent Soviet infiltration into underdeveloped areas. Fifth, it appraises the Soviet economic potential under the current Seven-Year Plan and the projection of the targets to 1970.

Material and topics have been selected with the purpose of producing a book which could be used as a general textbook for courses in Soviet Economics, as a reference source, and for supplementary reading assignments in political science, history, and geography. Since the purpose of this volume is manifold each chapter has been written with the objective of providing a comprehensive account of the subject matter under the title. However, I am aware that in a volume like this one it would not be humanly possible to avoid repetition in evaluation.

The idea for this volume stemmed primarily from the absence of a textbook for my courses in Soviet Economy. The research for it took a number of years and the manuscript was revised twice to include the 1956, 1958, and 1965 statistics which became available with publications of the Soviet Statistical Handbooks and the 1959-1965 Plan.

During the research and writing of this project many kind people have taken the trouble to advise me. For this I am deeply grateful. I am particularly indebted to M. Gardner Clark of Cornell, Holland Hunter of Haverford, Tobia Bressler of the Bureau of the Census, John P. Hall, of the University of Kentucky and Bryce W. Shoemaker of the University of Baltimore. My thanks must also be tendered to my students at the American University in Washington, D. C. who were the first exposed to this book and served as its critics. Many of them were highly trained specialists in Soviet affairs with the government, and their criticism was scholarly and profound.

VLADIMIR KATKOFF

Baltimore, Maryland

# Table of Contents

~~~~~~~~~~~~~~~~~~~~~

# CHAPTER 1

# Geography

~~~~~~~~~~~~~~~~

## INTRODUCTION

Economic geography is a dynamic and very real subject. It is made up of many physical and human elements which constitute the economic fiber of a country.

The Soviet Union, larger than the United States and possessing huge natural resources, is a comparatively poor country because of the dispersion and inaccessibility of many resources. Nevertheless, the vast Soviet territory, with its wide variety of climates and resources, can be considered economically self-sufficient in most of the minerals currently needed by industry. The largest part of the Soviet Union is located in the north where severe climate, poor soils, and mountainous terrain are preventive elements in the expansion of population and hence in industrial development. But as the technical knowledge of the Russian people expands, they remove many barriers imposed by their physical setting. This is a difficult task, for it requires not only the will of the people to conquer nature but also the skill and the means with which goals can be achieved.

In Tsarist Russia over 80 per cent of the total population was engaged in agriculture, mainly in the southern part of the country. The northern and eastern parts of the country were underpopulated and their rich mineral resources remained unexploited. Since 1914, however, there were many marked changes with accelerated industrialization leading the economic life of the country; many resources were discovered and extracted, and many are still to be developed.

As industrialization expanded, greater emphasis was laid on the opening of northern and eastern regions, previously considered useless. Consequently, with industrial growth, better land utilization in agriculture was introduced and new mineral and energy resources were developed. With ever-increasing industrial expansion, there are trends not only to adjust the geographic pattern, but also to influence the economic and political life of the country.

1

Since the early days of Russian history, agriculture has been a predominate factor, dependent upon the availability of cultivated land. Controlling forces in agricultural expansion were, and still are, climate and topography of the USSR. At present, the Soviets have reached the point of optimum expansion in agricultural land. Now the drive is to uncover the hidden mineral wealth without which industrialization cannot be diffuse. But it is the scarcity of agricultural land, peculiar to Soviet geography, which makes the huge territory of the USSR so unique.

## LAND

The Union of Soviet Socialist Republics occupies an area of over 8.6 million square miles, approximately 2.8 times the territory of the continental United States. It covers about one-seventh of the earth's inhabited land area. Its borders extend from the Baltic Sea 7,000 miles to the Bering Straits near Alaska—nearly half-way around the world—and from the Arctic Ocean at Cape Chelyuskin to the settlement of Kushka on the Afghanistan frontier, a distance of about 3,000 miles.

### Distribution of Land by Republic

The USSR consists of 15 Soviet Socialist Republics. The largest of the constituent republics is the Russian Soviet Federated Socialist Republic (RSFSR) which takes about 79 per cent of the total territory of the Soviet Union. This republic extends about 5,000 miles from the Gulf of Finland to the Pacific Ocean and south from the Arctic Ocean for a distance up to 2,500 miles. The next largest republic is Kazakh SSR, occupying about 12 per cent of the total territory of the Soviet Union. This republic is slightly smaller than Argentina. The other 13 constituent republics share approximately nine per cent of the total territory of the Soviet Union.

Since the end of World War II, the Soviet Union has increased its territory mainly by occupying the areas of Kaliningrad in East Prussia, Southern Sakhalin Island, the Kurile Islands and some other minor adjustments. During the 1947-51 period the Soviets surveyed their territory, which resulted in inclusion of ice-covered land areas of several Arctic gulfs and bays and land from the receding water level of the Caspian Sea. The White Sea, which covers about 35,000 square miles and the Sea of Azov (some 15,000 square miles) are not included in territories of any constituent republic, although they are part of the Soviet Union territorial possessions.

In land area, the territory of the USSR in 1959 was about the same as it was in 1913 and only slightly larger than it was at the beginning of World

War II. Over 60 per cent of the total territory in 1959, as in 1913, was located in the North and Siberia, and is not as sparsely populated as it was in the earlier period. But the arable land is situated in the southern part

TABLE 1—*Territory, Percentage of Arable Land and Density of Population of Region in 1959*[1]

| Republic and Region | Territory (in thousands of square miles) | Per cent of arable land | Average density per square mile |
|---|---|---|---|
| USSR | 8,649 | 100.0 | 24.2 |
| RSFSR: | 6,593 | 60.3 | 17.8 |
| North | 444 | 0.6 | 7.6 |
| Northwest | 204 | 1.2 | 34.7 |
| Central | 371 | 17.3 | 116.4 |
| Volga River Valley | 190 | 9.8 | 58.5 |
| Northern Caucasus | 137 | 7.2 | 84.0 |
| Urals | 291 | 9.0 | 56.8 |
| Western Siberia | 964 | 10.6 | 12.7 |
| Eastern Siberia | 2,790 | 3.4 | 2.5 |
| Far East | 1,202 | 1.1 | 3.6 |
| Kazakh | 1,065 | 14.0 | 8.7 |
| Ukraine | 232 | 15.7 | 180.6 |
| Turkmen | 188 | 0.2 | 8.1 |
| Uzbek | 158 | 1.4 | 51.3 |
| White Russia | 80 | 2.7 | 100.7 |
| Kirghiz | 76 | 0.6 | 27.0 |
| Tadzhik | 55 | 0.4 | 34.2 |
| Azerbaydzhan | 34 | 0.7 | 108.8 |
| Georgia | 27 | 0.5 | 150.0 |
| Lithuania | 25 | 1.2 | 108.5 |
| Latvia | 25 | 0.7 | 83.7 |
| Estonia | 17 | 0.4 | 70.4 |
| Moldavia | 13 | 0.9 | 221.5 |
| Armenia | 12 | 0.3 | 147.3 |

of the country with 60 per cent of it in the Central Industrial Region of the European USSR, the Ukraine, Kazakh SSR, and Western Siberia. These areas are the largest producers of Soviet agricultural commodities.

## Agricultural Pattern

Shortly before World War II Soviet agriculture was placed on a basis of self-sufficiency, requiring each region to be independent in any major farm imports that could be produced locally. Under this policy the principle of comparative advantage was ignored and low-yielding crops were grown in regions for which they were poorly adapted, replacing more profitable crops. It was contended by the Soviets that transportation facilities for shipping bulky agricultural commodities were scarce and that these facilities were needed for industrial and military purposes. By making every region self-sufficient, the central government washed its hands of any regional complaints of potential shortages. This policy existed until 1955. But in 1956, the principles of regional comparative advantage was adopted and the low-yielding crops were replaced with high yielding crops, a policy which exists today.

The new policy is based on "rational" rather than "optimum" utilization of all agricultural resources and is aimed at a full satisfaction of all local demands, state stockpiling requirements, and the need for foreign trade. Although the principle of comparative advantage has become an important issue, complete freedom in effecting it is limited by the State's interpretations, and large-scale regional import-export activities are not allowed. Nevertheless, a partial specialization and inter-regional import-export on farm commodities is possible in different volumes for different commodities. For example, inter-regional trading of only 18 per cent of grain output is permitted; 20 per cent of the wheat may be traded, and 17 per cent of the butter produced is subject to import-export. These percentages were recorded for 1952 and are still considered an accurate yardstick.[2] In general, the type of agricultural specialization now found in the USSR is a kind of diversified competitive advantage which can be attained regionally, but not on a nationwide scale.

## Soils

To assist in regional agricultural planning, the USSR Academy of Sciences has established 20 soil zones suitable for 18 agricultural zones producing a variety of crops. If the USSR is divided by latitude, a broad soil classification and type of agricultural crops may be described in general terms.

All soil between 75°and 55° north latitude is composed of polar desert and arctic tundra on the north and podzol soils to the south. Polar desert and arctic tundra are not adapted for field crops. The podzol soils occupy the bulk of Soviet territory. They cover the Baltic republics, White Russia and stretch from the Finnish border to the Urals and on to Western and Eastern Siberia. The Far East consists mainly of mountain forest soils as do parts of the Caucasus and other highly elevated regions.

Between 55° and 50° north latitude is located the irregular belt, called the forest-steppe or brown soil. It extends from the western frontier of the USSR to the Urals. Just below this belt is the famous "chernozem" belt or black soil which is abundant in humus and has moisture preservation characteristics. The belt starts in the Western Ukraine and stretches eastward to Siberia, a distance of about 3,000 miles. It is on the chernozem and the forest-steppe types of soils that about 70 per cent of the Soviet plowed land is located.

Below the chernozem belt is the chestnut soil belt which starts at the middle of the Don River and pushes to Western Siberia where it merges with mountain forest soils and podzols. Most of this belt is located in the Kazakh SSR. To the south of the chestnut belt lies the desert and loose sand belt which covers all of the Turkmen SSR, Uzbek SSR and lower Kazakh SSR. The Kirghiz and Tadzhik SSR's are located in the mountain meadow and steppe soils. Desert, mountain meadow, and steppe soils are also found in the Caucasus.

In general the podzol soils, predominant in the Soviet Union, are located mainly above the 55th parallel. In the European USSR, podzol soils occupy more than half of the territory. Podzol covers most of Western Siberia and the central part of Eastern Siberia. Next in magnitude are the mountain forest soils located in Eastern Siberia and the Far East. Mountain-meadow and mountain-steppe types of soil are in southeastern parts of Central Asia and the Caucasus. Chestnut soils cover the northern half of the Kazakh SSR, and part of the northern Caucasus. The most fertile chernozem soils extend from the Moldavian SSR to the Ob River and are below 55° north latitude. A few pockets of chernozem soil are found in the southern parts of Eastern Siberia. Brown soils also stretch from White Russia to the Ob River, with a few locations in Eastern Siberia. The desert and semi-desert lands are concentrated in Central Asia with the greatest share of them below the 46° north and between 54° and 70° east.

## Agricultural Belts

Regional agricultural patterns depend upon climatic conditions, soil types, and the topography of the given region. In Western Siberia, winter lasts 180 to 190 days; in the Northern Caucasus, only 20 to 70 days. The large area of chernozem, with its mild continental climate, has different types of agriculture than the semi-desert areas of the Kazakh SSR or the rough topography of the Caucasus. Again, economic considerations show that wheat production costs in the steppes and forest steppes of the Ukraine, Northern Caucasus and Northern Kazakhstan are lower than in any other parts of the Soviet Union. The cost of production of spring grains in White Russia and the Baltic States is higher than in Northern Kazakhstan and Western Siberia. On the other hand, the cost of production of potatoes in White Russia, the Baltic States and southwestern parts of the RSFSR is much below that of the Ukraine or the Northern Caucasus. For these reasons, the Soviet Union has regional concentration of production of certain agricultural commodities.

All regions above 60° latitude are devoted to agriculture in only a limited way—to reindeer breeding and small-scale production of fast-growing crops for their urban centers. However, rye, oats, and flax are grown in the European parts at that latitude.

Between 50° and 60° latitude a more intensified type of agriculture is possible. European parts of this zone are the major producers of rye, potatoes, flax, sugar beets, milk, and meat. The eastern parts of the USSR lying in this belt produces rye in the north and wheat, sunflowers, flax and livestock products in the south.

Although grain crops are grown throughout large areas of the Soviet Union, the greatest production of winter wheat is in the Ukraine followed by White Russia and the Baltic States. Production of spring wheat, on the other hand, is concentrated in the Urals and Western Siberia. The coarse grains such as corn, millet, oats, and barley are grown throughout the European USSR, with production concentrated between the Dnieper and Volga rivers, the Northern Caucasus, Northern Kazakhstan, and Western Siberia.

Sugar beet production is concentrated in the Ukraine and to lesser degree in the Central Industrial Region, Western Siberia, Central Asia, and the Northern Caucasus.

Potatoes are a northern crop, and production extends from the Baltic States to the Urals and from Leningrad to northern parts of the Ukraine. In other words, potatoes are produced in regions of greatest urban concentration. However, there are isolated small centers of potato production in the Caucasus, Central Asia, and in urbanized Siberia.

The sunflower belt stretches from Odessa through all the Ukraine and then forks out into the Northen Caucasus and the Urals. This belt crosses the Volga River between Stalingrad and Kuybyshev, bypasses the Urals and moves on to Omsk and almost reaches the Ob River. This is the longest crop belt in the Soviet Union.

Flax (grown for fiber) is a northern crop. Over 60 per cent of its acreage is located in the RSFSR, of which over 70 per cent is in the Central

Industrial Region. Second in importance are White Russia and the Baltic States. The cotton belt lies in Central Asia, especially in the Fergana Valley of the Uzbek SSR, Northern Caucasus and the southern Ukraine.

Vegetable crops are directly related to the density of population and for this reason their production is closely associated with urbanization. The greatest production of vegetables is in the European parts of the USSR. The RSFSR, with its population of over 56 per cent of the Soviet total, produces over half of all vegetables in the nation. About 40 per cent of the RSFSR's vegetable crop is produced in the densely populated and urbanized Central Industrial Region. Next in importance are the industrialized Northern Caucasus, Urals, and the Volga River Valley. The Ukrainian SSR, with 20 per cent of the total Soviet population, produces about 30 per cent of the Soviet vegetable crop, thus becoming an exporting region. Over 80 per cent of the Soviet vegetable crops are producd by two republics—the RSFSR and the Ukraine. The Central Asia and Transcaucasus, being poorly adapted to vegetable crops, are deficit regions and import vegetables from surplus areas.

Like vegetable crops, the livestock industry tends to follow concentrations of population. Since the Central Industrial Region is densely populated, its demand for milk, meat and eggs is the greatest, followed by the Northern Caucasus and the Urals. The centers of milk production for the European parts of the USSR are the Baltic States, White Russia, and the Central Industrial Region. The secondary center of milk production extends from the eastern boundary of the Urals, passing between Tobolsk and Omsk and then reaching Krasnoyarsk. Western Siberia, especially the Novosibirsk Oblast, is the major producer of milk and butter in Siberia. These are the two specialized milk producing belts while the rest of the USSR, excluding Central Asia and the Transcaucasus, has mixed production of milk and meat. Central Asia, Transcaucasus, and parts of southern Siberia produce considerable amounts of veal, wool, and karakul skins, in addition to dairy products.

The greatest concentration of hogs is in the European parts of the USSR especially in the Ukraine and Northern Caucasus. Sheep are the main animals in the Northern Caucasus, Transcaucasus, Urals, and Eastern Siberia.

## Usage of Land

Land utilization in the Soviet Union is quite different from that of the continental United States. Geographically, almost all the territory of the continental United States is located below the latitude of Kharkov, in the Ukraine, and more thar half of the United States is located south of Baku in the Soviet Union. It is this difference in the latitude and its effect on climate and topography that make land utilization in the Soviet Union less efficient than in the United States.

Table 2—*Land Utilization in the USSR*[3]
(*in millions of acres*)

|  | 1940 | | 1958 | |
|---|---|---|---|---|
|  | Area | Per cent | Area | Per cent |
| Total territory | 5,486 | | 5,535 | |
| Total sowed area: | 372 | 100.0 | 483 | 100.0 |
| Grain corps: | 273 | 73.5 | 309 | 64.0 |
| Wheat | 99 | 26.8 | 164 | 34.1 |
| Rye | 57 | 15.4 | 44 | 9.1 |
| Oats | 50 | 13.5 | 37 | 7.6 |
| Barley | 26 | 7.0 | 21 | 4.4 |
| Millet | 15 | 4.0 | 9 | 1.9 |
| Corn | 9 | 2.4 | 20 | 4.2 |
| Buckwheat | 5 | 1.4 | 4 | 0.9 |
| Industrial crops: | 29 | 7.9 | 30 | 6.3 |
| Sunflowers | 9 | 2.4 | 10 | 2.0 |
| Flax | 5 | 1.4 | 4 | 0.8 |
| Cotton | 5 | 1.4 | 5 | 1.1 |
| Sugar beets | 3 | 0.8 | 6 | 1.3 |
| Hemp | 1 | 0.4 | 1 | 0.2 |
| Truck garden crops: | 25 | 6.6 | 29 | 6.0 |
| Potatoes | 19 | 5.1 | 23 | 4.9 |
| Vegetables | 4 | 1.0 | 4 | 0.8 |
| Fodder crops: | 45 | 12.0 | 115 | 23.7 |
| Grasses | 41 | 10.8 | 92 | 18.9 |
| Silo crops | 4 | 1.2 | 23 | 4.8 |

The 1940-58 period was notable for the shift in land use. Grain crops in 1958 occupied 36 million more acres than in 1940. In 1958 the Soviets had larger wheat and corn acreage than in 1940 while other crops were reduced. Whereas the total acreage for industrial crops remained practically the same in both years, sugar beet area was doubled. The truck garden crops increased by 16 per cent, all potatoes. The greatest increase occurred in fodder crops—approximately 2.5 times larger in 1958 than in 1940. In their attempt to increase livestock, the Soviets more than doubled their grass acreage, and silo crops increased by almost sixfold.

## Topography

One of the outstanding features of Soviet topography is its great plains, described by Russian poets and novelists as "the dangerously lonely and endless bosom of Mother Russia," particularly desolate in winter. In broad geographic terms, over one-half of the Soviet Union consists of lowlands, which are divided by the Ural Mountains into the European and Siberian plains. The Western Siberia Lowland unites with the Central Siberian Plateau when the Yenisey River is crossed and then merges into the highlands of the Far East. These highlands and mountains extend along the country's southern frontiers from the Far East to the Caucasus and again appear in the western parts of the Ukraine.

## Lowlands

The immense lowland of the USSR extends from the Baltic Sea and Western Ukraine eastward to the Yenisey River and from the Arctic Ocean southward to the Caucasus and the Afghan border. This lowland is marked by several hilly regions. The most northwestern of the uplands is located in the Kola Peninsula at the border of Finland, stretching southward to the Ukraine between the Dnieper and Volga rivers, bypassing the Baltic states, Leningrad and Moscow. The Ukraine and Moldavia are generally lowlands with some elevted regions located in the western parts of the Ukraine.

The RSFSR is divided into several lowlands; the European plain stretches from Archangel and Moscow to the middle of the Volga River where it gradually merges with the moderately higher elevation of the Ural Mountains. The eastern slope of the Urals drops sharply to form another lowland which extends to the Yenisey River. This area is called the Western Siberian Lowland and is the largest of its kind in the world. The European Lowland has elevations of 1,000 feet in several areas while the highest elevation (270 feet) in the Western Siberian Lowland is in the Omsk area. The northern Caucasian lowland is located between the Don and Volga rivers north of the Caucasian Mountains. This lowland rises rapidly as it approaches the Caucasian Mountains. There are other pockets of lowlands found in the Lena River Valley, the Amur River Valley, and in several other places of Eastern Siberia and the Far East.

In the Central Asian lowlands, semi-deserts and deserts occupy the largest part of the territory. In the western part of the Kazakh SSR is located the Prikaspiysk Depression which is below sea level, encircles the northern Caspian Sea, and reaches the Caucasus. In the central part of the Kazakh SSR lies the Turansk Depression which slopes southward to the Sea of

Aral and extends to the Turkmen SSR. The sandy desert and semi-desert areas of Kyzyl-Kum cover southern Turkmen SSR, central Uzbek SSR and southern Kazakh SSR. The sands of the Kara-Kum desert cover most of the Turkmen SSR. Areas of lowest elevation in the Soviet Union, both in the Kazakh SSR, are the Karagye Depression, some 430 feet below sea level and the Batyr sink of 426 feet below sea level in the Mangyshlak Peninsula.

The Caucasian republics of Armenia, Azerbaydzhan and Georgia are located in elevated areas with 43 per cent of their combined territories situated in elevations of up to 1,970 feet above sea level and the remainder of the territory in elevations of about 2,000 feet. Only the Azerbaydzhan SSR has plains sloping from Tbilisi in Georgia to the shores of the Caspian Sea.

## Mountains

The vast lowland areas and areas of medium elevation in the Soviet Union are ringed along the western, southern and eastern borders by high ranges. In the southwest are the Carpathian Mountains, which slope down to the Ukrainian and Moldavian plains from Hungary and Rumania. These plains are interrupted by the Donets Ridge in the southeastern Ukraine. In the central Moldavian SSR is an elevation called the Kodry which reaches 1,310 feet.

The Crimean Mountains in the south represent a strip of elevated shore line two to six miles wide which extends from Sevastopol to Feodosiya. The highest peak is Roman-Kosh, some 4,920 feet above sea level.

The Caucasian Mountains are dense and high, covering 36 per cent of the area at elevations ranging from 1,970 feet to 5,100 feet, and about 21 per cent of this territory is situated in an area over 5,100 feet above sea level. The highest peak in Europe is Mount Elbrus, in the Caucasus, reaching 18,530 feet above sea level.

Across the Caspian Sea to the east lies the Kopet-Dagh ridge on the border of the Turkmen SSR and Iran, reaching 980 feet above sea level at points. To the east of the Turkmen SSR are the republics of Uzbek, Tadzhik, and Kirghiz. The Uzbek SSR lies mostly on moderate elevation which slopes down from the Pamir Mountain System in the southeastern part of the republic. Both the Tadzhik and Kirghiz republics are located in the Pamir and Tyan-Shan systems. In the Tadzhik republic are found the highest peaks in Central Asia. Stalin Peak reaches 24,590 feet and Lenin Peak is 23,370 feet high—both in the Zaalaysk Ridge. Unlike the Siberian mountains, these mountains are without timber. The Kirghiz SSR is also a mountainous area in the same Tyan-Shan and Pamir systems, reaching in height from 13,120 feet to 16,400 feet. The highest peak is Pobeda, some 24,090 feet above sea level in the Khan-Tengri Ridge. Most of the Kazakh SSR is a lowland, but the average height of the elevated areas in the eastern parts reaches from 980 to 1,310 feet and the areas on the edge of the Tyan-Shan system reach from 3,280 to 4,920 feet above sea level.

To the north of the Kazakh SSR, the highest peaks in the Ural Mountains are the Yamantay Peak (4,370 feet) and Iremel Peak (5,200 feet). The Altay-Sayan Mountains in Western Siberia are of rugged topography consisting of high and sharp ridges covered with permanent snow. The highest peaks in southwestern Siberia are Beluka (14,760 feet) and Munku-Sordyk (11,480 feet).

To the east of the Altay-Sayan Mountains, stretching from the Yenisey River to the Pacific Ocean, lies a complex topographical region of uplands and mountains with many plateaus and high hills. Among the most important are the Central Siberian Plateau, between the Yenisey and Lena rivers; the Yablonovy Ridge to the east of Lake Baikal; the Verkhoyansk Ridge, east of the Lena River; the Stanovoy Ridge between the Olekma River and the Pacific Ocean; the Sikhote-Alin Ridge in the Far East and several other less important ridges north of Khaborovsk and in Kamchatka. Kamchatka and the Kurile Islands are the only areas in the USSR where active volcanoes are in existence.

## CLIMATE

The Soviet Union extends over several climatic zones. About 16 per cent of the USSR territory is in the subpolar zone, another four per cent in the subtropical zone, and the rest in the temperate zone. The coldest area in the USSR is located in Verkhoyansk in Yakutia, long considered the coldest spot on the earth, with an average temperature of —58° F. in January. Batumi, which is in the subtropical zone near the Turkish frontier on the Black Sea, has recorded +43° F. in January, the warmest temperature in the USSR in that month.

In the north, the perpetual ice fields of the Arctic area minimize any influence the warm air current of the Arctic Ocean might have on the land mass. For example, in the Murmansk region the effect of the gulf stream in winter results in much milder temperatures in areas close to the ocean than in areas farther inland. The average temperature in the Murmansk region is +12° F. for July, —12° F. for January.

In the south and the east, mountain ranges and highlands of Central Asia, Eastern Siberia and the Far East intercept the moisture-laden winds from the Indian and Pacific oceans. Thus three-fourths of the northeastern Siberian territory is much colder than Archangelsk, while the southern parts of Siberia are in climate similar to the northern parts of the European USSR. Being isolated from the Atlantic and Pacific oceans, Western Siberia has a more continental climate than the European parts of the Soviet Union. For instance, Tomsk, which is on the same latitude as Moscow, is 10° F. colder in January than is Moscow. Cold spells of —30° F. occur in Tomsk as often as —20° F. in Moscow. In Eastern Siberia the climate is milder than in Western Siberia and winter temperature of —40° F. occurs there as often as —30° F. occurs in Western Siberia.

The Far East is the region of monsoons. Winter monsoons blow cold and dry winds from Yakutia and summer monsoons from the Pacific Ocean bring precipitation—mist and rain. Vladivostok which lies on the same longitude as subtropical Sukhumi on the Black Sea in Georgia, has a colder winter than Arkhangelsk, yet the summers are warm enough for rice growing.

Central Asia has a climate full of contrasts. The high mountains are covered with perpetual snow, where the average annual temperature is below 0° F., whereas the lowlands, semi-deserts and deserts, have a dry climate similar to that of Egypt. The average summer temperature ranges from +70° F. to +75° F., while in winter considerable frost with snow in many agricultural valleys is recorded. The driest and hottest region in Central Asia is the Turkmen SSR with winters lasting only two or three months. The total annual precipitation in the lowlands is not more than three to six inches. All central and western parts, about nine-tenths of the total territory of the Kazakh SSR, has an annual precipitation of less than 11.8 inches, with the driest region being near the Aral Sea where less than three inches of precipitation is recorded. The highest July temperature recorded for Central Asia is 88.3° F. in the city of Termez on the Afghan frontier, and the lowest annual precipitation of 1.1 inches is recorded in the depression of Lake Karakul in the Tadzhik SSR.

Although most of the Caucasus is made up of hilly and mountainous regions, its valleys and lowlands have a subtropical climate where cotton, tea, grapes, citrus fruits and other subtropical products are grown. The most fertile areas are located in the western parts of Georgia and in the Kura River Valley of the Azerbaydzhan SSR.

The climates of the Ukraine and Moldavia are similar. Winters are mild and summers are long and warm. On the other hand, White Russian

climate is changeable from dry continental to an ocean-influenced climate
with abundant precipitation. In contrast to the Ukraine and White Russia,
the climate of the three Baltic republics is of a limited continental variety.
Winters are milder and summers are cooler than in Moscow. Winters in
these republics are unpredictable due to the nearness of the Baltic Sea from
which abundant precipitation and milder air is blown—at times causing
snow thaws in winter.

TABLE 3—*Most Important Rivers in the USSR*[4]

| River | Length (miles) | Basin area (square miles) |
|---|---|---|
| Amur, with Shilka and Onon | 2,800 | 788,000 |
| Ob, with Katun | 2,720 | 1,131,000 |
| Irtysh, with Black Irtysh | 2,760 | 614,000 |
| Lena | 2,650 | 934,000 |
| Yenisey | 2,370 | 1,004,000 |
| Volga | 2,290 | 533,000 |
| Syr-Darya with Naryn | 1,650 | 85,000 |
| Aum-Darya with Pyandzh | 1,630 | 88,000 |
| Kolyma | 1,620 | 249,000 |
| Ishim | 1,580 | 53,000 |
| Ural | 1,570 | 85,000 |
| Vilyuy | 1,510 | 190,000 |
| Olenek | 1,500 | 95,000 |
| Dnieper | 1,420 | 194,000 |
| Aldan | 1,390 | 271,000 |
| Kama | 1,260 | 201,000 |
| Don | 1,220 | 163,000 |
| Angara | 1,140 | 409,000 |
| Vitim | 1,130 | 88,000 |
| Indigirka | 1,110 | 139,000 |
| Pechora | 1,110 | 126,000 |
| Tobol | 1,040 | 152,000 |
| Kura | 941 | 73,000 |
| Oka | 920 | 95,000 |
| Dniester | 880 | 28,000 |
| Northern Dvina with Sukhon | 814 | 139,000 |

## RIVERS

The Soviet Union has approximately 100,000 rivers. One can best
described the Soviet rivers by dividing them into three regions. If one draws
a rough line across the European part of the USSR from Leningrad to the
southern boundary of the Komi ASSR, the rivers above this line are flowing

into the White Sea and the Arctic Ocean, while all other rivers in the European USSR flow southward to the Black and Caspian seas. In Siberia, most navigable rivers flow northward and in Central Asia, as in Siberia, they flow northward into the Sea of Aral or disappear into the sands of the desert.

The greatest rivers in the Soviet Union are in Siberia. The most important—the Amur, Ob, Lena, and Yenisey—are used as ice routes for hauling freight and passengers by motorized vehicles, horses, dogs and reindeer.

In the European parts of the Soviet Union, the greatest river is the Volga, the largest in Europe. The Volga is dear to the Russians as a source of folklore and the hub of industrial and commercial activities. Other major European rivers in the Soviet Union are the Dnieper, Dniester and Don, all of which flow to the Black Sea while the Volga flows to the Caspian Sea. In the north European parts of the USSR, the main rivers are the Onega and Northern Dvina, flowing to the White Sea, and the Western Dvina which flows into the Gulf of Riga.

Aside from the Volga, the most important Soviet navigable rivers are the Kama, Oka, Northern Dvina, Pechara, Don, Ob, Yenisey, Lena, and Amur. All of these freeze from three to nine months of the year, and during their short navigable period, they are used to transport many bulky goods such as timber, coal, grain and other products, as well as passengers. Despite the huge network of inland waterways, they carry less than six per cent of the total Soviet freight.

The major user of the inland waterways is the RSFSR. The Central European Industrial Region uses river transportation to the greatest extent, followed by the Volga River Valley and the Urals. These three regions shipped and received over 50 per cent of the total river freight in in the RSFSR in 1958. Western Siberia, Eastern Siberia and the Far East with their many great rivers, handled only about ten per cent of the total river cargo of the RSFSR. Next in importance is the Ukraine, followed by White Russia. Their share of the total river freight is insignificant.

## SEAS AND LAKES

The Soviet Union is surrounded by 12 seas and oceans. The Arctic Ocean includes the following Seas: The White Sea, Barents Sea, Kara Sea, Laptev Sea, and the East Siberian Sea. The Pacific Ocean includes the Bering Sea, Sea of Okhotsk, and the Sea of Japan. In the south are the Caspian Sea, the Sea of Aral, the Sea of Azov, and the Black Sea. In the northwest, the Baltic Sea reaches Leningrad. The most important of these is the

Black Sea, through which over 50 per cent of Soviet exports pass, followed by the Baltic and White seas in order of importance.

Among the thousands of lakes in the Soviet Union, the most important are those which serve as means of transportation, sources of fishing and other industries, and provide a balance in the otherwise dry climate of the region.

The Caspian Sea, the world's largest salt-water inland sea, is the most important. Its coastline totals 3,980 miles, of which 3,360 miles are enclosed by Soviet territory and the remaining 630 miles are bordered by Iran. The Caspian Sea lies in a depression about 92 feet below sea level and is divided into three zones of depth. The northern zone is located north of the 44th parallel. The average depth in the northern Caspian Sea is about 16 feet; the deepest point is about 33 feet. The middle zone extends to Baku and Krasnovodsk with an average depth of about 558 feet and the deepest point 2,618 feet. The southern zone has an average depth of 1,096 feet and reaches 3,215 feet at the deepest point. Only the northern zone of the Caspian Sea freezes, from about the middle of November to the end of March. The largest bay in the Caspian Sea, Kara-Bogaz-Gol in the Turkmen SSR, covers some 7,080 square miles and reaches an average depth of 33 feet. This bay is unique in its relationship to the rest of the Caspian Sea, for it lies from 17 to 42 inches below the level of the Caspian Sea and acts as a natural evaporating basin for the region.

The Caspian Sea is fed by several rivers: the Volga and its tributaries, the Ural, Terek, Kuma, Sulak, and Samur rivers. These rivers contribute about 92,457 million gallons of water to the sea annually, of which the Volga alone brings about 77 per cent. Most of the river water received by the sea is lost through high evaporation. Since many rivers divert part of their waters to irrigation and industrial uses, the water level of the Caspian Sea has been steadily declining since 1929. The Volga alone has reduced the volume of its water delivery by ten to 20 per cent during the past 20 years. At the present time, the water level of the Caspian Sea has fallen 8.2 feet and the water area of the sea has been reduced by more than 12,740 square miles when compared with 1929. This has created maladjustment in its economic value. The fishing industry located on the Caspian Sea has been reduced, the approach to the Volga has become hazardous due to shallowness, ice formation in the north has become much thicker, and during the thawing period heavy ice blocks flow to the south and endangers the oil derricks on the water near Baku. Settlements which used to be on the shore have now become inland settlements. The atmospheric conditions for agricultural purposes throughout the entire length of the Caspian's shores have changed considerably since 1929.

Next in size to the Caspian Sea is the Sea of Aral, which is fed by the Syr-Darya and Amu-Darya rivers. The strong southwestern wind from the Kyzyl Kum desert deposits a large volume of sand there, forming small

TABLE 4—*Large Soviet Inland Seas and Lakes* [5]

| Name | Area (square miles | Greatest depth (feet) |
|---|---|---|
| Caspian Sea | 163,706 | 3,215 |
| Sea of Aral | 26,525 | 223 |
| Baikal | 12,162 | 5,712 |
| Ladoga | 7,104 | 738 |
| Balkhash | 6,679 | 85 |
| Onega | 3,822 | 394 |
| Issyk-Kul | 2,394 | 2,303 |
| Rybinsk | 1,737 | 82 |
| Khanka | 1,699 | 33 |
| Chudsk and Pskovsk | 1,390 | 49 |
| Chana | 1,004 | 33 |
| Ala-Kul | 888 | 154 |
| Zaysan | 695 | 26 |
| Sevan | 540 | 321 |
| Beloe | 463 | 36 |
| Vygozero | 463 | 66 |
| Ilmen | 425 | 16 |
| Topozero | 425 | 184 |
| Imandra | 347 | 220 |
| Serozero | 309 | 318 |
| Pyaozero | 309 | 151 |
| Kara-Kul | 139 | 774 |
| Telesk | 89 | 1,066 |
| Elton | 58 | 3 |

islands, especially in the southeastern corner of the Sea of Aral. Like the Caspian Sea, the Sea of Aral is salty in varying degrees and freezes in the northern parts for about three months of the year. Its average depth is 55 feet, but it is shallower in the northern than in the southern parts. As a whole, the Sea of Aral is of limited importance to industry, transportation, and wild life, and its contribution to agriculture is insignificant. The major industry is fishing, but the total catch amounts only to about three or four per cent of the total Soviet figure.

The third largest body of water in the Soviet Union is Lake Baikal. This is the world's deepest fresh-water lake. It occupies a depression bordered by high ranges and is fed by over 300 affluents, of which the Selenga, Barguzin, and Upper Angara rivers are the major sources. Its only outlet is the Angara River, which flows northward by the city of Irkutsk. Its economic value lies in the abundance of fish, especially goby, perch, pike, and white fish, and also as a means of transportation either by boats or frozen-surface vehicles. Its value for transportation is gaining in importance. It is expected that with the construction of the Irkutsk hydroelectric power works, the water level of Lake Baikal will be elevated, facilitating direct transportation from the Selenga River, with its source in the Mongol People's Republic, through Lake Baikal to the Angara and Yenisey rivers, and then by the Northern Sea Route to the North Sea.

There are 21 other lakes in the USSR which are used for transportation, fishing, irrigation, wild life, soil conservation, and recreation for the local communities. Some of them link the man-made canals in the European part of the Soviet Union.

## NATURAL RESOURCES

The most interesting aspect of the geographic location of Soviet natural resources is the recent discovery through an accelerated program of a number of important minerals and metals throughout the nation. The abundance of metallic and non-metallic raw materials is claimed to be the world's greatest, and permits maximum self-sufficiency in current Soviet needs. Many of these resources, although known, cannot be extracted because of lack of transportation and labor, adverse weather conditions, and investments in equipment and machinery. At the present time, resources are extracted only when economically justifiable, and although discoveries of new deposits are being rapidly mapped for future use, much remains to be done in surveying the hidden wealth of the USSR.

In metals and mineral resources, the Soviet Union may well be considered one of the richest countries of the world. The USSR claims a concentration of 41 per cent of the world's reserve of iron ore, 88 per cent of the surveyed manganese, 54 per cent of the potassium, almost one-third of the phosphorite and apatite, 60 per cent of the peat resources, 57 per cent of the world's coal deposits, and has the world's largest forest area. The USSR is the third largest producer of petroleum in the world, after the United States and Venezuela.

Every year new deposits of valuable metals and minerals are being discovered in Siberia, yet their economic exploitation is at a slow pace. Main

MAP 1—*Major Mineral Resources of the U.S.S.R.—Approximate Location*

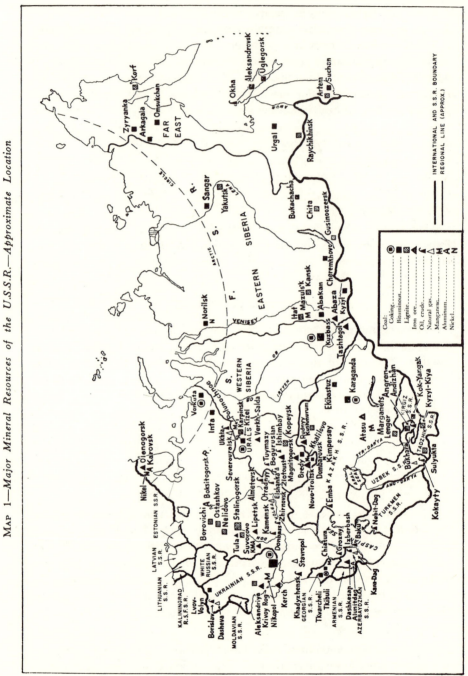

obstacles are the scarcities in transportation and manpower. The construction of a large industrial plant on permanently frozen ground creates problems not encountered in the Ukraine. A metallurgical plant producing one million metric tons of pig iron and rolled metal annually usually employs about 10,000 workers. To support this labor force, a city of about 100,000 inhabitants is required. For these reasons the development in the past of Siberian regions, with all their abundant deposits, was a slow process.

The anticipated increase in the use of mineral and metal resources during the current Seven-Year Plan calls upon Soviet geologists vigorously to survey the potential resources of all raw materials. According to this plan, geologists are to map 3.4 times more existing deposits of natural gas in 1965 than in 1958. They are assigned the task of surveying 50 per cent more possible petroleum deposits, 50 per cent more coal deposits, 40 per cent more iron ore and copper, 60 per cent lead, 25 per cent bauxite, 60 per cent nickel, 25 per cent mercury as well as other metals and minerals needed for the expanding economy.

## Coal

Among mineral deposits found in the Soviet Union, coal is more widely distributed than any other. The Soviets claim that there are nearly 50 coal basins but only seven are considered to be major basins. Of the known geological deposits of coal, 63 per cent is located in the northeastern parts of the Union, 29 per cent in the southeastern regions and only eight per cent in the European parts of the country.

It is claimed that out of the total known geological deposits of coal, said to be 8,669 billion metric tons, economically accessible deposits are estimated at from 1,000 to 1,200 billion metric tons. Assuming that the annual rate of production of coal is to be between 596 and 609 million metric tons, a goal which is to be reached by 1965, then the currently accessible coal deposits would last for the next 1,500 years, provided, of course, that distant deposits can be economically exploited. Since the European parts of the USSR have the greatest concentration of industry, their coal deposits provide 65 per cent of the total Soviet coal output, southeastern Siberia produces another 34 per cent and northeastern regions only one per cent. In other words, 7.6 per cent of the total Soviet geological deposits of coal in the Europen parts contribute 65 per cent of the total coal output—not a favorable ratio considering the rate of depletion of these deposits.

The largest coal deposits are in Siberia. But since Siberia is lacking oil, natural gas and peat deposits, about 70 per cent of currently produced coal is assigned to railroad transportation. Even the well publicized Karaganda coal fields allocate about 40 per cent of their total coal output to railroad transportation. European mines on the other hand contribute about 25 per cent of their coal to that purpose. The major users of coal are transportation, metallurgy and thermoelectric power plants. The combined coal consumption of these three industries amounts to about 66 per cent of the total Soviet coal output.

TABLE 5—*Geological Coal Reserves in the USSR* [6]
(in billion metric tons)

| Basin | Known Reserves | Per cent of Total Reserves | 1958 Output: Percentage to Total |
|---|---|---|---|
| Total  USSR: | 8,669.0 | 100.0 | 100.0 |
| European  parts: | 657.0 | 7.6 | 65.0 |
| Pechora | 344.0 | 4.0 | 3.4 |
| Donbass | 240.0 | 2.8 | 36.6 |
| Moscow | 12.0 | 0.1 | 9.5 |
| Urals | 7.5 | 0.1 | 12.3 |
| Others | 53.5 | 0.6 | 3.2 |
| Central  Asia: | 180.0 | 2.0 | 7.7 |
| Karaganda | 51.0 | 0.6 | 5.0 |
| Ubagansk | 36.0 | 0.4 | — |
| Maykubensk | 21.0 | 0.2 | — |
| Ekibastuz | 12.0 | 0.1 | 1.2 |
| Others | 60.0 | 0.7 | 1.5 |
| Southern Siberia: | 2,534.0 | 29.4 | 34.0 |
| Kansk-Achinsk | 1,220.0 | 14.1 | 7.3 |
| Kuzbass | 905.0 | 10.4 | 15.2 |
| Irkutsk | 87.0 | 1.0 | 6.0 |
| South-Yakutsk | 40.0 | 0.4 | — |
| Others | 282.0 | 3.2 | 5.5 |
| Northern Siberia: | 5,478.0 | 63.0 | 1.0 |
| Leninsk | 2,647.0 | 30.5 | 1.0 |
| Tungussk | 1,745.0 | 20.1 | — |
| Taymyrsk | 583.0 | 6.7 | — |
| Others | 503.0 | 5.7 | — |

The cost of production of coal, due to depletion in the older basins, is gradually increasing; and at the same time costs of its large-scale economic exploitation in eastern regions are still prohibitive. To overcome this situation the Soviets are rapidly expanding output of oil, natural gas and peat. Since cheap heat material is more abundant in the Eastern regions, there is a continuous relocation of industries to the east of the Volga River. However gradual this relocation may currently be, it still points to the East and especially to the southern parts of Western and Eastern Siberias where rail transportation is available.

## European Coal Basins

The most important European coal basin is in the Donbass. It covers an area of about 8,900 square miles of which 80 per cent lies in the Ukraine. Its deposits reach the depth of 1,800 meters (about 5,900 feet), which increases the cost of mining. Because of the prohibitive depths mining is possible only in an area where about 90 million metric tons of coal is concentrated. These deposits are equal to the combined coal reserves of Belgium, France, and West Germany.

Despite its unfavorable depth, the Donbass has an advantageous position by virtue of ample transportation and its proximity to consuming markets. It produces high calorific coal with about 30 per cent of the total output being anthracite and approximately 23 per cent coking coal. Because of the high quality of coal, this basin, possessing only three per cent of all reserves, produces about 37 per cent of the total Soviet coal—over 50 per cent of which is coking coal.

The hard coal industry in the Ukrainian Donbass is centered around Stalino. About 200 miles to the west of Stalino is Krivoy Rog, the center of Ukrainian iron ore mining. Since the distance between the two mining centers is not great, and since most of the metallurgical industry is located in the coal producing areas, the Donbass ships its coking coal to Krivoy Rog, which in turn supplies the Stalino complex with iron ore. Likewise, the Stalino exports its coke to Kerch in the Crimea and receives Crimean iron ore. And of course, the Donbass supplies the Central Industrial Region with coal, coke, and ferrous metals.

The second largest producer of coal is the Urals. The Ural mountains are very old and have been exposed to the elements for a longer period of time than other mountain ranges in the Soviet Union. For this reason the Ural mountains are relatively low and their metals and minerals are near the surface of the earth, facilitating extraction by the open-cast method.

The Urals are unique in that there is a concentration of a large variety of natural resources. It has been stated that the Urals possess over 1,000 different metals and minerals dispersed over 12,000 locations. The region has 17 hard and soft coal locations. In general, lignite coal is concentrated in the southern part and hard coal is in the northern part. About 30 per cent of the Soviet's coking coal is produced in the Urals.

As in the case of the Donbass, the Urals with their small geological deposits of coal supply over 12 per cent of the total Soviet coal, and since these deposits are being exhausted while industrial needs are rapidly expanding, the deficit is imported from the Kuzbass in Western Siberia and from Karaganda in the Kazakh SSR.

The Moscow coal basin, located south of the city of Moscow, is not only the oldest coal producer in the country but also the largest basin in the European part of the USSR. This basin covers 118,100 square miles and has widespread but not deep deposits. The geological reserves at a depth of 100 meters are estimated at 12 billion metric tons, producing about ten per cent of the total Soviet coal. The southern part of the basin occuping some 43,500 square miles is the center of coal mining. Only lignite coal of low grade is produced in the Moscow coal basin. However, despite this disadvantage, the basin has an exceptionally advantageous geographic location in the Central Industrial Region since the high cost of transportation from other coal basins serves as an incentive to use Moscow coal.

The second largest coal area after the Moscow basin is the Pechora basin covering about 74,600 square miles. Since this basin is not completely surveyed as the Donbass is, its current share in the total Soviet coal output amounts only to about four per cent. This basin produces different grades of coal of which about 26 per cent is hard coal. Only a small volume of coking coal is obtained there.

The European part of the Soviet Union has other small coal reserves, significant among which are the L'vov-Volynsk basin in the Western Ukraine and the Tkvarchel'sk basin in Georgia. The L'vov-Volynsk basin, recently developed, produces about 20 million metric tons of mostly hard coal per year. The Tkvarchel'sk basin annually mines only three million metric tons of hard coal from which coke of high grade is produced. Of these two, the L'vov-Volynsk basin is currently being surveyed for potential expansion in production.

## Central Asian Coal Basins

Important coal deposits in Central Asia are concentrated in the Kazakh SSR with reserves amounting to 140 billion metric tons. In addition, there are also small coal deposits located in the Kirghiz, Uzbek, and Tadzhik republics, the collective wealth of which is estimated at about 40 billion metric tons—less than one half of one per cent of the total Soviet geological deposits.

The Kazakh SSR has both large and small coal fields. Among the largest are the Karaganda, Ubagansk, Maykubensk and Ekibastuz basins with Karaganda and Ekibastuz most valued. In contrast with basins located in the European parts, Kazakh hard coal is not only of high grade but it also can be mined by the open-cast method.

The Karaganda coal basin has less than one per cent of the total geological reserves and produces about five per cent of the total Soviet coal. A relatively small area of 1,160 square miles, this basin has a high concentration of bituminous and anthracite-deposits and is a source of a considerable amount of coking coal. Being a relatively new coal producer, Karaganda, at the present rate of exploitation of 25 to 30 million metric tons, or even 100 million metric tons annually, with its estimated geological deposits, should last for the next 500 years.

To the north of Karaganda lies the Ekibastuz basin covering an area of 54 square miles. Since its coal layers are closer to the surface than those in Karaganda, the cost of production per ton of coal is the lowest in the Soviet Union. Hard coal produced here contains a large percentage of ash. Because of this drawback, the major users of Ekibastuz coal are the railroads and river steamboats, and only a small percentage of the total output is consumed by industry.

## Southern Siberian Coal Basins

Rich and accessible coal deposits are found in the southern parts of Siberia, roughly between Novosibirsk and Lake Baikal. Here are located the famous Kuzbass, Kansk-Achinsk and Irkutsk coal basins. The combined area of the three basins represents about five per cent of the total Soviet territory where about 30 per cent of the country's geological coal reserves are concentrated, almost fourfold the coal reserves of Western Europe.

The Kuzbass is second to the Donbass in the country's output of coal, even though its geological reserves are almost four times larger than in the Donbass; its coal output is about 41 per cent that of the Ukrainian Donbass. Kuzbass hard coal is of higher grade that that of Donbass, Karaganda, and Pechora. It is claimed that about 30 per cent of the Kuzbass geological deposit is coking coal, and because many layers are less than 2,000 feet below the surface of the earth, about 13 per cent of the total output is extracted by open-cast method.

Since the Urals are the major producer of iron ore but lack coal, and the Kuzbass is the prime producer of coal, the two regions supplement each other, even though they lie about 1250 miles apart. Under this arrangement, Kuzbass coal has been shipped by rail to the Urals since 1930, and in return the same transport facilities are used by the Urals to ship its iron ore to the Kuzbass. However, since the demand for Kuzbass coal has considerably increased at home, shipment to the Urals is declining. In addition, the Kuzbass no longer depends on iron ore from the Urals, and at present about 75 to 80 per cent of the iron ore required in the Kuzbass is being mined either in the Kuzbass itself or imported from areas closer than the Urals.

The Kansk-Achinsk lignite coal basin stretches some 430 miles along the Trans-Siberian railroad between the cities of Kansk and Achinsk. This basin has 23 coal locations, almost all of them with horizontal layers of coal close to the surface of the earth, suitable for open-cast mining. For this reason the cost of production per ton of coal in this region is much lower than in the Donbass. Although its coal reserves are 35 per cent greater than in the Kuzbass, its share in the total Soviet coal output is about one-half that of the Kuzbass. Because of its high grade coal, availability of rail transportation, and nearness to consuming eastern markets, this basin has been given priority for further expansion.

The Irkutsk hard coal basin also lies along the Trans-Siberian railroad covers about 13,500 square miles and has several deposits of coal. Among the most important are the Cheremkhovo, Novo-Metelkin, Karantsaysk, and Azeysk deposits. The Cheremkhovo coal fields contain about 30 per cent of all surveyed deposits in the Irkutsk basin and are the only fields commercially developed. With current rapid industrial expansion in the Irkutsk Oblast, it is expected that output of Irkutsk coal will be greatly increased to supply the needs of local railroads and the chemical industry. The Azeysk deposits, amounting to some 700 million metric tons adapted to open-cast mining, are also on the priority list for development during the 1959-65 period.

To the west of Lake Baikal, there are a number of scattered coal basins. Largest of these are the South-Yakutsk and Sakhalin Island deposits. The geological reserves of the South-Yakutsk are about 40 billion metric tons, but because of isolation these reserves cannot be developed without building transportation facilities. The Sakhalin reserves are estimated at 20 billion metric tons and are being mined to supply the Far Eastern industries. Other deposits in southern Siberia are considerably smaller, and some of them are being exploited to support local needs. The important thing about all of southern Siberia is that, although there are large coal deposits, it is a deficit coking coal region and therefore must import from the West, where reserves are on the decline.

## Northern Siberian Coal Deposits

To the north of Kansk-Achinsk basin and above the Sakhalin Island lies the huge and still unexplored coal wealth of northern Siberia.

The Tungussk hard coal basin is the largest, covering an area between 3,860 and 4,630 square miles. An incomplete survey of this basin revealed that the southern part of it has the greatest concentration of varieties of coal deposits, including anthracite. However, because of its isolated geographic location, its fuel wealth is not exploited.

The Leninsk hard coal basin embraces over 100 locations, covering about 154,400 square miles where over 30 per cent of the known geological resources of the country are concentrated. This is the largest coal area in the Soviet Union and equal to the territory of Paraguay. Like the Tungussk deposits, the precise wealth of the Leninsk basin is unknown, although the eastern parts of the basin, located near Yakutsk and Verkhoyansk are being modestly exploited to supply the local industries with fuel.

There are other large deposits of coal, some of which provide fuel to local industries, especially the Norilsk basin which supplies coal to its copper and nickel industries. However, most of the coal reserves are not economically accessible.

## OIL AND NATURAL GAS

It is claimed by the Soviets that their known petroleum reserves represent about 20 per cent of the world's known reserves. The Soviet Union has an abundant reserve of natural gas which in the main is found in areas producing petroleum. The actual geological wealth of petroleum and natural gas still is unknown. With the current intensive geological surveys of the Soviet ground wealth, the known reserves of both products no doubt will be enlarged by 1965. In connection with geological surveys undertaken now, the emphasis is on the "Second Baku" and Northern Caucasus since both regions have strategic advantages in transportation. Along with these main targets, the search for new deposits of petroleum and gas is to be accelerated in Central Asia and especially in the southeastern and central Turkmen SSR, the southwestern regions of the Uzbek SSR, and the western parts of the Kazakh SSR. This work is also to be extended to central and northern regions of Western Siberia, to Eastern Siberia, Yakutia, the southeastern parts of the European USSR, and the Ukraine.

The Soviet Union has 14 large areas of oil concentration but only seven of natural gas. The largest oil reserves are concentrated in the Second Baku where over 150 known and 250 possible oil deposits are located. These deposits are located in the Western Urals and extend to regions east of the Volga River. The first discovery of oil in the Second Baku in 1929; the most important oil producing regions at the present time are the Tartar ASSR, Bashkir ASSR, and the Kuybyshev Oblast. The Bashkir ASSR alone produces more oil than the old Baku oil fields in the Azerbaydzhan SSR.

The second largest producer of crude oil is the Azerbaydzhan SSR (Baku) with 16 main oil fields, but the most important deposits are located on the Aspheron Peninsula. The most intensive Baku oil extraction is on the shores of the Caspian Sea, where drilling reaches a depth of 16,400 feet. This region is significant, since the concentration of large oil reserves lies in a relatively small area where derricks are clustered in very much the same way as in some parts of Texas. The next important region is the Puta, southwest of Baku, followed by the Alyaty-Pristan and Neftechala reserves, both of which are south of Baku on the Caspian Sea. The inland reserves of oil are near Yevlakh, and are yet to be fully utilized.

Other oil reserves are located in the newly developed Turkmen fields, the Emba deposits in the western Kazakh SSR; in the Fergana Valley of the Uzbek SSR, the Termez in the Kirghiz SSR, and the Ukrainian oil reserves. Ukrainian oil is located near the city of Borislav in the west and also in the Poltava and Kharkov oblasts. Presumably these resources are considerable since the Ukrainians are already talking about the creation of the "Third Baku" in their republic.

The most important reserve of natural gas is located in the Northern Caucasus in Stavropol; its output is closely matched by the Stepnovsk reserves near Saratov. These two regions in 1958 produced 40 per cent of the total Soviet natural gas. Next in importance are two fields, the Dashev in Western Ukraine and the Shebelinsk in Eastern Ukraine, producing about 34 per cent of the total Soviet output of natural gas. Other reserves of natural gas are located in Central Asia, Azerbaydzhan and Yakutia. The Yakutian gas resources are not developed at present.

In Central Asia, the Gazlinsk natural gas of the Uzbek SSR is rapidly gaining in economic importance. Moreover, in 1958 about 125 miles southeast of the Gazlinsk a new reserve of natural gas was discovered at Yuzhnyy Mubarek. Other deposits were also uncovered in the Turkmen SSR and the Kazakh SSR. Thus, Central Asia is gradually emerging as a large producer of natural gas. Along with the intensified search for natural gas in Central Asia, similar efforts are to be made in discovering potential natural gas supplies the Moldavian SSR, the Baltic republics, White Russia, Siberia, and the Caucasus. All in all, commercial gas, including side recovery and shale, is being rapidly adopted by Soviet industries. Gas is economical fuel, requires less investment than in production of coal or oil, and may be conveniently piped at a low cost over long distances.

## IRON ORE

It is claimed that known iron ore reserves in the Soviet Union are the largest in the world, topping 85.5 billion metric tons. About 45 per cent of the total geological resources can be economically mined, and of this 44 per cent is located in the eastern parts of the Soviet Union.

Iron ore has different concentrations of iron. It is claimed that rich ore, on an average containing more than 55 per cent of iron, requires no processing and amounts to 6.2 billion metric tons or 16.2 per cent of the total industrial ore. The other 32.1 billion metric tons—83.8 per cent of the total—has from 30 to 37 per cent of iron and requires processing. However, of all the ores requiring processing, 21.5 billion metric tons can be processed by cheap methods. The eastern regions have about nine billion metric tons of such ores. The other 10.6 billion metric tons of the total consist of poor ore requiring expensive and complex methods of processing before it can be used for industrial purposes.

According to an incomplete geological evaluation of iron ore resources, the Russians think that they have another 147 billion metric tons of ore in addition to already surveyed deposits. Of the 147 billion metric tons, about 90 per cent lies in the eastern parts and over four-fifths of this consists of poor grade ore requiring complex processing. Thus known deposits plus geological estimates of possible resources amount to some 232 billion metric tons, over half of which is low grade ore. But the reserves accessible by current extraction methods amount to only 38.3 billion metric tons; over 85 per cent of the surveyed deposits are concentrated in the Ukraine, central parts of the European SSR, Urals, and the Kazakh SSR.

The largest sources of iron ore reserves and production are located in the southwest—in the Ukraine. There are three known reserves and the largest of them is the Krivoy Rog basin followed by the Kerch in the Crimea. Both basins have high-grade ore, much of which is being extracted by opencast method. The third basin, the Kremenchug, is located near the Krivoy Rog and was developed since 1955. Of the three basins, the Kerch holds about two billion metric tons, assuring future exploitation for many generations to come. Its current output of iron ore is under ten per cent of the total Ukrainian output; the remainder is produced in the Krivoy Rog.

The Krivoy Rog has been developed recently. Its deposits are located in a narrow strip of land 62 miles long and two to four miles wide. Recently it was discovered that the iron ore bed of the Krivoy Rog extends to the Dnieper River and reaches Poltava Oblast to the north, where the new

TABLE 6—*Known Commercial Iron Ore Reserves* [7]

| Region | Billion Metric Tons | Per cent to Total |
|---|---|---|
| USSR: | 38.3 | 100.0 |
| Southwest | 11.8 | 31.0 |
| Central West | 8.1 | 21.0 |
| Kazakh SSR | 6.8 | 18.0 |
| Urals | 5.9 | 15.2 |
| Siberia | 4.0 | 10.8 |
| Northwest | 1.7 | 4.0 |

Kremenchug iron ore base—similar in quality to the ore of the Krivoy Rog—has been established. The average percentage of iron in Krivoy Rog ore is about 60. However, the basin also contains poorer ores having 24 to 45 per cent iron. The Kerch ore is of poorer grade than Krivoy Rog ore, ranging from 33 to 42 per cent in iron concentration. Other deposits of poor grade iron ore are found in Carpathia, and the Dnepropetrovsk, Odesk, Kievsk, and Zhitomirsk oblasts.

In the Central European part of the USSR is the largest iron ore basin in the world, the so-called "Kursk Magnitnaya Anamaliya" (KMA) which was only recently discovered. The geological resources of this basin are not as yet known, but inconclusive estimates set its reserves at 25 billion metric tons. Extraction of the rich ore was started in 1958, and present total output is insignificant. But the planned output for 1965 is already set at 14 million metric tons or about 10 per cent of the country's total production. In 1958 practically all iron ore produced in central European regions came from the Tula and Lipetsk deposits.

In the Kazakh SSR, iron ore reserves are found in the Kustanay and Karaganda Oblasts. Kustanay Oblast has the largest deposits centered around the city of Kustanay. By 1965 this region which is located close to the Urals is to become one of the major suppliers of iron ore to Ural's metallurgy in addition to supplying its ore to newly created metallurgical industry in the Kazakh SSR. Karaganda Oblast has a few concentrated iron ore locations. Of these the Atasuysk basin with estimated resources of 330 million metric tons is the backbone of the Karaganda

Metallurgical Plant. It is estimated that Karaganda resources are large enough to supply iron ore of good grade to the Karaganda Metallurgical Plant for the next 30 years.

The Urals have seven major locations of iron ore, production of which is the basic mining activity in the region. The ore with a high concentration of iron is found in the lower Urals and the poor ore is in the upper Urals. About 70 per cent of the known reserves of the Kachkanar basin in the upper Urals contain ore with a low concentration of iron. Nevertheless, because of expanding industries in the Urals, the Soviets are building a large iron ore processing plant at Kachkanar which will have a potential processing capacity of 50 million metric tons annually. Another deposit located at Orsk is also expected to expand its output. The Orsk resources, at the present rate of extraction, are expected to last for only about 30 years.

The best known but already much depleted reserves of high-grade iron ores are located at the Magnitnaya Mountain near the city of Magnitogorsk and at the Blagodat and Vysokaya Mountains, both near the city of Nizhniy Tagil. These resources have been intensively exploited for a number of years. It is because of the depletion of high-grade ores in the Urals that the Kazakh SSR is rapidly developing its newly discovered deposits in order to supply Urals' expanding metallurgy with its good ore.

In Siberia the most important location of iron ore is in the Kuzbass, reserves of which are estimated at 950 million metric tons. These reserves extend to Kemerovo Oblast, Altay Kray and the Khakassk Autonomous Oblast. The Kuzbass ore is of high grade and easily accessible. The most valuable of all locations is the Gornoy Shorii which contains about 50 per cent of all known resources in West Siberia and is being intensively exploited. There are other locations at which the mining of ore has been conducted for a number of years. Currently a new reserve at the Abakansk is being developed.

Western Siberia has about ten iron ore locations, but prior to 1958 only the Abaza basin located near the Kazbass was of economic importance. Since 1958, however, many other locations were found. Among these is the large Angaro-Pitsk basin said to have about five billion metric tons of ore containing on an average 40 per cent of iron. Open-cast extraction is possible at this basin and its estimated potential annual output is valued at ten million metric tons. Another important location is at Angaro-Ilimsk, said to have about 600 million metric tons; the Yuzhno-Aldan iron ore base in the Yakutian ASSR is still being surveyed.

In the Far East, the Kimkan reserves of iron ore amount to 190 million metric tons and the Garinsk basin to 211 million metric tons. Both basins are not developed as yet. However, the Soviets are expecting to develop newly discovered and economically accessible locations of iron ore in order to assure Siberia and the Kazakh SSR an annual production of 30 to 35 million tons of pig iron. In general, during the 1959-65 period the Soviets are planning to survey new deposits of iron ore throughout the country, with an estimated increase of additional geological resources of 4.2 billion metric tons of iron ore.

## MANGANESE ORE

The largest reserves of manganese ore are the Chiatura in central Georgia and in the Nikopol in southeastern Ukraine. These two sites hold 32 per cent of all the Soviet geological resources and produce about 99 per cent of the country's manganese ore. Recently another source of manganese, as large as that of Nikopol, was located at the Bol'she-Takamsk which lies just east of the city of Nikopol. This newest addition is yet to be developed for commercial production.

Although Georgia has large reserves of manganese, it is the Ukraine's Nikopol that produces most of the Soviet manganese. This region produces about 65 to 70 per cent of Ukrainian manganese ore, which contains up to 30 per cent of manganese. Nikopol deposits lie from 66 to 262 feet below the surface of the earth with the average thickness of the seams being about six to seven feet.

In the Kazakh SSR manganese is found in the Dzhezdinsk in the Karaganda Oblast. This location currently is being developed. Another source of manganese is being rapidly developed in the Atasu mines, also in the Karaganda Oblast. Both deposits are to supply manganese to industries located in the Kazakh SSR and in Siberia.

In the Urals are several locations of manganese, among which are the Marsyatsk, Polunochnoye, Novo-Berezovo, Berezovo, and Yukin. All are located within the same geographic area in the northern Urals and all of their manganese output is consumed locally.

Western Siberia has the Nazulsk deposit which produces a small amount of manganese. Newly discovered, the large Usinsk source of manganese is being studied for potential production. Other small locations are found in the Far East but they are of no significance. Georgia and the Ukraine are the current major producers of Soviet manganese. However, since about 68 per cent of the geologic deposits of manganese are located in the eastern regions, the Soviets are planning to survey regions thought to have manganese. These potential producers are said to be located in Sverdlovsk region in the Urals, Karaganda and Semipalatinsk oblasts in the Kazakh SSR, Kemerovo Oblast in Western Siberia, and Krasnoyarsk Kray in Eastern Siberia. Since production of manganese in the eastern regions represents only about one per cent of the Soviet total, any expansion of ferrous metallurgy in the East logically leads to increased output of manganese there. It is for this reason that two-thirds of the planned geological increase of manganese resources during the 1959-65 period is assigned to eastern regions.

## CHROMIUM

Prior to 1937, almost all known resources of chromium were located in the Urals. A large percentage of Ural chromium was of a low grade, and the Soviets imported ferro-chrome from Turkey. Then in 1937 a new source of high-grade chromium, claimed to be the largest in the world, estimated at over 15 million metric tons, was discovered at Khrom-Tau in western Kazakh SSR. Since the development of open-cast mining of chromium in Khrom-Tau, the Soviets have not only become self-sufficient in this commodity but also export it to other countries.

The Urals have large chromium deposits at several locations, but mainly in the regions of Orsk, Kartaly, and Sarny. The Sarny deposits are the most significant. In general, the Urals are not the major producers of chromium and whatever amount they produce is consumed locally. However, the Soviets are searching for new chromium deposits in Siberia and in the Kazakh SSR. It is believed that new sources of economic significance will be found and developed.

## NON-FERROUS METALS

The Soviet Union claims to be the leading nation in reserves of the world's copper ore, lead, zinc, nickel, bauxite, mercury, and sulphur. Even diamonds are being extracted in Yakutia. With the aid of increased investments in development of their resources, the Soviets may well become a rapidly industrialized nation to a degree far beyond the expectations of Soviet leaders in their pronouncements.

### Copper

The Kazakh SSR ranks first in copper resources within the Soviet Union, representing about 50 per cent of all Soviet copper ore deposits. Mining of copper is centered mainly in the Dzhezkazgan in the Karaganda Oblast, said to be the second largest copper deposit in the world. Copper is also

mined at Kounradskiy on Lake Balkhash, in Bozshakul which is located in the northeastern part, and at Glubokoye in the eastern part of
the republic.

Next in importance is the Urals with seven major locations of copper
ore, the largest of which is the Revda, near the city of Sverdlovsk. Although
the Urals have lesser copper reserves and the ore is of lower grade than
in the Kazakh SSR, Ural copper mining has a definite advantage in
transportation costs to Ural smelting plants, which would have to pay
higher transportation costs for Kazakh copper ore.

Other copper deposits and their mining and smelting are at Kafon
and Alaverdi, both in the Armenian SSR, and provide the backbone of
the Armenian electronic and machine building industry. Almalyk near
Tashkent in the Uzbek SSR and Norilsk in the Far North also produce
copper on a small scale.

The main producers of copper are the Kazakh SSR, the Urals, Armenia
and Norilsk while the European part of the USSR and all southern Siberia
have little copper ore and therefore must import it from surplus areas.
In 1958 estimated production of refined copper in the USSR amounted
to about 400,000 metric tons.

### Lead and Zinc

Of these two metals, lead resources are the larger. Although lead and
zinc reserves are small in size and widely dispersed, the Soviets are self-
sufficient in both metals. Their most concentrated deposits are located
in the Kazakh SSR, mainly at Leningorodsk and Zyryansk in the eastern
part and at Achisay in the southern part of the republic. Next in importance are Kansay deposits in the Uzbek SSR, Aktyuz in the Kirghiz
SSR, and Kyugutan-Tau in the Turkmen SSR. Eastern Siberia and the
Far East have four small and scattered deposits. As self-sufficient as the
USSR may be in lead and zinc, during the 1959-65 period Soviet geologists are anticipating intensification of geological surveys of other regions
in order to discover and to develop many unknown deposits of lead and
zinc while improving the methods in recovering both these metals from
other metal ores.

### Aluminum

Bauxite ore is the main source of aluminum and is found in the RSFSR,
the Ukraine, the Kazakh SSR, and the Azerbaydzhan SSR. Present resources are large enough to satisfy Soviet needs; yet new deposits for

potential utilization are being mapped now in many regions. These sources are as dispersed as those of copper ore. Since the production of aluminum requires a large amount of electrical power, the construction of smelting plants is usually undertaken where cheap electric power in large volume, preferably hydroelectric power, is available. This points to the East.

Large supplies of raw material for production of aluminum are found at Severo-Yeniseyskiy in Krasnoyarsk Kray, at Karovsk on the Kola Peninsula, Baksitogorsk, near Lake Ladoga, Severouralsk in the Urals, Alunitdag in Armenia, Zaporozhe in the Ukraine, Arkalyk in the Kazakh SSR, and Alunitdag in the Azerbaydzhan SSR. Dispersion in the aluminum industry exists not only in raw materials but in smelting as well.

Since industrial expansion during the current Seven-Year Plan calls for greater consumption of aluminum, geological surveys are being intensified, especially in the eastern regions, in order to triple the output of aluminum by 1965. Known reserves of aluminum, at the current rate of consumption, should last for at least 30 to 40 years. Nevertheless, the Soviets are worried about the adequacy of their aluminum reserves; hence the intensive surveys.

## Nickel

Since the beginning of the second Five-Year Plan, the Soviet Union has been self-sufficient in nickel. Nickel ore is located in widely separated regions but the most important are in the Urals, the Kazakh SSR, and the Ukraine. In the Urals it is found at four locations, the most important of which are in Khalilovo and Kimpersay in the south. It is also produced at Nikel located near Murmansk and at Norilsk in the Far North. In the Kazakh SSR nickel is found in one location, at Batamshinsk near Orsk, and there are a few locations in the eastern Ukraine. In general the Soviets seem to have adequate known reserves of nickel for several decades and it is quite possible that new reserves might be found by 1965.

## WATER POWER

In the Soviet Union, river development is a multipurpose undertaking with prime emphasis on hydroelectric power. Next in importance is river transportation, aimed at relieving the heavy burden on railroads. Irrigation is significant in arid regions of Central Asia, where natural precipitation is low. Flood control, recreation, and other activities associated with river development are incidental.

The scarcity of water, needed for agricultural and industrial development of many of Central Asia's regions, is of a vital nature. The insufficient water supply in the Kazakh SSR, the Turkmen SSR, and the Northern Caucasus, and the receding water level of the Caspian Sea are factors which have long concerned Russian scientists. During the 1954-58 period the USSR Ministry of Geology and Conservation of Natural Resources, together with the USSR Ministry of Agriculture, drilled 10,152 holes in the ground, of which 9,217 yielded water for agricultural purposes and construction of artesian wells. Many revolutionary plans have been advocated, most recent of which proposes to divert the northern discharge of the Ob and Yenisey rivers to the southwest where water is more urgently needed.

Map 2—*Soviet Plans for Diversion of Irtysh and Yenisey Rivers*

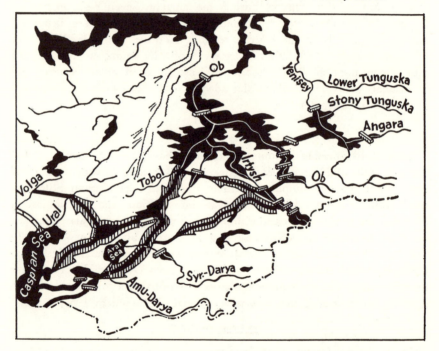

This plan proposes construction of a number of dams along the Ob and Yenisey rivers for the purposes of creating large lakes. Then, either by blowing up elevated obstructions or by construction of tunnels and canals through such obstructions, the northward flows of these great rivers could be turned to the southwest as shown in Map 2. Of course, this project would require huge long-term investments not available during the current Seven-Year Plan. However, scientific studies and the necessary calculations have been made, plans are formulated but set aside for consideration at the proper future time when economic and political justifications warrant it. Perhaps such undertaking may be considered after the completion of the current Seven-Year Plan.

The great rivers of the Soviet Union facilitate utilization of cheap hydroelectric power. Potential capacity of rivers for energy is estimated at 3,690 billion kilowatt hours. The main source of this energy is still mineral fuels. For example, in 1958 the total output of kilowatt-hours amounted to 233 billion, including 46 billion, or about 20 per cent, from hydroelectric installations. Nevertheless, in general, hydroelectric energy of the USSR has expanded at much faster rates than thermoelectric power. In 1940 the total electric power base of the Soviets was calculated at 11.2 million kilowatts and in 1958 it was increased to 53 million kilowatts, whereas during the same period of time, hydroelectric energy has expanded from 1.6 million killowatts to 10.8 million. It is expected that by 1965 Soviet hydroelectric energy will reach 500 to 520 billion kilowatt hours. However, 1959-65 plans call for the construction of cheaper thermoelectric facilities requiring less investment and yielding more rapid turnover of capital than for hydroelectric plants.

During the 1959-65 period, it is planned to unite the Kuybyshev and Stalingrad hydroelectric plants with the existing power systems in the Central Industrial Region and the Urals. The Kuybyshev hydroelectric power is currently transmitted to Moscow, some 560 miles away, and a lesser distance to the Urals. It is also planned to link the Stalingrad hydroelectric power with existing power systems of the south—that is, with Dnieper, Donbass, and Rostov-on-Don systems. The Soviets anticipate eventually creating a single united system for the European part of the USSR to supply power to new and yet unexploited areas lacking cheap electric energy for their development. In addition, a new energy system is to be formed in Central Siberia—a system from the Urals to Irkutsk—which would facilitate opening up the enormous resources of Western and Eastern Siberia and of the northern Kazakh SSR. Then it is planned that ultimately all these power systems may be merged into a single power energy system for the entire industrial parts of the USSR, covering the European part of the USSR, lower Siberia, and the upper part of Central Asia. This is to be a single grid power system merging all hydroelectric and thermal power plants. Because of the dispersion of industries in regions beyond Lake Baikal and in the lower part of Central Asia, these regions are excluded from this system.

## Bibliography—Chapter 1

[1] *Narodnoye Khozaystov SSSR v 1958 Godu,* Moscow, 1959, pp. 11-18, 38, 344; *Narodnoye Khozaystvo RSFSR v 1958 Godu,* Moscow, 1959, pp. 37, 48.

[2] *Planovoye Khozaystvo,* No. 4, 1955, p. 62.

[3] *Narodnoye Khozaystvo SSSR v 1958 Godu,* Moscow, 1959, pp. 386-393, 438-440.

[4] *Geograficheskiy Atlas SSSR,* Moscow, 1954, p. 65.

[5] *Ibid.,* p. 66.

[6] Antropov, P. Ya., *Perspektivy Osvoeniya Prirodnykh Bogatstv SSSR,* Moscow, 1959, pp. 25-33; Budnitskiy, I. M., *Ekonomika Ugol'noy Promyshlennosti SSSR,* Moscow, 1959, pp. 29, 30, 49.

[7] Antropov, *op. cit.,* pp. 39-40.

# CHAPTER 2

# Population and the Labor Force

∿∿∿∿∿∿∿∿∿∿∿∿∿∿∿∿∿∿∿∿∿∿∿∿∿∿∿∿∿∿∿∿∿∿

## INTRODUCTION

The population of the USSR may be considered as its most important economic feature. In a planned economy the skills of the people, their gross number, and geographic distribution must be related to the natural resources of the country in order to attain the economic goals desired. The growth of the population, as well as industrial development rests on the proper combination of people and resources by the planners. There is a direct relationship between population and the principles of non-proportional return. The Soviet Union, rich in natural resources, will grow in proportion to the effort it makes and ability it has to exploit these resources.

The growth of Soviet population came about as a result of several factors. On one hand the iron curtain created by the Soviets prevented mass emigration to other countries. On the other hand the Russian people were always restless and moved about within their own boundaries or to conquered regions. These factors were supplemented by the natural increase, that is, excess of births over deaths, and annexation of other populated regions.

However, the growth was erratic. At the time when the Soviets were established, the Civil War caused a considerable reduction in population. At the end of the Civil War and with the establishment of somewhat normal conditions, the rate of growth increased, only to be reduced during the hunger period of the early 1920's. This led to socio-economic adjustments, the creation of the New Economic Policy (NEP), and again the rate of population growth increased. Then came the period of brutal agricultural collectivization in the 1930's when the rate of growth fell below what it had been during the brief NEP period.

With the cessation of the upheaval of collectivization, the Soviet population increased rapidly, only to be checked by World War II. The second World War caused not only a decline in the rate of growth in the regions occupied by Germans, but also a decline in the total population. The 1950 figure was still below what had been reported for 1940. However, after 1950 the Soviets enjoyed peace and an increased volume of goods and services. Population growth was again on the increase. The annexation of populated regions in the West and in the East prior to and following the war boosted the Soviet population.

Within present borders, Soviet population has increased from 152.2 million in the peaceful year of 1913 to 208.8 million in 1959, an increase of 56.6 million. During the last 45 years and despite wars and socio-economic maladjustments, Soviet population increased at an average annual rate of some 1.2 million people.

Generally speaking, the Soviet Union cannot be considered "over-populated" in relation to its resources. There are still unknown and un-exploited resources which can be utilized to support a much larger popu-lation, provided these resources can be economically developed. In fact, Khrushchev in 1955 claimed that economically available resources can easily support a population of 300 million. Most likely this was a pre-tentious statement, since he did not mention how rapidly these resources might be developed in order to encourage an increasing rate of popula-tion growth. Nevertheless, claimed natural resources indicate that a much larger population can be supported without lowering the present standard of living.

An estimate of the size of the population can be obtained by several methods. The most popular method is, of course, the population census. Another general method is the use of permanent registers of births, deaths, residence, employment, and other records. However, this type of coverage is incomplete and may have many deficiencies. A complete enumeration of the population is most desirable.

The first Soviet population census, taken in August 1920, revealed a total population of 134.2 million persons, but it was an incomplete census because of the absence of the White Russian Armed Forces and the civilian population of the Far East.[1] The second census, conducted in 1923, was designed to cover the urban population alone. The first com-plete enumeration taken under peacetime conditions was on December 17, 1926, and it is the best census known to the West. Another census was planned for 1933, but the plan was abandoned before the enumeration was started because of the nearness of the 1930 collectivization drive.

After the turmoil caused by collectivization subsided and internal migra-tion became more stable, the Soviets launched a new census accompanied by a great deal of nationwide fanfare on January 6, 1937. Census district offices were established in every region, enumerators were trained, propaganda machinery was set up to explain and to educate the people regarding this undertaking, and in a few days the count was completed. However, the results of this census have never been published and all schedules were destroyed. It was claimed by the Soviets that there were gross violations of basic demographic and statistical principles as well as the instructions approved by the government. It was officially proclaimed that the 1937 census was "defective" and the work of "enemies of the people." The real reason for rejection lies in the fact that it was still too close to the impact created by forceful collectivization to give any comfort to the Soviets. Nevertheless, some Western observers estimated the 1935 population at about 160 million and the 1937 population at about 166 million persons. [2] Soon after the 1937 fiasco, plans were laid for a new census under proper state control and on January 17, 1939 it was taken to correct the errors made in 1937. But unlike the 1926 census, the results of the 1939 enumeration were not published in complete form.

The published 1926 census revealed all detailed information, including military personnel. The results of the 1939 census were published for certain age and sex groups only and excluded military personnel. Although statistically the 1926-39 population increase was favorable to the Soviets while the territory remained the same, it may be said that this was a spurious increase, actually resulting from differences in coverage.

Between 1939 and 1956, the Soviets did not publish many reliable statistics on population. In 1956, however, a population estimate of 200.2 million was published along with other demographic data which will be discussed later. In January 1959, the Soviets took their first population census in the last 20 years. The organizational pattern of this census closely follows the pattern developed for the 1939 census. The purpose was to avoid the errors made in the 1937 census. Preliminary population figures and regional distributions of the 1959 census were published in *Izvestia* on May 10, 1959. The figure of 208.8 million for the total population was released at that time. The final publications of this census will consist of 400 volumes, each of 500 pages, to be released sometime in 1960. Despite such promises, it is not certain that these volumes will be made available to Western scholars. In this chapter the author attempts to present some preliminary population estimates to indicate the general magnitude of the figures to be expected from the 1959 census. Many of the base population estimates have been derived from the Campbell and Brackett article cited as source 2.

## TOTAL POPULATION

The history of Soviet population growth is a history of erratic changes. Both the domestic socio-economic adjustments and the violent conditions of wars caused fluctuations of an immeasurable character. Given such unstable conditions, the student of population finds its difficult to estimate population size with accuracy and confidence. Even a census of the population, however accurately it may be conducted, is still an estimate, for it is not made under laboratory conditions. The demographer is not alone with this problem. The planners in a centralized economy would be responsible for an imbalance between population distribution as compared with the resources if their population estimates were unreasonable.

Table 1—*Total Population* [3]

| Date | Millions |
|------|----------|
| 1920 | 134.2 |
| 1926 | 147.0 |
| 1930 | 155.0 |
| 1935 | 160.0 |
| 1939 | 192.6 |
| 1941 | 200.0 |
| 1947 | 175.0 |
| 1950 | 180.0 |
| 1955 | 195.9 |
| 1956 | 200.2 |
| 1959 | 208.8 |
| 1960 | 211.4-215.1 |
| 1965 | 225.4-237.0 |
| 1970 | 237.2-259.2 |
| 1976 | 250.4-285.3 |

The most rapid growth of the Soviet population took place between 1920 and 1930—between the end of the Civil War and the beginning of agricultural collectivization in 1930. The collectivization drive caused a decline in the rate of growth of the population. For example, during the ten-year period of 1920 to 1930 the average annual increase in population was about two million people, whereas during the five-year period of 1930 to 1935 it was only one million. The total population rose slowly after 1935 and the annual rate of growth appeared to have climbed to the 1920-30 level with an average annual increase of some two million.

The 1939 population census reported 170.6 million people in the Soviet Union. With the annexation of the Baltic states and parts of Poland,

Rumania and Finland, the total Soviet population increased by about 22 million. Thus, the 1939 population is estimated at 192.6 million, and at the beginning of World War II the Soviet population, within present territory, reached about 200 million.

The German attack on the USSR in June 1941 resulted in a drastic drop in population and by 1947 it had fallen to about 175 million. After the end of World War II there was again a gradual increase in the growth of the population, and by 1950 it reached approximately 180 million. According to Campbell and Brackett, the total Soviet population, if there had been no World War II, would have been 220 to 225 million in 1950. Thus, because of the ravages of war on human resources, the 1950 Soviet total population was 40 to 45 million less than it might have been.

During the war population losses occurred in three broad classifications: first, military losses consisting mostly of young men in prime reproductive ages; second, civilian losses caused by violence of the military activities; and third, civilian losses resulting from a scarcity of food, lack of adequate shelter facilities, and overwork.

The number of military losses is difficult to evaluate. The estimates cited range from seven to nine million. The figures on civilian losses due to military activities, which also includes slave labor, range from 10 to 18 million people. Since many young people were denied normal reproduction, it has been estimated that during the war from 9 to 15 million children were lost because they were never born. These figures indicate the magnitude of Soviet human loss during World War II, especially in men. Campbell and Brackett estimated that the sex ratio in 1940 was 92 men per 100 women: by 1950 there were only 87 men per 100 women. They estimated that among the men 30 to 39 years of age in 1950, hit hard by the war, the sex ratio was 60 men to 100 women. There always have been more women in the Soviet Union but World War II increased their percentage from 52 per cent of the total population in 1926 and 1939 to 55 per cent in 1959. By 1959 the sex ratio of the group under 32 years of age had already reached equality of 50 per cent. This suggests that disproportion of sexes lies in the group 32 years of age and above and this aging group contains more women than men. In this aspect of population distribution, the Soviet Union is not unlike the United States where there is a disproportionate number of women in all of the older age groups.

In May 1956, the Soviets published an official total population figure of 200.2 million, with little indication of the reliability of the figure. The figure was given without explicit definitions of the groups which comprised the total. It was assumed, however, that the estimate was based on a population register including the recording of births, deaths, and residence, along with other items. Even with strict control, registrations of this type cannot in themselves provide complete or accurate data. For this reason many Western and Soviet students of population feel that the population figure of only 200.2 million in 1956 was an underestimate. Difficulty in estimating the post-war Soviet population lies in the fact that after World War II the USSR had acquired new territory located in East Prussia (Kaliningrad), the former Japanese possessions in the East (Southern Sakhalin and the Kurile Islands) ; also there were some minor adjustments in the Western borders of the USSR. However, if the official Soviet population of 200.2 million for 1956 is underestimated by about 3 million, it can be assumed that a difference of this small magnitude would have no great effect on conclusions drawn. Likewise, the 1959 preliminary census figure of 208.8 million will no doubt be adjusted upward when final tabulations are available.

Campbell and Brackett have accepted the official total population of 200.2 million for 1956 as a base for their own estimates of succeeding years. Using four different assumptions for rate of growth, they estimated the 1957 population at 202.3 million as the lowest projection, 202.4 million for the next projection, and 202.6 million and 202.9 million for the highest projections. It is interesting that the 1957 Soviet estimated population was 203 million.[4] This figure was derived by adjusting the 1956 estimate of 200.2 million. Still another Soviet source states that in 1957 the total Soviet population increased by "almost" 10,000 people every 24 hours.[5] In other words, the 1957 annual increase was about 3.6 million people or at the annual rate of 1.75 per cent. By using this annual rate of increase the 1959 total population may be estimated at 210.2 million. This makes the official 1959 preliminary figure of 208.8 million short by about 1.4 million. While this small difference is not significant, it strongly suggests that the 1959 figure as announced by the Soviets in May 1959 is somewhat low. In fact, Khrushchev in his report to the USSR Supreme Soviet on January 15, 1960 stated that at the beginning of 1960 the population was more than 212 million, an increase of 3.66 million during 1959.

As may be noted, Campbell and Brackett's total Soviet population as of January 1959 has been estimated in the range of 208.4 million to 210.9 million, depending on the growth rate assumed. This makes the preliminary Soviet total population of 208.8 million within the range of four estimates but somewhat closer to the lower limit.

Long-range population forecasts are dependent on the ability to project such variable components as fertility and mortality. Even with a thorough knowledge of historical trends, the job becomes difficult and complex. Cultural and economic development of the Soviet Union is rapidly expanding. Assuming that there are no wars or revolutions, the Soviet

FIGURE 1—*Estimates and Projections of the Total Population: 1939 to 1976*

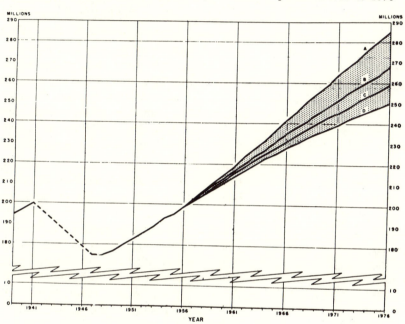

population will grow rapidly. Aided by an improving standard of living, better medical care, and stability of the economy, the estimates of growth as reflected in the projections prepared by Campbell and Brackett present a reliable picture of what can be expected in the future.

## POPULATION BY REGION

If we examine the distribution of the Soviet population by region, it will be noted that between 1939 and 1959 the Central Industrial Region of the European part of the RSFSR, White Russia, and Lithuania still have not recovered their prewar population. The greatest increase during these 20 years took place in Central Asia—the Uzbek, Kazakh, Kirghiz, Tadzhik, and Turkmen SSRs. These republics increased their population by 6.4 million, roughly 40 per cent. The Caucasus with its republics of Armenia,

Azerbaydzhan, and Georgia has boosted its population by only 1.4 million.

During World War II many workers and children were moved to these republics, notably in Central Asia, and after the end of the war a great many of them chose to remain there. Again, after the war, the

TABLE 2—*Population Distribution in the USSR by Region* [6]
1939-59
(in millions)

| Republic and Region | Population | | | Per cent of Total | | |
|---|---|---|---|---|---|---|
| | 1939 | 1956 | 1959 | 1939 | 1956 | 1959 |
| USSR: | 192.6 | 200.2 | 208.8 | 100.0 | 100.0 | 100.0 |
| RSFSR: | 108.4 | 113.2 | 117.5 | 56.3 | 56.6 | 56.3 |
| North and Northwest | 10.4 | 10.5 | 11.5 | 5.4 | 5.3 | 5.5 |
| Central | 47.4 | 43.4 | 43.2 | 24.6 | 21.7 | 20.7 |
| Volga | 9.8 | 10.0 | 10.9 | 5.1 | 5.0 | 5.2 |
| Northern Caucasus | 10.6 | 11.0 | 11.8 | 5.5 | 5.5 | 5.7 |
| Urals | 12.5 | 15.7 | 16.5 | 6.5 | 7.8 | 7.9 |
| Western Siberia | 9.9 | 11.8 | 12.3 | 5.1 | 5.9 | 5.9 |
| Eastern Siberia | 5.3 | 6.5 | 7.0 | 2.7 | 3.3 | 3.4 |
| Far East | 2.6 | 4.3 | 4.3 | 1.3 | 2.2 | 2.0 |
| Ukraine | 41.8 | 40.6 | 41.9 | 21.7 | 20.3 | 20.1 |
| White Russia | 9.2 | 8.0 | 8.1 | 4.8 | 4.0 | 3.9 |
| Uzbek | 6.3 | 7.3 | 8.1 | 3.3 | 3.7 | 3.9 |
| Kazakh | 6.1 | 8.5 | 9.3 | 3.2 | 4.2 | 4.4 |
| Georgia | 3.6 | 4.0 | 4.0 | 1.9 | 2.0 | 1.9 |
| Azerbaydzhan | 3.2 | 3.4 | 3.7 | 1.7 | 1.7 | 1.8 |
| Lithuania | 2.9 | 2.7 | 2.7 | 1.5 | 1.3 | 1.3 |
| Moldavia | 2.5 | 2.7 | 2.9 | 1.3 | 1.3 | 1.4 |
| Latvia | 1.9 | 2.0 | 2.1 | 1.0 | 1.0 | 1.0 |
| Kirghiz | 1.5 | 1.9 | 2.1 | 0.8 | 1.0 | 1.0 |
| Tadzhik | 1.5 | 1.8 | 2.0 | 0.8 | 0.9 | 1.0 |
| Armenia | 1.3 | 1.6 | 1.8 | 0.7 | 0.8 | 0.8 |
| Turkmen | 1.2 | 1.4 | 1.5 | 0.7 | 0.7 | 0.7 |
| Estonia | 1.0 | 1.1 | 1.2 | 0.5 | 0.6 | 0.5 |

Soviets laid great emphasis on the development of newly discovered natural resources and expanded agricultural activities in Asia while regions which had been under German occupation were still in the process of reconstruction. With greater exploitation of natural resources in Central Asia, the Urals, and Siberia, the Soviets encouraged workers and their families to remain there and encouraged others to migrate there.

The most densely populated areas in the Soviet Union are in its European region, which includes a part of the RSFSR, the Ukraine, White Russia, Moldavia, and the Baltic states. At the beginning of 1959, about 65 per cent of the total Soviet population lived in these regions. However, one of the most significant facts is that between 1939 and 1959 the Eastern regions of the USSR comprising the Urals and Siberia have increased their total population by approximately 9.8 million, while the European parts of the RSFSR, although still densely populated, decreased in population by 0.7 million. This indicates that migration to the Eastern parts of the USSR is a widespread movement involving all republics within the Union.

## URBAN POPULATION

In the main, urbanization in the Soviet Union indicates a degree of industrialization with the village being the main source of factory labor for the city. Between 1926 and 1939, the Soviet Union experienced a rapid industrial development and also inflicted a crushing blow to small independent peasants who refused to join the collective farms. During the same period the percentage of urban to total population rose from 18 in 1926 to 33 in January 1939, or in increase of 29.8 million persons, about 2.5 million annually. During the period covering September 1939 to August 1940, with the occupation of the Baltic states, the western parts of the Ukraine, Moldavia, and some areas in Eastern Poland and Karelia, the Soviet urban population increased by 4.5 million while nearly 80 per cent of the total increase was made up of rural population. As a result, the proportion of urban population declined from 33 per cent at the beginning of 1939 to 32 per cent in the middle of 1940.

Between 1939 and 1959, the urban population showed a real increase, totalling 39 million, or an average annual increase of almost two million. By 1959, the per cent of the population which was urban rose to 48 against 33 per cent in 1939.

During the last 20 years the greatest increase in urban population occurred in the Central Industrial Region, the Ukraine, the Urals, Western Siberia, the Volga Region, and the Kazakh SSR. Other republics and regions also increased their urban population. The Kazakh, Uzbek, Kirghiz, Tadzhik and Turkmen SSRs showed an increase in urban population of about 4.7 million people while the constituent republics in the Caucasus increased by only 1.7 million.

The Soviet urban population consists of people residing in cities, towns, and settlements classified as town-type settlements. Town-type settlements

Table 3—*Urban-Rural Distribution of Population
in the USSR by Region* [7]
(in millions)

| Republic and Region | Urban Population | | Rural Population | | Per cent of Urban Population to Total | |
|---|---|---|---|---|---|---|
| | 1939 | 1959 | 1939 | 1959 | 1939 | 1959 |
| USSR: | 60.7 | 99.8 | 131.9 | 109.0 | 32 | 48 |
| RSFSR: | 36.1 | 61.5 | 72.3 | 56.0 | 33 | 52 |
| North and Northwest | 5.3 | 7.4 | 5.1 | 4.1 | 51 | 64 |
| Central | 14.5 | 21.0 | 32.9 | 22.1 | 31 | 49 |
| Volga | 2.9 | 5.5 | 6.9 | 5.4 | 30 | 50 |
| Northern Caucasus | 3.1 | 5.0 | 7.5 | 6.8 | 30 | 42 |
| Urals | 4.7 | 9.8 | 7.8 | 6.7 | 38 | 59 |
| Western Siberia | 2.6 | 6.0 | 7.3 | 6.2 | 26 | 49 |
| Eastern Siberia | 1.8 | 3.7 | 3.4 | 3.3 | 34 | 53 |
| Far East | 1.2 | 3.0 | 1.3 | 1.3 | 46 | 70 |
| Ukraine | 13.8 | 19.1 | 28.0 | 22.8 | 34 | 46 |
| White Russia | 1.8 | 2.5 | 7.4 | 5.6 | 21 | 31 |
| Uzbek | 1.5 | 2.7 | 4.9 | 5.4 | 23 | 34 |
| Kazakh | 1.7 | 4.1 | 4.4 | 5.2 | 28 | 44 |
| Georgia | 1.1 | 1.7 | 2.5 | 2.3 | 30 | 42 |
| Azerbaydzhan | 1.2 | 1.8 | 2.0 | 1.9 | 36 | 48 |
| Lithuania | 0.7 | 1.0 | 2.2 | 1.7 | 23 | 39 |
| Moldavia | 0.5 | 0.6 | 2.0 | 2.2 | 13 | 22 |
| Latvia | 0.7 | 1.2 | 1.2 | 0.9 | 35 | 56 |
| Kirghiz | 0.3 | 0.7 | 1.2 | 1.4 | 19 | 34 |
| Tadzhik | 0.2 | 0.6 | 1.2 | 1.3 | 17 | 33 |
| Armenia | 0.4 | 0.9 | 0.9 | 0.9 | 29 | 50 |
| Turkmen | 0.4 | 0.7 | 0.8 | 0.8 | 33 | 46 |
| Estonia | 0.4 | 0.7 | 0.7 | 0.5 | 34 | 56 |

are those which have an adult population of not less than 1,000 persons and who derive not more than 25 per cent of their income from agricultural occupation.[8] These settlements comprise workers' residential areas attached to nearby cities, towns, or industrial enterprises located in rural areas, and summer residential settlements.[9]

Table 4—*Number of Urban Settlements by Type* [10]

| Type | Beginning of the year of | | | |
|---|---|---|---|---|
| | 1941 | 1955 | 1956 | 1959 |
| Cities and towns | 1,241 | 1,543 | 1,569 | 1,694 |
| Town-type settlements | 1,711 | 2,441 | 2,422 | 2,922 |

Between 1941 and 1959 the Soviets created 453 new cities and towns, but at the same time the number of town-type settlements was increased by 1,211. In 1939, the Soviet urban population comprised 60.7 million residents, of whom only 15.2 per cent were living in town-type settlements; in 1959 this percentage became 17.3 per cent. Many of these settlements are actually suburbs of large industrial centers such as those found around Moscow, Leningrad, and other metropolitan cities and industrial centers.

TABLE 5—*Distribution of Urban Population by Size of Settlements,* [11] *as of January 1959*

| Size of Settlement | Number of Settlements | Total Population (in millions) |
|---|---|---|
| Urban, total persons | 4,616 | 99.8 |
| Less than 10,000 | 3,024 | 14.3 |
| 10,000 - 20,000 | 810 | 11.3 |
| 20,000 - 50,000 | 483 | 15.1 |
| 50,000 - 100,000 | 151 | 10.6 |
| 100,000 - 500,000 | 123 | 24.4 |
| Over 500,000 | 25 | 24.1 |
| Cities and towns, total | 1,694 | 82.6 |
| Less than 10,000 | 506 | 2.9 |
| 10,000 - 20,000 | 440 | 6.4 |
| 20,000 - 50,000 | 449 | 14.2 |
| 50,000 - 100,000 | 151 | 10.6 |
| 100,000 - 500,000 | 123 | 24.4 |
| Over 500,000 | 25 | 24.1 |
| Town-type settlements, total | 2,922 | 17.2 |
| Less than 10,000 | 2,518 | 11.4 |
| 10,000 - 20,000 | 370 | 4.9 |
| Over 20,000 | 34 | 0.9 |

In 1959, 48.6 per cent of the Soviet urban population was concentrated in settlements of 100,000 persons and over. However, there were 25 cities of over 500,000 persons, with a total population for these cities of 24 million. Most of the town-type settlements are of small size (under 10,000 residents).

The most significant population increase with concentration of urban centers between 1939 and 1959 was in the eastern parts of the RSFSR (Urals, Western and Eastern Siberia, the Far East). The proportion of the total urban population in places of 100,000 persons or more living in the eastern parts of the RSFSR increased from 16 per cent in 1939 to 22 per cent in 1959. During the same period, the urban population living in centers of 100,000 persons and over in the Ukrainian SSR as well as in other regions decreased proportionately. In the main, during this period there was a noticeable shift in the urban population living in centers of 100,000 persons and over, with most of this shift resulting in a favorable balance for the eastern parts of the Soviet Union.

The largest segment of the urban population residing in cities with a population of 100,000 and over in 1959 was found in the European parts of the RSFSR, with about 40 per cent concentrated within a radius of 200 miles of Moscow.

Sprawling large cities in the USSR present a problem familiar in modern industrial centers elsewhere. As the population in the city increases, existing transportation facilities become overloaded, water supply for industry and people becomes scarcer, sewer systems often become inadequate, and housing and school construction never satisfy the need. As new housing facilities are built, decaying old houses and buildings require more and more attention and gradually become slums right before the eyes of the Soviet citizenry. Russians are desperately trying to relieve these conditions by building vertically in the cities and horizontally in the suburbs. For example, the city of Leningrad proper has a total population of 3.3 million of which some 400,000 people who are working in Leningrad's industries and offices reside in the suburbs. The city of Baku had to find dwellings outside its boundary for another 322,000 of its workers and their families. The outer fringes of many large industrial centers are made up of suburbs where sanitary conditions, schoolrooms, and other facilities are not as good as in cities.

### RURAL POPULATION

Between 1939 and 1959 the Soviet rural population declined from 131.9 million to 109 million, a reduction of 17.4 per cent. Khrushchev, in his speech of February 7, 1955, stated that during the 1950-54 period over nine million rural people migrated to the cities, about 1.8 million annually, whereas between 1939 and 1959 the rural population declined by 22.9 million. Based on the 1950-54 average rate of migration, 62 per cent of the total rural population decline during the 20-year period is concentrated in the period beginning with 1950. This decline in rural population is expected to continue up to 1975. Reasons for the decline are the need for an industrial labor force for the expanding economy, and the increased productivity of farm labor. In 1956 the Soviet agricultural labor force represented about 46 per cent of the total labor force against eight per cent in the United States. It is obvious that the Soviets have great opportunities to increase agricultural productivity and to reduce the farm population, provided there are other job opportunities for it. Such relocation of employment cannot be achieved rapidly, and Soviet planners are aware of this.

During the same 20 years, all regions except the Uzbek, Kazakh, Kirghiz, Tadzhik, and Moldavian SSRs lost rural population. The increase in rural population in these republics amounts to 1.8 million persons whereas the total increase was 6.6 million. The greatest increase in rural population was in the Kazakh SSR, amounting to 800,000 persons, and 500,000 persons in the Uzbek SSR. It is also interesting that during this period the Armanian SSR, Turkmen SSR, and Far East did not expand their rural population. In Western Siberia, even though large areas of virgin and unused lands are being plowed now, the rural population decreased by 1.1 million between 1939 and 1959. The figures show a shift to urban centers of 3.4 million during the same period. The excess of rural population in some areas in 1959 as compared with 1939 is due to agricultural expansion after 1939, especially during the war and postwar periods. This was most evident on irrigated lands of Central Asia.

The Soviet rural population includes all those persons who are actively participating in agricultural activities and those who are living in rural areas but deriving their livelihood from other sources. Out of 113.8 million in 1956, about 82 million were members of collective farms, rural handicraft workers organized into cooperatives, and their families. The number of independent peasants and non-cooperative handicraft workers with their families represented about a million.[12] Therefore, in 1956 approximately 30.2 million persons residing in rural areas were engaged in occupations other than those mentioned above. These were persons deriving their income from employment on the state farms, machine tractor stations (MTS), forestry, and soil conservation. Also included were the village intelligentsia, those who derive their livelihood from hunting, fishing, or part-time employment in urban centers, and those simply depending on other means of financial support.

## LABOR FORCE

Labor in the economic sense includes all human efforts, either physical or mental, which contribute to the production of goods and services. Thus, theoretically, the demand for labor arises because of its use in connection with other factors of production. When production of goods and services is increasing, the labor force expands also, and this state of affairs may be used as an indication of the welfare of the country and the potential for expansion of the labor force within a given total population. It is for this reason that the size of the total population is important as a factor in determining how large the labor force can be.

In the Soviet Union, all able-bodied persons, excluding small groups of independent peasants and handicrafters, students, aged persons, domestic servants, and some other minor groups, are employed by the State. Unlike the workers on state farms, members of collective farms cannot legally be considered as state workers since they derive their income from the proceeds of their work, and because they are allowed to keep small individual enterprises on their tiny plots of land. However, most of their income is derived from their relationship with the State, which is the chief purchaser of farm products. The possession of their individual plots depends upon the grace of the State. For this reason, peasants on collective farms must be included with the rest of the people working for the State, even though they do not receive regular wages, as do the other state employees.

## STATE-EMPLOYED LABOR FORCE BY REPUBLIC

This section, in the main, is confined to a discussion of the labor force employed by the State, excluding members of collective farms, members of industrial cooperatives, non-cooperative handicraft workers, independent peasants, and all others engaged by small enterprises or working as domestic servants.

In 1940 about 15.6 per cent of the total Soviet population was directly employed by the State. With the beginning of World War II, the 1940 state employment of some 31.2 million declined to 18.5 million by 1942, a reduction of 12.7 million. The impact of World War II caused a decline not only in the number of workers but also in the quality of the labor force. New and inexperienced recruits boosted the 1945 total number to 28.3 million, still short of the 1940 number by 2.9 million. At the end of the war the state employment was short by almost four million as compared with 1940. Even the agricultural labor force in 1946 had 29 per cent fewer able-bodied workers than in 1940.

World War II, of course, had the greatest impact upon persons of working age, 15 to 59 years. In 1940 this group numbered about 113 million, but only 112 million in 1950. At the same time the group of state employees increased by 7.7 million persons. This increase, in the main, came from the members of the Armed Forces who were reluctant to go back to the farms. For this reason, the 1949 number of able-bodied farm workers was still under the 1940 level. However, those born during 1935 to 1940 brought the working age population in 1956 to about 127 million. Thus, between 1950 and 1956 the working age group of 15 to 59 years was increased by some 15 million persons, and during the same period state employment increased by about 2.1 million and the scarcity of able-bodied farm workers was relieved. In 1959 the state employment numbered 54.5 million persons.

TABLE 6—*Average Annual State-Employed Labor Force by Republic* [13]
(in thousands)

| Republic | 1940 | 1950 | 1955 | 1956 | 1958 |
|---|---|---|---|---|---|
| USSR — total | 31,906 | 38,895 | 48,380 | 50,537 | 54,600 |
| RSFSR | 20,778 | 26,554 | 31,614 | 32,838 | 35,054 |
| Ukraine | 6,202 | 6,926 | 8,352 | 9,790 | 9,354 |
| White Russia | 1,062 | 999 | 1,237 | 1,316 | 1,490 |
| Uzbek | 695 | 852 | 1,057 | 1,102 | 1,361 |
| Kazakh | 915 | 1,461 | 2,236 | 2,186 | 2,598 |
| Georgia | 454 | 623 | 717 | 749 | 822 |
| Azerbaydzhan | 456 | 568 | 602 | 628 | 669 |
| Lithuania | 187 | 338 | 461 | 494 | 559 |
| Moldavia | 95 | 262 | 348 | 357 | 379 |
| Latvia | 264 | 442 | 534 | 576 | 644 |
| Kirghiz | 165 | 249 | 308 | 321 | 364 |
| Tadzhik | 139 | 174 | 232 | 248 | 275 |
| Armenia | 142 | 234 | 291 | 310 | 361 |
| Turkmen | 173 | 206 | 245 | 255 | 271 |
| Estonia | 179 | 289 | 346 | 367 | 399 |

As a result of the Civil War, collectivization, and other socio-economic maladjustments, the age group 60 years and over was small in 1940. As a group of least resistance to the hardships of the war, this group at the end of the war reduced its number from about 13 million to 12.4 million. But by 1956 their number increased to 15.2 million and under peaceful conditions and higher standard of living this group is expected to grow more rapidly. In fact the 1959 census indicates that there are more aged women than men, and the unbalanced sex ratio at ages over 60 in favor of the women indicates that the pattern for the Soviet Union is much like that of the United States.

The greatest concentration of state employment is in the three largest constituent republics: the RSFSR, Ukraine, and Kazakh. In 1958 they employed about 86 per cent of the total state employees. Although the distribution of state employment among constituent republics is not uniform because of the planned economy, there is a close correlation between the total population and the number of state workers. This is true for each republic and the central government of the USSR.

An analysis of individual republics reveals that during the 1940-58 period, the smallest increase in state employment occurred in White Russia—about 40 per cent. This republic was hard hit by World War II. Many of its plants, factories, and other industrial installations were destroyed or taken to Germany. Some of its plants and establishments were evacuated by the Russians themselves before the German occupation. Many Soviet citizens of working age migrated to other parts of the Soviet Union, perished during the war or were taken to Germany. These factors, aggravated by the severe drought of 1946, caused this republic to have a difficult and prolonged postwar recovery and rehabilitation period. On the other hand, Moldavia, which in 1940 was a more intensely agricultural republic than White Russia, had rapidly expanded its employment in state enterprises by 1958. A large share of this employment was being concentrated in state farms and in other state agricultural enterprises.

The greatest expansion in state employment during the 1940-58 period took place in the republics in Central Asia, especially in the Kazakh SSR. The Baltic republics, comprising Lithuania, Latvia, and Estonia, increased their State employment by 972,000 persons in the 1940-58 period. In 1940 these republics were still in the process of reorganization of their economics after the Soviets had occupied them in August 1940. The Caucasian republics of Georgia, Azerbaydzhan, and Armenia had increased their state employment during the 1940-58 period by about 76 per cent.

## AGRICULTURAL LABOR FORCE

Agricultural production in the Soviet Union is carried on not only by the collective and state farms but also by state organizations, enterprises, experiment stations, and non-agricultural workers and employees. A part of the total farm labor force which in the United States would normally be classified as agricultural workers, in the Soviet Union is grouped in the industrial labor forces. This includes such persons as employees of the state farms. Again, there are persons who are not permanent members of any farming organization, yet reside in rural areas. These individuals frequently work in the fields with the regular farm workers, especially during the heavy and intensive farming operations of planting and harvesting of the crops. In addition, many farming regions depend upon a seasonal farm labor force available from nearby urban centers. These seasonal farm workers are made up of housewives, industrial workers, office employees, school children and even members of the Armed Forces.

TABLE 7—*Average Annual Agricultural Labor Force* [14]
(*in thousands*)

| Category | 1940 | 1950 | 1955 | 1956 | 1958 |
|---|---|---|---|---|---|
| Total | 43,402 | 33,700 | 41,797 | 41,949 | 40,988 |
| Collective farms and household plots | 35,490 | 26,490 | 32,614 | 32,542 | 31,625 |
| State farms and supplementary enterprise | 1,760 | 2,425 | 2,832 | 2,949 | 4,627 |
| Machine Tractor Stations (Repair Machine Stations) | 530 | 678 | 3,065 | 2,880 | 1,262 |
| Independent peasants and non-cooperative handicrafts | 3,659 | 1,601 | 268 | 472 | 178 |
| Non-agricultural workers and employees work on their own small plots | 1,963 | 2,562 | 3,018 | 3,106 | 3,296 |

In 1940, of the total rural population of some 132 million in the Soviet Union, about 27 per cent of collectivized peasants were working in agriculture, excluding non-agricultural workers and employees working on their own plots. This is a strong indication of underemployment of the farm labor force. The surplus of the agricultural labor force in prewar years may be seen in the fact that in 1937 the number of able-bodied members of collective farms of 16 to 59 years of age was estimated at 34.7 million and the average annual requirement for work on collective farms and on the peasant's own plots was calculated at 26.7 million. At the same time it was shown that another 2.3 million able-bodied peasants were employed in nearby industrial enterprises and school enrollment in grades eight through ten was 373,000 persons. The surplus farm labor, therefore, was estimated at about 5.3 million.[15]

One of the reasons for the relatively low participation of the peasants in 1940 is that in that year the Baltic republics and the western parts of the Ukraine and White Russia were still in the process of being pooled into collective and state farms, whereas in 1958 very few independent peasants remained there. In 1958, the total rural population of the USSR was 109 million, of which 34 per cent, excluding non-agricultural workers, employees, and independent peasants, were working in agriculture, compared with 27 per cent in 1940. The 1939-58 period revealed a decline of total rural population and a reduction in the number of peasants on collective farms and among independent peasants and non-cooperative handicrafters, but, on the other hand, there was a remarkable increase in the state farms and the old machine tractor stations (MTS) and among non-agricultural workers and employees working on their own plots. To replace the lost farm labor on collective farms, the Soviets decided to strengthen the state farms and especially the MTS.

In 1953, without consulting the peasants on collective farms, by a stroke of the pen the Soviets decreed that all those members of the collective farms who had previously been employed as part-time workers in the MTS were to be transferred to permanent employment there. Since these people were skilled in the operation of mechanized equipment, it was no problem for them to find work with industrial enterprises where pay was higher. Consequently the machine tractor stations were frequently short of operators of farm machinery when they were most needed. In addition, various agriculture specialists such as agronomists, livestock specialists, and veterinarians were also transferred from their non-agricultural occupations to machine tractor stations. This was a drastic process of freezing to the job, forced assignment without protest on the part of the workers. Within a few months, between 1952 and 1953, the personnel of the machine tractor stations thus had increased by 1.4 million.[16] By 1955, some two million members of collective farms were transferred to permanent work with MTS and about 29,000 agricultural specialists were forced to accept jobs with them.

Permanent employment in state farms during the 1950-58 period increased by 2.2 million, mainly because of the 1954 policy of organization of new state farms in the eastern virgin and unused lands. Between 1950 and 1956 the independent peasants and non-cooperative handicrafters, hard-pressed by heavy taxes and low income, were obliged to abandon their independence by joining either the industry or socialized agricultural sector. But with relaxation in taxes and in required State deliveries in 1956 they again gained ground, only to be reduced in number again by 1958.

Non-agricultural workers and employees working on their own plots are really part-time farmers, growing mainly truck-garden crops or perhaps having a cow or a few hogs. Their contribution to the total production of Soviet agricultural products is of considerable significance, for they not only satisfy their own demands but also sell their surplus products to others, thus relieving the demand on collective farms. In summarizing the total agricultural labor force non-agricultural workers working on their own plots are excluded. They are, however, included in other sectors.

In 1940, the rate of civilian participation in the labor force to total population was 35 per cent, whereas in 1958 it was 41 per cent. In 1940 this rate was low because of large military requirements for manpower

TABLE 8—*Summary of the Total Employable Labor Force in the Soviet Union (in thousands)*

| Sector | 1940 | 1950 | 1955 | 1956 | 1958 |
|---|---|---|---|---|---|
| Total: | 71,055 | 66,930 | 80,994 | 83,551 | 86,403 |
| Non-agricultural | 29,616 | 35,792 | 42,483 | 44,708 | 48,711 |
| Agricultural | 41,439 | 31,138 | 38,511 | 38,843 | 37,692 |

as preparedness for war became necessary. There were a large number of independent enterprises in the newly occupied regions and also a considerable number of involuntary laborers who were included in the total population but not in the statistics for the civilian labor force. In 1958 conditions were normalized as a result of the reduction in non-civilian, non-state employment, and the rate of participation in the labor force was increased. A comparison with the civilian labor force participation rate in the United States at the beginning of 1957, which was about 40 per cent, reveals the similarity between the two countries.

In 1950 the non-agricultural labor force was about seven million more than in 1940, but the agricultural labor force was ten million less. In 1950 the Soviet Union still felt the effect of the last war with respect to manpower, and its total labor force was about four million less than in 1940. In comparison with 1950, the 1958 non-agricultural labor force participation increased by 13 million, and the agricultural labor force by some 6.5 million, but was about four million less than the 1940 level. As a whole, the civilian labor force participation during the 1940-58 period increased by some 21 per cent whereas the total population increased by approximately nine per cent. Increase in the labor force with a slight increase in the total population came about by enrollment of a large number of women who were in a position to stay home in 1940.

In 1965 state employment is expected to reach 66 million, or an average annual increase for the 1958-65 period of 1.6 million. Based on the 1950-58 annual average increase in total population of 3.2 million, the expected increase in employment by 1965 does not seem to be unreasonable. However, there appears to be a discrepancy in the reasoning. While it is true that a large part of the increase in the total population after 1950 will be made up of children born during this period, they will not be available to join the labor force until well after 1960. According to Campbell and Brackett, the low birth rates and high death rates during the war and immediately after it reduced the number of children under 15 years of age from 68 million in 1940 to 56 million in 1950 and to only 57 million in 1956. In addition, there are indications that the planned 1959-65 increase in the labor force of 11.5 million will not be large enough to absorb all persons who are already available or will be ready for jobs on the labor market. Unless the Soviets are able to put into operation the new industrial enterprises which they are now building by 1965 as planned, the increased labor force will not be totally utilized, and considerable unemployment may result.

### SOURCES OF THE SKILLED LABOR FORCE

With expanding industrial production which started with the First Five-Year Plan (1928-32), the Soviet government found itself in a dilemma in obtaining additional industrial manpower to maintain its new plants and factories, move goods to points of consumption, and distribute all the goods and services produced by the State. The urban population was not able to satisfy the increasing demand for new factory workers and the only untapped labor reserves were found in the rural areas. The shortage of industrial labor was felt as early as the days of the Second Five-Year Plan (1933-37).

In 1939 Stalin called attention to the scarcity of industrial labor and, to relieve this condition, he proposed that the rural areas should provide at least 1,250,000 village youths annually to be trained in schools to become skilled factory workers. In accordance with his wishes, a decree was issued on October 2, 1940 to meet the growing need for expansion of the industrial labor force.[17] As a result of this decree, each chairman of a collective farm was instructed to select two boys of 14 to 15 years of age from every 100 members of both sexes residing on farms and to send them for training in schools established by the railroads. Here they were to be trained for two years in the repair work of railroad stock and the movement of railroad equipment on the track. In addition, another two boys, aged 16 to 17, were to be selected for training in various schools organized by factories and plants (FZO), where six months training was to be given to boys who qualified for industrial work. In addition, every town and city was instructed to supply students for these schools, with an annual quota to be fixed annually by the government.

Selection of these boys was arbitrary, and it created many hard feelings and emotional tensions in families. In many cases the yardstick for selection was the scholastic standards of the students. Poor students were most likely to be trained in a vocational skill rather than in a general educational program. Later on, when the scarcity of workers intensified, 15-year-old girls were brought into this training program for the first time during World War II.

With the beginning of the first postwar Five-Year Plan (1946-50) there was a great demand for all kinds of skilled workers urgently needed for reconstruction and rehabilitation of the war-torn Soviet economy. It was planned that by the end of 1950 the Soviet Union would have additional 21.6 million skilled and semi-skilled young people. The training which these young people were to receive in schools and on the job was designed to qualify them for better jobs or to keep them on their old jobs. The postwar scarcity of workers was so great and it created such a serious bottleneck in the rapid rehabilitation program that the Soviets decided to include boys up to 19 years of age in training for heavy industry in 1947. Criteria for selection were similar to those for younger boys. Upon successful completion of the training programs, all trainees were subject to assignment to jobs for a four-year period. Assignment to a job was extended to all young people upon graduation from colleges, universities, or labor reserve schools. Refusal to accept the assigned job resulted in harsh punishment, and in some cases even the death penalty was imposed. However, the labor reserve training program in 1947 was not intended to be the main means of training of the new industrial labor force. It was expected that after a period of stabilization, factories, plants, and other state establishments would train needed workers on the job. It was believed that by the end of 1950 young people of both sexes numbering 5.4 million would receive training by means of individual and group training methods, 2.3 million would be trained as tractor and combine operators, and 13.9 million young people would get on-the-job training. The labor reserve schools were to train 4.5 million people.

Thus, during the 1946-50 period, on-the-job training, theoretically, was regarded as the fastest means of obtaining more and better qualified industrial workers. Since 1950, however, emphasis has been placed on the labor reserve schools, which train workers for more complex equipment than was available during the period ending with World War II. The labor reserve schools were expanded and their training program was improved. In 1952 the training program in some of these schools for 16 to 17-year-old students was lengthened from six to ten months in order to include training in more than one trade or specialty. Beginning with the 1953-54 school year the standards were raised, and only graduates of the seventh-grade were accepted in industrial and mining schools. To qualify as a tractor driver and to be able to do some minor repairs, the training period was increased to one year. Thus, after 1950 all labor reserve schools were emphasizing diversified training programs.

By 1956 the labor reserve schools had more than 500 different courses. Some of the courses given during the 1951-55 period had been abandoned and new ones set up to meet the demand of advanced technology. With the increased mechanization and improved technology, it was planned that during the 1956-60 period the labor reserve schools expected to install 20,000 units of new metal-cutting and forging-pressing equipment for training purposes. At the same time, plans have been made to permit new trainees in the labor reserve schools with seventh-grade educations to be taught a trade and to receive secondary education at the same time.

The importance of the labor reserve schools is increasing. More and more attention is given to their activities, not only because they provide the new and young industrial workers but also because they offer opportunities for those young people who might fail in their studies in general educational institutions. The growing significance of labor reserve schools may be seen from the fact that in comparison with the 1951-55 period the 1956-60 period anticipated an increase of approximately 44 per cent in the number of students. This means that the share in the total training programs in the USSR for the labor reserve schools will be increased from 15-16 per cent during the 1951-55 period to 25-26 per cent at the end of 1960. During the 1956-60 period, it was expected that the number of labor reserve schools will be increased by 632 new establishments with not less than 90 per cent to be located in the eastern parts of the Soviet Union, where industrial expansion is now taking place. The 1959-65 plan anticipates a considerable expansion of these training schools.

Beginning with 1954, the Soviet Union launched a program of best utilization of its skilled labor force which at times conflicted with personal choice. This program may well be called, "Get out and start working!" For example, in 1954 the Ministry of Production of Consumer Goods transferred 15,000 of its administrative employees holding college and university degrees in technical and specialized fields to actual production and construction jobs. The Ministry for Foodstuffs transferred 20,000 such workers, and the Ministry of Non-Ferrous Metallurgy transferred 17,000.[18] This suggests that at present the usage of manpower in the Soviet Union is based on the worker's training and specialization rather than on his preference. It seems to indicate a considerable underutilization of trained manpower and a reluctance of trained workers to go to jobs where they are most needed. For example, in 1940 there were 110 engineers and technicians to every 1,000 workers in the USSR, but only 106 in 1950 and 108 in 1956.[19]

On-the-job training was devised at the time when labor reserves schools were organized, and its importance since 1950 has increased. This program serves as an incentive for all workers who wish to improve their qualifications or to secure new skills leading to better jobs. Generally, the on-the-job training program covers workers who are already employed or who were recently hired by enterprises or establishments. There is no loss of working time.

In addition to direct training courses for individuals and groups, correspondence courses dealing with a variety of subjects are organized to help the workers improve their skills and efficiency. On the whole, on-the-job training programs in the Soviet Union do not differ from those practiced by industry in the United States. The main purposes of such programs are to train workers how to do the job better and to create opportunities for factory and office workers to improve their efficiency and earning power.

The training programs by higher educational institutions have been expanding alongside the labor reserve schools and on-the-job training. These higher educational institutions consist of universities and specialized schools of equivalent standards (tekhnikums).

In its goal to build a skilled labor force, the Soviet government has developed an intensive and extensive training program for young men and women. Although not all of the trainees are capable of completing the training program, the annual average number who do finish is staggering.

In 1958 the graduating class of all higher educational institutions was 812,500 persons, and at the end of 1958 the Soviet Union employed 7,476,-000 persons graduated from these institutions.[20] This means that in 1958, 10.9 per cent of all employable specialists were available for new jobs. However, between 1957 and 1958 the number of employable specialists had increased by only 655,000 persons, while the 1958 graduating class consisted of 812,500 persons. Thus, 157,500 young specialists had to find other ways to utilize their talents. Perhaps a token number of them were able to enroll in post-graduate schools, but the majority of this surplus labor force faced keen competition for jobs with older graduates and were forced to accept less desirable work or work outside their fields.

It has been estimated that the total 1955 labor participation was about 81 million persons, of which 32 per cent were skilled workers including graduates from higher educational institutions who were employed by

Table 9—*Average Number of Graduate
Professional and Skilled Workers* [21]

| Training Agency | Number of Workers (in thousands) | | |
|---|---|---|---|
| | 1950 | 1955 | 1958 |
| Total: | 9,334.6 | 9,132.3 | 9,030.3 |
| Universities | 130.4 | 224.2 | 290.7 |
| Specialized schools (tekhnikums, etc.) | 255.7 | 311.9 | 521.8 |
| Labor reserve schools: | 678.5 | 372.2 | 652.5 |
| Technical schools | —— | 5.4 | 98.0 |
| Railroad, mining, and repair schools | 204.8 | 143.8 | 109.0 |
| Factory and mining schools | 473.7 | 198.0 | 178.0 |
| Agricultural mechanization schools: | 513.0 | 578.0 | 422.0 |
| Tractor drivers | 329.0 | 286.0 | 306.0 |
| Combine drivers and repairmen | 49.0 | 66.0 | 59.0 |
| On-the-job training: | 7,757.0 | 7,671.0 | 7,143.3 |
| New workers | 2,626.0 | 2,593.0 | 2,604.5 |
| Training for the new job | 5,038.0 | 4,978.0 | 4,438.8 |
| Training by factory schools | 93.0 | 100.0 | 100.0 |

the State in actual production processes, transportation, and trading. They represented workers of various skills and "know how"—what Russians call "productive" workers—amounting to 20 million. In 1955 labor reserves schools and agricultural mechanization schools trained 925,200 new workers, or approximately five per cent of the already existing number of skilled "productive" workers. These newly trained workers also were looking for better opportunities. But the total increase in state employment of all workers and employees during the 1954-55 period had been only 1.1 million. All this suggests that in 1955 these newly trained workers, like their comrades with new college diplomas, had a difficult time in finding jobs for which they were trained.

Assuming that all training programs for new workers either in the institutions of higher learning or in other establishments during the 1956-60 period should be at about nine million annually, as it was in 1950 through 1958, then by 1965 the Russians will train about 63 million young workers of various skills. The annual average increase in state employment during the 1959-65 period is estimated at 1.6 million persons, whereas current training programs qualified about nine million workers annually. In fact, at the present rate of training of young people from higher educational institutions, about 40 per cent of the total annual increase in the labor force as planned for the 1959-65 period should be filled by new college graduates. This suggests a very high degree of automation to be developed by 1965.

It is because of the slow rate of expansion in the total state employment on the one hand and the intensive training programs of young workers in large numbers on the other hand that a number of new social and economic problems for the Soviet Union can be expected. These conditions would create dislocation in opportunities for many workers and dissatisfaction among those who were not able to apply their training to improve their earning capacity. They would force new workers to accept less desirable jobs and would also create keen competition on the side of supply in the labor market. On the other hand, because of competition among workers and better training, labor efficiency should be improved and costs production should be reduced, with perhaps an increase in the real wage as well. There also should be a problem of at least partial unemployment. But by 1965 there should undoubtedly exist a Soviet labor force which will be better trained and more efficient in a variety of skills than in the past. Already the official annual output per worker in heavy industry between 1950 and 1958 has been increased by about 9.2 per cent and further increases at a reduced rate may well be expected by 1965. Also, this may be seen in the fact that between 1950 and 1955 the Soviets organized highly specialized technical schools, which in 1955 graduated 5,400 technicians, whereas in 1958 this figure was 98,000.[22] This is a new and real challenge to the West.

## WOMEN IN THE LABOR FORCE

Women in every industrialized country are regarded as an untapped labor reserve which can be drawn into the labor participation to meet a national emergency or to increase meager family incomes. In the past the policy of the Soviet Union toward women seemed one of encouragement to participate in labor both for political and economic reasons. The administration was interested in working women, not only as a source of additional manpower but also as an opening wedge in destroying conflicting traditions regarding employment. It was to their benefit to "unmask" the veiled women living behind boarded doors in Moslem Central Asia.

Equality of opportunity was widely publicized, and millions of women joined the labor force. Women are taking an active part in all phases of the Soviet economy. According to the latest information, they constitute 65 per cent of all garduates from the institutions of higher learning. Women comprise 76 per cent of all physicians and 70 per cent of all teachers, and about one-third of all Soviet engineers and technicians are women. Thus, women in the Soviet Union are an important factor in running the socialized economy even though many of them devote all of their time to their own families after a brief experience in professional fields.

It is true that in the USSR more women work than in any Western country, but their advancement to higher wage levels is limited and even in occupations where they make up the majority of the workers they are in a minority in better paid jobs. Thus the "equality of opportunity" about which the Soviets boast is nothing more than equality for the low paying jobs.

TABLE 10—*Per cent of Women in Total State Employment* [23]

| Industry | 1940 | 1950 | 1955 | 1956 | 1958 |
|---|---|---|---|---|---|
| Total: | 38 | 47 | 45 | 45 | 46 |
| Industry | 41 | 45 | 45 | 45 | 45 |
| Construction | 23 | 33 | 31 | 31 | 30 |
| Machine tractor stations | 11 | 16 | 9 | 7 | 7 |
| State farms and supplementary enterprises | 34 | 49 | 46 | 43 | 40 |
| Transportation and communication | 24 | 34 | 33 | 33 | 33 |
| Trade, procurement, supply | 38 | 52 | 58 | 59 | 66 |
| Public catering | 67 | 80 | 83 | 83 | 84 |
| Education | 58 | 67 | 68 | 67 | 69 |
| Health | 76 | 84 | 85 | 85 | 85 |
| State apparatus, public organizations, credit and insurance | 35 | 45 | 49 | 50 | 49 |

Between 1940 and 1950 the percentage of women employed by state enterprises and organizations increased by approximately 21 per cent. This percentage, however, was much higher during the war. In 1950 a large number of skilled and unskilled workers were required in reconstruction, rehabilitation, and expansion of the Soviet economy at a time when Soviets maintained large Armed Forces. Only women were available for the task. As a result of demobilization, after 1950, the participation rate of women in state employment declined somewhat, especially in the agricultural sector and in transportation and communication. The proportion of women in the industrial labor force remained the same, but in the field of services the share of the total increased considerably, especially in commerce and administration. Although the participation rate declined between 1950 and 1955, the actual number of women employed in 1955 was about 3.5 million more than in 1950, or about 36.8 per cent of the total increase. In 1958 approximately 1.2 million more women were employed than in 1940.

The work participation rate of women on collective farms is difficult to estimate. For example, in 1938 total participation of them was 52.7 per cent of the total, or about 18.7 million.[24] However, of this total 23.2 per cent worked up to 50 days a year, 19.9 per cent of them worked between 51 and 100 days a year, and only 16.3 per cent of the women worked between 101 and 300 days a year. In 1938, 1.6 million women who were able-bodied members of the collective farms did not participate at all in communal work on farms. In that year, utilization of women on the farms was not nearly as complete as that for men, for women contributed only 37 per cent of all working days recorded on collective farms With the intensified agricultural production programs on the collective farms, the total 1940 participation of women in the work increased to 54 per cent, and there were fewer women members of collective farms who did not work at least four months of the year. During World War II their participation swelled and by 1950 the percentage of women to the total number of persons working on collective farms became 64. Since that year there has been a gradual decline in their participation and by 1958 women working on the farms constituted 58 per cent of the total.[25]

Since 1955 the Soviets have begun to withdraw women from certain occupations, such as work underground. This was justified on the grounds that recent increases in the real wage were received by family wage earners. But the competitive conditions in the Soviet labor market lead one to believe that withdrawal of women was due to scarcity of jobs for newly trained workers. Since 1956 the Soviet policy toward women employed in state enterprises and organizations has been that of reducing the number of women in employment. Only highly trained women workers may compete with men for a job. This reduction of women in the labor force was real, and even recently printed pictures in the Soviet newspapers and journals showed groups of workers with fewer women workers than they did during or immediately after the war. The reduction of the women's labor force was the official Soviet policy in 1956. It was believed that since the real wage for workers and employees is on the upswing in Russia, and since the Soviet Union is rapidly increasing its skilled manpower, the need for an additional wage earner in the family no longer present, and more and more women remained at home.

Since 1958, however, many Soviet officials have indicated that women in industry have a definite and important role. It is assumed that the initial phases of anticipated automation may not require a large number of women for the construction of automatic machinery. When the construction process is over there may be a considerable increase in the need for women in the labor force to run the already constructed equipment. Thus, the policy of diverting women from employment to the home is temporary, since in the long run automation creates more jobs than it displaces, with the result that unskilled workers are absorbed as specialists.

## Chapter 2—Bibliography

[1] *Planovoye Khozaystvo,* No. 5, 1940, p. 12.

[2] *Memorandum No. 27,* by the United States Embassy in Moscow, August 18, 1939, and Arthur A. Campbell and James W. Brackett, *Estimates and Projections of the Population of the USSR: 1950 to 1976,* Foreign Manpower Research Office, Bureau of the Census, U. S. Department of Commerce, Washington, D. C., May 1959, p. 3. (Hereinafter referred to as Campbell and Brackett).

[3] *Vsesoyuznaya Peripis Naseleniya,* Moscow, 1958, p. 13, gives the 1920 total population. *Izvestia,* May 10, 1959 has the 1926 and 1959 total population figures. Figures for 1939 and 1956 are from Michael Roof and Frederick A. Leedy, *Population Redistribution in the Soviet Union, 1939-1956. Geographical Review,* Vol. XLIX, No. 2, April 1959, p. 212. All other figures from Campbell and Brackett, pp. 3, 24, 45.

[4] *Voprosy Truda v SSSR,* Moscow, 1958, p. 389.

[5] *Vsesoyuznaya Peripis Naseleniya,* op. cit., p. 4.

[6] Roof and Leedy, *op. cit.,* p. 212, and *Izvestia,* May 10, 1959.

[7] *Ibid.*

[8] Polyanskaya, G. N. and Ruskol, A. A., *Sovetskaye Zemel'noye Pravo,* Moscow, 1951, p. 135.

[9] *Spravochnik Profsoyuznogo Rabotnika,* Moscow, 1949, p. 608.

[10] *Narodnoye Khozaystvo SSSR,* Moscow, 1956, p. 26, and *Izvestia,* May 10, 1959.

[11] *Izvestia,* May 10, 1959.

[12] *Narodnoye Khozaystvo SSSR,* Moscow, 1956, p. 19.

[13] *Narodnoye Khozaystvo SSSR v 1956 Godu,* Moscow, 1957, p. 207; *Narodnoye Khozaystvo SSSR v 1958 Godu,* Moscow, 1959, p. 661.

[14] Derived from *Narodnoye Khozaystvo SSSR v 1956 Godu,* Moscow, 1957, pp. 202, 203; *Narodnoye Khozaystvo SSSR v 1958 Godu,* Moscow, 1959, pp. 654, 655.

[15] *Gosudarstvenniy Plan Razvitiya Narodnogo Khozaystva na 1938-1942,* Moscow, 1938, p. 109.

[16] *Izvestia,* January 31, 1954.

[17] Barker, G. R., *Soviet Labour,* Bulletin on Soviet Economic Development, No. 6, Series 2, June 1951, p. 1.

[18] *Pravda,* February 8, 1955.

[19] *Voprosy Truda v SSSR,* Moscow, 1958, p. 384.

[20] *Narodnoye Khozaystvo SSSR v 1958 Godu,* Moscow, 1959, p. 673.

[21] Derived from *Narodnoye Khozaystvo SSSR,* Moscow, 1956, p. 197, 198, 228; *Narodnoye Khozaystvo v 1958 Godu,* Moscow, 1959, pp. 692, 694, 696, 837.

[22] *Pravda,* December 27, 1955; *Narodnoye Khozaystvo SSSR v 1958 Godu,* Moscow, 1959, p. 692.

[23] *Narodnoye Khozaystvo SSSR v 1958 Godu,* Moscow, 1959, p. 664.

[24] *Problemy Ekonomiki,* No. 7, 1940, p. 119.

[25] Embassy of the USSR, *Press Department,* No. 120, Washington, D. C., March 7, 1960.

# CHAPTER 3

## Administrative Apparatus

### INTRODUCTION

The emphasis placed upon the interrelation of Communist ideology and practice in the Soviet State should not be underestimated. To Soviet leaders the only basic theory to be applied in the administration of their State is the "scientific" explanation of socio-economic phenomena first developed by Marx and Engels and subsequently interpreted by Lenin, Stalin and Khrushchev. It is upon this basic "scientific" Marxian philosophy and numerous pronouncements of Marxists that the present Soviet society has been built. However, since communism emphasizes ideology in political terms, it cannot be considered as pure economic theory leading to the formation of an economic society as the classical economists advocated. In other words, the Soviet society is of a structure more political than economic. Moreover, Soviet Communist Party represents also leadership for the economic life of the country and establishes a status of monopolized legality which in turn formulates the autocratic system of the proletarian dictatorship itself. Under these conditions, no single important political or economic question can be resolved without direction from the Party.

However, Soviet leaders do not expect Marxism to exist unqualified forever. While many of his basic postulates may remain true and workable, others may become obsolete with rapid changes effected by socio-economic forces and may require revision in emphasis and application, and hence new principles are discovered for dealing more effectively with new conditions. Speaking of Marxism and its adaptability to creation of a new Soviet State, Lenin said: [1]

> We do not at all look upon the theory of Marx as something finished and untouchable; to the contrary, we are convinced that it only laid down the cornerstone of that science which the Socialists must push forward in all directions if they do not want to remain behind life.

Thus, to Lenin and his followers, Marx was a sort of mason who "laid down the cornerstone" for a new society but left to his students not only interpretation of his philosophies in the light of new socio-economic environments, but also the changing of these environments. However, under normal conditions socio-economic conditions do not change rapidly, and when changes take place there is a lapse in time between the introduction of the change and the results of its application. Since the monolithic structure of the Party does not permit criticism of its philosophy by individuals, all interpretations must come from a few men at the top of the Party's hierarchy. In short, any socio-economic adjustments in the USSR are determined by the single person who happens to be the leader at the time. As leader, he becomes both philosopher for the Communist Party, interpreting Marxian theory in the light of current events, and manipulator of the Soviet socio-economic pattern. Such dictatorship, powerful as it is, depends on the personality of the dictator and the goals set by him for the society, creating, in turn, a political environment in which free discussion cannot be conducted. Hence, economic theory cannot be developed to fit the convictions of the majority. Since Marxism is a rigid thoretical system describing a fixed and dogmatic socio-economic condition of the past, as such it becomes a myth to present generations. Theoretical Marxism, with its emotional appeal to all underprivileged workers of the 19th century, can no longer stir millions of people to blind, passionate devotion to the cause.

Since workers in so-called capitalist societies are no longer oppressed, enjoy a higher standard of living than they did a century or even 50 years ago, and have in general considerably improved their lot, theoretical Marxism has lost its emotional appeal, its traditional logic, and its value. For these reasons, the Soviet leadership, of necessity, tends to become more flexible in interpretation in implementation of Marxian theory to existing socio-economic conditions. Instead of winning workers to their cause by calling on revolution, the Soviet leaders become more realistic and attempt to show the workers the superior efficiency of their system which expectedly would bring a still higher standard of living, economic stability and peace.

## KARL MARX (1818-1883)

Karl Marx, as a philosopher, interprets the causes of social behavior, its changes and developments, with bitter and emotional appeal to the workers who are exploited by the propertied classes. He calls passionately upon all workers of the world to unite against their oppressors and take the means of production away from the rich. He proposes a new distribution of wealth and describes the capitalist process from a historical view-point so revolutionary in approach that it establishes him in a separate class from other socialists.

Basically, Marx was a follower of classical economists and was influenced by Adam Smith (1723-1790) and especially by David Ricardo (1772-1823), whose labor theory of value he practically accepted. However, it was the theory of biological evolution described by Charles Darwin (1809-1882) that provided the basis for the Marxian interpretation of history. He fitted classical economics and Darwin's evolution processes into one broad, historical framework, describing classical capitalism as one stage of a process of economic development. It became a materialistic interpretation of history, in which economic factors determined the course of historical events.

There are three bases of Marxian analyses: the doctrine of class struggle, the theory of labor value, and the economic interpretation of history. The doctrine of class struggle calls upon united workers to take means of production from the owners by force. Since workers and propertied classes no longer participate in bloody contests for the ownership of means of production, but rather settle their differences by peaceful agreements, the doctrine of class struggle has become obsolete. The theory of labor value, although supporting Marx's theory of exploitation, was discarded as baseless with the development of the theory of marginal productivity of labor. But his interpretation of history, which has survived to our times, has become the major cornerstone of the Communist philosophy.

In general, the economic interpretation of history suggests that the modes of production in material life determine the general character of the economic, social, political, and spiritual fiber of a society. Any new, important discovery or innovation tends to alter the socio-economic behavior of mankind. To Marx, the feudalistic system of ownership, which he calls "thesis," led to the establishment of serfdom, or "antithesis" and then emerged into a higher form of economic system, capitalism, or "synthesis." By devising this historical or dialectical process, Marx clearly expected communism to be the end of the dialectical process, because of the elimination of class struggle. However, despite his expectation, the Marxian "thesis-antithesis-synthesis" analysis gives rise to the theory that since historical progress produces change, then it is reasonable to assume that communism will also be changed into new socio-economic structures unless historical processes as described by Marx will cease to yield to the forces of modes of production.

Marx had no thoeries of socialism or planning systems and he did not even speculate about how the emancipated means of production should be used by the new owners. Nevertheless, it is upon his analysis of economic processes that modern theories of an authoritarian state are based. But whereas Marx was basically a socialist philosopher, his followers in the Soviet union are socialists to only a limited extent, even in theory, since they have abandoned the principles of economic equality and economic democracy. The principles are in conflict with public ownership of means of production and centralized planning, as the Soviet leaders have realized.

## NIKOLAI LENIN (1870-1924)

Marx's doctrine, like the Bible, has many interpretations, and the most gifted student of Marx, according to the Russians, was Lenin, who became the empire builder. Lenin, like Marx, sought the destruction of capitalism. Both men leaned heavily upon the overinvestment theory. To Lenin, as to Marx, capitalism depends on profit to provide new capital investment. Formation of new capital investment must take place at an increasing rate because each new increment of capital increases the old investment of capital from which the rate of profit is calculated. But Lenin could not wait until capitalism would choke itself by overinvestment.

Once in power, Lenin set to organizing a new society. He required authority and organization at any cost and by every means. He had to organize a legislature to establish a Communist State—his ultimate goal. He had to set up a body of laws and a means of law enforcement. Above all, he had to form a running economy to feed, clothe, and shelter his new subjects. Whereas Marx believed that social change would come from within the workers themselves, Lenin thought they had to be pushed into socialism.

Lenin saw his mission as that of savior of the mud-logged working class wandering aimlessly in a socio-economic quagmire. If they could not see their way out, he and his followers, well-trained in the theories of Marx, knew how to save them: the Marxists, the prophets of a new life, could lead suffering mankind to a new life under communism. But since most of the workers were ignorant of the benefits of communism, the magic words had to be spelled out again and again.

Lenin's interpretation of Marxism was flexible, requiring daring imagination, and it was necessary for him to interpret Marxism in the light of existing socio-economic conditions which he inherited from the Tsar after World War I and the Civil War. He had to be yielding to promote unity and to preserve the newly created society. For example, Lenin's solution of agrarian questions was based on two principles. Lenin, like Marx, was for nationalization of all the land, but as an empire builder, he had to compromise on distribution of land among the peasants since the peasants were not yet ready for socialism. Again, Lenin's NEP of 1922-28 and distribution of land among peasants are well-known examples of his adaptability to existing economic conditions.

Lenin and his followers had no fixed idea of what the new socialist state would be like. They improvised methods without the aid of theories and hence made many costly blunders in terms of human suffering. Moreover, neither Lenin's driving power nor his faith in Marxism were the sole forces behind the success of the Bolshevik Revolution. Slow advancement of capitalism in Tsarist Russia paved the way from semifeudalism to socialism. Although the Russian intellectual awakening had occurred many decades prior to the Bolshevik Revolution, there was a gap in common unity between the comparatively few intellectuals and the masses. Lenin was able to fill this gap with promises of a better life for the people. Using the Marxian doctrine of class struggle as a tool in uniting the workers, he crushed the weak resistance of the opposition and with the support of the workers rose to power as the undisputed benefactor of the oppressed.

His genius as a builder of a new society cannot be overestimated. Without historical experience to guide him in changing from one economic form to another, he led his followers to an entirely new society. Since Marx did not develop a positive theory of authoritarian or centralized planning, Lenin was forced to interpret Marx's political pronouncements to economic ends to achieve his goals. These interpretations became known as the so-called "Marxism-Leninism" keys in guiding the newly-established socialistic state. Unlike Stalin, Lenin used many ideas expressed by Marx in the earlier days of his career when Marx was more of a humanitarian than in his later years.

In general, neither Marx nor Lenin had developed a theory of central planning. After 43 years in power, the Soviets still lack an economic theory of authoritarian planning. The intellectual environment for Soviet economists is not conducive to scientific inquiry; and, at best, they are too concerned with the practical problems of planning to develop theoretical generalizations. Hence, they have contributed little pure economic theory. Although progress in this direction is slow, there are evidences that since Stalin's death Soviet economists have begun to realize their inadequacy in theory and devote more of their efforts to filling this gap.

## JOSEPH STALIN (1879-1953)

After Lenin's death, Stalin became the ruler of the country by success-fully manipulating intrigues. The Civil War and foreign intervention were over, danger of counterrevolution had decreased, the economy was func-tioning more or less without interruption, and Stalin became an autocrat carrying out ideologies professed by Marx and Lenin. He did not con-tribute anything new intellectually to Marx's nor Lenin's ideas. True, he had his own kind of ability, maligned as it may have been, and he did show talent for some adjustments—often wrong-minded—to problems which served to keep him in power. He was a militant ruler, a tyrant feared by his subjects, and lonely and uncertain of his personal ability to hold the power he had. A man with less than high school education, he dis-trusted the intellectuals and Marxian theoreticians around him, yet be-cause of fear of his ruthless methods, he was made the source of all the knowledge under the sun by others. His opinions became unquestionable and beyond criticism. Once this trend started, it was encouraged by Stalin, and like a pregnancy, development of which cannot be retarded, the trend (cult of personality) gathered its volume until his death.

He was a man without the intellectual vision required of great social reformers and leaders. He believed in a status quo which he was ready to defend with forces already mastered, and only when it was absolutely necessary did Stalin make adjustments in socio-economic relations to preserve his own powers. Even the theory behind the bloody collectivization was developed for him while Lenin was still alive. The brutality of the collectivization as it was carried out is too well known to describe, but it reflected Stalin's lack of creative thinking. The idea of five-year plans was borrowed from Trotsky. In politics he came up with slogans like "socialism in one country" and "social-fascism" which ran counter to the train of Marxist-Leninist tradition. During World War II, Stalin was forced to deviate from his prewar goal of complete communism. But it occurred at a time when the Soviet economy was unbalanced and with masses ceasing to fear his iron-fisted rules and demanding new values to replace the old ones.

After the war Stalin solidified his position to the extent that he alone was given credit for the winning of the war, and then, in the main, he picked up his socio-economic targets, temporarily abandoned at the be-ginning of the war. Like an old and stubborn despot, he proceeded to put them into effect as if the war had not altered the old values, failing to recognize the impact the war had made on mankind. Although by this time his powers extended beyond Russia, Stalin was still basically an isolationist enveloped in the original drive towards establishment of a pure Communistic State in Russia.

But the social picture never stands still. It generates ever new problems, the solution of which demand vision and theoretical awareness. Yet Stalin, instead of reaching the masses, isolated himself not only from the people, but also from his co-workers, and this gap widened as his death approached. Distrust and fear of all around him rapidly seized him. He rejected many new social adjustments proposed by his co-workers, considering them to be hostile ideologies directed against him personally. As a result, the lonely and friendless old man, motivated by the increasing fear of losing his powers, imposed his will upon others as a medieval autocrat, the "Red Tsar" of an empire.

### GEORGI MALENKOV (1901-    )

Malenkov has no important place in the history of the world, nor even in the history of the Soviet Union. His brief premiership of the USSR Council of Ministers, inherited upon Stalin's death in March 1953, was uneventful and was lost to Nikolai Bulganin in February 1955. Bulganin, in turn, lost his premiership to Khrushchev in March 1958 to become an obscure chairman of the Stavropol Sovnarkhoz. Essentially an isolated, conservative bureaucrat, Malenkov failed to replace the image of the all-powerful Stalin or to win the support of his colleagues, the other Soviet leaders. He inherited his master's domestic and foreign policies on the one hand, but on the other hand, he attempted an improvement of socio-economic forces, long overdue in Russia, under currently existing conditions. But he hesitated to secure power to support his new ideas. In general, he held no respect from the old Bolsheviks, and the average members of the Communist Party and the people in general did not know him. His leadership was the product of the one-man will of Stalin and was the legal heir of Stalin's empire for the short period during which other leaders were debating upon the course of a new leadership.

It is true that Malenkov made a modest attempt to win popularity by encouraging greater production of consumer goods. It was under him that negotiations with Great Britain for expanding trade in consumer goods were conducted and less emphasis was put on production of capital goods. This adjustment in capital-consumer goods relationship came too late to do him any good, and it was precisely this attempt which was used against him when his eventual demotion came. Having long been a "yes" man to Stalin, Malenkov was unskilled in protecting his own interests. He was too timid, too cautious, and too unsure of himself to stimulate the imagination of the restless citizens of the postwar USSR. People wanted dramatic events. They sought new values and goals, having tired of repeating the old slogans created by Marx, Lenin, and Stalin under different socio-economic circumstances. They were no longer satisfied with promises and wanted action to improve their standard of living.

Malenkov had failed to provide the changes sought by the people and eventually he was stripped of his power as Premier of the USSR Council of Ministers and in the Party Secretariat. Until July 1957 he maintained his place as a permanent member of the President of the Central Committee of the Party. Then, ousted from the Presidium, he became Minister of Electric Power Industry and finally was demoted to merely a manager of an electric power house at Ust-Kamenogorsk in the northeastern Kazakh SSR. It is doubtful that Malenkov and other ousted fellow leaders will rise from their obscurity. Malenkov has no talent to contribute in the field of science, and politically he is dead. Certainly current Soviet leaders will not bring him back to power and thus jeopardize their own safety. However, it is possible that some demoted leaders may be given more responsible positions than they now hold. Those with long experience in administrative fields may be utilized to better advantage without promoting them to a policy-making level.

## NIKITA KHRUSHCHEV (1894- )

Khrushchev, like his predecessor, Stalin, is a self-made man without college education. A die-hard Communist, Khrushchev is certainly no intellectual Marxist. More a Leninist than a classical Marxist, Khrushchev is an organizer, builder, and pusher. He is the kind of man who, in an expansive mood, can make a few casual remarks which would cause foreign governments to revise their foreign policies.

He is a man in a great hurry, a man of many uncontrolled and unpredictable moods, a man of seemingly endless interests—always making speeches, shaking hands, kissing babies, encouraging some and humiliating others. But he is not a killer of his enemies as Stalin was. Khrushchev disposed of his opposition by demoting all who questioned his wisdom in leadership and unorthodox programs. Just to remind his followers who is the boss, he has time after time denounced the so-called "anti-Party" group of Malenkov, Kaganovich, Molotov, Bulganin, and Shepilov and their followers. Khrushchev calls them "anti-Party" group because they opposed his proposals for revamping the whole economy of the USSR. The "anti-Party" gambled on support of the secret police (Beria) or the managerial class (Malenkov) against the masses within the Party, and Khrushchev defeated them by direct appeal to the masses of the Party However, he never accuses them of being "enemies of the people." To him they were insubordinate to his leadership and to his targets and therefore they were to be stripped of their political power and rendered harmless.

Energetic, bombastic, and outspoken, Khrushchev had made no binding pronouncements earlier in his career as Stalin had done, and thus he has no pronouncements to defend nor has he any promises to which he is held. Being free of earlier economic and political commitments, he has plunged eagerly into reforming the bureaucracy which was choking the entire Soviet system.

He became the leader of the Central Committee of the Communist Party on March 15, 1953 and then Premier of the Council of Ministers of the USSR in March 1958. At the age of 65, he has become a useful human symbol of the society which he leads and which looks upon him as a man who can cut through bureaucracy and stimulate the imagination of the younger people. The Russian people know that he is tough and has a talent for survival since he has acquired his present great position among them in a period of widespread intrigue when no man's life, no matter how great, was secure.

With disregard for his political safety, Khrushchev spearheaded the re-organization of collective farms, sent tens of thousands of young city people to develop new agricultural regions in the eastern parts of the USSR, attacked bureaucracy at every opportunity, and pushed a staggering and radical plan of administrative and economic reorganization of industry and construction. A man with a cautious nature or a man of uncertain political standing would not have acted as rapidly in a number of different fields as Khrushchev did. But Khrushchev is a calculating gambler who takes his chances with eyes wide open and who knows the consequences. As a gambler, however, he protects himself with a number of plays, and for this reason we see several programs sponsored by him at the same time. Should he lose one program, he may win with another, and since he moves fast, people are not permitted time to brood over a single failure, especially when new goals are set up for them. Moreover, whether it is domestic or international policy, Khrushchev hits hard, challenging the Russian people to follow him. In general they do follow him— they have no one else to follow.

## DE-STALINIZATION

There are many interpretations of the recent transformation in the socio-economic values in the Soviet Union. Most of them are centered around the personalities of Stalin and Khrushchev as if the two men belonged to entirely different schools of thought.

Upon taking over the leadership of the Communist Party, Khrushchev had two avenues of action open to him. He could try gradually to win the loyalty and trust of those who were devoted to Stalin's policies or he could attack Satlin and destroy the myth built around his personality. Waiting was a slow process for a man 65 years of age and Khrushchev chose the latter course, not because of personal weakness, but rather because of strong support from other Soviet leaders. Without majority support he could not have succeeded, and the masses of Russian people were ready and willing to go along with him. Khrushchev also believed that this was the time to destroy many of Stalin's policies and to launch his own. No doubt Khrushchev and other Soviet leaders gave the idea a lot of thought before attacking Stalin, for it was not in their interest to jeopardize their own positions, lives, or the future of the Communist State for which they had fought so long and so hard.

Building Stalin's "cult of personality" was a gradual process, and once it was started its pace was rapidly accelerated; once moving with a kind of inertial motion, it was difficult to stop. The Central Committee of the Communist Party foresaw the development of the "cult of personality" even before World War II, and in November 1938 it was decreed that education of Communists must not be based on biographical sketches of individuals but on general ideas of Marx and Lenin. However, this decree was ignored by many teachers, and Stalin's personality dominated all phases of Soviet life. Khrushchev's famous "de-Stalinization" outcry and his attack on the "personality cult" in 1953 were needed to break the backbone of stubborn Stalinists, who could have obstructed and even destroyed his own politics. By his dramatic appeal to communist parties at home and in the satellite countries and to non-communists in general, Khrushchev has shaken the pedestal, if not destroyed the image, of Stalin's assumed powers of wisdom and leadership throughout communist and friendly non-communist societies. It is true that many Russians were shaken by the destruction of their ideal and were hesitant to make Khrushchev their leader, but Party discipline soon overcame the temporary bewilderment in the minds of the average Soviet citizen. Gradually, most of them lined up behind the new "collective leadership" doctrine. The more unyielding ones were punished, the communist institutions remained intact, and Khrushchev won the leadership.

With the old ideal destroyed, many Russians became overenthusiastic about Khrushchev. The new ideal and eventually another decree de-

nouncing personality cults and encouraging "democratization" as expressed
in the Constitution of the USSR were promulgated. After an initial
outburst of criticism of Stalin, the passion subsided and he was pictured
as a man who made many mistakes in the latter part of his life but who
was a strong defender of Marxism prior to 1934, especially during the
bloody days of collectivization.

With the Stalin legend out of the way and with his leadership accepted
by the Party and people, Khrushchev launched his own reform in many
areas on a large scale. He reorganized the troubled agriculture industry,
merged small collective farms into larger units, moved production of
grain crops to the East, reduced agricultural taxes, and increased prices
paid by the State for agricultural commodities which it purchased. Industry, too, began to shift to the East. The centralized administrative apparatus in Moscow underwent reform with the result that people in the
provinces gained a greater share of management of their own affairs. The
Soviet populace in general was granted certain new rights and privileges
not enjoyed under Stalin, and the overall relationship of the people with
the State was improved.

In general, the "de-Stalinization" policy created conditions under which
the Russian people could begin to enjoy a restricted amount of freedom.
However, no matter how limited freedom may be, it creates a demand
for more freedom. It establishes a chain of reaction, resulting in differences
of opinion which require resolutions that in turn call for new resolutions.
This leads to decentralization of power and the destruction of rigid rules.
It leads to establishment of new institutional structures to manage the
differences of opinion, and hence the existing powers find themselves
granting more and more freedom of choice. The return to the monolithic
era of Stalin should the Kremlin decide on it now would be extremely
difficult and costly to the present leadership and the Russian people alike.
It would destroy faith not only in the existing leadership but in existing
institutions.

## COLLECTIVE LEADERSHIP

The "de-Stalinization" activity of Khrushchev was aimed at destruction
of the "cult of personality." This destruction basically was supported by
Lenin's idea of "collective leadership," or what the Russians call "democratization," under which the people supposedly could participate in national affairs, a right denied them by Stalin. However, mass participation in national affairs now permitted in the USSR is not devised for un-

controlled expression of opinion by all individuals. It is to be "creative" participation approved by the Party leaders. One cannot avoid noticing that in recent Soviet publications the old Stalinist formula of "bloc of communists and non-communists" as it was used in the description of Soviet managerial personnel is being mentioned less frequently and the "Party" is emerging as the leading intellectual and guiding power.

With the destruction of Stalin's one-man leadership, theoretical communism as such has lost its appeal to millions of Russians. Stalin was blamed for his neglect of the people's demands for more goods and services, and for his curbing of their freedom and right of choice. And the absence of the collective leadership in the Communist Party was of greater concern than the idea as applied to the rights of the people in general. It was used by Khrushchev as a tool in winning support of the rank-and-file members of the Communist Party.

The XIX Congress of the Central Committee of the Communist Party, held in July 1953 after "de-Stalinization," revealed that there were gross violations of collective leadership within the Party's hierarchy. It was shown that the masses did not participate in elections of the Party's leaders from top to bottom, in direct opposition to Lenin's ideas of democratic processes.

Lenin's idea of "collective leadership" was advanced at a time when differences of opinion were tolerated, and since the Bolsheviks were in a majority position and held the power in their hands, the principle of collective leadership could not have changed Lenin's main goals. Moreover, in Lenin's time many talents were needed and democratization was necessary if these differences of opinion were to be used to solidify the Communist Party. Hence, Lenin's idea of collective leadership was pronounced at a different time and for different reasons than Khrushchev's collective leadership.

Lenin felt that ideological and organizational unity of the Communist Party was a basic condition of its strength and stability and the source of its every success. To Lenin, all normal activities of the Party as a whole and of all its organizations could be carried out only if the principle of collective leadership was followed. He believed that it was a necessary condition for the proper interpretation and successful resolution of tasks undertaken by the Party. He realized that because of the lack of experience in theoretical and actual building up of the State, a variety of opinions was essential.

To Khrushchev, the principle of collective leadership has a different meaning. He uses this principle not as a tool of enriching the Party intellectually but as an instrument of efficiency by which the best leaders can be elected. Under the current interpretation of the principle, the duty of the Party organs is to hold required elections of the best and most trusted men and women, to render accountability reports of an organ's activities, and to analyze past performances of the "cadre," and self-criticism. These functions are looked upon as the most important conditions for the exercise of initiative in determining shortcomings in Party functions and finding means for improvement. Since the membership of the Party is a militant, voluntary association of Communists who think alike theoretically, the principle of collective leadership safeguards correct Party unity. Even the best-trained and experienced leader is not free from a one-sided approach in making decisions and, therefore, not exempt from mistakes. Thus, the collective leadership may serve as a watchdog for any deviations from the general Party line. In general, it is claimed that the current interpretation of collective leadership cuts bureaucracy to a minimum and is responsible for the solution of the most complex problems of domestic and foreign policies. It effects the discovery and removal of defects in economic and political goals and unites the masses under the leadership of the Party.

The principles of collective leadership, although mainly affecting the Party structure, has also penetrated the relationship between the general citizenry and the administrative organs. Citizens now have the right to criticize their local leaders in terms of a direct face-to-face complaint or through writing letters to their leaders or to the press. Unlike those under Stalin and his one-man rule, current local leaders must please all the citizens with their wide range of interests at the same time. Local leaders such as city councilmen and the management of industrial enterprises are more sensitive to the public voice now than in the past. Thus, theoretically, public criticism tends to point out where maladjustments exist, in order to improve efficiency and reduce bureaucracy, if such criticism is taken seriously. However, similar efforts were made in the past and were proved to be futile. Whether the "voice of the people" will receive lasting attention from the present leadership is a question for speculation. Nevertheless, at least temporarily, this "voice" is stronger than in the past.

The role of the Party as a link with the masses has also improved in effectiveness under the current interpretation of collective leadership. Higher echelons of the Communist Party stimulate the activity and initiative of the broad masses of members by informing them of all important decisions undertaken by the Party and administration. The lesser Party leaders call general meetings for the non-Party workers, explaining the goals of the government and asking their advice on the solution of the tasks assigned to them. This produces lively interest among the masses and inspires their enthusiasm in the successful implementation of tasks for which they are responsible. During the later years of the Stalin regime, direct appeals to workers were often ignored. The fact that the general public is not consulted upon the formation of new targets but merely asked how to accomplish them effectively does not enter the mind of the average Soviet citizen. He seems, at least at present, to be satisfied with his power as an advisor on how to use his own efforts to best advantage.

## DECENTRALIZATION

Khruschev's decentralization of industrial and construction management has brought about major changes in the structure of administrative organs throughout the Soviet Union. In accord with this program, the USSR Supreme Soviet decreed that on May 10, 1957, a "Sovnarkhoz" (Council of National Economy) be formed for the management of industry and construction in each economic administrative region of the USSR. These sovnarkhozy were to be formed by the Council of Ministers of each constituent republic.

The formation of sovnarkhozy in the USSR did not originate with Khruschev. In December 1917, a Supreme Council of the National Economy was established which in turn organized local sovnarkhozy. With the nationalization of industry in 1918, sovnarkhozy were entrusted with the direct supervision of nationalized enterprises. During the Civil War their role decreased in importance; operational administration of nationalized enterprises was transferred to central organs. After the end of the Civil War the power of local sovnarkhozy increased, and they were responsible for the redistribution of equipment, raw materials, supplies, and fuel among enterprises located in the areas. Then when industrialization began in 1932, administration of enterprises involved in heavy, light, and timber industries shifted to centralized management by People's Commissariats. As industrialization expanded, the administrative duties were distributed to newly formed organs, and by 1940 the Soviet Union had 18 commissariats directing industry under the Supreme Council of the National Economy of the USSR. In March 1946, all commissariats were named ministries and the Supreme Council of the National Economy of the USSR became the USSR Council of Ministers. Similar changes occurred in the administrative structure in all constituent republics.

The fluidity of Soviet socio-political arrangements was due to the absence of a prolonged period of normalcy required for massive stability in government, and since the Soviet leaders have been learning how to run the economy through trial and error, the development of administrative functions toward any kind of equilibrium has been a slow process and has taken place only when the old processes have ceased to function effectively. Moreover, as the economic activity of the country has expanded, new administrative organs have been modeled on the basis of the old organs; thus, often the same errors were repeated.

On January 1, 1956, the administrative structure of the Soviet Union consisted of 66 major ministries and independent agencies attached to the USSR Council of Ministries. Industrial production of the Soviet Union was entrusted to 36 All-Union ministries and agencies. The constituent republic had similar administrative ministers and agencies under supervision of their respective councils of ministers.

Serious shortcomings in the ministerial set-up became evident even before 1956. The remoteness and isolation of the ministries from their enterprises did not permit the necessary development of local initiative. It also hindered the use of the vast possibilities existing throughout the economy. In order to reduce centralized management of industry and construction, the Soviets changed several All-Union ministries into Union-Republic ministries, beginning in 1954. This was effected to stimulate initiative and responsibility through improving the administration of enterprises and establishing a principle of "collective management" by the local leaders. At the same time, many industrial enterprises were transferred from All-Union jurisdiction to jurisdiction of constituent republics. During the period 1954-56, some 15,000 industrial enterprises in all, mostly small, were transferred to the jurisdiction of constituent republics. Thus, even in 1956 constituent republics administered about 25 per cent of the nation's most important industrial goods and in some sectors this percentage was 50.[2]

Khrushchev's attack on centralized planning began in 1955. First he proposed that planning in agriculture should be conducted by the Gosplan together with agricultural ministries of constituent republics. These plans were submitted to the Central Committee of the Communist Party rather than to the USSR Council of Ministers. Then in 1957 Khrushchev proposed the establishment of the sovnarkhozy. By July 1, 1957, organization of 105 sovnarkhozy was completed. The RSFSR organized 70 sovnarkhozy, the Ukraine 11, the Kazakh SSR 9, the Uzbek SSR 4, and each of the other consituent republics formed one each.[3] However, due to the abolition of two sovnarkhozy in the RSFSR in November 1957 and the creation of an additional sovnarkhoz in the Uzbek SSR in January 1958, the total number of sovnarkhozy on March 1, 1958 was 104.[4]

In the past, the customary process was to form a new ministry or administration when a new industry was developed or when production under a single administration became so complex and cumbersome as to endanger the fulfillment of established production goals. In 1957 the USSR had more than 206,000 state industrial enterprises and over 100,000 construction sites, and since newly formed ministries and administrations were modeled after the old structures there were no improvements in efficiency of administration. With the Soviets' determined drive to increase their industry and construction according to their expectations, the tremendous tasks in centralized planning and management have become too cumbersome and too slow in the face of a dynamic development of technology, specialization and complex mechanization of expanding production. To keep the old forms of management, which were dependent upon minute production instructions from above, became impractical. The departmental barriers led to the weakening of normal production processes between enterprises of different ministries located in the same industrial city or economic region. The old vertical managerial responsibility was creating long delays in the settlement of important problems.

In his speech of May 7, 1958, to the Seventh Session of the USSR Supreme Soviet, Khrushchev illustrated many shortcomings in centralized management and departmental barriers. As an example, the Ministry of the Construction of Metallurgical and Chemical Industry in 1956 alone shipped to Krasnoyarsk Kray 20,000 square meters of prefabricated houses from Karelia. A large number of similar houses were also shipped to Krasnoyarsk by the Ministry of Construction from Kirov Oblast. At the same time, the Ministry of Timber Industry and the Ministry of Construction of Petroleum Industry shipped prefabricated houses with a total of 170,000 square meters of dwelling space from Krasnoyarsk Kray to other parts of the USSR. The cost of transportation due to departmental barriers alone amounted to hundreds of millions of rubles annually. Khrushchev emphasized that more horizontal managerial organizations in the form of sovnarkhozy would eliminate much inefficiency in production, reduce cost of production, and stimulate initiative of local leaders and workers.

Khruschev stressed that this reorganization would assist in removing many shortcomings, would bring administration nearer to production, and would help to reduce bureaucracy. However, he also cautioned the Russian people not to be so naive as to believe that under new management bureaucracy would be abolished completely, but that by bringing the management closer to the broad masses of workers the people could exert a greater influence in curbing bureaucracy. Basically, this is the principle of "collective leadership" mentioned above.

Not all industrial and production ministries were abolished. Some remained intact; others were merged. The Ministry of Defense Industry was merged with the Ministry of General Machine-Building Industry; the Ministry of Electric Power Stations was merged with the Ministry of Construction of Electric Power Stations; and the Ministry of State Farms was merged with the Ministry of Agriculture. Similar changes took place in constituent republics. Thus at the beginning of 1959, only the following ministries were still in existence:[5]

| *All-Union* | *Union-Republic* |
| --- | --- |
| Foreign Trade | Internal Affairs |
| Maritime Fleet | Foreign Affairs |
| Transportation | Higher Education |
| Medium Machine-Building | Geology and Conservation |
| Construction of Transportation | Health |
| Electric Power Station Construction | Culture |
| | Defense |
| | Communication |
| | Agriculture |
| | Finance |

The reorganization of management brought vast changes in the structures of Soviet society. It changed socio-economic values. It opened the door for individual initiative and self-expression no matter how disciplined or restricted it might have been. It called for massive participation of all citizens to improve their standard of living, to be guardians of new management, and to prevent development of greater bureaucracy.

The sovnarkhoz is an economic administrative region directly subordinate to the Council of Ministers of the constituent republic. Its reports are also made to the Councils of Ministers of the autonomous republics and to the executive committees of the kray or oblast, or to the council of workers' deputies of the city under jurisdiction. But the USSR Council of Ministers directs the sovnarkhoz through the Council of Ministers of the constituent republic. Most enterprises and organizations of the abolished ministries are subordinate to appropriate sovnarkhozy. Enterprises and organizations subordinate to the All-Union ministries but receiving allocation of materials from sovnarkhozy are assigned to these sovnarkhozy.

Enterprises under the jurisdiction of non-industrial All-Union ministries are also subordinate to sovnarkhozy in the same manner.

The basic task of the sovnarkhoz is to fulfill the required production norm established by the Gosplan. The sovnarkhoz develops and submits proposals on important economic problems to its .immediate supervisory body, the Council of Ministers of the constituent republic. It implements specialization and interindustry production so as to establish rational production both within the economic region and with other regions. It eliminates excessive and unnecessary long-distance cross-hauling and supervises the concluding of economic agreements and contracts made by individual enterprises. Sovnarkhozy organize the material-technical supply for their enterprises and the sale of products. In addition, the sovnarkhoz is empowered to introduce and to improve technology and automation and to develop new and improved machines and new types of instruments and materials. The sovnarkhoz directs financing of its enterprises, organizations, and institutions. It controls their financial operations and submits required proposals for loans. In general, sovnarkhozy deal with all economic problems under their jurisdiction. Creation of sovnarkhozy did not reduce the number of these problems existing under the old vertical administrative structure, but produced conditions under which they could be solved faster and more efficiently.

The establishment of a soznarkhoz is generally based upon the territorial-administrative-economic significance of an area. The size alone is not the yardstick. For example, the largest sovnarkhoz in the USSR is the Yakut ASSR. In 1959, this republic covered more than 1.9 million square miles, with a total population of some 489,000 persons and a budget of 853 million rubles. The smallest sovnarkhoz is the city of Moscow, covering some 127 square miles, with a population of over five million and a budget of approximately eight billion rubles.[6]

Because of variable economic factors, the functional organization structure of individual sovnarkhozy differs greatly. Highly industrialized sovnarkhozy have larger numbers of functional departments than less industrialized ones. But in the main, the structural organization of sovnarkhozy is similar. Inter-sovnarkhoz departments for economic planning, labor and wages, finance, central accounts, personnel and educational affairs, justice, transportation, and the like are found in each economic region. As can be seen from the two charts below, the Yakut Sovnarkhoz is much simpler than the Leningrad Sovnarkhoz. In Yakutia, there are seven functional departments whereas there are 17 in Leningrad. Yakutia has only five industrial and other administrations against 21 in Leningrad.

The Council of Ministers in each constituent republic is empowered to appoint the chairman of the sovnarkhoz, deputy chairman and the members of the council. Upon recommendation of the chairman of the Council

CHART 1—*Organizational Structure of the Yakut Sovnarkhoz*

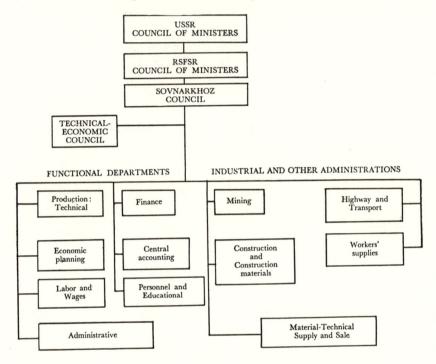

of Ministers of a constituent republic to its Supreme Soviet, the chairman of a sovnarkhoz may be designated a minister, and thus become a member of that Council of Ministers. The sovnarkhoz Council consists of a chairman, his deputies, and the chiefs of major divisions and industrial administrations.

The technical-economic council of a sovnarkhoz is a consulting body appointed by the council. Its duties are advising the sovharkhoz council on all important and complex problems. The size of the technical-economic council varies with the economic development of a sovnarkhoz. For example, the large and highly industrialized Kemerovsk Sovnarkhoz with its over 500 large-scale industrial enterprises has 220 members in its technical-economic council. Membership of the technical-economic council includes both men and women from all walks of life—educators, scientists, engineers, economists, plant managers, and workers from various industrial enterprises. The technical-economic council of the Kemerovsk is divided into specialized sections as follows: mining, power, metallurgy,

CHART 2—*Organizational Structure of the Leningrad Sovnarkhoz*

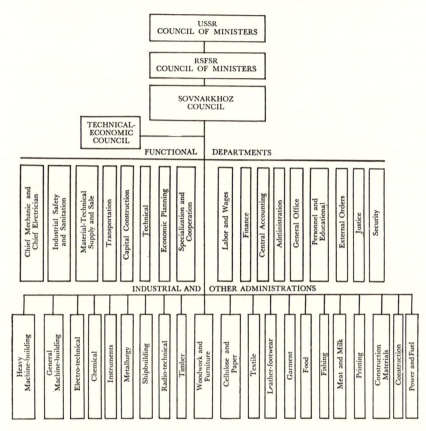

machine-building, chemical, economic, and automation.[7] Members of the technical-economic council are assigned to a section of their field of specialization where their theoretical knowledge and practical experience can be of most value for the development of all branches of the economy in the sovnarkhoz.

The sovnarkhoz has the right, within the limits of its own competence, to issue decrees and regulations based on the laws of the USSR, of its own constituent republic, and of the decrees and regulations either of the USSR Council of Ministers or of the Council of Ministers of the constituent republic. In addition, the decrees and regulations of a sovnarkhoz may be revoked by the Council of Ministers of the constituent republic, and the USSR Council of Ministers has the right to suspend the decrees and regulations issued by a sovnarkhoz.

Structural reorganizations of the management of Soviet enterprises have been common in the USSR since the establishment of centralized controls. However, reorganization of management and a resulting implementation of greater efficiency in production do not necessarily occur simultaneously. It is much easier to reshape the existing centralized administration than to improve the efficiency rate. Soviet leaders lack experienc in increasing efficiency of productive forces, and since the theoretical standards dealing with economic operations are poorly developed, many sovnarkhozy display an inadequacy in the theoretical approach in solving their problems. Reorganization of management was set up by decree, but what the sovnarkhozy have needed is not so much talent at reorganization as business executives and production administrators who have combined talents in organization and in administration and who have been trained in reaping the greatest possible profits.

In the past, economic problems had been solved or adjusted on a ministerial level. The sovnarkhozy created conditions of diversification and the old criteria could not be successfully used for the new economic organization. A sovnarkhoz has the economic power of a very large organization similar to that of General Motors in the United States in controlling variable and many fixed factors. A large sovnarkhoz having a considerable concentration of modern technology may develop diseconomies if production of a decreasing-cost enterprise and even of industries under its jurisdiction is suddenly reduced by government decision. Consequently, without a new basic theory to guide the activities of sovnarkhozy, a prediction of what may be accomplished in the future is impossible with the criteria at hand. Since the sovnarkhoz's power is similar to that of oligopolistic organization, its motives may change from short-run to long-run profit maximization, and its action may vary from rational to irrational as it seeks solutions to its economic problems through political channels alone. As a large industrial organization, a sovnarkhoz may develop greater opportunities for local interests to the detriment of national goals by using the input-output matrix in production planning. It even may show a tendercy to break away from micro-economics to regional macro-economics. Certainly there will be conflicts in interests between large and small enterprises.

Perhaps in the distant future at least some of the sovnarkhozy will acquire a combination of highly specialized professional management, productive labor, and efficient equipment. This combination of factors will tend to develop high output per person and effect a simultaneous increase in wages, production, and profit. This will explode the classical "iron law of wages" and "wages fund" theories and the Marxian doctrines of exploitation. In this event, there will be more demand for wide dispersal of powers and relaxation of direct regulation. This does not imply that anything like *laissez-faire* could be expected, but it may lead to new theoretical approaches yet to be found in the USSR. In the meantime, Soviet economists are most immediately concerned with devising theoretical tools for the management of sovnarkhozy and of individual firms; new concepts of costs determination, maximization of profits, supply and demand; and revision of the marketing system.[8]

The main advantage of the new management appears to be in the elimination of barriers that heretofore have isolated the Soviet industries under the ministerial system, each ministry handling all or most of its own requirements for housing, transportation, construction, sales, and in some cases even production of required raw materials. It also appears that the tasks for plant managers are much easier since they can settle specific problems and obtain permission to change plans by discussion at the sovnarkhoz council instead of going through Moscow.

Sovnarkhozy are responsible for a large share of national industrial and construction goals. But there is no political domination of the planning for agriculture, and production of agricultural commodities, which are not under their jurisdiction. If a sovnarkhoz is responsible for production of canning plants or sugar refineries, why should it not be responsible for collective farms supplying raw materials to those industries The current trend among the sovnarkhozy is to secure control over all enterprises located in their regions. This pressure upon government is seen in numerous articles in Soviet newspapers recently. However, collective farms are still undergoing reorganization, and it is quite possible that after this reorganization is complete they may come under the sovnarkhozy. Should this happen, the sovnarkhozy would become a powerful economic force able to control markets, competition, and prices. This would be a radical departure from the past, but it could be accomplished within the present flexibility of Soviet economic policies, and if such organizational structure should show rapid advancement in production and improvement in standard of living in the USSR, unorthodox Khrushchev, the instigator, might accept it. The decentralization of industrial management in 1957 and the announcement of the Seven-Year Plan indicate further moves toward liberalism in the marketing system of the USSR.

## HIERARCHY

As a monolithic state, the Soviet Union has one political party—the Communist Party of the USSR. There is no organized political opposition, and thus no political minority groups register dissatisfaction with the State. The Party runs a state where divergent interests are not expressed. The gigantic administrative apparatus is more complex than in non-communist societies because it is enlarged by planning, enforcement and data-collection organs on all levels of Soviet administrative structure.

### Administrative Hierarchy

At the beginning of 1959 the USSR consists of 15 constituent republics, 19 autonomous republics, nine autonomous oblasts, 117 krays and oblasts, ten national okrugs, 3,980 rayons of which 393 are urban rayons, and 48,675 village soviets. The large number of administrative subdivisions calls for a large number of deputies to the Supreme Soviets of the USSR, constituent republics, and autonomous republics, and deputies to the Soviet of workers in all other administrative subdivisions. In 1957 the USSR Supreme Soviet consisted of 1,347 deputies, 5,271 deputies were sent to the Supreme Soviet of constituent republics, 1,944 deputies to the Supreme Soviets of autonomous republics, and 1,549,777 deputies were in local workers' soviets—a total of 1,558,339 deputies.[9] All administrative subdivisions have the same model (on a reduced scale) of authority as the administrative organs for the USSR. All deputies, excluding workers' soviets, are elected for a period of four years and deputies to workers' soviets for two years.

As a federation of constituent republics the USSR has its constitution, and each constituent and autonomous republic has its own constitution. However, the citizens of constituent and autonomous republics are also citizens of the USSR. Moreover, the highest administrative organs of the USSR administer the whole territory of the USSR.

The USSR Supreme Soviet is the highest authoritative state power. It assumes all authority such as legislative, executive, and judicial control. It has unlimited power in control of activities of all other organs. The USSR Supreme Soviet consists of two bodies: the Soviet of the USSR, and the Soviet of Nationalities, each with equal power. The Soviet of the USSR represents the Soviet Union as a whole, and the Soviet of Nationalities represents constituents and autonomous republics. In general, the two Soviets are parallel in organizational structure and have similar jurisdictions and rights. In a case of disagreement between two bodies, the question is settled by a special committee representing both organizations. If agreement is not reached, then the Presidium of the USSR Supreme Soviet may dissolve the USSR Supreme Soviet and must call a new election for the Soviet of the USSR and the Soviet of Nationalities. It is on the floor of the Soviet of the USSR and the Soviet of Nationalities that statutory laws are enacted, the national budget is reviewed, state policies are discussed, and criticism of various administrative organs is made. The

CHART 3—*Supreme Organs of Soviet Government*

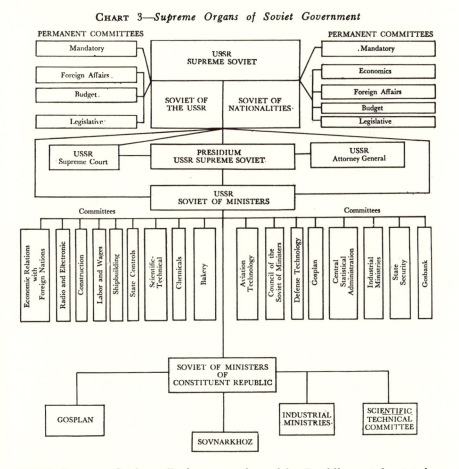

USSR Supreme Soviet calls for a meeting of its Presidium at least twice a year or in extraordinary sessions, when most important political and economic decisions are to be approved.

The highest executive and administrative state organ in the USSR is the USSR Soviet of Ministers, appointed by and responsible to the USSR

Supreme Soviet. The USSR Soviet of Ministers administers a number of committees which are headed by chairmen and chiefs.

In the constituent republics the highest state authority lies with the Supreme Soviet. The highest executive and administrative organ is the Soviet of Ministers. The highest authority on the local level is in the hands of the Soviets of Deputies of Workers and their executive committees.

## PARTY HIERARCHY

Despite impressive theoretical powers, the Supreme Soviets and Soviet of Ministers of the USSR and of the constituent republics are only weak functional organs, expressing the unity of the people behind the government. The real power in the Soviet Union is the Communist Party and primarily its leadership.

Article 126 of the Constitution of the Soviet Union states that "the most active and politically conscious citizens in the ranks of the working class and other sectors of the working people unite in the USSR Communist Party, which is the vanguard of the working people in their struggle to strengthen and develop the socialist system and is the leading core of all organizations of the working people, both public and state." This is the concept of "dictatorship of the proletariat" led by the Party which is completely dominated by its Presidium headed by Khrushchev.

The power of the Communist Party in the government comes from various sources. In the first place, the most important state offices are usually assigned to party members throughout all levels of the government hierarchy. Strong Party discipline and opportunity for political and economic advances keep them from deviating from the Party's policies. Non-Party officials also hold posts at the sufferance of the Party. Thus, the key positions in the government are held by persons whose first loyalty is to the Party rather than to the government or the nation. In the second place, the Party and its individual members have extraordinary powers of intervention in state affairs and power to criticize other officials, which may lead to personal advantage. In general, as in all dictatorships, the coercive powers of the Party assure the ultimate execution of its designs. But the Party does not trust its members; and Article 35(a) of the Statute of the Communist Party states that the Committee for Control of the Party "verifies maintenance of Party discipline of members and candidates, makes Communists answerable for violation of program and statute of the Party, Party and State discipline, as well as violation of Party's morale (deceiving Party, dishonesty and insincerity towards Party)." This makes every Communist a defender of the Party, its policies, and its leadership.

The Communist Party has a relatively small membership, but it is a closely knit, militant minority, which presents a united will of its leaders to the rest of the USSR.

TABLE 1—*Membership in the USSR Communist Party* [10]

|  | 1939<br>XVIII Congress | 1952<br>XIX Congress | 1956<br>XX Congress | 1959<br>XXI Congress |
|---|---|---|---|---|
| Full members | 1,588,852 | 6,013,259 | 6,795,896 | —— |
| Candidates | 888,814 | 868,886 | 419,609 | —— |
| TOTAL | 2,477,666 | 6,882,145 | 7,215,505 | 8,239,131 |

While some members and candidates are dismissed or die, others join the ranks. Between 1952 and 1956, a greater number of members joined the Party, and the number of candidates was reduced by more than 50 per cent. As compared with 1956, the 1959 total number of members and candidates increased by over a million, almost two-thirds of whom were workers and members of collective farms.

Between 1956 and 1959 the growth of the Party membership averaged 341,200 a year; the greatest increase occurred in 1957 and 1958. In 1958 the total membership increased by over 480,000 persons. The 1957-58 period was crucial for Khrushchev, and he stuffed the Party with loyal followers to help him publicize his industrial and agricultural drives. This job seems to be accomplished, and beginning with January 1959 the growth of new membership began to slow down. During the first six months of that year only about 127,000 were admitted. The next Congress is to be held in 1961, and it is very likely that the membership in the Party will be enlarged since the total population of the country will be considerably increased, especially the younger generation; but this increase will be at a reduced rate as compared with 1958.

Khruschchev encourages admission of younger people to membership. The fact that the younger generation is gradually taking over the leadership of the Party may be seen from the 1959 Congress. Out of 1,375 delegates present at the Congress, 63 per cent of them were members of the Party since 1940, but what is remarkable is that of the total number of delegates, 15 per cent were young, holders of Party cards since 1950.

New members of the Communist Party come from candidates and from the Komsomol (Young People's Communist League), whose membership in 1958 was over 18 million. Thus the total number of members, candidates, and members of the Komsomol represented about nine per cent of the total population, whereas Party members alone represented less than four per cent of the total population. It is a small party, indeed, that controls this country of more than 210 million persons. In actuality, it is not so much the Party that rules the Russian people as its Presidium, and particularly the Presidium's First Secretary, Nikita Khrushchev.

CHART 4—*Supreme Organs of Soviet Communist Party: 1959*

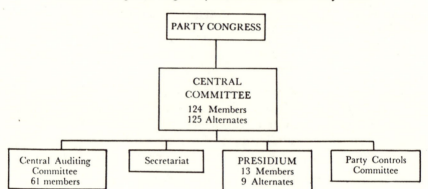

In 1959 there were 1,269 delegates to Party's Congress, each representing 5,000 members with full rights to vote and 106 delegates with consultative vote. As a rule, the delegates hear their First Secretary and other Party leaders on the state of domestic and international conditions as well as on other important economic and political issues at home and abroad; they approve proposals advocated by their leaders with only minor revisions. The delegates also elect the Central Committee, which operates the Party and through which the Communists direct the Soviet Union between congresses. The Central Committee elects its Presidium which decides policy between meetings of the committee. The Presidium is the most powerful group in the USSR, and its membership provides clues for eventual shifts in the fortunes of Soviet leaders and in political trends of Soviet government. The Presidium is the inner ruling circle of the Central Committee and the supreme political organ of the USSR.

In 1952, when Stalin was still alive, the delegates to the XIX Communist Party Congress elected 125 full members and 111 candidate members to the Central Committee. At the XX Congress in 1956, the Central Committee was enlarged to 133 full members and 122 candidate members.

Between 1952 and 1956, 47 full members and 51 candidate members were dismissed or died. Therefore, in 1956 the Central Committee was enlarged by 55 new members and 65 candidate members carefully selectd by Khrushchev. The XXIst Congress held in 1959 reduced the number of full members to 124 and of candidate members to 105. In 1952 the Presidium consisted of 11 persons, all of whom won seats on the Central Committee in the election of March 1956. They were Khrushchev, Bulganin, Mikoyan, Kaganovich, Voroshilov, Pervukhin, Saburov, Molotov, Suslov, Kirichenko, and Malenkov.

In June 1957 the purge of those who had committed so-called "ideological errors" began. Former Premier Malenkov was relieved of his duties as the deputy chairman of the USSR Soviet of Ministers and was ousted from the Party's Presidium. Molotov was dismissed from his job as First Deputy of the USSR Soviet of Ministers and from the Presidium. Kaganovich was removerd from the office of First Deputy of the USSR Soviet of Ministers and the Presidium. Saburov also lost his job as First Deputy of the USSR Soviet of Ministers and his place in the Presidium. Pervukhin was removed from his posts as Deputy of the USSR Soviet of Ministers and his seat in the Presidium. Zhukov won his seat in the Presidium only to lose it later when removed from his post as Minister of Defense. By the end of 1958 Khrushchev had greatly strengthened his position by placing his supporters at the top of the Soviet hierarchy groups. He abolished factional warfare between groups and actually acquired all of Stalin's power, if not more. Even former Premier Bulganin disappeared from the political scene and linked with the "anti-Party clique" in November 1958.

But as the old leaders disappeared, new faces appeared at the Presidium, among them Furtseva (a Communist since 1930), Koslov (a Communist since 1926), Aristov (Party member since 1921), Beliyev (member since 1921), Brezhnev (1931), Ignatov (1924), Shvernik (1905), and Kuusinen (1904). Thus, at the end of 1958 the Presidium of the Central Committee of the Communist Party consisted of 13 full members and nine alternate members, with Podgornyy (1930) and Polyanskiiy (1939) elected in June 1958—all were followers of Khrushchev. It is a closely united clique which must protect itself from any deviationists who might attempt to endanger its security and power. They cannot all be Premiers, and only one of them can become First Secretary of the Communist Party. Their elected leader is Khrushchev, whom they must protect in order to protect themselves. Although they are new in national politics, nevertheless they are old and trusted Communists of the older school, the Old Guard who survived the 1937 purge to become the purgers in 1958.

## Chapter 3—Bibliography

[1] *Bolshevik,* No. 19, 1938, pp. 90-91.

[2] Allakhergiyan, D., *Natsional'nyy Dokhod SSSR,* Moscow, 1958, p. 96.

[3] *Istoriya SSSR, Epokha Sotsialisma, 1917-1957,* Moscow, 1958, p. 752.

[4] *Vedomosti Verkhovnogo Soveta RSFSR,* No. 3, December 28, 1957, p. 162, and *Stroitelnaya Gazeta,* January 22, 1958.

[5] *Zasedaniya Verhovogo Soveta SSSR,* 5th Conference 2d Session, December 22-25, 1958, Moscow, 1959, pp. 694.

[6] *Narodnoye Khozaystvo RSFSR v 1958 Godu,* Moscow, 1959, pp. 37-48.

[7] *Sovetskiy Soyuz,* No. 2, 1958, p. 32.

[8] *Materialy Vsesoyuznogo Soveschaniya Zaveduyuschika Kafedrami Obschestvennykh Nauk,* Moscow, 1958, p. 44.

[9] *Narodnoye Khozaystvo SSSR v 1956 Godu,* Moscow, 1957, p. 21; *Washington Post and Times-Herald,* July 31, 1958; and *Forty Years of Soviet Power,* Moscow, 1957, p. 25.

[10] *Ezhegodnik Bolshoy Sovetskoy Entsiklopedii,* Moscow, 1957, p. 9; *Vneocherednoy XXI S'ezd Kommunicheskoy Partii Sovetskogo Soyuza* (I), Moscow, 1959, pp. 112, 468.

## CHAPTER 4

# Economic Planning

## INTRODUCTION

Economic planning in the Soviet Union is characterized by the absence of the consumer sovereignty of millions of men and women who independently make their economic decisions in Western countries. The Communists believe that they cannot permit individual freedom of choice since in the short run personal choice would reflect unrestricted self-interest and would not in the long run be in the best interest of the total society. The Communists fear that without economic planning people in the short run would consume too much of certain things and would not be able to accumulate resources adequate for the expansion of production in the long run. For this reason consumers' choice in the Soviet Union is of less significance than the balance of resources among various sectors. By this method overproduction in one sector and underproduction in another is expected to be controlled, if not completely eliminated.

Economic planning was not invented by the Soviets. Any enterprise, whether small or large, must under any social conditions have some kind of planning if it is to survive competition and to prosper. Moreover, it is important to understand that economic activities everywhere are governed by a few basic economic laws, such as the law of "comparative advantage," which is useful in planning. The Soviets have also adopted the "equilibrium" principle to fit their own needs. Therefore, Russians cannot claim any contribution in the theory of economic planning. But they have introduced large-scale planning and shown that large-scale investments, however painful they may be for the people, can be obtained without accumulating them from a few individuals. Thus, consumers' propensity to save is no longer of consequence in the USSR.

The Soviet planning mechanism is based on Lenin's broad interpretation of the government's and therefore of the Party's role in socio-economic building of a new society. The concept of "building of a new society" is the core of the planning mechanism, since the Communists believe that after destroying capitalist society they have to build their own State. This ultimate goal, Communists feel, can be reached only through rational planning. Consequently, as was noted before, the real power in economic planning in the USSR is concentrated in the Communist Party, which is controlled by a handful of individuals—the power elite.

During the early days of the Bolshevik State, socio-economic planning involved the people, and their direct participation which resulted in changes that were mainly of local significance. When a factory was nationalized its workers were consulted and were called upon to help run "their" new enterprise for "their" own benefit, for it was emphasized by the new regime that the workers were the new owners of the means of production. But today the magnitude of planning is so complex and the tempo of economic changes is so rapid that the interplay of economic events and decisions is far too indirect and distant to produce enthusiasm of mass participation similar to that evident in the earlier days.

In the past economic events often preceded economic planning and decisions. Such was the case in the formation of the NEP by Lenin, the main goal of which was to stimulate production. Now events are made by the power elite, as in their decision to produce a "sputnik," or to plow the virgin and unused lands. Now, all aspects of Soviet society are interlocking, and decisions made by the power elite are of major consequence to all sectors. Even the failure to reach decisions is itself an act that is often of greater consequence than the decisions the power elite do make, for they are in command of the hierarchies and pyramidal organizations, which cannot act on their own without command from above.

Planning in the Soviet Union embraces not only economic but also political, military and international domains. Other less important areas such as education and health are subordinate to more important realms. All significant areas are subjected to planning and coordinated in one master plan by the power elite. However, the power elite are not solitary rulers, since they are assisted by cohorts of advisers, consultants, spokesmen, and opinion-makers. They are all intellectually flexible enough to interpret the writings of Marx and Lenin to fit any of the current socio-economic phenomena with ready-made slogans and justifications. Since the decision-makers trust their advisers, the moral conception of the top planners, then, becomes a fact, since they are in the driver's seat and because their decisions are linked to the masses from which they assume their power.

All major economic targets are originated by a small group of individuals who are members of the Presidium of the Central Committee of the USSR Communist Party. Proposed targets are then submitted to the Central Committee for conformity and next presented to the General Congress of the Communist Party for its approval. By such a process, all Communists are held responsible for the proposed targets and their fulfillment.

The adopted goals are then passed over to the USSR Soviet of Ministers, which as an executive branch of the government legalizes them before submitting them for final approval by the USSR Supreme Soviet. Upon authorization of the targets, which is nothing but a formality, the Supreme Soviet declares the necessary decrees and orders for constituent republics and for any other economic sector, excluding, however, political organizations which are in the domain of the Party.

The planning organs and their subordinate organizations which assist the executive branches of the government are not policy-making bodies but rather working organs, the main function of which is to provide information required by the decision-making agencies. As in the case of the executive branch,' which starts from the top with the USSR Soviet of Ministers and ends with the smallest political-administrative unit of the rayon, the planning organs have a similar pyramidal structure in order to assist every administrative subdivision.

This is a cumbersome and expensive planning mechanism with many faults. It encourages inaction and submission to bureaucracy; yet it also encouraged ambitious, energetic, and self-assured men who are pushing retarded Soviet technology forward, revolutionizing production methodology, and building new industrial bases in the wilderness of Siberia and Central Asia.

## STATIC ECONOMY

Planned economy attempts to balance the supply and demand of resources in order to achieve some kind of long-run equilibrium. Such equilibrium is desirable for any society whether or not it has central planning. However, without central planning the equilibrium is decided by millions of consumers who, by exercising their rights in a free choice, determine the allocation of resources for the most desirable end. In the Soviet Union consumers are not free to express their wishes in allocation of resources which will bring them short-run benefits. This function is taken away from them by the State, which acts as a monopolist and seeks a long-run balance of all economic sectors.

The State controls all factors of production and determines what to produce, how much to produce and for whom to produce. Consequently, central planning destroys competition among producers, retards innovations, hampers improvement of goods, and obstructs reduction in the cost of production. It is this absence of competition on the market that makes the Soviet economy static. It is static because the country does not have independent producers who, as in non-planned societies, compete for the consumers' markets and thereby create a dynamic economy. By controlling all phases of the economy the Soviets have destroyed the free play of supply and demand on the market and consequently the dynamic nature of the market. True, the Soviet economy is rapidly expanding, but this does not mean that the economy is dynamic. No matter how high the rate of growth might be, the economy remains static because of the absence of competition on the market.

By setting up a planned economy, the State became a monopoly controlling a static economy. The planners, having limited, scarce resources to start with, must allocate enough resources to each economic sector to maintain some kind of balance for the normal production of goods and services needed for the country. Otherwise, under conditions of scarcity and in the absence of a free play of supply and demand factors on the market, some sectors will expand more rapidly and undermine the growth of others.

This economic balance is more than a mere input-output relation because the Soviets are defining it in terms of theoretical and, if possible, of actual equilibrium in all economic sectors. This means that a mining engineer must be employed at the mine rather than in the department store. It means that upon deciding to expand the chemical industry, the central planners must find means to train more chemists and to adjust existing conditions to prevent disequilibrium in other sectors. If the planners decide to produce two pairs of shoes per capita annually despite the consumers' wish for three pairs, the State, to maintain its balance, would produce two pairs of shoes. The static economy cannot be adjusted to the erratic demands of the consumer.

Even though the classical free play of supply and demand cannot be tolerated in a static economy, sovnarkhozy are permitted to make decisions in small-scale production of minor goods and services, thus creating competitive conditions among different regions. The State purchasing programs for agricultural commodities recognize cost differentials in production; hence the past inflexibility in planning is gradually yielding ground to the forces of supply and demand. True, this is a meager beginning; but it may be of greater significance later when immediate scarcities will be adequately supplied.

## PLANNING APPARATUS

In the early days of the Bolshevik regime, economic planning was of a hit-and-miss character because Communist leaders disagreed among themselves on theoretical issues involved in planning and because there was no adequate planning mechanism. However crude the early planning was, the consumers' demands were met only when those demands did not endanger the political institutions. Only with the beginning of the second Five Year Plan (1932-37) were the Russians able to strengthen their planning apparatus, to improve methodology, and to develop ways and means for the rational allocations of resources.

In building up their planning schemes, the Soviet planners were guided by pronouncements made by Marx and Lenin, and even though neither of them ever heard about macroeconomics, the broad concept of Soviet central planning fits many phases of macroeconomics. Finally the Soviets have developed the planning mechanism through which they have directed production by industries and for the country as a whole. With the formation of sovnarkhozy, however, the Soviets inadvertently entered the realm of microeconomics and equilibrium of the firm. This does not imply that the Soviets are moving from macroeconomics to microeconomics. Perhaps both will be used in future planning.

As stated, at the beginning of this chapter, all major planning targets are proposed by a few individuals in the Presidium of the Central Committee of the Communist Party. Krushchev, as the First Secretary of the Communist Party and the premier of the USSR Soviet of Ministers, is behind all major socio-economic plans undertaken after Stalin's death. He is the top decision-maker, but he is not an autocrat since he must justify his proposals in the light of pronouncements inherited from Marx and Lenin if he wishes to preserve the existing institutions.

Marx held that planning could be effective only in a highly industrialized economy, certainly not in a country such as Russia was in 1918 with some 20 million small-scale scattered farms, dispersed industry, and disorganized markets. Considering these conditions, Lenin, Trotsky, and other leaders realized that the classical Marxian theory could not help them to develop a comprehensive planning machine. Consequently, Lenin was forced to devise new schemes and principles for the planning mechanism from its birth and until his death.

But Lenin at the beginning of 1922 was already overworked and tired, and in May of that year he was struck down by his first attack of paralysis. Recovering, he returned to work and until his death in 1924 Lenin was deeply concerned with organization of a planning apparatus. As a prolific writer Lenin left about 30,000 pronouncements dealing with socio-economic problems. Many of these pronouncements were made at the time of his illness. Incapacitated as he was, Lenin kept on producing theoretical tools for those who would rule the new society after him. But many of his recommendations were less coherent and less analytical than those prior to his illness; they were sporadic and dealt with specific problems with no attempt to fit them into an overall scheme of things which could apply to the economy as a whole. In many instances they were corrective schemes to amend errors already made.

Krushchev, as the chief decision-maker, relies mostly upon Lenin's assertions; many of the recent socio-economic adjustments undertaken by Khrushchev are supported by recommendations made by Lenin in his last two years. These recommendations are incomplete and scanty but as such they are also more flexible in conditions than the classical Marxian pronouncements.

## The USSR Soviet of Ministers

The USSR Soviet of Ministers, the country's highest executive branch of the government, carries out the directives approved by the Central Committee of the Communist Party and the USSR Supreme Soviet. The USSR Soviet of Ministers conveys the wishes of the Party and the government to lower economic subdivisions through the Soviet of Ministers of each constituent republic; they in turn spell out these wishes to lower echelons under their jurisdiction.

To assist the USSR Soviet of Ministers in coordinating the economic activity of all constituent republics, there are a number of State Committees and Administrations whose tasks are to provide the information needed for decision-making by the USSR Soviet of Ministers.

The most important of these is the State Planning Committee, or the USSR Gosplan. Others are: the Committee on Labor and Wage, Committee on Science and Technology, Committee on Aviation Technology, Committee on Defense Technology, Committee on Radio-Electronics, Committee on Shipbuilding, Committee on Automation-Machine Building, Committee on Chemicals, Committee on Bread Grain, Committee on Construction. Committee on Foreign Economic Relations, and Committee on Professional-Technical Education. In addition there are a number of less important committees and administrations: the Committee on Innovation and Discovery, Committee on Industrial Safety; Committee on Standaids, Measurements and Weights; also the Main Administration of Natural Gas Industry, Civil Aviation, Atomic Power, Labor Reserves, and National Resources.

In 1959 another advisory body, the State Scientific and Economic Soviet, was organized by the USSR Soviet of Ministers. This organization is empowered to conduct a detailed study of the overall economic position of the country and to make recommendations to the USSR Soviet of Ministers regarding the course to be taken in order to speed the economic development of the country. In a sense this organization is the "brain-trust" of the Ministers.

Supported by such an accumulation of highly specialized and powerful organizations, the USSR Soviet of Ministers' main objective is to coordinate planned or proportional development of all constituent republics and their subordinate sectors. The USSR Soviet of Ministers systematically checks on progress reports submitted to it by the Soviet of Ministers of constituent republics, and when it is deemed necessary the USSR Soviet of Ministers takes compulsory action to assure the achievement of the established targets and even to develop new plans for the constituent republics.

The USSR Soviet of Ministers is the watchdog for economic development of the country. It is entrusted with tremendous power in the allocation of resources and capital and can move these allocations from one constituent republic to another. The complexity of forces entering into the administration of the economy inevitably creates maladjustments which may be due to wrong decisions or to indecision. For instance, in 1957 the USSR Soviet of Ministers decreed that the Soviet of Ministers of the constituent republics transfer the existing and newly constructed public housing under their jurisdiction to the jurisdiction of local soviets. It was also ruled that all newly constructed housing transferred to local soviets carry a guarantee for repairs. But the law failed to identify the financial source, and repair funds were not appropriated. Only in 1958 at the Congress of the USSR Supreme Soviet was this inequity brought up and corrected.[1]

## Gosplan

The USSR Gosplan was organized by Lenin in 1921 and throughout its stormy existence it withstood many skirmishes with the critics. Moreover, it survived numerous changes in its authority as the planning organ of the Soviet Union and, perhaps only because it was set up by Lenin himself, the agency preserved its original name and objectives.

Prior to 1940 the USSR Gosplan was empowered to devise and to compel fulfillment of detailed plans for the country as a whole and for individual enterprises. It was an unrealistic central planning mechanism, located in Moscow and isolated from the problems of individual enterprises scattered throughout the huge country. Such central planning often created disequilibrium in the allocation of resources among users and dissatisfaction among those who were responsible for the fulfillment of the plan. Because of mounting criticism on the inflexibility in planning by the USSR Gosplan, the USSR Soviet of Ministers in 1941 granted greater authority to gosplans of the constituent republics in devising and implementing their own plans. Similarly, the industrial ministries were permitted to expand their rights in planning. Consequently, beginning with 1941 the industrial ministries were empowered to devise plans for their respective industries which were coordinated by the USSR Gosplan on the national level.

However, this did not alter central planning, since all ministries were also located in Moscow, isolated from the local problems. Under the new planning system, ministries and individual enterprises, still faced with the scarcity of resources, attempted to safeguard the fulfillment of targets and often hoarded supplies and manpower, thus creating confusion in procurement activities and disequilibrium in the allocation of resources. Such multiformity existed until 1954 when Krushchev launched a bitter criticism on central planning in Moscow.

As a result of Khrushchev's criticism, the State Economic Commission for Current Planning under the jurisdiction of the USSR Soviet of Ministers was formed in May 1955. The USSR Gosplan was assigned to longrange planning only. This separation of short- and long-range planning authorities was found to be fruitless, and the Economic Commission was abolished in 1957 with the USSR Gosplan again being authorized to do all the planning. With the formation of sovnarkhozy, the USSR Gosplan underwent a new reorganization and emerged with greater power in the realm of long-range economic planning and technological development of the economy. However, the short-range planning activities were taken away from it.

As the country's planning organ, the main objective of the USSR Gosplan is to coordinate overall production of goods and services and to insure proportionate development of the economy including technological, scientific, cultural and all other areas which contribute to productivity of resources. On the basis of directives issued by the Party and the Government, the USSR Gosplan coordinates but does not plan normal short-range targets; it proposes long-term plans for supplying the country's demands for resources for the next 15 to 20 years. In addition, the USSR Gosplan proposes plans for shorter periods.

Since the 1957-58 reorganization, the USSR Gosplan, by virtue of its authority to allocate major resources among various users, controls the economy. Its functions are performed through gosplans of the constituent republics and their subordinate organizations. Through this network the USSR Gosplan not only controls the fulfillment of the plans and coordinates production throughout the country but also assigns to different sectors quotas for the most important resources such as raw materials, fuel, electric power, equipment, machinery, and consumer goods. In addition, the USSR Gosplan obtains goods and services required for the All-Union needs, establishes wholesale and retail prices, transportation rates and costs of services.

The 1957-58 reorganization of the USSR Gosplan also changed its structural organization. As of 1958 the Gosplan had ten overall planning departments:[2] Prospective Plans and Economic Development of Constituent Republics; Current Plans and Problems of Constituent Republics; Materials and Allocations; Labor and Wage; Cost of Production; Finance; Domestic Trade Turnover; Investments; Foreign Economic Relations; Specialization and Cooperation.

In addition, the USSR Gosplan has 21 industrial departments: Ferrous Metallurgy; Non-ferrous Metallurgy; Coal, Peat and Slate; Petroleum; Electrification; Timber, Paper and Woodworking; Construction Materials; Heavy Machine Building; Machine Building; Electro-technical and Instruments; Tractor and Agricultural Machinery; Consumer Goods; Foodstuffs; Transportation and Communication; Construction; Education and Health; Geology; Defense Industry; Chemicals; Agricultural Procurement; Fisheries.

All these departments are subdivided into sections, units, desks, and so on to facilitate detailed analyses of broad problems associated with the planning for the constituent republics and for each of the major industries. As can be noted from the list of industrial departments, the USSR Gosplan's main activities are directed to problems dealing with industrial production rather than with agriculture, even though the production of chemical fertilizers and farm machinery is planned by the Gosplan.

Aside from domestic problems, the USSR Gosplan is responsible for the coordination of the Soviet economy with countries within the Soviet bloc in order to reach the most advantageous division of labor among the bloc countries. The USSR Gosplan also proposes plans for exports and imports with the bloc countries and with non-communist countries. In short, the USSR Gosplan is responsible for the overall internal and external economic activities of the country.

While the USSR Gosplan watches for the fulfillment of the national targets, gosplans of the constituent republics perform similar functions, excluding international plans, within their own republics. Republic gosplans and their district offices establish annual plans for production and allocation of resources for enterprises located in their republics and coordinate the economic activities of sovnarkhozy and other large economic sectors within their republics. Being close to local problems, gosplans of the constituent republics are often influenced by local interests in their decisions. This creates disequilibrium in the national planning schemes. Some of the administrators within the USSR Gosplan have powers equivalent to that of the USSR Ministers, yet often they are unable to cope with strong localism practiced by some sovnarkhozy, especially in hoarding of supplies.

Planning procedures, either short-range or long-range, are nothing but "forward" planning. It is the coordination of all economic forces within the framework of the established plan that is hard to control. Once the decisions related to future production are formulated and become known to the USSR Gosplan, its machinery sets to work. As a starter, the USSR Gosplan analyzes the past performance of all important sectors. Individual industries are examined on their own merits and on their relations to the economy as a whole. The new national plan, then, includes the past achievements of every important sector plus anticipated additions to be realized through expansion of existing productive forces and greater usage of technology and improvement in labor productivity as decreed by higher authority.

Approved national targets are then assigned to constituent republics which in turn allot production quotas to sovnarkhozy, which hand over to individual enterprises their shares in production. All these planned production targets are called "Control Figures" and are used as minimum goals. Upon receiving the Control Figures, the individual enterprise devises its own planned outputs which may be above or below the targets established by the Control Figures. Depending on circumstances, the republic gosplan can adjust the original targets as given in the Control Figure for the enterprise, sovnarkhoz or even for the constituent republic. These adjustments are incorporated into the overall national plan. It is because of this procedure that the plans officially announced at the beginning of the period are often changed during the period.

Although the USSR Gosplan is responsible for the overall plan, the few remaining ministries still have authority in the development of their plans by their own planning departments. These planned targets are incorporated in the national Control Figures by the USSR Gosplan. The USSR Ministry of Finance develops its own annual plans for the State budget. The State Bank (Gosbank) works out the annual size of credits to be provided for economic expansion and estimates the volume of currency needed. The USSR Ministry of Foreign Trade estimates annual volume of exports and imports and the amount and type of convertible currency required for the operation of foreign trade. Other ministries, likewise, project their needs and potentialities in production within the framework of socio-economic consideration at home and abroad.

The USSR Gosplan, despite its great powers, is at times unable to correct unwise decisions made previously without adjusting other sectors, which might start a chain of reactions throughout the whole planning mechanism. This is a self-generating process. For this reason, blunders often occur and are difficult to avoid. For example, in the Latvian SSR in 1958 about 15 per cent of all its enterprises were submarginal and anticipated losses were planned and established. The presence of these enterprises was denounced by the Central Committee of the Communist Party and the USSR Soviet of Ministers and recommendations were advocated for the liquidation of all submarginal firms. Yet the USSR Gosplan and the USSR Ministry of Finance failed to take measures. To haul these enterprises out of the red would require adjustments in their cost of production as well as in wholesale and retail prices. Any of these adjustments would disrupt the currently existing cost-price relationship throughout the whole system. The best that regulatory agencies can do is to hope that other sectors will reduce their prices in order to enable submarginal firms to reduce their costs. Pooling of isolated Latvian peasant households into central areas of collective farms was approved many years ago but has achieved only token success. To speed up relocation of peasants, the republic needs construction materials and durable consumer goods. Requests by the Latvian Sovnarkhoz to the USSR Gosplan and the USSR Ministry of Trade for greater allocation of needed goods were ignored.

Another example of unwise decisions may be cited. The Lithuanian Sovnarkhoz was assigned agricultural targets for 1965 larger than those for 1958. To achieve the planned targets more chemical fertilizer is required. But the USSR Gosplan in 1958 allocated less chemical fertilizer to Lithuania than it was given in 1957 and the 1965 allocation for fertilizer is only slightly above the 1957 amount. Thus there is a constant tug of war between the USSR Gosplan and the individual sovnarkhozy which must have greater shares if they are to increase their outputs.

It is recognized that the allocation of scarce resources among various users cannot be precise and many poor decisions in allocation are likely to crop up, but planning in production can be more accurate. For example, the USSR Gosplan plans production of trucks, but not spare parts or tires for them. As a result many otherwise workable trucks are useless. In 1958 the Lithuanian Sovnarkhoz received an allocation of 475 rubles worth of spare parts for each truck on the collective farm whereas the minimum required under Lithuanian conditions is 1,300 rubles. Because of poor planning the Lithuanian SSR in 1957 had over 1,000 trucks out of use.[3] This was an unwise decision on the part of the USSR Gosplan, which still uses the macroeconomics approach in planning. It might be true that the average annual value of spare parts per truck for the country may be worth 475 rubles but such an average is overweighted by favorable conditions operative outside Lithuania.

## State Committees

State committees and administrations have replaced many abolished ministries, but their functions are quite different since they do not administer enterprises. The main task of these committees and administrations is to develop uniform scientific methodology and practices throughout the country in order to reach the fulfillment of economic and technological targets established by higher authority. There is a distinct division of labor, since each committee or administration engaged in a specific task is coordinated by the USSR Soviet of Ministers. They develop technology in order to increase production; they conduct scientific experiments to discover new products or to improve old ones; as a research and scientific organization they propose locations for the construction of new industrial sites, factories, and so on. They are responsible for all experiments and scientific work assigned to various industrial enterprises and scientific institutions. They are not administrative organs and therefore escape the pressure which the individual enterprises were able to put on their ministries in the past.

Since these committees and administrations are answerable only to the USSR Soviet of Ministers, there is a degree of separation between scientific and political targets, and consequently they are less influenced by political machinations than other institutions. In addition each committee has its own field of specialization. For example, the State Committee on Science and Technology is empowered to study scientific and technological accomplishments at home and abroad. To do this, the committee conducts research, makes experiments, constructs and tests new technology, and introduces standardized technology throughout the economy as a whole. The State Committee on Aviation Technology is made up of specialists dealing with their specific problems.

As organs of the USSR Soviet of Ministers, they have greater effect in obtaining information and cooperation from economic sectors than under the ministerial structure where local interests or disinterests were more common. Now these organs secure more complete required information more promptly and use facilities in many branches of the economy without arousing suspicion or jealousy among enterprises or administrative organs.

But what is significant is the fact that the specialists employed in these non-decision-making organizations do influence those whom they advise. Consequently, they shape indirectly the opinions of the top decision-makers. They do not represent the managerial group nor do they tangle with bureaucracy but they do sway the decisions of the high-ranking echelons. After all, even Khrushchev has to listen to atomic scientists.

Yet, being isolated from the local interests and having autonomy in their own spheres results in duplication of efforts and misunderstanding. For instance, in 1958 a scientific conference was called for the purpose of determining the usefulness of the metal-cutting machine NEIIMS, and it was discovered that over 100 different colleges, institutes, and experiment organizations were engaged in this problem without coordination of efforts. The water and sewer pipes used in the Ukraine in 1958 were of the same specifications as in 1882. These pipes were 10 to 25 per cent heavier than required and consequently more expensive.[4] Still, the State Committee on Standards, Measures and Weights has failed to devise less expensive pipes. True, new standards for water and sewer pipes can easily be found, but it would require adjustments in plants producing these pipes for the country as a whole and perhaps lighter pipes would not be suitable for colder climates elsewhere.

## Central Statistical Administration

In a society where the market is not controlled, decisions for production are made by individuals even though such decisions may be based on guesses, hunches, or statistical analyses. But as a planned economy, the Soviet decision-makers must have a large volume of diversified statistical information if some kind of balance between supply and demand of resources is to be attained. What is more important is that such information must be relatively reliable if disequilibrium in planning is to be avoided. This is especially true in the allocation of raw materials among various users, industrial capacity, manpower, transportation, and all other forces entering into a complex system of production of goods and services.

The USSR Central Statistical Administration was formed at the same time as the USSR Gosplan, in 1921, with its main purpose to gather statistics needed for the planners. At that early phase the young agency, without strong methodological concepts, failed to satisfy the political leadership, and in 1930 it was abolished and its functions were transferred to the more powerful USSR Gosplan. In 1948 the USSR Central Statistical Administration re-emerged as an independent agency answerable directly to the USSR Soviet of Ministers.

With the 1955 reorganization of the USSR Gosplan, the USSR Central Statistical Administration was assigned a greater role in gathering and analyzing statistical materials to be used for short-term and long-term planning and its findings were to be published. Strengthening of the USSR Central Statistical Administration was due to shortcomings of other planning organs, mainly of the USSR Gosplan and the State Economic Commission.

Prior to the formation of sovnarkhozy in 1957, individual enterprises were requested to supply statistical information to their ministries, to various planning, financial, and banking organizations, and at times even to local administrations. Since 1958, however, the USSR Central Statistical Administration became the sole agency in gathering and analyzing data pertaining to industry, agriculture, commerce, and education. At present the administration has 30 departments, about 4,000 permanent district offices throughout the Soviet Union, and approximately 80 per cent of all the workers are located at the major centers of industrial production and construction sites in order to obtain progress reports quickly for the higher authority.

The USSR Central Statistical Administration not only gathers and interprets the data, but also develops uniform statistical methodology. Beginning with 1958, uniformity of statistical methodology was introduced and definitions and statistical practices were spelled out. As a result of the new statistical methodology, the 1955, 1956, and 1957 data published prior to 1958 were adjusted in order to be comparable with the 1958 methodology. In addition, this administration develops various indices and indicators dealing with cost of production, labor productivity, utilization of materials; technological efficiency, prices, profitability, and savings. Last but not least the USSR Central Statistical Administration analyzes the effectiveness of automation, complex mechanization, and modernized equipment. The administration is not a policy-making organ, even though its statistics are used for economic, political, and scientific purposes by others.

Whatever statistical methodology and practices are adopted by the Russians, they are used for their own planning mechanism, and the reliability of their statistics becomes important to Western students of Soviet affairs in comparing the USSR with other countries. Undoubtedly, in the eyes of the West, Soviet statistics include unqualified, meaningless, evasive, and misleading information. But however noncomparable Soviet statistics may be, in most cases this can be traced to differences in statistical methodology and definitions rather than to a Soviet desire to mislead the West. After all, the same statistical material is used in national planning and in research at Soviet universities.

Consequently, statistical methodology and definitions of indices play an important part in this misunderstanding. For example, the production of iron ore in the United States is estimated in terms of iron content in the ore whereas in the Soviet Union output of all ores associated with iron ore mining is counted as iron ore. Such differences are causing more difficulty in agricultural than in industrial indices. The output of cotton in the United States is measured in terms of unginned cotton; in the Soviet Union it includes cotton seeds. The Soviet total sowed acreage is estimated in the spring; in the United States only the harvested spring acreage is counted, excluding crop losses sustained during the spring. The average milk yield for the USSR as a whole is calculated on the basis of all cows, including dry cows, whereas in the United States only the milking cows are included. It is such differences in methodology but mostly in definitions of indices that make Western students cautious and critical of Soviet statistics.

### Sovnarkhoz

The sovnarkhoz and its planning organs are responsible for the development and implementation of short-term and long-term plans for all industrial enterprises, construction sites, combines, trusts, and all other organizations under its jurisdiction. The sovnarkhoz is also authorized to devise plans for the specialized establishments organized for a specific purpose, cooperatives, and supply bases within the limits established by higher authority, in order that the national targets in all major items can be met.

Once proposed plans of each economic unit are assembled, their coordination falls in the realm of the gosplan of the constituent republic, while the managerial side remains with the sovnarkhoz. But it is the individual enterprise that originates the plans for actual physical production and for financial targets. Here we have dual responsibility. All physical plans devised by an enterprise are submitted for approval to the republic gosplan whereas all financial plans are approved by the republic Ministry of Finance. Under such division of authority, the physical plan may be approved while the financial plan may be rejected. This, of course, calls for revision of the rejected plan and causes a delay in coordination of both plans.

The individual enterprise receives its production targets through its sovnarkhoz. These plans have broad limits, spelling out the general goals. Based on these limits, more detailed production and financial plans are developed by the enterprise. For example, the government's planned targets of cotton fabric for a textile plant may be expressed in terms of total production; it is up to the textile plant to develop a plan for the production of different kinds of fabrics within the total production for all fabrics. Thus, plans proposed by the enterprise spell out quantity and quality indicators, contractual obligations agreed upon by the enterprise, ways and means by which the quality of goods is expected to be improved, timely fulfillment of all obligations and pledges. In addition, plans proposed by the enterprise include such items as estimates in labor productivity, reduction in the cost of production, efficiency of machinery, equipment and materials, and estimated profits or losses.

This requires not only the accumulation of a large volume of diversified statistical material but also an organization to do the planning. Every Soviet enterprise, no matter how big or small it may be, has a planning bureau, a department or a unit responsible for the development of physical production, technological, and financial plans—a so-called "Tekhpromfinplan."

The Tekhpromfinplan, therefore, is a detailed plan proposed by the enterprise but based on targets set in the overall Control Figures developed by the higher authority for the enterprises. It consists of seven major indices :[b]

> a. Plan for nomenclature, volume of each type of goods produced, gross and net outputs, daily, monthly, and quarterly production records, cooperation with other enterprises, usage of all indicators of productivity.
> b. Technological plan—showing existing technology, proposed installation of new technology and its efficiency in improving quality of goods produced.
> c. Manpower plan—including number of workers in each category of skills, their wages, plans to improve skills of the workers and the growth of labor productivity.

d. Cost of production—indicating reduction in costs of production and overhead.

e. Material-technical supply plan—showing the demand for raw materials, fuel, power, new equipment, and sources to cover these costs.

f. Capital construction plan—spelling out the size of work to be undertaken, time schedule for the completion of the undertaking, estimates for manpower and construction material needed, and proposed ways and means by which construction costs may be reduced.

g. Financial plan—describing the detailed expenditures for the above plans plus estimated profits, taxes, needs for credit and all other payments to the State.

Formulated plans are submitted to the sovnarkhoz, and upon their approval they are incorporated in the national plan of the USSR. These plans provide the sovnarkhoz with a full picture of economic standing of each enterprise and enable the sovnarkhozy to measure the progress of each enterprise. In addition, these plans can and often do reveal the extent of hoarding of resources or lack of them and their utilization. At least from a theoretical viewpoint these plans provide the sovnarkhoz with enough information to foresee and take necessary measures to prevent interruptions in production. However, the management of an enterprise often underestimates its productive capacity in order to cover up its own inefficiency. Of course, under ideal conditions and with sufficient resources to cover any eventualities, there should not be underestimation of plant capacity. But since this is not the case, the management of many enterprises does hoard manpower and materials to safeguard the fulfillment of assigned production targets.

### VERIFICATION

Even in the early stages of the Soviets, the machinery for verification was established for checking the accounting and practices of state establishments and the loyalty and efficiency of the workers. Later on, in 1921, instruments of verification were established for the Party membership in order to check the faithfulness and fitness of individual members. At present, economic participation of the Soviet worker overshadows the significance of this loyalty to the State because of the disappearance of the mass resistance which existed in 1918.

Verification is conducted by numerous state organizations and the Party and is reinforced by complaints from individuals. In the main, verifying organs check upon efficiency of enterprises, abuses, personal injustices, distortion of Party and State decrees and targets, red tape and similar deviations from decisions of the higher authority. In this way, economic and political verifications are intertwined and overlapping and are continuously undergoing alterations in scope, emphasis, and methods of application.

Under this complex system of checks and balances the USSR Soviet of Ministers, the USSR Gosplan, the USSR Ministry of Finance and the USSR Gosbank check on the rightful use of allocated resources and finances by the constituent republics. Similarly the corresponding organs in the constituent republic verify economic activities of individual enterprises and organizations.

The concept of verification as it is implemented now is quite different from the early days of the Soviet State. Nevertheless, the State allocates resources in order to avoid disequilibrium in utilization of such resources. A complete State policing of the economy in precise use of the resources would require a huge number of officials and large monetary expenditures. This is why the Soviets encourage the local Party organs and individual members of the Trade Union to participate in reporting to higher authorities all noncompliance with official decrees. But this does not create friendly feeling between the workers and their immediate supervisors, especially when management knows who the informers are. Therefore, only the unusual cases of deviations from the official line are brought to attention of higher authorities.

The Soviets claim that verification is a necessary tool by which many errors are detected and quickly corrected. But the system is not perfect, and during the XXth Party Congress in 1956 it was stated that verification is the weakest link in supervision of individual enterprises and their compliance with established production targets. This is true because no administrator would want to advocate a strong verification apparatus empowered to check his activities. Again, the priority of values of things devised by central planners often may be of no consequence to an individual manager or administrator—hence violations of official directives are widespread.

These violators are on both low and high levels of Soviet managerial strata. For example, during eight months of 1959, seven enterprises in the Kharkov Sovnarkhoz spent 2.8 million rubles for field trips of their employees and illegally appropriated this sum to administrative and procurement accounts. Similar unauthorized transfers of funds were found in other sovnarkhozy.[6] In 1958 the Chairman of the Mordovsk Sovnarkhoz transferred 10.5 million rubles from accounts assigned for the construction of the Saransk Power Plant, the power line, and the medical instruments factory to the account committed for the reconstruction of the Mordovsk

State University. Other unauthorized transfers of funds were also exposed in 1958.[7]

The fact that from the viewpoint of local leaders unauthorized use of resources in the long-run would yield greater returns is of no consideration to higher authority, which attempts to maintain economic discipline in order to obtain a planned balance in the utilization of resources. But it also suggests that many Soviet managers and administrators have imagination and daring in noncompliance with directive when values of greater importance to them conflict with official interests. It indicates that the weakness lies not in the people but in the system, because there are many violators attempting to improve their economic position or that of their enterprises.

## DISEQUILIBRIUM IN PLANNING

The Western meaning of "equilibrium" is generally described by Soviet economists as "proportionality." Both terms imply uniformity of growth in the economic framework with the purpose of attaining an optimum allocation of resources among alternative uses. Both terms include a desired balance between various magnitudes and coherence in continuous growth of all economic sectors free of important maladjustments.

The national plan of the Soviet Union is an attempt to ease the continuous growth of the economy. To maintain rational expansion of the economy, every enterprise becomes a part of the whole system in the same manner as the unborn child is a part of its mother by the umbilical cord. The overall plan is schemed on the assumption that given resources will produce given products without consideration of unforeseen forces causing disequilibrium. In a sense, the Russians are using the principle of "other things being equal" which existed in the past and extended in the planning for the future, with a hope of correcting some of the seeds which produced past maladjustments. However, future sources for disequilibrium may be of greater magnitude than in the past and more difficult to control. All this makes planning uncertain and often irrational.

Certainly World War II caused a tremendous disequilibrium in resources. After the war a rapid increase in urban population and the industrial labor force, as well as the destruction of housing, were responsible for the present housing shortages. Again, changes in military and political considerations have created disequilibrium in the allocation and usage of resources. In general, in the long run, one major economic disturbance such as a war would tend to accelerate maladjustments in all other sectors; while these sectors change their plans and practices, the disequilibrium develops.

War is not the only reason for disequilibrium. Changes in institutions also bring major maladjustments, as happened with the formation of sovnarkhozy. With the abolishment of ministries, the old supply channels were destroyed and new channels, although spelled out in directives, were not put into immediate operation by sovnarkhozy since they were in the process of setting up the new distribution machinery. Moreover, in the process of organization of their economies, many sovnarkhozy ceased to produce many items upon which other sovnarkhozy depended, thus causing disequilibrium in production.

The short-run disturbances such as droughts, floods, heavy snowfalls, fires and so on also create maladjustments in many areas. For instance, a heavy snowfall might disrupt normal transportation, forcing many enterprises with short inventories to reduce their normal production or to shut off production altogether, setting off interruptions of work in other enterprises not affected by weather. A drought covering a large area such as in 1946 will generate disequilibrium in many industries. Again, disequilibrium in resources might simply be because industrial growth advances too rapidly while agriculture lags behind.

Then, too, human miscalculations in planning result in disequilibrium. Enthusiastic planners, in their attempt to please the higher authority, often devise exceptionally high targets which when put into effect give rise to disparity. An example of such planning is found in the 1956-60 plan, the targets of which were so high that it was necessary to extend the time for their achievement to 1962; then it was finally replaced by the 1959-65 plan.

It is claimed by the Soviets that to avoid unnecessary disequilibrium in any sector of the economy the planners of the 1959-65 plan took into consideration all the eventualities which might cause such disparity. In other words this plan supposedly is a masterpiece of Soviet planning without overstrain on the economy, one which will enable all sectors to receive enough resources for the successful accomplishment of their targets.

Assuming that this is true but remembering that the Soviet Union has many submarginal firms, one can conclude that under these conditions efficient enterprises would create surpluses while inefficient one would produce just their quotas. The Russians anticipate just that and state that efficient producers with their surpluses would help their less fortunate compatriots. But while these theoretical anticipations were defended, some of the 1959-65 targets were revised downward because of increased emphasis on some of the sectors such as chemicals.

Generally speaking, central planning in a large country such as the USSR which produces diversified goods and services under different geographical conditions cannot devise a perfect long-term plan without disequilibrium. But it must be recognized too that under central planning short-run disequilibrium can be corrected much quicker than without any control of resources.

## Bibliography——Chapter 4

[1] *Zasedaniya Verkhovnogo Soveta SSSR*, Chetvertogo Sozyva (devyataya sessiya), Moscow, 1958, p. 134.

[2] Efimov, A. N., *Perestroyka Upravleniya Promyshlennost'yu i Stroitel'strom v SSSR*, Moscow, 1957, p. 85.

[3] *Zasedaniya Verkhovnogo Soveta SSSR*, Pyatogo Sozyva (pervaya sessiya), Moscow, 1958, p. 289.

[4] *Vneocherednoy XXI S'ezd Kommunisticheskoy Partii Sovetskogo Soyuza*, January 25-February 5, 1959 (I), Moscow, 1959, p. 121.

[5] Evenko, I. A., *Voprosy Planirovaniya v SSSR na Sovremennom Etape*, Moscow, 1959, pp. 49-50.

[6] *Zasedaniya Verkhovnago Soveta SSSR*, Pyatogo Sozyva (vtoraya sessiya), Moscow, 1959, p. 39.

[7] *Vneocherednoy XXI S'ezd Kommunisticheskoy Partii Sovetskogo Soyuza*, January 25-February 5, 1959 (II), Moscow, 1959, p. 48.

## CHAPTER 5

# Organizational Structure in Industry

## INTRODUCTION

Soviet industry is overwhelmingly mining and capital production. While the Soviet Union is building up capability for future production of consumers' goods, the distribution and service functions are of secondary significance. The central planners of the iron society, even at the beginning of the Bolshevik regime, had a better understanding of the industrial than of the agricultural sector. Industrial facilities and factory workers were then, as now, concentrated in urban centers. It was much simpler to organize, to control, and to discipline the industrial sector than the millions of dispersed peasants.

To produce goods and services for the country's needs, some sort of organizational structure for command of production must exist. This led to the establishment of administrative domains from the highest to the lowest levels of authority with power to make long-run decisions for the country as a whole and daily decisions by which an enterprise could be run effectively. Hence a pyramidal organizational structure was developed to run the Soviet central-planned industry.

At the beginning of Red control, the organizational structure of the economy was loose and flexible, regulated with decrees issued by the Supreme Soviet of the People's Economy. Since this highest authority suffered from controversial theoretical interpretations among its own leaders as to how the emancipated economy was to be organized and administered, its effectiveness was not complete. To run the economy successfully, the delegation of power to make decisions on the spot was then assigned to economic regions. Later a more centralized control developed, and economic regions were replaced by specialized commissariats from which greater efficiency was expected. It was anticipated that no single specialized industry administered by a commissariat could be completely self-sufficient; therefore it could be controlled by the higher central planning authority more effectively.

But as the country's industrial complexity increased, the relationship between individual enterprises and commissariats (ministries later on) became cumbersome; coordination among specialized industries became confused, and industrial expansion was retarded. As a result, the Soviets in 1957 again delegated the power to make decisions to sovnarkhozy, which are expecting to improve efficiency.

At present, industrial organizational structure is focused in four broad sectors: (1) the All-Union sector which includes large economic regions such as the Urals; (2) homogeneous industries such as transportation, agriculture, fuel; (3) industries which are still under the jurisdiction of various ministries and administrations; and (4) sovnarkhozy. This system of authority is not perfect and further organizational changes and adjustments will come, not because of political necessity but because of economic and technological developments within the economy itself.

## ALL-UNION SECTOR

From the early days of the Soviet State, its leaders were faced with problems of industrial production. The nationalized means of production had to be expanded; the industrial labor force had to be fully employed. Since the free market was destroyed, decisions dealing with industrial production had to be centralized. But at that early period the Soviet leaders lacked the theoretical knowledge for successfully organizing industrial production; they also lacked loyal and trusted industrial administrators. They did know that if their system was to survive and the expected economic equilibrium was to be achieved, industry had to be put under central administration.

Accordingly, in December 1917 the Soviets organized the RSFSR Supreme Soviet of Peoples' Economy (VSNKh) whose functions were to regulate the economic life of the country and to administer industrial production. Under the 1917 directive, the VSNKh was to organize the economy and finance; to develop the average norms of production for industry; to plan production; and to coordinate industrial activities of the centralized and local administrative spheres of influence. This was the beginning of central planning and administration for industry.

At this stage, formation of the early economic regional administrations or so-called sovnarkhozy was encouraged, and through these the VSNKh regulated the economy. As noted in Chapter 3, these early sovnarkhozy were much larger in territory than the present ones and included all of the Northern Region, the Urals, the South, and other regions. By 1920 there were 86 sovnarkhozy where 37,000 industrial enterprises were located. About 25 per cent of the total number of enterprises were merged into an industrial trust, while the rest were under the jurisdiction of main administrations or supervised by local sovnarkhozy.

Although this system provided some decentralization of decisions, it did not last long. Shortages of consumer goods and foodstuffs forced the Soviets in 1919 to establish the War Communism, under which control of the economy became highly centralized. The role of sovnarkhozy in the management of industry declined and many industries were reorganized into industrial administrations with homogeneous characteristics. The highest authority was still the VSNKh, which organized a number of industrial bureaus for each economic region. Shortly after the formation of the USSR in December 1922, the status of the VSNKh was changed to that of an All-Union organ.

With the formation of the VSNKh of the USSR, the Soviet industrial sector was divided into three jurisdictions: the All-Union sector, primarily heavy industry; the republic sector; and the local sector. Under this separation of authority, the enterprises of All-Union significance were pooled into trusts, which in 1924 numbered over 70. To coordinate the economic activities of these trusts a new agency, the Central Administration of All-Union Industries, was established. Small trusts under republic jurisdiction likewise were merged into larger industrial trusts, and responsibility for their coordination was delegated to the Main Economic Administration of each constituent republic, which was answerable to the VSNKh and to the local sovnarkhoz. The local industry was liable to the republic VSNKh and the sovnarkhoz. And the VSNKh was accountable to the Soviet of Labor and Defense and the Soviet of Peoples' Commissars.

By 1926 the VSNKh of the USSR, through numerous main administrations and departments, administered the following twelve fields: metallurgy, defense, textiles, electro-technical, chemicals, agriculture, timber-paper, solid fuels, geology-geodesy, printing, leather, and scientific-technical. Meanwhile the Central Administration of All-Union Industries and the Main Economic Administration were supplanted by a new organ, the USSR Planning Administration. For a short period this agency encouraged expansion of industrial syndicates, but because of their unsuccessful record they were merged with local administrative organs.

Instability in the administration of the All-Union sector existed until 1928, when the Soviets were able to gear their economy to the long-range five-year planning schemes. As industrial output increased and as new industries were developed, the administrative apparatus also expanded. This created the need for further changes, and in January 1932 the VSNKh of the USSR was changed to the Peoples' Commissariat of Heavy Industry. Simultaneously the timber and light industries were separated into the All-Union and Republic jurisdictions and a few new commissaries were formed. In 1940 there were 39 Peoples' Commissariats of the USSR which, according to the Russians, facilitated central planning and administration for each specialized industry. By the end of 1940 these commissariats were transformed into All-Union, Union-Republic, and Republic ministries and each ministry controlled more or less specialized industry such as coal, petroleum, chemicals, and so on. Other less specialized industries such as consumer goods, food, and the like were administered by less specialized ministries.

It would be erroneous to assume that the industrial organizational pattern on the national level can remain unchanged. The need for flexible organization stems from different causes. Rapidly expanded industrial production would be cause for alteration in the pre-expansion organizational structure. New industries, new products, new technology also tend to have their impact on organizational structures. Indeed, from 1917 to 1940 the All-Union industrial organization was systematically adjusted in its forms and methods to fit the new socio-economic conditions. For example, before the Revolution Russian metallurgy was a very simple industry and was considered as one branch of the economy. Now, with technological advancements, metallurgy is classified and subdivided into more than 40 sectors such as machine-building, metal processing and so on, with each sector producing a different commodity. The chemicals and plastics industries provide other examples of how new products can force the existing organizational patterns to alter their forms.

The huge, diversified industrial sector of the USSR cannot have a dormant organizational structure. As the number of industrial enterprises increases and their output expands, a new and more flexible administrative organization has to be found. It requires diffusion of authority rather than concentration of it as in 1920. The 1960 planned production covers 133 major industrial branches producing some 11,000 different products.[1] It is a tremendous task for any central administrative organ to supervise the planned production of diversified goods ranging from matches to sputniks.

Imagine, if you can, 306,000 industrial enterprises and construction sites, plus other state industrial and agricultural establishments, stores,

warehouses, schools, banks, post-offices, and the like, which are administered by the vertical organization located in Moscow. At the end of 1958
the participating industrial labor force in the USSR was over 20 million
persons. Such a concentration of decision-making power over investments
and workers is bound to develop bottlenecks. Correction of bottlenecks,
because of overlapping authority, was often delayed at best; and finally
the Soviets were forced to delegate decision-making power to smaller and
more flexible administrative organs—to sovnarkhozy.

As of 1960 the All-Union sector is organized to administer only 14
basic industries:[2] ferrous and non-ferrous metallurgy, petroleum and natural gas, coal, electric power stations, machine-building, agriculture, defense, radio-technology, construction sites and materials, timber, paper,
woodworking consumers' goods, and foodstuffs. Production in these industries is planned in the light of domestic and international political and
economic conditions and is closely controlled through a pyramidal network of All-Union administrative organs extending to individual enterprises. Such an organizational structure is not perfect; it cannot be perfect, for it is in a state of continuous modification. Perhaps by 1965 the
existing All-Union industrial sector will be further disentangled to meet
the new economic conditions.

This trend already may be seen in the fact that beginning with 1959
the establishment of annual plans for industry has been abandoned and
replaced by more detailed planned targets which are no longer limited
to one year, but are for the time required to attain the goal. This applies
also to new technology, utilization of which cannot be accomplished within
a specified period of time.

## REPUBLIC SECTOR

Prior to 1957, the heterogeneous industrial sector of each constituent
republic was administered by a large number of All-Union, Union-Republic and Republic ministries. Even the Uzbek SSR, considered to
be the most homogeneous region within the Soviet Union, with over 70
different industrial branches, was supervised by 52 ministries, often unable
to coordinate activities of major economic branches. A host of ministries
ran the economies of other constituent republics.

With such pyramidal organizational structure on three different levls
of authority, industrial specialization was difficult to develop and to expand. Each ministry, no matter how large or how small, attempted to
be self-sufficient in all its supplies. This was especially true in the machine-

building industry, where a large number of enterprises under different ministerial jurisdictions produced the necessary equipment and supplies. Of course, such a diffusion in production did not improve efficiency in authority. For example, the production of agricultural machinery was concentrated in the hands of 24 different ministries, each supervising a certain branch producing certain parts needed in assembling the machines. Metal-cutting equipment was produced in 171 enterprises under the jurisdiction of 19 ministries while the Ministry of Metal-Cutting Industry totally supervised only 55 enterprises.[3] The outcome of such organizational structure resulted in a large number of small-scale establishments producing small volumes of goods for their parent enterprises, retarding both the development of technology and the improvement of labor productivity.

This organizational structure was ended in 1957 with the formation of sovnarkhozy and the abolishment of 141 All-Union, Union-Republic and Republic ministries. The number of employees in the All-Union ministries was reduced by 33,000 and in the Republic ministries by 47,000, a total of 80,000 persons, most of whom were absorbed by sovnarkhozy or by individual enterprises. As of 1959 there were still six All-Union and ten Union-Republic ministries.

In fact, with the formation of sovnarkhozy the role of constituent republics in matters of actual management of their industries has been curtailed. The republics still have authority above sovnarkhozy only in a few exceptional cases where such administration is absolutely necessary. The Uzbek SSR, for instance, has the Ministry of Cotton Production simply because this republic produces and processes cotton in four of its sovnarkhozy. To coordinate the production of cotton among all four sovnarkhozy, which do not administer agricultural enterprises, the republic runs this industry through the ministry. Since the growing of cotton is concentrated in Central Asia only, there was no need for a USSR Ministry of Cotton Production.

The only agencies which gained greater authority are the Ministries of Finance of each constituent republic and their subordinate regional offices. This additional power came in a roundabout way and through increased power of the central control of the All-Union financial sector. Since the All-Union sector controls the production of basic industries, the USSR Soviet of Ministers prohibits the USSR Gosplan and consequently gosplans of constituent republics from altering planned capital investments in these industries. However, supervision of financial expenditures of any enterprise is entrusted not to the gosplan but to the Ministry of

Finance. Hence it is the power to investigate, to approve, or to reject any unusual expenditure proposed or already undertaken by individual enterprise or even by the sovnarkhoz that makes the Ministry of Finance so powerful.

Despite measures designed to enforce the rightful utilization of appropriations, violations still presist. An investigation of 89 sovnarkhozy showed that in 1958, 29 of them disobeyed the State investment directives and illegally transferred funds amounting to 318 million rubles earmarked for All-Union sectors to other uses.[4] It is for this lack of financial discipline among enterprises (which, if not encouraged, is at least ignored by the sovnarkhozy) that greater authority was vested in the Ministry of Finance. This, of course, increases the animosity between the Ministry of Finance on the one hand and individual enterprises and sympathetic sovnarkhoz on the other, while all these organizations are under the jurisdiction of the Soviet of Ministers of the same constituent republic.

## REGIONAL SECTOR

The regional administrative system in the Soviet Union has always been prominent in the planning and control of industry. This is the basis for the comparative advantage of one region over another—the maximum planned exploitation of every region and theoretical and practical scheming for regional specialization.

The principle of regional comparative advantage was used in planning by the Russians as early as 1920 when eight economic regions were organized for the most rational use of local resources and manpower. Since the Soviet economy at that time was less complex than now, each of the regions occupied a huge territory with more or less homogeneous industries. These regions were: the Northern, Central-Industrial, Volga River Valley, Southern, Urals, Caucasus, Turkestan, and Western Siberia. Eastern Siberia and the Far East were excluded because the Civil War was still unsettled there.

At the end of the Civil War in 1921 the territories of the established economic regions were reduced, Eastern Siberia and the Far East were included, and the number of economic regions was increased to 21. These regions had greater homogeneity in resources and industrial specialization, exploitation of which were controlled by local inexperienced talent, hemmed in by central planners in Moscow.

With the establishment of the first Five-Year Plan in 1928 the central planners anticipated creation of 24 economic regions, and 32 in the second Five-Year Plan.[5] At that time it was felt that as the industrial production of each economic region increased, the region could be reduced in size in order that each region could become a true homogeneous industrial complex. Along with this idea, it was also proposed that every industrial complex could eventually become an administrative unit of the territory it occupies. Moreover, since communication and transportation facilities between Moscow and many distant regions were poor, such administrative organizations could facilitate the decision-making mechanism in all less important aspects of regional production on the spot, rather than bothering Moscow with a host of minute details. In short, at the beginning of the Soviet central planning era, the leaders visualized some delegation of decision-making authority to the economic regions with overall supervision of the central organs located in Moscow. But while these theoretical considerations were debated, the unloved-by-Marxists reality forced them to adopt the more specialized industrial controls.

One of the reasons for the difference in industrial control through economic regions or through specialized industries is that the establishment of economic regions with even a mild kind of autonomy leads to horizontal organizational structure. Under such an arrangement several regions, united in their efforts to improve their own economic position, might undermine the overall national plan; and the USSR was not ready to grant such powers to regions.

Although the formation of a regional structure was undermined by specialized industrial commissariats, the concept of regional industrial controls has never been completely destroyed. Between 1928 and 1957 regional planning, construction, and production were limited to few economic activities such as mining (Donbass), reforestation, irrigation, transportation, agriculture, and some other sectors. During this period territories, because of changing economic conditions, became flexible. Fluidity in territories came about through regional industrial growth, increased transportation network, growth of the total population, development of new resources, and administrative-territorial changes within the constituent republics.

Perhaps the main reason for the existence of a regional problem in the Soviet Union is its huge territory. Were the USSR as homogeneous a country as Sweden, for example, it would not have this problem. Moreover, the regional organizational pattern as an alternative to the specialized ministerial system has never been fully developed by the Russians and was opposed by the ministerial clique, who protected their own interests.

In 1956 the USSR Gosplan, facing increased criticism of centralization, again proposed the formation of 24 basic economic regions with power to administer their own economies. This proposal was advanced as the solution to the bureaucratic system of ministerial administration. But the proposal was rejected on the ground that regions were too large in territories, in population, and in industrial production to make them different. It was also claimed that since many of the proposed economic regions overlapped territory of more than one constituent republic cooperation among different republics would be difficult to maintain. Nevertheless, the idea of the regional industrial structure was adopted with some modification in 1957 and resulted in the formation of sovnarkhozy.

At the 1958 Communist Party Congress it was stated that with the formation of sovnarkhozy, many functions performed by the State in the past would gradually be transferred to sovnarkhozy in order to speed up economic development of the country. However, it was emphasized that this does not mean that the role of the central authority as a builder of a pure Communist State is being undermined. This goal is not set aside, but by changing the organizational structure the same goal is expected to be pushed ahead at a more rapid pace. If this is correct, then the leaders of the Communist Party foresee further adjustments in the organizational set-up.

## SOVNARKHOZ

With criticism of a centralized ministerial administration mounting, the Soviets have searched for a more efficient system ever since the end of World War II. The general idea of the early regional administrative apparatus, which was not very successful in 1920, was re-examined and again became prominent in 1957. The old idea was renovated and modified to fit present conditions and was centered around the old concept of the sovnarkhoz in which the Soviets have found an economically desirable and politically feasible system of regional administration or a large array of establishments, combines, and trusts, situated in a relatively compact industrial complex.

As of now, sovnarkhozy are responsible for the production of three-fourths of the total industrial output. They account for the entire output of iron ore, pig iron, metallurgical machinery, steam and gas turbines, automobiles, chemicals, and general purpose machinery. They produce almost all Soviet steel, rolled ferrous metals, non-ferrous metals, coal, petroleum, cement, textiles, plus 81 per cent of the total production of leather footwear.[6] Therefore a sovnarkhoz administers not a single-line industry as under the ministerial system, but a whole industrial complex producing a variety of goods and services.

The establishment of sovnarkhozy had an impact on administrative functions of the State. The central planning system was drastically reduced, permitting sovnarkhozy greater power in decision-making and planning. For example, the 1957 All-Union Plan contained 4,200 economic indicators of which 1,700 were related to major industrial items of All-Union significance; in 1958, 2,450 indicators were specified and only 1,042 of them were major industrial goods. The 1959-1962 All-Union Plans spell out production of about 820 different items.[7]

The sovnarkhoz has the power to increase its planned production by utilizing non-controlled or local resources. It can produce goods from resources provided by a customer which may be another sovnarkhoz or its individual enterprise. In a sense, the sovnarkhoz sells its services to others. It plans production for its enterprises in the realm of major items, leaving the more detailed items to individual enterprises. It has the authority to keep for its own use up to five per cent of the total new investment in capital goods, materials, wage fund and manpower. This amount is to be used for any emergency arising from any changes in planned production or for stimulating production of lagging enterprises.

Another change was the reduction in the number of small-scale and inefficient enterprises. In the 1955-56 period, 25 to 30 per cent of all industrial enterprises under the ministerial administration failed to fulfill their quota production. In 1957-58, the number of such submarginal enterprises was reduced to 15 per cent. Moreover, many still existing submarginal enterprises have improved their efficiency and recorded smaller losses than prior to 1957.[8] With the establishment of sovnarkhozy only two administrative systems remain. The sovnarkhoz runs the industries of All-Union and Republic significance; the local soviets administer local industries.

It is claimed by the Soviets that with the establishment of sovnarkhozy, the old centralized ministerial system was replaced by a more flexible organization. However, some of the sovnarkhozy produce different volumes of the same commodities. There is a degree of decentralization of a single industry which, in the past, was administered by one ministry. Three sovnarkhozy (Ivanovo, Moscow, and Vladimir), all with connecting boundaries, produce about two-thirds of the USSR cotton fabrics. The Ivanovo Sovnarkhoz produces over 30 per cent of the total cotton fabrics; the Vladimir, only 13 per cent. To Ivanovo this industry is of major economic significance and Ivanovo would certainly strive to improve and to expand it. Vladimir, where the textile industry is of lesser significance, might find it more profitable to invest in other industries. Under these conditions, the development of a single industry such as textiles by many sovnarkhozy may be of an irrational nature, with some sovnarkhozy expanding it while others maintain "status quo" or even curtail it.

## LOCAL SECTOR

It was stated previously that the local industries are organized for the purpose of producing goods utilizing local resources to supply the local markets. For example, a collective farm having excessive labor for its normal needs during its off-season may organize a small brickmaking enterprise. Its clay is there and free, simple hand implements can be made by the peasants, and unused farm transportation facilities can be fully utilized by such an enterprise. The peasants can be organized to use their spare time in production of harnessing equipment, sledges, wooden shovels,. and a number of other handicraft items.

In the city the local authorities organize small-scale enterprises producing items for local markets—foodstuffs, toys, garments, footwear, and other handicraft articles. In addition, the city provides public services such as housing, bath houses, barber shops, and many others. The main objectives are to utilize local resources and skills and to provide goods and services for local markets and jobs to disabled or retired citizens who still can contribute to the national production while improving their own earning power.

In comparison with state-owned enterprises, the local producing units are not only small but are inefficient and lack technology. As a result their productivity is low. In the RSFSR, for example, the average number of workers per enterprise is under 100 persons, and many of them have only 30 or 40 workers. But it is the absence of mechanization rather than the few workers that makes many of them unprofitable to operate; yet, since they are essential for the public welfare, they are often permitted to function at a loss.

The present importance of local industries to the country as a whole is greater than it was prior to the transfer to local authorities from ministerial jurisdiction. In 1956 the total output of local industries was about 15.4 billion rubles; in 1958 their planned production was estimated at 100 billion rubles, with 15.5 billion rubles in anticipated profit.[9]

To stimulate improvement in the efficiency and profitability of local enterprises, they may retain up to 60 per cent of their gross profits in order to increase their output of goods and services. The other 40 per cent, taken by the local authority, can be used for any purposes, not necessarily connected with improvement of local industries. However, since profits from local enterprises are small and the cost of new technology is high, the management of local enterprises cannot use their profits for that purpose as the larger state-owned enterprises do. During the 1954-56 period, for example, some local enterprises spent as little as 23 per cent of profits for improvement of their efficiency; the other part was spent for non-productive activities such as paying higher wages to workers to keep them on the job. Consequently, the application of the small profits obtained by such enterprises often interferes with the planned expansion schems devised for them by higher authorities.

## ORGANIZATION OF AN ENTERPRISE

A Soviet enterprise is just one cog in the State machinery that produces goods and services, the quantity and quality of which, in the main, are determined by officials rather than by consumers. But the enterprise is not entirely a puppet; it may without approval of higher authority alter its operations to produce better goods, to lower the cost of production, to maximize its profits, or even to lower the quality.

As a business organization, a Soviet enterprise is engaged not only in production of goods and services but also in purchases of raw materials, sales of its goods, rendering services, to others and hiring and firing workers. However, it is not solely a profit-seeking undertaking as in other economic systems, and although the profit motive does exist, it is regulated by the State to prevent the development of losses. It is because of these profit opportunities, however uncertain they may be, that a mild form of competition among enterprises producing similar products does exist.

The administrative structure of a Soviet enterprise patterns itself on a vertical combination of authority. The highest authority is represented by the director of the enterprise. Under his direct supervision, depending upon the size and the purpose of the enterprise, are a number of departments. In most industrial enterprises there are a few basic departments: planning; bookkeeping; labor, wages, and training; safety controls; production and servicing, to name a few.

Every director has at least one assistant who helps him run the enterprise; generally he heads the procurement and selling departments. In addition, every industrial enterprise has a chief engineer whose duties extend to the supervision of production, construction, technology, mechanization, and power departments. Under these highest administrative officers of the enterprise are the heads of sub-departments, shops, and sections and many minor administrative, technical and office personnel.

The production function of an enterprise is also framed after the vertical combination of authority and basically consists of three types of organization: (1) the production shop or department, which is usually comprised of a score of specialized production sections; (2) the technological shop which is made up of stock, processing, and distribution sections; and (3) the mixed shop, the least specialized of the three, which has a stock section, a single-line products section, and a diversified products section. Second in importance to the production shop is the technological shop which supervises transportation and warehousing. Next in importance are the repair, instruments, and power shops. The last is the complementary shop, which utilizes waste.

In addition to production and distribution functions the Soviet enterprise provides services to its workers such as training, clubs, housing, nurseries and kindergartens for workers' children, cafeterias, medical aid and plots of land for the workers' gardens. Consequently, the Soviet enterprise represents a small community with a multitude of problems, the welfare of which depends upon the management of the enterprises.

The shop (tsekh) in a Soviet enterprise is the administrative unit producing finished or semi-finished goods or performing services for other shops. Every shop has a number of sections and each section is represented by floor space where a number of workers with tools at their disposal collectively produce a given type of goods or services. Actually, the section is the lowest link in the chain of administrative apparatus of the enterprise.

As a rule, a section is divided into working places for each worker. These places may be specialized to the point where only one type of goods is produced or where a single operation is performed, or it may be a place where at different times the output of goods or operations is diversified.

Prior to 1957 many enterprises, hoping to maintain self-sufficiency in spare parts and simple equipment, kept a large number of workers assigned to their production. For instance, a survey made in the machine-building industry showed that the number of workers in supporting activities ranged from 55 to 60 per cent of the total labor force. In the automobile and tractor plants more than half of the total labor force was in supporting occupations producing bolts, nuts, and services, often functioning with simple tools or hand labor. With the formation of sovnarkhozy, however, this self-sufficiency and consequent small-scale specialization was replaced by multi-purpose shops which produced many items by their own efforts. This was especially true in heavy industry, where the needs for diffusion of production were not as acute as in other areas. No sooner was it adopted by many industries than a new trend developed. The new trend is for the abolishment of shops as such and for the increasing importance of sections. The new trend in the organizational structure is taking form as a result of increased automation in many industries. Already many tool and instrument-producing industries and some automobile plants, especially the ones located in big cities such as Moscow and Leningrad, have eliminated shops in favor of sections. It is claimed that this change resulted in simplification in planning and reduction in the cost of production; it also relieved the burden in accounting and documentation. However, replacement of shops by sections coincided with a recent increase in their size in certain industries. Other industries still have sections subordinated to shops.

## Director

The director of Soviet enterprise is a trusted and loyal servant of the State. He has to be in order to hold his post. He is a trustee of his plant's facilities, supplies, and all things, including the manpower for the production of goods and services. He is responsible for the production of a share of the gross national output, and the success with which he runs his enterprise is a measure of his own success.

He is personally accountable to a host of higher authorities for all unwise decisions made by him, yet his power to make decisions is restricted by them. He is not a fool, but he is a product of a society which does not encourage deviations from the approved modes of conduct. As a member of this society he forms the habit of looking straight ahead but not into the distant future. His immediate duties are spelled out for him by the State, and he tries to perform them intelligently. Once immediate duties are completed he waits until results appear. With the accomplished results, either good or bad, a new action is taken by him again in the prescribed manner. He is like a chess player who has in his head no moves beyond the one he is about to make. Since he is functioning in a society of scarcity with his ability to make decisions tied up by the system he represents, he is often dumbfounded when things go well for any length of time.

Moreover, since he is a respected and highly paid official with power to make the less fortunate do what he wants, he naturally protects his position. To be able to do this he must have flexible morals, learned not in Soviet schools but in blunders, observations, and association with persons who already have traversed the rough course in the art of survival. Self-protection within the limited scope of available actions is a vital motive in his decisions, for he cannot quit his job for another with the same employer—the State.

The State itself is responsible for many of the undesirable characteristics that go with the management of an enterprise. Many obsolete laws passed prior to World War II and even some enacted in 1955 cause difficulty for the director. Many regulations dealing with the delegation of power are confusing, overlapping, and fraught with different interpretations. Even though the duties of a director are prescribed by the State, discrepancies in laws often compel him to take unauthorized courses of action. What is more important is that whatever action he takes may be deemed improper if it does not please the higher authority.

Profits, one of the prime phases in administering Soviet enterprise, are important to both the State and the director. In 1958 over 20 per cent of the total All-Union budget was made up from this source. It is from profits that the director's "fund" is derived. The director's fund is established by plan for the anticipated profits. When planned profits materialize they serve as indicators of the economic position of the enterprise. It is true that enterprises may have profits and losses simultaneously, because while the physical production plan may be fulfilled and also show profits, the financial plan, because of variations in such factors as material costs, wages, or the price of produced goods, may show losses.

Assuming that both plans were profitable, the enterprise could set aside a given percentage of profits for the fund. This fund may be used to cover losses, to improve services to workers, to increase turnover capital, to expand production facilities, to pay interest on loans, to buy modern technology, as well as other things.

The director's fund usually stems from three sources—the fulfillment of planned physical production, planned reduction in the cost of production, and planned profits. In the first instance, the fund ranges from one to six per cent of the planned total value of all goods produced, but from 20 to 50 per cent from the amount produced over the planned value. In the second instance, when planned reduction in the cost of production is achieved, the enterprise may form a fund amounting from four to 40 per cent of the total reduced costs. In the last case, a fund range from one to 20 per cent of the total gross profits is permitted.

Although expenditures of these funds are prescribed by the State, the director has a free hand in spending them, for he is not accountable for their precise allocation. In this sense, he has the ultimate power either to increase services for his worker, for example, or to invest them in new technology.

Of the three sources, only the fund derived from overplanned profits carries more detailed regulations. This fund can be used for premium payments to workers participating in the All-Union competition for highest production records. This source is also used to establish the general fund for the enterprise and for the construction of housing for the workers; it may take up to 30 per cent of the total profits. Overplanned profits are used to pay debts on capital borrowed for the purchase of new technology and to cover the increased cost of production as decreed by the State.

All in all, the director's fund is a powerful economic factor which can be used to improve the standard of living of the workers, who are closely watching its expenditure by the director.

## Foreman of the Shop

The foreman is responsible for all activities of his shop and answerable to the director or the assistant director. Usually the shop consists of several sections, each headed by a section chief or "master." It is the duty of the foreman to arrange available resources for maximum production in each section. With powers granted by the director, he hires and fires many workers, promotes them to better jobs, and in general acts as any shop foreman elsewhere in the world.

Many foremen are experienced workers but lack general education. Thus they experience keen competition from new workers who are now entering industrial labor with seven to ten years of schooling background. To keep their jobs the older men must study and be better qualified. This, of course, creates ill feeling between the old-timers and the younger men.

Again, many foremen are not interested in the development of new products. Their bonuses depend on fulfillment of monthly outputs in terms of norm-hours spent for the old items, the production cycle of which has been mastered by the workers in the shop. Consequently, an unhappy foreman can be a hindrance in the production of new items or in the installation of new equipment because on the short run he and his men will be receiving lower take-home pay. It is in such cases that the director's fund may be successfully used to overcome the foreman's reluctance and the apathy of the workers over whom he has jurisdiction.

## Master

The "master" or the section chief is responsible to the foreman of the shop. The success or failure of an entire enterprise rests on the efficiency of each section where actual production takes place. In a small enterprise without shops the master is under the direct supervision of the director of the enterprise. He organizes the production processes. With the approval of the foreman he can hire a worker and assign him to a job. He maintains working discipline, organizes competition among workers for higher production, and in general tries to improve the efficiency of men and equipment. In many enterprises where bonuses are permitted the master is given three per cent of the total monthly money wage received by the section. This becomes his fund, and from it he pays bonuses to workers for their productivity. This system of incentives in terms of bonuses starts at the lowest level in the administrative pyramid of the Soviet enterprise and works up to the director. And one cannot avoid the conclusion that while the leaders of the Soviet Union boast about their dedication to the great course of communism and equality, men in the shops and sections have developed a distinct sense of materialism which is maintained through a complex vertical system of authority and bonus payments.

## Bibliography—Chapter 5

[1] Evenko, I. A., *Voprosy Planirovaniya v SSSR na Sovremennom Etape*, Moscow, 1959, pp. 67-68.

[2] *Ibid.*, p. 66.

[3] Efimov, A. N., *Perestroyka Upravleniya Promyshlennost'yu i Stroitel'strom v SSSR*, Moscow, 1957, p. 22.

[4] *Finansy SSSR*, No. 7, 1958, p. 12.

[5] Efimov, *op. cit.*, p. 30.

[6] Efimov, *op. cit.*, p. 136; Evenko, *op. cit.*, pp. 16-17.

[7] Evenko, *op. cit.*, pp. 77-78.

[8] *Ibid.*, p. 181.

[9] *Finansy SSSR*, No. 7, 1958, pp. 27, 30.

## CHAPTER 6

# Industrial Output

### INTRODUCTION

The spectacular growth of Soviet industrial production is centered around rapid increase of production in mining, capital goods, and construction activities. Any method devised for the purpose of measuring credibility of official Soviet statistics showing high increase in industrial production would probably show a rapid rate of industrial expansion, even though it might be below the official rate.

In many cases the great achievements claimed by the Soviets are the result of statistical methodology, quite different from the West, and it would be a difficult task to calculate one's own indices. Moreover, official Soviet statistics reveal many shortcomings by which industrial growth can be analyzed without complete rejection of Soviet statistics. Therefore, to avoid statistical guessing games, use of Soviet data in this chapter, as in others, is not intended to be a bland acceptance of the boastfulness of Soviet achievements; rather, it represents a basis for certain conclusions associated with industrial expansion that goes on in the Soviet Union.

Despite any exaggeration, it is clear that industrial output has grown markedly since 1930—a growth made possible by the construction of many new factories and other installations using modern technology. Along with physical expansion of facilities, the Soviets have stimulated the people's interest. All the prejudices, customs, traditions, inadequacy in leadership, as well as the apathy of the people, had to be overcome. These adjustments in themselves created new problems which in turn had to be solved by an inexperienced political and economic leadership—a slow process despite a favorable economic setting between 1930 and 1940, and again after 1953.

With abundant natural resources and manpower, largely unskilled, the will of the Russian people to improve their standard of living and to expand production was strong. One might even justly argue that regardless of what kind of government existed in Russia prior to 1917 the potenti-

133

alities for industrial development were present. It would even seem safe to assume that without the socio-economic maladjustments created by the nationalization of capital, collectivization in agriculture, and the general economic upheaval created by a change in the ownership of factors of production—and even without Lenin, Stalin and Khrushchev—Russia might have been rapidly industrialized if there had been an incentive to stimulate people's creative imagination under dynamic leadership.

Unfortunately, this leadership was provided by the Bolsheviks whose theoretical conceptions were based on the development of heavy industry, which was in turn expected to stimulate output of consumer goods. Thus, the growth of heavy industry—the increase in production of industrial raw materials, machinery, chemicals, electric power facilities, transportation equipment, armament, and the like—was rapid indeed. But the growth rate in production of consumer goods, although it increased with the years, was below that of capital goods.

Nevertheless, as output increased in volume and in variety of goods, more complex goods were produced, such as jet airplanes, automatic production machinery, sputniks, chemicals, and wonder drugs. Much of Soviet industrial development has been geared to building of military and economic strength for the purpose of achieving maximum self-sufficiency. As a result, the relatively high cost of domestic production compared to the prices of imported goods has been ignored. Despite many blunders during the last 20 years, Soviet industry has been transformed from a backward to a highly advanced technological power, in many instances up to or but little behind the United States. True, this technological progress has not been equal in all fields. Some phases such as interplanetary development gained more rapidly in importance than the production of consumer items of good quality. One thing to remember is this: if the Russians have the talent and resources to produce a sputnik, they also can improve the quality and increase the quantity of consumer goods, provided that goals for heavy industry are satisfactorily met.

The new Seven-Year Plan for economic development of the Soviet Union from 1959 through 1965 is a mixture of deadly serious economic planning and propaganda. To write it off as only the latter would be foolish. Even acceptance of the partial expansion of Soviet industrial production during the next seven years calls for certain modification of Western courses of action. No matter what evaluation of this plan might be reached by the West, its impact on the West will be felt during the next seven years.

In many ways the figures for the Seven-Year Plan are projections of production of the USSR for a 15-year period running to 1972-73 and indicate diminishing rate of growth compared to immediate postwar years. Yet Khrushchev predicted confidently that in the next 15 years the Soviet Union would "take first place in the world not only in total output but also in per capita production." His boastful claim that countries in the Soviet orbit will account for more than half of the world's production by 1965 can be dismissed as propaganda. However, the rapid growth of the Soviet economy and its success in steadily narrowing the gap between Soviet output and that of the West must be accepted as a real challenge. Much of the world's socio-economic stability depends upon the success or the failure of the Seven-Year Plan. Khrushchev is gambling on it but like any crafty gambler, he is keeping his cards close to his chest.

## INDUSTRIAL DEVELOPMENT UNDER FIVE-YEAR PLANS

The history of Soviet industrial development is a history of gradual expansion with many political and economic adjustments. Even in its early stage the Soviets had numerous conflicts between theoretical Marxism and practical economic goals. Perhaps political considerations were more important at the beginning of industrial development than they were in the later years. Economic considerations seem to have priority over political issues in the current Seven-Year Plan. But even here the Party organizations are charged with watching the performance of managerial personnel. The main difference between the past and the present is that in the past the Party's loyal members ran the economy whereas now they seem to be watchdogs over managerial experts.

Soviet planners do not have an easy job in determining short-run or long-run production of goods and services. They must answer a number of key questions before volume of output is decided. First, they must determine the total volume of goods and services to be produced. Then they must determine the volume of each major commodity. Assuming that with the tools at hand they might find answers to these questions within a few years, they still cannot be sure that the discrepancy between economic and political ends will not change during the process of reaching the planned goals. In addition, they must consider the location and specialization of industry. How rapidly can one sector be permitted to grow and what impact will such growth have on other sectors? All these questions and answers profoundly influenced the economic history of the USSR, as they have that of other societies.

True, with accumulated experience in planning, the Soviets could make reasonable estimates to be attained on a short-run, especially in defense and in heavy industries which are better controlled than consumer goods. Yet, as in the case of the 1956-60 plan, the disproportions in investment and in output in certain sectors created real problems in relation to overall expectations. It is not that more accurate planning cannot be done. Soviet planners are constantly improving their methods. In fact, the Russians are now in the process of adopting "input-output" methodology for the purpose of more balanced development of their economy. The important factor interfering with Soviet planning is the socio-economic adjustments decided upon by political leadership. It would not be incorrect to say that if the USSR had socio-economic stability for a certain period of time industrial planning even with present tools would not be too impossible, and perhaps even desirable to avoid misuse of natural resources and manpower. Nevertheless, even with imperfections in planning methodology and errors in projections the rate of growth of Soviet industry, according to official statistics, increased rapidly after the end of the war, but then declined in 1951; and it is expected to continue to decline during the current Seven-Year Plan.

## FIRST FIVE-YEAR PLAN

Soviet industrial growth started with its First Five-Year Plan (1928-32). During this period investment in industry amounted to 24.8 billion rubles, with about 80 per cent allocated to heavy industry; the Soviets planned to build 1,138 new plants and factories—they completed 1,500. Large enterprises such as the Kharkov Tractor Plant, the Saratov Grain Combine Plant, the Machine-Building Plant at Gorki, the Frezor Plant in Moscow, the Azov Steel Plant, were built ahead of schedule. Even so, they were needed to provide goods for further expansion of other economic sectors.

Investments for the First Five-Year Plan came from an accumulation of turnover taxes and other sources rather than from collectivized agriculture. The latter was still in the process of adjustment to new conditions under collectivization, and industry was not yet efficient enough to accumulate reserves. Only at the end of this period did collectivized agriculture became a major source of capital formation for industrial development, as it was in all subsequent Five-Year plans until 1958.

At the end of the First Five-Year Plan Soviet ferrous metallurgy, nonferrous matellurgy, machine-building, and chemical industry was considerably increased. It was claimed that during this period the production of capital goods increased 2.3 times and consumer goods 1.9 times, with a total industrial output amounting to 36.8 billion rubles (priced in 1926-

27 rubles).[1] In general, industrial output in terms of investment was increased by about 50 per cent.

With the year 1928 providing a low starting base, and with the introduction of Western techniques and equipment, the First Five-Year Plan reflected a rapid growth in industrial output. Since the emphasis was on capital goods, production of consumer goods, although increased, was still about 25 per cent below the increase shown in heavy industry and construction.

## SECOND FIVE-YEAR PLAN

The Second Five-Year Plan (1933-37) is notable for a greater degree of industrial expansion than the First Five-Year Plan. In 1937 gross industrial output according to official data reached 95.5 billion rubles, (priced in 1926-27 rubles) or 2.2 times greater than in 1932; production of capital goods had increased 2.4 times.

During the First Five-Year Plan efforts were made to produce capital goods, the production and use of which were already known to the Russians. During the Second Five-Year Plan the Soviets began to produce new types of goods, using recently acquired technology. This created considerable economic maladjustment. The most difficult problems were in the development of new industries, in the mastery of technological innovations, and the training of a labor force capable of operating new kinds of machinery. Since the industrial speed-up process during the second Plan was so rapid, numerous industrial "ills" developed. Many plants and factories failed to train the needed skilled workers and those who were already employed were largely inefficient. They were careless, endless breakdowns occurred, and sometimes machinery even became useless. The disenfranchised peasants and other factions sabotaged equipment and in general tended to resist forced industrialization, objecting to the high pressure for maximum output per worker. Work stoppages occurred in many plants and factories; production of defective goods was widespread. Thus, despite great increases in output of all kinds of industrial and consumer goods as reflected in statistical data, the quality was poor and the actual gain during the whole second Plan was far less than indicated.

To overcome sabotage and production of low quality goods the Soviets launched a program designed to improve workers' skills, to improve the organization of production, to reduce the cost of production, and to utilize available raw material and the labor force more efficiently. It was the beginning of an efficiency drive throughout the Soviet Union. In 1935 the Stakhanovite movement was created; by the end of 1936 it embraced

25 to 30 per cent of the industrial labor force, and the Soviets claimed that in 1936 alone the productivity of the industrial labor force was increased by 21 per cent in heavy industry and by 30.2 per cent in the production of consumer goods. It is because of this efficiency drive that the Soviets were able to reach the goals for their Second Five-Year Plan nine months before the end of the period.

Although industrial output more than doubled, production of consumer goods was still about 17 per cent below the increase recorded for heavy industry.

## THIRD FIVE-YEAR PLAN

The Third Five-Year Plan (1938-42) lasted until the German attack on the Soviet Union in June 1941. By 1940 Soviet industrial output had reached 138.5 billion rubles. The greatest expansion was realized in the machine-building and metal-working industries, which increased by 76· per cent between 1937 and 1940. Between 1938 and the beginning of 1942 the average annual increase in industrial production was 14 per cent. But this increase was 15.7 per cent in the production of capital goods, and only 11.5 per cent in consumer goods.

During the first three years of the third Plan, 2,900 plants, factories, mines, electric power stations, and other enterprises were added to existing facilities. However, in spite of these increases, several sectors experienced a poor showing, because construction of new plants and facilities had consumed resources without adding to total output. For example, the output of pig iron increased only three per cent, cement by four per cent, output of wood for fuel was not increased to any extent, and there were deficits in textile, food, and light industries while new facilities were expanding. Also, many industries failed to lower their costs of production.

In comparison with 1928, the 1940 total industrial output increased sixfold. But production of capital goods increased tenfold whereas that of consumer goods only fourfold. Even with heavy military investments, however, the standard of living of the Russians in 1940 was considerably higher than it was in 1928.

## WORLD WAR II

The Germans forced the Soviets to intensify the past slow relocation of their industries. Within a few months of the German attack, over 1,360 large-scale industrial enterprises had moved from the western parts of the Soviet Union to the East, beyond the reach of German armies and planes. The Urals became the arsenal for the Soviet Armed Forces, and industrial output sharply increased in Western Siberia and in Central Asia. However, as a result of the war, destruction of industrial enterprises was heavy, and the total investments in industry sharply declined. It was only after the relocation of industrial enterprises to the East took effect that investments in industry again increased. Of the total investments in 1942, 79 per cent was allocated to plants producing military goods. Thus the eastern regions in 1942 increased their output by 35 per cent compared with 1941. In 1943 the eastern regions received 75 per cent of the total Soviet investments and by 1944 investments in eastern region industry were 1.5 times those of 1943. By the end of World War II, the total Soviet industrial investments in rubles were at the prewar level, but at highly inflated prices.

As industrial relocation adjustments were made, labor productivity improved among women, youths, and aged workers, who replaced the skilled labor taken by the Armed Forces. Between May 1942 and May 1945 official labor productivity increased about 40 per cent in industry as a whole. During the same period labor productivity in the aircraft industry increased by 47 per cent, in heavy armament by 48 per cent, and in light dustry were 1.5 times those of 1943. By the end of World War II, the output and only the most efficient facilities were used.

The immediate impact of the war caused heavy losses in industrial production. This may be seen in the fact that in December 1942 industrial output of the existing facilities was increased 50 per cent over that of January of the same year. By the end of 1942, all industrial enterprises which had evacuated to the East were well established. Yet in 1943 the overall gross industrial output increased only 17 per cent. Confusion in relocation of the evacuated enterprises, installation of equipment by unskilled workers without labor-saving devices, shortages of raw materials, parts, and numerous other problems associated with rapid large-scale industrial relocation contributed to the poor showing in 1943.

With evacuation of industrial plants to the East, the western parts of the USSR reduced their industrial production; eastern areas showed an increase. During the first six months of 1945, the total industrial output of eastern areas doubled as compared with the first six months of 1941. During the same period of time the industrial production in the Urals increased 3.6 times and in Siberia 2.8 times. Even parts of the Volga River Valley near the battlefront but not damaged by war increased industrial output 3.4 times. But during the 1941-45 period the Soviet budget was officially in the red by 39.7 billion rubles.[2] All stockpiles of industrial and agricultural reserves were exhausted, and the country's industry subsisted on current production of raw materials. At the end of the war the metal-processing capacity of the USSR stood at the level of 1933-35, and output of tractors was at the 1930 level.

TABLE 1—*Annual Growth of the Soviet Gross Industrial Output* [3]
*(In per cent of preceding year. Minus = decline)*

| Year | Total | Capital Goods | Consumer Goods |
|------|-------|---------------|----------------|
| 1940 | 12 | 15 | 8 |
| 1945 | — 8 | 12 | —41 |
| 1946 | —16 | —27 | 14 |
| 1947 | 22 | 23 | 22 |
| 1948 | 26 | 29 | 21 |
| 1949 | 20 | 25 | 8 |
| 1950 | 23 | 26 | 15 |
| 1951 | 17 | 17 | 16 |
| 1952 | 11 | 12 | 10 |
| 1953 | 12 | 12 | 12 |
| 1954 | 13 | 14 | 13 |
| 1955 | 12 | 15 | 8 |
| 1956 | 11 | 11 | 9 |
| 1957 | 10 | 11 | 8 |
| 1958 | 10 | 11 | 7 |
| 1959-65 (annual rate) | 9 | 9 | 7 |
| 1966-72 (annual rate) | 5 | — | — |

Table 1 shows a considerable industrial decline between 1940 and 1948. Using the 1944 figure as a base of 100, the postwar maladjustments caused by shifting from war to peace production were responsible for still further drops in output. Only in 1948 were the Soviets able to reach the 1944 level of production. From 1948 on, the growth rate was at a slower pace than during the whole reconstruction period of 1945-50. However, it must be remembered that postwar production was geared to the replacement of industrial facilities destroyed during the war and to the restoration of production to the prewar level. It might be mentioned that in 1945 the output of oil, pig iron, and steel amounted to the average output during the 1931-37 period, or considerably below 1940 production.

In connection with average annual growth rates of Soviet industrial output, it is interesting to note that during the 1928-55 period the official Soviet index was 11.9 per cent, whereas Professor G. Warren Nutter calculated index ranges from 5.1 to 7.3 per cent, or about half the official Soviet index.[4] Considering the wartime destruction, even Nutter's over-cautious index indicates a favorable growth of Soviet industrial production, in comparison with 3.7 per cent for the same period in the United States.

## FOURTH FIVE-YEAR PLAN

The Fourth Five-Year Plan (1946-50) was generally a period of reha-bilitation of the devastated Soviet economy, especially in areas occupied by the Germans. It is claimed that the Germans and their allies destroyed 31,850 industrial enterprises which employed about four million workers in 1940. Because of this, while the 1944 output of capital goods, mainly military, increased by 36 per cent, the output of consumer goods was 54 per cent below that of 1940. Most scarce during the war were food, clothing, and housing. For this reason, the main objective during the 1946-50 period was to rehabilitate weakened Soviet productive facilities and to speed up output of all kinds of goods in order to reestablish stockpiles and satisfy the demands of the people.

Rehabilitation and reconstruction of destroyed and damaged plants, fac-tories, mines, and urban settlements was rapid indeed and was started as soon as the occupied areas were liberated. In 1946, many of the damaged or destroyed enterprises were already in partial operation, producing 28 per cent of their prewar output. At the same time, with the end of the war, military contracts were drastically reduced and plants and factories were authorized to shift to production of non-military capital and consumer goods.

Since many skilled young workers were released by the demobilization in 1946, the factory labor force was augmented and existing labor pro-ductivity was increased. However, because of problems in the conversion from wartime to peacetime production—shortages of spare machinery parts and equipment and of skilled labor for peacetime production, and a drastic reduction in the production of military materials—the 1946 gross industrial output was 17 per cent below that of 1945 and reached only about 77 per cent of the 1940 volume. The year 1946 was a year of industrial decline and a year of a severe drought in western parts of the USSR.

By 1947 Soviet industry was able to increase its production 22 per cent and by 1948, 26 per cent. At the end of 1948, industrial output was 18 per cent above the 1940 level.[5] Since the immediate need was for machinery and equipment, the machine-building and metal-working industries were very much expanded. Newly manufactured machinery and equipment was installed in many plants and factories to replace machinery and equipment in use since 1930. To some extent, destruction and damage to old factors of production had its own compensation, inasmuch as it made necessary new machinery and equipment which yielded far higher productivity than could ever have been expected from prewar equipment.

An important achievement claimed by the Fourth Five Year Plan was an increase of 48 per cent in gross industrial production, while the output of heavy industry was twice as great as in 1940. However, the increase in the light industries was only 23 per cent. During this period over 6,000 large-scale state-operated enterprises were rehabilitated, rebuilt and put into operation.

It also must be remembered that in 1940 and then from 1946 through 1950 the Soviets gained much from annexation of Western Ukraine, parts of Poland, and other regions, the industrial production of which was not included in the 1940 official statistics By 1948 these regions were able to organize production in a wide range of goods, from mining equipment to consumer durable goods. The contribution of these regions to the total Soviet gross industrial output is of considerable volume. At the time of the occupation of these regions their gross industrial output was disrupted by Soviet nationalization of factors of production. Then during World War II their industrial facilities were either destroyed or confiscated by the Germans. It was not until the end of the war that their industries were revamped and their skilled labor force reorganized. Since then these regions have passed through a much more rapid expansion than any region within the USSR itself. This was not a problem of developing new regions, but rather of rehabilitating already existing facilities. Still another source from which the Soviets gained much is the so-called "war booty" from occupied regions, which consisted of capital and consumer goods.

With the postwar emphasis on rehabilitation of industrial facilities, production of consumer goods lagged. As compared to 1940, the 1945 official Soviet index of consumer goods stood at 59. It was 1949 before the Soviets were able to reach the 1940 level. Since physical output rather than quality was stressed, many capital goods and most consumer goods were of poor quality and required replacement after a short use. Precisely because of this, 1950 production of consumer goods almost doubled compared with 1946. Yet in 1950 the official figures show that it was only 23 per cent above the 1940 level; but production of capital goods and construction more than doubled.

## FIFTH FIVE-YEAR PLAN

Emphasis during the Fifth Five-Year Plan (1951-55) was on internal reorganization of industry. The statistical methods by which many sectors of industry concealed their inefficiency were exposed. The unequal distribution of workload for many enterprises during the fiscal year as a whole was also criticized by the central administration. Intensifying production at the end of each quarter or annual period to fulfill production quotas was widely practiced. This did not increase overall efficiency among the large number of workers, and did nothing to stimulate production; it actually increased unit production costs.

During this period more attention was given to production of farm machinery and equipment, especially tractors, which had been neglected in the previous Five-Year Plan. But perhaps the 1951-55 period is most notable for its socio-economic adjustments in industry and in agriculture. Controls in industry were tightened and real attempts were made to reduce costs of production and waste in materials and human energy. In agriculture, small collective farms were merged into larger units and their relationships with the government and the planning apparatus took a new turn for the better. The administration of Machine Tractor Stations (MTS) was improved for the purpose of stimulating a more effective use of their machinery. Despite these adjustments the average annual increase in the gross industrial output during the 1951-55 period was only 13.1 per cent, but production of capital goods increased 13.8 per cent, and consumer goods 11.9 per cent; 1955 gross industrial output was 3.2 times greater than in 1940. The largest increases occurred in production of cement, electric power, crude oil, pig iron, chemical fertilizer, rolled metal products, steel, and coal even though the official labor productivity was increased only 44 per cent, rather than the 50 per cent goal. This deficit in labor productivity resulted from the general confusion created by reorganization of industry and agriculture undertaken after 1950.

With the end of the war, reconstruction of heavy industry was the most vital problem faced by the Soviets. All efforts were directed to that end. Even prisoners of war were used for construction of new or rehabilitation of damaged plants. It is claimed that during the Five-Year plans before the war (that is, during 13 years) the Soviets constructed 9,000 large industrial enterprises. But during the postwar eight years (1946-54) over 8,000 large industrial enterprises became operative, either by reconstruction of damaged facilities or building of new ones. Thus an average of one large enterprise was put into operation every eight hours.[6] Of course, the postwar reconstruction of industry was made on sites where other related facilities already existed or were partially disabled. The damaged railroad track or highway was easier to repair than to replace. Nevertheless, considering postwar shortages in raw materials and equipment, the rehabilitation of industry was swift.

The Fifth Five-Year Plan was confused by the death of Stalin. His heir Malenkov attempted to increase production of consumer goods, but was overruled by Khruschchev, who replaced Malenkov. Production goals were often revised, creating confusion among managerial personnel and planners. This accounts for a somewhat reduced rate of growth in total industrial production during this period as compared with the Fourth Five-Year Plan. But despite this confusion the production of consumer goods narrowed the gap to about eight per cent below the growth rate in heavy industry.

## SIXTH FIVE-YEAR PLAN

With Khrushchev in power, emphasis of the Sixth Five Year Plan (1956-60) was on preferential treatment of heavy industry, continuous improvement in technology, and increased labor productivity. The overall goal for industrial output during this period was set at an increase of 65 per cent. This unrealistic plan included excessive expectations for industrial output and anticipated too high increases in efficiency of equipment and manpower. For example, the planned average increase in labor productivity was set at 50 per cent, whereas planned output of capital goods was expected to be increased by 70 per cent and consumer goods by 60 per cent. The Soviet planners set their 1960 industrial production at three times that of 1950. These figures indicate that the makers of the 1956-60 Plan expected to speed efforts of workers, who were against being pressed at the time when the post-Stalin era promised betterment of their lot.

The efficiency drive upon which the planners of the Sixth Five-Year Plan so much relied for the attainment of their goals was started in 1953. The drive strove to improve the planning mechanism and to emphasize managerial leadership through an introduction of more decentralized responsibilities on the part of the constituent republics, ministries, administrators, and individual managers. In December 1956 additional rights were granted to all constituent republics, ministries, and enterprises to simplify the management of industry. With the formation of sovnarkhozy the Soviets seem to have completely departed from the planning and administrative processes of the past. Because of this radical change in socialized planning and administration, the sixth Plan was first extended to 1962 and then completely abandoned, to be superseded by a new Seven-Year Plan (1959-65).

A review of the Sixth Five-Year Plan shows that it was not the natural fruition of previous successful planning but rather a replacement for unsuccessful past planning. It was Khrushchev who was largely responsible for the unrealistic high rates of growth contained in the 1956-62 plan. Before 1956 ended it was clear that these demands were overtaxing Soviet resources. In December 1956 the Party called its first retreat by scaling down the output and investment targets for 1957.

The whole period between 1953 and 1958 might be called "samba-like"— one step forward, one step backward but in a new direction. Only by 1957 did the Soviets finally decide on a firm course. By forming sovnarkhozy and concentrating on production bottlenecks for the remainder of the year, they were able to evolve the Seven-Year Plan 15 months before it was released in November 1958. The last nail was driven into the coffin of the never-completed Sixth Five-Year Plan. The 1958 planned targets of 8.3 per cent increase in capital goods and 6.1 per cent increase in consumer goods were claimed to be reached with 11 per cent in capital and seven per cent in consumer goods over the 1957 level.

The sixth Plan was the result of overenthusiastic planners to please the new Soviet leaders, and especially Khrushchev. To preserve their jobs, those who were responsible for the planning and for actual production (ministries) hoped that by increasing production of both capital and consumer goods they might be untouched by the purge of industrial management. The lower echelon was accused of poor discipline in planning and of lagging in fulfilment of high production quotas. They were blamed for high production costs and failure to deliver the goods on time. Meantime the rate of industrial growth since 1956 declined, especially in capital goods. By extending the Plan to 1962 and by forming sovnarkhozy the Soviets actually provided encouragement to workers and management alike in their productive efforts. As a result the 1957 gross industrial output was fulfilled by ten per cent instead of the planned seven per cent. Moreover, it was in the second half of that year that sovnarkhozy were able in increase their output.[7]

In general, the rate of industrial growth in 1958 was 70 per cent below the 1951 rate. The rate in capital goods was 54 per cent and in consumer goods only 44 per cent. In the case of consumer goods it must be remembered that many small-scale enterprises producing consumer goods, especially food items, were not included in the official Soviet statistics. With the transfer of these enterprises to sovnarkhozy, production of these enterprises, however small, is now included in the official statistics. At the meeting of the Plenum of the Central Committee of the Communist Party of the USSR, December 15-19, 1958, several regions were criticized for claiming the fulfillment of planned quota production only because they purchased livestock products from individual workers, employees, and peasants. By eliminating the private sector contribution from the state-owned sector, the production of consumer goods by the state-owned enterprises alone should be much lower than shown for 1958.

## SEVEN-YEAR PLAN

Now that some broad comparisons have been drawn for the past years, what does the new Seven-Year Plan call for, and what are its chances for success? The new Plan reemphasizes the priority of heavy industry over consumer goods, as did all other plans. However, its annual growth rate ranges from 9.2 to 9.4 per cent in production of capital goods and from 7.1 to 7.4 per cent in consumer goods. Significant is the fact that with the slowdown in the growth rate of industrial production other key indices too will be slowing down. The rates of capital investment, national income, and the like will be reduced in proportion to the decline in industrial activity. Nevertheless, it is the continued preference for capital goods over consumer goods that stimulates more rapid expansion than in the so-called matured economics of the West. Although the growth rate of the USSR still exceeds that of the West, it is diminished as a result of the larger base from which the Soviet Union now operates. Even these rates, reduced by 50 per cent as by Nutter, are still substantial.

Moreover, the USSR has reached a sufficiently larger base to begin to narrow the absolute gap in production which separates the Soviets from the West. The ratio of producer goods to consumer goods with the new Plan is roughly the same as it was in the past Five-Year plans. Obviously, the consumer will benefit more in the next seven years than in the past seven years because of the ever-expanding output base.

In connection with expanding output of capital goods and consumer goods it must be noted that many goods produced in the USSR now differ greatly from those produced in prewar days; many were not produced at all in 1940. Among these commodities are nuclear power, hydrogen bombs, jet airplanes, and cotton-pickers. Among consumer goods not produced in 1940 are washing machines, television sets, plastic goods. The Russians have a wider range of goods available to them; yet the priority is still with capital goods. In his speech introducing the 1959-65 Plan, Khrushchev stated that between 1940 and 1958 output of capital goods increased five-fold, against a 2.5-fold increase in consumer goods, with a total population increase of four to five per cent. Even if these figures are exaggerated for political purposes they still suggest that the standard of living of the Russians has improved.

The general target, as expressed in the Second Seven-Year Plan (1966-72), suggests an overall increase in Soviet industrial production of two to two and one-half times the 1959 level. Most striking is the considerable decline in the annual rate of growth, from an official ten per cent recorded for 1958 to a range as low as 4.7 to 6.3 per cent per year for the Second Seven-Year Plan.[8] Perhaps the 1972 goals do not represent the usual specific figures and rates given for shorter periods and may be altered later.

But what is the true rate of Soviet industrial growth? Since Soviet statistical methodology differs from Western methodology, every Western student of the Soviet economy arrives at a different rate. For instance, the Director of the Central Intelligence Agency, Mr. Allen W. Dulles, in 1959 estimated that Soviet industry grew at a rate of 9.5 per cent during the 1950-57 period, compared to the claim of over 11 per cent in official Soviet statistics. During the same period of time, it was noted, the American growth rate was only 3.6 per cent. A few months later Dr. R. V. Greenslade and Miss Phyllis A. Wallace, also of the CIA, arrived at the following average annual growth rates for the United States and the USSR:[9]

| Period | United States | Soviet Union |
|--------|---------------|--------------|
| 1913-1957 | 2.5 | 3.8-4.3 |
| 1928-1957 | 2.2 | 5.9-6.5 |
| 1939-1957 | 3.3 | 4.8-5.4 |
| 1950-1957 | 1.8 | 8.3-9.2 |

The main purpose of Dr. Greenslade and Miss Wallace was twofold: to elaborate on the figures presented by their chief, Mr. Dulles, and to point out the unrealistic conclusions derived by Dr. Nutter. The above comparisons do not support Dr. Nutter's finding that industrial growth in the United States has kept pace with that of the USSR and that the two indices cannot be compared because of a considerable difference in samplings. These are challenging thoughts, and require much more evaluation before any reduction in Soviet claims can be made. In any event, the rate of growth favors the Soviet Union. Too, the Soviets devote a far higher part of their total resources to heavy and defense industries, and the general target of the Seven-Year Plan does not indicate any noticeable curtailment of military outlays.

How much more realistic the 1959-65 Plan is than the unfortunate 1956-60 Plan! On June 30, 1959, the Communist Party's Central Committee was told by its leaders that the task of installing modern equipment in Soviet industry is too difficult a task to be managed in the current Seven-Year Plan.[10] Many short cuts are taken and a greater emphasis on short-term investments producing quick results is stressed. It was already realized that retooling in many backward Soviet industries cannot be effected by the end of 1965. Of 80 steel-rolling mills in the RSFSR only three are modern; the others date to the last century.

These shortcomings are not necessarily an admission of failure to reach the original goals; rather, they indicate the recognition of powerful economic facts. This calls for a revision of long-run goals and emphasis on short-run targets. It means larger investments in automation and in labor-saving machines, diverting urgently needed manpower elsewhere. It means priority to open-pit mining rather than construction of expensive mines. It means relocation of investments for the purpose of higher turnover. Since this relocation of investments and capital is designed for the removal of bottlenecks in the production of raw materials, it suggests that other branches of industry must also make adjustments. In short, faults of the 1956-60 Plan are already coming to the surface of the new Seven-Year Plan.

However, planning for a large and expanding economy such as the Soviet Union is a gigantic task. Moreover, with imperfect tools available to planners plus interference from political sectors, there are bound to be errors and miscalculations in projections. The early recognition of the miscalculations is remarkable. This grace in time should be a valuable asset in redirecting efforts to other fields, while the original goal in the race with the United States for world industrial leadership will remain unchanged. Even assuming that these shortcomings will continue to crop up through the next seven years, forcing the Soviets to alter their timetable in reaching the volume of the United States for a year or two, it should not decrease the danger of a challenge to the West .

The June meeting of the Central Committee revealed many miscalculations in the Seven-Year Plan. But what is more interesting is the increasing disregard by the lower echelons of the Party's orders to cease practicing relocation of funds and materials from planned production to local needs. Again and again Khrushchev denounced this trend, yet it seems to be more prevalent throughout the Soviet Union than ever before.

## INDUSTRIAL IMPORTANCE OF INDIVIDUAL REPUBLICS

The industrial importance of each constituent republic depends upon the availability of local raw materials, labor force, electrical energy, and transportation; the import of raw materials from other regions; and other factors of production needed for industrial output. Since the RSFSR is the largest in size of all constituent republics, its population and labor force are larger too. The RSFSR is also rich in raw materials, which have been used by industry for many generations. In general, this republic possesses about two-thirds of all industrial investment and produces about two-thirds of all Soviet gross industrial output. The industrial production of this republic is not evenly distributed among its vast economic regions. Some of them are more industrialized than others, and industrial investments in means of production, e. g., buildings, machinery, equipment, power, vary greatly from region to region.

Second in importance is the Ukrainian SSR, which in 1955 possessed about 20 per cent of the total Soviet industrial investments. In 1955 these two republics accounted for about 84 per cent of the industrial investments in the Soviet Union, as shown in the following table. Their 1959-65 share in the total Soviet industrial output is somewhat below that of 1955.

TABLE 2—*Percentage Distribution of Industrial Investments by Republic* [11]

|  | 1950 | 1955 | 1957 |
|---|---|---|---|
| USSR: | 100.0 | 100.0 | 100.0 |
| RSFSR: | 65.0 | 63.8 | 65.5 |
| Central Industrial Region | — | 18.8 | — |
| Urals | — | 13.8 | — |
| Siberia and Far East | — | 12.7 | — |
| North and Northwestern regions | — | 8.1 | — |
| Volga River Valley | — | 5.4 | — |
| Northern Caucasus | — | 5.0 | — |
| Ukraine | 20.1 | 20.2 | 20.2 |
| Kazakh | 3.0 | 3.4 | 3.3 |
| Azerbaydzhan | 2.9 | 3.1 | 2.8 |
| Georgia | 1.5 | 1.8 | 1.7 |
| Uzbek | 2.0 | 1.7 | 1.6 |
| White Russia | 1.4 | 1.6 | 1.6 |
| Other republics | 4.1 | 4.4 | 4.3 |

The above table shows the distribution of investment in means of production, excluding labor force, for the production of industrial goods. Since the means of production and their output are calculated in rubles, there is a very close relationship between the two. The above percentages are also very close to the distribution of industrial labor force for each constituent republic and region.

Between 1940 and 1958 the RSFSR's industrial output increased about four times. The heart of the RSFSR's industrial production is the Central Industrial Region around Moscow, followed in importance by the Urals and the eastern parts of the RSFSR. However, since 1940 the greatest industrial expansion has taken place in the Urals, and in Siberia, where a coal-metallurgical base second only to the Donbass in the Ukraine has been created. Major machine-building centers are in Novosibirsk, Omsk, and Krasnoyarsk. Other regions also expanded. For example, in 1955 the Cherepovets Steel Works, was constructed and put into operation to supply the industry of the northwest. The Chelyabinsk Steel and Iron Works put in operation its fourth blast furnace which is claimed to be the largest in the world. The Krasnoye Sormovo Works in Gorki with its automatic controls in production of steel was also commissioned. In general, the largest increase in industrial production in the RSFSR during this period was in coal, natural gas, crude oil, electric power, tractors, automobiles, cement, pig iron, steel, rolled metals, radio and television sets, bicycles, paper, dry goods, as well as other capital and consumer goods.

As the second important industrial producer, the Ukrainian SSR has completely recovered from the devastation of World War II. Its 1958 production of industrial commodities included raw industrial materials, and finished products, with emphasis on pig iron, steel, rolled metals, and coal. Diesel railroad engines are produced in the Ukraine alone, and over 70 per cent of the total Soviet output of refined sugar is produced there. An intensified industrial expansion has taken place since 1940 in the western parts of the Ukraine which were occupied just before World War II and which did not have large-scale industries. But the main concentration of industrial production in the Ukraine lies in the eastern parts, mainly in the Donbass, Krivoy Rog, and around Kiev. The entire economy of the Ukraine itself is compact and better balanced than that of the RSFSR. Ukrainian industries are not only concentrated in a few well-known regions, but they range in a favorable combination of heavy and light industries producing raw materials, capital goods, and an abundance of consumer goods and food items. The Ukraine can easily be self-sufficient in a great many capital and consumer goods.

Other constituent republics are specialized either because only a certain number of raw materials are available or because they are not self-sufficient and must depend on importation of scarce raw materials from other parts of the Soviet Union. Azerbaydzhan, for example, specializes in oil production. White Russia's main products are dry goods items, paper, and food products, and the Kazakh SSR produces coal, non-ferrous metals, and oil in addition to food items. However, within each republic there is a tendency gradually to expand industry according to the abundance of certain raw materials and regional specialization in production.

TABLE 3—*Investment and Gross Industrial Output* [12]
*by Republic: 1959-65*

| | Investment | | |
|---|---|---|---|
| Area | (1959-65) Billion Rubles | Per cent Increase over 1952-58 | 1965 Gross Industrial Output In Percentage to 1958 |
| USSR: | 1,940–1,970 | 81–84 | 80 |
| RSFSR | 954– 974 | 86–90 | 80 |
| Ukraine | 214– 219 | n.a. | 77 |
| White Russia | 32 | 150 | 80 |
| Uzbek | 35–36 | 140 | 80 |
| Kazakh | 116–119 | 130 | 170 |
| Georgia | 16.8 | 75 | 75 |
| Azerbaydzhan | 29 | 60 | 90 |
| Lithuania | 12.5 | 100 | 80 |
| Moldavia | 8.8 | n.a. | 100 |
| Latvia | 10.8 | 100 | 60 |
| Kirghiz | 10.5 | 130 | 120 |
| Tadzhik | 8.6 | 160 | 80 |
| Turkmen | 15.7 | 140 | 100 |
| Armenia | 12 | 120 | 120 |
| Estonia | 8.1 | 90 | 80 |

n.a. = not available

The Seven-Year Plan emphasizes new industry in and beyond the Urals. By 1965 the eastern regions are expected to be major producers of many basic industrial commodities such as copper, aluminum, coal and steel. Copper is to be produced entirely in the Kazakh SSR; its contribution of coal is also to be significant. Aluminum is to come from the Irkutsk Aluminum Plant, claimed to be the largest in the Soviet Union, using electric power from the Bratsk and the Krasnoyarsk hydroelectric plants. In general, new discoveries of iron ore and coal, plus expanding hydroelectric power capacity in Eastern Siberia should essentially change the economic structure of Siberia and the Kazakh SSR. New iron deposits, claimed to be five times as large as those of Krivoy Rog in the Ukraine, have been found between Kustanay and Magnitogorsk in the Kazakh SSR. These deposits are to be exploited during the current Seven-Year Plan and economic development of these regions should benefit other branches of the economy. However, since newly discovered deposits cannot be fully utilized at the beginning of their exploitation, utilization of them is carried out mainly through government subsidies. This also applies to new facilities.

About 456 billion rubles of the total Soviet investment during the current Seven-Year Plan are not allocated among constituent republics. This accounts for the fact that the sum total for all 15 republics, as shown in Table 3, is about 23 per cent below the given figure for the USSR. Presumably this sum is for All-Union requirements by the ministries and other agencies since it is too large a sum to consider as a statistical omission or error in rounding out. The total for 15 republics ranges from a low of 1,484 billion rubles to a high of 1,513 billion rubles.

About 80 per cent of the total investment in the constituent republics is allocated for the RSFSR and the Ukraine to increase their industrial output by some 80 per cent. Next in importance is the Kazakh SSR with an allocation between 116 to 119 billion rubles. However, it is in the Kazakh SSR where the greatest industrial growth is to take place. Collectively, the Kazakh SSR, the RSFSR, and the Ukraine represent about 86 per cent of the total investment of all 15 republics. White Russia, the Uzbek SSR, and the three Baltic republics have approximately the same investments in each area. Other republics are of lesser economic significance.

## PHYSICAL OUTPUT OF BASIC COMMODITIES

The development and exploitation of major raw materials in the Soviet Union has been very rapid indeed. Increasing production of these resources is considered a "derived" demand, that is, these materials are required by plants and factories which produce capital and consumer goods. But their output is "administered" by the planning apparatus of the USSR, which eliminates the competitive forces. Nevertheless, the principles guiding the expansion of Soviet industrial production are basically those of any long-run expanding economy where considerations are given to minimum cost in production and maximum profit.

The rapid expansion in industrial output, and especially production of raw materials, is due to two basic factors. One is partial automation and extensive technological reconstruction of many basic industries, including modernization of equipment followed by more efficient utilization of other factors of production; the other is the relocation of many basic industries to areas abundant in raw materials. As technological improvements are rapidly realized, production of raw materials and electric power are also accelerated. This is especially true in the new areas of the East and in old industrial regions of the southern European parts of the USSR, notably in the Northern Caucasus, below Moscow, and the Volga River Valley. The increased output of raw materials will inevitably increase production of capital and consumer goods.

The greatest increase in the output of basic industrial commodities during the 1940-58 period was realized in fuel, with natural gas expanding at a much faster rate than either electrical power or oil output. Growth rates of coal, iron ore, steel, and pig iron were more uniform than those of fuel supplies. Production of coke was closely associated with the growth rate of pig iron and steel.

Growth in production of metallurgical equipment was 2.6 times higher than that of machine tools. Since metallurgical equipment is needed not only for newly constructed plants and factories but also for the replacement of the old equipment, its production growth rate was much more than that for machine tools, durability of which is longer.

An interesting point, however, is that according to the Soviets their industry was reconstructed and technologically advanced by 1950. Yet despite the youth of most of their industries, as compared with the West, there are individual industries which are still utilizing old equipment long overdue for the scrap pile. Old equipment breaks down often and requires repair, and according to Soviet sources twice as many metal-cutting machines are being kept busy on repair jobs as in the United States. Thus, even though the growth rate of Soviet industrial production might show phenomenal advances and might even be statistically correct, its total contribution to the expanding economy may not be as spectacular as statistics would indicate. But to measure this diversion of metal-cutting machines to repair work or to make a percentage allowance for spoiled or wasted metal in the shops is a very difficult task indeed. The repair plants employ as many workers and as many metal-cutting machines in the process of repairing other machines and equipment as there are workers employed in the production of new machines and equipment. In the machine-building industry, repair work and servicing of new machines amounts to from ten to 20 per cent of their original cost. The outlay for maintenance of capital repair work for one million motor vehicles amounts to about two billion rubles for the space and another billion rubles for spare parts. This type of capital repair requires about 100,000 workers. As to the waste in metals, it has been estimated that annually about 5.5 million metric tons are being wasted.

Khrushchev's industrial leap forward in an attempt to reach the in-

TABLE 4—*Physical Output of Main Raw Materials and Industrial Goods in the USSR* [13]

| Commodity | Unit | 1940 | 1950 | 1955 | 1956 | 1958 | 1965 Plan |
|---|---|---|---|---|---|---|---|
| Coal | Million metric tons | 165.9 | 261.1 | 391.3 | 429.2 | 496.0 | 596-609 |
| Coke | Million metric tons | 21.1 | 27.7 | 43.6 | 46.6 | 50.9 | 81-84 |
| Crude Oil | Million metric tons | 31.1 | 37.9 | 70.8 | 83.8 | 113.0 | 230-240 |
| Iron Ore | Million metric tons | 29.9 | 39.7 | 71.9 | 78.1 | 88.8 | 150-160 |
| Pig Iron | Million metric tons | 14.9 | 19.2 | 33.3 | 35.8 | 39.6 | 65-70 |
| Steel | Million metric tons | 18.3 | 27.3 | 45.3 | 48.6 | 54.9 | 86-91 |
| Natural Gas | Billion cubic meters | 4.0 | 6.2 | 10.3 | 13.7 | 29.8 | 50 |
| Electrical Power | Billion kw-hours | 48.3 | 91.2 | 170.2 | 192.0 | 233.0 | 500-520 |
| Machine tools (lathes) | Thousands | 58.4 | 70.6 | 117.8 | 121.3 | 138.0 | 190-200 |
| Automobiles, trucks and buses | Thousands | 145.4 | 362.9 | 445.3 | 465.0 | 511.0 | 750-856 |
| Cotton fabrics | Million meters | 3.9 | 3.9 | 5.9 | 5.4 | 5.8 | 7.7-8.0 |
| Refined sugar | Million metric tons | 2.1 | 2.5 | 3.4 | 4.3 | 5.4 | 9.2-10.0 |

dustrial production of the United States by 1965 is already snarled. The only thing which might improve conditions is a fuller application of automation, which is still in its infancy in the Soviet Union. In June 1959 scientists and efficiency experts were given six months for the purpose of devising a plan for large-scale introduction of automation in industry and to train the required labor force to man automative equipment. Six months is too short a time for the solution of this important problem, and if the experts do have some recommendations, they would require further refinement later, creating maladjustments in the goals. Problems of retooling and installation of new equipment necessarily require production stoppage at individual plants and factories, and if these breaks in production are prolonged, the planned production quotas will suffer.

## FINANCING OF SEVEN-YEAR PLAN

An interesting point in financing the current Seven-Year Plan is that it does not rely heavily on siphoning agriculture as in the past Five-Year plans. The largest share of the total investment is expected to be derived from industrial yields and turnover taxes. In addition, it is expected that fast turnover of investments will stimulate further availability of additional capital. In short, Soviet planners are anticipating that the acceleration process will help them to finance the current Seven-Year Plan.

TABLE 5—*Distribution of Investments by Industries: 1950-65* [14]
(*Billion Rubles*)

|  | Rubles |
|---|---|
| Total USSR: | 1,940–1,970 |
| Construction of capital goods: | 1,488–1,513 |
| Oil and natural gas | 170–173 |
| Electric power | 125–129 |
| Railroads | 110–115 |
| Building materials: | 110–112 |
| Cement | 75–81 |
| Chemicals: | 100–105 |
| Plastic and synthetic | 50 |
| Ferrous metallurgy | 100 |
| Consumer goods and food | 85–85 |
| Coal | 75–78 |
| Timber, paper and wood processing: | 58-60 |
| Cellulose and wood processing | 35–36 |
| Public housing, schools, hospitals, etc. | 375–380 |
| Agriculture | 150 |

The greatest portion of the total investment in industrial development is assigned to the oil and natural gas industries, with emphasis on natural gas. The Soviets expect that the percentage of oil and gas in the total fuel supply of the USSR will be increased from 31 in 1958 to 51 in 1965. Although production of oil by 1965 is anticipated to be over 2.5 times that of 1958, it will not be entirely consumed at home. According to recent agreements with satellite countries, the Soviets will supply Czechoslovakia, East Germany, Hungary, and Poland with oil produced at "Second Baku." [15] It is not clear how much will be diverted to these countries but it should be a considerable amount, since the Russians are planning to construct a pipe line 2,500 miles long through which the oil is to be delivered. To these, other foreign commitments, including Cuba, must be added.

Next in importance is the expansion of electric power, mainly through the construction of thermoelectric power stations utilizing cheap coal resources and natural gas. However, combined investments in the coal, oil, and gas industries are in priority. Peat and wood, which have been furnishing about ten per cent of the heat energy, will drop to six per cent. In general, total fuel production in 1965 is expected to be double that of 1958. The continued growth of industry will demand such expansion. But even if this is achieved, it will still mean only 65 per cent more energy-supply for an industrial growth of 80 per cent by 1965.

The chemical industry is expanding rapidly in the USSR. A tripling of its output is envisaged by 1965, with synthetic fibers and plastics in priority. This is to relieve the dependence on agriculture for raw materials and to benefit consumers as quickly as possible. Based on past performance of the Soviet chemical industry, the target set for 1965 is quite ambitious, and may not even be realized by 1972.

The targets for other sections of industry, excluding pig iron and steel, seem more conservative than those for fuel and chemicals, though some will still require all the skill and ingenuity in political and economic propaganda of Soviet leaders. The engineering and metal-processing sectors alone are scheduled to double their output. And the Soviets are expecting to intensify the usage of plant capacity by re-equipping many existing plants and increasing automation wherever possible.

The 1965 goals for pig iron and steel production are an increase of 24 to 30 million metric tons of pig iron and 28 to 36 million metric tons of steel—tremendous increases in Soviet pig iron and steel capacities. Moreover, it was announced by the Soviets that by 1972, the production of pig iron is to be 75 to 85 million metric tons and 100 to 120 million metric tons for steel. If the minimum range figures are accepted, they are not much higher than the maximum range figures set for 1959-65. Also, it might be true that the Soviets would not need a great increase in pig iron capacity because of the possible excess of pig iron over steel. The steel production output would show a definite slowing down.

All in all, although the steel target is severe, it is not unreasonably exaggerated. The main problem in steel output will probably arise in connection with the supply and treatment of sufficient amounts of iron ore, the most accessible deposits having been overworked for decades. This is the "tie-in" concept of the economic process, the interdependence links in the chain of producing and using a product as described by Jasny.[16]

The 1959-65 investment in the coal industry is a very conservative one indeed. This investment amounts to about 75 to 78 million rubles, somewhat below the cement industry allocation. Investment in the coal industry, in the main, may be considered as an act to complete current mine construction and fuller exploitation. In 1957 the coal industry was in the process of constructing 320 mines. Many of these mines require heavy long-term investment, and at times it takes from seven to ten years before mines can be fully developed. No doubt there will be expansion in the capacities of existing mines, but current emphasis is on open-pit mining which requires less investment and yields profit faster.

The phenomenal increase in non-ferrous metallurgy is not particularly significant except for the fact that more attention is devoted to it. By 1965 the production of aluminum is planned to be 280 per cent more than in 1958, and refined copper is to be increased by 190 per cent. A considerable increase is expected to take place in the output of nickel, manganese, titanium, and other metals. An increase in precious metals is also anticipated during the 1959-65 Plan, but amounts are not specified, probably because in an absolute sense these increases are not significant. The 14-fold increase in the production of diamonds in Yakutia does not mean much since the mining of Yakutian diamonds started in 1958 and the 1965 output is calculated at a very low base.

Targets for production of agricultural machinery, equipment, and other items have been cut down considerably, from 11 per cent per year in the Sixth Five-Year Plan to 7.8 per cent per year for 1959-65. But agriculture is still considered overoptimistic. It would mean a 70 per cent rise in production of agricultural commodities over the seven year period and for this reason mechanization of agriculture has a permanent place in the development of industry.

With so much emphasis on increased and improved supplies of the basic industrial materials, it is not surprising that the remaining sectors are relatively low on the priority list. These are not, however, forgotten. Expansion and modernization of railroads is to increase about 50 per cent. In connection with transportation, freight capacity is stressed by enlarging the number of electric and diesel engines, expansion of railroad lines, construction of new oil pipe lines some 3,250 miles long, and increased services by airlines. These changes are devised to modernize and to improve rather outdated transportation systems.

The output of consumer goods is expected to be increased by 60 per cent; much of this increase is assigned for the rapidly developing chemical industry. Moreover, a further betterment in the standard of living is to come from the individual and communal housing construction.

## LABOR PRODUCTIVITY

In any society, a worker merits more consideration than a commodity, yet workers rent out their efforts for a price. The wage or salary paid to a worker must be "worth" at least as much to the one who pays it as to the worker who receives it. Labor productivity, in the main, depends upon the availability of natural resources, technology, the degree to which applied science is utilized, and the will of the workers. In the USSR, as in any other country, growth in labor productivity is calculated on the basis of increased physical output of goods and services at any given period of time.

Since the beginning of the First Five-Year Plan, the Soviets emphasized industrial production by building new plants and factories, by modernizing industrial facilities, and by acquainting workers with advanced technology. The Soviets claim that since the beginning of their industrialization drive, the greatest share of their growth in industrial production has come from improvement in labor productivity. During the First Five-Year Plan 51 per cent of the total increase in industrial production was derived from the increase in labor productivity. During the Second Five-Year Plan growth in labor productivity was responsible for 69 per cent of the total industrial increase, and in the 1950-55 period 68 per cent of the total industrial growth was attributed to improvement in labor efficiency. Planned 1956-60 labor productivity was set at 80 per cent of the total increase in industrial output. During the current Seven-Year Plan industrial productivity is expected to be increased by another 45 to 50 per cent.

The abundance of natural resources influences the level of labor productivity, but since volumes of these resources cannot change very rapidly, they do not affect movement in labor productivity. The most important factors in the growth of labor productivity—other factors being equal—are investments in advanced mechanization, improvement in technology, and skill of the labor force. Between 1940 and 1955 investments in technology per industrial worker increased by 52 per cent, while industrial labor productivity increased by 98 per cent. This suggests that a small increase in technology results in greater labor productivity even in the USSR.

Since a large share of Soviet industrial investment is assigned to large-scale industrial facilities, production of small labor-saving devices which tend to increase the productivity of labor is neglected. These supplementary and complementary mechanized pieces of equipment are in short supply in the USSR. For example, 44 per cent of the workers in the coal industry in 1955 were using simple hand tools such as shovels and hauling coal to the earth's surface by hand, and 68 per cent of the timber industry workers used hand tools. Another example of the scarcity of labor-saving devices is notable in the construction industry, which in 1955 used about 900,000 workers in loading and unloading occupations with insufficient mechanized equipment.[17] The Soviets have estimated that as a whole in 1955 five to six million workers were employed with inadequate technological means.[18]

An example of poor work organization is found in the construction industry in which an average of about one and one-half hours was spent in process of changing from one shift to another. Each shift, and individual workers, must have detailed records of what has been accomplished by other shifts and of what supplies are left for the new shift. In addition, there are other stoppages of work due to lacks in materials and adequate supervision over the workers, many of whom are taking "long smokes."

Inefficient utilization of manpower is one of the main reasons for the high cost of Soviet production. Only recently an attempt was made to increase production of labor-saving devices to replace manual labor. But this is only a partial solution. Theoretically, Soviet workers are the owners of means of production, and as long as this concept is emphasized by the government, any improvement in labor discipline will be difficult to maintain.

Another major factor in the growth of labor productivity is the skill, training, and general education of the labor force. In pre-World War II years, the largest part of the industrial labor force in the Soviet Union had an average of three to four years of schooling. By 1952, over one-half of the industrial workers had five to six years of general education and younger workers who joined the industrial labor force in 1952 had seven to ten years of general education. These younger workers now represent a considerable portion of the industrial labor force.[19]

Table 6—*Growth of Industrial Labor Productivity* [20]

| Year | Per cent |
|------|----------|
| 1940 | 100 |
| 1950 | 137 |
| 1951 | 150 |
| 1952 | 161 |
| 1953 | 171 |
| 1954 | 183 |
| 1955 | 198 |
| 1956 | 212 |
| 1957 | 226 |
| 1958 | 240 |

Between 1940 and 1950, the official average annual labor productivity in industrial enterprises rose by about 37 per cent, or by 3.7 per cent annually. However, between 1950 and 1958 this average annual increase was 7.5 per cent. As was noted, the 1940-50 period was an abnormal one which included Warld War II, and during which labor productivity in armament industries considerably increased; yet labor productivity as a whole remained below the 1940 civilian industrial production level. According to some indications, 1945 industrial labor productivity as a whole was 25 per cent above that of 1940.[21] This leads to the conclusion that during the five years of the war the average annual increase in labor productivity was about five per cent, and during the reconstruction period, it was about 2.4 per cent. But these wartime increases are largely for the plants producing military material where high productivity was stimulated by the speeding-up process, by attractive incentives to the workers and by the general feeling of contributing to the war effort. It also should be noted that during the 1950-56 period Soviet industrial labor productivity increased by 55 per cent. During the same period the labor productivity in manufacturing industries of the United States increased by only 16.2 per cent.[22] However, an increase of one per cent in labor productivity in industries of the United States represents a greater physical volume than a corresponding share in the USSR.

In general, comparison of industrial labor productivity of the United States and the Soviet Union is very unsatisfactory. It requires qualification of such troublesome factors as what consitutes an industry, or how productivity should be calculated. In the United States, government-owned enterprises such as dockyards are excluded from the private economy, whereas in the Soviet Union they are included in calculating industrial labor productivity. On the other hand, many services are omitted in the USSR but included in the United States. Again, the mode of computation of industrial labor productivity may be based on average annual output per worker, per man-hour or per man-hour worked. Generally, all productivity indicators are devised for specific purposes, to picture a given set of factors. The Soviets have chosen to use the average annual output per man as their indicator of labor productivity although it is less sensitive than the one based on man-hours worked. It may be well to add that however interesting and important the above-mentioned questions may be, because of space limitations they cannot be justly analyzed in this chapter. Normally, such questions are dealt with in articles rather than in general purpose books such as this.

Labor mobility from job to job, absence from work, and defective production of goods in the Soviet Union reduce productivity per man. In some Soviet enterprises, annual turnover of labor force fluctuates from two-to-three to eight-to-twelve per cent of the total labor force. In 1954 alone, over 40 million man-days were lost through mobility of workers and absence. Based on an eight-hour workday, this represents five million workers, of which 4.2 million workers were in the timber industry. In 1953 alone, production of defective goods amounted to 3.2 billion rubles, or over 190 rubles per worker of the total industrial labor force.[23]

Growth in Soviet industrial labor productivity is not uniform among various industries. Those industries which are important for national security or for further economic expansion of the country or relatively new industries have higher rates of growth than others.

In Table 7 productivity index, numbers show changes in output per worker on an average annual basis, including paid holidays, vacations, sick leave, etc. Labor productivity has advanced more rapidly in machine-building, chemicals, cement, pig iron, steel, and electric power than in coal mining, timber, food processing, and crude oil. The most rapid advance occurred between 1953 and 1958, especially in machine-building, cement, chemicals, crude oil, and electric power. The least advance is shown in coal, timber, food processing and in consumer goods.

Since 1950, the end of the rehabilitation and reconstruction period, Soviet labor productivity has exhibited a considerable capactiy for sustained growth, especially in the machine-building and chemical industries. Larger numbers of machines will inevitably increase the output per worker in the future. Recent adjustments in the management of industrial enterprises, increases in actual income of the workers, and a general propaganda drive for greater efficiency should provide additional incentives for greater productivity of the labor force. In short, opportunities for increasing labor productivity in the Soviet Union are not limited to additional investments

TABLE 7—*Official Growth of Average Annual Labor Productivity Per Man in the USSR* (1940=100)[24]

| Industry | 1950 | 1951 | 1952 | 1953 | 1954 | 1955 | 1956 | 1958 |
|---|---|---|---|---|---|---|---|---|
| Machine-building | 169 | 193 | 213 | 231 | 257 | 296 | 325 | 387 |
| Chemicals | 176 | 200 | 219 | 239 | 260 | 293 | 305 | 351 |
| Cement | 122 | 136 | 152 | 168 | 193 | 225 | 235 | 282 |
| Pig iron | 133 | 146 | 165 | 176 | 191 | 204 | 230 | 237 |
| Steel | 143 | 153 | 162 | 172 | 183 | 200 | 215 | 216 |
| Electric energy | 132 | 142 | 156 | 164 | 175 | 195 | — | — |
| Consumer goods | 122 | 133 | 139 | 147 | 156 | 165 | 173 | 186 |
| Rolled metals | 121 | 126 | 133 | 137 | 146 | 157 | 168 | 173 |
| Crude oil | 82 | 91 | 95 | 99 | 110 | 131 | 156 | 198 |
| Food processing | 97 | 105 | 113 | 118 | 125 | 131 | 138 | 151 |
| Timber | 90 | 95 | 96 | 97 | 107 | 109 | — | — |
| Coal (total) | 98 | 106 | 110 | 114 | 119 | 124 | 125 | 132 |
| Coal (pits) | 93 | 100 | 103 | 104 | 107 | 109 | — | — |

alone. More and better mechanization and automation will undoubtedly increase productivity, but the real opportunity lies in more efficient management and labor organization in production and in stabilizing the labor force. Simply by reducing mobility and absence of the workers and by eliminating waste in the use of raw materials, labor force, and equipment, the Soviets can greatly increase their industrial productivity per worker.

In his speech made in Kiev on May 11, 1959, Khrushchev emphasized the urgency of automative development.[25] But automation needs skilled workers  According to the Soviets, for every graduate engineer at least three skilled workers or so-called "technicians" are needed. Most of these skilled workers are in heavy industry and especially in metallurgy, where labor productivity is much higher than in production of consumer goods. Training programs for youg workers are rapidly expanding, with emphasis on programs for the eastern parts of the USSR. As these newly trained workers are taking part in industrial production, more and more enterprises show improvement in the fulfillment of state plans. A decline in the number of plants showing a production quota deficiency began in 1957 and it is expected that this downward trend will continue.

## Chapter 6—Bibliography

[1] *Ekonomika Sotsialisticheskoy Promyshlennosti,* Moscow, 1957, pp. 34, 37.

[2] *Sovetskaya Sotsialisticheskaya Ekonomika: 1917-1957,* Moscow, 1957, p. 581.

[3] *Narodnoye Khozaystvo SSSR v 1956 Godu,* Moscow, 1957, p. 52; Valodarskiy, L. M., *Statistika Promyshlennosti i Voprosy Planirovaniya,* Moscow, 1958, p. 91; W. K., *Reaching for the Moon,* The World Today, February 1959, p. 47; Khrushchev, N. S., *Kontrolnye Tsifry Razvitiya Narodnogo Khozaystva SSSR na 1959-1965 Godu,* Moscow, 1958, p. 29 (hereafter referred to as *Kontrolnye Tsifry*).

[4] *Science,* Vol. 130, July 31, 1959, p. 253.

[5] *Ekonomika Sotsialisticheskoy Promyshlennosti,* op. cit., p. 44.

[6] Maevskiy, I., *Ekonomicheskaya Osnova SSSR,* Moscow, 1956, p. 28.

[7] *Pravda,* May 6, 1958.

[8] Grossman, G., *Thirty Years of Soviet Industrialization,* Soviet Survey, October-December 1958, p. 15.

[9] Dulles, Allen, *The New York Times,* April 9, 1959; *The American Economic Review,* September 1959, p. 693.

[10] *Pravda* and *Izvestia,* June 30, 1959.

[11] *Ekonomika Sotsialisticheskoy Promyshlennosti,* op. cit., p. 308; *Narodnoye Khozaystvo SSSR v 1958 Godu,* Moscow, 1959, p. 134.

[12] *Kontrolnye Tsifry,* pp. 63, 77-90.

[13] *Narodnoye Khozaystvo SSSR v 1956 Godu,* Moscow, 1957, p. 60; *Sovetskaya Sotsialisticheskaya Ekonomika,* op. cit., p. 284; *Ekonomika Sovetskoy Promyshlennosti,* op. cit., p. 361; Embassy of the USSR, *Press Department, No. 37,* Washington, D. C., March 6, 1959; *Kontrolnye Tsifry,* pp. 39-43.

[14] *Kontrolnye Tsifry,* pp. 63-69.

[15] *Sovetskiy Soyuz,* No. 5 (III), 1959, p. 32.

[16] Jasny, N., *Interpreting Soviet Statistics,* Soviet Survey, October-December 1958, p. 12.

[17] Shass, M. E., *Ekonomika Stroitel'noy Promyshlennosti SSSR.* Moscow, 1958, p. 30.

[18] *Voprosy Politicheskoy Ekonomii,* Moscow, 1957, p .47.

[19] *Ekonomika Sotsialisticheskoy Promyshlennosti,* op. cit., p. 453.

[20] *Narodnoye Khozaystvo SSSR v 1958 Godu,* op. cit., p. 111.

[21] *Dositzheniya Sovetskoy Vlasti za 40 Let v Tsifrakh,* Moscow, 1957, Diagram No. 6.

[22] *Economic Report of the President,* transmitted to the Congress, January 20, 1958. U. S. Government Printing Office, Washington, D. C., p. 108.

[23] *Ekonomika Sotsialisticheskoy Promyshlennosti,* op. cit., pp. 456-57.

[24] *Promyshlennost SSSR,* Moscow, 1957, pp. 26-27; *Narodnoye Khozaystvo SSSR v 1958 Godu,* op. cit., pp. 153-54.

[25] *Pravda,* May 14, 1959.

# Organizational Structure
# In Agriculture

## INTRODUCTION

The organizational structure of Soviet agriculture is primarily the result of the interplay of three basic factors: the historical servitude of Russian peasantry, the nature and topography of the major agricultural regions of the Soviet Union, and the Marxian doctrine of ownership of means of production and its adaptation by Soviet agricultural policy-makers.

The Russian peasant was under servitude for most of the years of his recorded history. Only during a brief period between 1860 and 1930 was he able to escape virtual slavery; but with the establishment of collectivized agriculture in 1930, the peasant again yielded his freedom to a landowner—the State.

The present agricultural setting in the Soviet Union is the result of Marxian theory developed principally to correct industrial rather than agricultural ills. With this system the peasant is only a secondary consideration; it is not the system itself but the adaptations and manipulations within the system which can be attributed to his outwardly submissive but inwardly resistant nature.

The present system was produced by loud slogans of Marxism-Leninism, plus the urgency of Stalin's program for "building socialism in one country" surrounded by a hostile world. Assumptions used in the formulation of the policy were few, and the mathematical equation was simple.

Emphasis on industrialization with a limited investment demands a greater labor force. The source of this labor force is the farm population. As the urban population increases and the rural population declines a gradually increasing amount of foodstuffs must be produced by fewer peasants. In the absence of agricultural incentives for greater output a larger share of the peasants' total production must be taken away so that they will have to produce more to meet growing demands. The answer to this dilemma was found in the basic Soviet agricultural organization.

To produce a larger amount of foodstuffs and raw materials for industry the Soviets relied upon increasing mechanization, adaptation of scientific farm practices and more efficient large-scale farm organization. The availability of great plains suitable for large-scale farming methods, the collective heritage of Russian village communities, the collectivist Marxian doctrine, and the militant nature of Party organization made a program of agricultural collectivization an obvious solution for Soviet policymakers.

It was the speed of industrialization, plus the attachment of peasants to the land they had won in the preceding 50 or 60 years, that made force a handmaiden of this solution and has thereby necessitated the retention of force, open or veiled, in the preservation and operation of a collectivized agriculture.

The early history of collectivization is the history of peasants' resistance to the State force which created suspicion and fear on both sides. However, in the main, it was repulsion of the peasants which forced the State to make concessions to their underprivileged status. The strong desire for profit among collectivized peasants has finally been accepted as their basic characteristic by the State. This motivation is now being utilized by Soviet leaders as a means to increase agricultural output and to win the loyalty of the peasants. Realization of an economic motivation among the peasants is the major break from the harsh treatment of the past; a return to past policies is unlikely in the near future.

## COLLECTIVE FARMS

In its agricultural adjustments the Soviet government has, at one time or another, experienced three types of socialized farming. First came the agricultural communes, where all factors of production were pooled for common use and the produce thus derived was equally shared among all participants. This was an ideal communistic approach, practiced only at the beginning of the Red Revolution on a small scale. Second were the various cooperative organizations (TOZ), with only the land and labor pooled together, while the implements and working stock, although commonly used for field work, were privately owned. The produce of the common labor and land was then distributed among members in accordance with contribution in land, labor, and other factors of production. This type of agricultural organization has also ceased to exist. Third was the agricultural organization known as the "artel," or collective farm, where the produce is distributed according to the contribution in labor by each member. The land in the collective farm is state owned and cannot be sold, rented, or mortgaged. Thus, the century-old dream of the peasant to own the land they work on is still only a dream.

## A. INTERNAL STRUCTURE

From the legal point of view, a collective farm is a voluntary organization and requires approval of all major activities by the membership which includes all persons over 16 years of age. To some degree, then, officially the collective farm resembles the cooperative organization where the membership decides upon activities or proposals presented by the management or by the State. More often, of course, these proposals are rigidly enforced by the government or by local Party organizations. But at times the membership of the collective farm, especially if it has excellent past political and economic records, can manage its affairs under the principle of "collective leadership" which was in existence even prior to Khrushchev's recent pronouncement of it.

The supreme organ of the collective farm is the general meeting of the members. The general meeting "elects" the chairman of the collective farm. The chairman may be nominated from the membership or, as in most cases, he is recommended by the State. In any case, he has to be approved by the local Party organ. He is elected for a two-year period, with the prerogative of dismissal before the expiration of his term by the membership, provided there is no interference from the Party on his behalf. The duties of the chairman are sharply defined: he is respeonsible for the direction of everyday work on the collective farm. However, he is not held responsible before the law for failure to use the land to best advantage.

The general meeting approves the proposed annual plan for business activity, the annual budget estimates, and plans for new construction. It establishes the minimum norms of work to be performed by each member for each task, ratifies contracts with other organizations, and endorses the annual report of the Board of Directors and the reports of the most important Executive Committees. It establishes the size of various funds in cash or in kind to be set aside and the amount of cash and produce in kind to be paid for each "labor day" to the members. And, of course, the genreal meeting ratifies the by-laws and rules on the size of the individual plots of land and the number of livestock owned privately by the members on the basis of State recommendations, which are seldom violated.

The Board of Directors is elected by the general meeting and has wider powers than the chairman. The Board approves or rejects the plans and practices proposed by the chairman or by committees. It has power to hire any farm specialist or skilled worker not found among members and it enforces the by-laws in the charter of the collective farm.

The general meeting elects an auditing committee, which looks after the books of the collective farm and checks on the progress of the business activity four times a year. Another function of the general meeting is the election of brigadiers or a straw boss, who serve for a two-year period or more.

## B. ORGANIZATION OF WORK

The most profound changes made by collectivization were in the organization of farm work. Prior to collectivization each farmer made his own plans, in most cases using family labor and following the traditional pattern of small-scale family-type farming practices. The system which exists now was created gradually, experimentally, after many trials and errors, and it is still not perfected as far as the Communists are concerned. Nevertheless, although the principle of collectivization now has the same goal as in 1930, the farm work methods have been changed. Experience and new discoveries in social and economic relationships between the peasant and the State have adjusted the organizational structure of the work.

Work participation in collective farms is calculated in terms of a labor day which is a unit of human effort with given factors of production devoted to a given task during the working day. At the very beginning of collectivization, every collective farm established its own norm of work per labor day. Under these conditions the peasant reduced the workload per labor day in order to get as many such days as possible. Then in 1933-34 the government "recommended" the establishment of norms for the 35 most important agricultural tasks fitted into seven labor days, the value of which ranged from one-half to two labor days per task.

With increased mechanization of the farms and the pressure from the State in 1940-41 for greater output, most regions increased norms of work per labor day. Then in April 1948 the USSR Council of Ministers established a scale consisting of nine labor days ranging in value from one-half to two and one-half labor days.

The minimum participation in farm work varied from region to region, depending on the type of agriculture. For instance, in 1955, in the cotton-growing regions of Central Asia the minimum requirement was 150 labor days a year. In the Ukraine it was 120 and in Siberia and northwestern parts of the RSFSR it was 100 labor days for every able-bodied adult member. Children of 12 to 16 years of age were required to work not less than 50 labor days annually, usually in the summer. However, the local government had the right to increase or decrease the required minimum number of labor days by 20 per cent when warranted.[1]

The concept of labor days is really based on the principle of piecework. The more one produces under adverse conditions, the more labor days he earns. A watchman on a collective farm gets only one-half of a labor day for a full working day, whereas a man taking care of ten horses receives three labor days for eight hours of work. In some cases a worker engaged in performing a difficult task is able to accumulate ten to 12 labor days per working day; if he works overtime, this number may be increased.

Farm production currently, with its increased mechanization, its improved scientific practices, and its better work organization, enables many peasants to earn the required minimum number of labor days in a shorter period of time than in the past. By working beyond the minimum number, they are able to accumulate a greater number of labor days annually.

Yet, the labor day as such has no standard value. Its value is expressed only in terms of units into which the farm net profit is divided. Thus the more peasants on the collective farm accumulating a large number of labor days, the less is the "worth" of the labor day. On the other hand, when a given net profit of the collective farm is divided by a fewer number of labor days, its "worth" is greater.

During the XX-th Communist Party Congress of February 1956, many Soviet leaders criticized the outdated scale for labor days and suggested that the general meeting of each collective farm re-evaluate labor days. The first reaction to this criticism came from a collective farm located in the Far East.[2] The general meeting of this farm ruled that in 1956 all able-bodied men must report for work 270 times a year and earn 400 labor days a year; women without children must report 270 times a year and earn 300 labor days; women with as many as three children or disabled dependents must report 150 times a year and earn 180 labor days; and women with more than three children or dependents must report 100 times annually and earn 125 labor days. The children aged from 12 to 16 years were to report for work 50 times a year to earn 25 to 50 labor days. In cases where the minimum number of labor days was not attained, the general meeting had the right to reduce or take away entirely the plot of land assigned to the member.

Soviet leaders recognized that the old requirement of a minimum number of labor days had become obsolete in 1956. Yet in general the peasants were cautious about committing themselves to any action which might backfire. Since the initial change in the structure in work participation in the Far Eastern collective farm, not many other farms came forward with specific proposals and there seems to be a "wait-and-see" attitude on the part of the peasantry. Eventually the government will be forced to issue a directive dealing with the problem of required participation in farm work by its members. In the meantime the pressure to increase participation in farm work is in the hands of the local Party and government organs. The pressure is real and already during the 1950 to 1955 period peasants have increased their participation in work in terms of labor days by 35 per cent.[3] The problem with labor day payments is that similar tasks performed on different collective farms are being paid by a different scale of labor days. Since the labor day cannot be used as a measurement of labor productivity, the Soviets are gradually adopting a new method based on "mandays" participation which can be calculated in monetary units for each task performed.

The basic working unit on the collective farm is the brigade. In 1940 the average brigade consisted of 56 workers of both sexes.[4] In that year, on an average, every collective farm producing field crops had 2.2 brigades, each having 62 workers.[5] But with the merging of collective farms after 1950 their sizes were considerably increased and there are now many multiple-purpose brigades, in which the members produce field crops for the livestock assigned to them. This is a new trend to get away from specialization, and under certain conditions one brigade is able to manage several small-scale farming enterprises. For example, raising a small number of hogs may easily be combined with production of feed for them. Now that the collective farms have the right to own farm machinery, the trend in formation of multiple-purpose brigades is on the increase and their size in manpower is on the decline.

Withdrawing from one brigade and joining another is permitted only under certain conditions, as in the case of a quarrel between a brigadier and a member, or inability of a brigadier to organize for greater output. Under such conditions, the average worker would try to join the ranks of the best brigade and the records often show that one brigade having the same allocation of scarce resources as the next is nevertheless more productive. This creates ill feeling among the peasants, and at times a change in personnel is necessary. For more flexibility in working assignments the field brigade is divided into links, which in most field work consist of ten to 12 workers who handle specific tasks suitable for a small group of workers. Other types of links, such as in livestock, are smaller. Again, since peasants now own farm machinery, the size of a link is also being reduced by about half. Since links are given the necessary machinery, their productive power now resembles the brigade of the earlier years.

## C. LAND AND CAPITAL EQUIPMENT

The collective farm's land is given to it by the State for permanent use, without charge. It may be taken by the State for its own use, but theoretically the collective farm will be given other land. Legally, once the land has been granted to a collective farm, it cannot be given to another collective farm, except in the process of merging several collective farms or when decreed by the State.

There are two methods used in the creation of capital on the collective farms. During the early period of collectivization, buildings, implements, and livestock were confiscated from the wealthy peasants, the so-called "kulaks," and were given to collective farms in addition to some assistance that the government was able to spare from its own reserves and the meager resources contributed by the members themselves. Later, when the collective farms became going concerns, from one-fourth to one-half of the total capital in produce and cash income was set aside in "undivided funds," used for the purchase of livestock, building materials, farm equipment, seed, and all the other factors of production needed by the collective farms. In addition to these sources, farm credit from the State and Agricultural Banks became available in increasing amounts.

The argument that a society under socialism will save little, because of the consumers' great tendency to spend and the lack of opportunities for investment of individual savings, does not apply to the collective farms, for their savings are required by law and the rate of savings can easily be increased. In many instances it may be said that some of the collective farms, especially in the cotton-growing regions, save too much instead of too little, for there is still a scarcity of the goods and services which wealthy collective farms would like to have. But it is also erroneous to assume that all collective farms save too much, either in kind or in cash. There are many marginal and submarginal collective farms which are barely able to fulfill their required obligations, let alone accumulate necessary funds for desired improvements. These collective farms received state assistance in the form of subsidies or credit on an assumption that once their economic condition improves they too will show a profit and save in order to continue the cycle of constant amelioration of their economic status.

## D. THE INDIVIDUAL ECONOMY OF THE MEMBERS

Every peasant household on the collective farm has a right to have its own small enterprise. Every household has, besides a place for the house, the right to a plot of land which ranges from 0.6 to 2.5 acres in size. This plot might become a garden or be put to other use. In regions of intensive cultivation such as around Moscow, or in densely populated rural areas such as the Ukraine, or in irrigated regions of Central Asia, between 0.6 and 1.25 acres are allowed to every household. In the cattle range areas the individual is allowed as much as 2.5 acres. The plot is given to the household for its personal use only. It cannot be sold or rented, and if not used it is taken away. If a family is divided into two households the plot cannot be divided. A new plot is given to each new family when it becomes a member of the collective farm.

Besides having the plot, every household has a right to own livestock. In regions where grain, cotton, sugar beets, flax, hemp, vegetables, tea, and tobacco are grown, each household is permitted to have one cow, or two heifers, or two calves, or one sow with all her sucklings. In some cases the household may be allowed to have two sows with all their sucklings, or ten sheep and goats, or an unlimited number of poultry and rabbits, or 20 beehives. In regions where livestock is important for livelihood, each household may have two or three cows with all their young stock, or two or three sows with their sucklings, or 25 sheep and goats. In regions where the nomadic type of agriculture still prevails each household may have four or five cows with all their young stock, or two or three sows with their sucklings, or 30 to 40 sheep and goats, or one horse, or two camels, or two asses, or two mules.

In regions where intensive range and pasture practices prevail, as in the Buryat ASSR, each household is permitted to have 18 cows with their growing stock, or 100 to 150 sheep and goats, or ten horses, or five to eight camels, or an unlimited number of poultry.

The private enterprise of the members of the collective farm was, and still is, allowed to exist because not all collective farms can satisfy all the needs of their members. Many collective farms are highly specialized in cotton or sugar-beet growing, for example. Others are primarily livestock or fruit farms, but their members need vegetables and other produce not grown on the collective farms. Originally this was to be a temporary expedient, not designed either to undermine the purpose of collectivization or to free the collective from caring for its members. In the face of the recent trend in farm specialization, it is doubtful that the Soviets will abolish the individual peasant enterprises. They are important, not only as a source of additional foodstuffs for the peasant families, but also as suppliers of local urban markets.

The government is not so much against the possession of these private enterprises as it is against ingenuity on the part of the peasants in creating profitable private enterprises on these plots and avoiding work on the collective farms. An example of peasants' cleverness in creating private enterprises is the case of a woman who planted on her quarter-acre plot grapes for wine, sale of which produced enough income so that there was no need for her to work on the collective farm at all.[6] There are many exceptional cases such as this, and the Soviets bitterly oppose the peasants' irrepressible urge to create profitable enterprises yielding more profit from their plots at the expense of the work on the collective farms.

Until March 1956 the rights and privileges of the members of the collective farms were safeguarded by the Model Statute for the Collective Farm adopted in 1936 and revised in 1942. The principles laid down by the Model Statute were protected by the government and any violation of these principles was severely punished. At the session of the Central Committee of the Communist Party and the USSR Council of Ministers held in March 1956 these principles were revised. It was pointed out that between 1936 and 1956 many major changes had taken place in the life of collective farms, and in view of those changes it was decreed that the individual plots of the members of collective farms should be fixed, not on the basis of the member's right to the plot as stated in the early Model Statute, but on the basis of the labor contribution of the able-bodied members of the household to the communal work. Those households whose able-bodied members contribute more working time on the collective farm may receive larger plots than those who work less. The number of livestock privately owned by the members is also to be determined by labor participation and by local conditions. An interesting point of the 1956 decree is that although it requires the collective peasants to abide strictly by the land nationalization laws, it does not hold them responsible for fulfilling the planned production quota devised for them.

By virtue of the annexation of western parts of the Soviet Union, the number of collectivized households between 1940 and 1950 was increased by about two million. With the increased number of households, the land in private lots also increased, whereas the number of livestock declined.

From 1950 to 1956 the number of households remained practically unchanged as was the case in their total sowed area. But the number of peasant-owned livestock—especially cattle, sheep, hogs, and goats—increased. Only a slight increase is shown for cows, the most important and valuable animal to a household. On an average of one cow per household, there were six million farm families without cows in 1940,

TABLE 1—*Significant Data on Individual Economy of the Peasants* [7]
(*at the end of the year*)

| Item | Unit | 1940 | 1950 | 1954 | 1955 | 1956 | 1958 |
|---|---|---|---|---|---|---|---|
| Total number of households | Million | 18.7 | 20.5 | 19.7 | 19.8 | 19.9 | 18.8 |
| Total sowed acreage: _____ | Million | 11.1 | 14.6 | 14.1 | 14.3 | 13.9 | 13.6 |
| Grain crops _____ | Million | 2.1 | 4.8 | 3.8 | 4.1 | 3.7 | 3.3 |
| Industrial crops _____ | Million | 0.4 | 0.3 | 0.3 | 0.3 | 0.3 | 0.2 |
| Truck gardening crops _____ | Million | 7.7 | 8.8 | 9.2 | 9.1 | 9.1 | 9.1 |
| Fodder crops _____ | Million | 0.9 | 0.7 | 0.8 | 0.8 | 0.9 | 1.0 |
| Total number of livestock: | Million | 59.4 | 40.8 | 48.7 | 52.8 | 62.0 | 57.9 |
| Cattle: _____ | Million | 19.2 | 18.3 | 17.5 | 18.8 | 25.5 | 20.3 |
| Cows _____ | Million | 12.7 | 11.5 | 10.9 | 11.1 | 11.7 | 12.7 |
| Hogs _____ | Million | 8.6 | 6.3 | 11.2 | 11.2 | 11.7 | 11.1 |
| Sheep _____ | Million | 25.4 | 10.8 | 12.4 | 15.5 | 17.8 | 22.1 |
| Goats _____ | Million | 6.2 | 5.4 | 7.6 | 7.3 | 7.0 | 4.4 |
| Per household: _____ | Number | | | | | | |
| Sowed acre _____ | Number | 0.59 | 0.71 | 0.72 | 0.73 | 0.70 | 0.72 |
| Cattle: _____ | Number | 1.03 | 0.89 | 0.89 | 0.95 | 1.27 | 1.08 |
| Cows _____ | Number | 0.68 | 0.56 | 0.55 | 0.60 | 0.60 | 0.68 |
| Hogs _____ | Number | 0.46 | 0.31 | 0.57 | 0.57 | 0.59 | 0.60 |
| Sheep _____ | Number | 1.36 | 0.53 | 0.63 | 0.78 | 0.90 | 1.13 |
| Goats _____ | Number | 0.33 | 0.26 | 0.39 | 0.37 | 0.35 | 0.24 |

nine million cowless households in 1950 and seven million in 1958. Thus, between 1940 and 1958 the number of collectivized households was increased by 100,000 whereas the cow population remained the same.

An intresting trend in ownership of livestock by members of collective farms and others has developed since 1953. At the beginning of this period emphasis was on ownership of smaller animals, but later a greater number of cows was owned by this sector. For example, in 1953 the members of collective farms and others in the Azerbaydzhan SSR owned 145,000 cows, and 235,000 in 1958.[8] True, during this period the total number of socialized livestock of this republic was also increased, but not in cows. It is claimed that a large number of cows in a private sector reduces the participation of members in communal work. With the abolition of required meat deliveries to the State from private owners of livestock and with increased prices on meat products, the members of collective farms have increased their cow population. As a result, many oblasts in 1958 were able to fulfill their state delivery requirements in meat only by purchasing livestock from the members of collective farms and other owners at high prices.

The problem became so important that Khrushchev, in his speech to the Central Committee in December 1958, proposed the creation of specialized meat-producing state farms. Without condemning private owners of livestock, he criticized poor organization of the livestock industry by the socialized sector. He felt that instead of direct interference by the government, the local Party organs should indirectly force the collective farms to purchase livestock from their members.

## E. MERGING OF COLLECTIVE FARMS

In the history of Soviet collectivization of agriculture the problem of the merging of small collective farms into larger economic units has been ever-present. As the availability of agricultural machinery increased, small collective farms were at a disadvantage. In 1936 there were many collective farms, often having five to ten households which did not possess enough land for new large-scale farm machinery and depended to a large extent upon hand labor in their major farm operations, thus reducing the yield. These small farms, by a decree of December 19, 1935, were merged into larger units.[9] Then with the occupation of the Baltic states and western parts of the Ukraine and White Russia in 1939-40, many small collective farms were organized there and it was only after the end of World War II that the Soviets turned their attention to pooling them into larger units.

But the most dramatic attack on small collective farms came from Khrushchev in late 1949 when he proposed the formation of "agrogorods" or village towns comprising about 5,000 people each. The main idea in the creation of agrogorods was to pool several small collective farms into a centralized place under one administration, thus providing greater opportunities for using large-scale farm machinery. It was assumed that the peasants themselves would build new houses with their own resources and labor at the time when their efforts and resources were needed for the reconstruction and rehabilitation of the country as a whole. This plan required huge long-term investments not only on the part of peasants themselves but by the government as well. Nevertheless, some collective farms have begun to develop plans for construction of agrogorods. For example, four collective farms located in Ukraine devised a plan for the construction of an agrogorod where 2,000 brick houses were to be constructed, streets were to be asphalted, and bus and automobile services were to be provided. It was planned to build the main office for the collective farm, a club, a moving picture house, hotel, school, several stores and shops, a stadium and park. The time required for the construction of this agrogorod was to be between five and seven years.[10] It was because of the length of time required and the large investments to be tied up in the building of the agrogorods that the venture was dropped shortly after its introduction.

However, the idea of merging small collective farms into larger economic units without construction of agrogorods took deep root in the minds of the Soviet leaders. They felt that merging several collective farms into one and permitting the peasants to live, when possible, at their old homesteads would serve the same purpose as building an agrogorod. Moreover, it was assumed that when conditions were favorable, the collective farms would relocate their members to a centralized place of residence.

The program was vigorously launched by the Party and by the press. It was explained that by merging of several collective farms into a single unit, the land use would be better organized, large-scale farm machinery would be employed to better advantage on larger fields, and the total land area would be increased; while other factors of production, previously divided among several collective farms, would remain the same. Meanwhile, the labor force would become more efficient and more productive. For example, while one milkmaid was employed for eight cows in each of three merging collective farms, under the reorganization she could take care of 12 cows and thus eliminate the extra worker for employment elsewhere. There would be no need to have three chairmen, three bookkeepers and three watchmen. Horses and implements would be more fully and efficiently utilized. Centralized administration would be more economical to operate. The standard of living of the members would be improved and schools, clubs, and other social improvements could be established on a larger collective farm whereas on the small farm these services were denied because of lack of funds.

At the same time merging would strengthen political control over the collective farms. Party organizations would have better propaganda machinery installed to control the moods of the peasants. The lack of Party control within collective farms was looked upon as an inexcusable phenomenon. Even in 1954, with merging programs almost completed, only 85.4 per cent of all farms had communist apparatuses of some kind, even though the total number of Communists on the farms was a little over a million and the number of rural Komsomols was over two million.[11] There were not enough loyal cadres to guide the Party line among the peasants;

and prior to the merging program, conditions were even worse. By 1958 the number of Communists on collective farms was 1,350,000. With an average Party cell consisting of 20 members, in 1958 only 67,500 collective farms had such communist cells.[12]

From the early beginning of the merging program it was looked upon as an efficient drive to tighten economic and political controls over the collectivized agriculture. The merging also harmonized with the basic conception of the Communists of bringing the peasants closer to the status of factory workers in the cities.

In a small collective farm without strong political control, the peasants had closer contact with the problems of their farm and of protecting their own interests, whereas in a large one they lose personal touch with affairs. The new farms became big business, with several independent enterprises such as field crops, livestock, vegetables, and the like. Management of a large-scale farm enterprise requires knowledge of many more things than management of a small farm where every member knows everyone else. Again in the process of merging, some good "dirt" farmers were assigned to work with livestock or with truck gardening crops. In many instances peasants' households were relocated to new living quarters leaving behind them all the improvements they had made on their homesteads. It might have been a new fence around the plot or a few carefully tended fruit trees in which the peasants took pride. All this created dissatisfaction and resentment.

At the beginning of the merging program in 1950 there were 121,400 collective farms, but in 1952 their number was reduced by 26,600. In the main, the merging program was not uniform throughout the USSR. During a single year (1950) the Moscow Oblast reduced its number of collective farms from 6,000 to 1,668; the Kalinin Oblast from 7,500 to 1,800; the Leningrad Oblast from 2,000 to 600; and the Smolensk Oblast from 5,486 to 2,300.[13] These four oblasts contributed more than half of the total Soviet reduction in collective farms. The rapidity with which the Soviets conducted merging suggests that it was an intensive drive, perhaps of the same magnitude as the early collectivization program of 1929-30 but involving fewer peasant households. But even in 1958 there were still small collective farms. In the Chita Oblast, for example, there were 33 small collective farms, some of them consisting of 20 to 25 households. Similar conditions existed in mountainous regions of the Caucasus. These small farms contribute little to the State, but they receive state subsidies. Yet the cost of relocating them would be high for the local governmen.[14]

There are two types of collective farms in the Soviet Union. The predominant type is the agricultural collective farm, engaged in cultivation of the land or in raising of livestock. The other type consists of those which do not cultivate land but devote their efforts to maintaining beehives, fishing, breeding of precious fur-bearing animals, reindeer, and the like.

TABLE 2—*Significant Data on Collective Farms* [15]
(*at the end of the year*)

| Item | Unit | 1940 | 1950 | 1954 | 1956 | 1958 |
|---|---|---|---|---|---|---|
| Total number of collective farms: | Thousand | 236.9 | 123.7 | 89.0 | 87.8 | 69.1 |
| Agricultural collective farms | Thousand | 235.5 | 121.4 | 87.1 | 83.0 | 67.7 |
| Total sowed acreage: | Million | 290.8 | 299.0 | 343.2 | 375.8 | 483.3 |
| Grain crops | Million | 224.9 | 222.6 | 245.3 | 253.0 | 309.4 |
| Industrial crops | Million | 25.9 | 28.7 | 27.7 | 30.5 | 30.4 |
| Truck gardening crops | Million | 10.6 | 11.6 | 13.1 | 13.8 | 13.6 |
| Fodder crops | Million | 29.4 | 36.1 | 57.1 | 78.5 | 114.9 |
| Communal livestock: | | | | | | |
| Cattle: | Million | 20.1 | 28.1 | 27.8 | 26.9 | 32.1 |
| Cows | Million | 5.7 | 7.0 | 8.7 | 10.0 | 11.5 |
| Hogs | Million | 8.2 | 12.3 | 13.6 | 12.8 | 23.1 |
| Sheep | Million | 39.1 | 60.8 | 73.7 | 70.7 | 73.8 |
| Goats | Million | 2.8 | 7.5 | 4.1 | 2.0 | 1.3 |
| Horses | Million | 14.5 | 11.1 | 12.1 | 10.2 | 8.0 |
| Average per collective farm: | | | | | | |
| Households | Number | 81 | 165 | 224 | 238 | 276 |
| Sowed acres | Number | 1,216 | 2,389 | 3,828 | 4,446 | 6,965 |
| Cattle | Number | 85 | 225 | 312 | 317 | 464 |
| Cows | Number | 24 | 56 | 78 | 118 | 166 |
| Hogs | Number | 35 | 98 | 153 | 151 | 334 |
| Sheep | Number | 165 | 487 | 828 | 834 | 1,068 |
| Goats | Number | 12 | 60 | 46 | 23 | 19 |
| Horses | Number | 61 | 89 | 135 | 121 | 116 |

In comparison with 1940 and 1950, collective farms in 1958 had a larger total number of households, as well as more land and livestock. Growth came not only as a result of the merging program but also because of reorganization in the land utilization pattern. And despite all the bewilderment, confusion, and hardship on the part of a great many peasant families, as an economic organization the collective farms emerged in 1958 as a larger enterprise than they were in 1940 or in 1950.

The year 1956 was a turning point in agricultural land expansion. The total grain acreage in 1958 was about two per cent below that of 1956.[16]

The current Seven-Year Plan does not anticipate spectacular land expansion on the collective farms, since between 1950 and 1958 their land already had been increased by about 67 per cent. This is not, however, a relaxation period for the peasants. During the next seven years the collective farms are expected to increase their efficiency in production of field crops and livestock on the land which they already have. Moreover, they are to improve their farms, undertake necessary construction of homes for the peasants, and in general to improve their standard of living. With increased efficiency they are expected to supply about 60 per cent of the total national grain requirements in 1965, the same share as it was in 1958. The task is not easy, since in the past any increase in agricultural output came mainly through expansion in the land; and the "efficiency" concept is still rather new for the peasants to cope with.

## STATE FARMS

Although large state farms were organized as early as 1918, prior to 1954 they were not an important source of the food, fiber, and the fats and oils needed by the nation. The concept of large-scale state farms is inherited from the early days of the Soviet regime. At that time it was believed that the shift to a large-scale farming system was in harmony with the ideological beliefs of the Communists, who were very much impressed with the superiority of large-scale methods of production. This belief was inherited from Marx and reinforced by the new faith in the advantages of tractor, combine, and irrigation farming. The ideal agricultural organizations would be, according to Marx, state farms where private ownership, no matter how insignificant it might be, could not exist, and where all the workers were to be paid by the State on the same basis as the factory workers.

Although the collective and state farms are quite different within their internal structure, both are governed by one management—the State. In this they are not independent or isolated from each other, but united by overall state planning, especially when such large undertakings as production of foodstuffs, reclamation, irrigation, drainage, reforestation, construction of railroads, highways, usage of modern technology on the farm, selection of seed, and improving breeds of livestock are concerned. Unlike collective farms, which have a more flexible internal structure, the state farms are strictly state-operated organizations.

The state farm, like any other state enterprise, is a government-owned and operated enterprise. Its annual budget and annual operation plans are developed by the State and all its lands, equipment, livestock, buildings and machinery are supplied and owned by the State. The state farm hires permanent workers and pays them a wage established by the State. Many state farms are highly specialized, devoting their efforts to raising only corn, sugar beets, cotton, citrus fruits, or livestock, while others are diversified such as those engaged in dairying and vegetable growing. The state farms

TABLE 3—*Significant Data Relating to State Farms* [17]
(*at the end of the year in thousand*)

| Item | 1940 | 1950 | 1953 | 1955 | 1956 | 1958 |
|---|---|---|---|---|---|---|
| Total (number) _____ | 4,159 | 4,988 | 4,857 | 5,134 | 5,098 | 6,002 |
| Total sowed acreage: | 28,545 | 31,861 | 37,448 | 63,852 | 77,873 | 129,606 |
| Grain crops _____ | 18,980 | 18,624 | 19,353 | 44,018 | 55,229 | 91,707 |
| Industrial crops ____ | 815 | 818 | 912 | 1,302 | 1,522 | 3,368 |
| Truck garden crops__ | 687 | 670 | 798 | 1,171 | 1,238 | 2,122 |
| Fodder crops _____ | 8,063 | 11,710 | 16,385 | 17,361 | 19,884 | 32,409 |
| Total number of livestock: | | | | | | |
| Cattle: _____ | 2,462 | 2,802 | 3,404 | 3,348 | 3,778 | 8,217 |
| Cows _____ | 952 | 848 | 1,128 | 1,280 | 1,461 | 2,833 |
| Hogs _____ | 1,910 | 2,494 | 3,502 | 3,320 | 6,292 | 8,127 |
| Sheep _____ | 5,841 | 7,544 | 10,047 | 10,297 | 10,758 | 26,193 |
| Goats _____ | 67 | 89 | 77 | 41 | 38 | 205 |
| Average annual permanent workers ____ | 1,373 | 1,665 | 1,844 | 2,101 | 2,168 | 3,835 |
| Total number of tractors _____ | 74 | 74 | 90 | 136 | 154 | 279 |
| Total number of combines _____ | 27 | 33 | 42 | 63 | 83 | 168 |
| Number of trucks _____ | 21 | 33 | 40 | 55 | 69 | 140 |

are considered as socialist schools for young city people who come during the harvest seasons to learn about large-scale agricultural production. During the 1955-58 period over three million students and young workers and employees from the cities were participating in the harvest on state farms.

The basic business organizational unit in the state farm is a section (otdelenye) and the state farm may have several sections such as for grain, industrial crops, or vegetables. A large state farm producing a single commodity such as corn may have several sections. In livestock the section is called "ferma." Each section has a given amount of land, labor force, equipment, and machinery.

For those who are permanent employees, small individual plots of land are provided for the duration of employment of each worker. The size of these plots varies from region to region and depends upon the type of farming undertaken by the state farm. In dry farming areas, plots are from 0.7 to 1.2 acres in size and in irrigated regions they are about 0.4 acre. As in the case of the members of collective farms, state farm workers are also permitted to keep a limited number of livestock.

Unlike the collective farms, which are administered by the USSR Ministry of Agriculture, the state farms prior to 1957 were under the jurisdiction of four different ministries. Often the same types of state farms located in different areas were organized and administered by two different ministries as in the case of tea, orchards, truck gardening crops, sugar beets, poultry, and a few other specialties. With the abolishment of many ministries in 1957, all state farms were finally transferred to the USSR Ministry of Agriculture.

The size of state farms varies with the type of specialization; but an average sowed area per state farm in 1958 was about 21,600 acres against about 7,000 acres for the collective farm. During the whole 1940-58 period, the total number of state farms increased by 1,843, mainly because of the formation of new state farms in the eastern regions of the USSR. By January 1, 1960 there were 6,500 state farms in the country. In 1959 they delivered to the State 38 per cent of the total grain required by the government, 22 per cent of the total livestock and poultry, 25 per cent of the milk and 28 per cent of the wool.

Prior to 1953 state farms were neglected and criticized for their inefficiency, high cost of operation, and poor leadership. Yet, the government had subsidized them since 1934. This subsidy was high indeed. For example, in 1953 the actual cost in production of grain was 66 per cent above the planned cost of production; 57 per cent in milk; 77 per cent in production of beef; and 73 per cent in pork.[18] In 1954 direct subsidies were abolished, and the state prices paid to the farms were increased in order that they might be operated on a "pay-as-you-go" basis—a different type of subsidy.

Then with the opening of virgin lands in the East, state farms became increasingly important. Consequently, the share of their sowed land to the total Soviet sowed land area increased from ten per cent in 1953 to about 27 in 1958. This rapid rise in economic importance of state farms was due to heavy investment in the formation of new state farms, supplying them with farm machinery and equipment, and construction of farm buildings and housing projects for the workers, at a cost of 35 billion rubles.[19] During the 1954-58 period the government invested 30.7 billion rubles in the development of state farms in the virgin lands. And according to Khrushchev, during this period, the state farms on virgin lands produced 48.9 billion rubles worth of grain, showing a net profit of 18.2 billion rubles.

The organization of state farms in the eastern regions had political repercussions in the Presidium of the Central Committee of the Communist Party and may be considered as one of the most important "issues" in the ouster of the so-called "anti-Party" group of Bulganin, Kaganovich, Malenkov, Molotov, and Shepilov. Even at the beginning of the development of virgin lands and expansion in the number of state farms the anti-Party group was against it. In 1954 Malenkov, who was a Chairman of the USSR Council of Ministers, signed a decree forbidding the establishment of state farms on virgin lands located in the Altai Kray. As a result, the organization of ten new state farms was delayed until 1955. The USSR Gosplan, upon pressure from Kaganovich, claimed that it had no money or resources for the development of virgin lands in supplying new state farms with farm machinery, equipment, housing, and other necessities.[20] It is claimed that the anti-Party group attempted to prove to Khrushchev and his followers that the virgin land venture has no economic significance. True, during these debates Bulganin sat silent but his silence is now interpreted as agreement with the anti-Party clique.

Since winning the battle over the development of virgin lands, Khrushchev is less critical of the state farms' performance than he was in the past. But he still condemns their mismanagement and low productivity. The status of the state farms has the ideological inheritance derived from the Marxism-Leninism doctrines of socialized ownership. The question of the existence of state farms and collective farms and their importance in socialized agriculture is being debated among Soviet economists. Which organization is the more socialistic—the state farm or the collective farm?

Khrushchev in his report to the Supreme Soviet in March 27, 1958 declared that state farms and collective farms are only different forms of one and the same method of socialist production.[21] He stated that the only distinction between the two organizations is that the state farm is entirely socialized and more technologically advanced than the collective farm, which is organized on a cooperative principle. At present both organizations have their own places in socialized production. How long will this duality in ownership exist, especially should a real drive toward a completely communist society be developed? From a theoretical viewpoint, in the pure communist society collective farms have to be converted to state farms. But theoretical interpretation of the social value of one organization over the other is in the hands of Khrushchev and his followers, who are no longer classical Marxian theoreticians. To them economic justifications seem to be of more importance than Marxian theoretical considerations.

Assuming that the gulf between theoretical Marxism and practical considerations will continue to exist among present and future leaders of the Soviet Union, it would also be reasonable to assume that collective farms might even swallow the state farms. The average size of the collective farms is now greatly increased. They are permitted to own farm machinery, equipment, and supplementary enterprises. The concept that the state farms are the model of farming efficiency is no longer valid. Collecttive farms have similar advantages in large-scale farming as state farms. Moreover, farming is not only an occupation but it is also a way of living for millions of peasants which would be dangerous to uproot.

Another point is that the collectivized peasants are less mobile than the workers on state farms, which in the main depend on a seasonal labor force. And as the farm population increases more land will be needed for new collective farms or for the expansion of the existing collective farms. If the collective farms during the next seven years could manage to improve their efficiency in production and if there would be the need for expansion of their total land area, it would be possible that some land might be taken from state farms. It is true that at present the Soviet government favors state farms in virgin lands, but this may be considered as a temporary measure devised not only to boost the agricultural output but also to prove to the peasants that the virgin lands are not deserts and to stimulate migration of collective farms as a unit to the eastern regions.

## SUPPLEMENTARY STATE-OPERATED AGRICULTURAL ENTERPRISES

Supplementary state agricultural enterprises are organized by many institutions and establishments. In this category are found non-agricultural cooperative organizations, health establishments, research, education, and penal institutions. The land is given free of charge to sponsoring organizations rather than to a group of workers or to individuals. The produce yielded from such undertakings is distributed by the organization among participating members, but most frequently the produce is pooled for common consumption. Some of these enterprises, such as experiment stations, are state owned and organized on a permanent basis.

There is no overall law in regard to land use by supplementary agricultural enterprises. The annual planning of farm operations is decided by the organization, and in this respect these organizations enjoy more freedom in determining land utilization than do the state and collective farms.

Between 1940 and 1950 the number of state supplementary agricultural enterprises (mainly as a result of the war) increased 2.7 times. Between 1950 and 1958, their number was considerably reduced; yet the total sowed area increased by about 46 per cent, of which 64 per cent was

TABLE 4—*Significant Data on*
*State Supplementary Agricultural Enterprises* [22]
*(at the end o fthe year in thousand)*

| Item | 1940 | 1950 | 1953 | 1956 | 1958 |
|---|---|---|---|---|---|
| Total (number) _____ | 45,836 | 124,536 | 114,064 | 116,336 | 107,894 |
| Number of tractors _____ | 13 | 38 | 39 | 46 | 47 |
| Number of combines _____ | 1 | 5 | 11 | 6 | 10 |
| Total sowed acreage: _____ | 4,218 | 7,519 | 7,589 | 9,312 | 10,971 |
| Grain crops _____ | 2,300 | 4,188 | 3,606 | 4,543 | 5,510 |
| Industrial crops _____ | 25 | 143 | 94 | 116 | 151 |
| Truck gardening crops ____ | 455 | 895 | 741 | 894 | 796 |
| Fodder crops _____ | 1,438 | 2,293 | 3,148 | 3,759 | 4,514 |
| Cattle: _____ | 608 | 1,074 | 906 | 819 | 1,000 |
| Cows _____ | 249 | 332 | 301 | 333 | 367 |
| Hogs _____ | 990 | 891 | 767 | 1,402 | 1,787 |
| Sheep _____ | 840 | 1,092 | 1,003 | 717 | 768 |
| Goats _____ | 11 | 51 | 32 | 20 | 12 |

taken by fodder crops. During the same period of time, the number of cattle, sheep and goats declined, but cows and hogs increased, with hogs almost doubled in number.

This sector may be regarded as a kind of state subsidy program for state institutions such as sanatoriums, homes for aged and retired persons, disabled veterans, and the like. On the other hand, these enterprises may be considered as a source of additional income for workers who otherwise would have to pay higher prices for goods they produced themselves. Again, institutional inmates have the opportunity to increase their subsistence rations from such undertakings. The pupils in educational institutions are not only trained in farming practices, but also provide foodstuffs for themselves and divert a part of their yield to other state institutions.

## MACHINE TRACTOR STATIONS

Prior to 1958, the heart of collectivized agriculture was the Machine Tractor Station (MTS). It was organized, financed, and managed by the State, and all its employees were hired personnel, receiving monthly payments in cash, or in a combination of cash and kind. Theoretically, the collective farms had the land and labor force and the MTS had the large-scale farm machinery which the collective farms prior to 1958 were not permitted to own. Both organizations were engaged in agricultural production but under different ownership.

The MTS not only directed the major farming activities of the collective farms but also helped the peasants in developing new enterprises. It trained peasants in the use of new machinery and equipment and supervised the political life of the peasants.

There were two types of MTS: one provided services only for collective farms; the other was a special-purpose MTS working in land reclamation, irrigation projects, soil conservation, reforestation, and in the construction of artificial lakes and water holes. All MTS were under the jurisdiction of the USSR Ministry of Agriculture, except those located in cotton-growing regions and administered by the Ministry of Cotton Production of the individual constituent republic.

The main function of the MTS was to provide farm machinery to the collective farms, for which the latter paid in cash and in kind. Since payments in kind were large, the MTS were also collecting points of agricultural commodities from which the national demands were supplied. But the MTS did not possess any cultivated land.

Services to the collective farms were available on a contractual basis. The contract specified in minute detail what the MTS must do during any specified period of time and the time for each task to be performed. Plowing contracts specified not only the size of the plot to be plowed and the time of starting and finishing, but also the depth of the plowing. On the other hand, the collective farm named its own obligations, as to when the field was to be ready for the tractors, and how many farm workers were to be available on the field. A typical contract between the MTS and the collective farm was designed by the government and covered every item associated with farming operations, either in the field or in the barn.

There were more MTS created during the 1940-50 period than between 1950 and 1956. With the expansion of state farms in the East, the number of MTS in 1957 was considerably reduced since their machinery was transferred to new state farms. In the main, between 1950 and 1956 the MTS increased not only their equipment but also their labor force. The most revealing fact, however, is that prior to 1958 the MTS were better equipped for cultivation operations than for harvesting, especially in industrial crops and vegetables where human toil is still predominant.

The reorganization of labor force in 1953, as described in Chapter 2, did not bring about desired result. The whole program of transferring specialists to the MTS caused a reduction in efficiency not only in the farming operation but also in other sectors of the national economy. Never-

TABLE 5—*Significant Data on Machine Tractor Stations* [23]
(*at the end of the year*)

| Item | Unit | 1940 | 1950 | 1953 | 1956 | 1957 | 1958 |
|------|------|------|------|------|------|------|------|
| Total number of MTS ___ | — | 7,069 | 8,414 | 8,985 | 8,737 | 7,903 | 345 |
| Permanent labor force ____ | Thousand | 537 | 705 | 1,167 | 2,953 | 2,626 | 136 |
| Number of tractors _____ | Thousand | 444 | 483 | 615 | 670 | 628 | 670 |
| Number of grain combines _____ | Thousand | 154 | 173 | 265 | 283 | 322 | 322 |
| Total sowed area in collective farms | % | | | | | | |
| Grain crops _____ | % | 56 | 73 | 91 | 95 | 96 | 96 |
| Cotton _____ | % | 81 | 92 | 97 | 98 | 98 | 98 |
| Sugar beets _____ | % | 93 | 92 | 95 | 96 | 97 | 98 |
| Per cent of total harvested area: | | | | | | | |
| Grain crops_____ | % | 43 | 51 | 78 | 85 | 87 | 89 |
| Sugar beets _____ | % | — | 2 | 6 | 43 | 57 | 54 |

theless, the program, painful as it was, rooted out many agricultural specialists from their non-agricultural occupations and sent them to the farm where their training was more valuable.

Confusion created by staffing the MTS with specialists and then releasing them did not stabilize conditions in agriculture. Something new had to be offered. The solution was found in reorganization of the MTS. This problem was debated at the meeting of the Plenum of the Central Committee of the Communist Party in February 1958. Then on March 27, 1958, at a session of the USSR Supreme Soviet, Khrushchev delivered a report "On the Further Development of the Collective Farm System and the Reorganization of the Machine Tractor Stations." The Presidium of the Central Committee of the Communist Party together with the USSR Council of Ministers developed a new program. [24]

Under this program, the MTS were to be reorganized as Repair Technical Stations (RTS), and the collective farms were permitted to buy farm machinery and equipment from the MTS. The newly organized RTS were to keep the old sites of MTS and their workers were encouraged to stay with RTS, whose main tasks were to provide repair services for farm machinery purchased by the collective farms and to supply the collective farms with spare parts, fuel, oil, and other materials. Along with abolishment of the MTS, the government in June 1958 freed the collective farms of all past indebtedness to MTS. At the same time it was expected that by 1959 most collective farms would be able to purchase needed farm machinery. Poor collective farms were given credit for up to five years for that purpose.

Reorganization of the MTS was not smooth. One problem was the pricing of purchased machinery. Some MTS insisted on the original price, others sold at current value, and because of this confusion new Evaluating Offices were organized. Again, the MTS received all their supplies through state channels, whereas collective farms used eight different suppliers. As a result there was the usual indecision as to which agency would supply things for collective farms. In addition, many collective farms demanded repair equipment for their machinery which was to remain with the RTS.

Although the collective farms may buy combines, tractors, and other farm machinery from MTS, RTS, and from the Office of Agricultural Supplies (Selkhozsnab), such purchases are not based on the principle of supply and demand and contracts do not bear a clause for violations. As usual there are shortages of machinery, differences in quality, and variations in prices.

In December 1958 about 80 per cent of all MTS were already reorganized into RTS and over 55,000 collective farms (81 per cent of the total number) had purchased agricultural machinery at a cost of 21 billion rubles. During the 1958-59 period, collective farms bought 32 billion rubles worth of farm machinery and equipment. Of this, 18 billion rubles were spent for the used machinery bought from MTS and 14 billion rubles for the purchase of new equipment. Altogether, the collective farms bought about 660,000 tractors and 300,000 grain harvester combines. On an average each collective farm at the end of 1958 owned about ten tractors and four combines.[25] At the December 1958 meeting of the Central Committee of the Communist Party many speakers complained that in some regions the RTS serve two or three collective farms, and in the absence of competition many RTS accept only repair jobs which are more profitable to them. Questions were raised whether it would be possible for the collective farm to purchase the repair shops from the RTS, and to let the RTS keep its functions of selling machinery, repair parts, and supplies.

In general, Khrushchev was not against such proposals, but he cautioned of the effect it might have on poorer collective farms. He also suggested that the establishment of inter-collective farms repair shops serving several collective farms is desirable; but again he emphasized the fact that such organizations must be introduced gradually without creating disequilibrium among other factors. To support his guarded proposal he cited the fact that there are many poor collective farms still dependent upon farm machinery from the MTS, especially in White Russia, the Kazakh SSR, the Kirghiz SSR, and in other regions. Nevertheless, it is relatively certain that in a few years the MTS will completely disappear, the original role of the RTS will be changed, and the collective farms will own not only farm machinery but their own repair shops. As of April 1959, there were only 112 MTS, and about 4,000 RTS.

## INDEPENDENT PEASANTS

In 1959 the Soviet Union counted about 60,000 independent peasant households. They are permitted to exist for a number of reasons. Many independent peasants are located in sparsely populated areas where the formation of collective farms is not economically justified. Many natives in the Far North and the Caucasus living in small settlements composed of a few households still preserve their independence as in the past. Again, some independent peasants are located close to industrial centers where they work part time to supplement their scanty income derived from farming. And there are a number of peasant craftsmen who combine their skill and farming to maintain independence.

The land allocated to independent peasant households is free of charge. It belongs to the household collectively even though some of the members may be temporarily employed elsewhere. The head of the household represents the family in all transactions with the State. The land which has been granted to the household, let us say in 1930, is still in the possession of the same household and cannot be taken away except when all members of the household waive their right to the land, or in case of discontinuation of farm operation, death of all members, a court order prohibiting possession of the land, or repossession of the land by the State for national or social purposes.

Utilization of the land possessed by independent peasant households is supervised by the local soviet. The amount of land which the household may possess varies from region to region depending on the type of farming in a given region. In the intensively irrigated cotton regions, the plot is about 0.25 acre, in sugar beet growing regions it is about 1.4 acres, and in other regions it is about 2.5 acres.[26]

On November 1, 1958, the independent peasants occupied 247,100 acres of land area. Of this, 123,500 acres were suitable for agricultural purposes but only about 49,000 acres were sowed crop area. The sowed area represented about 20 per cent of the possessed land.

In 1940, independent peasants represented 15.7 per cent of all Soviet peasant households, mainly because of the occupation of the Baltic states and western parts of the Ukraine and White Russia. Excluding the occupied territories for that year, independent peasants represented only 3.1 per cent of all Soviet peasant households. By 1950 they comprised 3.3 per cent of

Table 6—*Significant Data on Independent Peasants* [27]
(*at the end of the year in thousand*)

| Item | 1940 | 1950 | 1955 | 1956 | 1958 |
|---|---|---|---|---|---|
| Total sowed acreage: | 34,866 | 4,720 | 99 | 99 | 49 |
| Grain crops | 24,512 | 3,385 | 30 | 30 | — |
| Industrial crops | 1,829 | 173 | — | — | — |
| Truck gardening crops | 3,707 | 791 | 52 | 52 | 49 |
| Fodder crops | 4,818 | 371 | 7 | 7 | — |
| Cattle: | 6,733 | 433 | 95 | 108 | 81 |
| Cows | 4,657 | 263 | 67 | 57 | 46 |
| Hogs | 4,704 | 250 | 53 | 54 | 36 |
| Sheep | 5,628 | 253 | 65 | 59 | 61 |
| Goats | 299 | 126 | 61 | 50 | 40 |

all Soviet peasant households, 0.7 per cent in 1953 and only 0.3 per cent in 1958. All of their land is used for truck gardening crops such as vegetables, melons, berries, and grapes. For all practical purposes the independent peasants are nonexistent in Russia.

## WORKERS AND EMPLOYEES

Use of agricultural land by workers and employees who are not members of collective farms but who reside in rural areas or in urban settlements such as state farms is permitted. Many of them comprise the village intelligentsia: teachers, agronomists, physicians, and other professional personnel. They are allowed to possess individual plots of land for their own use and to use state-owned hay and pasture land for their livestock.

In many rural areas there are industrial enterprises such as mining, with many workers and employees living close by. They, too, have the right to possess plots of land. And there are numerous organizations which pool their small plots and efforts in production of agricultural products for themselves. These organizations often represent the veterans of World War II or trade unions and the like who collectively cultivate their merged plots.

The land which is free of charge may not be over one-half an acre and pasture and hay land may be allocated from the state land fund, state timber land, the land belonging to railroads, the land in possession of the village soviets or any unused land. If pasture land is not available from those sources, the collective farms may lease unused pasture for a payment which must cover only the cost of the upkeep of fences and water holes.

TABLE 7—*Significant Data on Supplementary Agricultural Enterprises Possessed by Workers and Employees* [28]
(*at the end of the year in thousand*)

| Item | 1940 | 1950 | 1953 | 1956 | 1958 |
|------|------|------|------|------|------|
| Total sowed acreage: _____ | 2,026 | 3,856 | 3,533 | 4,026 | 4,522 |
| Grain crops _____ | 371 | 643 | 420 | 395 | 445 |
| Industrial crops _____ | 49 | 74 | 49 | 74 | 99 |
| Truck gardening crops ____ | 1,557 | 3,114 | 3,015 | 3,508 | 3,904 |
| Fodder crops _____ | 49 | 25 | 49 | 49 | 74 |
| Cattle: _____ | 4,932 | 6,085 | 5,697 | 6,635 | 8,855 |
| Cows _____ | 3,538 | 4,248 | 3,933 | 4,064 | 5,776 |
| Hogs _____ | 2,705 | 1,897 | 3,893 | 4,481 | 4,037 |
| Sheep _____ | 2,624 | 1,836 | 2,078 | 3,235 | 6,508 |
| Goats _____ | 2,204 | 3,120 | 3,690 | 3,292 | 3,319 |

In some cases trade unions organize their own enterprises in truck gardening, orchards, poultry, and honey production for their members residing in urban centers. In this case the land is granted to a sponsoring agency. The land for such organizations comes from unused land belonging to urban settlements, state land funds, railroad and highway unused strips, and free land possessed by various industrial enterprises and administrative organizations. Up to 600 square meters of land is permitted per plot within city limits; up to 1,200 square meters outside city limits.

Between 1940 and 1958 the sowed area cultivated by workers and employees was more than doubled. Most of this land is used for truck gardening. During the same period, cattle (including cows) and other livestock were also considerably increased. An interesting point is that between 1950 and 1958, the land utilization of this sector was practically unchanged, but as a result of lower taxation and required delivery rates since 1953, the number of livestock, especially sheep and hogs, was considerably increased.

Although the total sowed acreage cultivated by workers and employees in 1958 represented less than one per cent of the total Soviet sowed acreage, the importance of this sector cannot be overlooked. In 1940, the number of non-agricultural workers cultivating their own plots was about two million. But during the war period of 1942-45, their number increased from 5.0 to 18.5 million and the total plot area increased from 1.2 to 3.7 million acres.[29] The 1958 acreage occupied by these plots has slightly increased since 1945, but the number of people engaged in cultivation of these plots has been reduced to three million. This is probably due to the reduction in grain acreage and an increase in the number of livestock kept in barns.

The economic significance of this sector lies in the fact that these workers (especially during the war and immediately after) not only produced food for their own needs but also sold to others. To some degree they relieved the pressure on other sectors which otherwise would have had to supply an additional volume of products, not to mention the related demands for transportation and distribution services.

## MECHANIZATION

The main problem with agricultural mechanization is its narrow specialization. A survey made by the USSR Institute for Agricultural Mechanization revealed that even with the most favorable agricultural practices, utilization of farm machinery in terms of days on an annual basis is limited. In addition, there is a gap between utilization and life expectancy of equipment. Maximum utilization of equipment during a short period of time causes frequent breakdowns, resulting in high repair cost. Again, because of a general scarcity of farm machinery, it is often necessary to move it about. For example, during the 1956 grain harvest in the Kazakh SSR, there was an acute shortage of farm machinery and 12,700 grain combines with their operators, 29,000 reapers, and 52,000 truck and other farm machinery were dispatched to the Kazakh SSR from other parts of the Soviet Union.[30] The cost of transportation of this machinery, of course, increased the cost of production. This was one of many reasons for disbanding the MTS and permitting the collective farms to own farm machinery.

Draft animals, as a source of power on the farm, in 1958 was minimal. The greatest increase was in motorized transportation; and with increased electrical and mechanical installations, the use of tractor power in other than plowing and harvesting activities has declined. Of all constituent republics, only the Kazakh SSR between 1940 and 1958 increased its number of horses by 33 per cent.

Criticism of the inadequacy and inefficiency of farm machinery and equipment have always been favorite subjects among farm leaders and peasants. With the merging of small collective farms into larger units, the problem of mechanized farming became even more acute than in the past. And by allowing the collective farms to own farm machinery and equipment this problem was intensified by an increasing demand for the labor-saving devices.

TABLE 8—*Mechanization of Soviet Agriculture in Percentage to Total* [31]
(*at the end of the year*)

| Item | 1940 | 1950 | 1953 | 1956 | 1958 |
|------|------|------|------|------|------|
| Total: | 100.0 | 100.0 | 100.0 | 100.0 | 100.0 |
| Mechanized power: | 77.7 | 88.3 | 91.7 | 94.6 | 95.7 |
| Tractors | 37.1 | 35.8 | 33.3 | 32.3 | 30.5 |
| Combines | 12.2 | 12.9 | 15.3 | 13.7 | 16.2 |
| Motorized transportation | 25.1 | 34.3 | 36.3 | 41.5 | 42.1 |
| Electrical installations | 3.3 | 5.3 | 6.8 | 7.1 | 6.9 |
| Animals in terms of mechanized power | 22.3 | 11.7 | 8.3 | 5.4 | 4.3 |

In the past the uniform design of farm machinery disregarded regional needs. The same tractors and combines were produced for the flat lands of the northern Caucasus and for the mountainous regions of the Far East. Since emphasis was on output of large pieces of machinery, smaller farm equipment was neglected. Even in 1958 the Soviets produced only 12 types of seeders. In that year 12,000 grain-cleaning machines were produced, as compared with 67,000 pianos.[32]

What the peasants need now is not so much large-scale farm machinery but more grain-cleaners, grain-sorters, grain-dryers, and loading and unloading equipment. In many collective farms handling of grain and straw requires more labor than for all operations in growing and harvesting.

An abundance of farm machinery promised during the current Seven-Year Plan in itself cannot greatly reduce manpower requirements without a corresponding increase in electrical power requirements. In 1958 about 49 per cent of all collective farms had electricity. Because of the lack of electric power, mechanized watering for collectivized livestock is only 27 per cent and the use of milking machines on the collective farms represents only 3.6 per cent of the total. While one milkmaid in many collective farms is able to milk only ten to 12 cows, with milking machine she could milk 30 to 40 cows. This is one of the reasons the current Seven-Year Plan anticipates a fourfold increase in electrical power as compared with 1958.

## SHEFSTVO

The word "shefstvo" is a Russian word meaning patronage or auspices. Under conditions of scarcity such as exist in the USSR, the importance of patronage is significant and it extends not only to agriculture but to other sectors of the national economy as well. In this way non-agricultural workers may indirectly participate in agricultural production. In general, workers and employees of any large factory or any other establishment organize the patron-association with the purpose of helping the adopted farming enterprise in fulfilling its production goals. The patron-association is an unincorporated organization, but it has public pledges to assist the adopted enterprise, which may be a collective farm, a state farm, the rayon, oblast, another state-operated enterprise, or even a part of the Armed Forces. For example, the members of the Komsomol have pledged to provide patronage for construction of atomic electric plants. They pledged to supply the needed labor for construction, as well as to provide other services to all atomic electric plants.[33]

Any assistance pledged by a patron-group, of course, depends upon the character, size, and location of the patron-association and the adopted enterprise. Basically, these associations have two functions. First, they strengthen the relationship, understanding and common unity between two different economic groups of workers. Second, they actually help adopted organizations by providing needed manpower, materials, and other assistance not available to the adopted enterprise. But the most important economic function of the patron-association lies in improving the efficiency of the adopted enterprise. For example, during the rush harvesting season, the patrons may organize their members to go to the farm to help the peasants with harvesting. When the collective farm is late in repair work on its farm machinery, the patron-association may send them a few of their own mechanics. If the collective farm decides to put in new electrical installations, an appeal may be forwarded to the patron-association for experts. When the collective farm is short of fertilizer, the patrons may organize collections of ashes and manure in urban settlements and deliver them to the farm.

Assistance of this kind cannot be seen in statistics, but it is a powerful instrument in bringing together non-agricultural workers and peasants, especially at times when collective farms are unable to cope with problems by themselves or without an additional heavy investment, or when there is no time to spare. It may be a little thing like having an additional three to five trucks working for a few days and nights in transporting harvested grain, which in itself does not seem very impressive, but which may become an important factor for the peasants in harvesting and transporting grain to storage on time.

With current reorganization of the whole Soviet economy earnestly underway, even greater effort is being made to expand the work of patron-associations in agriculture. In May 1956, the workers of the Voroshilov Plant located in Vladivostok issued an appeal to all the workers and employees in the Far East to enlarge the scope of patron-associations. In 1954 the workers of this plant assumed patronage over several collective farms. They have built a silo on one collective farm, a barn on another, and dug a silo storage trench for 1,000 tons of feed for a third. By helping the peasants in non-agricultural occupations the patrons freed the farmers to devote more of their time to crops and livestock and thus indirectly assisted in increased productivity of the collective farms.

The reaction of individual industrial workers to patronage of other organizations is difficult to evaluate. However, one may assume that not all of the workers are enthusiastic about spending their free time working for others. But there is nothing they can do when the local Party proposes it. They must show the right enthusiasm and willingness simply to avoid misunderstanding with the Party.

## REQUIRED DELIVERIES TO THE STATE

The Soviet leaders have always thought that the peasants must be able to support the country with foodstuffs and raw materials in addition to satisfying their own demands. Agriculture as an industry has been exploited and squeezed of any large savings to finance the expanding industrialization. Economic relationships between the government and the peasants were based on short-run adjustments. Whenever the amount of food and raw materials needed for the country became inadequate, the government would relax its demands upon the peasants. For example, when the Soviets needed, let us say, more flax, the economic squeeze would be relaxed and short-run incentives would be introduced to stimulate the production of flax. Incentives may take the form of reduced tax on that part of the income derived from production of flax, or in the form of additional goods obtained at lower prices for any additional amount of flax delivered to the State, or in higher prices paid by the State. When the scarcity of flax is relieved, the government ends these incentives and new ones are devised for another short commodity. The method of short-run incentives is extremely flexible and advantageous to the government.

The Soviet government obtains its domestic foodstuffs and raw materials from two main channels: state farms, and collective farms. The other channels consist of members of collective farms, independent peasants, and all others who grow agricultural products to be sold.

The state farms, being state-owned organizations, deliver all their produce to the State after covering the required need for livestock, seeds for next year's operation and foodstuffs for the workers.

The collective farms must produce enough to satisfy the State demands and to supply their own needs. The history of the government's dependence on foodstuffs and raw materials from collective farms has been flexible, depending on development of agricultural production.

Prior to collectivization, the government obtained required agricultural commodities by contracting with farm enterprises and cooperatives for the production of a given volume at specified prices. With the beginning of collectivization, and especially during 1932-33, when agricultural output was drastically reduced, the contractual agreements were replaced by required deliveries (zagatovka) of the basic commodities to the State. Along with the introduction of required deliveries, the payments in kind to MTS were also established. The required delivery norms were set at firm rates based on planned sowed acreage and planned livestock on the farm. These were harsh requirements, disregarding economic and growing conditions. The amounts of agricultural commodities taken away from the collective farms at low prices did not stimulate efficiency in farming. In fact, efficient farms have been penalized more than less efficient ones because they had to deliver a greater volume, and the income of the peasants in terms of effort expended in production was lowered.

In March 1940 the method of calculating required deliveries to the State was changed and rates were attached to the acreage of land possessed by the collective farms. The impact of this policy forced the peasants to intensify the utilization of their land. In 1947 norms for required deliveries within a given region were set at differing rates, forcing the large collective farms with ample mechanization and manpower to pay higher rates than others. Those collective farms not using the services of the MTS were to pay higher rates.

With reduced agricultural production during World War II, the state-required deliveries were insufficient and many peasants boosted production of their individual plots, the produce of which they sold at high prices. Not wishing to increase the required delivery rates nor to increase prices paid, the Soviets devised a new purchasing program (zakupka) at higher prices than paid for the required deliveries. Simultaneously contractual agreements were reintroduced in the purchase of major industrial commodities such as cotton, sugar beets, flax, and hemp. All these prices, of course, were state-controlled and amounts which the collective farms had to produce were also controlled by the State.

Thus, in 1958 the Soviets obtained their required agricultural commodities through four channels: required deliveries (zagatovka) ; payments in kind to MTS; purchasing program (zakupka) ; and contractual agreements with the collective farms. The complexity of these programs was mainly due to the large number of prices required to stimulate agricultural production. This proves that the planned economy was not successful in stabilizing its own procurement programs.

True, in September 1953 the state-required delivery prices were increased, but it was a meager increase amounting in total to about 50 billion rubles annually, adequate to cover the cost of production of some collective farms. The aim of this price increase was to overcome the apathy of the livestock growers. Accordingly, prices for required deliveries for livestock were increased 5.5 times and doubled for milk and meat. Simultaneously the purchasing prices (zakupka) also were increased by 30 per cent for meat and 50 per cent for milk. Smaller price increases became effective in grain, vegetables, flax, and hemp. The required delivery norms to the State were stabilized on the basis of acreage under plowed land, hay, and pasture lands for the whole region; and all collective farms, poor and wealthy alike, were required to deliver the same amounts.

Then in September 1957 another price increase took place on all basic agricultural items, agricultural taxes were reduced and, beginning with 1958, the required delivery from individual plots of members of the collective farms and workers and employees was abolished entirely. Under the latter program the members of collective farms gained about three billion rubles in 1958.

Finally in June 1958 Khrushchev proclaimed the abandonment of the state-required deliveries and the payments in kind to the MTS, and the purchasing system (zakupka) was to be the sole method of obtaining state requirements in agricultural commodities.[34] He stated that the state required delivery norms were unrealistic since they violated the law of comparative advantage. For example, the Baltic states are better adapted to production of livestock, yet collective farms were forced to grow grain and to pay grain to the MTS. In 1957, for instance, Latvia's planned grain output was established at 93,000 metric tons but its delivery to the State amounted to only 18,000 metric tons.

Contractual agreements between the State and the collective farms for the production of industrial crops contained an array of variations in terms of premium. One price was paid when contractual obligations were fulfilled; the same commodity delivered in greater volume than planned carried premium payments. For example, the average price which the government paid for one unit of flax produced in the Kalinin Oblast in 1957 ranged from 445 to 2,971 rubles. The higher price was the result of premium payments.

Beginning with 1959 the state procurement program for agricultural commodities was to depend upon several factors. To guarantee availability of required agricultural commodities for the State, procurement plans are to be devised for a number of years for each state farm and collective farm. Depending on growing conditions in each particular region, the annual production plans may be adjusted up or down. In devising these production plans the growth of demand for various commodities is also to be considered. It is claimed that this system affects only that part of the total agricultural output which is needed by the State, and the other part is to be disposed of by the collective farms on the collective farm markets at higher prices.

The price structure is to be stable when yields of particular crops are normal; this is a kind of guaranteed price based on yields within a given region. The average price of any commodity is to be calculated on the basis of average yields and cost of production of the past few years. Thus, with a good yield and abundant crop production the price is to be lowered, and with low yield the price is to be increased to cover the cost of production. In other words, the system provides subsidy payments in terms of higher prices or in terms of seeds for marginal collective farms.

The new state procurement program is more simplified than previous methods. Its basic principle relies upon state demands as in the past, but its methodology is more fitted to the type of planning to be expected from the central planning economy. By the same token, it is not mathematical as is calculating for the industrial sector. Errors made in the old agricultural planning method are found in the fact that the planners attempted to produce a precise amount of potatoes just as they planned the production of a certain number of radio sets. After 43 years of planning, only now the Soviets realize that agricultural production cannot be planned in the same manner as factory output, where labor and capital can be controlled with greater effectiveness than the land productivity on the farm.

## Chapter 7—Bibliography

[1] *Pravda,* April 17, 1942.

[2] *Tikhookeanskaya Zvezda,* May 20, 1956.

[3] *Narodnoye Khozaystvo SSSR,* Moscow, 1956, pp. 128-29 excluding managerial personnel and workers in supplementary industrial farm enterprises.

[4] *Sotsialisticheskoye Selskoye Khozaystvo,* August 1943, p. 12.

[5] Kolesnov, S. G., *Organizatsiya Sotsialisticheskikh Selskokhozaystvennykh Predpriatiy,* Moscow, 1947, p. 231.

[6] *Selskoye Khozaystvo,* May 1, 1955.

[7] *Narodnoye Khozaystvo SSSR v 1958 Godu,* Moscow, 1959, pp. 349, 394-95, 447-48.

[8] *Plenum Tsentral'nogo Komiteta Kommunisticheskoy Partii Sovetskogo Soyuza,* December 15-19, 1958, Moscow 1958, p. 231 (hereinafter referred to as *Plenum,* December 15-19, 1958).

[9] Kraev, M. A., *Pobeda Kolkhoznogo Stroya v SSSR,* Moscow, 1954, p. 650.

[10] *Izvestia,* January 1, 1950.

[11] Koralev, A. I., *Pravovoye Polozhenye Predsedatelya Kolkhoza,* Leningrad, 1954, p .16.

[12] *Plenum,* December 15-19, 1958, p. 87.

[13] *Voprosy Ekonomiki,* No. 9, 1950.

[14] *Plenum,* December 15-19, 1958, p. 211.

[15] *Narodnoye Khozaystvo SSSR v 1958 Godu,* Moscow, 1959, pp. 349, 386-89, 447-48, 457.

[16] *Plenum,* December 15-19, 1958, p. 14.

[17] *Narodnoye Khozaystvo SSSR v 1958 Godu,* Moscow, 1959, pp. 518-19.

[18] Benediktov, I. A., *Sovkhozy Nashey Strany,* Moscow, 1959, p. 9.

[19] *Plenum,* December 15-19, 1958, p. 52.

[20] *Ibid., pp.* 318, 408.

[21] *Zasedaniya Verkhovnogo Soveta SSSR,* Pyatogo Sosyva. Pervaya Sessiya, March 27-31 1958, Moscow, 1958, p. 79.

[22] *Narodnoye Khozaystvo SSSR v 1958 Godu,* Moscow, 1959, pp. 518-19.

[23] *Ibid.,* pp. 349, 487, 505, 509-10, 535.

[24] *Pravda,* April 20, 1958.

[25] *Plenum,* December 15-19, 1958, p. 59; Embassy of the USSR, *Press Department,* No. 71, Washington, D. C., Febbruary 8, 1960.

[26] Polyanskaya, G. N., and Ruskol, A. A., *Sovetskoye Zemelnoye Pravo,* Moscow, 1951, p. 110.

[27] *Narodnoye Khozaystvo SSSR v 1958 Godu,* Moscow, 1959, pp. 394-95, 447-48.

[28] *Ibid.,* pp. 394-95, 447-48.

[29] Aksenenok, G. A. *Pravo Zemlepolzovanya Sovkhozov, MTS i Podsobnykh Khozaystv,* Moscow, 1953, p. 124.

[30] *Ogonek,* No. 42, October 1956, p. 2.

[31] *Narodnoye Khozaystvo SSSR v 1958 Godu,* Moscow, 1959, p. 486.

[32] Embassy of the USSR, *Press Department,* No. 37, March 6, 1959.

[33] *Nauka i Zhisn,* No. 11, 1956, p. 2.

[34] *Izvestia,* June 20 1958.

# Agricultural Production

## INTRODUCTION

After the collectivization and with improved technology the Soviets anticipated a rapid rise in production of crops and livestock. Agricultural production plans were devised basically on the same principle as production for steel mills. Opposition from the peasants was brutally crushed during the collectivization period. But increased investment in farm mechanization did not produce the desired results, even though antiquated practices were replaced by large-scale modernized farm machinery. From the early days of the collectivization until 1953 the Soviets battled the peasantry, attempting to force them to produce more. The conflict of interest between the two was basically centered around the method by which the State tried to make the peasants increase their productivity. Without incentives, the peasants refused to comply with the wishes of the State.

As disparities between industrial and agricultural growth increased the Soviets became more alarmed at the poor showing of their agricultural sector. Various short-run devices to boost agricultural output were hastily introduced, but without much benefit. For example, between 1940 and 1952 official industrial output more than doubled, whereas agricultural output increased by only ten per cent, even though the 1952 total sowed area and the number of livestock were at prewar levels. This called for a drastic revision of agricultural policy. Foodstuffs and raw materials had to be increased to supply rising demands of the growing population and industry.

In September 1953 the Central Committee of the USSR Communist Party met in Moscow, at which time various measures were recommended to stimulate sluggish agricultural production; one type of stimulant was soon followed by other types. Consequently, during the 1954-58 period many basic adjustments took place; mechanization was increased, the state prices paid for agricultural commodities to the collective farms were raised, the peasants received greater amounts of credit on better terms, subsidies expanded, taxes and required state deliveries were reduced, the small collective farms were merged into larger units, and the virgin and unused lands were opened to boost total output.

These measures not only created incentives for the peasants but also changed land utilization practices and strengthened the principle of comparative advantage. These rapid changes were confusing to the peasants, but they also brought benefits and gradually the peasants realized that these incentives were not of a short-run nature. In response to the improvement in their lot, the peasants increased their productivity sufficiently to supply the state's requirements and their own needs.

## SOVIET LAND UTILIZATION

Land utilization is significant from the point of view of specialization. It explains the concentration of the crops where they can be produced at the lowest cost. In the main, this is based on the principle of comparative advantage, but this principle as applied to agriculture is not as inelastic as in the mining industry. The lowest cost of production of a single agricultural commodity is not the prime objective when diversified agriculture is practiced. This can be observed in a number of farm operations such as corn-hog production and fodder-meat-milk production.

Today in the Soviet Union the great bulk of staple crops is produced primarily in the specialized areas. Cotton is grown exclusively in the southern parts of the Soviet Union, particularly in Central Asia. The Kazakh SSR with its abundant pasture and grazing land takes a leading place as the sheep grower. The Ukraine possesses about 60 per cent of the total Soviet sugar beet acreage. Tea leaves are grown exclusively in the Caucasus, especially in the Georgian SSR. Tobacco, flax, and hemp are grown in the limited areas where their production has greatest advantage over other crops. On the other hand, grain is grown in areas where it can successfully be produced either as a major crop or as a supplementary crop for other uses. In general, the principle of Soviet land utilization is not greatly different from that in the United States, or any other country for that matter.

The total Soviet sowed area in 1950 as compared with 1940 was reduced by about eight per cent. The impact of World War II and the 1946 drought were still felt by the peasants in 1950. Grain acreage, especially under winter wheat, oats, and spring barley, was considerably reduced but acreage under industrial crops, truck garden, and fodder crops was somewhat increased. However, despite these adjustments in individual crops, overall land utilization was practically unchanged.

The total sowed acreage in 1958 as compared with 1940 was increased by about 30 per cent, although the total Soviet territory during this period was enlarged by less than one per cent. The 1958 acreage under industrial crops increased by approximately four per cent over that of 1940. There was 16 per cent increase in truck garden crops but the fodder acreage more than doubled. The bread grain acreage (spring and winter wheat and rye) increased by 33 per cent; corn, by 1.9 times. The greatest increase occured in spring wheat, annual grasses, and silage crops.

In 1940, as it was in 1950, primary emphasis was on the production of crops for human consumption with less stress on fodder for livestock. To produce a unit of livestock for human consumption requires a larger acreage than production of crops for direct human consumption. And only in 1956 were the Soviets able to produce sufficient foodstuffs for direct human consumption and also to allocate an increased acreage for fodder in order to produce more livestock products. As the livestock population, especially cattle and hogs, increased, the increasing demand for fodder followed. However, the increase in fodder acreage was at a higher rate than that of livestock. This suggests that during the period in question the Soviets attempted not only to increase the livestock populaion by providing them with minimum feed subsistence but also to increase animals' productivity in terms of meat and milk.

Although land is immobile it can be shifted from one use to another. It is true that such shifts do not take place as readily in agriculture as they do in industry. Elevation, topography, climate, and rainfall may place important limitations upon how land may be used; usually there are several alternatives left within the limitations. Certainly, the Far North of the Soviet Union is not adaptable to grain farming but it may be used for reindeer breeding.

Full utilization of land for agricultural purposes, of course, depends upon the limitations discussed above. The Ukranian SSR, having good soil as well as favorable climate and rainfall, uses 54 per cent of its territory for sowed crops, but only 0.8 per cent is utilized in the Turkmen SSR, which is largely desert. The Moldavian SSR, like the Ukraine, uses 56 per cent of its territory; the Kazakh SSR, only 10.5 per cent. In general, the four per cent of the total Soviet territory occupied by the six republics (the Ukraine, White Russia, Moldavia, and the three Baltic republics) sowed over 46 per cent of their total territory. The five Central Asiatic republics, occupying about 18 per cent of the total Soviet territory, sowed only about nine per cent of their land area.

The well-developed agricultural regions of the European parts of the Soviet Union are fully utilized. These regions cannot greatly expand their sowed acreage without considerable investments in drainage and reclamation work. At the same time, it is most unlikely that they would convert their orchard, hay, and pasture lands to sowed areas. The Caucasian regions are fully utilized for sowed crops; and considering the mountain terrain of the Caucasus there cannot be any substantial expansion in sowed areas even with extensive irrigation and reclamation ventures. The only areas left which can be expanded for sowed crops are in the regions located east of the Volga River, particularly the southern parts of Siberia and the northern Kazakh SSR.

Because of its vastness, Siberia, including the Urals, must be given special attention. Siberia occupies about 60 per cent of the total Soviet territory but has only about 23 per cent of the total sowed acreage. Cultivated land, or even hay and pasture land, in these regions is not necessarily as good as that in the Ukraine or in the Northern Caucasus. Climate, topography, and the availability of moisture limit utilization of eastern regions to fewer crops than in more favorable locations.

Soviet agriculture and industry have different characteristics. Agriculture is sluggish, slow in its expansion; industry is sensitive and can be erratic. The rapid rise in Soviet industrial output is well known, but production efforts in farming and the resulting output of food, feed, and fiber have increased at a very slow pace indeed. Even a single bumper crop cannot create large bulges in total output. The reason is that any increased production has to be allocated to so many users for so many purposes that the final benefits represent only a slight increase.

The old agricultural regions of the Soviet Union are already producing their share with existing technology, irrigation, machinery and farming practices. Any increase in output in these regions would require additional heavy investments. One may speculate about the regions which until recently were not used for crops. One may ask: "Why weren't these regions cultivated by the land-hungry peasants in the past?" The answer may be found in the cost of production and the relative price on the market. But the Soviets often ignore production costs of many enterprises. It is the unique calculation of social cost, no matter how uneconomical it may be in other societies, which enables the Soviets to undertake dubious ventures at high costs. In a large country such as the USSR many crops are grown at the same time in different regions, and when disaster such as a drought strikes one part of the country other parts escape it or may even produce a bumper crop, and the total loss for the country may be minimized. Moreover, marginal and submarginal producers do not leave the industry and receive subsidies while attempting to improve their economic conditions.

TABLE 1—*Total Sowed Acreage by Republic* [1]
(*in millions of acres*)

| Republic | 1940 | | 1950 | | 1956 | | 1958 | |
|---|---|---|---|---|---|---|---|---|
| | Area | % | Area | % | Area | % | Area | % |
| USSR: | 371.7 | 100.0 | 361.5 | 100.0 | 481.2 | 100.0 | 483.4 | 100.0 |
| RSFSR: | 227.5 | 61.2 | 219.8 | 60.8 | 282.7 | 58.7 | 283.4 | 58.6 |
| North | 3.5 | 0.9 | 3.2 | 0.9 | 2.9 | 0.6 | 2.8 | 0.6 |
| Northwest | 4.7 | 1.3 | 4.1 | 1.1 | 4.4 | 0.9 | 5.1 | 1.1 |
| Central | 78.3 | 21.0 | 75.5 | 20.9 | 83.0 | 17.2 | 77.8 | 16.1 |
| Volga River Valley | 33.8 | 9.1 | 31.2 | 8.6 | 40.0 | 8.2 | 45.7 | 9.5 |
| Northern Caucasus | 32.6 | 8.8 | 32.1 | 8.9 | 38.8 | 8.1 | 37.3 | 7.5 |
| Urals | 31.2 | 8.4 | 30.3 | 8.4 | 42.5 | 8.8 | 41.0 | 8.5 |
| Western Siberia | 31.1 | 8.4 | 30.4 | 8.4 | 51.2 | 10.6 | 52.5 | 10.9 |
| Eastern Siberia | 9.7 | 2.6 | 9.7 | 2.7 | 15.5 | 3.2 | 16.4 | 3.5 |
| Far East | 2.6 | 0.7 | 3.2 | 0.9 | 4.4 | 0.9 | 4.8 | 0.9 |
| Ukraine | 79.9 | 20.7 | 75.7 | 21.0 | 80.5 | 16.7 | 80.4 | 16.6 |
| White Russia | 12.9 | 3.5 | 12.1 | 3.4 | 13.5 | 2.8 | 13.5 | 2.8 |
| Uzbek | 7.5 | 2.0 | 6.9 | 1.9 | 7.5 | 1.6 | 7.5 | 1.6 |
| Kazakh | 16.8 | 4.5 | 19.4 | 5.4 | 68.9 | 14.3 | 70.8 | 14.6 |
| Georgia | 2.2 | 0.6 | 2.3 | 0.6 | 2.2 | 0.5 | 2.2 | 0.5 |
| Azerbaydzhan | 2.8 | 0.7 | 2.6 | 0.7 | 3.1 | 0.6 | 3.1 | 0.6 |
| Lithuania | 6.2 | 1.7 | 5.7 | 1.6 | 5.5 | 1.2 | 5.5 | 1.2 |
| Moldavia | 5.1 | 1.4 | 4.7 | 1.3 | 4.7 | 1.0 | 4.7 | 1.0 |
| Latvia | 4.8 | 1.3 | 3.5 | 1.0 | 3.6 | 0.7 | 3.6 | 0.7 |
| Kirghiz | 2.6 | 0.7 | 2.6 | 0.7 | 3.0 | 0.6 | 3.1 | 0.6 |
| Tadzhik | 2.0 | 0.5 | 2.1 | 0.6 | 1.9 | 0.4 | 1.8 | 0.4 |
| Armenia | 1.1 | 0.3 | 1.1 | 0.3 | 1.1 | 0.2 | 1.0 | 0.2 |
| Turkmen | 1.0 | 0.3 | 0.9 | 0.3 | 0.9 | 0.2 | 1.0 | 0.2 |
| Estonia | 2.3 | 0.6 | 2.0 | 0.6 | 1.9 | 0.4 | 1.8 | 0.4 |

Table 1 above shows that the 1958 total Soviet sowed acreage was considerably above the 1940 level, with the Kazakh SSR showing the largest increase. But sowed acreage in a few regions declined. Among these are Lithuania, Tadzhik, Armenia, and Estonia. These reductions may be considered as postwar adjustments whereby unprofitable land usage was abolished. The eastern regions of the RSFSR (the Urals and all of Siberia) maintained their sowed acreage in 1950 as in 1940. But by 1958 their acreage was increased by 54 per cent over 1940. The greatest increase occurred in Western Siberia, followed by the Urals, Eastern Siberia, and the Far East.

## WORLD WAR II CHANGES IN LAND UTILIZATION

The Germans attacked the Soviet Union before harvesting time. In their swift mechanized advance they occupied the most productive agricultural regions of the Ukraine, White Russia, and the European parts of the RSFSR. By autumn of 1942 the Germans and their allies had occupied the following percentage of Soviet agricultural land located in p ewar boundaries:[2]

| Land use | German-occupied percentage |
|---|---|
| Sowed area _____ | 41 |
| Grain acreage _____ | 38 |
| Winter wheat and corn area _____ | 75 |
| Barley and buckwheat area _____ | 66 |
| Truck gardening crops _____ | 50 |

It is interesting to note that during the first two years of World War I, Russia lost about 31.1 million acres of total sowed acreage to the Germans. In World War II the most productive land (which was practically intact in Russian possession during the first World War) was largely occupied by the Nazis. It was not only the occupation of the land that caused slow rehabilitation of Soviet agriculture, but the scarcity of a labor force, machinery, livestock, fertilizer, and seeds.

To overcome the wartime reduction in acreage in the West, the Soviets encouraged cultivation of land in the East. But there again were shortages of farm equipment, seed, livestock, and labor force. It was with high enthusiasm that the peasants in unoccupied regions responded to the national emergency. Peasants introduced new crops in regions where they had not been grown before, but yields were low. The old farming practices suitable for these regions were readjusted, scientific methods were abandoned, weeds invaded many fields, and the state requirements for production of bread grain were ignored. The peasants planted grain crops such as millet when wheat and rye were needed. The influx of industrial population in the East created obstacles in planting more grain in the face of an increased local demand for vegetables. In general, although the sowed acreage in unoccupied regions considerably increased, the crops grown there were mostly products locally demanded which did not necessitate overloading of scarce transportation facilities.

The increase in sowed acreage occurred in the eastern regions in 1942 and 1943. In addition, the liberated regions contributed to the total Soviet sowed acreage in 1943. Thus, actually there were two factors contributing to the increased sowed acreage: the expansion of unoccupied cultivated land and the acreage liberated from the Germans. But by this time Soviet agriculture was so dislocated that the law of comparative advantage was difficult to maintain. Intensively irrigated cotton regions turned their fields to production of grain. High-yielding millet replaced more valuable spring wheat in Central Asia. Crops requiring less cultivation than wheat increased in acreage. In fact, only the liberated regions hauled the Soviet Union out of catastrophic failure as far as the production of bread grain was concerned. The Germans planted the bread grain crops and in many instances they failed to destroy them prior to their retreat.

The course of Soviet agricultural output during World War II and immediately after it is a sad one. Dr. Jasny describes this period in terms of a "collapse." [3] The 1942 total sowed acreage was about 55 per cent of the 1940 level and by 1946 this percentage was up to about 75.[4] However, because of low yields, the effective 1946 production of grain as estimated by Dr. Harry Schwartz was 50 per cent that of 1940.[5] After the war it took the Russians six years to restore their prewar sowed acreage. The average annual increase in sowed acreage was about five per cent, and when the prewar level was reached in 1951, the further increase was at a slower rate until 1954, when Khrushchev launched his famous program for cultivation of virgin and unused lands in the eastern parts of the USSR. This program may be titled "Go East, Young Man."

## "GO EAST, YOUNG MAN" POLICY

The abolition of serfdom in Russia took place in 1861, 56 years before the October Revolution of 1917. Under the land reform of 1861 the peasants were allocated the plots which they had been using before 1861 without any title to them. They received the same land which they had been cultivating half the time for the landlords and half the time for themselves. Under this arrangement, the peasants had used only one-half of their working capacity and were thus forced to seek additional income elsewhere. As free members of the Russian society many of them migrated to other regions.

After the Soviets had taken power in 1917, the government issued the "Statutory Law Concerning Land" in February 1918, under which all land was nationalized and plots of land were given to all Soviet citizens who were prepared to work them. The size of each plot was based on the size of the peasant's family. But while the plots remained static, the size of the family in many cases increased, causing migration of peasants either to industry or to parts of the country where ample land was available.

Collectivization started after the harvest in December 1929, and within a few months the traditional Russian individualistic peasants became members of a socialized agriculture. Yet, while the peasants were collectivized, the basic question of land distribution remained unsolved. The availability of agricultural land per peasant household still depended on the density of population.

The disparity in land distribution created problems in income distribution and the standard of living, and caused underemployment of peasants. To overcome this maladjustment in land distribution, the Soviet government encouraged migration of peasants to the eastern regions. In 1939, over 10,000 members of European collective farms migrated to Siberia.[6] This was not a forced migration such as that of 1929-30. The peasants themselves organized their migration. The selection of places for settlement was made by special delegates who were elected for that purpose by the peasants. In many cases migrated peasants joined previously established collective farms in the East or organized new collective farms there. But these migrants settled close to urban centers or on the railroad lines where they could sell their produce. Instead, the government wanted to settle uninhabited regions, calling for a pioneer spirit in building up potentially valuable new industrial regions.

The government intended to accelerate the tempo of migration in 1940. Extensive plans were laid to absorb 20,000 migrants in the Altai Kray.[7] The Novosibirsk Oblast expected another 20,000 peasants.[8] The Primorsk Kray was ready to accept 4,500 peasants.[9] The densely populated Ukraine made plans for migration of 30,000 peasant households to the East.[10] In 1940, a total of over 100,000 peasant households was expected to migrate from the West to the East, and in 1941 the plan was to increase this number to 111,000 households.[11] It was the Soviet policy at the time to unload the densely populated western regions of excessive farm labor force, to populate sparsely settled regions of the East, and to divert a greater part of the land in the western parts to other crops than bread grain. Even during and after the war, peasant migration to the East was encouraged; but the process was too slow to suit the impatient Soviet leaders.

Economic pressure was created by specialization in farming of cotton flax, vegetables, and the like, requiring grain for people and fodder for livestock in increasing amounts. In the densely populated regions of general purpose farming the peasants obtained low incomes and were unable to satisfy the increasing state demands for grain and livestock products. It was a semi-static condition which could only be altered with a radically dynamic approach. In addition, there were other socio-economic conditions which also had to be solved in a general readjustment of socialized economy which could not be delayed too long if further economic gains were to be achieved. These multiple-purpose adjustments came in 1954.

The decree issued on March 2, 1954, encouraged expansion of grain production on virgin and unused lands located east of the Volga River and the northern Caucasus, but mainly in the northern parts of the Kazakh SSR. The decree also provided ways and means of constructing new collective and state farms, and providing additional equipment, livestock, technical personnel, and housing facilities. Certain laws dealing with social security provisions were amended to facilitate transfer of workers and employees from urban centers to new rural settlements. Khrushchev spearheaded this drive despite opposition from the "anti-Party" group mentioned in Chapter 7. Molotov called this program an "adventure." Malenkov and Kaganovich echoed Molatov, insisting that the program would leave the Soviet Union without bread and that the country does not produce enough fodder to increase the proposed number of livestock in order to reach the per capita production of the United States. Khrushchev, on the other hand, insisted that if out of five years they could get two good harvests, one average, and two poor ones, the comparatively small investment would justify the establishment of agricultural production in new regions.

The official Soviet explanation for the opening of new agricultural regions in the East was based on scarcities of grain needed for food, feed for the livestock, increased foreign trade obligations, and the need to increase domestic consumption, boost state grain reserves, and provide industry with raw materials. Primary emphasis was on production of additional feed for livestock (grain, silage crops, or green feed). Moreover, this program superseded Stalin's "Transformation of Nature" program devised for the purpose of minimizing droughts and to be carried out from 1949 to 1965. Stalin's program provided for the planting of eight huge forest shelter belts covering about 14 million acres. But the whole program failed because of high costs and lack of interest on the part of peasants who wanted immediate improvement of their lot.

For the purpose of definition, *virgin* land was land not cultivated for the past 25 years; *unused* land was land not cultivated for at least two years.

As Table 2 shows, over 54 per cent of the total plowed virgin and unused lands during the 1954-56 period was concentrated in the Kazakh SSR,

TABLE 2—*Plowed Virgin and Unused Lands: 1954-56* [12]
(*in million acres*)

| | 1954 | 1955 | 1956 | Total 1954-56 |
|---|---|---|---|---|
| USSR: _____ | 46.9 | 35.6 | 7.1 | 89.6 |
| RSFSR: _____ | 24.8 | 10.2 | 1.9 | 36.9 |
| Volga River Region _____ | 2.2 | 1.6 | 0.05 | 3.8 |
| Urals _____ | 5.0 | 1.7 | 0.2 | 6.9 |
| Northern Caucasus _____ | 1.2 | 0.9 | 0.1 | 2.2 |
| Western Siberia _____ | 11.4 | 3.0 | 0.5 | 14.9 |
| Eastern Siberia _____ | 2.4 | 1.3 | 0.3 | 4.0 |
| Far East _____ | 0.5 | 0.2 | 0.3 | 1.0 |
| Kazakh SSR _____ | 21.1 | 23.3 | 4.7 | 49.1 |

41 per cent in the RSFSR, and the remaining five per cent in other regions. Between 1950 and 1956 the total Soviet sowed area was increased by 119.4 million acres; of this total 75 per cent came from expansion of virgin and unused lands during the 1954-56 period. In 1958 another 2.6 million acres were added, mainly in Western Siberia, the Volga River region, and the Kazakh SSR while other areas reduced their acreage.

As compared with 1956, the 1958 total Soviet sowed acreage increased by about 2.2 million acres—an increase of less than half of one per cent. During the same period, the grain acreage was reduced by some 7.7 million acres; industrial crops declined by about two million acres; truck garden crops remained unchanged; but fodder crops increased by 28.4 million acres.[13] In their drive to increase the livestock population the Soviets are allocating more of their land for production of fodder and at the same time intensifying grain production on reduced acreage.

The 1959-65 agricultural plan does not anticipate another large increase in new land. Only about 15 to 17 million additional acres can be put to agricultural use, mostly in dry farming areas of the southern parts of the European USSR.[14] Instead, the Soviets are expecting some adjustments in land utilization. For example, the Ukraine plans to increase its sunflower area by some 740,000 acres. Sugar beet acreage in the Ukraine and the Kazakh SSR is to be increased, but most of the increase will occur in corn replacing other crops. In 1958, the Soviets established a new grain-producing base in the Kazakh SSR, Volga River Valley, Urals, and southern regions of Siberia. These regions will maintain large grain acreage, especially of wheat. As wheat producers they possessed 48 per cent of the 1953 total Soviet wheat acreage, but 69 per cent in 1958. The main goal for these regions during the current Seven-Year Plan is to produce more hard wheat, more fodder, and more livestock.

The significance of this huge increase in sowed acreage in so short a time cannot be expressed solely in terms of increased production of grain and fodder crops. It has a much deeper relation to the socio-economic conditions existing in the Soviet Union.

At the beginning of this chapter it was shown that the Soviets in the past encouraged migration of peasants to the East. The past movement was too slow. In most cases the cost of moving was paid by the peasants themselves. What the Soviet leaders wanted was not a piecemeal migration but a mass eastward movement by peasants and urban workers. They desired a plan which would catch the imagination of the people and move them to discover a new frontier for their efforts. The whole Go East, Young Man policy was based on the strength, not the weakness, of the Soviet society. Certainly a monolithic government such as that of the Soviet Union could have brought about increased production of grain and fodder without pushing into the virgin and unused land of the East. This could have been accomplished through a more relaxed monetary-fiscal policy or importation of grain from the West.

On the other hand, there were other factors which contributed to the eastward movement of the population. With the opening of the eastern plains to agriculture the Soviets actually adjusted farming practices in the old agricultural regions. The land-use pattern of these old regions has already changed. By 1958 they produced a greater volume of sugar beet, potatoes, cotton, vegetables, and other crops than in 1954.

Settlement of uninhabited regions, especially in the eastern parts, is also closely related to industrial expansion in these parts. The migrating peasants and urban workers, in addition to growing grain and fodder, established settlements and built roads and communication lines which would be important for industry when plants and factories began to mushroom there. With industry following agriculture, factory workers would have locally produced food, means of transportation, and communication with the civilian administration already established there.

In relieving the concentration of skilled and semi-skilled labor in the cities and providing opportunities for those who were unable to find jobs of their choice, the Go East, Young Man movement was a powerful force. That is why skilled factory workers, so indispensible only a few years before, were sent in 1954 to become farmers in the East. Stimulated by propaganda, textile workers from Ivanovo Oblast, shoemakers from the Ukraine, graduating students from specialized institutes, demobilized personnel of the Armed Forces, automobile workers from Moscow, and others went to the East. Wnole trainloads of them were sent with bands and flowers from various industrial centers. Many of them, after a brief stay in the East, returned home disappointed, but replacements for these were readily available, and many remained in the East. The outcome of this movement was better job opportunities for those who remained behind.

A large number of these urban workers signed up to work on virgin or unused lands. In 1954 the Kazakh SSR received 140,000 of these workers, and 20,000 persons were sent to the Altai Kray. In 1955, about 100,000 new settlers arrived in the new agricultural regions. Of this number, 60,000 persons were from urban factories and offices. In 1955 the Kamsomol organization alone sent 350,000 of its members to work on the virgin and unused lands. In 1956 Siberia expected 36,000 households of new settlers. It is estimated that the total rural population of the eastern regions between 1954 and 1955 increased by more than two million persons, most of whom were adults. The Kazakh SSR increased its rural population during this period by almost one million persons, also mainly adults.[15] The major flow of these migrants has declined now, and the further movement of population will be on a reduced scale, but the ice has been broken for others to follow.

True, development of industrial enterprises on newly cultivated land is still embryonic, but the potentialities are there. On his visit to the Kazakh SSR, Khrushchev proposed construction of industrial enterprises there. He claimed that a fuller utilization of the labor would result from such undertakings, mainly in the processing and packing of agricultural commodities, production of construction materials, furniture, and the like. Since the government spends huge sums for transportation of urban workers for the harvesting of crops grown on these new lands, Khrushchev felt that it is better to reduce the dependence upon seasonal workers and to increase permanent residents, who must be employed throughout the year; hence, development of local industries is desirable. The Altai Kray in 1957 employed 50,000 students from other regions for the harvest of its crops, but in 1958 this region was able to do the job with its own local workers. Consequently it is expected that during the next seven years more regions will stabilize their agricultural labor force. To achieve this, fuller manpower utilization is required which in turn leads to the establishment of new or supplementary industrial enterprises.

## PRODUCTION OF MAJOR CROPS

The subject of agricultural output in the USSR is as controversial a matter as the Soviet total population, labor force, and industrial output. In the past there were more statistics on acreage than on production of individual crops. Many Western students at one time or another have attempted to estimate Soviet crop production, since it is believed that scattered data published by the Soviets are meaningless in themselves. It is only natural that with inadequate statistical information many factors were either excluded or completely ignored and each Western student could arrive at a different estimate for the same commodity. These factors, among other limitations, consist of differences of opinion in relation to definitions of Soviet terminology, yields of individual crops, lack of information to variety of crops planted, methods of cultivation and harvesting. The most troublesome factor was the "biological" yield used by the Russians until 1954. Since that year the Soviets again adopted the "barnyard" yields in their calculations of the harvested crops and adjusted all previously published biological yields to barnyard yields.

In the table below, only the Soviet published figures are used, since they have to be fitted to information available for the current Seven-Year Plan. This controversial subject has a wide range in differences of opinion among Western students of Soviet agriculture. For example, one investigator gives the 1950 Soviet wheat output of some 30.2 million tons while the Soviets announced 31.1 million metric tons.[16] The figures are close to each other, providing no ground for quarrel. Another source gives the 1952 total grain output of 112 million metric tons.[17] The official Soviet 1952 barnyard grain production was only 89.6 million metric tons.[18] Even the Soviet press differed in opinion. For instance, in 1952 Malenkov declared that the problem of grain production had been solved by the Soviet Union. He claimed that the 1952 grain output amounted to 128 million metric tons. In 1958, Khrushchev accused Malenkov of giving out misleading information since this figure was expressed in biological yields.

No doubt some Western investigators, especially the ones whose estimates differ from the official Soviet outputs, would question the figures given in Table 3. However, it is believed that eventually these statistics would have to be accepted by all non-Soviet agricultural experts simply to avoid confusion and controversy similar to that now existing in the fields of Soviet industrial, scientific, and military potentials.

TABLE 3—*Total Barnyard Production of Major Crops* [19]
(*in million metric tons*)

| Commodity | 1940 | 1950 | 1953 | 1954 | 1955 | 1956 | 1957 | 1958 | 1965 Plan |
|---|---|---|---|---|---|---|---|---|---|
| Total grain: | 95.5 | 81.2 | 82.5 | 85.6 | 106.8 | 127.6 | 105.0 | 141.2 | 164.0–180.0 |
| Wheat | 31.7 | 31.1 | 41.3 | 42.4 | 47.3 | 67.4 | 58.1 | 76.6 | – |
| Corn | 5.1 | 6.6 | 3.7 | 3.7 | 14.7 | 12.5 | 7.0 | 16.7 | – |
| Sugar beets | 18.0 | 20.8 | 23.2 | 19.8 | 31.0 | 32.5 | 39.7 | 54.4 | 76.0–84.0 |
| Cotton | 2.2 | 3.5 | 3.8 | 4.2 | 3.9 | 4.3 | 4.2 | 4.4 | 5.7–6.1 |
| Flax | 0.3 | 0.2 | 0.2 | 0.2 | 0.4 | 0.5 | 0.4 | 0.4 | 0.6 |
| Sunflowers | 2.6 | 1.8 | 2.6 | 1.9 | 3.8 | 3.9 | 2.8 | 4.6 | 5.0 |
| Potatoes | 75.6 | 88.6 | 72.6 | 75.0 | 71.8 | 96.0 | 87.8 | 86.5 | 147.0 |
| Vegetables | 13.7 | 9.3 | 11.4 | 11.9 | 14.1 | 14.3 | 14.8 | 14.9 | 21.6 |

Production of grain depends not only upon men who work the land but also on growing conditions. For example, in 1951 a drought existed in the Kazakh SSR, Volga River region and in Western Siberia, and the total output of grain was below that of 1950. The year 1952 was a good year, and grain output increased. In 1953 there was a drought in Western Siberia, but the most important factor attributing to low grain output in that year was turning grain lands to grass production. As a result of this policy, the 1953 grain acreage was 9.6 million less than in 1940. The year 1953 was a hard year for the Russians. The grain procurement program was short 4.8 million metric tons required for the national needs, and the State was forced to cover this deficit from its grain stockpile.

In 1954 another drought hit the Ukraine and Volga River region, but with expanding grain areas in the East the Soviets managed to harvest a larger crop. The 1955 drought damaged grain crops in the Volga River region, Urals, and Western Siberia, but the Kazakh SSR enjoyed good weather and the total output of grain was considerably increased. In 1956 adverse growing conditions were experienced by the southern parts of the Soviet Union in their planting of winter crops. There was also poor weather in the Urals and Western Siberia. The greatest damage to grain crops in 1956 occurred in the Ukraine and the lower Volga River region, but with expanding acreage in the East, the USSR produced a larger harvest than in 1955. In general, the 1956 grain harvest was considered good. The growing conditions in 1957 were very poor, and the total production of grain was 22.6 million metric tons below the 1956 level. The year 1958 was a good year with the largest grain output in the history of the USSR. The gross grain harvest in 1959 was lower than in 1958 because of the drought in some areas, and the State purchased 1.8 million metric tons less of grain but enough to meet all the government needs.

Between 1940 and 1958 the total grain acreage was increased by 13 per cent, whereas grain production was up 48 per cent. This suggests that during this period there was a considerable improvement in grain productivity, mainly since 1954, when Soviet agriculture was revamped.

It is expected that the total Soviet grain output is to be increased from 141.2 metric tons in 1958 to 164 or 180 million metric tons by 1965 or an increase of between 23 and 39 million metric tons. To achieve this goal, Khrushchev spelled out the means: he proposes an increase of average grain yield by three to four centners per hectare (less than three bushels per acre), more timely field works, improved scientific farm practices in rotation, improved seed selections, increased production of chemical fertilizer, and a greater utilization of barnyard manure. The production of chemical fertilizer is to be greatly increased from 10.6 million metric tons in 1958 to a 1965 level of 35 million metric tons,[20] sufficient not only for industrial crops, potatoes, vegetables, and fodder crops but also for grain. The increased amount of barnyard manure is to come from the increased livestock population, and the seed growers are to extend their output of better seeds.

An interesting point is found in the proposed boost in yields of 1965 grain output. Assuming that in 1965 the same grain acreage and growing conditions prevail as in 1958, an increase of three or four centners per hectare would produce an additional 38 to 50 million metric tons of grain. But the plan anticipates an increase of only 23 to 39 million metric tons by 1965. There are two answers to this discrepancy: it might be that Khrushchev does not really believe that the peasants will increase their yields as expected; on the other hand by having a larger target to meet, they might intensify their efforts in order to reach it. Even if the expected increase in the yield is only 75 per cent the 1965 planned grain production will be assured. It might also be that the Soviets are actually expecting a full increase in planned yields. If this is the case, then less grain acreage will be required by the country and excess acreage may be allocated to other uses, especially for fodder crops to feed the planned increase in the number of livestock.

The rate of growth in grain production during the current Seven-Year Plan is less than it was during the 1955-58 period at which time great land expansion occurred. Nevertheless, the 1965 grain target is still far from modest. The soils of the dry farming regions have already begun to lose fertility, and Khrushchev is opposed to heavy investments in irrigation projects. Even the anticipated output of chemical fertilizer will be insufficient to have any visible impact in grain production. The Lenin Academy of Agriculture estimated that an output of 45 million metric tons instead of the planned 35 million metric tons would be necessary before it would improve grain yields.[21]

During the 1954-58 period, improvement in the institutional structure and the socio-economic environment in Soviet agriculture improved productivity of lands and peasants. Grain output was considerably increased, mainly through expansion in cultivated land. Prices paid by the State were increased and there were favorable changes in the labor supply, technology, capital investment, and perhaps better management in agriculture and planning. These forces have been important in stimulating production in the past, but it does not follow that they will continue to push the peasants to greater production in the future. The value of these forces is not as notable now as at the beginning of the period; but perhaps Khrushchev will find new incentives to drive the peasants on to desired targets.

Adverse growing conditions do not affect production of wheat as much as other grain crops. Since the Soviets grow both winter and spring wheat, with spring wheat, with spring wheat representing about 72 per cent of the total wheat acreage, there are the alternatives of intensifying the sowing of either spring or winter wheat when growing conditions are unfavorable, or even of replanting the same crop. Again, wheat is grown throughout all the vast Soviet Union, and no single drought could possibly affect the whole country. When one region has poor growing conditions other regions intensify their production of wheat. For this reason wheat production is less erratic than that for grain crops as a whole, which includes all kinds of grain commodities.

Soviet wheat production for 1958 increased by 2.4 times over 1940. The Soviet Union now produces enough wheat to meet all its requirements. In 1958 Khrushchev boasted that now the Russians can eat wheat bread, whereas in the past rough feed grain and potatoes were added in baking of bread. It is also claimed that the current production of wheat is double that of the United States.

As in the case of grain in general, wheat production has also shifted to the eastern parts of the Soviet Union. Between 1953 and 1958 the Kazakh SSR alone increased its wheat acreage almost fivefold. Western Siberia and the Urals, too, expanded their wheat acreage and production. These eastern parts are the new Soviet breadbasket.

Grain which the State obtains is used for supplying the population with grain products, for foreign trade, and for stockpiling. This is only a part of the total grain production. The other part is kept on the farms for livestock, for seeds needed for the next year's planting, for payments to members of collective farms, and so on. The amount of grain received by the State varies from year to year depending on the area under various grain crops and yields.

In 1940 the State took 36.4 million metric tons of grain, or 38.1 per cent of the total output. The State also took 15.6 million metric tons, or 49.2 per cent of the total wheat production. In 1950 the Soviets produced less total grain and wheat than in 1940, and the State's share of the total grain increased to 39.8 per cent, but only to 48.5 per cent for wheat. With larger gross production of grain and wheat in 1956 the State took 42.4 per cent of the total grain and 55.2 per cent of the total wheat. In 1958 the output of total grain was above that of 1956, therefore the share of total grain taken by the State was reduced to 40.2 per cent, but 55 per cent for wheat.[22] In 1958 the amount of total grain and wheat obtained by the State was the largest in the history of the Soviet Union.

Apparently in 1958 the state's stockpile of grain was low, even though it was the best year. Khrushchev in his speech in December 1958 stated that if Soviet agriculture during the 1959-60 year would produce as much grain as it had in 1958, then with increased stockpiles by 1960 the government's share in the total grain output by 1965 could be reduced to about 48 million metric tons, 27 to 29 per cent of the expected 164 to 180 million metric tons.[23] Consequently, with the increased total output of grain a larger part of it is expected to be left on the farms for livestock. Unlike grain, crops such as cotton and sugar beet, except for small amounts left on the farms, are entirely delivered to the State.

No doubt the Russians are taking steps to increase their stockpiles of foodstuffs because of the high concentration of radioactive fallout in bombed areas after a nuclear attack, during which soils would be contaminated and crops could not be grown for a considerable period. It is reasonable to assume that the Soviets, to avoid possible starvation in the event of a nuclear war, are already stockpiling surplus agricultural commodities.

Along with further development in agricultural production, the Soviets are also adjusting their procurement practices. Khrushchev in December 1958 stated that in 1958 prices paid for one centner (100 kilograms) of grain to the collective farms averaged 63 rubles, whereas only 44 rubles were paid to the state farms. The price for a like amount of cotton was 242 rubles at the state farms and 340 rubles at the collective farms. Thus, in 1958 the State subsidized grain production on the collective farms. By allowing the collective farms to possess farm machinery the State purchasing practices are being adjusted to encourage rapid advances in efficiency. Khrushchev stated that during the current Seven-Year Plan the State will buy grain where it is cheaper, that is, in Siberia, the Ukraine, the Kazakh SSR, the Volga River region, and the Northern Caucasus.

## THE SOVIET LIVESTOCK INDUSTRY

In 1958 Soviet leaders claimed that they had licked the problem of supplying the country's demands for grain. It was said that they had at last caught up with the United States in grain and wheat production. The next stage is catching up with the United States in the production of meat, milk, and butter. Khrushchev, in his historic television interview of June 2, 1957, boasted that in per capita production of milk and butter the Soviet Union would match the United States in 1958; in meat, in 1961. Yet in December 1958 he admitted that the 1958 per capita production of milk and butter in the USSR was still below that of the United States. By admitting the lag in Soviet production of milk and butter in 1958 he repudiated his 1957 boastful claims.

Khrushchev estimated the 1958 Soviet per capita production of milk at 279 kilograms, against 330 kilograms in the United States, per capita production of butter at 3.7 kilograms against 4.0 kilograms in the United States.[24] Without reference to the growth in total population in both countries, Khrushchev stated that to catch up in per capita production of milk, the Soviet Union must produce 70 million metric tons of milk against 58.8 million metric tons in 1958 and 840,000 metric tons of butter instead of 778,000 metric tons as in 1958. The actual 1958 per capita production of meat in the Soviet Union was 38 kilograms against 94 kilograms in the United States; 284 kilograms of milk in the USSR against 326 kilograms in the United States; and Khrushchev does not expect to "catch up" with the United States even by 1965. He claimed that to catch up with the United States in per capita production of meat the USSR has to produce 20 to 21 million metric tons annually. The 1958 Soviet commercial meat output was only 7.7 million metric tons, and the 1965 target is set at 16 million metric tons.

The "catching up" concept is dear to the hearts of the Communists, and it has a historic background. One of the reasons for launching Five-

Year plans was to "catch up" and to "overtake" production of the so-called "capitalist" nations. It served as a whip to push on and on to greater production in order to prove to the world that socialized economy is as efficient as the economy in the capitalist world. But it also serves as a double-edged sword. With abundant production of foodstuffs the standard of living for the Russian people will be improved, and since the early intellectual approach to conversion of other nations to communism failed, the ability to produce as much as the capitalist countries is used as a bloodless instrument in convincing other nations of the value of socialized economy.

In this section, only the cattle, cows, hogs, sheep, and poultry are being discussed. It is realized that goats and other animals are also used for meat, but since their contribution to the total Soviet meat production is insignificant only the major meat-supplying animals are being considered.

The leading livestock republics in 1940 as in 1958 were the RSFSR, the Ukraine, White Russia, and the Kazakh SSR, and their share in the total Soviet was 82 per cent in 1940 and in 1958. During the 1940-58 period their number of cows grew from 80 to 86 per cent; hogs increased from 87 to 90 per cent; but the number of sheep somewhat declined from 80 to 76 per cent. During this same period other Central Asian republics considerably expanded their sheep population.

It is only natural that the RSFSR, the largest constituent republic, with its concentration of population and industry, has the largest number of livestock by specializing regions. The leading livestock region in the RSFSR is Western Siberia, with about 14 per cent of the republic's total livestock population, 16 per cent of the cattle, 14 per cent of the hogs, and 12 per cent of the sheep. Next in importance is the Northern Caucasus, followed by the Volga River region, and Eastern Siberia. The Central Industrial region, with its population of 43.2 million, in 1959 possessed about 30 per cent of all the cattle, 35 per cent of all the cows, 36 per cent of the hogs, and 22 per cent of the sheep. The northern regions and the Far East are least abundant in livestock.

The largest number of cattle is found in the Central Industrial region, followed by Western Siberia, the Northern Caucasus, and the Urals. The same distribution applies to hogs. The Northern Caucasus leads in the number of sheep, followed by the Central Industrial region, lower Volga River region, and Western Siberia.

While the industrial sector is totally socialized, livestock is not. Since the socialized agricultural sector is not capable of supplying the urban population and the peasants with meat and dairy products, the Soviets were

TABLE 4—*Total Number of Livestock by Republic on January 1 of Each Year* [25]
(*in million head*)

| Republic or Region | 1941 | | | | 1957 | | | | 1959 | | | |
|---|---|---|---|---|---|---|---|---|---|---|---|---|
| | Total Cattle | Cows | Hogs | Sheep | Total Cattle | Cows | Hogs | Sheep | Total Cattle | Cows | Hogs | Sheep |
| USSR: | 54.5 | 27.8 | 27.5 | 79.9 | 61.4 | 29.0 | 40.8 | 108.2 | 70.8 | 33.3 | 48.7 | 129.9 |
| RSFSR: | 27.8 | 14.2 | 12.1 | 46.7 | 31.6 | 15.3 | 19.8 | 63.0 | 36.1 | 17.3 | 24.0 | 60.9 |
| North | 1.1 | 0.6 | 0.3 | 1.0 | 0.7 | 0.4 | 0.2 | 0.3 | 0.8 | 0.5 | 0.3 | 0.5 |
| Northwest | 1.2 | 0.7 | 0.7 | 1.3 | 1.1 | 0.7 | 1.0 | 0.7 | 1.3 | 0.7 | 1.0 | 1.0 |
| Central | 7.9 | 4.8 | 4.6 | 12.4 | 9.5 | 5.3 | 7.3 | 11.8 | 11.0 | 6.0 | 8.6 | 13.3 |
| Volga River | 2.9 | 1.3 | 1.0 | 7.1 | 3.5 | 1.5 | 1.8 | 9.7 | 3.9 | 1.7 | 2.3 | 11.1 |
| Northern Caucasus | 3.8 | 1.5 | 1.9 | 8.4 | 4.2 | 1.7 | 3.6 | 11.7 | 4.8 | 1.9 | 4.4 | 13.9 |
| Urals | 3.5 | 1.8 | 1.2 | 5.8 | 3.9 | 1.9 | 1.9 | 5.4 | 4.5 | 2.1 | 2.4 | 6.3 |
| Western Siberia | 4.6 | 2.2 | 1.3 | 7.2 | 5.3 | 2.4 | 2.5 | 6.9 | 6.1 | 2.7 | 3.3 | 7.6 |
| Eastern Siberia | 2.4 | 1.0 | 0.7 | 3.4 | 2.7 | 1.1 | 1.2 | 6.0 | 2.9 | 1.2 | 1.2 | 7.0 |
| Far East | 0.4 | 0.2 | 0.4 | 0.08 | 0.7 | 0.3 | 0.5 | 0.2 | 0.8 | 0.4 | 0.6 | 0.2 |
| Ukraine | 10.7 | 5.8 | 9.1 | 6.6 | 13.4 | 6.6 | 14.2 | 9.1 | 16.0 | 7.7 | 15.8 | 10.7 |
| White Russia | 2.8 | 2.0 | 2.5 | 2.5 | 2.9 | 1.7 | 2.4 | 1.4 | 3.4 | 1.9 | 2.7 | 1.4 |
| Uzbek | 1.7 | 0.6 | 0.1 | 4.2 | 1.7 | 0.6 | 0.2 | 6.7 | 2.0 | 0.8 | 0.3 | 7.8 |
| Kazakh | 3.4 | 1.3 | 0.4 | 7.0 | 4.3 | 1.6 | 0.7 | 18.4 | 5.2 | 1.9 | 1.3 | 25.5 |
| Georgia | 1.6 | 0.6 | 0.6 | 1.7 | 1.4 | 0.5 | 0.5 | 1.4 | 1.5 | 0.5 | 0.6 | 1.7 |
| Azerbaydzhan | 1.4 | 0.5 | 0.1 | 2.3 | 1.2 | 0.4 | 0.1 | 3.7 | 1.4 | 0.5 | 0.1 | 4.3 |
| Lithuania | 1.0 | 0.8 | 1.1 | 0.6 | 0.9 | 0.5 | 1.0 | 0.4 | 1.0 | 0.7 | 1.2 | 0.4 |
| Moldavia | 0.5 | 0.2 | 0.3 | 1.4 | 0.6 | 0.3 | 0.8 | 1.7 | 0.7 | 0.3 | 1.0 | 2.0 |
| Latvia | 1.0 | 0.8 | 0.6 | 0.6 | 0.8 | 0.5 | 0.5 | 0.5 | 0.8 | 0.5 | 0.7 | 0.5 |
| Kirghiz | 0.6 | 0.2 | 0.1 | 1.8 | 0.7 | 0.2 | 0.1 | 4.4 | 0.7 | 0.3 | 0.2 | 5.7 |
| Tadzhik | 0.6 | 0.2 | 0.02 | 1.0 | 0.6 | 0.2 | 0.05 | 2.0 | 0.6 | 0.2 | 0.06 | 2.2 |
| Armenia | 0.6 | 0.2 | 0.06 | 1.0 | 0.6 | 0.2 | 0.1 | 1.4 | 0.6 | 0.2 | 0.1 | 1.8 |
| Turkmen | 0.3 | 0.1 | 0.04 | 2.0 | 0.3 | 0.1 | 0.03 | 3.9 | 0.4 | 0.1 | 0.05 | 4.7 |
| Estonia | 0.5 | 0.4 | 0.3 | 0.3 | 0.4 | 0.3 | 0.4 | 0.2 | 0.4 | 0.3 | 0.4 | 0.2 |

forced to compromise and accept private ownership of livestock along with the socialized ownership concentrated in communal livestock herds on collective and state farms and in other state-operated supplementary livestock enterprises. It was pointed out in the preceding chapter that in 1958 private sectors owned 56 per cent of the total number of cows in the Soviet Union. Consequently this sector is largely responsible for the breeding of horned animals and for the production of milk.

The Germans occupied an area where about 38 per cent of all the cattle, 28 per cent of all the sheep and goats, and 59 per cent of all the hogs were located.[26] At the same time, the demand for grain for human consumption reduced the grain acreage for livestock in the unoccupied regions. Therefore, beginning with the second half of 1941, the livestock industry depended entirely upon the amount of feed which was available in any one particular region or on any one particular collective or state farm. The overburdened transportation system stopped hauling bulky livestock feed soon after the beginning of the war, and on the whole, during the war, livestock expanded where feed was available and decreased where feed was short. Most of the increase in livestock population took place in the Kazakh SSR and Siberia, where hay land, pasture, and range were abundant. However, the increase in the number of livestock in these regions was insufficient to satisfy the demand of both the Armed Forces and the civilian population.

During the war, the Soviets were proud of the fact that the Soviet Armed Forces did not experience the "meatless days" of the "capitalist" armies. But the meat supply afforded the army during the war meant further belt-tightening for the civilian population. For example, in a besieged Moscow in January 1942, each adult in an essential occupation received about 2.5 pounds of meat, and in February this allotment was reduced by about 50 per cent. Undoubtedly the reduction of meat distribution in regions far from the front lines was not as drastic as in Moscow. Nevertheless, to relieve the meat shortage in 1942, the government devised a plan by which the collective and state farms were to increase their livestock during 1943, but the plan did not fully materialize, although there were small increases. In the absence of feed and proper care, the death rate among matured and growing stock increased considerably, and since many collective farms used cows during the plowing and harvesting activities, the milk yield, too, was drastically cut.

When the Russians counterattacked the Germans and forced them to retreat, the liberated regions had from 31 to 43 per cent of their prewar number of cattle, 22 to 30 per cent of sheep and goats, and ten to 12 per cent of the 1940 number of hogs. With the liberation of the occupied regions a slow recovery of the Soviet livestock industry started, which was interrupted by the 1946 drought in White Russia and the Ukraine. Sluggishness in the recovery of livestock may be seen in the fact that even on January 1, 1951 the Soviet Union increased its total cattle population by 2.6 million head and its sheep population by 2.7 million, in comparison with January 1941, but the number of cows was 3.5 million head below the 1941 level and hogs were short by 3.1 million head. Slow as the recovery was, it was abruptly stopped by the merging of collective farms. Confused and bewildered peasants began to slaughter their own stock, as they had during the early days of the collectivization rush. Care of the livestock owned by collective farms was disorganized, causing low yields of young stock and higher mortaility rates for the older animals. In 1952 alone the number of cattle was reduced by 2.2 million head, 550,000 of which were cows. The number of cows in the socialized sector alone was 3.5 million below the 1940 level.[27]

To stimulate the livestock industry, the Soviets in 1949 developed a Three-Year Livestock Plan. This plan completely failed because of its unrealistic expectation in planned yields of meat and milk, shortage of fodder, and lack of incentives for the peasants to increase their livestock. Because of fodder shortages during January to March 1951 (the last year of the Three-Year Plan) 895,000 head of cattle, 1.3 million hogs, and 4.8 million sheep died of starvation.[28] In 1952 conditions were still bad, and fodder shortages caused a large number of deaths among animals. Only the intensified purchasing campaign by collective farms from their members and other private owners somewhat boosted the 1952 total socialized livestock population. As a result of these conditions the state meat and milk procurement programs in 1953 and 1954 also failed.[29] In September 1953 a new attempt was made to revive the Soviet livestock industry by increasing production of fodder, improving plans for livestock expansion, and increasing the price paid by the State. But it was not until 1955 that there was a real improvement in the socialized livestock industry.

The decree "On Increase of Livestock Products," issued on January 31, 1955, was designed to correct past errors. It reorganized the old practices in livestock breeding, required deliveries, increased prices paid by the State, and generally attempted to encourage expansion of livestock in the nation. The additional incentives of this decree stimulated the peasants to devote more of their efforts to livestock, and the 1955 number of livestock was considerably increased in comparison with the period 1941-51, particularly in hogs and sheep. Encouraged and relieved of pressures, the peasants received higher incomes from livestock and in 1956 increased their attention to animal husbandry.

With increased emphasis on livestock the 1959 number of cattle was increased to 74 million head, 34 million cows, 53 million hogs, and 136 million sheep.[30] However, as the total number of livestock increased in both socialized and private sectors, the socialized sector showed a greater increase in cows than did the private sector because of the sale of its animals to collective and state farms.

The 1965 planned number of cattle is set at 106 to 110 million head, or an increase of 26 to 31 per cent over the 1958 level.[31] But the 1965 targets in state procurement programs for meat, milk, wool, and eggs call for more than doubling the 1957 level. However optimistic this increase may be, the Soviets are determined to meet their targets by adjusting plans and practices within the livestock industry.

Artificial insemination practices are to be intensified. In 1958 about 5.5 million cows and heifers and 29.1 million ewes received artificial insemination.[32] This is about 15 per cent of the total cow population and 17 per cent for the sheep. The Ukraine, the leading republic in the use of artificial insemination, in 1958 had 47 per cent of its total cows and heifers artificially inseminated. Other figures are 8.4 per cent in White Russia, 6.4 per cent in Estonia, 6.2 per cent in the RSFSR, 5.3 per cent in Latvia, and 3.1 per cent in the Kazakh SSR. In general, the western parts of the USSR are more advanced in these practices than Central Asia.

To expand artificial insemination among large animals the number of bulls must be increased. In 1958 the Soviet Union had about 550,000 breeding bulls of which only 190,000 may be considered to be thoroughbred. In 1958, on the average, each bull in artificial insemination stations served about 35 to 65 cows, approximately the same number as they would under natural practices. Consequently, if artificial insemination is to be greatly expanded, the number of bulls must be considerably increased, and this takes several years. On the other hand, the Soviets have a larger number of thoroughbred rams than bulls. They are more successful with artificial insemination in sheep, and the aim of reemphasizing artificial insemination is mainly directed to sheep.

Since the 1965 targets for livestock are expected to be greatly increased, the question of fodder supply becomes very important. The current Seven-Year Plan underlines production of silage, especially from corn, followed by better utilization of hay, pasture, and range lands. In 1953, the USSR had 32 million metric tons of silage but 148 million metric tons in 1958 of which 108 million tons was corn silage. By 1965 total silage is planned to be about 222 million metric tons.[33] Assuming that the Russians, just to please Khrushchev, will increase corn acreage for silage, there still will be the problem of constructing silos or similar storage facilities, failure to solve which might undermine the whole silage expansion program.

Along with the silage program, increases in the acreage under annual and perennial grasses are also anticipated, provided that mechanization in hay production is considerably improved. Moreover, it is uncertain whether farm machine-building enterprises can produce more machinery for hay. Even assuming that production of hay is achieved as planned, there is no certainty that this hay can be transported hundreds of miles from producing to consuming regions. As to utilization of natural pasture, there are about 864 million acres, mostly located in the Kazakh SSR, Northern Caucasus, Western Siberia, Volga River Valley, and Far East. These regions are too far away from areas of intensive production of livestock. The main problem is increased production of hay and better utilization of pasture and range lands depends upon availability of mechanization, additional manpower, the price of hay and livestock, and the willingness of the peasants to change to pasture and range practices, which were not popular in the past.

Another problem closely associated with an attempt to increase livestock is the Russian practice of slaughtering young animals. Since the planned targets for meat production are usually established at high rates, the collective and state farms, in their effort to fulfill the planned norms, often slaughter young animals. Annual slaughter of young cattle is expressed in million heads. The current Seven-Year Plan recommends that young animals be kept on the farm until they are one and one-half or two years old. With proper feeding, the contribution of young stock to the total meat supply is estimated to be an additional 30 to 40 per cent.

In the case of sheep, which in the past were slaughtered at full maturity, the 1965 plan calls for about 40 per cent of all the sheep to be slaughtered at the age of seven to nine months. By changing slaughtering practices it is expected to increase the number of slaughtered sheep by 1965. As to an increased number of hog slaughterings, the 1965 directive decrees a better utilization of sows and a reduction in time for feeding piglets by sows to five or six months only. This change in practice anticipates an increase in the weight of sows and also a speed-up in the feeding of piglets and in their growth.

All these measures were used in the past without much success. They are good economic measures for any society, provided that the peasants have additional incentives. Khrushchev admits the task will not be easy. His grain production policies have raised grain and especially wheat production so that people have enough bread. Now the problem is more fodder to expand livestock herds so that more meat and dairy products will be available. But as he stresses livestock, new problems are cropping up. He admits that only a few years ago, the state procurement programs in livestock products, in the main, were achieved because of the large number of livestock purchased from members of collective farms, workers, and employees. By 1965 he wants collective and state farms, that is, the socialized sector, to be the main supplier of livestock products. The 1965 targets for livestock are indeed optimistic. If in the meantime the lower echelon of the Communist Party would attempt to force private owners to sell their livestock to the socialized sector, then the 1965 targets may not be reached at all. There even may be a decline in the total number of livestock, as happened in the past when the government became too ruthless with private owners.

## PRODUCTION OF LIVESTOCK PRODUCTS

In the Soviet Union, meat milk and eggs are produced by all who own livestock, but the largest percentage of these commodities is obtained from the collective and state farms. Availability of livestock products during any one year depends upon the number of animals slaughtered and the average yield per animal.

In 1940 the average yield per 100 cows and ewes on collective farms was 61 calves and 57 lambs.[34] One may assume that the average yield for the country as a whole was somewhat higher, because privately owned cows and ewes would have had better care during the period of labor, and newborn stock also would have had more attention. Their death rates also would be lower for the same reasons. The death rates of newborn stock has wider range than the birth rate, and since the death rate depends more upon climatic conditions than the birth rate, the northern regions have a higher death rate among newborn animals than the warmer climates.

The amount of meat produced per hundredweight of liveweight for cattle 1957 was 43.8 per cent, the same as it was in 1940. A hundredweight of liveweight hog produced 60.6 per cent of pork in 1940, and 59.0 per cent in 1957. Sheep and goats on an average yielded 40.6 per cent of meat in 1940, and 40.2 per cent in 1957. Thus, Soviet animals between 1940 and 1957 did not increase in weight; the average weight of cattle slaughtered for beef in 1957 was about 516 pounds, 187 pounds for hogs, and 84 pounds for sheep on the hoof.[35] In general about 30 per cent of all the animals delivered to the State for slaughter in 1957 were underweight, which of course reduced the average yield per animal. Even during the first nine months of 1958, 36 per cent of all livestock delivered to the State was underweight.[36] This suggests that in attempting to fulfill the meat production norms in 1958 many head of young stock were slaughtered.

Urban populations obtain livestock commodities from state-operated retail establishments or from collective farm markets. The share of collective farm markets in the total supply of livestock products varies from city to city, depending on prices and on how well the state retail stores are stocked with particular goods.

With reorganization of the administrative structure of the economy, state procurement activities for agricultural products were centralized. Yet, there are still a number of agencies which obtain their meat not only through state-operated channels but also from collective farm markets. These are mainly local institutional buyers who buy animals from private owners for slaughtering purposes to supplement their meat allotments.

State pocurement programs for livestock products after 1953 were considerably improved, particularly so after 1955 when prices for agricultural goods were raised. With this incentive in mind and with promises that livestock would not be taken away, the peasants intensified their efforts in production of livestock and its products. As production increased, the collective farms and their members accumulated higher incomes. The 1952 cash income of all collective farms amounted to 42.8 billion rubles; by 1957 it was 95.2 billion rubles. During the same period the income of collective farm members in terms of cash and kind also increased from 47.5 billion rubles in 1952 to 83.8 billion rubles in 1957.[37] There were greater monetary gains by the collective farms than by their members. The larger income shown by the collective farms resulted not only from an increase in price and production but also from improvements in efficiency in operating larger farms. In connection with the increased prices on agricultural commodities, Khrushchev in 1958 cautioned Party leaders not to increase the income of collective farms by further increases in prices. He recommended that any further increase in income must come through increased labor productivity and better administrative organization on collective farms. Nevertheless, the incentives which the peasants have at the present time are much higher than they were in 1952. Whether the peasants will be satisfied with them in the future is a question for speculation.

As was previously noted, the State obtains the required livestock products from various sources, but the main source is the socialized sector—the collective and state farms.

TABLE 5—*1958 Sources for Livestock Products* [38]
(*in percentage of total*)

| Product | Collective Farms | State Farms | Members of Collectives | Others |
|---|---|---|---|---|
| Total Meat: _____ | 5̶1̶ | 26 | 21 | 2 |
| Pork _____ | 4̶6̶ | 35 | 18 | 1 |
| Milk _____ | 62 | 22 | 15 | 1 |
| Wool _____ | 62 | 28 | 10 | — |

These percentages indicate that even after merging small collective farms into larger units and expanding the number of state farms, the private sector was still important, supplying 23 per cent of all meat, 19 per cent of all pork, and 16 per cent of the milk. And because of its value in the total supplies of livestock, the Soviets are cautious about destroying this channel.

Estimating production in livestock products is difficult, since a considerable amount of it is directly consumed by the producers, especially by the members of collective farms and workers and employees possessing livestock. The State acquires its share in terms of raw materials such as dressed meat, milk, and wool, and also in terms of living animals. Animals on the hoof are delivered to state enterprises where they are fed until a specified weight is reached; then they are slaughtered. In 1940, 920,000 cattle and 800,00 hogs were delivered to these enterprises; in 1956 the number of cattle increased to 2.3 million head and 2.4 million hogs. By intensified feeding of these animals the State in 1940 gained 120,000 metric tons of meat, and in 1956 weight increased to 203,000 metric tons,[39] indicating that a larger number of young animals were used in 1956 than in 1940.

Since information relating to the production of livestock products excludes direct consumption by independent owners, the statistics in livestock production from the socialized sector are underestimated for the country as a whole. At any rate, the state procurement programs in livestock represent the bulk of all production. What is more important is the State's changing policies in obtaining products which have an impact on private ownership of livestock. This may be seen from the fact that in 1956 the share of livestock products in the state's procurement of the total agricultural output was calculated at 37 per cent; it became 41 per cent in 1958.[40] The share in 1965 probably will be still greater.

It was previously stated that the state procurement programs for livestock products consist of two channels: the slaughtering of livestock obtained on the hoof; and the procurement of livestock products either in terms of dressed meat such as poultry or semi-finished goods such as raw milk and wool. Table 6 shows that the planned 1965 State slaughtering program is set at 16.0 million tons for all meat, twice as much as in 1958 or 3.4 times larger than in 1940. The 1965 industrial use or the commerical processing of meat also expects to be almost twice the volume recorded for 1958.

TABLE 6—*State Procurement Programs on Livestock Products* [41]
(*in million metric tons*)

| Commodity | 1940 | 1950 | 1953 | 1956 | 1957 | 1958 | 1959 | 1965 (plan) |
|---|---|---|---|---|---|---|---|---|
| Total meat, slaughter weight: __ | 4.7 | 4.9 | 5.8 | 6.6 | 7.4 | 7.7 | 8.6 | 16.0 |
| Pork _____ | 1.7 | 1.5 | 2.3 | 2.7 | 3.3 | 3.3 | — | — |
| Industrial use: ___ | 1.5 | 1.6 | 2.2 | 2.7 | 3.1 | 3.4 | — | 6.1 |
| Beef _____ | 0.8 | 0.9 | 1.2 | 1.2 | 1.3 | 1.4 | — | — |
| Pork _____ | 0.3 | 0.3 | 0.5 | 0.8 | 1.1 | 1.2 | — | — |
| Lamb _____ | 0.2 | 0.2 | 0.2 | 0.3 | 0.3 | 0.3 | — | — |
| Poultry _____ | 0.05 | 0.03 | 0.09 | 0.1 | 0.1 | 0.1 | — | — |
| Others _____ | 0.1 | 0.1 | 0.2 | 0.3 | 0.3 | 0.3 | — | — |
| Total milk _____ | 33.6 | 35.3 | 36.5 | 49.1 | 54.7 | 58.8 | 62.0 | 100–105 |
| Industrial use: ___ | 6.5 | 8.5 | 10.6 | 17.3 | 20.3 | 22.6 | — | 40.6 |
| Butter _____ | 0.2 | 0.3 | 0.4 | 0.5 | 0.6 | 0.7 | 0.8 | 1.5 |
| Eggs (billions) _____ | 12.2 | 11.7 | 16.1 | 19.5 | 22.3 | 23.1 | 24.8 | 37.0 |
| Wool _____ | 0.2 | 0.2 | 0.2 | 0.3 | 0.3 | 0.3 | 0.3 | 0.6 |

Prior to 1953, the main source of state meat reserves was cattle and cows but since 1957 a greater emphasis was put on pork, and the current Seven-Year Plan calls for still greater emphasis on pork and poultry. In 1958 pork represented about 40 per cent of the total meat supplies against 23 per cent in 1940, and in 1965 it is to provide a still greater per cent of the total meat. The 1965 share of poultry in the total meat supply is also to be increased. Consequently the 1965 share of beef in the total meat supply is to be considerably reduced in order to increase the cattle population.

By 1965, the Soviets expect to increase its poultry, especially ducks, not only as a source of meat but also for increased output of eggs. The 1965 production of eggs is to be increased by 60 per cent and poultry meat by 5.4 times over 1958. Similariy, with the decline in slaughtering of cattle, especially cows, their total number is expected to be greatly increased and hence a 73 per cent increase in the milk yield is anticipated. Lamb and wool are complementary products, and in general, any increase in wool production would follow a similiar increase in lamb. As compared to 1958, the 1965 output of wool is expected to increase by about 67 per cent.

The 1965 output of meat is to double the 1958 output; production of milk is to be increased by some 70 per cent and eggs by 60 per cent. To reach these tremendous targets, each constituent republic is required to match the national goals.

In 1965 production of meat, only Georgia, Lithuania, Latvia, and Estonia are planning to increase their meat output by less than 100 per cent. Other republics are expected to more than double their meat production. The Kirghiz SSR is to triple its meat output while that of the Kazakh SSR is to be increased 2.5 times. In comparison with 1958, the Kazakh SSR in 1965 is pledged to increase its sheep population by threefold or to 75 million head, cattle by 58 per cent or to 7.5 million head, hogs by 2.5 times and poultry by 84 per cent in order to increase its meat output by 2.5 times and milk output 80 per cent.[42] It is planned that by 1965 over 100 million hogs are to be slaughtered whereas in 1957 their number was only 17.6 million head.[43] Indeed, this is a tremendous and overoptimistic target to achieve.

TABLE 7—*Production of Meat in Slaughterweight in Centners per 100 Hectares of Land* [44]

| Republic | 1958 Actual | 1965 Plan | Increase Percentage |
|---|---|---|---|
| Ukraine | 49 | 101 | 106 |
| Lithuania | 46 | 75 | 63 |
| Latvia | 44 | 80 | 82 |
| Moldavia | 42 | 103 | 145 |
| White Russia | 41 | 89 | 117 |
| Estonia | 40 | 81 | 102 |
| Georgia | 31 | 64 | 106 |
| Armenia | 26 | 53 | 104 |
| RSFSR | 17 | 54 | 218 |
| Azerbaydzhan | 17 | 40 | 135 |
| Tadzhik | 10 | 22 | 110 |
| Kirghiz | 8 | 26 | 225 |
| Uzbek | 6 | 11 | 83 |
| Kazakh | 3 | 9 | 200 |
| Turkmen | 1 | 2.6 | 160 |

(one hectare = 2.47 acres; one centner = 100 kilograms or one-tenth metric ton)

Calculated increases in livestock production are based on the availability of agricultural land possessed by collective and state farms.

According to Table 7, the greatest increase in meat production is to take place in the Kirghiz SSR, mostly through expansion of sheep herds. The smallest increase is to take place in the Lithuanian SSR, maily in pork. In genreal, increased output of beef is expected to take place in the abundant pasture land regions of the Kazakh SSR, Northern Caucasus, Siberia, and the Volga River Valley. Lamb is to come mainly from sheep-growing Central Asia and pork from the Baltic states, White Russia, parts of the RSFSR, and the Ukraine. Most of the poultry increase is anticipated in the western regions of the RSFSR.

To accept the percentage increases in Table 7 is to be too naive. True, some of the republics and certain regions having low meat yields now could fulfill their targets, since their required increase is so much smaller than for most efficient meat-producing regions. It would be a virtually impossible task for the Ukraine, Moldavia, and White Russia to double their already high meat output norms.

Mechanization in the livestock industry is low. It was estimated that with present mechanization in the livestock industry an additional five million workers will be needed to produce the 1965 meat targets, provided that there is a considerable increase in the number of livestock. Problems related to an increase in meat production are so numerous that confusion and misuse of resources are bound to occur. The peasants are supposed to increase the number of livestock, and at the same time to increase their average weight. This is a difficuilt, if not impossible, task since even in 1957 the country lost about 500,000 metric tons of meat through slaughtering of underfed cattle. In rushing to increase the number of livestock, there will be more underweight animals delivered to the State. Artificial insemination is still in its infancy, and promises of increased concentrated feed production of 20 to 21 million metric tons and of allocation of 80 to 90 million metric tons of grain for the livestock by 1965 are still nothing but promises.

Enthusiastic Khrushchev, in his drive to catch up with the United States in meat production, is reshaping Soviet agriculture to reach this goal. It has become a mania with him, and the "white horse" on which he dreams to ride to this goal is corn. More corn means more feed for livestock which means better fed, more productive animals. To push this principal, he forgets or ignores other factors such as willingness on the part of the peasants to shift to new production methods or to production of new crops. However, if his targets are only 50 per cent realized, it would still be a great achievement.

As to milk production, Khrushchev is also overoptimistic. Again, using the input-output formula, he expects by 1965 to get 70 per cent more milk than in 1958. The average yield of milk per 100 hectares of farm land in 1957 was 11,100 kilograms, and the anticipated 1965 yield is estimated at 20,000 to 21,000 kilograms. As with the total meat output, planned production of milk is not realistic. In 1957 the average annual milk output per cow in the Soviet Union was 1, 858 kilograms; the anticipated 1965 milk yield per cow in the collective farms is set at 2,600 kilograms. This is an increase of 40 per cent instead of 70 per cent for the total milk. To produce the other 30 per cent for the national target, the Soviets are expecting to increase the cow population so that major milk-producing regions would have not less than 20 to 25 cows per 100 hectares of farm land. Thus, to produce the 1965 milk target of 100 to 105 million metric tons, the Soviets are anticipating an increase in the average milk yield per cow as well as an increase in the cow population. In 1958 the average annual yield of milk per cow on 20 per cent of all collective farms was less than 1,300 kilograms. What is to be done with these low-yielding cows? They are poor producers because of their breed. Would these low-yielding animals produce more milk with additional feed? How much increase in feed would be required to boost their output? These problems are not answered by Khrushchev. His solution is to increase milk yields per cow, by any means, to expand the cow population, and to increase milk fat in fluid milk.

To increase yields of milk per cow, it is not as much environment that matters as the breed of cows. Most Russian cows are of a poor milk-yielding breed. Expansion of a similar breed of cows would produce a larger total volume of milk for the country, but they would cut deeply into available feed supplies. To replace low-yielding cows with better species would be an expensive process which would take several years at the time when Khrushchev is in a great hurry to outproduce the United States. The content of fat in milk now ranges between 3.6 and 3.7 per cent. Calculations by Soviet dairy scientists show that an increase of 0.01 per cent in milk fat content would produce an additional 20,000 metric tons of butter. To produce that much butter would require 250,000 cows under current conditions.

Considering all the limiting factors related to milk production, it is doubltful that the Russians will be able to reach their assigned target for 1965. Nevertheless, the peasants and farm leaders, awakened from the lethargy of the past, are willing to learn new tricks in production, especially methods used in the United States.

Whatever increases in production of meat and milk in the Soviet Union might occur by 1965, a part of this success may be attributed to the United States. During his speech to the Central Committee of the Communist Party in December 1958, Khrushchev time after time referred to American farm practices and high productivity, especially the value of corn in production of livestock. In fact he admits that there is much the Russians can learn from American farmers and he looks with awe on American farm operations.

It is estimated by the Soviets that annual per capita consumption of all meats and pork fat would be about 160 kilograms (353 pounds) and 540 kilograms (1,190 pounds) of milk, butter and cheese. It is also estimated that to supply the above amounts of meat and milk, for every five persons there must be one cow and for every 25 persons there must be one sow.[45] This means that, based on the official population report of 208.8 million persons, the Soviet Union should have been able to produce 36.8 million metric tons of meat and 124.3 million metric tons of milk in 1958. Assuming that the rural population supplies its own requirements of meat and milk, the State is basically obliged to supply the urban population only. The urban population at the beginning of 1959 represented 48 per cent of the total Soviet population and its requirement for meat amounts to 17.7 million metric tons, and 59.6 million metric tons for milk. But in 1958 the State procured only 7.7 million metric tons of meat and 57.8 million metric tons of milk. Consequently, in 1958 the Soviets were unable to supply the minimum requirement of these products to the urban population. At the end of the current Plan in 1965, the Soviets will still be short in their supplies of meat and milk, even if one makes an assumption that there will not be an increase in the total Soviet population.

Since the State is unable to supply the urban population with livestock products, the existence of the collective farm markets is essential, for here the city people buy meat and milk at higher prices. Will the peasants be as enthusiastic about putting greater efforts into production of livestock as Khrushchev wants them to be? Will they be induced to follow his planning programs to catch up with the United States? Do they want to catch up with the United States at the expense of greater effort?

In general, the movement in catching up with the United States is rapidly spreading throughout the Soviet Union and it has a political implication. In his speech in Leningrad on May 22, 1957, Khrushchev said: "If we catch up with the United States in per capita production of meat, butter, and milk, we will have hit the pillar of capitalism with the most powerful torpedo yet seen."

## LABOR PRODUCTIVITY IN AGRICULTURE

Labor productivity in agriculture depends on men, nature, technology, organization for farm work; and length of working time would naturally increase production of farm labor. But it also may happen that when growing conditions are bad, additional input of factors of production may not result in increased output.

The general improvement in the management of Soviet agriculture has been reflected first of all in more timely sowing. The central problem here is not so much mechanization and livestock as the efficiency of labor. The government tries to improve the quality of labor by every available means: propaganda, training of young peasants, incentives, better leadership, additional farm machinery and fertilizer. But this is a slow process. Century-old traditions are deeply ingrained in the Russian village. In many parts, hand labor is still considered the most effective method of farming, and many peasants are still skeptical about the advantages of mechanized farming.

The efficiency of tractors and other mechanized equipment varies from region to region, and although a given region may have a sufficient number of tractors and combines, there are breakdowns, and valuable time is spent on repairs. It may be added that the deep-rooted inefficiency of Russian agriculture lies not in the lack of equipment, but rather in inefficient use of the existing machinery and in the shortage of skilled workers. This can be seen in the fact, that during the harvest of grain in the Kazakh SSR in 1956, many college girls who had no more than two weeks of training were allowed to handle complex farm machinery.

The efficiency or inefficiency of the Soviet's farm labor, machinery, and livestock cannot be analyzed by statistical methods only, for the inefficiency of labor is not an inherent quality. It ties in with government policies and planning, and the resistance of the peasants to these plans. But statistical evidence shows that, as a whole, labor and machinery on the Soviet farms are inefficient, though they may be improved by training of labor, and better workmanship on the machinery, as well as an increased variety of farm labor-saving devices.

According to Soviet official figures, labor productivity between 1940 and 1958 increased 56 per cent for the collective farms and 40 per cent for the state farms. However, there were differences in the growth rates, as can be seen from the following table.

As Table 8 shows, the average annual increase in labor productivity on the collective farms during these 17 years was three per cent, while for state farms it was 2.3 per cent. The Table also shows that even in 1950 both collective and state farms were below the 1940 level, with the state farms lagging behind the collective farms in their productivity. By 1953 as compared with 1940, the collective farms increased their labor productivity by 15 per cent, whereas the state farms only by four per cent. Between

TABLE 8—*Agricultural Labor Productivity in the USSR* [46]
(*in per cent to 1940*)

| Year | Collective Farms | State Farms |
|------|------------------|-------------|
| 1940 | 100 | 100 |
| 1950 | 99 | 91 |
| 1952 | 112 | 100 |
| 1953 | 115 | 104 |
| 1955 | 130 | 116 |
| 1956 | 146 | 149 |
| 1958 | 151 | 139 |

1953 and 1956 the state farms caught up with labor productivity of the collective farms, but in 1958 they again dropped behind the collective farms.

The smallest increase in labor productivity for the collective farms was in the troublesome year of 1953 when their productivity advanced only three per cent; the largest increase, 15 per cent, occured in 1955 when prices were increased and required deliveries to the State were lowered. The increase in labor productivity on the state farms between 1950 and 1953 averaged 4.3 per cent. There was no increase in labor productivity on the state farms at all in 1954, the year when expansion of the state farms in the East took place. With reorganization of the state farms in 1955 there was an increase of 12 per cent. The greatest increase in labor productivity in the state farms took place in 1956—33 per cent. In general, beginning with 1955, farm labor productivity was considerably increased through expansion of agricultural lands, raised prices paid by the State, reduction in required delivery norms, relief in taxation, and other incentives which stimulated labor productivity.

In comparison with 1958, the 1965 labor productivity for the collective farms is expected to be doubled, but to increase only 55 to 60 per cent of the state farms.[47] During the current Seven-Year Plan, the average annual labor productivity of state farms is to be increased at the rate of 7.8 to 8.5 per cent against 7.7 per cent recorded for the 1955-58 period. More than likely at the beginning of the Seven-Year Plan this rate will be smaller than in later years. Generally, the 1959-65 growth in labor productivity on state farms is below the 1950-58 rate.

The 1965 target for collective farms (to double their labor productivity) is in itself meaningless, since in 1958 collective farms were not permitted to own farm machinery, whereas in 1959, with the abolishment of MTS, they may buy it. Consequently, with ownership in farm machinery on the collective farms, their labor productivity is bound to increase tremendously if we compare it with prevailing conditions in 1958.

Considering the lack of experience in maximum utilization of farm machinery by the collective farms, it is reasonable to assume that the performance of farm machinery will be less efficient at the beginning of the ownership period. Moreover, in comparison with 1955-58, the growth in labor productivity for the state farms in about the same as for the 1959-65 period. From this, one may assume that the growth in labor productivity in the collective farms will also tend to be similar to what it was during the 1955-58 period. Therefore, based on these assumptions the growth of actual labor productivity on the collective farms may be estimated at about seven per cent annually, and the total increase by 1965 might amount to only 49 per cent over 1958 instead of doubling. Even this increase, if achieved, would provide a tremendous boost in the total argicultural output. Certainly these figures are much closer to the anticipated total agricultural increase of 70 per cent.

The Soviet leaders realize that the farm labor is a long way from being efficient. But any improvement in the efficiency of labor and equipment must start from the bottom. Directives, decrees, and rules are easy to write, but compliance with them is difficult to maintain when the human element exists and is as crafty as it is. There is no doubt that under private ownership the same labor and equipment could be more efficient because of competitive forces, but as long as the majority of the peasants are not wholehearted socialists the farm labor force will be inefficient, without increasing incentives. The Soviets must consider not only the quality of existing labor and equipment, but also the quantity, with emphasis on quality if the rapid increase in production of agricultural products is their goal. This goal is set at a high level, and attempts are made to improve the quality of labor and equipment, but there are unforseen factors which may disturb the programmed goal, since the efforts are spread in every direction and only the minimum requirements are allocated for each sector. Since the collective farms are now larger and are allowed to possess all the necessary machinery and equipment required for successful operation, the emphasis has shifted to leadership of them. Many Communists are in managerial positions on the collective farms, and many of them are not professional farmers, which creates conflicts between them and the peasants.

Khrushchev, in his speech to the Central Committee in December 1958, admitted that many of these comrades are not qualified farm managers, and must be replaced with better personnel. Thus, farm leadership is also undergoing a drastic change, a trend which might develop a new "farm managerial class," similar to that in industry; and Khrushchev might be faced with a new problem of crushing it later, as he has done with ministerial bureaucracy.

## Chapter 8—Bibliography

[1] *Narodnoye Khozaystvo SSSR v 1958 Godu,* Moscow, 1959, p. 398. (hereafter referred to as *Narodnoye Khozaystvo*)

[2] Katkoff, V., *Soviet Agriculture Since 1940,* a Ph. D. dissertation, The Ohio State University, 1950, p. 7.

[3] Jasny, N., *The Socialized Agriculture of the USSR,* Stanford University Press, 1949, p. 69.

[4] Katkoff, V., *op. cit.,* p. 79.

[5] Schwartz, Harry, *Russia's Soviet Economy,* 2d Edition, Prentice-Hall, 1954, p. 358.

[6] *Pravda,* February 7, 1940.

[7] *Izvestia,* June 15, 1940.

[8] *Pravda,* April 26, 1940.

[9] *Ibid.,* February 15, 1940.

[10] *Izvestia,* June 15, 1940.

[11] *Pravda,* April 26, 1940.

[12] *Narodnoye Khozaystvo,* p. 433.

[13] *Ekonomika Sel'skogo Khozaystva,* No. 3, 1959, p. 30. (hereafter referred to as *Ekonomika*)

[14] *Plenum Tsentral'nogo Komiteta Kommunisticheskoy Partii Sovetskogo Soyuza,* December 15-19, 1958, Moscow, 1958, p. 424. (hereafter referred to as *Plenum*)

[15] *Ogonek,* No. 42, October 1956, p. 2.

[16] U. S. Department of Commerce, Bureau of Foreign Commerce, *Basic Data on the Economy of the USSR,* Washington, D. C., February 1956, p. 18.

[17] De Huszar, G. B., and Associates, *Soviet Power and Policy,* Thomas V. Crowell Co., 1955, p. 105.

[18] *Plenum,* op. cit., p. 13.

[19] *Narodnoye Khozaystvo,* pp. 71, 369-82, 418-19; *Plenum,* pp. 9, 12-14, 25 27, 71-72.

[20] *Ekonomika,* p. 35; *Narodnoye Khozaystvo,* p. 67.

[21] Hoeffding, O., *Substance and Shadow in the Soviet Seven-Year Plan,* Foreign Affairs, April 1959, p. 404.

[22] *Narodnoye Khozaystvo,* p. 357.

[23] *Plenum,* p. 79.

[24] *Plenum,* p. 73.

[25] *Narodnoye Khozaystvo,* pp. 447-48, 451-53, 455.

[26] Karnoukhova, E. S., *Kolkhoznoye Proizvodstvo v Gody Otechestvennoy Voyny,* .Moscow, 1947, pp. 49-50.

[27] *Izvestia,* September 13, 1953.

[28] *Plenum,* p. 31.

[29] Khrushchev's speech to the Communist Party Session held on January 25-31, 1955.

[30] Embassy of the USSR, *Press Department,* No. 71, Washington, D. C., February 8, 1960.

[31] *Planovoye Khozaystvo,* No. 4, 1959, p. 46. (Hereafter referred to as *Planovoye*)

[32] *Ekonomika,* p. 68.

[33] *Planovoye,* p. 48, and *Ekonomika,* p. 35.

[34] *Sotsialisticheskoye Sel'skoye Khozaystvo,* April 1942, p. 3.

[35] Zotov, V. P., *Pischevaya Promyshlennost Sovetskogo Soyuza,* Moscow, 1958, pp. 26, 194.

[36] *Plenum,* p. 429.

[37] *Ibid.,* p. 62.

[38] *Narodnoye Khozaystvo,* p. 468.

[39] Zotov, V. P., *op. cit.,* p. 27.

[40] *Zasedaniya Verkhovnogo Soveta SSSR,* Chetvertogo, Sozyva (devyataya sessiya), December 19-21, 1957, Moscow, 1958, p. 27.

[41] *Narodnoye Khozaystvo,* pp. 65, 306-07, 467; Embassy of the USSR, No. 37, March 6, 1959 and No. 71, February 8, 1960; *Kontrol'nye Tsifry Razvitiya Narodnogo Khozaystva SSSR na 1959-1965 Gody,* Moscow, 1958, p. 52.

[42] *Izvestia,* March 18, 1959.

[43] *Planovoye,* pp. 44-45.

[44] *Plenum,* p. 445.

[45] Ioffe, Ya., *Ob Osnovnoy Ekonomicheskoy Zadache Sovetskogo Soyuza,* Moscow, 1956, p. 37.

[46] *Narodnoye Khozaystvo,* p. 108; Grigor'ev, A. E., *Ekonomika Truda,* Moscow, 1959, pp. 77-78.

[47] *Plenum,* p. 72.

# CHAPTER 9

# Monetary and Fiscal Policies

~~~~~~~~~~~~~~~~~~~~~~~~~~~~~~~~~~~~~~~~~~~

## INTRODUCTION

Basically, monetary policy consists of the expansion and contraction of the volume of money in circulation to match the volume of goods and services available on the consumers' market. The object of this policy is the maintenance of a balanced economy and the Soviets are using monetary policy for the planning of employment and as a stabilizing tool in an expanding economy. It also facilitates the planning and control of the volume of consumers' saving, the rational production of enterprises, and the allocation of money among territorial sectors.

Fiscal policy is the tax and government financial system. It determines the amount of tax and levy revenues and the volume and direction of central government expenditures for specific objectives such as the maintenance of a certain level of consumers' incomes and purchasing power, or an expansion in the production of guns instead of butter. As with monetary policy, fiscal policy is closely associated with overall planned development of the economy. The instruments of fiscal policy include the multitude of direct or indirect taxes which are or may be levied; they are flexible, and include the detailed features of all the taxation mechanism such as inclusions and exclusions, exemptions, particular, progressive, proportional, and regressive rates. It includes all the modes and procedures of government spending and subsidies.

From the viewpoint of classical communism, both policies are not desirable or necessary. However, the Soviets claim that they are still in the transitional stage from socialism to communism, during which money, prices, credits, and banks are needed because they facilitate production and exchange functions in the socialized and non-socialized sectors alike. Thus in general money performs many of the same functions in the USSR as it does in the United States. It is a medium of exchange representing purchasing power, used in transactions between different enterprises and with foreign countries and as a measure of productivity.

The Soviets have accepted the indispensible role of money in the planned economy. Along with other devices, money simplifies the integration and coordination functions of the many different parts of the complex production and distribution mechanism of the Soviet Union. But the Russians were not as sophisticated in this area at the beginning of the present regime as they are now.

At the beginning of their power, the Soviets were apologetic about the existence of money, and plans were made to wipe it out entirely in the forthcoming communist state. And while Soviet leaders planned to abolish money, runaway inflation infected the country. The value of the ruble declined, prices soared, and the printing presses turned out a flood of paper money which further contributed to the velocity of the spiral. Only the revival and rapid growth of production and trade during the New Economic Policy (NEP) made it possible to stop inflation and to stabilize currency through monetary and credit reforms. It was the fear of another "galloping" inflation after Warld War II which caused the Soviets to hasten the 1947 devaluation of the ruble and to wrest hoarded money away from the people.

At the beginning of the Soviet regime, monetary and fiscal policies were not considered as major regulators of economic stability and normal development of the country. Originally it was thought that direct physical planning and controls would be sufficient. However, with the rapid growth and increasing complexity of the Soviet economy, it was extremely difficult to control through physical devices alone. As a result, the Soviets, along with physical production and distribution plans, also use monetary-fiscal plans, each supplementing the other.

The main objective of Soviet fiscal policy is to collect excessive income from the people. Because it is not sufficiently flexible as a tool to control the money market, its dependence upon a monetary policy logically follows. Money is useful in the socialized sector of the economy because it serves as an indicator of industrial progress, efficiency, and as a basis for calculating reductions in production costs. Money allocated to the nonsocialized sector equals wages and all welfare payments, and is a much smaller percentage of the gross national product (GNP) than in the United States. This topic will be more fully examined later.

Capital formation in the USSR is fully controlled by the government through direct and indirect means in every sector of the economy. About 96 per cent of the national revenue is derived from the activities of state-operated enterprises and establishments. The more important sources of government revenue are the turnover tax and the profits of state enterprises, together comprising over 65 per cent. Part of the profits and savings of enterprises are invested directly and are not shown in government revenue, but they are an important part of the capital formation plans. Direct taxes on the non-socialized sectors of the Soviet economy consist of income taxes, fines, licenses, and so on. They are used as methods of regulating consumer supply and demand as well as sources of revenue.

The role of money is increasing in importance in the Soviet Union. The 1959-65 plan emphasizes the so-called "control by ruble," or the efficient utilization of investments in production of goods and services and in reduction of the cost of production. Moreover, the Soviets hesitantly are beginning to consider pushing the ruble on the world money market, where the Soviets hope it would compete with the dollar's leadership. Whether the ruble would become a truly international currency is hardly a question for serious consideration at this time. Nevertheless, this thought shows the growing importance of money as an economic tool in the Soviet Union.

## MONETARY REFORMS

With the fall of the Tsarist empire in March 1917 the Kerensky government was established, and Tsarist rubles were replaced by new notes printed in the United States. Then the Bolsheviks replaced the Kerensky government, and the Civil War broke out. During the Civil War, the Bolshevik government and almost every warlord of the White Russian movement printed their own paper money. The value of the ruble depreciated, often hourly, and the barter system became the major measure of the value of exchange.

Under so-called War Communism, which lasted until 1921, market relationships virtually disappeared and foodstuffs were requisitioned forcibly from the peasants, often without payment. The peasants, unable to purchase the goods they needed and reluctant to accept Soviet worthless money, reduced their output, which stimulated inflation still further. During this period the volume of currency in circulation increased from 28 billion rubles in January 1918 to 1,169 billion rubles on January 1921, and the price index rose from 1 in 1913 to 21 in January 1918 and jumped to 16,800 in January 1921.[1]

To combat this astronomical inflation, the Soviets devaluated the ruble in 1921, and again in 1922. In 1921, because of peasant opposition to War Communism, Lenin instituted the New Economic Policy (NEP) as a tranquilizer for the capitalist elements, under whom revival and rapid growth of production and trading took place. The NEP lasted until 1924. But even as production in the countryside and in the cities increased, inflationary forces were difficult to control. Between January 1921 and March 1924 the volume of currency in circulation increased from 1,169 billion rubles to 809,625,217 billion rubles; the 1913 price index rose from 16,800 to 61,902,000,000.[2] As one would expect, during the 1918-24 period the government operated with enormous deficits.

In their frantic attempts to stabilize the ruble the Soviets in October 1922 authorized the State Bank (Gosbank) to issue a new unit of currency, the "chervonets," which was equal to ten Tsarist gold rubles. But the Treasury still continued to issue paper money, the "sovznak," the value of which was still declining. The chervonets was not a legal tender, and was used only in transactions where gold payments were required by law; the sovznak served as "change" money since the country was short of small currency notes and coins.

The issuance of the chervonets was backed by 25 per cent of the value in gold and foreign currencies and the remaining 75 per cent by short-term notes and by easily marketable goods. To increase its gold reserves and foreign currency the government intensified foreign sales, and as a result increased its volume from 10.9 million rubles on January 1, 1923, to 153.6 million rubles on February 1, 1924.[3] Despite the increase in gold reserves, they were still but nine per cent of the Tsarist reserves in 1914. Nevertheless, the rate of exchange of the chervonets throughout its existence until 1930 was remarkably stable, holding at $1.94 to $1.95, or having approximately the same rate of exchange as the Tsarist ruble.

The year 1924 was the end of Soviet monetary reform and inflation. New Treasury notes of one, three, and five ruble denominations were issued in 1924 and printing of the sovznak was discontinued. Silver and copper coins were increased in circulation, and the sovznak issued in 1923 was redeemed by new Treasury notes on the basis of 50,000 rubles for one new gold-supported ruble. Along with monetary reforms, the Soviets in the 1930-32 period revamped their credit institutions. Thus, by 1936 State budgetary deficits were ended, the ruble was stabilized, control of credits was strengthened, prices were leveled off, and rationing was abolished. Many of these reforms were made early in the 1930-34 period, when the Western world was fighting a depression.

After the shaky economy was somewhat stabilized, the foreign exchange rates of the new ruble underwent adjustment, too. During this period the ruble was valued in terms of the French franc. In April 1933 the exchange rate was 13.15 francs to one ruble and by April 1936 this rate had changed to three francs to one ruble. Then, because of the devaluation of the franc in November of the same year the value of the ruble increased to 4.25 francs. Consequently, as a result of the general valuation of foreign currencies, the official gold content of the ruble was reduced from 0.774234 gram of pure gold in 1933 to 0.176850 gram in 1936, and in July 1937 it became 0.167674 gram.[4] As an aftermath of devaluation of the ruble and the instability of the French franc, the ruble was linked to the American dollar in June 1937 at the official rate of exchange of 5.30 rubles to one dollar.

The next monetary reform occurred in 1947 as a direct impact of World War II. Disregarding the destruction of physical property caused by the war, direct military expenditures during the war amounted to 551 billion rubles in prewar prices. Immediately after the German attack on the USSR, government expenditures sharply arose, while receipts drastically declined. By the end of 1942, revenue from turnover taxes dropped 38 per cent from the 1940 level and profits from state-operated enterprises was reduced by 29 per cent. A wide gap was created between revenues and expenditures, with the deficit covered mainly by printing additional paper money and, to some degree, by reserves. Thus, during the first three war years, the volume of paper money in circulation increased 2.4 times.[5] The scarcity of consumer goods, especially foodstuffs, caused collective farm market prices to rise ten to 15 times above the 1940 level. Since the shelves in the state stores often were bare, consumers had to pay exorbitant prices on the collective farm market. Workers were receiving so-called "bread" subsidies, which were insufficient, and forced them to supplement their meager rationings at the collective farm markets.

World War II inflation was not as tremendous as it was during the 1918-24 period, when retail prices rose many thousands of times. Unlike the early period, the Soviets had control over wages, and over prices in state stores. Nevertheless, the Soviets feared that the 1941-47 inflation might lead to disequilibrium in economic and political spheres as it did before, and they launched a vigorous movement to curb it.

On December 14, 1947 a decree was issued devaluating the ruble, decreasing prices, and abolishing rationing. About six months prior to the devaluation decree, on May 5, 1947, the Soviets announced a state loan amounting to 22.9 billion rubles.[6] And a few days before devaluation, the state internal lottery loan at three per cent was announced. Those who watched the Soviet press during that period could not have failed to notice the names of prominent Soviet leaders and professors who signed up for large amounts of the 1947 bonds. Undoubtedly many of these people knew about the coming devaluation and hastened to convert their paper money into state bonds. The masses were caught by surprise.

First, the Soviets printed new notes. Those who did not exchange old notes for new ones could not use the old notes at all. Cash on hand was exchanged on the basis of ten old rubles for one new ruble. Savings up to 3,000 rubles were exchanged ruble for ruble. Savings up to 10,000 rubles were exchanged ruble for ruble for the first 3,000 rubles and two new rubles for three old ones for the remainder. Amounts over 10,000 held by individuals were exchanged on the basis of ten old rubles for one new ruble. Deposits of cooperative organizations were redeemed at the rate of five old rubles for four new ones and all the deposits of state enterprises and organizations were exchanged ruble for ruble. The greatest impact of the devaluation was upon the peasants who had hoarded paper money, and collective farms which failed to deposit their funds with banks. It may be added that in large cities where rumors of coming devaluation were heard there was a rash of buying sprees before the deadline. As a result of devaluation of the ruble, its purchasing power by April 1948 increased by 41 per cent, with the wage level remaining unchanged.

In May 1960 the USSR Supreme Soviet adopted a decision to devaluate the ruble again (on January 1, 1961). The law is intended to raise the value of the ruble, to increase the gold content of it, and to revise the price level tenfold. By increasing the value of the ruble tenfold, the Soviets will reduce all wholesale and retail prices tenfold simultaneously. The exchange of old money to new units will be effected at the ten to one ratio—one new ruble for ten old rubles—without restriction as to the amount of cash on hand or of savings, during the first three months of 1961, during which time both the old and new currency will be in circulation.

Along with these actions, wage levels, pensions, grants and all other forms of income received from the State will be recalculated accordingly to the 10:1 ratio. Simultaneously, the exchange rate of the ruble with regard to foreign currency will also be changed on the same basis.

It is claimed by the Soviets that the expected 1961 devaluation of the ruble will have no impact on the economy at all. It certainly should reduce the cost of printing a large amount of cheap money as now in circulation, and it would stabilize the ruble by bringing its official value closer to the American dollar. At the same time it would have an impact on the value of currency of the Soviet bloc countries, which would also be forced to devaluate their own currency. The proposed devaluation of the ruble seems to have stemmed from the expanding industrial output rather than from any economic weakness of the USSR.

Since 1937 the exchange rate of the ruble has been based on the value of the American dollar. On May 1, 1950, the Soviets increased the official gold content of the ruble to 0.222168 gram of pure gold, and the exchange rate was reduced from 5.30 to four rubles per American dollar. At the same time the price of gold purchased by the USSR Gosbank was established at 4.45 rubles per gram. Fearing another devaluation of the ruble, people rushed to the stores, causing a mild, short-run inflation, and forcing the government to make an official statement that no further devaluation of the ruble was contemplated. Then on April 1, 1957 the Soviets announced that foreign currency exchange rates for personal, tourist, and non-commercial transactions were to be increased by 150 per cent, although official exchange rates were to remain unchanged. Presumably in January, 1961 the above rates will be adjusted at the 10:1 ratio.

At present the bulk of physical currency is made up of Treasury notes of one, three, and five ruble denominations printed by the USSR Ministry of Finance for the Gosbank. These notes do not require backing by gold since officially they are insured by all the wealth of the USSR. As small bills they are serving as "change" currency. The Gosbank issues bank notes of larger denominations (10, 25, 50 and 100 rubles). The law requires that at least 25 per cent of all new notes printed by the Gosbank must be covered by gold, other precious metals, foreign currency, and short-term credits which can easily be converted into cash. Domestically, both types of notes are legal tender. The main difference between the two kinds of notes is that the Treasury notes serve as a source for short-term credits, while the Gosbank notes support transactions with foreign firms. In addition, the USSR coining house produces nickel coins (10, 15 and 20 kopeks) and bronze coins (1, 2, 3, and 5 kopeks). Silver and copper are no longer coined in the USSR. No changes in denominations are anticipated with the devaluation of the ruble in 1961.

## THE ROLE OF MONEY IN A PLANNED ECONOMY

The role of money in the Soviet Union is similar to its role in other societies, where it is used as a medium of exchange, being something for which every other commodity will be exchanged, except in its conversion to capital goods for private exploitation. Since the Soviets print and distribute the money, its market both for the people and the government is controlled in accordance with planned requirements.

The main purpose of Soviet fiscal policy is to obtain money from the people in order to reinvest it in enterprises, to cover all state expenditures, and to maintain a balance between purchasing power of consumers and availability of goods and services on the market. But even in this endeavor, the fiscal policies must be selective, for they may conflict. Direct taxation in the Soviet Union is not an important source of State revenue. Some measures, such as pension payments, stipends to students, and other social welfare benefits cannot be greatly reduced. For these reasons, certain fiscal measures must of necessity be rigid. Only the turnover tax provides an adequate supply of revenue; but in a planned economy all monetary channels, however insignificant they may be, must be controlled if a balanced budget is to be attained.

Being a tool in a planned economy, money serves as an indicator of the progress of the socialized sector. Supplying money to this sector is a simple matter of bookkeeping in transferring funds. Every enterprise needs capital, not only to pay wages but also to purchase finished or semi-finished goods needed in the normal process of activities. In addition, cash is used for repair work on buildings and equipment, fuel, electric power, water, and amortization.

Aside from its direct function, the amount of money serves as an indicator of efficiency. In some instances the cost of production may be calculated by considering the costs of labor alone. But there are other instances in which one enterprise may be dealing with another and in which the cost of labor is not the primary cost and will not, in itself, show accomplishments of the given enterprise. Consequently, monetary values must be used to determine the costs.

Still another facet of the use of money is its convenience in calculating reduction in the cost of production and in calculating profits. It is true that not all state operations produce profits. The efficiency of educational and health institutions cannot be measured in terms of input alone; but in the production of consumer goods, money coordinates all elements involved in production. And since money is used to determine not only the cost of production but also reduction in the costs, it becomes an important tool in determining the efficiency of the economy as a whole.

In the main, the amount of money allocated to the socialized sector is controlled by state financial plans. Each state enterprise and establishment receives an overall financial plan; many have financial and physical plans supplementing each other. It is clear that a hospital would have a financial plan rather than a plan for physical output. For the country as a whole, the financial plan is an integral part of the overall economic plan. It parallels and is merged with the production and distribution plans. But of necessity, the financial plan is calculated prior to the production plan, because it determines the income and expenditure patterns of all important sectors of the Soviet economy.

The amount of money which is allocated to the non-socialized sector is equivalent to the cost of social welfare, and of goods and services. Wages include the money received by workers digging ditches, salaries of executives, and all other compensation for services rendered. Compensation also involves payments "in kind" to the members of collective farms or to those who have meals at their place of employment. In contrast to the United States, the share of the national income allocated for the use of the people in the Soviet Union is much smaller, because of different taxation measures. In the United States, disregarding the level of living, compensation for production of goods and services is much higher, since individual earners pay many taxes and make contributions from their gross earnings; in the Soviet Union these are already included in the price of any product or service the Russian buys. Even the cost of so-called "free" Soviet medical service is considered in the wage the Russian worker receives.

## BANKING FACILITIES

During the period of War Communism, the Tsarist system of banking and finance was wiped out and a new system was loosely organized. In November 1921 the State Bank of the RSFSR, the Gosbank, was organized; it later became the USSR State Bank. Tasks assigned to the Gosbank were many, but the most important ones dealt with the stabilization of the national accounting system and the development of a new credit system with appropriate measures for safeguarding against misuse of credits by individual borrowers. The Gosbank was empowered to collect money for the government and to regulate the amount and velocity of money within the country. It was intended that the Gosbank would be the only credit agency in the country.

Since a single banking institution could not be effectively geared to supplying the diversified demands of the growing economy, soon many specialized banks were established. The Gosbank became a short-term credit institution, while specialized banks provided long-term credits. All the activities of these banks were coordinated by the Gosbank. Thus, the Gosbank became the "banks' bank."

As the Gosbank gained experience and intensified its financial influence upon the economy, many specialized banks were abolished and their functions were transferred to the Gosbank or to other banking systems. By 1936 only these banks remained: the Indusrial Bank (Prombank), the Agricultural Bank (Sel'khozbank), the Commercial Bank (Torgbank), the

Municipal Bank (Tsekombank), and the Savings Banks. In January 1957 the commercial banks were abolished, and in April 1959 the long-term credit functions of the agricultural, municipal and communal banks were transferred to the Gosbank and the Industrial Bank was renamed the Construction Bank (Stroybank).

## The Gosbank

The Gosbank acts as the government's fiscal agent. It receives all revenues payable to the government and pays out budgetary appropriations to enterprises and institutions having approved budgets. In addition to issuance or withdrawal of money from the money market, the Gosbank performs all the transactions between state-owned enterprises and institutions and maintains accounts of every enterprise having a budget. It is also entrusted with purchases of precious metals and foreign currencies and with settlement of foreign accounts. And, of course, the undivided funds of collective farms are received by the Gosbank.

In August 1954 the role of the Gosbank in control over credits received by enterprises was greatly strengthened, especially in dealing with excessive wage expenditures. It has the power to deny credit to anyone whose wage fund exceeds the planned level or when authorized funds are shifted to unauthorized uses. Since credit plans are calculated on a quarterly basis, at the end of which accounts must be submitted to the Gosbank, misuse of budgetary expenditures is not difficult to detect.

With the formation of sovnarkhozy, the Gosbank underwent a reorganization to fit the new managerial pattern. Many departments which previously served numerous ministries were abolished and new credit departments were formed to provide services and control mechanisms for industries and enterprises under the jurisdiction of sovnarkhozy and local administrations. Along with this, the Gosbank also merged credit facilities serving the state and collective farms, RTS and state procurement programs.

The Gosbank is the largest financial institution in the world. In 1957 it employed 7,728 persons having college degrees in economics in 90 regional offices, plus 4,690 branches throughout the Soviet Union.[7] It maintains correspondence with almost 300 foreign banking institutions located in 60 countries.

Since the Gosbank provides mainly short-term credits at the rate of one to two per cent interest, its capital turnover is rapid. Beginning with May 1957 the Gosbank altered its standing as a short-term credit agency and initiated credits to collective farms for up to one year. During the 1941-45 period the average annual short-term credit total amounted to 311 billion rubles, and in 1956 it was 2,483 billion rubles.[8] But as the volume of credit increased, the indebtedness to the Gosbank also rose from 55 billion rubles on January 1, 1941, to 243.6 billion rubles in January 1957. The major users of short-term credit are the trading establishments which need additional capital to stack their inventories. Next in importance is heavy industry, which uses short-term credit for the replacement of old equipment. The food-processing industry and light industry are also large users of short-term credits. The Gosbank is required to make sure that the credit it has granted is used in accordance with the state physical and financial plans. In general, the Gosbank is the watchdog of the entire financial structure of the USSR.

### Specialized Banks

The specialized banks were under the jurisdiction of the Ministry of Finance. They were long-term credit banks limiting their activities to specialized areas, such as investment in production or installation of new capital goods. They used special cash resources derived either from the savings of individual enterprises or from the USSR budgetary surpluses. Like the Gosbank, specialized banks were required to be vigilant on the right use of granted credits, in accordance with state plans. In addition, they actively participated in the reduction in the cost of production.

Since a greater degree of uncertainty surrounds long-term loans than short-term, many enterprises and organizations were in the past, as they are now, reluctant to use long-term credits. If equipment is purchased today at a high cost, it may be purchased at a lower cost later. The opportunity cost is more important in the long rather than the short run. And although long-term credit is being encouraged by the State, it is far from desired. For example, the largest of all specialized banks in 1952 was the Industrial Bank, now called the Stroybank. On January 1 of that year this bank had 67.4 billion rubles of unused funds that no one wanted to borrow. In 1958 these excess reserves increased to 89.2 billion rubles even though the rate of interest is between one and two per cent annually.

### BUDGETS

The budgetary mechanism is simple enough, and the main channels of income and expenditures are known. But complexity is in the definition and classification of national accounts which are often shifted from one purpose to another.

The USSR budget is composed of about 60,000 accounts, so that every organization operates within known appropriations. There are two main budgets. Upon approval of the USSR budget by the USSR Supreme Soviet, it is divided into two. One becomes the All-Union, or centralized, budget; the other is allocated among the constituent republics, each receiving its budget. The constituent republic in turn holds part of it for its own needs; but most of the allocated funds are assigned to local budgets. The local budgets are for autonomous republics, oblasts, krays, rayons, cities, and village soviets. Each of the above budgets supports its own administration and distributes authorized budgetary appropriations among subordinate enterprises, establishments, and organizations. This is a pyramidical structure, similar to that of other couutries.

The USSR budget is made up annually, and consists of the projected programs of government expenditures and the planned volume of government revenues during that period. All state expenditures are met in the main by taxes paid directly or indirectly by the people. In addition to projected programmed government expenditures and revenues, the budget includes financial activities of banking institutions, international investments, and foreign trade. Although the USSR budget and budgetary practices somewhat resemble those of the United States, there are some fundamental differences in political and economic concepts by which government revenues are collected and spent. The USSR budget covers many budgetary functions which in the United States are performed by private means. These would include investments in plants and factories, education, distribution functions, and the like, which in the USSR are performed by the State.

The basic laws on the budget devised more than 30 years ago were outmoded by the present socio-economic conditions of the USSR and were amended in 1959. The underlying principle of the new budgetary law is the uniformity of budget structure among constituent republics, copied after the budget of the All-Union structure. This provides a greater centralization of funds for specific targets desired by Moscow rather than by the local administration. The new law also provides broader power for the constituent republics in obtaining adequate revenues to meet the financial outlay required for implementing the USSR socio-economic program and their own republican programs as well.

## A. THE USSR BUDGET

National economic policies are formulated by the leaders of the Party. These policies are then spelled out by directives, decrees, and rules which may or may not be publicly announced. Based on planned goals, which in most cases cover a number of years, the financial position of the country is examined. In the light of these targets the USSR budget is made up each year for the calendar year. The groundwork in collecting required information for the budget is delegated to the Ministry of Finance, and begins many months before the final appearance of the budget.

The Ministry of Finance assembles all the necessary data for the proposed USSR budget, which includes tentative budgets of all constituent republics and local budgets. These are preliminary steps in order to see how these will fit in the overall USSR budget, to determine the volume of contributions from the centralized or all-Union budget to republican and local budgets, and the size of potential revenue. At this preliminary stage the Ministry of Finance, without consultation with republican or local authorities, submits its rough budgetary draft to the USSR Gosplan, the USSR Council of Ministers, and the Council of Ministers of each constituent republic.

The USSR Council of Ministers analyzes the budget, including recommendations made by the Gosplan; upon approval by the USSR Council of Ministers it is sent to the Budgetary Committees of the USSR Supreme Soviet and the USSR Soviet of Nationalities, which may make changes. Then the budget is submitted to the USSR Supreme Soviet for final approval by its delegates before it becomes the law of the land and is published.

Since the published budget is condensed, there are many gaps in the channels of revenues and in specific allocations. On the other hand, this leaves the planners a free hand in transferring funds from one account or use to another. On the receiving end of the budget are actual revenues as well as sums which have value only on paper and to bookkeepers, such as amounts representing transfers of funds. Among the expenditures listed are actual expenses and also involuntary and unpaid labor contributions by the Soviet citizens. Among fluid items which are included in the budget are the potential reductions in the cost of production, increased labor productivity, and all the funds in the banks and in other state-controlled organizations. Thus, as a whole, the USSR budget is made up of a number of items, and the actual values of some are difficult, if not impossible, to estimate. How these items are priced by the Russians is not known, but directly or indirectly they are included in the budget just the same.

TABLE 1—Total Industrial Investments in the USSR [9]

(in billion rubles)

| | 1951-55 (average) | | | 1956 | | | 1957 | | | 1958 | | |
|---|---|---|---|---|---|---|---|---|---|---|---|---|
| | Total | USSR Budget | By Enterprises | Total | USSR Budget | By Enterprises | Total | USSR Budget | By Enterprises | Total | USSR Budget | By Enterprises |
| Total: ———— | 293.6 | 197.6 | 96.0 | 355.3 | 245.2 | 110.1 | 387.8 | 256.3 | 131.5 | 412.9 | 257.2 | 155.7 |
| Production and construction | 152.7 | 91.1 | 61.6 | 201.2 | 128.2 | 73.0 | 208.9 | 125.9 | 83.0 | 226.0 | 129.0 | 97.0 |
| Agriculture and forestry —— | 49.6 | 41.0 | 8.6 | 57.1 | 49.1 | 8.0 | 58.7 | 49.7 | 9.0 | 65.2 | 53.4 | 11.8 |
| Transportation and communication ———— | 34.1 | 16.8 | 17.3 | 40.6 | 21.6 | 19.0 | 37.8 | 18.8 | 19.0 | 32.2 | 14.4 | 17.8 |
| Commerce ————— | 2.1 | 0.7 | 1.4 | 2.4 | 1.2 | 1.2 | 4.4 | 0.6 | 3.8 | 5.4 | 0.6 | 4.8 |
| Others ————— | 55.1 | 48.0 | 7.1 | 54.0 | 45.1 | 8.9 | 78.0 | 61.3 | 16.7 | 84.1 | 59.8 | 24.3 |

## BUDGETARY RECEIPTS

Financial investments in Soviet industry are derived from two major sources. The prime source is the USSR budget; the other source is the part of the total profit, real or potential, accumulated by enterprises and organizations, amortization, and other sources. In addition, the reserves of the USSR Council of Ministers, the Council of Ministers of constituent republics, and the long-term loans from specialized banks are used for industrial investment. In 1958 the USSR Council of Ministers held 16.7 billion rubles in reserves and three billion rubles were allocated for long-term credit; in 1950 this source is anticipated to be 21.8 billion rubles.

Table 1 (p. 248) shows an interesting development in USSR industrial growth. In 1958 the total industrial investment in comparison with the 1951-55 average increased by 40 per cent. A similar increase prevails in production and construction. Investment in agriculture and forestry increased by only 32 per cent, even though by 1958 the Soviets considerably enlarged their sowed acreage. Investment in commerce more than doubled, but investment in transportation and communication was reduced by some 12 per cent.

Another interesting point is the investment from the USSR budget.

TABLE 2—*The National Budgetary Revenues of the USSR* [10]
*(in billion rubles)*

| Account | 1940 | 1950 | 1956 | 1957 | 1958 | 1959 (Approved) |
|---|---|---|---|---|---|---|
| Total: _____ | 180.2 | 422.8 | 585.9 | 626.9 | 672.3 | 723.3 |
| Turnover tax ____ | 105.9 | 236.1 | 258.6 | 277.3 | 304.5 | 332.4 |
| Profit from enterprises _____ | 21.7 | 40.4 | 102.9 | 116.0 | 135.4 | 154.9 |
| Income tax _____ | 9.4 | 35.8 | 50.5 | 53.2 | 51.9 | 56.0 |
| State loans and lottery _____ | 9.0 | 26.4 | 32.8 | 18.4 | 3.2 | 10.0 |
| Saving deposits ___ | 0.2 | 3.1 | 10.0 | 14.0 | 6.5 | 13.4 |
| State insurance____ | 8.6 | 19.6 | 28.3 | 31.0 | 33.1 | 36.0 |
| Taxes, non-socialized sector____ | 3.2 | 5.5 | 14.1 | 15.5 | 16.6 | 21.7 |
| Revenue from MTS (RMS) ____ | 2.0 | 3.6 | 10.6 | 13.9 | 9.7 | 0.5 |
| Other revenues____ | 20.2 | 52.3 | 78.1 | 87.6 | 113.4 | 98.4 |

Average contribution during the 1951-55 period was 63 per cent, just as it was in 1958. In 1958 the USSR budget allocated 57 per cent to production and construction against 60 per cent during the 1951-55 period.

Budgetary investment in agriculture and forestry remained practically unchanged at 82-83 per cent. In 1958 transportation and communication received 45 per cent from the USSR budget against 49 per cent in 1951-55. Investment in commerce for 1958 amounted to only 11 per cent against 33 per cent in 1951-55. In general, excluding commerce, the Soviet investment policy during the 1951-55 period and in 1958 was remarkably stable, but expanding nevertheless.

TABLE 3—*The National Budgetary Expenditures of the USSR* [10]
(*in billion rubles*)

| Account | 1940 | 1950 | 1956 | 1957 | 1958 | 1959 (Approved) |
|---|---|---|---|---|---|---|
| Total: _____ | 174.4 | 413.2 | 563.5 | 607.3 | 642.7 | 707.6 |
| *Industrial sector*: _____ | 58.4 | 157.9 | 245.2 | 256.3 | 290.3 | 308.9 |
| a. Production and construction _____ | 28.6 | 79.2 | 128.2 | 125.9 | 145.1 | 162.1 |
| b. Agriculture and forestry _____ | 12.6 | 33.9 | 49.1 | 49.7 | 58.0 | 30.3 |
| c. Transportation and communication ____ | 8.2 | 16.9 | 21.6 | 18.8 | 17.4 | 25.0 |
| d. Commerce and procurement _____ | 2.0 | 10.1 | 18.6 | 27.3 | 32.0 | 32.7 |
| e. Others _____ | 7.0 | 17.8 | 27.7 | 34.6 | 37.8 | 58.8 |
| *Social services*: _____ | 40.9 | 116.7 | 164.4 | 188.4 | 214.2 | 232.0 |
| a. Education _____ | 22.5 | 56.9 | 73.6 | 79.0 | 86.0 | 94.3 |
| b. Health and physical education _____ | 9.0 | 21.4 | 35.7 | 38.0 | 41.2 | 44.0 |
| c. Social insurance _____ | 5.0 | 12.7 | 18.6 | 19.3 | 24.4 | 20.7 |
| d. Social welfare _____ | 3.2 | 22.1 | 31.5 | 60.1 | 57.3 | 67.3 |
| e. Subsidies to destitute mothers _____ | 1.2 | 3.6 | 5.0 | 5.2 | 5.3 | 5.5 |
| *National security* _____ | 56.8 | 82.8 | 97.3 | 96.7 | 93.6 | 96.1 |
| *Government apparatus* _____ | 6.8 | 13.9 | 12.1 | 11.9 | 12.0 | 11.5 |
| *Loan expenditures* _____ | 2.8 | 5.1 | 16.3 | 11.0 | 3.7 | — |
| *Others* _____ | 8.7 | 36.8 | 28.2 | 62.6 | 56.4 | 59.1 |
| Budgetary surpluses _____ | 5.8 | 9.6 | 22.4 | 19.6 | 29.6 | 15.7 |

As tables 2 and 3 show, between 1940 and 1959 the Soviet budgetary revenues and expenditures underwent a fourfold increase. The fulfilment of the 1959 budget will depend upon the tempo of economic development in the current Seven-Year Plan. The bulk of the Soviet revenue comes from the so-called socialized sector, that is, through state-owned enterprises and organizations. In 1940 this sector supplied 95 per cent of the total budgetary revenue. During World War II and in the postwar period the contribution of the so-called non-socialized sector (i.e., direct income tax, consumers' savings deposits, state loans, etc.) has increased from five. per cent in 1940 to 17 per cent in 1950; in 1959 its contribution was about ten per cent. This distinction between the two sectors is more of a convenience for propaganda purposes because all channels of revenue in the USSR are state controlled.

The most important source of revenue is the turnover tax which in 1940 made up 59 per cent of the total budgetary receipts. In 1950 it was 56 per cent and in 1959 it is anticipated to be 46 per cent. Next in importance is profit from enterprises and organizations which in 1940 amounted to 12 per cent of the total revenue and ten per cent in 1950. With the rehabilitated and expanded economy in 1956 its share became 17 per cent and the 1959 target is set at 21 per cent. These two sources accounted for 71 per cent of the total Soviet budgetary revenues in 1940; this figure may be reduced to 67 per cent in 1959.

The preliminary 1960 State budget is made up of total revenues in the sum of 773 billion rubles, and total expenditures of 745.8 billion rubles, the revenues exceeding expenditures by 27.2 billion rubles.

## Turnover Tax

The turnover tax was established in 1930 at the time when Soviet industry, unable to support itself, needed additional investments for further expansion. Although many leading Marxists at the time regarded sales and excise taxes as an inequitable burden on low-income groups, the Soviet government of necessity accepted the concept of turnover tax as the main instrument in raising revenues and in controlling the purchasing power of the people. Since the volume of profits from state-owned enterprises and organizations was inadequate, and a direct income tax was not politically desirable, the Soviets were forced to adopt indirect taxation. But heavy turnover tax favors the higher-income groups over the lower-income groups. Moreover, as an anti-inflationary measure, either direct or indirect taxes could be used with similar success.

Turnover tax is collected by wholesale distributing organizations, individual enterprises, and procurement organizations dealing in consumer goods and foodstuffs. Prior to 1957, about 57 per cent of the total amount of turnover tax was derived from enterprises and procurement organizations and 43 per cent from wholesale distributors. With the formation of sovnarkhozy, however, many Soviet writers recommended a new policy in shifting the responsibility for collection of turnover tax to individual enterprises.

The purpose of turnover tax is to provide funds for state-wide investments and to sap the purchasing power of the people. Since individual consumers are not allowed to own capital goods, most of these goods do not carry turnover tax at all. But every item produced for the consumers' market has a turnover tax rate. For example, the footwear industry produces 1,443 different items for identical purposes, yet each item has a different turnover tax rate. In synthetic fabrics, the rate of taxation ranges from 16 to 83 per cent. Often the same article has different rates because of the flexibility of its supply in different regions. With such a fluid system, the Soviets are able to control purchasing power, to push certain goods on the market while retarding the sale of others, and by so doing, to control the so-called consumers' "choice."

As Table 2 shows, between 1950 and 1956 turnover taxes increased by 22.5 billion rubles, whereas profit from enterprises leaped by 62.5 billion rubles. This was the period of socio-economic change which witnessed plowing of the virgin and unused lands, reduction in prices, lowering in agricultural taxation, and similar measures devised to stimulate enthusiasm of the workers for greater output. But these adjustments came late in the period; then the growth of turnover taxes slowed down. To overcome this loss, the Soviets, beginning with January 1, 1956, introduced the tax on trucks and busses and other durable goods previously sold untaxed.[11] As a result of this and other increases, the amount of turnover taxes between 1956 and 1959 is expected to be boosted by 73.8 billion rubles, while profit from enterprises and organizations increases by only 52 billion rubles.

### Profit from Enterprise

Tables 1 and 2 show that in 1956 state enterprises retained 7.2 billion rubles for their own use; in 1958 they retained 24.4 billion rubles, or an increase of more than three times. Part of this increase was due to increased efficiency, but most of it came through expansion and modernization of facilities. It may be added that allowing greater authority to management was also a contributing factor in increased efficiency.

With the formation of sovnarkhozy a larger share of the net profit received by an enterprise was permitted to remain there. This increased economic power in the hands of local administration created new problems for the Soviets. It not only reduced the state revenue but also provided management with flexibility in decision-making, which often may run counter to the wishes of centralized authority. To curb this power, a new turnover tax on goods which previously were purchased tax-free is now assessed. This is the result of a new policy (khozrazchet) under which every enterprise must cover its costs and show a profit. As a result, beginning with 1956, turnover taxes began to rise.

## Income Tax

Direct taxation in 1940 amounted to about five per cent of the total revenue; in 1959 it is expected to rise to eight per cent. The Soviet income tax system is progressive in structure: the more one makes, the more one pays. It ranges from a minimum of 0.15 per cent to a maximum of 13 per cent of monthly earnings, withheld by the enterprises. Direct taxation is closely associated with the planned growth of the national wage fund payable by the State and including other incomes received by consumers. In an effort to stimulate production, the Soviets were forced to increase incomes as the surest way to greater output. This created disequilibrium in earnings among various groups and triggered the rise of the new elite society comprised of artists, writers, high officials, managers of enterprises, educators, scientists, and others. Although a wage and salary reform undertaken by Khrushchev a few years ago to reduce the wide gap between the highest and lowest earnings is still in the making, it will not eliminate all inequalities in earnings received for different talents.

Khrushchev, in his Party Congress speech on January 27, 1959, promised to end direct taxation in the next few years. This is his follow-up in wage and taxation reforms which started with a reduction in income taxes for the peasants in 1953, followed by the abolishment of forced state loans in 1957 and elimination of taxation on single persons and small families in 1958. As a result, the 1953 collection of income tax was 1.3 billion rubles less than in 1957. However, the 1959 income tax revenue was expected to be 4.1 billion rubles more than in 1958. It is claimed by the Soviets that the 1959 increase will reflect higher profits by the peasants, and also greater participation in the labor force.

The declaration to abolish direct taxation is of considerable propaganda effect, both in the Soviet Union and abroad. While it is quite possible that collection of these taxes is costly, direct taxation cannot be ended without replacement by other revenues such as the turnover tax or profit from enterprises.

Theoretically, there should not be any taxes at all in the USSR. The State fixes incomes and prices to equal supplies on the market and the spread between costs and prices can be large enough to satisfy the needs for investment and for public services. If direct taxation is to be abolished, it would bring greater benefit to the new Soviet "aristocracy" receiving high incomes rather than to the low-income groups. Khrushchev is no doubt aware of this; and taxation of the high-income group may take a different form. Along with this, many Soviet writers recommended establishment of some kind of a control over inheritance. There is no inheritance tax in the USSR, and since the end of the war large inheritances are appearing more frequently. Abolishment of direct income tax without some other form of taxation would increase inheritances, would be inflationary in nature, and would not remedy the problem of unequal income distribution.

## State Loans and Lottery

State loans were introduced at the beginning of industrialization in 1928 as an additional source of revenue for development of the economy. They were forced loans, collected as a percentage of individuals' incomes through a subscription quota. It was as compulsory as taxes. From the beginning until World War II the Soviets received 50 billion rubles from state loan drives. During the war these drives were intensified and amounted to 76 billion rubles covering about 15 per cent of all military expenditures. The postwar recovery and rehabilitation period was even more forceful in the collection of state loans. During the 1946-50 period state loans amounted to 133 billion rubles; during the 1951-55 period another 137 billion rubles were collected. From 1928 to 1958 state loan contributions to the USSR budgetary expenditures amounted to nearly 350 billion rubles.

But as state loan bonds began to mature, interest payments on them rapidly increased. Between 1937 and 1957 the State paid about 260 billion rubles in interest and it was estimated that by 1967 these payments would equal receipts. As a result, in April 1957 the Soviets stopped interest payments on state bonds and through its moratorium decree postponed repayment on principal for the next 20 to 25 years. The issuance of state loan bonds was abandoned.

With the abolishment of state loans, the Soviets in May 1957 established another money-making scheme, a 12 billion ruble state lottery. This is a straight lottery—a much better scheme than loan bonds for there is no obligation to repay the money and the government stands to make a clear profit of 60 per cent.

But by abolishing state loans by a stroke of the pen, the government also angered and frightened the public. In 1958 the combined income from state loans and lottery amounted to 3.2 billion rubles, of which 2.6 billion rubles came from previously purchased and pledged loans. Reactions of anger, fear, and hesitancy on the part of the public because of lost investments in bonds and the new scheme are temporary. Since a lottery has greater gambling appeal than the old bonds, the new money-making scheme undoubtedly will be successful and more profitable for the government.

## Savings

Savings deposits are encouraged by the government and are used as a weapon for combating shortages of consumer goods and as a source of additional revenue. The total savings deposits increased from 7.3 billion rubles in 1941 to 53.7 billion rubles in 1956, and in 1959 are expected to be 94.2 billion rubles.[12]

As Table 2 shows, the greatest saving deposits were made in 1957 when state loans ended. During 1958 the public deposited seven billion rubles of their savings but the State siphoned 6.5 billion rubles to its budget. This suggests that many deposits are of a long tenure. The expected new savings for 1959 are estimated at 7.2 billion rubles and the contribution of savings balances to the 1959 budget is calculated at 13.4 billion rubles.

In 1959 there were 58,600 savings banks in the USSR with 47 million accounts. They pay an interest rate of two per cent on current accounts and three per cent on time deposit accounts; there is no limit on the size of deposits. The average deposit at the beginning of 1959 was about 1,850 rubles. But there are large savings deposits which yield a considerable amount of so-called "unearned" income. This presents a paradox: on one hand the Soviets enshrined the motto that "he who does not work, neither shall he eat," but on the other hand the constitution protects "the personal property right of citizens in their income and savings from work."

In theory, all citizens must work. But suppose he who has saved a large sum of money, say 500,000 rubles, and deposited it with a savings bank can earn between 10,000 and 15,000 rubles a year, about double the average Soviet wage, without any work at all? Suppose he dies and his money is inherited by his only child? With such an unearned income the legatee can live without working. This is the real problem creating social, economic, and political inequality in the State which proclaims the equality of all, except in regard to earnings and opportunity to live on unearned income.

## State Insurance

State insurance is another money-making scheme. Originally devised for collective farms and cooperative organizations, state insurance now extends to the life and property of individuals.

The collective farms are required to insure their crops, livestock, and other farm property. The cooperatives insure their own property. Individual citizens insure their possessions such as homes and furniture, and also take life insurance to supplement the state social payments. In 1957 almost ten million persons had life and accident insurance policies.

The profitability of this undertaking is real indeed. In 1957, payments for state insurance contributed 31 billion rubles to the USSR budget whereas payments to policyholders amounted to two billion rubles to the collective farms and some 600 million rubles to individual citizens, a total of 2.6 billion rubles or about eight per cent of the total contribution. In 1958, the state insurance fund contributed 33 billion rubles to the USSR budget but paid out only three billion rubles.

With the formation of sovnarkhozy, state insurance was transferred to the jurisdiction of the constituent republics. Since most collective farms hold some kind of insurance, the present emphasis is to expand insurance coverage to individuals. It is expected that local authorities could do a better job than the old centralized insurance administration. Potentially this source of state income could be greatly expanded since only about five per cent of the total Soviet population have individual coverage.

## Taxation of Non-Socialized Sector

The non-socialized sector is mainly represented by collective farms and cooperative organizations. A small tax revenue is also derived from independent entrepreneurs, but their contribution to the USSR budgetary income is negligible.

Between 1951 and 1957 the collective farms paid flexible rates on their gross profits. Flexibility of rates depended upon income sources. A six per cent tax was levied on all products that a collective farm used for its own needs, such as seeds, fodder for livestock, and for the establishment of funds. A 12 per cent tax was assessed on the volume of commodities distributed among members of collective farms for their labor contributions. In both cases the tax was calculated on the basis of the cost of production.

In addition, collective farms paid income tax on cash received. A nine per cent tax rate on cash received from contractual sales to the government and a 15 per cent tax was attached on the cash received from sales made on the collective farm markets.

This system was designed to encourage maximum deliveries to the State, but since collective farm markets paid higher prices, the government competed with it by reducing taxation. The system was crude and provided an opportunity for juggling of collective farm accounts in an effort to reduce taxation payments. Besides, the government did not like the idea of competing with prices in the free market.

Along with streamlining agriculture, all of these rates were abolished by a decree of September 1957 and replaced by a uniform rate of 14 per cent to become effective January 1, 1958. Taxation was calculated on the basis of net cash income received from the sale of commodities either to the State or on the collective farm market. It is not clear what basis was used to calculate net cash income for commodities left on the farm and distributed among members. Comparing rates existing before and after January 1, 1958, it is obvious that the new rate was unfavorable for the collective farms, and reduced their incomes at the time when they needed more cash to pay for farm machinery.

To provide greater incentives for collective farms, the 14 per cent rate was reduced in 1959 to 12:5 per cent. It is expected that the new rate will create enough profit for collective farms to expand their economics, to provide additional income among their members, and to induce them to devote greater efforts to socialized farming. Even with the reduced tax rate of 1959 the Soviets anticipate a larger collection because of higher income left on the farm. It is also interesting that although the 1958 harvest was good, the high rate of taxation did not produce large revenue for the State.

Cooperatives, either producers' or consumers', pay income tax on the basis of net cash profit. Producers' cooperatives pay a tax of 20 per cent of income provided that their net profit does not represent over five per cent on the investment. If their net profit is higher than five per cent, the taxation rate might go as high as 90 per cent of the total net profit. Since consumers' cooperatives do not show flexibility in profit, as the producers' cooperatives do, their rate of taxation is a straight 25 per cent of the total profit.

The members of collective farms pay tax for the use of their individual plots on the basis of area possessed, disregarding the volume of income obtained from it. The land tax was lowered in 1953 along with the reduction in norm deliveries to the State. In 1951-52 this source produced ten billion rubles of revenue; in 1954-56 it was reduced to four billion rubles. Presumably the 1959 revenue will be similar to the 1954-56 level.

## BUDGETARY EXPENDITURES

As has been previously stated, the total investments in the Soviet economy come from budgetary expenditures and also from profits reinvested by enterprises and organizations, credits from the banks, and emergency funds of the USSR Council of Ministers.

Budgetary expenditures of the USSR represent the bulk of all state investments. These may be broken down into four major categories: industrial investments, consumption, national security, and administration. These four broad accounts represent 92 to 95 per cent of the total budgetary expenditures and represent the Soviet gross national product (GNP).

Table 3 shows that between 1940 and 1959 total state expenditures increased fourfold. The greatest increase occurred in production and services, both being increased over fivefold. National security increased by about 85 per cent and administration expenditures by 70 per cent. Categories lumped in the "others" classification increased by 6.8 times. One of the major categories in others is the net foreign investment, but this will be discussed in Chapter 17. The industrial sector represents national investment and consumption accounts. Consumption is also included in the social service account.

### Production and Construction

Investment in production in the USSR rose from 33.5 per cent of the total budgetary expenditures in 1940 to 43.6 per cent in 1959. It is hardly necessary to mention that in the Soviet Union public investments are the prime source. As can be expected, capital goods and construction industries are the major consumers of budgetary funds. In 1940 they received about 16 per cent of the total budget, and 20 per cent in 1959. The Soviet government concentrates on growth-inducing investments in areas that constitute the bases of economic power—manufacturing, mining, metal processing, public utilities, and the like. For example, in 1959 the chemical industry, which currently gets special attention, was allocated 71 per cent more funds than in 1958; machine-building 33 per cent; ferrous metallurgy 32 per cent; and petroleum and natural gas industries 23 per cent. It is also true that in 1959 about 25 per cent of the total investment in production and construction was appropriated for the enterprises under All-Union jurisdiction and the other 75 per cent to enterprises administered by sovnarkhozy.

Heavy industry and machine building are increasingly taking a greater share of total budgetary expenditures. In 1956 they received about 17 per cent of the total budget, as against 11 per cent in 1940. The construction industry in 1940 as in 1956 was allocated the same share of the total budget—three per cent. Although investments in heavy industry and machine building have considerably increased, priority is given to the construction industry. Housing construction in 1958 was granted about 37 billion rubles, six per cent of the total budgetary expenditures. In addition, in 1958 another 3.2 billion rubles in credits became available to individual home builders.

Since abolition of MTS, investments in agriculture and forestry are on a decline and only the state farms still continue to be a major recipient of budgetary funds. The collective farms provide their own investments. In 1959 budgetary investments in state farms amounted to 14 billion rubles; another eight billion rubles were allocated from the budgets of constituent republics. But as agricultural investment declined in 1959, revenues from farm machinery purchased from MTS by collective farms increased. Although investments in transportation, communication, commerce, and procurement have been increased more than fivefold during the 1940-59 period, their percentage of the total state expenditures has remained practically unchanged.

Other categories of investments are too numerous to mention. Among them are various semi-public organizations such as those for maintenance of small airports for training of non-military personnel, maintenance of highways, and so on. However small this investment was in 1940, by 1959 it increased by better than eight times and represents eight per cent of the total budgetary expenditures.

## Social Services

These are consumption categories in the Soviet GNP and they have been gradually increased as the total population of the USSR has grown. As in other consumption categories, investments in social services come from the USSR budget and from budgets of the constituent republics. Needless to say, since the USSR Supreme Soviet approves both budgets they are a part of the same source but transferred to the republics for administrative purposes. For example, in 1940 about 25 per cent of the total investments in education came from the All-Union budget; the other 75 per cent came from budgets of the constituent republics. In 1957 All-Union investments amounted to about 86 per cent.

Investment in education includes the cost not only of maintaining schools and students but also of constructing new schools and providing salaries for teaching personnel. The annual per capita educational expenditure for 1959 in the Soviet Union is about 450 rubles.

The largest share of Soviet educational investment in 1959, amounting to 50.5 billion rublies, (53 per cent of the total), is devoted to general education and training of children and teen-agers. Maintenance of kindergartens and nurseries in 1959 took 9.4 billion rubles. Between 1958 and 1959 investments in these two categories rose by 900 million rubles. Of course, increase in investment includes construction of new kindergartens, nursery homes, summer camps, and so on. The maintenance of higher educational institutions takes about 23 per cent of total educational expenditures; vocational schools take seven per cent.

Educational investments also include scientific research, propaganda, and development programs. This allocation cuts across all major categories of budgetary investments. The real investments in it are difficult to estimate, not because of Soviet secrecy alone but because the boundaries of "research and development" are so fluid that correct and consistent statistics are hard to find. In 1957 total investment in research and development amounted to 13.9 billion rubles of which 11.7 billion rubles came from the USSR budget.[13] In 1958 it was increased to 23.9 billion rubles, of which 15 billion rubles came from the budget. In 1959 the expenditure in research and development was set at 27.3 billion rubles which includes a budgetary investment of 23.1 billion rubles.[14]

Health and physical education expenditures cover outlays for medical and hospital care, construction of new medical establishments, training of medical personnel, research, funerals, and similar services. These combined expenditures in 1959 represented six per cent of total budgetary expenditures. Although the social insurance fund is included in the USSR budget, its distribution is entrusted to the trade unions. In 1940 as well as in 1959 this category represented 2.9 per cent of the total Soviet expenditures.

Social welfare and subsidies as a whole represented 2.5 per cent of the total budget in 1940, and 10.3 per cent in 1959. As a result of a decree issued in 1956 the Soviet pension law was streamlined, low-paid pensioners received larger payments, with a minimum of 300 rubles per month, and high-priced pensions were reduced to a maximum 1,200 rubles per month. Thus beginning with 1957 social welfare benefits almost doubled as compared with 1956 and as the Soviet population rapidly grows older, the need for expenditures for the old-age group increases. Out of the total expenditure of 67.5 billion rubles in 1959, benefits for temporarily disabled persons were estimated at 11.2 billion rubles or about 16.6 per cent of the total social welfare fund.

## National Security

This category covers all aspects of national security. It covers Soviet overt and covert military outlays; and it should be understood that these expenditures represent inputs rather than outputs. This account represents the destructive power of the USSR, which includes pay and maintenance of military personnel, hardware, operational expenditures, food, and so on. Although the armament industry is the most efficient among Soviet industries, Soviet lower military personnel receive quite a modest pay as compared to American standards. In other words, the Soviet military machine requires fewer resources to produce the same destructive power as its American counterpart.

Military investments in the USSR are considered as a total loss in regard to natural resources and human efforts because military goods do not increase the country's wealth and cannot be consumed as consumer goods. Nevertheless, the 1959 budgetary expenditures for national security as compared with 1940 were increased by 39.3 billion rubles. True, though the share of military expenditures to the total budget was reduced from 32.6 per cent in 1940 to 13.6 per cent in 1959 and there was a gradual reduction in actual outlays, the Soviet Union still maintains a larger Armed Force than the United States.

Military decisions of any country are not subject to any market mechanism, competitive or otherwise. They are made administratively under conditions where today's targets often have little to do with yesterday's. Moreover, the incommensurability of military inputs and outputs, as well as the difficulty of comparing various outputs, makes it almost impossible to arrive at valid tests in regard to efficient decision-making. What seems to be happening in the Soviet Union (and one may only guess) is that the Soviets are replacing their military manpower with mechanized and electronic destructive weapons requiring less manpower. Certainly Soviet leaders would not reduce their military manpower if they expected a war or if there were no cheaper yet more effectively destructive weapons.

Apparently the Soviets reached the point of safety in reduction of military personnel in 1958. Between 1956 and 1958 military manpower was reduced by 2.1 million men, whereas expenditures decreased by 3.7 billion rubles. Assuming that the 1956-58 reduction in military expenditures was caused solely by reduction in manpower, then there was a saving of some 1,760 rubles for each demobilized man. However, in 1958 the Soviets announced a reduction of 300,000 men and military expenditures were cut by 3.1 billion rubles or at the rate of some 10,300 rubles per man. Obviously, along with the reduction of manpower, other cuts were made within the Soviet war machine.

### Administration

Government expeditures are minor in size. In 1940 they represented about four per cent of the total USSR budgetary spending, only 1.6 per cent in 1959. Although they are a minor item, they are important for domestic propaganda and as an endless conversation topic.

Between 1940 and 1959 the cost of administration increased by 4.7 billion rubles. This rise is due to an expanding administrative apparatus and also to increases in salaries and wages. The postwar inflation and mushrooming of administrative organs in 1950 resulted in doubling its cost. Reduction in administrative staffs started in 1953 and is still continuing. Between 1950 and 1959 a reduction of 2.4 billion rubles took place. It is claimed that in 1956 alone personnel in administrative branches of the government, enterprises, and other organizations was reduced by 200,000 persons, saving 1.7 billion rubles.

### Surpluses

The budgetary surpluses represent the difference between the total receipts and expenditures and form a cushion for decision-making, dependent upon the size of the national budget. It is interesting to note, however, that with the reorganization in taxation and social services systems prior to 1957 there was a drop of 2.8 billion rubles in surpluses in 1957. Then again, with decentralization of industrial management and the abolishment of MTS along with other socio-economic adjustments, 1959 surpluses are expected to be 15.7 billion rubles or a drop of 13.9 billion rubles in a single year. The 1959 surpluses amount to about two per cent of the total expenditures.

The 1959 surpluses would have been still smaller if the USSR Supreme Soviet did not increase the receipts for the USSR budget. Upon recommendations of the Budget Committees, the USSR Supreme Soviet increased the total USSR budgetary receipts by 696 million rubles, of which 592 million rubles were to come from increased rates in the turnover tax, 44.5 million rubles from profits of enterprises, and another 59.5 million rubles from other sources.

## B. THE BUDGET OF THE CONSTITUENT REPUBLICS

Establishment of budgets for each constituent republic and for local administrations is authorized by Article 14 of the USSR Constitution of 1936. Prior to 1956 the USSR Supreme Soviet authorized budgets for constituent republics and local administrations. Beginning with the transfer of many small-scale local enterprises to jurisdiction of the constituent republics in 1956, the USSR Supreme Soviet included local appropriations with those of the constituent republics. By this act the old practices of spelling out minute and specific expenditures for the local administrations was ended. In turn, republics gained a greater flexibility in using their appropriations. As of now, a broad classification of expenditures is decreed for constituent republics. These categories are the production sector, social services, and administration. No funds are appropriated for national security, since this category is in the hands of the central government.

Upon receiving its budget, the constituent republic allocates it among its recipients on a quarterly basis in order to maintain financial control over individual sectors and to control expenditures of individual establishments under it jurisdiction. Appropriated funds for the use of a given branch of industry or even a large enterprise are then deposited with the USSR Gosbank. Along with this, funds from the USSR budget assigned for the same recipent are also deposited with the USSR Gosbank. Thus a large-scale enterprise might have two accounts, each for a definite purpose, which cannot be used for any unspecified expenditures. It is here where the USSR Gosbank becomes so powerful in controlling expenditures of an enterprise by periodic checking of accounts of enterprises.

Now that the center of gravity in the management of Soviet enterprises has shifted to sovnarkhozy and constituent republics, budgets of constituent republics have considerably increased. These increases come from revenues collected by republics from their own population and industries but which only the authority of the USSR Supreme Soviet can permit them to retain. For example, in 1957 the percentage of turnover taxes which constituent republics were allowed to keep ranged from 9.7 to 73.9 per cent of the total collection. In 1958 this range was from 23.6 to 100 per cent and in 1959 it was 17.6 to 100 per cent. Whereas retention of income tax receipts by republics in 1957 was a straight 25 per cent, in 1958 and 1959 it was increased to 50 per cent. The retention of agricultural tax was 75 per cent of the total receipts in 1957 and 100 per cent in 1958 and 1959. The share of the 1958-59 savings deposits accumulated by republics was permitted to remain there at 50 per cent of the total deposits. The whole system by which budgets of the constituent republics are authroized is flexible and, depending upon interests of the centralized planners, monetary and fiscal policies are adjusted to meet targets.

As Table 4 shows, beginning with 1957 the importance of constituent republics in the USSR budgetary expenditures has rapidly increased. In

1958 better than 50 per cent of Soviet GNP was allocated to accounts of the constituent republics. Now, since the centralized government of the USSR has control over all major sources of revenue, the constituent republics, except in minor cases, do not have their own revenue, and whatever revenue they obtain must be turned over to the centralized government.

TABLE 4—*Budgets of thhe Constituent Republics of the USSR* [15]
(*billion rubles*)

| Year | Total | Per cent of Budgetary Expenditures of the USSR |
|---|---|---|
| 1940 | 42.1 | 24.1 |
| 1950 | 95.9 | 23.2 |
| 1956 | 139.6 | 24.8 |
| 1957 | 194.1 | 32.0 |
| 1958 | 319.7 | 50.1 |
| 1959  (approved) | 343.5 | 48.5 |

In a sense, the constituent republics represent administrative organs in distribution of the GNP for the centralized government. Moreover, the centralized government with 50 per cent of the total investment funds at its disposal maintains a pretty firm hold on local authorities.

### Bibliography—Chapter 9

[1] Schwartz, Harry, *Russia's Soviet Economy,* 2d Edition, Prentice-Hall, 1954, p. 471.

[2] *Ibid.*

[3] *Denezhnoye Obrashcheniye i Kredit SSSR,* Moscow, 1957, p. 50.

[4] *Ibid.,* p. 117.

[5] *Ibid.,* p. 121-22.

[6] *Gosudarstvenuyy Zaymy v SSSR,* Moscow, 1956.

[7] *Gosudarstvennyy Bank SSSR,* Moscow, 1957, pp. 44, 48.

[8] *Ibid.,* p. 62.

[9] Allakhverdiyan, D. A., *Ekonomicheskoye Soderzhaniye Raskhodov Sovetskogo Byudzheta,* Moscow, 1958, p. 28. *O Gosudarstvennom Byudzhete SSSR na 1959 God i ob Ispolnenii Gosudarstvennogo Byudzheta za 1957 God,* Moscow, 1959, p. 10.

[10] Allakhverdiyan, *op. cit.,* pp. 28, 49. *O Gosudarstvennom Byudzhete SSSR na 1959 God,* op. cit., pp. 4, 7-8, 9-10, 20, 22-23, 37-38. *Narodnoye Khozaystvo SSSR v 1958 Godu,* Moscow, 1959, pp. 899-900, 905.

[11] Kanter, L. M., *Sebestoimost v Sotsialisticheskoy Promyshlennosti,* Moscow, 1958, p. 253.

[12] *Finansy SSSR,* No. 4, 1957, p. 33 and No. 1, 1959, p. 5. *O Gosudarstvennom Byudzhete SSSR na 1959 God,* op. cit., p. 9.

[13] Allakhverdiyan, *op. cit.,* p. 48.

[14] *O Gosudarstvennom Byudzhete SSSR na 1959 God,* op. cit., p. 23.

[15] *Ibid.,* p. 38.

# CHAPTER 10

# Wage Determination and Incentives

## INTRODUCTION

The Soviets have often said that human labor is not a commodity which can be bought and sold on the market; nevertheless, the wages and salaries paid to Soviet workers are essentially the prices paid for their services. Except for members of collective farms and a few other minor groups, Soviet workers are employed solely by the State, which buys the services of millions of workers in a buyer's monopolistic market.

The State, as monopolist, owns the natural resources but not the talents of the people. Since workers have different skills the question of equalization of wages was never considered as a solution in distribution of gross national income among all the workers on equal bases. True, since the early days of their power, the Soviets have emphasized the concept of equality, but it was equality of opportunity rather than equality of income. In 1921 Lenin himself laid the rule that materialistic interests of the workers must be stimulated in order that greater national output may be obtained. When the total of all the goods and services produced by the whole country is increased, only then can wages also be increased. Even in the early days of the Bolshevik regime highly skilled and trained workers such as physicians and engineers received higher wages than janitors or watchmen.

Equalization of wages was strongly attacked by Stalin, and he emphasized the "worth" of the worker in production rather than his "needs." Although the Soviets do not officially accept the theory of marginal productivity of labor, it is nevertheless being generally used as a means of controlling the wage-price relationship. The present leadership is also against wage equalization as such, emphasizing the so-called "fringe" benefits of all workers rather than those in industry only.

The wage system of the Soviet Union was formulated by Lenin who, in an effort to increase production of goods and services, adopted differential payments. The white collar and supervisory workers in administration, education, health, and so on were basically salaried personnel. Only the industrial workers benefited from differential payments. And with improvement in technology and in skills of the workers new types of incentives were devised; finally the system became a monstrosity under which workers were more interested in incentive payments than in basic wage scales.

The whole incentive system became cumbersome and confusing; its original aim was lost in misuse of its principle. In 1956 the average share of the basic wage for piecework represented 40 to 55 per cent of the total earnings, and the share for time work was 65 to 75 per cent.[1] Reform of the system started in January 1957; the share of basic wage payments for piece rate workers was set at 70 to 75 per cent of their total earnings and at 80 to 85 per cent for the time rate workers. Any further increases in workers' earnings are anticipated in the form of basic wage payments rather than in additional incentives. Although the system has been improved it is still far from perfect. It cannot be perfect or completely equalized as long as the Soviets have different wage policies for industrial workers, for the so-called "unproductive" white collar sector, and for collectivized peasants.

The 1957 reform was caused by a widespread misuse of the piece rate payments received by about 50 per cent of the total state employed workers. Yet the principle of piece rate is still being employed and justified on the basis that it pursue its aim of determining the relation between incomes but not the size of it. That is, since the basic wage scales are more or less uniform throughout the country and represent the minimum wage level, the size of earnings depends on the worker's productivity. The more he produces, the larger share of the gross national income he is entitled to. This policy, of course, penalizes all unproductive workers and fails to equalize the earning opportunities for many Soviet citizens.

## PRODUCTION NORMS

Basically the norm of production represents a unit of time necessary to produce a given unit of a commodity or to perform a specific operation with a given set of tools or skill. This facilitates the planning of labor requirements for a given industry and for the country as a whole. It helps to estimate labor productivity, to establish the so-called "wage fund" from which workers receive their wages, and to balance the volume of goods and services on the market with that of workers' expenditures. Therefore, the norm of production is one of the major tools in the planning mechanism, and serves as a regulator in the wage system of the Soviet Union.

Karl Marx, and his early followers as well, considered only one kind of utility: form utility. They regarded productive activities as only those which lead to the physical creation of goods. Consequently, there are many kinds of human activities which the Soviets classify as so-called "unproductive," although they recognize them as useful and necessary. Lacking the theoretical understanding of the function of labor in general, the Soviet economists even now debate whether passenger train porters are productive or unproductive.

Such unrealistic classification of workers creates many conflicting problems. With many workers engaged in unproductive activities, any enterprise may calculate its norms of production per man by excluding unproductive workers. This may show high labor productivity per worker, but at the same time the total cost of production per unit of output may be high. Similarly, there are many methods of production which are extremely wasteful of both human and natural resources. The fact that some other method of production might be more efficient does not imply that a particular method or activity is unproductive. It is merely inefficient.

In the light of these statements it would be helpful to keep in mind that production norms in the Soviet Union may be, and often are, calculated on several bases which depend on the type of goods produced and the purpose of such norms. In the cement industry the output for different grades of cement is estimated on the basis of an investment, say one million rubles, for each kind of cement. The norm of production is then established on the basis of the efficiency of equipment at each cement plant and the availability of labor required to reach the planned output. However, there are technical limitations requiring a fixed amount of labor per unit of output. In the baking industry, half a pound of flour, let us say, is required for making a pound of bread. It is this simple physical "input-output" relationship which was adopted during the early Red regime.

This physical input-output relationship was used in the calculation of norms of production per worker during the First Five-Year Plan, simply because the Soviets did not have the necessary data to establish other measures of productivity. But with expanding industrial production and with complex mechanization the norms of production could no longer be based on the physical input-output principle. Since the scarcity of productive resources varied considerably from enterprise to enterprise, the physical input-output principle became valueless, and a new set of measures had to be devised for determining whether an enterprise was profitable and how to correct the bottlenecks created by the misuse of available resources.

Later, with the planning mechanism firmly established, the norms of production were linked to other factors measuring the worker's contribution to the national income, the availability of goods and services on the market, and his purchasing power. In this way, production of goods and services was at least theoretically linked to the cost of production, wages, and prices. But these adjustments came only in 1932, when official norms of production were established for the first time for industry and agriculture. Moreover, since the socialized economy was still young and operating on two separate levels—one for the socialized sector and another for collective farming—a great flexibility in norms was permitted. As a result, the Soviets were faced with the problem of society paying the cost for inefficiency as greater volumes of goods were produced.

### Industry

As was stated above, prior to 1932 only a rough input-output relationship was used to determine norms of production. But as the Gosplan accumulated more statistical material on labor productivity the Soviets were able to see more clearly what the average norms of production should be. Consequently, beginning with the Second Five-Year Plan, firmer norms of production were established which were tied in to the input of labor per unit of output in homogeneous occupations.

However, by 1935 these norms became obsolete with the spread of the "Stakhanovite" movement. Alexei Stakhanov, a coal miner in a mine with abundant resources and with good equipment, by dividing tasks among his three-man team during the night of August 30, 1935, was able to produce a record output of 102 metric tons of coal. This output was many times the average tonnage produced by other miners. His achievements were well publicized throughout the country, and soon other miners and industrial workers began to produce greater output. The principle of piece rate, previously denounced as capitalist exploitation of workers, thus became a part of the socialized economy.

To induce workers to increase their productivity a variety of incentives, both monetary and social, were devised in 1936. The basic wage rates were still in effect, but the practice of paying a piece rate in addition to the basic wage was widely adopted in industry. These payments were calculated for work exceeding planned output and varied with the quality and quantity of goods produced.

One must realize that increased productivity was not achieved through greater physical effort of workers alone. By this time industry had more and better machinery, and newly trained workers had joined the ranks of the industrial labor force. These factors influenced the frequent upward revision of work norms between 1936 and the beginning of World War II. On the other hand, upward revisions of work norms per worker demanded greater efforts from those who were not in possession of efficient equipment or were not in a position to reorganize their factors of production for larger output. Their maximum effort was required to produce even the minimum required norms. Bitterness of these workers against the Stakhanovites increased, and sabotage occurred frequently.

Since the beginning of the Second Five-Year Plan the Soviets have had three norms of production for overall planning. The first and highest norm was calculated on the experience of the most efficient workers in any given plant. This was used for propaganda purposes as an example of what could be achieved when the proper combination of factors of production and the will of the workers was present.

The second norm was called "the average-progressive" norm and was calculated on an average based on production records for the most efficient plants—the upper half of all enterprises within a specific industry. Such norms were used in annual and five-year production directives for industry, agriculture, transportation, and construction. They were used in planned increases in labor productivity in all enterprises, and included such items as potential reductions in cost of production, waste of materials and labor, and other indicators of efficiency. It is because of these high planned work norms that so many plants in the lower bracket of the efficiency scale constantly failed to fulfill their planned targets.

The third norm of production was the so-called "experimental-statistical." This was a special-purpose norm devised for plants and industries without previous experience in production, for old plants producing new commodities, for plants in new locations, or where new and untested equipment was installed. There was not time limit for the use of this norm by the enterprise. In the absence of data on efficiency and productivity, these norms were considerably lower than the average-progressive norms, yet many plants were continuously using experimental-statistical work norms just because a small amount of new machinery was installed or some minor new product was produced. The divergence between these last two norms was great. For example, in 1955 the Kharkov Machine Tool Plant, using experimental-statistical work norms, fulfilled its average production by 190 per cent, where as the same output calculated on the basis of average-progressive norms represented only 86 per cent of the planned output.[2] In this example the average-progressive norms were twice as high as the experimental-statistical ones.

The experimental-statistical norms are important both to the workers and to management in regard to overfulfillment of required production quotas. By having low work norms workers not only fulfill their required norms more easily but also receive extra payments for the amount produced above required norms. Management was able to attract the best workers and to stabilize its labor force by offering larger gross income to the workers. Many plants deliberately lower work norms to provide greater differences between the established basic wage levels and the actual incomes which their workers earn for additional output. But larger earnings are only a part of a worker's consideration. By having a job at a plant with lower norms the worker can fulfill his norm in a shorter period of time and take time off the job if he wishes.

The experimental-statistical norms, despite governmental objections, were used by many enterprises. For example, in 1956, over 50 per cent of all industrial enterprises in the Sverdlovsk Oblast were using these norms, and in some enterprises they represented 60 to 80 per cent of all the norms employed to determine the earnings of the workers.

Theoretically, the norm of production must be "progressive" in the sense that any additional dose of technology or increased skill of the workers would tend to increase labor productivity and thus would call for a new and higher norm. However, norms also must be low enough to be applicable to the masses of workers in the country. Since labor productivity depends on many factors, the state-established progressive norms can be too high for some enterprises or below the actual productivity for others. For example, the Stalingrad and Kharkov Tractor plants have similar machinery and equipment for producing the same type of tractors. Nevertheless, in 1953 the Kharkov plant spent 2.4 per cent less for labor per tractor than the Stalingrad plant. Labor productivity at the Kharkov plant was ten per cent higher, the cost of production was ten per cent below that of the Stalingrad plant, and waste in materials was 41 per cent less.[3]

However, it should be remembered that damage to many plants during World War II was considerable. Though rehabilitation of many industries and regions was rapid, it was not fast enough to permit equalization in efficiency, even by 1953. Postwar investments and allocations of manpower and materials were conducted under imperfect conditions, causing many production maladjustments. Nevertheless, in their efforts to boost industrial production norms, the Soviets invested 26 billion rubles in new machinery and equipment annually during the 1950-55 period.[4] As investments in mechanization increased, the average output per worker was considerably increased.

As Table 1 shows, metal-processing industries in 1950, disregarding the increased cost of production, had recovered their prewar annual production per worker. On the other hand, production of coal per worker for the country as a whole and for some individual coal basins was below the 1940

TABLE 1—*Annual Average Production per Worker* [5]

| Industry | Unit | 1940 | 1950 | 1955 | 1958 |
|---|---|---|---|---|---|
| Pig iron per blast furnace worker____ | Tons | 1,061 | 1,416 | 2,169 | 2,518 |
| Steel per open hearth worker ____ | Tons | 524 | 747 | 1,048 | 1,133 |
| Rolled ferrous metal products, excluding pipes and forging from ingots__ | Tons | 226 | 274 | 354 | 391 |
| Cement _____ | Tons | 224 | 273 | 504 | 632 |
| Coal for USSR: _____ | Tons | 367 | 361 | 454 | 484 |
| Eastern Siberia _____ | Tons | 619 | 571 | 924 | 1,294 |
| Urals _____ | Tons | 527 | 527 | 733 | 880 |
| Karaganda basin _____ | Tons | 527 | 485 | 749 | 974 |
| Kuznetsk basin _____ | Tons | 517 | 436 | 560 | 641 |
| Far East _____ | Tons | 415 | 482 | 581 | 689 |
| Moscow basin _____ | Tons | 389 | 422 | 504 | 541 |
| Donets basin _____ | Tons | 313 | 272 | 310 | 357 |
| Central Asia _____ | Tons | 266 | 288 | 418 | 543 |
| Georgia _____ | Tons | 269 | 290 | 410 | 455 |
| Petroleum _____ | Per cent | 100 | 82 | 131 | 198 |
| Electric power _____ | Per cent | 100 | 132 | 195 | 267 |
| Chemicals, including minerals-chemicals _____ | Per cent | 100 | 179 | 284 | 351 |
| Machine building _____ | Per cent | 100 | 90 | 109 | 141 |
| Timber at point of origin _____ | Per cent | 100 | 90 | 109 | 141 |
| Light industry, gross per worker ____ | Per cent | 100 | 122 | 165 | 186 |
| Food industry, gross per worker ____ | Per cent | 100 | 97 | 131 | 151 |

level. In the petroleum industry, because of obsolete and worn-out equipment, output per worker in 1950 was 18 per cent below that of 1940. In the timber industry the average production per worker in 1950 was ten per cent below prewar norms, and in the food industry it was three per cent.

With improvement in technology during the period between 1950 and 1958, annual production per man in all industries listed in Table 1 was increased. Even the sluggish timber industry was able to improve. It also might be added that as output per worker increased, the cost of production declined; but not in a direct relationship to the increase in output per man. Higher prices for raw materials and capital goods as well as higher wages were responsible for this gap.

The trouble with establishing norms of production is found not so much in the principle as in the bureaucratic approach to the problem. With technological advances, new tasks appear and older ones become obsolete. Any change in administrative or organizational arrangements calls for new terminology, and new jobs have to be defined—a time-consuming operation. In 1956 for only six operations in the metal-working industry there were definitions of 6,000 different tasks, covering about 10,000 pages.[6] Since a worker may at one time or another perform several tasks, calculation of his earnings becomes a complex and costly procedure. Moreover, today's task may be differently defined tomorrow or not defined at all.

Even after the 1957 reform, complexity in norms was very much in evidence. For instance, in 1957 the metallurigcal plant "Serp i Molot" had about 43,000 different norms of production for which different payments were made. The accounting job was so enormous that the plant was forced to organize a special branch to do the job. This of course increased the cost of production and reduced the plant's profits.[7]

Khrushchev inherited the methodology in determination of working norms. The original planners excluded the impact of technological advances upon productivity of labor. The methodology was devised by Lenin; Khrushchev cannot criticize him for his lack of vision, as he criticized Stalin. This means that whatever improvement in the system can be made must come through a slow process, one which does not pull Lenin from his pedestal. Khrushchev had already begun the process with the 1957 reform; further adjustments in that direction can be expected. Technological advances and the skill of the workers cannot be kept static even for Lenin's sake.

### Agriculture

The industrial worker's production norm and his earnings can be measured in monetary units and related to the gross national income. Monetary units are also used in establishing work norms for state farms, since they are state-controlled enterprises.

As a rule, collectivized peasants have two sources of income: one from work on collective farms and another from their own small private plots of land. Consequently, production norms, and therefore peasants' earnings on the collective farms, represent only a part of their efforts and earnings. And unlike the industrial worker, who receives his wage in terms of cash, the peasant on the collective farm is paid in cash and in kind, both calculated in terms of labor days at the end of the farming season.

The whole problem of work norms on collective farms may be reduced to a few major issues: (1) the considerable underemployment of the peasants, (2) the annual fluctuation in the cost of production, (3) the attempted adjustment of wages to the cost of living rather than to marginal productivity of farm labor, (4) misuse and inefficiency of manpower and farm equipment, (5) bureaucracy in the management of collective farms. All of these factors are related to each other in the determination of production norms on collective farms. Perhaps underemployment is the most important problem and should be considered as voluntary underemployment. Since earnings from work on collective farms are low in comparison with industrial earnings, the peasants reduce their participation in communal work. It is this reluctance to participate more fully in farm work which the Soviets are attempting to overcome by additional incentives, revision in work norms, and other economic stimuli in order to achieve the 1959-65 targets set for agriculture.

Determination of work norms for members of collective farms is even more complex than for industrial workers. Theoretical considerations of input-output values are loosely included, as well as differences in other factors associated with performance of the task. But instead of measuring the norms in monetary units, they are measured in terms of the so-called "labor days" concept which was developed in 1928.

A labor day, as described in Chapter 7, represents the unit of human effort plus other factors of production required for the accomplishment of a given task within a given period of time. Needless to say, the value of a labor day depends upon the skill and efficiency of the worker and his equipment. But the labor day is not a measure of working time, since the number of labor days is often not related to production. For example, a peasant might spend a considerable amount of time and effort in planting and cultivating a given crop. Because of a drought, his efforts might fail to yield the harvest. Still he must be paid in order to survive, even though the value of the labor day in such a case might be reduced to a minimum. Therefore, the labor day cannot be used as a measure of labor productivity.

Because of the peculiarity of the agricultural industry, with so many uncontrolled factors influencing production from year to year, many Soviet economists advocate abandonment of labor days and adoption of the concept of "man-days." A modest experiment has already started in this direction, which is deemed by some Soviet economists to be a more accurate measure of labor productivity. No doubt in the near future calculation of work norms on collective farms will take a new form. In the meantime, the labor day is still used to measure the peasant's earnings.

In the industrial sector work norms are established by the government. On the collective farms, as was noted, they are fixed, with broad State guidance, by the general meeting of the members. In a sense the peasants have a wider flexibility than industrial workers in determining how hard or how long they should work at any one task to receive a certain number of labor days. Since the number of labor days for any task is set by the government, the general meeting is empowered to set the norm of work only. To protect their own interests the peasants often increase the time required to accomplish a certain task in order to obtain a larger number of labor days. It is this flexibility in time which causes the difference in the payment for labor days for similar tasks among different collective farms. To illustrate, in 1955 three collective farms paid a different number of labor days for every four tons of manure moved from the barn to the field, located at similar distances. These payments were 1.25 labor days in one case. 2.55 labor days in another case, and 3.25 labor days in still another case. Similar differential payments exist in other farm activities.

In an attempt to equalize the wide spread in payments for the same task, many collective farms adopted a new procedure requiring each able-bodied member to put in 25 working days per month. If he fails to show up 25 times a month or if he does not fulfill the work norm assigned to him, his payments are reduced and he loses his right to three weeks paid vacation. For reporting 25 times a month for work and for fulfilling his work norms the peasant receives three rubles per day in advance with final settlement at the end of the season. By showing up between 15 and 25 times his cash advance is reduced to 2.15 rubles per day; for less than 15 working days the cash advance is only 1.50 rubles per day. In addition, for failure to report 25 times a month for work the collective farm charges the worker 15 rubles per month per head of cattle when he uses pasture belonging to the collective farm. In a sense, therefore, the new procedure penalizes those peasants who do not wish or are unable to work the prescribed time and fulfill the norms.

The problem of determining the work norm per member of collective farms is closely connected with the merging of collective farms which started in 1950. As small collective farms were pooled into larger units, means of production per farm worker were greatly increased and unnecessary costly activities were eliminated. As a result, participation of the peasants in work on collective farms increased considerably, and the income of individual members was also increased. Since the greatest part of the member's income is now derived from work on the collective farm, and since other members of the peasant household contribute to the household's income by working on the collective farm at one time or another, the calculation of the work norm and income received per household would be a better economic unit to consider than the income per member. There are members of collective farms who are too old or disabled to participate at all in farm work, and there are minors and temporarily disabled adults who work only part time. Moreover, the average size of the peasant household for the country as a whole cannot vary greatly from region to region.

In 1958, the average able-bodied peasant on a collective farm contributed 342 labor days against 254 in 1940. In 1950, because of confusion created by the merging program and the postwar opportunities for employment elsewhere at higher wages, work participation on collective farms declined by three labor days.[8] Assuming that under normal conditions a full-time farming occupation requires about 270 working days annually, only 1.4 members of a household participated in collective farm work in 1940, 1.6 members in 1950, 1.7 members in 1956, and 1.8 members in 1958.

Norms of production on collective farms are closely associated with prices paid for agricultural commodities by the State. Higher prices bring higher incomes to the peasants and encourage peasants' participation in farm work. However, it does not mean that their efficiency increases. It simply means that they work more often or longer hours in order to yield higher wages.

TABLE 2—*Significant Data on Collective Farms* [9]
(in percentage)

|  | 1940 | 1950 | 1956 | 1958 |
|---|---|---|---|---|
| Gross agricultural output _____ | 100 | 99 | 137 | 153 |
| Number of households _____ | 100 | 110 | 106 | 100 |
| Cash income _____ | 100 | 165 | 457 | 637 |
| Labor productivity _____ | 100 | 99 | 146 | 170 |
| Number of labor days earned _____ | 100 | 99 | 130 | 135 |

As Table 2 shows, norms of production on collective farms depend upon every factor associated with income. Between 1940 and 1958 the gross agricultural output increased by 53 per cent. Most of this increase took place after 1953 when the virgin and unused lands were put to cultivation. True, during the 1950-58 period the number of peasant households declined by ten per cent and to produce an extra 54 per cent of the gross agricultural output the peasants increased work participation in terms of labor days by 36 per cent. Along with this their labor productivity advanced, mainly through improved technology, by 71 per cent, and since prices paid by the government increased cash income was boosted more than sixfold.

In general, the peasants in 1958 increased their work participation. A man receiving two to three labor days per day could earn the minimum in four to five months. No wonder many peasants with overtime pay and bonuses for good work were able to earn over 400 labor days. But this can happen only on efficient collective farms.

As to labor productivity, Russian peasants spend more time in the production of a given unit of output than farmers in the United States. In 1956 it took one man-hour to produce one centner (100 kilograms) of grain in the United States and 7.3 man-hours on the collective farms of the USSR. This great disparity in time results from the lack of small farm machinery on the collective farms plus the time devoted in selection, cleaning, and drying of seed; American farmers in most cases buy their seed from specialized producers.

### INCENTIVES

If wages and working conditions were the same in every industry or occupation, then workers would distribute themselves in such a way that there would be no advantage for them in the selection of their occupation. However, because of differences in occupations, the Soviets adopted an incentive payment to make some difficult jobs more attractive financially than less difficult jobs.

At the beginning of the industrialization drive the problem of incentive payments was simple enough—payments were made for the time spent in production of a given unit of goods and services. But with expanding industrial output and an increasing labor force the incentive payments were rapidly expanded while the basic wage increased sluggishly. New incentives were devised to attract workers to new occupations and to stimulate their productivity.

Generally, piece rates are more popular than any other kind. Piece rates may consist of straight scales, with the same rate paid for any additional output. They may be "progressive"—a worker producing from one to five per cent over his production quota would receive 30 per cent more pay, while for extra output of six or ten per cent he would get 60 per cent or more in income. Premium payments are allowed only when a worker has produced a given volume assigned to him, or for overfulfillment of his quota, or when he has lowered the cost of production or reduced waste in raw materials.

As shown in Table 3, basic piece rates for the workers were well stabilized in 1950 and 1955, representing roughly 60 per cent of the total earnings.

However, progressive piece rates have increased considerably and the proportion of basic time rates in 1955 has declined in importance in comparison with 1940. The proportion of the basic salary payments for engineers and technicians to the total earnings was higher in 1940 than in 1950 and 1955, but these specialists received higher bonuses in 1950 than in 1940 and seniority payments in 1955 accounted for almost seven per cent.

TABLE 3—*Composition of Income for Industrial Workers and Technical Personnel* [10]
(in percentage of total)

| Item | 1940 | 1950 | 1955 |
|---|---|---|---|
| **Workers:** | | | |
| Total: _____ | 100.0 | 100.0 | 100.0 |
| Basic piece rates _____ | 57.9 | 59.4 | 59.5 |
| Basic time rates _____ | 19.9 | 16.3 | 15.6 |
| Paid vacations _____ | 5.4 | 5.8 | 6.3 |
| Premiums for time and piece work _____ | 4.8 | 6.1 | 4.1 |
| Progressive piece rates _____ | 3.3 | 5.2 | 5.5 |
| Seniority payments _____ | 1.2 | 3.1 | 3.7 |
| Overtime payments _____ | 1.2 | 0.3 | 0.2 |
| Cost of services and payments in kind _____ | 0.7 | 0.3 | 0.2 |
| Payments for stoppages and changes in shifts ___ | 0.7 | 0.2 | 0.2 |
| Payments for differential working condtions | 0.5 | 0.3 | 0.4 |
| Other payments _____ | 4.4 | 3.0 | 4.3 |
| **Engineers and technicians:** | | | |
| Total: _____ | 100.0 | 100.0 | 100.0 |
| Basic salaries and payments _____ | 78.3 | 71.0 | 70.0 |
| Seniority payments _____ | — | 4.9 | 6.8 |
| Other payments _____ | 12.0 | 8.3 | 11.0 |

The main point that can be derived from Table 3 is that a greater opportunity wage exists for a worker's efforts than for those of the members of supervisory staffs. It is a complex system, but workers with favorable combinations of factors of production have greater opportunities for expanding their norms of production and enlarging their earnings. Since many industrial plants are being constructed and operated in the eastern parts of the country, workers receive higher earnings simply because they work in sparsely populated regions, where incentives are considerably increasing their earning power.

During the 1940-55 period basic piece rates for industrial workers increased only slightly, but the average cash earnings more than doubled. It was this disparity between the basic piece rates and the actual earnings of many of the workers that forced many industrial enterprises to reduce their work norms in order to provide an additional incentive to their workers and to bring them to the average level of the others. For example, because of various incentives the average coal miner in the USSR received about 200 to 300 rubles more per month than the lumberman who floated logs down the river. Since the log-man has no incentive, as the coal miner does, reduction of his work norm could be the only possible incentive. There are a number of other industries where incentives for greater output are limited, such as shoe manufacturing, tobacco, meat, and baking industries, the outputs of which are limited by physical input-output phenomena.

Moreover, workers with similar skills may be getting different wages. In 1955 a lathe operator of Grade 4 classification in the radio-technical industry received 817 rubles a month, and 839 rubles in the heavy machine-building industry. A Grade 5 lathe operator in the same industries received 930 and 1,092 rubles respectively.[11] Thus, even though workers may be in the same job classification, their wage might be different because of dissimilar working conditions. The metallurgical industry is especially noted for its high wage rates.

TABLE 4—*Types of Incentives Received by One Worker at the Steel Mill "Verkh-Isetsk" Plant in September 1956* [12]

| | |
|---|---|
| Total payment—in rubles: | 2,635.60 |
| Piece rates for production of steel | 1,005.08 |
| Progressive rates for overproducing norm | 295.11 |
| Premium for production of 90 percent of plan | 220.00 |
| Premium for conservation of fuel | 252.00 |
| Premium for uniformity of oven | 345.44 |
| Payment for repair work of oven | 148.00 |
| Payment from "Master's fund" | 275.00 |
| Payment for overtime | 94.87 |

In this table the basic piece rate for this worker represented about 40 per cent of his total earnings. Perphaps this is an unusual case, but the point is that under favorable conditions a worker has an opportunity to earn far above his basic pay.

If this worker were in the Far North or in Eastern Siberia instead of in the Urals, he would have been entitled to additional payments in equalization of real income between geographic regions. As a rule, differential payments are allowed not only because of geographic differences but also for different industries. Coal, metallurgical, and petroleum industries pay higher rates than others.

A worker who signs up to work for three years in the Far North or in Eastern Siberia receives a ten per cent increase in income every six months, but he cannot double it. For instance, if a worker signed up for four years at a basic pay of 1,000 rubles per month, during four years he can increase his earnings by 80 per cent only. His transportation costs are paid by the State. With each year employed there the worker accrues double credit for his experience, pension, and length of service. Thus, by working ten years in Eastern Siberia, he would accumulate 20 years of accreditable experience and 20 years toward retirement. In addition, his vacation is longer than if he were in the European parts of the USSR.

The question of incentives has its drawbacks, too. Assume that two workers, working side by side, make eight pieces of certain parts per shift at the piece rate of four rubles for every finished part. Here each of them would receive 32 rubles per day. Suppose they increased their norms to ten parts per working day; their wage would be increased to 40 rubles a day. Now, one of them develops a method enabling him to produce 16 parts a day. His daily wage becomes 64 rubles while the other man still would receive 40 rubles. If the other man adopts the new method within six months, both men are then producing 16 parts per day each and their piece rate payments would be reduced by 50 per cent or to two rubles and their daily wage would become 32 rubles instead of 40 rubles. To increase their wage they would have to speed up production or to discover a more efficient method of production. It is for this reason that many workers are shy of any rapid increase in output, and they try to reduce their norms, since any increase in efficiency leading to greater output is of a short duration only.

## WAGE STRUCTURE

A complete wage equalization program under which all workers with different talents would receive equal rewards for their efforts has never been seriously considered by Soviet leaders. Wage differentials have always existed among branches of the Soviet economy, as well as among regions and workers. Salaries, wages, additional compensations, and their ranges are directly established by the government as a part of its complex overall economic planning. Wages are not determined by bargaining processes between workers and employers. Only the workers who are signed up for a specific period of time to work in the Far North or in Eastern Siberia have contract agreements with the employing enterprises in which wages and various compensations are spelled out in detail. The rest of the workers are hired without contractual agreements at the prevailing wage scales, which are determined in collaboration with the government and the Central Trade Union Council. They are for a specific time, usually one year. In this way, the central planners are able to estimate the country's total wage bill (wage fund) required for the economy and for each sector in particular. Needless to say, the estimated wage fund is derived from the planned number of workers of various grades and the established rates of payments for each grade plus the cost of additional payments. Wage scales can be changed by the government to meet certain targets, such as the stimulation of production of goods in short supply, rather than in response to direct pressure from workers. For this reason, wage scales might be raised in one or in a number of economic sectors while other sectors keep the wage scales firm.

Within the planning mechanism of the USSR, planned physical output is determined along with planned cost of production. Wage funds are included in the cost of production of each enterprise. During the 1928-29 period, wages and all other additional payments represented 34.3 per cent of the total cost in industrial cost of production. In 1940, as a result of an increase in labor productivity, this percentage was reduced to 22.4 per cent and then to 20.9 per cent in 1955. Excluding the sum for additional payments received by workers in 1955, their basic wage payments represented 19.5 per cent of the total cost of industrial production. Moreover, there are considerable differences among industries in which the basic wage payments vary with the type of products obtained.

TABLE 5—*Percentage of the Basic Wage
in the Total Cost of Production by Industry in 1955* [13]

| Industry | Percentage |
|---|---|
| Total: | 19.5 |
| Sugar refining | 9.1 |
| Textile | 10.2 |
| Ferrous metallurgy | 19.1 |
| Crude oil | 23.5 |
| Machine building | 30.9 |
| Coal mining | 59.0 |

According to Table 5, the cost of labor excluding incentive payments in the coal industry in 1955 represented the greatest bulk of all expenditures in production, whereas in the textile industry, where wages are relatively below those in mining, the labor cost was only ten per cent of the total cost. The percentages in this table represent the size of the wage fund for these industries. Similar wage funds are established for every constituent republic, sovnarkhoz, enterprise, and organization. These wage funds are planned but not necessarily do they include all payments received by the workers.

## Wage Scales

Generally speaking, the wage system of the Soviet Union is organized on principles similar to those of the Civil Service of the United States. All workers are classified in accordance with their education, experience, and longevity by grade and rate of basic payment. Members of collective farms determine their own earnings at the general meeting of the membership under the restrictive policy set by the government. Similar restrictions are provided for the cooperative organizations.

Workers employed by the State are paid on the basis of a general wage schedule consisting of several grades. Each grade represents a wage or salary coefficient of the lowest rate of payment considered as one. Depending upon a worker's qualifications, his wage rate is then established by multiplying the lowest rate (one) by the wage coefficient.

All Soviet workers receive their wages either on the basis of time or piece rates. Time rates are usually lower in the belief that piece rate would provide encouragement for the workers to produce more in order to earn higher wages. This is a paradox. Marx visualized conditions under which social productivity could be increased by the whole society. Lenin, on the other hand, advocated the concept of individual materialistic interests which must be stimulated by a system of incentives, and thus he deviated from Marx and his belief in an increase in the social product through social productivity.

There are three basic component parts in the determination of wage scales: the general wage schedule, the wage coefficient, and wage rates.

1. General Wage Schedule (tarifno-kvalifikatsionnyy spravochnik) is the backbone of the Soviet wage scales. This schedule consists of a detailed description of qualifications and requirements for the successful performance of every job or task within a given sector of an industry. Qualifications include education, skill, training, and experience in handling of machinery, equipment, and instruments; also in selection of raw materials. Requirements cover physical and personal adaptability to perform a given task or an assignment, responsibility in supervision, and so on. In general this schedule covers all functions associated with performing the job, no matter how simple or how complex it may be. The schedule is divided into several broad categories which include similar jobs, such as operation of a lathe, blast furnace, open hearth, and the like, where the task of an individual worker ranges from simple to more complex responsibility.

2. Wage Coefficient (tarifnaya setka) is the basic wage rate for the task performed within any category of related occupations described in the

General Wage Schedule. This coefficient starts with one for the simplest assignment and by multiplying the lowest wage rate by the coefficient, the wage rates for more complex tasks are determined. A coefficient of more than one depends upon the worker's qualifications and establishes the worker's grade.

In general, there are eight different grades which cover 75 per cent of all industrial workers. About 12 per cent of the workers are divided in seven grades, but mining, glass, and a number of branches of the chemical industry have ten to twelve grades. During the First Five-Year Plan the range of wage coefficient varied from 1:3.2 to 1:3.6 and for some heavy work it ranged from one to 4.5. Currently, in the effort to narrow the wide spread in wages the high coefficient has been pulled down to 2.8. However, although the gap between high and low grades has been somewhat diminished, there are still variations within the coefficient which determine the wage of the worker.

Table 6—*Variations in Wage Coefficient* [14]

| Wage grades | I | II | III | IV | V | VI | VII | VIII |
|---|---|---|---|---|---|---|---|---|
| First coefficient _____ | 1.0 | 1.15 | 1.32 | 1.52 | 1.77 | 2.06 | 2.40 | 2.80 |
| Per cent increase ____ | – | 15 | 15 | 15 | 16 | 16 | 16 | 16 |
| Second coefficient _____ | 1.0 | 1.12 | 1.26 | 1.44 | 1.66 | 1.96 | 2.34 | 2.80 |
| Per cent increase ____ | – | 12 | 12 | 14 | 15 | 18 | 19 | 20 |

The above table shows that a worker in the Grade 8 receives a wage 2.8 times more than the worker in the first grade. The Soviets claim that these differentials stimulate workers to improve their skills and to earn greater incomes. Moreover, with this flexible system the government may increase or decrease the coefficient in order to encourage or to discourage the entrance of workers to any one grade.

Among the shortcomings in past wage coefficient structures were too many coefficients. In 1956 industry and transportation maintained about 1,900 different coefficients. The ferrous metallurgy industry had 170 different coefficients, the chemical industry maintained 140, the machine-building industry 152, the shipbuilding industry 100, and the construction industry 83. The Ural Machine Building Plant in 1956 alone had 32 different coefficients. In addition some industries had zone coefficients paying different wages for similar jobs. For instance, the petroleum industry had four such zones and the timber industry three zone coefficients. True, since 1957 there has been an improvement in the system, but rapid advances in technology cause the existing coefficient system to be outdated as soon as the new coefficient is devised by the government.

3. Basic Wage Rate (tarifnaya stavka) is the lowest wage time or piece rate per hour or day. However, the lowest basic wage rates differ among individual enterprises. Highly mechanized industries, mining, and work requiring strenuous physical efforts usually have a higher and wider range in basic wage rates as follows: [15]

a. Time rates under normal working conditions but of different complexity range from 14.0 to 39.2 rubles per day.

b. Piece rates under normal working conditions and time rates for work in mild heat requiring some degree of physical effort pay from 16.45 to 46.06 rubles per day.

c. Piece rates for work in heat or requiring considerable physical effort range from 19.25 to 53.90 rubles daily.

d. Piece rates for work in extreme heat and requiring strenuous physical effort range from 20.44 to 57.26 rubles daily.

## Wages for Technical and Administrative Workers

Persons in administrative and executive positions are paid on a monthly basis, depending on their qualifications and the degree of responsibility attached to the position. Like the manual workers, managerial staffs are divided into a number of grades carrying different basic salaries. However, the number of grades for administrative personnel is smaller and less confusing than for the manual workers.

The director of the enterprise establishes the minimum and maximum salaries for each type of position in order to compensate for qualifications, experience, and the degree of responsibility associated with the position. For example, in 1956 in the building materials industry all enterprises were placed in four groups, and depending upon the volume of their output executive monthly salaries varied from group to group as follows: [16]

|  | Director and Chief Engineer (rubles) | Head of the Department (rubles) |
|---|---|---|
| Group I | 1,400 - 1,600 | 1,000 - 1,200 |
| Group II | 1,200 - 1,400 | 980 - 1,100 |
| Group III | 1,000 - 1,200 | 880 - 1,000 |
| Group IV | 880 - 1,000 | 790 - 980 |

As can be observed from the above table the gap between salaries received by directors and chief engineers in the first and the fourth groups is much greater than among heads of departments. The difference in the basic salaries is due to responsibilities associated with the larger volume of output. Similar grade differentials, but not necessarily of the same magnitude, are established in other industries.

Supervisory personnel of the lower ranks are also paid monthly salaries. Prior to 1955 their incomes were linked to the incomes received by the workers under their supervision. In 1955 salaries of section chiefs in factories were increased by 15 per cent above the wage level of workers under their supervision. All managerial personnel in addition to their salaries receive premiums for overfulfillment of planned production norms and for reduction in the cost of production. Premium payments to these employees are complex because of the variety of functions performed by them in extra production or in the reduction in the cost of production, and each enterprise may have different premium payments.

Between 1940 and 1946, as a stimulant for greater production, premium payments to employees mushroomed to such a degree that basic salaries became meaningless as such. Moreover there was no uniformity in premium payments, creating confusion and undermining the original purpose. As as result, between 1946 and 1948 these payments were stabilized and narrowed down to fewer types of payments. The 1946-48 reform spelled out who is entitled to premium payments and how much when planned targets are overfilled. These employees who were not responsible for overfillment of the planned targets in any way were paid an additional 25 per cent from the total premium fund.

It is claimed that the 1946-48 premium payments for managerial personnel are outmoded. The established premiums for the introduction of modern technology have already outlived their usefulness because of rapid technological changes which are not necessarily associated with replacement of yesterday's equipment and skills. It might involve a replacement of technology inherited from 1930 or 1940. It also might occur when a cheaper substitute for raw material is found while old equipment might be still in operation. These changes are taking place so rapidly, especially since 1956, that the whole concept of their significance in the reduction of the cost of production tends to become increasingly elastic, whereas premium payments have a tendency to be static or at least less dynamic than the changes in production methods.

## Money Wage

Prior to World War II money income received by industrial workers was based on the principle of "higher pay for higher output," and piece rates were encouraged by the government. During the war, to replace the workers drafted for military services, millions of new workers, mostly unskilled youths and women were hired. Since their productivity and earnings were low, it was necessary to reduce the work norms while the basic wage scales remained practically unchanged. As a result lowered work norms at stable wage rates increased the use of piece work. Consequently by 1944 the average money earnings of the workers as compared with 1940 had increased by 53 per cent. In regions such as the Urals this increase amounted to 65 per cent; in the Volga River region and in Western Siberia, to 79 per cent. These differentials remained after the war.

Postwar industrial reconstruction was not uniform throughout the country, and bottlenecks developed which retarded overall efforts, especially in the glass and pulp and paper industries. To stimulate output of these industries the liberal usage of progressive piece rates and various premium payments were permitted. By 1955 as compared with 1940 the average money wage, and labor productivity doubled, but the share of the basic wage payment was reduced to as low as 30 to 35 per cent of total earnings. This divergence resulted in a further reduction in the work norms. Consequently, workers were able to fulfill their work norms with ease and great numbers of them produced 50 to 100 per cent above the established norms. In cases where work norms were impossible to reduce, various additional payments were introduced. Thus, with the beginning of World War II and until 1947 the Soviet money wage policy was a compromise and incentives were used to spur greater output in the face of inflationary pressure. It is possible that the Soviets considered increased incentives as a temporary measure which could be checked when economic conditions improved. Yet even in 1958 the gap between the basic wage payments and the total workers' earnings was still wide and not to the liking of the government. The process of narrowing this gap was slow and met resistance on the part of management and workers alike.

In their efforts to narrow the gap between basic wage payments and the earning power of the workers, the Soviets adjusted the incomes of various workers who were on straight monthly salaries. In 1947 wages and salaries of low-paid workers receiving less than 900 rubles per month were increased. Wages ranging up to 300 rubles per month were increased by about 37 per cent, whereas workers in the 701-900 ruble wage bracket got a nine per cent increase.

In July 1955 a further increase in the wages of low-paid workers took place in order to narrow the disparity between high and low earnings. It was felt that there was no longer the urgency to stimulate greater output per worker by additional incentives. Along with these adjustments, the salaries of the highest paid members of the Soviet professional and administrative personnel were drastically reduced in 1956. In some cases these cuts were 50 per cent in order to eliminate the wide gap between high and low-paid personnel and at the same time to provide greater incentives for those who wish to transfer from administrative positions to production jobs.

During the XXth Congress of the Communist Party in February 1956 it was recommended that the existing complex system of regulating wages be revised in order that the disparity in earnings be reduced and the system itself be simplified. It was proposed that new basic wage scales be introduced which could be used by enterprises with similar production functions, irrespective of the departments to which they might be subordinate. The proposed basic wage scales were to insure a higher level of pay for workers in heavy industry, machine building, and construction, as well as for workers in the eastern and northern parts of the country. At the same time, these scales were to be high enough to promote high productivity among the workers. It was proposed that the number of grades be limited and that the multitude of coefficients, bonuses, and premiums be reduced to a minimum. Along with this the salaries of professional personnel were to be linked to the average wage structure of the country.

Then in January 1957 a minimum wage of not less than 300 to 350 rubles became effective for the low-paid workers and office employees in industrial enterprises, building sites, transportation, and communication. The low-paid workers in urban centers and industrial settlements were put on a minimum wage of 300 rubles per month with a minimum of 270 rubles in the rural areas. As described in Chapter 18, the average monthly money wage for workers and employees, excluding members of collective farms, was twice as high, and since most of the households have more than one wage earner the average per household was approximately 1,000 rubles per month. By 1959 the 1957 decree had considerably reduced the disparity in incomes and, at the same time, it reduced the bidding power of workers previously receiving high incomes for scarce goods and services on the market.

The actual money wage reform started in October 1956, and by January 1957, a new basic wage scale for underground workers was established. By the middle of 1957 wages for workers and engineers in the ferrous metallurgical, coking, and iron ore mining industries were more or less equalized. Along with these measures many coefficient and piece rates were abolished and the share of basic wage rates was considerably increased in the total earnings received.

Still, the 1957 basic wage rates tend to benefit workers exposed to heat, working underground, or in jobs requiring considerable physical effort by 15 to 20 per cent. Despite this disequilibrium, the general wage level was stabilized throughout industry even though heavy industry was still paying higher wages. What is more important is that the 1957 reform called for a revision of the General Wage Schedule and simplification of the whole system. Since the incomes of professional staffs are calculated on the basis of time rates, and in the absence of piece rates for this group of workers incentives in terms of premiums are still allowed for reduction in the cost of production and for increase in profits by enterprises. Regional differentials, although reduced in number, are still in effect as a means to assure the required labor for the distant regions.

The 1957 reform in the wage system was still incomplete in 1959 among scientific personnel. No longer did the mere possession of a Ph.D. degree entitle one to a lifetime of luxury in the country's top salary brackets. Drastic changes in the system of wages and payments to scientists, providing for payment based on the quality of work rather than on an academic degree, were drafted in 1959. This draft attempts to close the large gap between the salaries of academicians and others who teach and do research on the one hand and scientists and engineers who participate in production on the other.

During the current Seven-Year Plan, the Soviets anticipate an increase in the wage of low-paid workers to 500 to 600 rubles per month. In general, during the 1959-65 period the average monthly money wage of workers and employees is expected to be increased by 26 per cent but the wage increase for workers in the lower brackets should amount to 70 per cent. Undoubtedly wage equalization is now seriously considered by the Soviets and earnest attempts are being made in this direction. However, it must be added that during the next few year there are many economic factors which might upset all hopes in wage equalization, and the possibility of a return to higher incentives cannot be completely eliminated, should a severe scarcity in the labor force become apparent.

## COMPETITION

Since the introduction of piece work the Soviets have claimed that the principle of competition would have a decisive role in the increase of labor productivity. This made a favorable impression upon the masses, for it was clear to them that the government did not intend to take all the fruit of the workers' efforts, and that the more and better the goods one produced, the more one would receive. This confidence in the good intentions of the government curtailed the workers' fear of losing the gains of their labor, reduced the passive resistance of the masses, and lessened sabotage.

Many energetic and ambitious factory warkers and peasants produced more than the required minimum norms, not for the sake of maintaining their jobs, but because they wanted to increase their earnings, to have more and better goods and services, and to have first place among their comrades. The early system of incentives was both dynamic and flexible, with new incentives being introduced as soon as the old ones became obsolete. When the incentive system became workable for individuals, it was adopted by groups of workers who than began to challenge each other in a race of overproduction. Therefore, by providing incentives and encouraging competition among the workers, the Soviet government achieved two things: (1) it created incentives for willing and energetic workers to produce more, and (2) it forced many unwilling workers to work a little harder in an attempt to raise their incomes.

To encourage competition between enterprises and regions, the Soviets devised the so-called "Red Banner," a flag which was ceremoniously transferred from one plant to another, or from region to region, for records of excellent output and exceptional speed. This banner was significantly important during the war, and possession of it meant certain privileges, but it was most valuable as a psychological boost to the moral of the workers.

Until about the time of Stalin's death, competition among plants, factories, collective farms, rayons, and even oblasts was common. Each plant or region proudly announced its production goals, challenging others during the coming year. They received wide publicity in the Soviet press, with names of outstanding workers and even photographs published. Since these were the pledges for the coming year, good intentions often were not fulfilled, and it was then that the government began to criticize those who could not fulfill their pledges. But there was no machinery to force the plants and farms to produce what they had pledged. And as more and more official criticism came from Moscow, the local Party organizations became less and less eager to promote pledges. Since 1950, however, fewer unrealistic pledges have been announced.

Moreover, as the old method of pledges gradually died, a new trend was already developing. It was called "socialist competition" and was expressed in more and better products, more efficient services, or in more attractive displays of goods in the retail stores. Under socialist competition, emphasis was placed on the volume and reliability of products rather than on the gross output, often made up of low quality goods. At the same time, challenges for greater output by individual industrial enterprises, collective farms, and even entire regions have been limited to only those who actually could realize their planned goals while continuing to pledge for a still higher productivity of individual commodities, such as grain, meat, and milk per 100 hectares of land, or a greater volume of consumer goods.

A. I. Kirichenko, the Secretary of the Ukrainian Communist Party, speaking at the XXth Congress of the Communist Party on February 16, 1956 stated that socialist competition for certain commodities already exists between constituent republics and between regions of different constituent republics At the same time he challenged the RSFSR to compete in the production of livestock and milk per 100 hectaes of land. This was the beginning of challenging of one large economic region to match the production of many agricultural commodities produced in another region. Because any important agricultural commodity is normally grown on the land of different political and administrative subdivisions, challenges for competition for any crop usually involve the whole economic region.

Competition in the Soviet Union was introduced because it was necessary to provide incentives for workers to stimulate their interest in greater production associated with larger incomes. This principle is well known by the Russians and accepted by them as a part of their economic system. At the beginning, one worker competed with another, both being employed at the same enterprise. Later, individual enterprises challenged each other for the honor of being the "first" in the USSR. Soon large economic regions and constituent republics were competing for greater output of certain commodities. Finally, Khrushchev in 1957 established international competition, challenging the United States in per capita production of basic agricultural commodities and in some industrial goods. Perhaps the actual gains derived for poularization of competition between the USSR and the United States are the stimulation of the Russians to produce more than they would have produced without the hope of international leadership. This may not bring them large additional payments, but it encourages them to work harder; and even if they do not reach the goal, the country will benefit from their extra efforts in terms of greater production in general and in increased labor productivity in particular.

## TRADE UNIONS

Soviet trade unions have different functions and objectives from those in the Western countries. In the Soviet Union, trade unions are creations of a monopolistic state and have passed through many stages of organization. They never were in the past and never will be in the future wage-bargaining organizations. Since they are supervised by the ruling hierarchy of the Communist Party, mass strikes and organized strikes have been virtually unknown since 1928.

At the beginning of the Red regime, trade unions were important in the participation in management of industrial enterprises and in the establishment of wage scales and work norms. Later, with increased industrial production, their role in many activities was curtailed. During the postwar years, as a result of the adoption of piecework payments on a large scale, the All-Union Central Trade Union Council and the Central Committee of the Trade Unions have almost completely discarded their functions in questions related to wage scales and work norms.

The Soviet trade unions are organized on the industry principle. All workers employed by the coal industry have their trade union, transportation employees have their own trade union, and so on, industry by industry. Nominally, membership in trade unions is voluntary. There is a small group of temporary or seasonal workers who are non-members, but much pressure is placed on all of them to join the trade union since membership provides certain advantages such as greater social insurance payments, larger maternity payments, leave of absence due to pregnancy, perference in admission to rest homes and sanatoria, free legal aid at court, and other such benefits. New members pay an initiation fee of one per cent of their monthly wages, and monthly dues have recently been established at 50 kopeks for every 100 rubles up to 500 rubles of monthly earnings. Workers earning between 500 to 700 rubles per month pay somewhat less in dues than those who earn over 700 rubles and pay a straight one per cent of their income.

One of the most important functions of trade unions is to increase the labor productivity of their members. To achieve high productivity, leading workers with outstanding production records become "aktivists" or group organizers who, by their personal example, exercise influence among the masses. In 1955, 1.3 million of these men and women promoted socialist competition among other members, disseminated information leading to greater output, and actually trained over 1.6 million workers. The trade unions also print posters and pamphlets and organize reciprocal visits of the best workers to various enterprises with the view of exchanging the most advanced methods of production.

In 1956 Khrushchev criticized the inactive role of the All-Union Central Trade Union Council and its Central Committee in questions of norm and wage systems. As a result, beginning with 1956, the role of trade unions in policymaking decisions dealing with the labor was strengthened, and they were empowered with greater responsibility in devising new basic wage scales and other payments in the Soviet complex wage system. The All-Union Central Trade Union Council was directed to set a new wage and work norm system, to simplify bonus payments in accordance with technological advances, to safeguard against accidents, and to increase labor productivity. With an anticipated reduction in working hours, unions were instructed to improve and to expand educational services. In establishing new basic wage schedules for salaried persons, the All-Union Central Trade Union Council, together with the USSR Ministry of Finance, was delegated to work out various salary scales. Thus by 1957 the All-Union Central Trade Union Council again became an important factor in determining basic wages and work norms, and especially in training and educational programs to increase the skills and productivity of workers.

In 1957 the role of trade unions was strengthened still more. They were to be reorganized to fit the requirements of each sovnarkhoz and to make every worker aware of the importance of the new managerial organization. In the event of any misconduct by the sovnarkhoz, it is the duty of the local trade union to prevent any deviations which are contrary to overall national interests. In other words, the trade union is a sentinel for any sign of the development of localized interests as opposed to concern for the country as a whole. They were given power to work out the details related to workers' benefits when they are transferred from an abolished ministry or agency to a sovnarkhoz, and to protect workers from unlawful dismissal. But the most important aspect of the reorganization of trade unions was their increasing importance in assisting the State Committee for Questions of Labor and Wages. The fact that N. M. Shvernik, the head of the All-Union Central Trade Union Council, was elevated to full membership in the Presidium of the Communist Party in 1957 suggests the increasing importance of trade unions. Another decree, in July 1958, further increased the role of the unions. Today the firing of any worker for reasons not specified in the decree can occur only with the approval of the local union.

Perhaps one of the reasons for the recent significant growth in power of trade unions is the increase tempo of industrialization by sovnarkhozy, which requires workers of every skill. Since a great number of union members are not Communists, the sheer necessity for many workers to do a job well forces the Soviets to put more faith than ever before in union membership, for the union serves as a group which can be influenced, directed, and controlled through its meetings. In this way, trade unions would provide mass propaganda media in questions dealing with production targets, pointing out short-comings in management of enterprises, fulfillment of contracts, and pledges for higher output, stimulating the interests of workers in a greater and better level of production, and improving the standard of living of the workers. This is what Khrushchev calls "collective leadership," to be guided and controlled from above.

In 1957 there were 47 million members of trade unions; and if they are wisely directed they can exercise an important force in the management of enterprises, increase of labor efficiency, reduction of cost of production, elimination of bureaucracy, and similar endeavors. During the 1951-55 period alone the trade unions spent ten billion rubles for improvements in safety and hygiene.

In 1957 trade unions had 11,000. clubs, 115,000 local exhibiting and meeting places (red corners), 18,000 libraries, 11,000 film projectors, and 8,200 sport platforms and fields. Throughout the country trade unions maintained some 416,000 local units which covered 96 per cent of all trade union organizations and which were members of 47 national trade unions. With the reorganization of industry and construction, trade unions also underwent a reorganization, pooling into 23 trade unions on the basis of industrial classification. At all events, new importance fell to Soviet trade unions because many of the tasks performed by agencies and ministries which were abolished were assumed by the unions. In a sense, the strength of unions became a factor only when managerial responsibilities were transferred from ministries to sovnarkhozy; certainly Soviet leaders do not hold that organized labor's main function is to protect its workers' interests.

## Chapter 10—Bibliography

[1] Chigvintsev, I. N., *Zarabotnaya Plata pri Sotsializme*, Moscow, 1958, p. 17.

[2] Kisman, N. and Slavnyy, I., *Sovetskiye Finansy v Pyatoy Pyatiletke*, Moscow, 1956, p. 45.

[3] Leont'ev, L. A., *Osnovnaya Ekonomicheskaya Zadacha SSSR*, Moscow, 1956, pp. 156-57.

[4] Kisman and Slavnyy, *op. cit.*, p. 43.

[5] *Promyshlennost' SSSR*, Statisticheskiy Sbornik, Moscow, 1957, pp. 26-27, 105, 135, 191, 281; *Narodnoye Khozaystvo SSSR v 1958 Godu*, Moscow, 1959, pp. 153, 154, 199, 202, 212, 215, 228; *Narodnoye Khozaystvo RSFSR v 1958 Godu*, Moscow, 1959, p. 88.

[6] Grigor'ev, A. E. *Ekonomika Truda*, Moscow, 1959, p. 296.

[7] Lomonosov. V. and Klement'eva, A., *Znat' Konkretnuyu Ekonomiku*, Moscow, 1957, p. 43.

[8] *Narodnoye Khozaystvo SSSR v 1958 Godu,* op. cit., p. 495.

[9] *Ibid.,* pp. 100, 113, 349-50, 494-95.

[10] *Promyshlennost' SSSR,* Statisticheskiy Sbornik, Moscow, 1957, p. 28.

[11] *Voprosy Politicheskoy Ekonomii,* Moscow, 1957, p. 110.

[12] Chigvintsev, *op. cit.,* p. 14.

[13] Grigor'ev *op. cit.,* p. 338.

[14] Ibid., p. 300.

[15] *Ibid.,* p. 301.

[16] *Ibid.,* p. 317.

# Bureaucracy

## INTRODUCTION

Bureaucracy and red tape are inherent in any government or other large organization where laws, regulations, and restrictions hamper decision-making of individuals. Moreover, administrations and managers must depend upon an ever-expanding body of scientific knowledge and government policies in their decision-making. The nineteenth-century manager with daring imagination who depended upon his experience and hunches in his economic activities has no place in the USSR. The individualist is replaced by the bureaucrat—the "apparatchik."

The bureaucracy of the administrative hierarchy of the USSR mushrooms in every aspect of human activity, creating conflict of interest between government and the people even though, theoretically, there should be no conflicts between the economic interest of these sectors. Then too, as the economy of the USSR has expanded, those in government have become more resourceful in the invention of reasons for more controls and bureaucracy, intensifying feelings of envy, hate, fear, and competition for survival of individuals and organizations. The principle of "divide-and-conquer," employed in the early phase of the State formation, is still being used to create conflicts among the lower echelons of hierarchy, to be umpired by higher authority.

The main causes for bureaucracy are the people and the State itself. From the beginning of the formation of the Soviet State, the people were not trusted to carry out the socio-economic transformation, and hence a complex system of checking and counter-checking was set up to protect the interests of a new state. Since the people, on the other hand, did not trust the State, they developed indifference to state demands. When the two interests—public and individual—clashed, new regulations were devised to correct the maladjustment; these in turn led to other violations and more laws and regulations. Thus were created conditions under which the State, the owner of the economy and the builder of new institutions, accuses its own administrators of bureaucracy and inefficiency. But only the higher authority of the Presidium accuses the lower heirarchy of wrong decision-making and there is no one to criticize the Presidium, which represents the Communist Party and can do no wrong. All the decisions or indecisions made by the Presidium have immediate impact on the economic system, requiring an increased amount of bureaucratic processes without which the central planned economy cannot exist.

## Administrative Bureaucracy

The administrative bureaucracy in the Soviet Union extends to some 400,000 large and small industrial enterprises, construction sites, collective and state farms, and other state organizations. To coordinate their planned production, distribution, and services, the Soviets were forced to set up a myriad of administrative organs throughout the whole system. The higher authorities (the USSR Supreme Soviet and the Presidium of the Party) provide centralized policymaking and administrative leadership. To the peripheral administrative organs responsibility is delegated for decision-making of secondary importance which at times may be interpreted wrongly and not consistent with the wishes of the central authority. Since the administrative hierarchy is based on a vertical combination of authority, passing down the wishes of the central organs to subordinates is time-consuming and often reqires additional interpretation, amendments, and special clauses to meet the local conditions.

Since the decision-making of the countless individuals acting independently in a competitive market such as in the United States is not permitted in the USSR, these decisions are made by a few planners for millions of individuals. Under such a system maintenance of coherent production and distribution is based on sharply defined responsibilities throughout the whole system. The central planners, therefore, not only plan economic activity of the country but constantly check on its fulfillment.

In a huge country such as the Soviet Union with dispersed, diversified production under different economic and physical conditions, adjustments in one sector tend to have an impact on other sectors, requiring a new co-ordinated goal. Such a process is bound to be slow and bureaucratic while revisions in plans are made. All such delays even under perfect conditions would create confusion. In February 1957, 52 ministries supervised the activities of 8,500 construction organizations which directed over 100,000 projects. The administrative apparatus dealing with procurement, supply, and marketing employed 850,000 persons.[1] Such centralized administrative structure would inevitably create confusion in decision-making. Bureaucracy even leads to arbitrary decisions affecting the intellectual life of the country. At the second All-Union Congress of Soviet Writers the following objections to such practices were made:[2]

> As is known, publishers determine the quality of poems in terms of three categories of honorariums. The highest fee is for excellent work, the middle for good work, and the lowest for mediocre work. . . . In the Bashkiria Publishing House the 1953 production and finance plan called for publication of five per cent excellent poems, 25 per cent good poems and 70 per cent mediocre poems. The 1954 plan did not provide for any excellent poems but allowed for up to 25 per cent good poems. The 1955 plan did not provide at all for excellent or even good poems by Bashkir poets!

It is true that since 1955 the Soviets have carried out a number of measures for the reduction of superfluous centralization of power; yet there seems to be no serious improvement. Whatever changes in authority have been made represent a shift of the same responsibilities to other areas. As long as the Soviet Union is a planned economy it cannot tolerate independent decision-making. Collectivism is one of the major goals of the Communists.

## All-Union Bureaucracy

The most important economic decisions are formulated by the small group of men in the Presidium of the Communist Party. They are the top policymakers, the product of Marxian ideology, generated to the top by the system itself on a highly competitive basis but without participation of the masses. Even though they may now be called "flexible" in comparison with the earlier "rigid" leaders, they all have in common Marxian "puritanism" of righteousness in their cause and the coming of the classless society. They are preoccupied with running the rapidly expanding economy, and they know that if their system fails their cause is doomed to failure. Mistakes and blunders they may make but seldom are they repeated; many of the top men do not have second chances to err, as in the case of the "anti-Party" group.

Since the scope of decision-making by the Presidium is based on social, economic, and international considerations at home and abroad which may require immediate adjustments or revision in overall policy, the subordinate organizations do not know exactly what the Presidium's wishes may be in advance or when they may be changed. These changes may occur because of military considerations, new agreements with other communist countries, discovery of new sources of raw materials at home, establishment of new industries, or any other event that necessarily would lead to the amendment of the existing goals. Examples are Khrushchev's reemphasis on production of capital goods after he replaced Malenkov, the scrapping of the Sixth Five-Year Plan (1956-60), and the installing of the Seven-Year Plan (1959-65).

Needless to say, any such changes in policies would affect all responsible administrative levels. The USSR Gosplan and the gosplans of the constituent republics would have to revise their plans for overall production for every constituent republic and sovnarkhoz, which in turn would have to alter the old goals previously assigned for their subordinate organizations and individual enterprises. This would tend to create misuse in factors of production, to disrupt investments, to cause hoarding of materials and labor in some enterprises and shortages in others, and to intensify violations of the lower managerial hierarchy. But once a decision, wise or unwise, has been made by the Presidium, it would be molded into new working plans through existing bureaucratic processes.

## Republic Bureaucracy

The Council of Ministers of a constituent republic, the highest authority there, is answerable to the Council of Ministers of the USSR. As the highest authority, the Council of Ministers of the SSR has the responsibility to coordinate planned production of its sovnarkhozy, ministries, and the local organizations within the limits prescribed by the USSR Constitution.

Since the Council of Ministers of a constituent republic is located on the spot, it is assumed that it has clearer understanding of the economic problems within the republic than the USSR Council of Ministers and the USSR Gosplan. But because of local pride or to improve their own popularity or political powers, the republic ministers often favor local interests, especially when the management of a large enterprise puts pressure on them. This result in conflicts between the republic Council of Ministers and the USSR Council of Ministers and especially with the USSR Gosplan, which is entrusted with allocation of scarce resources.

The power of the USSR Gosplan is not to be underestimated. Even the so-called "decentralized" investments, which amount to about ten per cent of the total Soviet industrial investment, are determined within general targets set by the USSR Gosplan. Within the so-called "centralized" investments, financed from the All-Union budget, the Council of Ministers of a constituent republic may authorize projects of less than 50 million rubles. Even here the USSR Gosplan or the USSR Council of Ministers reserves a veto power through financial controls if the overall magnitude for such investments is not consistent with the intended goals set by the higher authority. By such separation of authority only the smaller projects can be authorized by republic Councils of Ministers, but the value of such projects is determined by higher authority, the USSR Gosplan. Even the coordination of production efforts among several sovnarkhozy within a constituent republic must have the stamp of approval of the USSR Gosplan.

In general there is more confusion in planning, more conflict, and more misuse of scarce resources on the republic level. It is here the enthusiastic plans for the expansion of local resources are made, causing deviations from the All-Union goals. All such maladjustments are eventually corrected by the USSR Gosplan or the USSR Council of Ministers. And since certain aspects of the development of the local economy are more important to the individual republic than to the USSR as a whole, frequent frictions, misunderstandings, and violations of the All-Union goals occur.

### Ministerial Bureaucracy

Imagine bureaucracy if the economy of the United States were run by a central apparatus from Washington, D. C.! Such bureaucracy has been concentrated in many specialized ministries of the USSR since its early formation. The interdependence of soviet enterprises on the State and on each other became so complete that it seriously threatened the entire economic system. To correct this, many ministries were abolished or merged, resulting in a bitter fight among apparatchiki, who either attempted to protect their own positions or who honestly believed the new set-up to be non-Marist.

Dissatisfaction with centralized planning and management was evident even before 1940, and in 1941 the USSR Council of Ministers granted to constituent republics a greater voice in planning. Similar cries against central planning and bureaucracy came from Khrushchev in 1954, but it was not until 1957 that decentralization in management took place and the shackles of ministerial bureaucracy were loosed.

Prior to the formation of the sovnarkhozy every ministry independently collected economic data from each enterprise under its jurisdiction, using 50 to 60 different forms. Some ministries had over 200 forms. Thus each enterprise had to prepare two sets of data: one for its ministry and the other for the Central Statistical Administration. In addition, the USSR

Gosplan required about 60 to 70 different forms for All-Union planning. In general about 100 different forms were filed with all higher authorities.

Since ministries acted as independent organizations interested in specific areas, parallelism and duplication of effort occurred on a large scale. Geologists of one ministry were looking for coal; geologists of another ministry for iron ore; and still another ministry was interested in oil only. As a result many existing resources were missed. Procurement of raw materials by many ministries was poorly coordinated with the needs of their enterprises. Some ministries hoarded raw materials and labor while other ministries experienced shortages. Many ministries were reluctant to specialize in production (especially of spare parts) and to establish cooperation among various ministries or even among individual enterprises for fear of causing a certain break in the already established forms of production and in organizational structures. No one ministry wanted to part with its authority or even share it with another.

But most important was the unnecessarily large administrative personnel force in Moscow. Khrushchev on May·7, 1957, speaking of ministerial bureaucracy, stated that industrial enterprises located in the RSFSR were run by 84 ministries and organizations, 80 of which were located in Moscow. They were responsible for the operation of 64 per cent of the country's total industrial investments and employed about 11 million workers. This breeded departmental barriers and prevented coordination. Even the problems of technological improvements in production within ministerial jurisdictions were often in the hands of several different authorities.

Bulganin, speaking in February 1955, mentioned that many constituent republics establish unnecessary ministries. In the Tadzhik SSR a Ministry of Light Industry was set up with a staff of 27 persons supervising six enterprises. The Moldavian SSR had a Ministry of Timber Industry with a staff of 32 persons directing eight enterprises, four of which were lumber camps. In 1954 the Department of Bee Products of the USSR Ministry of Agriculture employed 40 persons in the Tambov Oblast for the purpose of purchasing bees wax. In that year about one ton of bees wax was purchased. Again, the State Procurement Administration employed in the Poltava Oblast 13,000 workers and in the Tambov Oblast 8,429 persons who bought farm commodities from the collective farms. For each collective farm in Poltava the State employed 16 persons; in Tambov 12 persons. Such organizational structure created overlapping responsibilities, confusion, and conflicts not only between collective farms and administrative organs but also among the organs themselves.

The bureaucracy indeed had fertile ground for apparatchiki. In 1955 each state farm received 1,897 written directives and orders from the USSR Ministry of State Farms mostly containing unnecessary recommendations and advice. The Ministry of Urban and Rural Housing Construction of the Kazakh SSR during the first five months of 1955 sent 11,220 telegrams and 3,648 letters to its construction enterprises.[3] Interference with enterprises by ministries created conditions under which an individual manager was forced to spend a considerable amount of his time in answering all requests, no matter how trivial. He had to justify his decision-making, to clear himself of wrong-doing when things were bad, and also to compete with others in similar positions for favor from ministries which held coercive power over his head.

Since the abolishment of many ministries took place, only a few remain. Their power in planning has been curtailed and their main activities now lie in the planning of new technological and scientific developments and in construction of new enterprises. Moreover, these functions are now executed by the sovnarkhozy. Nevertheless, since the remaining ministries are of All-Union stature, they still have powerful influence with the USSR Council of Ministers and the USSR Gosplan and have priority in their demands. This again creates friction between remaining ministries and sovnarkozy and requires umpiring of all conflicts by the higher authority. Since the power held by the higher authority depends upon the Party regime and since the Party's cohesion depends on its ideology, no one can criticize the higher authority of the Presidium.

### Sovnarkhoz Bureaucracy

The reasons for decentralization of industrial management were many. The whole idea focused around centralized and vertical ministerial detailed planning which made economic maneuverability difficult, with the unnecessary flood of paper work and accounting. Planning without adequate knowledge of local conditions was cumbersome, and the production potential and financial means were unsatisfactorily coordinated. However, not all enterprises fell under the jurisdiction of sovnarkhozy. As an example, in the Ukraine they were charged with administering 2,752 enterprises; the other 767 enterprises were to remain under control of the local soviets or were directly subordinated to Moscow.[4]

Transfer of the management was rapid. Many sovnarkhozy were hardly formed before they were deluged with administrative apparatuses, and coordination channels were slowly worked out. Moreover, as one problem was solved another developed, and there were, and still are, continuous conflicts between higher authority and the sovnarkhozy and between individual enterprises and sovnarkhozy. These problems usually arise from misinterpretation of the authoritative power within each administrative unit.

The national interests and those of the sovnarkhoz may not be the same. Although the All-Union plans are known to the sovnarkhoz, such plans do not guarantee that the interests of the sovnarkhoz will not be treated preferentially by the local administration. Such localization (mestnichestvo) may be due to scarcity of both materials and labor to fulfill the national demands when demands under local strong political and economic pressures may be more urgent.

There are many cases of mestnichestvo leading to dispersion of funds (raspyleniye) among non-planned undertakings by sovnarkhozy. This is a clear violation of the state's planning and financial discipline and an illegal usage of funds which undermines the central planning. For example, the Permsk Sovnarkhoz used 11 million rubles assigned for the construction of a prefabricated housing combine for the construction of its own administration offices, a house, and the summer camp for the "pioneers." The Saratov Sovnarkhoz shifted ten million rubles from the construction of new enterprises to be used for the construction of a housing project. The Karaganda Sovnarkhoz illegally transferred funds appropriated for the construction of the Karaganda Metallurgical Plant, largest of its kind in the USSR. Other funds were diverted from coal mines under construction in Karaganda to the construction of a theater, a circus, a rest home, office buildings, swimming pools, and other non-planned projects. There are many other violations undermining the production of planned goods.[5] Reasons for mestnichestvo are many and the most frequent abusers of it are the sovnarkhozy created to reduce bureaucracy and to improve efficiency.

In some instances the sovnarkhoz might find it difficult to fulfill the demands imposed by its constituent republic. The sovnarkhoz and its oblast planning commissions are empowered to devise production plans for their respective regions to be included in the plan of their constituent republic. But the plans for the development of individual industrial sectors are in the hands of the USSR Gosplan. Such double planning responsibility for a single region would inevitably create conflicts. Furthermore, the USSR Gosplan is unable to stimulate cooperation among several regions producing specialized goods such as instruments, supplies, and parts. This, too, creates frictions between the USSR Gosplan and sovnarkhozy.

Unsatisfactory working coordination and cooperative among sovnarkhozy forces them to expand production of local raw materials, to expand output of materials previously imported from other regions, and to invest in too many supplementary enterprises for the purpose of securing needed materials and supplies. For example, the Omsk Sovnarkhoz, because of unsatisfactory deliveries, had planned in 1958 to terminate business relations with five economic regions. The Leningrad Sovnarkhoz launched a program of new construction and reconstruction of some 3,000 projects even though there were shortages of materials and investment to complete these projects. As a result the investment of over two billion rubles was "frozen" in unfinished projects. Such unwise investment on the part of enthusiastic sovnarkhoz planners resulted in a new law prohibiting the construction of new projects if sovnarkhozy do not have enough capital and materials to finish the undertakings.[6] But even if the sovnarkhoz is able to persuade the local bank to provide the credit for a new undertaking, the USSR Gosbank may deny the construction of the project. In 1957 the Tula Sovnarkhoz received two billion rubles in appropriations, yet the bank refused to release it and insisted on a special decree from the RSFSR Ministry of Finance.[7]

The organizational structure of the sovnarkhoz closely resembles an oligopolistic structure. Like any large organization, the sovnarkhoz operates largely according to general plans, rather than on the basis of individual judgment to meet a specific problem. Theoretically, the sovnarkhoz is an advisory body to its enterprises with an umbrella of mass research, investments, planning, development, and the like. It does not run the daily operations of the enterprise. Yet there is a constant flow of endless statements, reports, and demands arising from the accounting, production, sales, legal, and other activities of the region. Then there is the shortage of modern tabulating installations such as punchers, verifiers, and sorters to stabilize the accounting system. The sovnarkhoz simply is incapable of knowing all the details of a region's complex and diversified production from personal observations.

Since each sobnarkhoz has small and large industrial enterprises, some considered more important than others, the sovnarkhoz is bound to be influenced in its decision-making by pressure groups. Certainly problems of giants such as the Magnitogorsk Metallurgical Combine in the Chelyabinsk, which produces about 50 per cent of the total profit for the sovnarkhoz, would have priority over the subsidized enterprises or enterprises showing losses.[8]

Sovnarkhozy attempt to solve their specific problems by flexible interpretation of the existing laws. There is no uniformity in dealing with questions of the arrangements of the sovnarkhozy such as the organization of technology, documentation, and the training of new administrative personnel. In the absence of standards in these instances, many sovnarkhozy tend to develop their own, which often prove to be in error in the eyes of the higher authority or unfavorable to the lower hierarchy. All of this, of course, intensifies the old bureaucratic processes or establishes a new type of bureaucracy.

No doubt some of the problems that arose from the transformation of management will be ironed out. Many sovnarkhozy are still in the process of internal organization. The Latvian Sovnarkhoz, for instance, was criticized for its structure based on the old departmental line. Instead of solving problems directly the central administration of this sovnarkhoz depended on decisions by its own Division of Technical Production as the main operative organ. In general, every sovnarkhoz is trying to solve its problem without help from Moscow, often by creating greater bureaucracy than before.

## Local Bureaucracy

The so-called "local" industry consists of small-scale enterprises such as bakeries, beer and non-alcoholic bottling plants, canning plants, small garment and shoe repair shops, and bath houses, among others, which supply goods and services to local communities. Direct administration of such enterprises is in the hands of special administrative organs established by the Executive Committee of the Soviet of Deputies of the Workers (Ispolkom). Such organs exist in every oblast, kray, and city. Coordination of production of the local industry within any political-administrative unit such as the oblast or city is in the hands of the Main Administration of Local Industry. Depending upon the economic magnitude of each branch of local enterprises, they are administered by special organs. For example, production of local construction materials in the Moscow Oblast is run by the Main Administration of the Local Construction Materials, production of furniture by the Administration of Furniture, bakeries are administered by their own trust, and so on.

In the past most of the enterprises in local industry utilized local resources. With the formation of the sovnarkhoz many larger enterprises, formerly administered by the ministries, were transferred to the local sector, and dependence upon raw materials from other sectors has considerably increased. With the magnified importance of local industry many of these enterprises set up similar administrative structures as in the larger units with several departments and sections. As a rule they maintained a larger number of administrative personnel per thousand workers than in the larger organizations. Yet decision-making on the part of management of local industries has not been improved. Every decision of the local enterprises must be approved by its supervising organ, which in turn must seek approval from the main administration, which must obtain permission from the Executive Committee, which depends upon the grace of the sovnarkhoz. The decision-making process on the local level indeed is limited. At best the director of a local enterprise tries to fulfill his production quota and to supply the required economic information to higher authority.

Since local administrative structures are copied from larger administrative units, many heads of administrations and trusts tend to concentrate on management of their subordinate organizations without delegation of decision-making to the management of the enterprises, even though such decisions may easily be made by the management.

The USSR has a large number of small rayons each with a total population of about 30,000 persons. Here too, their administrative structure is modeled on the larger units. If the large rayon has bureaucracy because of its complex economy and large population, the smaller rayon has the same degree of bureaucracy because of its bureaucratic organizational structure. However, in an attempt to reduce the cost of administration and to increase the size of local enterprises a trend is underway to merge small rayons with others. In the Moldavian SSR, for example, all small rayons already have been merged into larger units in an effort to reduce cost and bureaucracy.[9]

The main reason for bureaucracy on the local level is the national emphasis upon heavy industry. Local industries, although dear to the hearts of their people, cannot do much. Since these industries are of secondary importance and must depend largely upon local resources, their relations with the higher authorities are those of a stepchild who has the right to exist but not to make decisions.

Almost all urban centers have an administrative structure modeled after larger organizations. Many cities have numerous trusts and departments maintaining their bridges, roads, and streets. Often maintenance of one street is assigned to different agencies. The repair and upkeep of the thoroughfare is charged to the Department of Roads; garbage collection and removal of snow from the street is assigned to the Department of Cleaning; planting of trees on the street is in the hands of the Department of Tree Planting. Many of these departments are small and operate on a seasonal basis, yet they are independent organizations without central coordination of efforts or costs.

In some small rayons which might have only one urban center there would be parallelism in organizational structure. The city of Kuybyshev, for example, has its own Public Health Department as does the Kuybyshev Rayon. In other instances, two different banking organizations would be engaged in providing credits for similar types of loans. Even the distribution of plots of land to urban populations for "victory gardens," although distributed by the rayon, must be approved by the oblast authority. In general all decisions made by local authorities must be approved by the higher authority as before.

### Management of Industrial Enterprise

The giant industrial enterprise in the Soviet Union, although state-controlled, basically performs the same functions in production and distribution as the giant enterprise in the United States. As the enterprise grows larger its physical assets become more decentralized, and its products more diversified, and the usual risk of unwise managerial decisions tends to decrease. The large enterprise with many components can move its resources from one place to another; it has greater flexibility in avoiding the many costly errors in decision-making that plague small-scale enterprises. Although the Soviets are claiming that bureaucracy is an inherent principle in the management of the capitalist system, they, too, recognize the problem of unwise decision-making within their own system. Efforts, of course, are made to correct them, but under the central planning system remedies often lead to increased bureaucratic processes.

### Responsibility

Prior to the formation of sovnarkhozy, the director of an industrial enterprise had limited responsibilities because practically all decisions were made for him by the higher authority. His main task was to follow the minute instructions. Now the director has greater opportunity to exercise his talents in fulfillment of the goals assigned to him, but under increased supervision. He establishes technical, production, and financial plans based upon instructions from the sovnarkhoz. Within the limits of the existing laws, he may now change these plans in order to obtain higher production or better goods. He has the power, upon agreement with the buyer, to establish prices on goods not established by higher authority. He has the authority to change technological processes in production of many goods and in utilization of excess materials and equipment, and to reorganize the labor force for greater efficiency. He is even permitted to set up and to buy materials and equipment for research work.

A considerable part of his efforts are devoted to such questions as organization of labor and wage scales, training of new workers, industrial safety, housing and supplies for the workers, and organization of child care. In short, the director of a large industrial enterprise is responsible for the production of goods and for the welfare of a small community.

Since many of these responsibilities were shifted to him from other authorities, he is no longer devoting all of his time to the management of productive forces. New duties are time-consuming, requiring numerous meetings dealing with production and also with items not directly related to it. All major measurements and plans for the enterprise must be discussed with departmental heads, at the meetings of all workers, with the leaders of the party organizations at the enterprise, with his superiors, and so on, before final decision may be reached. In fact, the director's responsibilities are so numerous and so diversified that it is difficult for a single man to know all the details under his administration, and his decision-making must be aided by numerous departments and advisory committees.

Since the director is separated from first-hand contact with the workers, at times certain actions such as the installation of new equipment may be accomplished without knowledge of the foreman. This usually creates friction between the foreman and his superiors. Eventually conflicts within the organization must be settled by the director, perhaps at a time when he is preoccupied with other problems.

In the past, strict production discipline encouraged the mediocre, the conformist, the timid, and inefficient persons to become directors. With expanding decision-making powers, many of them accept new power hesitantly, fearful of making errors and thus paying the penalty. All this, of course, tends to increase indecision and conflicts.

### Limitations

Essentially the director is interested in the present and future performances of his enterprise. But most of all he is interested in the fulfillment of the annual plans which have a direct relation to his monetary gains. Any potential disequilibrium between his income and the plan fulfillment is met by the director's resistance to higher authority. Such localization (mestnichestvo) is bound to create tensions between supervising authorities and the director of the enterprise.

With centralized allocation of scarce resources, the director trys to make sure of the availability of raw materials or semifinished goods for his own needs. With legal reserves of supplies being small, hoarding, even at higher prices, is not unusual. This may increase the cost of production, reduce profit, or even necessitate obtaining credit from the Gosbank. He might ignore installation of new equipment, or at least delay it, until the price of such equipment is lowered. In the race for fulfillment of the planned goal, he might even start production of expensive items. By so doing his production fulfillment, in monetary value, may be easier to attain, thus assuring him of premium payment for completion of the plan. But even if he is flexible in adjusting his production to high-priced items his dependence upon suppliers from different organizations is not assured, and so hoarding of supplies and labor, though illegal, becomes important to him.

Contractual obligations between producers and consumers are more complex and confused now than in the past. It may be temporary, caused by "growing pains" inherent in any large-scale reorganization, but in the short run it delays production and creates maladjustment in the production schedule. In Armenia in 1957 it was revealed that many enterprises failed to deliver contracted goods to consumers located within that republic and even to other regions.[10] Between June and September of 1957 Armenia received 417 telegrams and letters from diffrent enterprises and organizations located elsewhere requesting that measures be taken to force Armenian enterprises to fulfill their contractual obligations in deliveries, since nondelivery created shortages which hampered production in their enterprises. Lack of dependability and erratic delivery of contracted goods cause real problems for many directors, making them fearful of not fulfilling their planned output on schedule hence hoarding. It is true that attempts are made to equalize allocation of supplies among enterprises, but hoarding may be due to changes in production goals after the supplies were received and not reported to the higher authority. In the Gorki Sovnarkhoz on January 1, 1958, the value of hoarded materials was over 300 million rubles above the normal reserve requirements.[11]

Many directors are uninformed about the supply market, and to help those unable to find supplies some sovnarkhozy have established market days for recovered goods from hoarders and from other sources. Other sovnarkhozy publish bulletins to provide information on the availability of supplies. However, such measures do not prevent hoarding. Instead they intensify conflicts between directors and the sovnarkhoz. All such conflicts are settled by arbitration boards appointed by the higher authority. This increases bureaucracy and does not assure the consumer of timely delivery. Conditions were so bad that the USSR Council of Ministers on May 22, 1957, decreed that non-fulfillment of contractual delivery would carry a penalty of non-payment of premiums for the fulfillment of overall planned production by the violator of the contract. Then on April 24, 1958, the USSR Supreme Soviet decreed that the violation of contractual deliveries would lead to disciplinary actions, fines, or even criminal prosecution to be imposed on all persons and organizations responsible.[12]

The director of a Soviet enterprise spends a large part of his efforts in paper work, writing and answering various requests. For instance. such giants as the Gorki Automobile Plant have 300 to 500 suppliers situated in almost every sovnarkhoz and deliver goods to every region and even ship goods abroad. This requires voluminous correspondence, various meetings, and other administrative activity. The Novo-Kramatorsk Plant, for example, must have about 300,000 recorded items during the year from which various reports are made. The Ural Machine-Building Combine has 2,000, primarily documents, from which other reports are made.[13] Such a mass of data inevitably includes errors which need verification and adjustments in the final reports.

Maintenance of these reports is essential, since they are systematically checked by the Financial Department of the sovnarkhoz. When errors are found either in the use of allocated materials or in financial appropriations the Financial Department tells the director to correct the shortcomings, and at the same time the sovnarkhoz and the local communist organ are notified. Thus, the director who is not careful in his decisions might find several higher authorities using their own methods in attempting to correct his errors.

Last but not least, by the establishment of "democratic" leadership, the Soviets encourage individual workers of the enterprise and the general public to advise the director in the methods to be used to increase production and to reduce bureaucracy. The outcome of this policy is an increased flow of various individuals and mail into the director's office. Thus, the present director of a Soviet industrial enterprise is not only the administrator of the enterprise and the community of its workers but he also becomes a politician who must be courteous to all visiting citizens, be they with or without any suggestions. No wonder many directors are "too busy" or "at a conference" when visitors come to see them.

## Conflict of Interests

With the formation of sovnarkhozy the responsibilities of the director were considerably expanded. From a theoretical viewpoint this was aimed primarily at the reduction of departmental barriers, increased specialization in production, fuller utilization of all factors of production, and increased cooperation among enterprises. Reduction of personnel was the most important task since it meant reduction in the cost of production. Many enterprises have already reorganized their departmental structures thus increasing efficiency while reducing their labor costs.

The decentralization of decision-making, however, does not guarantee that local decision-making can be more judicious and less bureaucratic than the centralized planning apparatus of the past. In fact it may be as bureaucratic as the planning from Moscow, even though bureaucracy takes a different form. The attack on bureaucracy, in the main, was not an attack upon unwise decisions of the higher authority *per se* but rather an attack on the high cost of its maintenance.

As was noted, in the past the director received detailed goals expressed either in physical or monetary values. If, for example, the plan called for production of ten tons of nails made of Grade No. 2 steel, the director had the choice of producing the size of nails which would bring him the greatest profit. Again, if a plan called for production of 100,000 rubles worth of a certain commodity, he could produce goods which could be manufactured at lower cost, even though such goods were high-priced and less socially desirable. Nevertheless, since the state plans were fulfilled, the director was not subject to criticism, and he earned additional premiums for the fulfillment or even for overfulfillment of the plans.

By empowering the director to plan his own production his responsibilities were expanded, but the higher authorities have at their pleasure the right to adjust or completely reject his proposed production goals. In other words, the higher authorities can easily put the director in a disadvantageous position by changing the types or assortments of goods he had planned to produce. He can be forced to produce goods, the prices and profits of which may be a hindrance to him. His choice in different cost-price ratios in production of a variety of the same goods is restricted, and his profit motivation is more limited now than in the past. Since the government emphasizes reduction in the cost of production, the director has fewer opportunities for premium payments. To receive a premium, the director must lower the cost of production each quarter and every year. This is difficult because he must meet the important plan targets, and his combination of factors of production is not based on the concept of the least cost but is made to meet planned requirements. It is for these reasons that many directors are indifferent about reducing their cost of production. Once costs are reduced the next year's production quotas and profits are established at higher levels.

But even if the director is able to reduce the cost of production and achieves the profit for the enterprise and premium for himself, there is no assurance that he can repeat this the next year. Profit for the enterprise is also less of an incentive now than in the past since 70 per cent of it is spent on housing projects of the enterprise and the remainder goes to the sovnarkhoz, to the ministry, or to other higher authority. These authorities have the right to interfere in financial operations of their enterprises, especially in obtaining a part of turnover capital and profits to be allocated for other ends not benefiting the enterprise at all. In many cases such funds may be used to subsidize submarginal enterprises. Even when profits are planned by the soznarkhoz they are often established at a low level so that they may be larger and a greater sum can be retained by the sovnarkhoz. In short, the profit motivation of the director is less important now than in the past, and this limits his freedom of choice in arranging the factors of production to his own advantage.

He might or might not know the reasons for any action taken by the higher authorities. But he surely knows ways and means by which the higher authorities protect their own interests. To guard his own interests he must be alert to any potential changes in his production plans, to find a loophole to get around the law, or even to violate the regulations. This requires imagination and bureaucratic experience since any emergency decisions are still in the hands of the higher authorities who are reluctant to release direct control over the enterprise to its management. The Rostov Sovnarkhoz, for example, checks daily on the fulfillment of the most important items of every enterprise. When the daily production is disrupted or lagging behind it is the sovnarkhoz and not the director who takes the necessary measures to correct maladjustments.

To avoid criticism or penalty from higher authority the director must by threat or trick arrange the factors of production in order to insure the fulfillment of planned goals. The fulfillment of the plan is the most important single fact on his mind. He must be resourceful to preserve his position. He often presents to higher authorities facts which are favorable to him (ochovtiraniye). To obtain larger allocations of materials or credit he becomes knowingly overenthusiastic about the plant's capacity potentials (blat). To insure his requirements in supplies he often hoards manpower, raw materials, equipment, and the like (strakhovka). When unforeseen shortages of supplies endanger planned production goals the director dispatches one of his employees (tolkach) whose task, like that of a lobbyist, is to present the urgent problems to higher authorities in order to obtain immediate assistance.

These ways and means have developed because of conflict of interests between individual enterprises and higher authorities and are important forces in the running of enterprises. These practices are accepted by the Soviets and only unusual misuse of them is condemned by the government. For example, the Alapaevek Metallurgical Combine located in the Sverdlovsk Oblast spent half of its assigned appropriation to cover field trips of the officials and payments for tolkach. Some of them were on a "field trip" to the capital for over 80 days. To prevent extravagant expenditures on such matters the Sverdlovsk Sovnarkhoz issued a decree for economizing but not abolishing such outlays for 1958.[14] From the director's viewpoint, it pays to know the right people in the Gosplan, sovnarkhoz, trust, or other organizations with whom he deals. The "red carpet" treatment of high officials pays, even if it increases his costs.

The separation of physical and financial plans is of great importance. Physical production, even in defective goods, may reach the planned goals. These goods must be replaced at some future date. Meantime on the short run, especially during the last quarter of the year, such action might help to fulfill the quota. This compels many directors to be in a continuous "rat race" manipulating plans and practices. Other reasons for non-fulfillment of plans may be beyond the director's control. Acts of nature such as heavy snows paralyzing transportation, heavy rainfalls, earthquakes, and fires cannot be prevented or avoided; yet the plan must be fulfilled and goods must be delivered on time.

The director of Soviet enterprise must have "socialist" responsibility towards the society for which he works. He is exposed to criticism from higher authorities, from his workers, from the local Communists, and from the public in general. The principle of "democratic leadership" empowers all people to criticize shortcomings of the director but not to correct them. In 1959 during the construction of a well-publicized thermoelectric plant in the Kirghiz SSR drunken workers reported to duty. The management was unable to dismiss the offenders, and the Secretary of the communist cell of the enterprise, when the matter was brought to his attention, dismissed it lightly by stating that he would "soon" take up the problem of education and propaganda to correct it. Meanwhile, production was lagging and the director was responsible for it.

The director may be attacked by all and is answerable to all. In many respects his authority has been greatly reduced while his responsibilities have increased. He no longer belong to the elite class of managerial personnel which, before the formation of sovnarkhozy, was answerable only to the ministery. It may be a temporary setback, and he eventually may reemerge as a member of a more powerful managerial clique than before.

## Management of Agricultural Enterprise

This section is devoted mainly to the management of collective farms because state farms and other state-operated agricultural enterprises are, in general, similar to the industrial enterprises in their relations with the higher authority. As was noted in Chapter 7, the collective farms are considered by the Soviets as cooperative organizations of peasants who are collectively responsible for their business, but because of their importance to the welfare of the country, the State, through its numerous administrative organs, holds a strong control over the collective farms.

The bureaucracy in the management of collective farms originates from restrictive measures devised by higher authorities to provide "guidance" for the peasants. Such guidance is expressed in recommendations or decrees which collective farms, even against their own interests, much follow. This concept of guidance may deal with broad or specific problems extending to production, political, organizational, technical, and all other activities of collective farms.

Since 1953 the bureaucracy on collective farms has been somewhat reduced: detailed production plans are now devised by the collective farms themselves, the MTS have been abolished, and prices have been stabilized. Yet there is still a considerable amount of waste in human effort. Indolence and mismanagement in most cases lead to ignorance on the part of higher authority of the local conditions, and as a result the higher authority is unable to solve the problems in the light of the Marxian concept of agriculture on the one hand and the pecularities of farming on the other.

## Agencies in Control

All plans dealing with economic activities of the collective farm are originate by the peasants themselves under the general guidance of state's overall requirements for major farm items. The former guidance activities of MTS were transferred to the Rural Executive Committee (Rayispolkom) which enlarged its sphere of influence over the farms located within regional jurisdiction of the Committee.

Plans proposed by the collective farm are submitted to the village soviet as the first link of the higher authority. Although having somewhat limited powers, the village soviet may recommend certain adjustment in the plans. Plans for the whole village district are dispatched by the village soviet to the Rayispolkom, which check all the plans from the rayon's collective farms, makes necessary corrections and sends them to the Oblast Executive Committee (Oblispolkom). Plans from every collective farm are verified by the

Oblispolkom and then sent to the Ministry of Agriculture of the constituent republic. All these levels of authority have the power to interfere with planned activities of collective farms. They may cause a major change in the plans, creating conflict of interests between the individual collective farm and the higher authority.

The state requirements for production of major farm commodities such as a grain and livestock must reach the collective farms not later than September 1, and all plans must be devised by the farms and approved by the Rayispolkom and Oblispolkom by October 1. There is hardly time for the collective farms to analyze the state requirements and to adjust their production for greater advantage to them, nor is there time for the Rayispolkom and Oblispolkom to make sound recommendations. In most cases, both the collective farms and the Rayispolkom tend to make hasty decision which often are corrected later on. The responsibility of Rayispolkom is to see that the plans of the collective farms cover all required state demands, that all commodities specified in the plans are delivered to contracting agencies, and the amounts of the planned purchases by other organizations are included. The Oblispolkom verifies not only the proper economic activities of the collective farms but also the duties performed by the Rayispolkom.

The role of Rayispolkom in the guidance of economic activity of the collective farm is manifold. It is responsible for the right organization of farm work and the distribution of farm machinery among collective farms, provides technological assistance, introduces scientifice methods, watches the quality of work performed by the peasants, helps to build supplementary enterprises on the farm, and finally, attempts to increase the role of the village soviet as the first link between the collective farms and the Rayispolkom. The importance of the Rayispolkom lies in the fact that it is gradually taking greater responsibility in guiding farm production, and plays a role in farming activities similar to that of the sovnarkhoz in the industrial sector. It is true that the sovnarkhoz has more authority over its enterprises, but considering the cautious approach taken by the Soviets in dealing with the peasants the role of the Rayispolkom in the agricultural sector will no doubt be increased.

However, at present the Rayispolkom is not the sole authority dealing with diversified needs of the collective farms. Other organs are responsible for construction projects and installation of equipment on the collective farms. For instance, in 1957 in the Novosibirsk Oblast eight different organizations provided guidance in these tasks. Each of these independent organizations is answerable to its own higher organs and each acts without coordinating its efforts with others.[15]

Under such division of authority, interests clash not only between collective farms and guiding organizations but among authorities themselves. Often decisions are accepted not because they are good but because they are better than no decisions at all. Nevertheless, once decisions, good or poor, are made, they are verified and adjusted by the higher authorities, and the never-ending process of bureaucracy continues to flow.

Even an application for credit by the collective farm must be approved by a host of higher authorities, although the collective farm is not a state-operated organization. Often requests for credit move from rayon to rayon before being received by oblast authorities. The Rayispolkom may approve the credit, but the Oblispolkom may deny it despite the fact that the bank is outside its jurdiction. Bureaucracy creates bitterness and retards efficiency on the farms, but there is no way to avoid it.

## Limitations

With the abolishment of MTS the dual possession of factors of production ceased to exist and collective farms became holders of land, labor, and capital goods. But by gaining in ownership of machinery collective farms also lost self-protection, since they no longer could blame MTS for poor or untimely work. In the past the Rayispolkom guided economic and political activities on the farms through MTS which often would side with collective farms in protection of their interests. Under the present arrangement collective farms are more restricted in their arguments with the more powerful Rayispolkom than with MTS, which were closer to problems of the collective farms.

All the changes that have occurred since 1953 have perhaps had the greatest impact on the chairman of the collective farm. As a hired employee, the chairman is often expected to do an impossible task, especially when the cooperation of all the members is needed. He must satisfy the Rayispolkom and at the same time please the members. Although a hired employee, he gives orders to and verifies the performances of those who hired him. This, of course, often creates friction, misunderstanding, conflict, and bitterness between the chairman and individual members. Conditions of emotional irritability are usually strongest when things are bad and the scapegoat would usually be the chairman.

In 1953 out of some 91,200 chairmen only 2,400 of them had college or equivalent education; 14,200 had high-school training. Over 81 per cent of the chairmen in 1953 had less than high-school education. Yet, as chairman of a large economic unit, he signs contracts with other organizations, buys and sells commodites in large lots. The knowledge of small-scale peasant-type farming has become inadequate to run the collective farm successfully. Moreover, no matter how efficient the chairman may be, the general meeting of the members may overrule his proposals. For instance, the general meeting, to follow the examples of construction of huge nationally propagandized projects, might agree to build a large, expensive clubhouse or "livestock place" when a kindergarten, school, or hospital is more urgently needed. They might authorize hiring of an excessive number of workers such as recreation directors or cooks from the outside without economic justification; yet the chairman must follow their instructions against his own recommendations.

Theoretically the chairman can be dismissed at any time by the members, but even if he is inefficient, inexperienced, or unsuitable for the job, often members would have difficulty in firing him were he recommended by the higher authority and especially were he a Communist. In such a case the chairman finds himself surrounded by antagonistic and non-cooperative peasants. Consequently, blunders are committed resulting in serious impact on the economic and political stability of the collective farm. Appointments of Communists to managerial posts on collective farms were increased during the merging program. Many appointees were inefficient, arrogant, and even hostile to peasants. In December 1958, speaking to the Communist Congress, Khrushchev stressed the need for replacement of such Party members by more qualified persons.

But even if the chairman is good he no longer can personally supervise all the farming operations because of bureaucratic intervention. In 1953 the collective farm had to file an average of 60 to 70 forms. Twelve of these forms covered about 100 different items.[16] In 1957 the RSFSR Council of Ministers approved 11 forms with 260 basic items of information to be filed by each collective farm.[17] Of course not all items are filed by every farm; nevertheless it suggests the extent of the paper work required in preparation of various reports, graphs, charts, and other documentation. This is important since most decision-making by higher authorities is based upon such reports and any errors in the reports might lead to major changes in the plans of the collective farm.

## Conflict of Interests

Conflict of interest is a widespread phenomenon in any organized society. On the collective farm such conflicts are found between individual members and the general meeting where the majority rules. There are conflicts between the chairman on the one hand and the Board of Directors or the general meeting or the individual members on the other, or conflicts between the management of the collective farm and higher authorities. There are many reasons for conflicts but they can be narrowed down to two major factors: personal antipathy and violation of the rules. Personal dislike of the chairman might arise when a member is assigned to hard, dirty, or low-paid work. If the chairman is found to be biased in assigning well-paid jobs to his friends, the dissatisfied members are apt to do a poor job and will try to embarrass him or even demand his dismissal. And many collective farms, in defiance of the rules, distribute all their cash profits among their members.

In general, the causes of conflict between the peasants and higher authorities lie in the Marxian approach to the agrarian question. Farming is a specialized and highly skilled occupation. The majority of collective farm members still think of themselves as individuals possessing a wide range of skills associated with agriculture. Yet the Soviets are determined to equate them to the level of factory workers with a single skill. It is this interference with personal choice of occupations that leads to conflicts between the peasants and the State. However, crafty as they are, the peasants cannot compete with the State and are gradually losing ground in their fight for individualism.

## Chapter 11—Bibliography

[1] *Voprosy Ekonomiki*, No. 5, 1957, pp. 5, 22.

[2] *Literaturnaya Gazeta*, December 24, 1954.

[3] *Pravda*, September 12, 1955.

[4] *Izvestia*, May 31, 1957.

[5] *Voprosy Ekonomicheskoy Effektivnosti Kapital'nykh Vlozheniy i Novoy Tekhniki v Stroitel'stve*, Moscow, 1959, p. 72.

[6] *Finansy SSSR*, No. 1, 1959, p. 65.

[7] *Pravda*, August 17, 1957 and *Trud*, October 11, 1957.

[8] *Teoriya i Praktika Khozaystvennogo Rascheta*, Moscow, 1958, p. 105.

[9] *Finansy SSSR*, No. 1, 1959, p. 12.

[10] *Kommunist*, August 6, 1957 and September 27, 1957.

[11] *Finansy SSSR*, No. 1, 1959, p. 50.

[12] *Teoriya i Praktika Khozaystvennogo Rascheta*, op. cit., p. 74.

[13] Efimov, A. N., *Perestroyka Upravleniya Promyshlennost'yu i Stroitel'strom v SSSR*, Moscow, 1957, p. 94.

[14] *Teoriay i Praktika Khozaystvennogo Rascheta*, op. cit., p. 133.

[15] *Izvestia*, March 17, 1957.

[16] *Vestnik Statistiki*, No. 2, 1953, p. 39.

[17] *Planirovaniye v Rayone*, Moscow, 1957, pp. 116-21.

# CHAPTER 12

# Transportation and Communication
~~~~~~~~~~~~~~~~~~~~~~~~~~~~~~~~~~~~~~~~~~~~~~~~~~~~

## INTRODUCTION

Low-cost transportation, essential where regional division of labor exists, is of decisive importance in the exchange of agricultural and industrial goods produced in specialized regions. In a country with as widely dispersed natural and human resources as the USSR transportation is an important factor indeed. Coal from the Donbass and oil from the Bashkir ASSR must be hauled to consuming regions near Moscow and Leningrad some 900 to 1,500 miles away. The two-way exchange of grain and timber along the Volga River and the exchange of iron ore and coal between the Urals and the Kuzbass are other examples of region interdependence. Without expansion in transportation facilities, Soviet plans for industrial growth will not materialize. The Soviets know this, and during the last 43 years they have constructed new railroad lines, added second rail tracks, linked waterways with railroads, improved river transportation, and extended their air and highway traffic facilities to relieve the ever-growing demands of the rapidly advancing economy.

The Russians are already thinking in terms of new means of transportation to be introduced by the advent of sputniks. However, consideration of earth-bound forms of transportation is less visionary but more realistic for everyday transportation service. The actual expansion of industrial and agricultural production will depend on inexpensive, reliable, all-season transportation. While products of industry and agriculture are being hauled from source to consumption areas in increasing volume, the passenger services are also being increased. Therefore, because of the relative importance of freight and passenger service in the growth of the economy, the industrial expansion of the USSR is closely tied to the transportation services and their efficiency.

World War II caused considerable destruction to the transportation system, especially in areas occupied by the Germans, even though some expansion took place in the unoccupied regions. The Soviets claim that in World War II, 26 main railroad lines were destroyed and another eight were seriously damaged. About 40,000 miles of main railroad track and some 311,000 miles of secondary rail and sidings were destroyed. About 13,000 railroad bridges, 4,100 railroad stations and 317 repair shops were destroyed. Some 15,800 railroad engines and pieces of motorized equipment as well as 428,000 railroad cars were captured by Germany or damaged.[1] Though exaggerated, these claims indicate the degree of damages caused by the war. As a result, the years since the end of World War II have been devoted to rehabilitating the reduced transportation facilities and to new expansion in order to meet the still-growing demands of the industrial life of the country.

The railroad transport system is the most important of all forms of transportation. The Soviets claim that their rail network handles 40 per cent of the world's total freight turnover, as compared to ten per cent in 1929. During the 1950-55 period alone, the additional increase in rail freight turnover was equal to the total rail freight turnover of Great Britain and France combined. Expansion in means of transportation other than by rail has been even more spectacular, but its combined share in the total Soviet traffic load is only 19 per cent, and the railroads remain the major carrier of freight and passengers.

## LOCATION OF RESOURCES

Industrial expansion to new economic regions would have been impossible without an extension of the transportation network. In Tsarist times the Russian rail network was the largest in Europe, but its uneven distribution made it less effective. As much as 83 per cent of the total Russian rail network was in the European parts where most of the population and industrial activities were concentrated. Vast as it is, Siberia had only ten per cent of the total rail network, and the remaining seven per cent was in Central Asia. But as the natural resources were exploited, transportation facilities were expanded in the eastern regions where these resources were abundant. Thus, the average distance of freight traffic per metric ton increased from 435 miles in 1940 to 500 miles in 1958.[2] Now coal from the Kuzbass and iron ore from Magnitogorsk in the Urals are brought together for making steel in the Ural's Chelyabinsk Tractor Plant. The tractor, in turn, may be shipped to the Ukraine, Central Asia, or the Far East. Each of these regions must receive oil from the Baku (Azerbaydzhan) or the Second Baku fields (RSFSR) to operate their tractors and other machinery. The grain planted and harvested with these tractors is sent to consuming regions, sometimes thousands of miles away. The extent of regional interdependence may also be emphasized by the fact that the European parts of the USSR consumes annually not less than 14 billion matric tons of coal much of which is hauled from distant mining regions located 1,500 to 2,200 miles away. The cost of hauling coal alone by rail amounts to 800 million rubles, not considering depreciation of facilities and the impossibility of using them for other urgently needed freight traffic. The European parts of the Soviet Union produce over 80 per cent of all automobiles and almost all grain combines. But Central Asia and Siberia consumed most of the chemical fertilizer produced in the western parts of the USSR. Over 80 per cent of the total volume of cotton fabrics, about 70 per cent of the woolen fabrics, and 75 per cent of the leather footwear in the Soviet Union are produced in the Central Industrial Region of the European USSR for distribution throughout the country.

TABLE 1—*Regionalization of Rail Freight Traffic* [3]
(in percentage of total)

|  | Originated | | Received | |
|---|---|---|---|---|
|  | 1940 | 1955 | 1940 | 1955 |
| Total USSR: | 100.0 | 100.0 | 100.0 | 100.0 |
| European north | 1.9 | 3.1 | 1.3 | 1.7 |
| Northwestern | 5.5 | 2.9 | 7.8 | 4.4 |
| Western | 1.8 | 3.5 | 2.3 | 4.9 |
| Central Industrial Region | 16.0 | 14.4 | 22.6 | 19.3 |
| Southern | 32.9 | 27.5 | 27.2 | 24.8 |
| Caucasus | 9.7 | 7.5 | 8.1 | 6.7 |
| Volga River Valley | 4.9 | 1.4 | 5.2 | 4.6 |
| Urals | 9.3 | 14.7 | 9.4 | 14.7 |
| Central Asia | 4.8 | 6.6 | 4.5 | 6.5 |
| Western Siberia | 6.5 | 8.2 | 4.5 | 6.5 |
| Eastern Siberia | 3.2 | 4.8 | 2.9 | 3.1 |
| Far East | 3.5 | 2.4 | 4.2 | 2.8 |

Between 1940 and 1955 Central Asia and Siberia increased their freight shipments to other regions, whereas shipments from the central and southern regions decreased. The same trend is noted for freight received. The European central and southern regions, the Caucasus, and Volga River Valley reduced their share in the total tonnage originated from 63.3 per cent in 1940 to 50.8 per cent in 1955. On the other hand, the Urals, Central Asia, and the whole of Siberia increased their shipments from 27.3 per cent in 1940 to 36.7 per cent in 1955.

By 1965 the Soviets are planning to convert Siberia into the major base for coal and electric power output in order to produce all types of machinery, equipment and instruments. The Russians put their hopes in the eastern parts of the USSR as the Americans looked to the West during westward expansion. Central Asia, especially Northern Kazakhstan, and Siberia are the industrial frontier lands to which the young minds and imagination of Soviet school children are directed. It is not an El Dorado; it is a land of challenge, discovery, and exploitation of still unmapped resources by which the Russians hope to advance their standard of living.

With increased exploitation of eastern resources the demand for additional transportation facilities for hauling increased freight and passenger traffic must be met, and the Soviets are constructing new rail branches linking new resources with the main rail system, already in existence. On the established rail networks the freight turnover is being increased. Among these are the Karaganda, Omsk, Turkestan-Siberia, Krasnoyarsk, East-Siberia, Sverdlovsk, and South-Ural networks. By 1965 the Soviets expect to switch over about 43,500 miles of rail lines to electric and diesel traction in order to increase the traffic capacity. By concentrating on freight movements, the Soviets are attempting to make their limited rail transport capacity go further in serving the goal of increased production in new economical regions.

## FREIGHT TRANSPORTATION FACILITIES

With prewar and particularly wartime relocation of industry from west to east many consumers of raw materials moved closer to their sources. New industrial enterprises established during World War II and later in the eastern regions could not have expanded without transportation facilities sufficient to bring raw materials to factories and to ship finished products to consumers' markets. The extended transportation brought men and machinery for the exploitation of natural resources. It accelerated the establishment of new settlements. At the same time, increased use of local resources, especially coal, considerably reduced the volume of imported raw materials from older regions, and in many cases, the cost of production was reduced. Yet expansion in the output of local raw materials has not been equal to the demand, and the rate of consumption of them has been greater than their production; thus, eastern regions still have to import a considerable amount of raw materials from other regions.

### Railroads

The Soviet rail network is the largest of any country in Europe and is being constantly expanded as industry moves closer to raw material sources

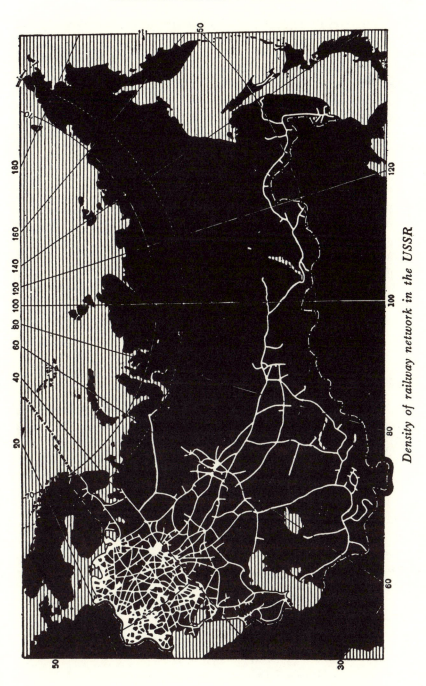

*Density of railway network in the USSR*

in the East. In 1940 the total rail length in use under all jurisdictions and of all types, including narrow-gauge lines, was about 85,100 miles, and and 131,300 miles in 1958. By 1965 the Soviets expect to build another 1,700 miles of trunk and secondary rail lines, making a total of about 133,000 miles. The most dense rail network, as stated above, is found in the European parts. Availability of the total Soviet railroads per 10,000 persons in 1940 was 3.4 miles, and by 1958 it had become less.[4] There are still tens of thousands of Soviet citizens who have never seen a railroad track and have never ridden on a train, especially in the Far North.

About 42 per cent of the total Soviet rail network is operated by organizations such as coal mining and timber enterprises for their own use. The importance of narrow-gauge track should not be underestimated. In developing new economic regions the first problem is the supply of materials and equipment, and since it is easier and cheaper to construct narrow-gauge track, especially on flat land, it may be quickly put into use. Narrow-gauge track was used in the vast grain-growing regions of the Kazakh SSR, for example. Now the Russians regret that they did not build wider track at the start; they must replace it with wider gauge standard track. Moreover, utilization of narrow-gauge tracks naturally requires additional expense in unloading from narrow-gauge sidings and reloading on wider gauge track lines, but under certain conditions, such as exist in the timber industry, the wide-gauge tracks are not as economically desirable as the narrow-gauge ones.

In 1940, the Soviet Union had about 63,400 miles of wide-gauge track, 72,000 miles in 1956, and by 1965 there should be some 78,000 miles. During the 16-year period from 1940 to 1956 the Soviets had replaced a large part of their narrow-gauge track with wide-gauge rails. As this replacement took place a program of electrification of railroad lines was intensified. In 1940 the USSR Ministry of Transportation administered about 1,200 miles of electrified trackline; by 1958 it was 5,900 miles. By the end of 1965 the Soviets expect to have about 18,600 miles of electrified rail track.[5] Most important freight routes and main passenger railroad lines have been electrified, as has rail service in suburban sectors of large industrial centers. The 1959-65 plan anticipates that the following routes will be completely electrified:[6]

> Moscow-Kuybyshev-Irkutsk-Far East
> Moscow-Gorki-Sverdlovsk
> Moscow-Kazan-Sverdlovsk
> Karaganda-Magnitogorsk-Ufa
> Moscow-Kharkov-Rostov-Mineralnye Vody

Some other, shorter routes serving the north and west are also to be electrified. In general by the end of 1965, the Soviets hope to have about 62,140 miles of rail track adaptable to electric or diesel traction. In 1959 electric and diesel traction already exceeded 40,000 miles.

TABLE 2—*Rail Network and Freight Traffic
Under the USSR Ministry of Transportation* [7]

| Indices | 1940 | 1950 | 1956 | 1958 |
|---|---|---|---|---|
| Length of network (miles) _____ | 65,900 | 72,600 | 75,000 | 76,300 |
| Freight turnover (billion metric ton miles) | 257.9 | 374.3 | 670.5 | 809.1 |
| Freight originated (million metric tons): | 592.6 | 834.3 | 1,371.0 | 1,616.9 |
| Coal and coke _____ | 153.0 | 266.0 | 422.0 | 478.8 |
| Mineral construction materials _____ | 112.0 | 158.0 | 263.0 | 324.2 |
| Grain for bread _____ | 45.0 | 39.0 | 68.0 | 71.5 |
| Timber _____ | 43.0 | 72.0 | 96.0 | 121.5 |
| Ores _____ | 35.0 | 48.0 | 89.0 | 108.1 |
| Oil products _____ | 30.0 | 43.0 | 87.0 | 112.5 |
| Ferrous metals _____ | 27.0 | 43.0 | 77.0 | 88.3 |
| Firewood _____ | 27.0 | 19.0 | 15.0 | 18.1 |
| Others _____ | 120.6 | 146.3 | 254.0 | 293.9 |

In 1940 coal, coke, and mineral construction materials represented about 45 per cent of the total freight traffic moved by the USSR Ministry of Transportation; in 1958 this figure increased to 50 per cent. It is interesting to note that, although the total length of railroad network under the USSR Ministry of Transportation increased only by about 16 per cent between 1940 and 1958, the freight turnover was 3.1 times greater, and freight originated increased by 2.7 times. The grater efficiency came as a result of better internal organization in the use of modernized equipment.

In 1958 freight turnover was 809.1 billion metric ton miles, an increase of 20 per cent over the 1956 volume. By 1965 the Soviets expect to increase their rail freight turnover by 40 to 45 per cent over the 1958 figure, reaching between 1,132.7 and 1,173.2 billion metric ton miles.[8] These are optimistic hopes. During the 1950-58 period the average annual increase in freight turnover amounted to 54.3 billion metric tons miles, whereas during the 1959-65 period it is expected to be 159.7 billion metric ton miles, a 300 per cent increase. Assuming that conversion to electric and diesel traction materializes as planned, the planned 1965 freight turnover would still be difficult if not impossible to achieve. The Soviets expect to increase their freight turnover by electric and diesel traction from 26 per cent of the total rail freight turnover in 1958 to 85 to 87 per cent in 1965. Such a rapid shift to electric and diesel traction would call for adjustment in other sectors of freight hauling activities, and maladjustments inevitably would crop up. Electrification of main rail systems is to be given special attention during the current Seven-Year Plan.

By increasing the number of electric and diesel locomotives, the Soviets during the 1959-65 period expect to reduce the cost of freight and passenger transportation. This, it is claimed, would save between 270 to 275 million metric tons of coal and would reduce the cost of fuel by 45 to 47 billion rubles.[9] However, with a reduction in coal consumption by railroads the demand for electricity is to be increased from 4.6 per cent in 1958 to eight per cent by 1965 and the fuel for diesel engines is to be expanded from 4.6 to 14.3 per cent.

The Soviets claim that on an average one electric engine can replace the combined capacity of two steam engines; on some systems, such as the Omsk, every electric engine would replace 4.6 steam engines. It is also claimed that on an average one diesel engine can replace 1.8 steam engines and on the Orenburg, Tashkent, and South-Eastern lines every diesel engine would be equal to two or three steam engines. The Soviets have estimated that by utilization of electric engines as compared with steam engines the average cost of transportation would be reduced by 34.5 per cent; diesel traction would be reduced by 29 per cent. In addition, the Soviets are expecting to install automotive equipment on 11,200 to 12,400 miles of rail systems. This would displace many workers and thus would reduce the cost.

As a result of these improvements, by the end of 1965 electric engines are expected to carry between 45 to 46 per cent of the total Soviet freight turnover. Similarly, diesel engines are to carry between 40 and 41 per cent of freight turnover. The other 13 to 15 per cent of the freight turnover is to be carried by the steam engines.

To achieve the 1965 targets assigned to the railroad industry is a difficult task. At the end of 1958 the length of railroad lines converted to electric and diesel traction was some 12,400 miles, and by 1965 it is expected to be fivefold—a tremendous task indeed. In 1958 electric locomotives were used in hauling 15.8 per cent of all freight turnover while diesels transported 10.2 per cent, for a total of 26 per cent.[10] To increase this percentage to 85 to 87 per cent by 1965 would require unusually strenuous concentration of efforts. Moreover, in comparison with 1958 the Soviets expect to increase their total rail freight turnover in 1965 by 39 to 43 per cent.

In 1957 the Soviets built 271 trunk-line electric and 400 diesel locomotives. In 1958 they produced 344 electric and 712 diesel engines. By 1965 the Soviets expect to construct between 2,500 and 2,700 electric and diesel locomotives having a combined capacity of between 8.4 and nine million horsepower. During the 1959-65 period the average annual production of electric and diesel locomotives is expected to be 375 engines against 1,056 engines produced in 1958. Even at the reduced rate in production of these locomotives during the current Seven-Year Plan the Soviets will most likely be forced to revise their planned target downward as they have done in the past. Of course, the Soviets might buy them from other countries. Soviet economists do realize that the anticipated increase in freight turnover during the next seven years is possible only by rapid and timely reconversion of main trunklines from steam to electric and diesel engines. During this period of time the Southern-Siberian line, extending some 4,350 miles, is to be fully utilized by the Kuzbass, Altay, Kazakhstan, and Central Asia. The Middle-Siberian line is also expected to be completed, and new main lines are planned for construction in the Kazakh SSR, the Urals, and the Volga River Valley.

Despite considerable improvements made on the rail network during the past few years there are notable strains on it, especially in the Urals, Siberia, and Donbass, and at outlets from these main lines. These lines are the bottlenecks in the Soviet rail network, and increasing streams of traffic pass over these points on a gigantic scale. To relieve the pressure, increased electrification and the introduction of diesel engines are considered the key factors in increasing the rail traffic potential. It is claimed that a new eight-axle electric locomotive with a capacity of 5,700 horsepower will pull trains weighing as much as 4,000 metric tons while developing a speed of up to 62 miles per hour. It is also claimed that trunkline two-section diesel engines would have a freight-carrying capacity ranging from 2,500 to 3,000 horsepower per section at increased speed. Thus, by increasing the speed and load on the existing main rail lines, the Soviets expect to increase the efficiency of their railroads.

The busiest multiple track is the Trans-Siberian line, where trains on the main sections run about every five to seven minutes. One of its most important sections runs between Omsk and Novosibirsk and is entirely electrified. From Omsk, electrification extends to the west towards Moscow and to the east towards Irkutsk; by 1965 it is expected to reach Vladivostok. Thus, slowly but surely the Soviets are fulfilling their plans to improve their railroads. And even though the 1965 plan may not be fully realized, the Soviet railroads at the end of that year will be more efficient and more powerful than they were in the past.

As was noted above, over 80 per cent of all Soviet freight is handled by railroads. They transport almost all ores produced in the country, 90 per cent of the coal, 80 per cent of the pig iron and steel, and about 40 per cent of the grain. Since about 75 per cent of their income is derived from freight, the Soviet railroads are geared mainly to carry freight rather than passenger traffic. Consequently, current industrial expansion requires greater emphasis on freight-carrying capacity, without which the development of distant economic regions and increasing output of the older industrial areas would not be possible.

### Rivers and Canals

The Soviet Union has a vast network of inland waterways. The total combined length of all rivers is some 248,600 miles, yet only one-third is usable for transportation, even during the navigation period.

As was shown in Chapter 1, practically all major rivers in the European parts of the USSR flow to the south and the eastern rivers flow to the north, without cross-country (east-to-west) inland waterways. However, many rivers in the western parts are close enough to be linked with man-made canals. As a result, the Soviets have created a continuous waterway uniting the Black, Azov, and Caspian Seas in the south with the White and Baltic Seas in the north, using the Volga River as a major artery. The main canals are the Moscow Canal, linking the White and Baltic Seas, the Dnieper-Bug Canal, the Volga-Don Canal, and the canals in the Mariinsk system, which connect Leningrad with the Volga River. By 1965 another canal linking the Volga River with the Baltic Sea is expected to be in operation. In 1957 about 4,400 miles of canals were used.

In the Asiatic part of the USSR, rivers are not connected for commercial navigation by canals as they are in the European part, although there are large canals such as the Great Fergana Canal, the Great Turkmen Canal, and others which are used primarily for irrigation and secondarily for transportation. But in Western Siberia and Eastern Siberia the tributaries of many rivers are close to one another, making it practical for certain freight to be moved from one river to another. This is especially true in the case of larger rivers such as the Ob, Irtysh, Yenisey, Angara, and Lena. The rivers located in southern parts of the USSR are least navigible because of mountainous terrains in the Caucasus and the lack of outlets to the open seas or to other navigible rivers. The rivers of Central Asia are shallow and have rapidly changing channels so that all navigation is difficult, even with specially constructed flat-bottomed barges.

The advantages of river over rail transportation are many, despite freezing during long winters. Construction and maintenance costs of tugs, motorized and non-motorized barges, and other types of boats are considered by the Soviets inexpensive in comparison with costs of railroad engines. Loading capacities of barges are greater than those of railroad cars and the means of traction used are less expensive. These major cost factors make river freight traffic cheaper than rail, even though river transport is much slower. Such bulky goods as timber, grain, salt, and oil comprise more than 90 per cent of the total river freight turnover, whereas the same goods account for less than 60 per cent of the total rail freight turnover.

TABLE 3—*River Transportation Freight Traffic* [11]

| Indices | 1940 | 1950 | 1956 | 1958 |
|---|---|---|---|---|
| Length of network (miles) _____ | 66,700 | 80,900 | 82,200 | 82,700 |
| Freight turnover (billion metric ton miles) | 22.4 | 28.7 | 43.8 | 53.1 |
| Freight originated million metric tons)__ | 72.9 | 91.5 | 146.8 | 178.3 |
| Timber and firewood _____ | 40.2 | 50.5 | 72.4 | 82.5 |
| Oil products _____ | 9.7 | 11.9 | 15.0 | 16.2 |
| Mineral construction materials _____ | 7.6 | 11.7 | 33.9 | 49.8 |
| Grain for bread _____ | 5.2 | 4.5 | 5.6 | 6.9 |
| Coal _____ | 2.2 | 4.3 | 8.8 | 10.7 |
| Salt _____ | 1.4 | 1.7 | 2.0 | — |
| Others _____ | 5.9 | 6.9 | 39.1 | — |
| Average length of haul per metric ton (miles) _____ | 306 | 312 | 298 | 298 |

As in the case of railroads, the efficiency of Soviet river transportation has also considerably improved during the 1940-58 period. Its total mileage increased by 24 per cent, while freight turnover and traffic each increased by 2.4 times.

In 1940 timber and firewood represented 55 per cent of the total freight traffic volume of Soviet river transportation but only 46 per cent in 1958. Mineral construction materials represented ten per cent of the total capacity in 1940 and 28 per cent in 1958. Transportation of oil products in 1940 represented 13 per cent and only nine per cent in 1958. It is interesting to note that between 1940 and 1956 the average distance of all freight traffic per metric ton decreased by eight miles, and for oil products by 125 miles, although the distance of transported timber and firewood increased by 25 miles. The decline in the volume of oil and oil products transported by river is the result of the expansion of oil production in the Second Baku and the construction of pipe lines. These two factors have reduced the significance of Baku in oil shipping via the Caspian Sea to Astrakhan and then upstream on the Volga River.

In 1958 river transportation represented only 5.3 per cent of Soviet freight turnover as compared to 81 per cent represented by railroads. About 93 per cent of the total river freight turnover is concentrated in the RSFSR. The Soviets are expecting to increase river freight turnover traffic during the 1959-65 period by 1.6 times, mainly by reconstruction of the river fleet, by tripling the capacity of river carriers, and by improving port efficiency in loading and unloading. It is anticipated that during the current Seven-Year Plan reconstruction of existing navigation facilities on the Volga, Kama, Dnieper, and especially on Siberian arterial waterways will be intensified, and mechanized loading and unloading will be increased by 75 per cent. A considerable increase in the repair facilities is also expected, mainly for the Siberian waterways. Because of seasonal operations on inland waterways the use of loading and unloading installations cannot, on an average, be employed to more than 30 per cent of their capacity. Nevertheless, by increased mechanization the Soviets expect to reduce costs, to speed up loading and unloading, and therefore to boost freight turnover.

## Maritime Transportation

The Soviet Union's ocean and sea frontiers are more than twice as long as its land frontiers. The long water boundary includes the Arctic and Pacific coastlines as well as the shores of the Black and Caspian Seas in the south. Despite the tremendous ocean and sea coastline neither the Soviet Union nor Tsarist Russia before it has ever been a major maritime power. The importance of maritime transportation is limited by severe climatic conditions. With many ports frozen for as long as nine months of the year maritime shipping faces problems similar to those of the river transportation system.

The most important transportation system is located in the Black and Caspian Seas. They transport about 63 per cent of the total Soviet maritime freight—mostly oil, timber, cotton, grain, coal, and cement. Over 50 pe rcent of the total Soviet maritime cargo is shipped on the Black Sea alone. Timber and fish are the major items hauled on the Baltic, Northern, and Pacific waters. Marine transport between domestic ports located on different seas is of relatively small significance, but freight shipping between ports of the same seas, such as on the Black, Azov, and Caspian Seas, has been greatly expanded. Maritime transportation of oil from Baku to Astrakhan comprises nearly half of the country's total sea freight turnover. The freight hauls in the northern and eastern seas are limited by freezing of the ports and because of the sparse population and underdeveloped economies of the regions. However, the northern seaway is getting more attention by the Soviets as an area potentially valuable for military and economic development, especially with the construction of the atomic icebreaker "Lenin" in 1959.

TABLE 4—*Maritime Transportation System* [12]

| Indices | 1940 | 1950 | 1956 | 1958 |
|---|---|---|---|---|
| Freight turnover (billion metric ton-miles) ____ | 12.8 | 21.4 | 44.5 | 57.4 |
| Freight originated (million metric tons): _____ | 31.2 | 33.7 | 57.7 | 70.8 |
| Liquid freight _____ | 19.6 | 15.8 | 24.9 | 31.1 |
| Non-liquid freight _____ | 11.0 | 17.2 | 31.1 | 37.8 |
| Timber and firewood _____ | 0.6 | 0.7 | 1.7 | 1.9 |
| Average length of haul per metric ton (miles)__ | 411 | 636 | 711 | 811 |

Table 4 excludes freight hauled by the fishing and non-ferrous enterprises which transported 2.8 million metric tons in 1956. It also excludes the volume of Central Asian fleet, whose maritime tonnage is of minor significance.

In 1940, maritime freight transportation handled about five per cent of the total Soviet freight turnover. World War II caused considerable damage to the maritime shipping facilities. It is claimed by the Soviets that over 1,400 passenger and cargo seagoing vessels were sunk or damaged and many ports were completely destroyed or badly damaged, especially Sevastopol, Odessa, Nikolaev, Leningrad, Murmansk, and Novorossiisk. After the war maritime shipping facilities were restored, expanded, and modernized. As a result, the 1958 freight turnover increased by almost 4.5 times in comparison with 1940, and origination of cargo doubled. The postwar rehabilitation and expansion of marine transportation, though fast, was not as rapid as that of the railroads. In 1955 about 56 per cent of the time was spent in tying up at the ports for repairs, loading, and unloading. Even the most efficient of all fleets, the Sakhalin fleet, failed to fulfill the planned targets in tonnage and ton-miles, showing losses in operation.

The 1959-65 plan for the expansion of marine transportation calls for doubling of the freight turnover. During this period the tonnage capacity is to be doubled; a large part of the increase is to come from other countries. The efficiency of port facilities is to be increased 60 to 70 per cent and mechanized loading and unloading equipment by 75 per cent. It is interesting to note that while an increase in cargo hauling is anticipated during this period in the Far East, Black Sea, Sea of Azov, the northern seas, and other waters, the Caspian Sea, with its lowering water level and its hazardous approach to the mouth of the Volga River, is declining in importance. Many sea ports are being enlarged to increase their capacities, and new warehouses and modernized piers are being constructed or improved, especially in the Black and Baltic Seas. The main emphasis is on faster seagoing vessels.

### Trucking

Despite the vast plains which facilitate construction of highways, the trucking facilities in the USSR are limited. Great distances between industrial centers and heavy winter snowfall in most parts of the Soviet Union are retarding factors in the development of a cross-country hard-surfaced highway system. For these reasons the Soviet trucking industry is limited to hauling freight over short distances connecting neighboring districts and to moving freight from manufacturing bases to railroad stations or river wharves. Only in regions lacking rail and river transportation such as the North, the Far East, and Central Asia does inter-regional feight trucking serve long distances. The cost of trucking over long distances is greater than by river or rail, and in many parts trucking is too seasonal to be practical. Still, many perishable goods are moved over highways between Moscow and Kharkov as well as over other well-maintained routes.

The development of the Soviet trucking industry depends on production of trucks, on availability of hard-surfaced roads, and on the ability of allied industries to produce equipment and materials for the construction and maintenance of highways under adverse climatic conditions. Thus, the immediate expansion in Soviet hard-surfaced road networks is limited to urbanized regions and to newly developed areas where construction of railroads is not economically feasible. Major hard-surfaced highways are located in the European parts of the Soviet Union, linking Moscow with Brest, Minsk, Kharkov, and Simferopol and connecting Kiev with Kharkov, Rostov, Mineralnye Vody, and Ordzhonikidze. Several shorter side-routes of main highways are located in the Urals, Caucasus, Central Asia, and in Siberia. Naturally, the RSFSR, because of its size and industrial development, has the greatest concentration of the Soviet trucking industry—45 per cent of the total hard-surface highway mileage is located there.

According to Table 5, the total road mileage in 1958 was about 55,100 miles less than in 1940. This is due to replacement of secondary and "dirt" roads by other means of transportation such as railroads. However, the combined length of hard-surfaced roads between 1940 and 1958 increased by some 57,500 miles, and although concrete-asphalt roads increased by

8.2 times it is the gravel roads that carry most of the Soviet overland freight and passengers, especially between isolated points in the North and in the East.

TABLE 5—*Overland Motor Vehicle Road Network* [13]

| Indices | 1940 | 1950 | 1956 | 1958 |
|---|---|---|---|---|
| All network mileage (thousand) _____ | 951.5 | 963.4 | 935.8 | 896.4 |
| Had-surfaced total: _____ | 89.1 | 110.1 | 133.3 | 146.6 |
| Concrete and asphalt _____ | 4.4 | 11.9 | 29.3 | 36.3 |
| Gravel _____ | 41.3 | 52.3 | 60.8 | 66.8 |
| Freight turnover (billion metric ton-miles) ____ | 5.5 | 12.5 | 30.1 | 47.7 |
| Freight originated (million metric tons) _____ | 858.6 | 1,859.2 | 4,200.9 | 6,474.4 |
| Average haulage per metric ton (miles) _____ | 6.5 | 6.7 | 7.1 | 7.4 |

Trucking freight turnover during the 1940-58 period increased 8.7 times, and the increase in freight originated increased 7.5 times, whereas the average shipping distance per metric ton increased only 14 per cent. There are several reasons for this. In the first place, the 1958 main and secondary roads were much better than they were in 1940, and an improvement in trucking turnover and length of haul was realized correspondingly. The greatest increase in trucking freight turnover between 1940 and 1958 took place in the Kazakh SSR. In general, over four-fifths of all trucking freight turnover is concentrated in three republics—the RSFSR, Ukraine, and the Kazakh SSR.[14]

The Soviet trucking industry comprises two sectors: the state-controlled trucking enterprises administered by sovnarkhozy, which provide services to their industrial, trading, and other organizations; and trucks belonging to individual enterprises such as factories, collective and state farms, mining and other industries, which haul products from their establishments to other destinations.

At the end of the 1956 the Soviet Union counted about 2.45 million trucks. One-fourth were concentrated in various agricultural enterprises; the rest were in the hands of state organizations and industrial enterprises. Many of these owners have from three to nine vehicles, but others have fleets of 100 or more. The efficiency of the larger trucking organizations in hauling freight is 86 per cent higher than that of the smaller fleets, and the cost of hauling per mile is much lower in larger motor pools. For example, hauling charges per metric ton-mile in 1954 ranged from 8.06 rubles by small trucking organizations to about 48 kopeks by the larger organizations.[15] Prior to 1952 there were many trucking freight rate scales.

Beginning with January 1952 their number was reduced, and in July 1955 stable rates for short hauls and regional differential rates were established. The basic rate was calculated on the basis of a two to 2.5 metric ton load for each ton-mile. All truck-hauled goods fall into four types of freight now. The first type consists of goods occupying the full capacity of the truck such as stones, bricks, books, metals, and so on; the second type, goods such as garments, using 71 to 99 per cent of the capacity; the third type, goods such as bottled commodities, furs, etc., taking 51 to 70 per cent of the carrier's capacity; and the fourth type, goods such as hay, raw cotton, and the like which use 50 per cent or less of the truck's capacity. Each type of goods hauled up to a distance of 62 miles has a different rate per metric ton-mile. In addition zone differentials ranging between five and 60 per cent may be added to the ton-mile rate. Rates per metric ton-mile and zone differentials are considerably higher in Siberia and Central Asia than the average charges for the USSR. In some instances freight rates for short hauls are fixed on an hourly basis.

The Soviets expect that between 1959 and 1965 freight turnover by the trucking industry will increase 1.9 times. To achieve this target they are planning to construct 2.8 times more road mileage than was constructed during the past seven years. New highways are to be mainly of cement surface, but considerable mileage of gravel for secondary roads of local importance, especially in the newly opened agricultural regions, is also anticipated. It is also planned that by 1965 the freight capacity will increase by 40 per cent over 1958. This target is to be attained by increased production of new trucks.

In 1940 the Soviets produced 136,000 trucks and buses, and in 1958 they turned out 389,000.[16] Since the main emphasis during the current Seven-Year Plan is to increase production of buses by 4.4 times, the anticipated output of new trucks probably will be at the same level as in the past, if not lower. Nevertheless, the Soviets expect that by 1965, freight shipping by motor road transport will be almost doubled as compared with 1958.

This will involve nearly five million trucks using about 100,000 miles of hard-surface roads. Although the number of trucks is expected to double by 1965, animal-drawn transportation will remain an important factor in rural areas. Animal power is used when roads are covered with deep snow or are too muddy for motor vehicles, and in deserts. Nevertheless, as industrial expansion develops, better motorized freight facilities are also being improved, with special emphasis on hard-surface roads. In 1940, there were 4.7 miles of hard-surface road per 10,000 persons, and seven miles in 1958. Nevertheless, because of unfavorable climatic condition and sparsely populated areas separated by long distances the Soviet trucking industry will always be of local rather than transcontinental importance.

## Airlines

Soviet air transportation may well be termed an infant industry and as such it has grown rapidly. This is the fastest but most expensive freight carrier of all. It links large urban and industrial center with remote regions lacking other fast transportation facilities. The importance of the airlines in the development of the Arctic cannot be ignored. Soviet airlines specialize in distant freight hauls of valuable or highly perishable products. The vastness of the country and the widely dispersed population force a rapid expansion of air transport. Because of the scarcity of refrigerator railroad cars and trucks, fruits from central Asia are shipped by air to Moscow, and flowers are flown from the Crimea to Leningrad. Precious furs from Yakutia and gold from Magadan are shipped to Moscow by air. Spare parts and equipment needed by remotely located enterprises are also moved by the airlines.

The Soviet Union prossesses the longest air routes over land areas, and there are many large and well-equipped airports in major cities as well as hundreds of smaller airports and landing strips. In remote regions landing facilities consist mainly of crude landing strips with inadequate repair or radar facilities. This requires skill at bush flying and landing on frozen rivers.

The total mileage of overland air routes was about 54,000 miles in 1940 and approximately 131,200 miles in 1958.[17] The volume of freight transported by the Soviet Civil Air Organization (Aeroflot) has steadily increased from 60,000 metric tons in 1940 to 486,000 metric tons in 1958. By 1965 originated tonnage is expected to be more than a million metric tons.

Between 1940 and 1958 the freight turnover by airlines increased by about 17 times and the increase in the tonnage originated was approximately 8.1 times, but it is the growth in passenger traffic that takes the lead with an increase of about 21 times.

During the current Seven-Year Plan the Soviets expect to increase air freight and passenger traffic. Passenger traffic alone is to be increased six-fold. Moreover, a large-scale replacement of older aircraft by new and heavier planes is planned. Consequently, old airports are to be enlarged and 90 new ones are to be built to accommodate new airplanes. There will also be construction and enlargement of airports of local significance. Currently the Soviets are producing five different jet and turbo-prop models for civilian use in long distance flights. These will form the backbone of

Aeroflot's new fleet. For suburban air transportation the Soviets are introducting helicopters. The trial was made in 1959 using about 6,000 machines for the convenience of the public residing in large urban centers. The largest helicopter is the YAK-24 "flying wagon."

The new TU-114 four-engine turbo-prop airliner can carry up to 220 passengers with a payload of 75,000 pounds. On longer hops it can carry 170 passengers and 35,000 pounds of freight. It can fly non-stop from Moscow to New York, some 4,660 miles via the Arctic route, and its top speed is 600 miles per hour. The TU-110 is a four-engine jet which can carry 100 passengers at a speed of 515 miles per hour. There is a smaller model of similar construction, the TU-104. The IL-18 Moskva, another four-engine turbo-prop, can handle a 100-passenger or 14-ton payload. The AN-10 Ukraina turbo-prop engines are similar to the IL-18 Moskva and the plane carries a heavier payload, up to 25 tons; it can operate on dirt or grass runways. Of course, there are numerous older models used off the main air routes which carry cargo and passengers. In 1958 the Soviet Civilian Air Transportation overfulfilled it freight targets by three per cent and its passenger traffic by 17 per cent. It is expected that by 1965 air passenger traffic will lead air freight by a considerable margin.

## Pipe Lines

The utilization of pipelines in Russia, started in 1906, has greatly expanded. They are used to move crude oil and natural gas from fields of production to major refining, shipping, and consuming points. The most important are the oil pipelines concentrated largely in the Caucasus, Volga River Valley, Ural, and Western Sibera. In 1958 pipelines handled about 75 per cent of the total transport of oil—about two per cent of the total Soviet freight turnover.

The greatest expansion in the use of oil pipelines has taken place since 1950. The cost of construction of pipelines is below that of railroads. The cost of each mile of constructed pipeline ranges from 249,000 to 373,000 rubles, or approximately 40 to 50 per cent of the cost of constructing a mile of railroad. Moreover, a mile of pipeline requires about the same amount of metal as a mile of railroad.[18] Therefore the use of pipelines is justifiable economically, and once pipelines are laid the cost of transporting oil is considerably less than by rail and even cheaper than shipment by river. The cost of maintaining pipelines is considerably less than for any other transportation means, and because of the greater all-round economy, use of oil pipelines is expanding rapidly, leaving other means of transportation free for hauling other goods.

TABLE 6—*Oil Pipelines Network* [19]

| Indices | 1940 | 1950 | 1956 | 1958 |
|---|---|---|---|---|
| Length in miles (thousands) _____ | 2.5 | 3.3 | 7.2 | 8.9 |
| Freight originated (million metric tons) _____ | 7.9 | 15.3 | 65.3 | 94.9 |
| Turnover in billion metric ton-miles _____ | 2.6 | 3.3 | 13.9 | 31.0 |
| Average length of haul (miles) _____ | 299 | 199 | 195 | — |

As can be seen from Table 6, the length of the oil pipeline network increased by 3.6 times between 1940 and 1958, and origination of freight increased over twelvefold. Moreover, as the length of the entire pipeline network increased the average length of haul has declined by more than 100 miles as a result of relocation of production of crude oil from Baku on the Caspian Sea to the Second Baku between the Volga River and the Urals. Among the pipelines constructed before World War II are the Gur'ev-Orsk, Groznyy-Tuapse, and Baku-Batumi oil pipelines. The Tuymazy-Omsk and Okha-Khabarovsk pipelines are notable results of the great expansion which took place after the war.

During the current Seven-Year Plan the oil pipelines are to be tripled. It is expected that by 1965 oil freight turnover will be increased by 5.6 times. The RSFSR is to construct six or seven new oil refineries and to lay some 7,520 miles of new pipelines. By 1965 oil piplines should extend from the Second Bauk to Irkutsk in the east and across the European part of the USSR some 2,500 miles long, to Poland, Eastern Germany, Czechoslovakia, and Hungary.

Among the pipelines transporting natural gas the Sverdlovsk line in the Urals from which natural gas is piped to Berezovo on the lower Ob River is notable. Saratov pipes its gas to Moscow. The Stavropol gas fields supply Moscow and also Groznyy, Tiflis, Sukhumi, Rostov-on-Don, and Stalino. In the far western part of the European USSR, gas pipelines are to link the Minsk gas fields with Leningrad, Wilno, Riga, and Drogobych. These are the main gas pipelines, but shorter ones have already been constructed or are under construction in the Urals, the Ukraine, Central Industrial regions, and on the upper Volga River.

In their industrial expension plan for 1959-65 the Soviets expect to intensify construction of pipelines for oil and gas products as the cheapest means of transportation. By 1965 it is planed to construct some 16,200 miles of natural gas pipelines. The rich Dashava natural gas deposits in the Western Ukraine and Stavropol in the Northern Caucasus are planned to become major suppliers of natural gas to the Baltic regions, Leningrad, and Moscow. The Kuybyshev natural gas is to be piped to Gorki and

Cherepovets; the Saratov gas to be delivered to Gorki, Yaroslav, and Zlato-ust; the Bukhara gas developed since 1958 is to be piped via Aralsk to Chelyabinsk and to other parts of the Urals and Central Asia.

It is anticipated that the largest new natural gas pipelines will originate from Dashava-Kiev-Moscow and extend some 820 miles, the Saratov-Moscow pipeline to extend some 500 miles, and the Mannibaevsk-Kazan-Gorki pipeline to extend about 400 miles. Because of the greater use of natural gas, by 1965 the number of workers employed in this and in related industries is expected to be increased four times more than in 1958.

## PASSENGER TRAFFIC

Most passengers on all types of state-controlled carriers are traveling on official business or commuting to and from their places of employment. Vacationists and those who travel to change their residences are of secondary importance.

TABLE 7—*Production of New Land Transportation Facilities* [20]

| Indices | 1940 | 1950 | 1956 | 1958 |
|---|---|---|---|---|
| Railroad freight cars, two-axle units ____ | 30,900 | 50,800 | 40,200 | 40,300 |
| Railroad passenger cars _____ | 1,051 | 912 | 1,799 | 1,800 |
| Passenger automobiles _____ | 5,500 | 64,600 | 97,800 | 122,000 |

The greatest wartime damage was sustained by freight and passenger cars, and although the 1958 construction of freight cars was 10,500 below that of 1950, output in 1958 was 30 per cent more than that of 1940. In pas-senger railroad cars the 1950 output was under that of 1940, but in 1958 it was 70 per cent above the 1940 production level. There was only token production of automobiles in 1940, mostly for official use, but production in 1958 increased considerably. At the end of 1956, the number of non-military motor vehicles in the entire USSR totalled about 3.1 million, in-cluding approximately 2.4 million trucks, 600,000 passenger cars and jeeps, and 55,000 buses. However, with emphasis on urban and suburban public transportation networks, the Soviets considerably increased production of buses. In 1957 they produced 452,000 buses and 475,000 in 1958. By 1965 the number of buses is expected to be 4.4 times greater than in 1958, and the number of taxis is also to be increased.

Of the total number of trucks and automobiles about 300,000 are owned by private citizens and collective farms. About 50 per cent of all auto-mobiles are owned by private citizens. Despite the rapid increase in pas-senger transportation facilities aside from railroads, it is the rail passenger traffic which is the most important. In 1956 over 40 per cent of the passenger rail cars were of obsolete design; local and suburban trains included many old, worn-out cars without even minimum conveniences, not to mention air-condtioning. In 1957 the Soviets tested a new type of air-condtioned train capable of a speed of up to 110 miles an hour.

TABLE 8—*Passenger Traffic Turnover* [21]

| Indices | 1940 | 1950 | 1956 | 1958 |
|---|---|---|---|---|
| Total (billion passenger-miles): __ | 66.1 | 61.1 | 109.9 | 131.7 |
| Railroad _____ | 60.9 | 54.7 | 88.5 | 98.4 |
| River _____ | 2.4 | 1.7 | 2.2 | 2.5 |
| Bus _____ | 2.1 | 3.2 | 16.4 | 26.5 |
| Maritime _____ | 0.6 | 0.7 | 0.9 | 0.9 |
| Airline _____ | 0.1 | 0.8 | 1.9 | 3.4 |

In 1940 the rail passenger turnover represented 92.9 per cent of the total; in 1958, only 75 per cent. River passenger traffic in 1940 accounted for 3.6 per cent of the total; by 1958, only two per cent. On the other hand, bus passenger traffic increased from 3.2 per cent of the total in 1940 to 20 per cent in 1958. The percentage of maritime passenger traffic turnover remained unchanged in both years. But air passenger traffic turnover increased from a mere 0.2 per cent of the total in 1940 to two per cent in 1958. In general, during the 1940-1958 period passenger traffic turnover on all means of transportation almost doubled; railroads increased 61 per cent, maritime 50 per cent, bus service 12.6 times, air service 34 times, and river transportation alone remained practically unchanged.

Most Russians travel by bus and by railroad. In 1958 the average length of travel by bus was 3.2 miles per person, but in intra-urban travel the average distance was only 2.4 miles.

Between 1940 and 1958 the total number of passengers using public transportation increased by 5.1 times, with the greatest increase taking place in the use of bus service. Most rail passenger traffic is handled in three constituent republics: the RSFSR, the Ukraine, and Azerbaydzhan, which transport about 90 per cent of the total turnover. Of the total number of rail passengers, about 85 per cent use intra-urban systems for commuting to their jobs, for shopping, for reaching sources of entertainment, or for any other reason. Since the RSFSR, Ukraine, and Azerbaydzhan have the largest concentrations of rail passenger traffic, their intra-urban passenger traffic amounts to 92 per cent of the nationwide total.

Since the cost of rail transportation per passenger-mile is twice as great as that per freight-mile, the Soviets have increased their bus service by many fold since 1940. About 65 per cent of all bus passenger traffic is

TABLE 9—*Number of Passengers Transported by Public Carriers Excluding Airlines* [22]
(in millions)

| Carrier | 1940 | 1956 | 1958 |
|---------|------|------|------|
| Total: | 2,009.6 | 7,206.4 | 10,325.0 |
| Rail | 1,343.5 | 1,658.3 | 1,834.0 |
| Bus | 590.0 | 5,458.2 | 8,376.7 |
| River | 73.0 | 81.7 | 102.2 |
| Maritime | 3.1 | 8.2 | 12.1 |

handled in the RSFSR, and about 11 per cent in the Ukraine. Of all bus passenger in the USSR approximately 90 per cent used bus service for inra-urban transportation. Buses are the cheapest of all facilities, and their popularity is reflected in the fact that they are always packed to capacity. Even in 1940 the average single bus handled 5,000 persons per day; in 1956 each bus accommodated 9,250 persons per day—an increase of 85 per cent. The average speed of a bus is 11 miles per hour, suggesting that because of the great number of passengers, time spent in loading and unloading of passengers takes a large percentage of the driver's time.

The importance of river transportation lies in freight rather than in passenger traffic. Between 1940 and 1958 passenger traffic on rivers increased 40 per cent. The average length of river travel per person in 1958 was considerably shorter than in 1940. About three-fourths of the total passenger traffic turnover is concentrated in five of the 19 river traffic organizations. These five organizations are the Volga, Volga-Tanker, Kama, Dnieper, and Moscow river routes. In addition to state-owned and operated river facilities, there are a number of self-propelled and non-propelled river boats owned by industrial enterprises and establishments, which carried about 2.2 million passengers in 1955. These are not public carriers but are used for freight and passenger movements of the respective organizations. Those collective farms which are located on rivers on seashores and have boats also carry their own freight and passengers, but their contribution to the total river traffic is negligible as compared to public carriers. In general, over 96 per cent of the total river passenger traffic is moved by publc carriers and is concentrated in the RSFSR (82 per cent), the Ukraine (12 per cent), and White Russia (two per cent).

Maritime passenger traffic is less seasonal, especially in the southern seas, than river traffic. Because of this, maritime passenger traffic between 1940 and 1958 increased by four times. However, with the increase passenger traffic the average length of travel on the sea has declined from 153 miles in 1940 to 61 miles in 1958, mainly because of the greater number of people making short pleasure trips. Most maritime traffic now is devoted to coastline needs. Only along the Northern Sea Route is the length of maritime passenger traffic greater, due to sparse population in related areas. In addition to state-owned and operated maritime carriers, industrial organizations such as fishing and non-ferrous enterprises maintain carriers to transport their own employees, but this share of the total public maritime shipping carriers is less than four per cent.

At present, the Soviet Union has a number of modern river and maritime passenger liners, especially on the Volga River and on the Black Sea. Many of the seagoing vessels carry both freight and passengers, especially in the Far Eastern and Far Northern routes. One of the reasons for recent expansion in maritime traffic is the availability of larger number of icebreakers used in regions where ports are frozen during the winter. The atomic icebreaker "Lenin" will undoubtedly increase maritime traffic, especially on the Northern Sea Route.

Commercially scheduled airline passenger service was inaugurated in 1923 between Moscow and Gorki. Between 1940 and 1958, the length of airline routes increased by 2.4 times while the number of passengers flown increased by 21 times. The Soviet Union has a number of large and comfortable passenger airliners used in scheduled transportation of passengers and mail which almost reach the speed of sound. Regular air transportation has been established with every country in the Soviet bloc and with a number of other countries.

The vastness of the territory within the Soviet Union makes necessary the expansion of the airlines. Traffic of mail and passengers from the western boundary of the Soviet Union to the eastern parts can be made in 12 hours. Regular air transportation has been established between Moscow and Irkutsk in six hours' flying time. From Moscow one may fly to Tbilisi in 2.5 hours, to Tashkent in four hours, to Peking in 8.5 hours, and to Prague in three hours.

Travel by air costs more than any other means and for this reason it is normally used only for urgent official business or for missions of mercy. In Siberia and Central Asia, especially during the winter, air transport serves regions on non-scheduled routes, and since these regions lack good maintenance and landing facilities flying requires considerable skill and knowledge of the area. A large number of the planes serving distant regions are old propellor-driven models without the conveniences of the main internationally scheduled airliners. Although the Soviets first started airline passenger service 40 years ago, the number of Soviet citizens using such facilities is still relatively small—only about one million passengers. However, the rapid expansion of the airlines during recent years suggests that air travel will increase considerably in the next few years and be particularly valuable in linking the West with the East and with Central Asia. Then, too, the Soviet Civil Air organizations are closely linked with military and could provide a ready-trained force when needed. In addition to the above services, facilities of the civil air organizations located in the eastern regions are used in performing tasks such as geological surveying, spraying of crops with chemicals, aiding in forest firefighting, transporting persons needing urgent medical attention, carrying valuable animals to distant places, and many other services.

The rapid expansion of Soviet Civil Air Transport is obvious in many fields. Construction of new and reconstruction of old airports is being intensified so that larger aircraft may be landed in regions heretofore inaccessible. The number of larger and faster passenger airplanes is also being increased. As a result, the cost of transportation per passenger in the larger airliners (over long distances) in still much higher than the third-class rail transportation, but only slightly higher than first-class. With the expansion and improvements in air transportation underway the Soviets foresee handling the bulk of passenger traffic through Civil Air Transport in the near future. As recently as December 1956 a regular air passenger service was inaugurated between Moscow and Khabarovsk, taking about 11 to 12 hours of actual flying time instead of four to five days by rail.

## COMMUNICATION

As a part of the socio-economic complex, the Soviet non-military communication system is administered by the State and by isolated industrial enterprises which need communication facilities for their own uses. The socio-economic complex in communications embraces not only facilities for transmitting of orders, information, and personal messages, but is also used as a vehicle for propaganda, education, and entertainment. The facilities used by the masses are directly administered by the State. Specialized services required by the railroads, airlines, seagoing vessels, and for weather forecasting have their own radio, telegraph, and telephone networks to meet their own needs. To these special users of communication facilities the cost of service is free after the instruments have been installed, but private citizens pay for it through the purchase of stamps, telegraph and telephone charges, and through annual taxes imposed for private use of telephones, radios, and television sets.

The Soviets have vigorously pushed expansion in all fields of communications since 1928. It was essential to have a wide and efficient communication network in order to run the heterogeneous planned economy which was unevenly distributed throughout the country. As Moscow is the hub of centralized policymaking activities, it has a direct telephone network with all of the capitals of the constituent republics and with many distant urban and industrial centers such as Vladivostok and the Kuzbass.

Most telephones are allocated for official uses only; relatively small numbers of private citizens, in high income brackets living in large urban centers, possess private telephones. The masses use the cheaper postal services for communication with their relatives and friends living in distant places. However, although postal and wire facilities increased and improved between 1940 and 1958, their services are unreliable. In general, mail is delivered to urban and rural homes; during harvest time it is delivered to the fields. But mail delivery to remote areas is often delayed, and in many instances letters and packages are lost.

As Table 10 indicates, state-operated communication offices increased by almost 8,500 establishments between 1940 and 1958. In 1958, the Soviets had about 4,000 large and small urban centers. Thus, urban centers averaged 3.2 offices, and the large centers such as Moscow were served by many more. The wartime damage to communication establishments was completely repaired by 1950, and since then facilities in both rural and urban areas have been expanded. About 80 per cent of all establishments were centered in the rural areas. Many rural offices are small, especially if the office serves distant collective farms. The greatest concentration of communication facilities is in the RSFSR, Ukraine, White Russia, and Kazakhstan, in which the concentration of population on one hand and the presence of a large number of industrial and agricultural enterprises on the other requires a good communications network. Between 1940 and 1958 the total number of communication establishments increased by 16.5 per cent, whereas the length of mail routes increased by 34 per cent, suggesting that the Soviet postal services in 1958 had expanded considerably.

The greatest expansion in mail delivery during the 1940-58 period took place in automobile, airline, and rail routes, while the river postal services have been reduced. Means of delivery by reindeer, horses, and dogs, have also been reduced, but animals are still used in mail delivery to isolated places, especially in the winter and in rough country-side. The total expansion in number of post office boxes between 1940 and 1956 amounted to 61 per cent. But, most of these boxes were in rural areas and, correspondingly, the greatest increase took place in rural postal service. This

Table 10—*Soviet Public Communication Network* [23]

| | 1940 | 1950 | 1956 | 1958 |
|---|---|---|---|---|
| Total Number of Postal, Telegraph and Telephone Offices: | 51,353 | 50,955 | 56,947 | 59,838 |
|    In rural areas | 44,234 | 42,888 | 46,023 | 47,000 |
|    In urban and industrial centers | 7,119 | 8,067 | 10,924 | 12,838 |
| Length of mail routes (thousand miles): | 881.1 | 957.6 | 1,093.0 | 1,180.6 |
|    Rail | 151.0 | 176.5 | 266.6 | — |
|    River | 125.5 | 94.4 | 103.4 | — |
|    Air | 110.6 | 259.1 | 259.7 | — |
|    Automobile | 79.5 | 72.7 | 170.3 | — |
|    Others | 414.5 | 354.9 | 293.0 | — |
| Total postal boxes (thousands): | 216 | 160 | 348 | — |
|    In rural areas | 174 | 120 | 281 | — |
| Total letters mailed (millions) | 2,580 | 2,607 | 3,896 | 3,985 |
| Total packages mailed (thousands) | 45,377 | 34,529 | 76,344 | 88,000 |
| Total money orders mailed (millions) | 96.0 | 204.7 | 261.7 | 293.0 |
| Total telegrams sent (millions) | 140.7 | 153.9 | 206.2 | 223.0 |
| Total telephones (thousands): | 1,225 | 1,410 | 2,067 | 2.370 |
|    In urban centers | 1,044 | 1,231 | 1,770 | 2,030 |
| Total radio receiver sets (thousands): | 1,123 | 1,767 | 7,380 | 9,600 |
|    In rural areas | 338 | 352 | 1,855 | 2,500 |
| Total television sets (thousands): | — | 15 | 1,324 | 2,500 |
|    In rural areas | — | — | 98 | 187 |

does not mean that the peasants in 1956 wrote more often to their relatives and friends than in 1940. Many rural and local post offices sell stamps and state bonds, handle money orders, furnish savings deposit services, receive taxes, and provide many other services needed in isolated areas. In the cities many of these services are performed by employers of large industrial or administrative establishments.

In 1940 about 13.5 letters per capita were handled by Soviet postal services; in 1958, this figure was 19.5 pieces. The great bulk of the letters, and also telegrams, originate through government business, and with the expanding industrial activities the volume of official correspondence has increased. However, most of the package mailed and money orders handled originate with the general public. Since members of many families have gone to distant industrial sites, relatives and friends mail varieties of goods unobtainable in remote areas. In return, those working away from home in isolated places have limited ways to spend their earnings, and send their savings back home. The hub of postal service is Moscow. It handles between 400 and 500 metric tons of mail daily. As any other country, the Soviet Union has different rates for first-class mail and for bulky items such as newspapers and magazines. Reduced postal rates are also given to state organizations such as the Gosbank.

The number of telephones in use during the 1940-58 period increased by 93 per cent, with the greatest increase taking place in urban centers. In rural areas, every collective and state farm and other agricultural enterprise have telephones with which they are linked to local soviets. Individual peasant households do not have private telephones. City residents have private telephones and there are a number of telephone booths on the street, in hotels, and in other public places.

Since 1940, the Soviets have improved their telephone and telegraph transmission networks, teletype communications, radio telegraphy, and direct two-way radio systems to speed their communication service. Actual ownership of radios by the public is less than production, amounting to about four million sets. Nevertheless, almost every rural settlement has a radio transmitter and receiver set. On collective and state farms at least one radio receiving set may be found at the club. Many urban citizens have their own radios at home. "Radiofication," the system by which many loudspeakers are installed at points where groups gather for work or recreation, is also used. Individual loudspeakers cannot be turned off, nor can the volume or station be changed. By this means the Soviets can insure that all the citizenry is exposed to a full dosage of propaganda and required information at a minimum cost.

The television network, still in the process of development, is rapidly expanding, and Soviet specialists are working on a program for adopting color television. In the meantime, most television sets are in the hands of urban populations. However, wealthy collective farms close to large urban centers also have television sets at their clubhouses. Expansion of the television network is not centralized, and there is no linkage of Moscow with Vladivostok as exists with radio. Thus, the Soviet television network is expanding locally, and even such far-away places as Sakhalin Island have been introduced to the wonders of television. There is no doubt that the radio-television network, serving as an instrument of government propaganda, education, and entertainment, will be greatly expanded by the Russians in the near future in order to reach the various ethnic groups in their own native languages.

## Chapter 12—Bibliography

[1] *Dostizheniya Sovetskoy Vlasti za 40 Let v Tsifrakh*, Moscow, 1957, p. 226.

[2] *Narodnoye Khozaystvo SSSR v 1958 Godu*, Moscow, 1959, p. 545 (hereafter referred to as *Narodnoye Khozaystvo*).

[3] *Sovetskaya Sotsialisticheskaya Ekonomika: 1917-57*, Moscow, 1957, p. 383.

[4] *Transport i Svyaz SSSR*, Moscow, 1957, pp. 27, 31; *Narodnoye Khozaystvo*, p. 544.

[5] Vedishchev, A. I., *Chto i Gde Budet Postroeno v 1959-1965 Godakh*, Moscow, 1959, p. 74; *Narodnoye Khozaystvo*, p. 544.

[6] *Kontrol'nye Tsifry Razvitiya Narodnogo Khozaystva SSSR na 1959-1965 Gody*, Moscow, 1958, p. 60; Embassy of the USSR, *Press Department*, No. 74, Washington, D. C., February 9, 1960.

[7] *Transport i Svyaz SSSR*, op. cit., pp. 28, 34-38; *Narodnoye Khozaystvo*, p. 549.

[8] Embassy of the USSR, *Press Department*, No. 37, Washington, D. C., March 6, 1959.

[9] *Voprosy Ekonomiki*, No. 2, 1959, p. 66.

[10] Embassy of the USSR, *Press Department*, No. 37, Washington, D. C., March 6, 1959.

[11] *Transport i Svyaz SSSR*, op. cit., pp. 115-16, 120; *Narodnoye Khozaystvo*, p. 565.

[12] *Transport i Svyaz SSSR*, op. cit., pp. 95, 97, 100; *Narodnoye Khozaystvo*, pp. 561-62.

[13] *Transport i Svyaz SSSR*, op. cit., pp. 155, 195-96; *Narodnoye Khozaystvo*, p. 573.

[14] *Voprosy Ekonomiki*, No. 2, 1958, p. 87.

[15] Birman, A. M., *Finansy Otrasley Narodnogo Khozaystva SSSR*, Moscow, 1957, pp. 141, 151.

[16] *Narodnoye Khozaystvo SSSR v 1956 Godu*, Moscow, 1957, p. 62; Embassy of the USSR, *Press Department*, No. 37, Washington, D. C., March 6, 1959.

[17] *The USSR and Eastern Europe*, Oxford Regional Economic Atlas, Oxford University Press, 1956, p. 81; *Transport i Svya SSSR*, op. cit., p. 208; *Narodnoye Khozaystvo*, p. 600.

[18] *Sovetskaya Sotsialisticheskaya Ekonomika* op. cit., p. 372.

[19] *Transport i Svyaz SSSR*, op. cit., p. 210; *Narodnoye Khozaystvo*, p. 572.

[20] *Narodnoye Khozaystvo SSSR v 1956 Godu*, op. cit., p. 62; Embassy of the USSR, *Press Department*, No. 37, Washington, D. C., March 6, 1959.

[21] *Transport i Svyaz SSSR*, op. cit., pp. 12-13; *Narodnoye Khozaystvo*, pp. 541, 601.

[22] *Dostizheniya Sovetskoy Vlasti za 40 Let v Tsifrakh*, op. cit., pp. 224, 231, 234, 238; *Transport i Svyaz SSSR*, op. cit., pp. 44, 134, 175, 209; *Narodnoye Khozaystvo*, pp. 552, 561, 584.

[23] *Transport i Svyaz SSSR*, op. cit., pp. 217, 219, 220, 221, 222, 223, 225, 227, 233, 243; *Narodnoye Khozaystvo*, pp. 602-03.

## CHAPTER 13

# Marketing Structure

## INTRODUCTION

The term "marketing" embraces all normal business activities involved in the flow of goods and services from physical production to consumption. The main marketing functions are exchange of goods (buying and selling), transportation, storage, standardization, and grading of goods. This broad concept of the functions of marketing exists in every organized society, even though they may differ in performance from society to society. Though the essence of the universal marketing structure exists in the Soviet Union, it has unique aspects in actual application.

The marketing system in the Soviet Union differs from others in that it does not involve the transfer of title of goods produced. The State is the sole producer and distributor of consumer goods either by state-owned organizations or by cooperative associations. Since practically all marketing functions are undertaken by the State, the only transfer of title occurs when ultimate consumers pay for a commodity. Even on the collective farm market transfer of title takes place only at the time when the consumer pays for the purchased commodity.

The present Soviet marketing system differs greatly from the early system used when the regime was new. Marx and Lenin did not spell out the precise policies of the marketing function once the means of production had fallen into the hands of the workers. However, Marx, Lenin, and their followers agreed that the role of the middlemen in the exchange function was a capitalistic invention to gain profit, and could not be tolerated. By eliminating the middlemen, the Soviets did not reduce the number of steps in the exchange function. The middlemen were replacd by the State and cooperatives, which not only produced goods but also provided services in assembling, sorting, grading, storing, transporting, distributing, and in risk taking.

With the nationalization of means of production the Soviets established monopolistic structures in production and distribution of industrial goods and for a large part of the farm produce. By destroying the existing marketing system the State was impelled to organize its own system. With centralized industrial ownership it was much easier for the Soviets to organize new wholesale networks, but the task of replacing the old retail network was so enormous that only in 1932 was it possible to abolish private retailing by law. Thus, until 1932 the Soviet marketing structure consisted of two systems. Wholesale distribution was concentrated in the state-controlled syndicates, joint-stock organizations, and consumer cooperatives which distributed goods through privately owned retail networks and through their own expanding channels.

When private retailers were completely abolished the Soviets expected that that part of the goods sold by independent retailers would move to the state or cooperative stores. Nothing of the sort took place. Instead, sales on collective farm markets increased, forcing many state and cooperative stores to close  Goods became scarce and expensive. To supply state-employed workers with goods the Soviets were forced to organize departments for supplying workers (Orsy) for each major industry.

In general, the Soviets were able to formulate the main aspects of the exchange function suitable for their society by 1933, and whatever adjustments have taken place in their marketing system since there were changes in delegation of power rather than basic revisions of the entire marketing system itself.

The basic problem in Soviet exchange functions has been, and still is, the scarcity of consumer goods. This problem cannot be solved until Soviet economy is able to produce all goods and services desired by the consumers. However, the Soviets are giving less attention to this problem than to transitory problems related to functions, institutions, or specific activities in the field of marketing. As a result, the present Soviet marketing system, in the absence of competition among producers and distributors, is less efficient than it would be in non-planned economies.

## STATE PURCHASING PRACTICES

The Soviet pricing system relies on Marxian analysis that the only cost of production of any commodity is that of labor. Thus the price of a ton of coal is traced to direct and indirect costs of labor required to mine and to deliver it to the consumer. Such is the broad theory behind the Soviet pricing mechanism which emphasizes condemnation of middleman's profit even though the State profit is considered to be just by the Communists.

As a rule, wholesale prices on industrial goods are calculated as an average for all enterprises producing similar commodities for the country as a whole or for a given economic region. This is a kind of forwarding price system to assist individual enterprises in their calculation of costs. As a result, the actual cost of production in one enterprise, particularly one with the most favorable combination of factors of production, may be lower as compared with a less efficient one. But since all enterprises are state-controlled business failure is impossible because the efficient enterprises subsidize the others. For this reason, the Soviets argue, profit must come not through an increase in wholesale prices but through a reduction in the cost of production.

The Soviet Union has two wholesale prices. One is calculated for the individual enterprise and includes the cost of production and profit. The other is established for the industry as a whole and includes the average cost of production, profit, and turnover taxes. As explained in Chapter 14, the turnover tax is the most complex phase in the wholesale price structure and may be distributed among various stages in production. For example, turnover tax on textiles is distributed among other industries such a machine building (textile machinery), fuel, electric power, chemicals, raw materials, and the like. For this reason the turnover tax does not originate at the place of production, because prices on capital goods, as a rule, though they exclude turnover taxes, might include subsidy, and also because other prices may be different from the actual costs of production.

The amount of turnover tax varies from item to item and from industry to industry. For small enterprises the amount of turnover taxes is established on the basis of percentage of cost of production and distribution accrued by the enterprise. Many items produced by such enterprises have lower turnover tax than the large enterprises, and many commodities exclude turnover tax altogether as a stimulant to sales turnover.

## THE SOVIET MARKETING NETWORK

Supplying the needs of the ultimate consumer is the final social objective of all production and marketing. However, a part of the total production of capital goods is allocated to the distribution phase. For this reason, the Soviets have separated their marketing system into two distinct phases, one the supplying and the other the distributing services within the same marketing process. The difference between the two is organizational rather than functional since distribution of goods produced by one economic sector became the supplies of another. As a result of this specialization, the USSR in 1957 had over 5,700 supplying establishments, excluding small-scale supplying establishments.[1]

## Wholesaling Structure

In the USSR few goods (mainly the farm produce) move directly from producers to consumers through the collective farm markets. Thus, practically all consumer goods are disposed through state wholesale channels. Producers sell their goods to wholesalers which in turn sell to institutional buyers or to some other wholesaling organizations for resale to the general consuming public. However, some institutional buyers, such as hospitals, may buy directly from producers, wholesale establishments or from the retail market.

Soviet wholesale establishments do not take title to goods because production and distribution are owned by the State and in main they buy and sell in large quantities. Normally, they do not sell over the counter to any substantial degree and are not open to the general consumer. They assemble goods produced in small lots by producers throughout the country and provide services in sorting, packing, storing, and transporting of goods to the retail market.

## Gosplan

To improve efficiency in the supply machinery the Soviets abolished the old system in February of 1957 and delegated supplying functions to the USSR Gosplan and its subordinate organizations. To perform its new responsibilities the Gosplan set up its own machinery, consisting of 18 main distributing organizations (Glavsbyty) throughout the country. These are specialized organizations devised for each broad category of goods such as shoes, garments, and so on. Together with their subordinate organizations in each constituent republic and with networks of wholesale bases, local offices, and warehouses they provide producers with needed supplies, machinery, and equipment. Basically, however, what took place was a change in administrative structure rather than a revolutionizing of the supply function of Soviet marketing. Then with the formation of sovnarkhozy in May 1957 the supplying organizations established a few months before were again reshaped to meet the new economic reorganization. The responsibility of supplying industries located within sovnarkhozy has been transferred from the jurisdiction of the Gosplan to that of the sovnarkhoz.

In order to fulfill their new duties the sovnarkhozy organized supply departments with a network of peripheral bases, warehouses, and supply houses which are responsible for supplying raw materials, fuel, electric power, equipment, and transportation facilities to all enterprises and organizations located in their regions. However, since sovnarkhozy produce goods for the other regions, their supply organizations have a dual supervision. The

USSR Gosplan has retained its rights to give orders concerning the method and priority of shipments, as well as to make changes in production of certain goods assigned for delivery to particular buyers located in other regions.

The importance of the sovnarkhozy in the matters of supply for their own enterprises and others is increasing, and the local supply bases are being transferred to sovnarkhozy from other organizations. This is especially true when administrative boundaries of the sovnarkhozy coincide with those of constituent republics, in which cases there is no division or responsibilities.

There is an increasingly important movement among individual enterprises to enter into contractual agreements for direct supply from producers. If this trend is to continue to expand, it will revolutionize the entire Soviet supplying system. In the meantime, since sovnarkhozy are responsible for supplying their enterprises, they are organizing large supply establishments to replace the small one which existed in the past. Since the new supply bases are large, it is expected that ultimately all individual enterprises will discontinue the hoarding of raw materials for their own needs.

## Ministry of Trade

The USSR Ministry of Trade was formed in 1917, and by 1957 it had passed through numerous reorganizations. With the establishment of the sovnarkhozy the Ministry became the Union-Republic Ministry of Trade. Despite its structural changes, the Ministry was the main agency in the Soviet marketing system, especially in the realm of urban retailing, until December 1958 when it was abolished and its duties were transferred to the Central Administration for Cooperative Associations (Tsentrosoyuz) and the sovnarkhozy.

But prior to 1953 the wholesaling of industrial goods was, in the main, conducted by various industrial ministries which built up their own main wholesale organizations (Glavsbyty) with large numbers of subordinate wholesale establishments. The entire system was cumbersome and inefficient. In an attempt to improve the distributing system, the Soviets transferred all Glavsbyty and their subordinate establishments from ministerial administration to the USSR Ministry of Trade in the middle of 1953. In all, 2,512 wholesale establishments were transferred.[2] Of these, 752 wholesale establishments were engaged in the distribution of consumer goods, 733 specialized in grocery items, 304 in meat and butter, 208 in fish products. As a result, the producing functions of industrial enterprises were separated from the distribution functions, and the Ministry organized ten of its own specialized main wholesale organizations with a larger number of subordinate establishments assisting in assembling and distribution. The Soviets claim that the 1953 reorganization of the wholesale network resulted in simplification of the whole structure and saved about one billion rubles annually.

The main wholesale organizations (Glavsbyty) are found in every constituent republic, as they were in 1953, and have a network of subordinate establishments which supply local retailers and also sell to institutional buyers. The subordinate establishments are made up of regional and local wholesale bases, offices, and warehouses providing the main link between the suppliers and the retailers.

The most important wholesale establishments are the specialized wholesale bases (Vykhodnye bazy) which perform different functions. They are located in the regions where the goods are produced. The region may consist of a single large producer, or a number of smaller enterprises whose products are sold to specialized wholesale bases which in turn sell to the trading bases (Torgovye bazy) or the retailers. The main functions of the specialized wholesale bases are to assemble a variety of goods and to safeguard the normal flow of goods to trading bases and to large retailers.

The trading bases are smaller organizations than the specialized wholesale bases and are located in the midst of the retail markets rather than near producing centers. They form the backbone of wholesale operations. The trading bases may be specialized, handling a single line of goods, or they may handle a number of different lines. There are, however, more specialized bases. The main task of the trading base is to supply the urban and rural retailers located in the areas assigned to the base.

Both specialized and trading bases have double functions, and are engaged in the wholesaling of consumer goods produced within a given republic or region through local channels and also in the shipment of goods to regions beyond their normal sphere of activity. There are, however, some exceptions. In the wholesaling of fishery products, for example, these functions are performed by a specialized buying-selling office located in the region where the fishing and processing are conducted without channeling these products through specialized and trading wholesale bases. Again, products such as ice cream or dry ice are distributed to the retailers directly. These goods, however, are the so-called "non-fund" goods, meaning that they are not included in the national plans. They are produced by small-scale local producers using local materials. Some of these goods may be shipped to the main wholesale administrations, to be specialized or trading bases of the respective administrations, or to other regions.

Beginning with January 1957, the constituent republics were permitted to plan the trade turnover for their respective areas and to allocate the most important consumer goods to the wholesale establishments. By this act, a closer relationship between producers and customers within the constituent republic was established. However, goods produced for export to other republics were contracted by the wholesale organizations of the Ministry of Trade and the Central Administration for Cooperative Associations (Tsentrosoyuz).

Then in 1958 another reorganization occurred in the wholesale network, and wholesale bases of the abolished Ministry of Trade were transferred to the jurisdiction of the Tsentrosoyuz. Since the wholesale bases of the Ministry of Trade were organized for the purpose of supplying consumer goods to urban markets only, the transfer of these bases to cooperative associations enabled the same organizations to supply consumer goods to both the urban and rural markets. Along with these changes the Tsentrosoyuz reduced their number of bases either by merging the transferred bases with their own or by eliminating small bases altogether.

## The Central Administration For
## Cooperative Associations (Tsentrosoyuz)

Consumers' and producers' cooperatives flourished in Tsarist Russia and the Soviets recognized their value as instruments of marketing. Basically membership in all cooperative associations is voluntary and for the benefit of the members in accordance with the principles established by the Rochdale pioneers. Although cooperative associations are not a branch of the State, nevertheless they are controlled by the government by the fact that the State controls all the factors of production, prices, wages, and allocates goods and services to producing and consuming channels. For these reasons cooperative associations cannot be isolated from the State marketing system since their function is to supplement the state-owned marketing channels.

The Tsentrosoyuz unifies all activities of consumers' and producers' cooperative associations. The consumers' cooperatives are the most important, and in 1956 their turnover of sales amounted to 97 per cent of the total turnover made by all cooperatives.[3] In that year the facilities of producers' associations were transferred to the State, and for all practical purposes they have ceased to exist.

It is claimed by the Soviets that in 1958 membership in 21,000 associations numbered 35 million persons.[4] The cooperative associations perform a number of valuable functions in the marketing. Basically they serve the rural population. In addition to retailing, the cooperatives are engaged in the purchase of farm produce from collective farms, individual members of collective farms, independent peasants, and from all others who grew farm commodities. Since many of the purchases are made in small lots, the cooperatives also do the grading, sorting, processing, packing, storing, and transporting of farm produce. In short, cooperatives perform the wholesaling functions as well as supplying the goods to their own marketing channels.

Consumers' cooperatives are organized vertically, each level performing specific functions in marketing. The Tsentrosoyuz has seven main wholesale administrations (Glavtorgi). These are specialized organizations limited to marketing functions not undertaken by the state wholesale system. All their functions are performed through a network of subordinate organizations.

In 1958 the direct trade turnover of the main wholesale administrations represented over 30 per cent of the total turnover recorded for all consumers' cooperatives. Basically, the wholesale trade of the main administrations is devoted to supplying the collective farms with farm implements, construction materials, power-driven farm equipment, and the like. Buying and selling activities of the main wholesale administrations are conducted through their own network of 470 wholesale bases throughout the USSR which in turn distribute their goods to smaller wholesalers.

The wholesale operations of the cooperatives are carried out by associations established in each constituent and autonomous republic. The republic associations have subordinate organizations in every populated area. The main task of these associations is to obtain goods for their subordinate establishments through contractual agreements with local producers, suppliers, and state-operated wholesale establishments. Frequently many larger associations located in different regions trade among themselves.

The Rayon's Consumers' Cooperative Associations (Raypotrebsoyuzy) are the most numerous and they represent the lowest link within the wholesale structure of the Tsentrosoyuz. Since many rural cooperatives are unable to obtain goods from state enterprices or from wholesale bases, the rayon's associations are the only channel through which goods may be obtained, especially in the isolated regions. The rayon's associations, however, are not only suppliers of their subordinate network but they also process raw materials obtained from local markets. In many cases these associations through their own buying offices purchase farm produce and raw materials and receive goods from collective farms and peasants on a commission basis. Although they are smaller than other associations, their wholesale turnover is about 60 per cent of the total wholesale turnover of all associations combined.

The complexity in the structure of cooperatives lies in the numerous associations having similar functions. For example, the republic association perform similar functions as the oblast or the kray associations do. Each of these associations has a network of wholesale bases, warehouses, and field offices. They are isolated from the purchasing public and deal mostly in durable and producers' goods rather than in goods which consumers would like to have. But it is the rayon's associations that provide a link between producer sand consumers. Being small-scale organizations, they are responsible for the complex task of contracting big producers for small orders which producers frequently are reluctant to accept. It is the rayon's associations which perform the duties of local wholesalers supplying individual consumers' cooperative associations.

The most important local consumers' associations are the rural cooperatives (Selpo) which act as the retailing outlets. Different cooperatives are set up for various members. There are cooperatives primarily for workers and employees of the state farms (Sovkhozrabkoop); others serve the members of collective fishing farms; still others are set up for the workers and employees of industrial enterprises located in the rural areas who are engaged in the production of construction materials; urban cooperative associations (Gorpo) serve members residing in urban centers; lastly, regional associations (Raypo) are established in the regions where the rural cooperatives cannot be organized either because of a sparse population or because it would not be economically feasible. The most decentralized organization dealing with a variety of commodities is the regional consumers' cooperative association (Raypo) which has a network of retail outlets including general purpose stores, book stores, store-warehouses for selling, building, and repairing materials, restaurants, and tea houses.

With the formation of sovnarkhozy and the abolishment of the required deliveries to the State, the role of the consumers' cooperatives, especially on the lower level, has become increasingly important in the purchase and distribution of farm produce from producers to consumers and in establishing a closer relationship with the sovnarkhozy. Along with this, the role of local associations in receiving farm produce on a commission basis is also being emphasized more than before. The role of the cooperative as the agent of the State has grown, for it is their task now to provide the urban sector with the major share of farm produce, and they assume a larger responsibility in marketing, which was previously administered by the Ministry of Trade.

## SOVIET RETAILING

Soviet retailing embraces several types of establishments. It includes the state-operated small and large retail establishments, consumers' cooperative stores, public catering establishments, repair and servicing shops, and collective farm markets. Only small amounts of the commodities, mainly farm produce, are now being purchased directly from the producers, bypassing wholesale channels. Despite the recent structural adjustments, Soviet retailing is still organized on the basis of task or service performed.

TABLE 1—*Per cent of the Total Soviet Retail Turnover* [5]

| Channel | 1932 | 1940 | 1950 | 1955 | 1958 |
|---|---|---|---|---|---|
| Total USSR: | 100.0 | 100.0 | 100.0 | 100.0 | 100.0 |
| State-operated | 34.4 | 62.7 | 63.9 | 63.2 | 65.2 |
| Cooperatives | 53.9 | 23.0 | 24.1 | 28.1 | 29.1 |
| Collective farm markets | 15.7 | 14.3 | 12.0 | 8.7 | 5.7 |

In 1932 cooperatives led urban and rural retailing. Cooperatives together with collective farm markets shared almost 70 per cent of the total Soviet retail turnover, mainly in foodstuffs. However, the role played by these channels has been overshadowed by the expanded state retail network and in 1958 the state stores took the lead, handling 65 per cent of the total Soviet retail turnover while cooperatives recorded only 29 per cent.

The Soviet retail network is divided into two broad classifications—the permanent and the temporary, or seasonal establishments. In 1958 the permanent retail establishments represented 74 per cent of the 519,300 state-controlled retail outlets. Of all the retail outlets, 52 per cent were concentrated in rural areas, which had more permanent establishments but fewer seasonal stores than the urban areas.

Between 1932 and 1940 a considerable expansion in the retail network took place in both urban and rural areas. During World War II the retail network, along with other sectors of the Soviet economy, suffered a considerable reduction, and although by 1950 the urban areas had increased the number of selling establishments the rural areas had fewer than in 1940. This number, however, increased in both areas in 1958, particularly in the urban centers.

On the average, one retail establishment (excluding public catering) in 1958 served about 402 customers and in the large cities they served about 600 to 700 customers daily despite a store capacity of about 220 to

TABLE 2—*Number and Types of Retail Establishments* [6]
(*in thousands*)

| Establishments | 1932 | 1940 | 1950 | 1955 | 1958 |
|---|---|---|---|---|---|
| Total USSR: | 340.2 | 494.8 | 511.2 | 605.6 | 650.2 |
| Stores | 208.5 | 307.1 | 298.4 | 352.5 | 383.1 |
| Stalls, stands, etc. | 75.9 | 100.1 | 117.4 | 135.0 | 136.2 |
| Public catering | 55.8 | 87.6 | 95.4 | 118.1 | 130.9 |
| Total urban areas | 148.4 | 212.6 | 258.9 | 304.0 | 344.0 |
| Stores | 67.8 | 90.7 | 108.7 | 134.7 | 154.2 |
| Stalls, stands, etc. | 48.4 | 62.7 | 80.4 | 86.2 | 93.1 |
| Public catering | 32.2 | 59.2 | 69.8 | 83.1 | 96.7 |
| Total rural areas | 191.8 | 282.2 | 252.3 | 301.6 | 306.2 |
| Stores | 140.7 | 216.4 | 189.7 | 217.8 | 228.9 |
| Stalls, stands, etc. | 27.5 | 37.4 | 37.0 | 48.8 | 43.1 |
| Public catering | 23.6 | 28.4 | 25.6 | 35.0 | 34.2 |
| Collective farm markets | – | 6.3 | – | 8.7 | – |

250. It is clear that Soviet retailing is overloaded and cannot perform its function well. The plan which the Soviets have devised for the expansion of retail outlets during the next seven years calls for the opening of some 90,000 additional establishments, thus considerably cutting down the number of consumers per store.[7]

In the past, the Ministry of Trade served urban customers and cooperatives served rural areas, but there was some overlapping of functions so that many cooperatives were found in urban centers while the Ministry of Trade had been extended to the rural areas. The 1957 and 1958 reshuffling of the wholesale and retail systems is still in process, causing confusion in pinpointing of responsibilities. To say that Soviet retailing is experiencing growing pains is a mild statement because expansion in retailing still cannot catch up with the growth of consumers' demand, particularly in the urban sector. In 1940, for instance, retail turnover of goods per capita was 914 rubles and in 1958 it was 3,275 rubles.[8] Because of the increasing purchasing power of the population the growing pains in retailing in 1965 will become more acute than ever, with an expected increase of 57 to 62 per cent in the retail trade above the 1958 records. The most interesting phenomenon, however, is the fact that between 1950 and 1957 rural demand for goods increased at a higher rate than in urban centers. Average purchases per urban family increased from 8,970 rubles in 1950 to 15,146 rubles in 1957 but the purchases of rural families increased from 1,923 rubles to 4,623 rubles.[9]

TABLE 3—*Total Retail and Catering Turnover in the USSR* [10]
(*in billion rubles*)

| Channel | 1932 | 1940 | 1950 | 1955 | 1958 |
|---|---|---|---|---|---|
| Total State controlled: | 40.4 | 175.1 | 359.6 | 501.9 | 677.2 |
| Urban | 27.6 | 123.5 | 273.0 | 368.7 | 503.2 |
| Rural | 12.8 | 51.6 | 86.6 | 133.2 | 274.0 |
| Total state stores: | 14.6 | 128.1 | 261.1 | 347.3 | 467.9 |
| Retailing | 13.0 | 109.6 | 223.2 | 302.1 | 417.5 |
| Public catering | 1.6 | 18.5 | 37.9 | 45.2 | 50.4 |
| Total cooperatives: | 25.8 | 47.0 | 98.5 | 154.6 | 209.3 |
| Retailing | 22.5 | 42.6 | 89.0 | 141.0 | 195.4 |
| Public catering | 3.3 | 4.4 | 9.5 | 13.6 | 13.9 |
| Collective farm markets | – | 29.1 | 49.2 | 48.9 | 40.7 |

In this table retail turnover of the collective farms is excluded from the total socialized sector. Beginning with 1955 the retail turnover for the co-operative associations included goods sold on a commission basis amounting to 4.9 billion rubles, and in 1958 it was 8.7 billion. In 1932 the turnover of collective farm markets was not significant in comparison with the socialized sector. It is interesting to note that between 1940 and 1958 the share of retail turnover for the state stores remained constant in relation to the total Soviet retail turnover. But the share of turnover for cooperatives increased from 23 to 29 per cent while the share of the total turnover by collective farm markets declined from 14 to about six per cent. The 1958 reduction in total sales by collective farm markets is due to the increased volume of sales on a commission basis by the cooperatives.

As the table shows, the turnover of state stores has greater significance than that of cooperative and collective farm markets, although the 1950 and 1958 purchases were made at inflated prices as compared with 1940. The 1958 retail turnover of the socialized sector was 677.2 billion rubles; the planned turnover for 1965 is expected to reach 1,080 billion rubles, an increase of about 60 per cent. It is also claimed by the Soviets that whereas the daily public consumption in 1958 averaged about 1.8 billion rubles, by 1965 daily purchases are expected to average about three billion rubles, or an increase of more than 50 per cent during the seven-year period.[11]

Since the largest percentage of the total turnover in retail and public catering establishments is concentrated in urban centers, it is to be noted that the 20 largest cities in the Soviet Union, representing about 23 per cent of the total urban population in 1959, were responsible for about 24 per cent of the total urban retail turnover. Moreover the turnover in retail trade overshadowed the turnover in public catering establishments almost ten to one. Turnover of state and cooperative stores and public catering establishments per capita in these 20 cities ranged from 4,000 rubles in Omsk to 10,000 rubles in Moscow. In general, larger industrial and administrative centers have higher consumption power than the smaller urban centers, not only because of the presence of a large number of persons with high incomes but also because they are buying centers serving suburban areas and visitors.

Prior to 1957 planning in retailing of the state-operated retail network was concentrated in the hands of ministries. Beginning with 1957 these responsibilities were shifted to the Supreme Soviets of each constituent republic and to sovnarkhozy, which direct their own retail administrations established in every populated area. The most important of these are local administrations for retailing (Torgi) in large cities, in oblasts, and in rayons. If the Torg is of sufficient size it may have branches. In 1957, there were 971 Torgi and 293 branch houses in the USSR.[12] The Torg operates within the limits set by the planned retail turnover, and its duties are to administer its retail establishments and to supply goods and services required by them.

Another type of administrative organization which supervises retailing is the system of specialized departments which supplies industrial workers (Orsy). In 1957, there were 2,011 Orsy, whose supply bases accounted for 29 per cent of the state retail turnover. The main task of Orsy is to supply workers in a given industry with the goods at lower prices than can be obtained in regular stores. This is considered as an incentive to the workers and is used to combat excessive labor turnover and to increase productivity of the workers. However, with the establishment of sovnarkhozy, several constituent republics have taken steps to reduce the number of administrative organizations dealing with retailing, especially that of Orsy. Many administrative organs were merged into larger units, but the increasing demand for the transfer of urban retail stores from republic to city jurisdiction has not yet been effected by the government. Nevertheless, many retail stores are already under jurisdiction of the city's soviets or run by the Oblast's Executive Committees.

The State and cooperatives have several types of stores, including general, specialized, specialty, departmentalized specialty, variety, and department stores. Similar merchandise is sold in all of these stores, but general stores are most numerous. For example, in 1957 ready-to-wear garments were sold by 30,000 urban stores and by almost the same number of stores in the rural areas which handled other lines as well. Out of about 50,000 stores handling footwear, only 2,000 were specialized stores selling footwear. At the beginning of 1958 the USSR had about 40,000 specialized stores, handling food items mostly.[13]

The largest retail units are the department stores, which carry several lines of merchandise and provide services to the buyers. In 1958 there were 300 such department stores. The largest of them is Moscow's State Universal Store (GUM), which covers about 25.3 acres of total floor space—one-fourth is selling space, the rest is taken by warehouses and offices. The annual sales turnover of GUM is over two million rubles. It provides such services as a check room, delivery, post office, public telephones, savings bank, cafeteria, and a nursery with diaper-changing services.

Another type of a large store specializing in foodstuffs is the so-called "Gastronom" which handles a wide variety of food items. These stores have a large sales turnover and also provide certain services to the public. In addition, there are other specialized stores dealing in furniture, textiles, footwear, meat and dairy products. Self-service stores are a recent development. The first was opened in Leningrad in 1954 followed by the opening of similar stores in Moscow and other cities, and at the end of 1958 there were over 2,000 such establishments. The self-service stores handle specialized lines such as bakery items. Still another type of store of recent origin is the one formed in Kiev, where some 900 different items are sold at prices ranging from one to five hundred rubles. This type is similar to the "five and ten" chain stores in the United States.

The method of selling depends upon the merchandise. Consumer durable goods are sold from samples exhibited in the store and delivered to the consumer from the warehouse. In most cases goods are exhibited on the counter from which consumers select desired items. Once selection has been made, the clerk writes out the bill which the consumer takes to the cashier for payment and then returns to the clerk to claim the purchased item. However, the recently introduced direct payment to the clerk is now rapidly replacing the old system of payment to the cashier.

Since year-round stores are concentrated in the center of the cities, many cities established a number of stalls and stands at strategic points in the outlying areas easily accessible to the consumers who want consumer goods and foodstuffs; their greatest sales turnover, however, comes from seasonal fruit and vegetables. Workers going to or returning from work are able to buy the items they need. The individual purchases of such items as non-alcoholic drinks, ice cream, sandwiches, and so on may be made from vending machines. In 1956 there were only about 1,000 of them; in 1958 there were 35,000 and their number·is claimed to be over· 200,000 in 1960. During the summer season à large number of vendors sell ice cream and non-alcoholic drinks in the parks and on the streets.

Guarantee of the quality of purchased goods by the stores is limited to a few goods such as furniture, watches, television, radio sets, refrigerators, and others. The buyer has the right to return defective goods within seven days of their purchase. Return of ready-made garments, textile fabrics, and the like is permitted, although they are sold without a guarantee.

Home delivery for a small fee is limited to items such as washing· machines and television sets. However, home deliveries of bread, milk, and other farm produce are made in the major Soviet cities to regular customers residing within the store's radius of trade. Home deliveries of farm produce are rapidly expanding, especially in the larger cities. In 1958, for example, 68 stores in Moscow already were delivering bottled milk to some 200,000 families at nominal extra cost.

Packaging of certain commodities may be considered as part of the manufacturing and marketing operations and is inadequate in the USSR. In 1957 there were only about 680 retail outlets selling packaged food items. In 1955 only three per cent of the total retail sale of macaroni in the USSR was packaged, vegetable oil, five per cent; butter, six per cent; cubed sugar, ten per cent; and only 8.6 per cent of the milk sold was bottled. Refined sugar, cereals, starch, and a great many other items are still sold from larger containers, requiring weighing and wrapping by clerks. The main reason for the absence of packaged goods is that producers do not have the necessary equipment for packaging. For example, daily consumption of milk in Moscow is about 2,500 fluid tons; however, only in 1956 was milk bottled and then only 200 tons or some six million quarts were bottled daily. Deposits for the bottles are required, much to the annoyance of the customers; milk cartons are still unknown to the Soviet customers.

The greatest shortage, however, exists in the repair shops, especially for shoe repairing and for garment cleaning and repairing. In 1958 Kuybyshev, Novosibirsk, and Omsk each had one shoe repair shop per 8,000 to 10,000 persons. Kostroma did not have a single repair shop for refrigerators, and owners of broken refrigerators had to take them to another city for repairs to buy a new unit.

There is no large-scale installment buying; most goods are purchased for cash. A few items, however, such as musical instruments, radio sets, and others, can be bought on the installment plan. The down payment is fixed at 20 to 25 per cent, the balance payable in installments extended over a six-month period. Plans are now being made to introduce installment buying for certain expensive consumer goods such as furniture, despite previous criticism of such sales as an invention of capitalism. The super-markets found in the United States are unknown to the Russians, although a modest experiment already has been started with the establishment of self-service stores. Other improvements in retailing have also made noticeable headway.

In 1958 a new type of retailing—the renting of goods from retail stores—was introduced and is being rapidly installed in all large cities. A given article can be rented by a customer for an hour, a day, or a week. Demanded goods include items such as baby carriages, china, appliances, musical instruments, sport goods, beds, and cameras. Undoubtedly this new development in retailing is closely associated with the scarcity of consumer goods on one hand and increased incomes of the public on the other. In 1959 the Svardlovsk Oblast already had about 40 such rental departments run by large retailers.

Rental charges vary from store to store within a city, depending upon the jurisdiction over the store. For example, in Sverdlovsk the daily charge for a vacuum cleaner by a store under the jurisdiction of city's soviet is four rubles, and the store under the jurisdiction of the Oblast's Executive Committee charges 120 rubles; other stores charge 150. The retail price of a vacuum cleaner is 360 rubles.[14] The daily charge for a washing machine is ten rubles in one store, 48 rubles in another, and 93 rubles in still another. The hourly charge for an accordion is three rubles, or 20 rubles per day. If one wishes to enjoy a bicycle ride he can rent one at two rubles an hour. It should be clear that these rental charges are not controlled by the State, and stores charge as much as the market can bear.

## Consumers' Cooperatives

As was stated previously, the main task of consumers' cooperative associations is to supply rural consumers with goods and services. Rural areas have several types of stores. One type consists of general stores (Univermagi). There are stores with a variety of food and non-food items for sale to the whole rural population of the rayon (Raymagi). Other stores specialize in handling consumer goods only (Rayprodmagi). The village stores (Selmagi) handle a number of different lines. In addition, there are one-line stores selling ready-made garments, shoes, dry goods, books, bakery items, keresene, and other goods. Since rural stores have fewer customers than the city stores their volume of sales is smaller. In most cases they only sell standardized merchandise and do not provide customer services as the large city stores do. Since their selection of goods is limited some small village stores are being replaced by vending machines.

Consumers' cooperative associations also operate stalls and stands in small agricultural communities during the harvesting season, and maintain a considerable number of trucks which travel from farm to farm carrying a variety of goods to the farm workers. In 1957 there were about 1,200 stands organized for the duration of heavy field work on the farms.

Since many peasants are isolated from larger stores in the cities the cooperatives have organized mail order houses (Koopposyltorg). This is different from the Sears and Roebuck Company in the United States, though both have like functions. The Koopposyltorg does not send out catalogues but posts price lists in the local post offices or at similar places on the merchandise available in the warehouse located in the given region. The peasants consult the price list on the articles they wish to obtain, buy the equivalent money order, and mail it to the proper warehouse. Most goods sold by mail order are standardized and consist of such items as bicycles, radio receiving sets, musical instruments, hunting guns, watches, dry goods, and the like. Its modest beginning was in 1950, when only 27,000 packages were mailed to out-of-town customers. In 1956 the number of mailed packages reached 850,000 valued at 1.7 billion rubles.[15]

## Collective Farm Markets

Independent traders were banned entirely in 1931, and to replace them the collective farm markets were established. Since then peasants have been allowd to sell their surplus produce directly to consumers at the collective farm markets located in the urban centers and in rural areas, on railroad stations or piers, and to visiting consumers from the cities. The market place is built by the government, and the peasants share in the cost of maintenance by paying fees according to the sales method involved. Fees are set up on each animal or on the volume brought to the market, or on the stalls and stands, pushcarts, or trays. These fees are small in relation to the total value of the produce on sale and are used for the improvements on the market.

In 1956 collective farm markets consisted of 29,547 stands, 4,440 stores, 1,253 refrigerated warehouses, 1,031 storage establishments, 2,053 meat inspection and 1,925 milk inspection points, excluding the numerous tables on which peasants display their produce.[16] The use of these facilities is available to all sellers, and Sundays are usually the busiest days since the peasants not only sell their surplus produce but also buy other goods for themselves. Agents of the local producers also display and sell their wares there.

Since the sales of collective farm markets represent about six per cent of the total Soviet turnover, the State has a direct influence upon the price structure on the collective farm market. True, the price on the collective farm market is established by a free play of supply and demand, but the State can influence this price by increasing the volume of merchandise in its own or in cooperative stores. Since normally the state store prices are lower, prices on collective farm markets are thereby regulated or checked.

This narrowing of the price gaps between state stores and collective farm markets has been more evident since 1955. Nevertheless, prices on collective farm markets are still considerably above those in the state stores.

TABLE 4—*Difference in Prices Between*
*Collective Farm Markets and State Stores* [17]
*(in percentage of state stores' prices)*

| Commodity | 1955 | 1957 |
|---|---|---|
| Potatoes _____ | 257 | 150 |
| Butter _____ | 195 | 137 |
| Milk _____ | 160 | 126 |
| Vegetable oil _____ | 140 | 112 |

As the above table shows, the 1957 price of potatoes on the collective farm market was still 50 per cent above the price in state stores, and even vegetable oil was 12 per cent higher. Despite higher prices the government encourages sales on the collective farm markets not only to spur the peasants on to produce more but also to replace a large number of retail units which the State would otherwise have to establish. For these reasons the State builds and improves collective farm markets, sponsors farm fairs, and regulates the sale methods to prevent speculation. In many cases members of collective farms sell their livestock to collective farms. Collective farms in turn slaughter animals, dress the meat, transport it to collective farm markets and sell it there. For these services the collective farm charges ten per cent of the total income from the sales of meat, and the rest is paid to members.

Regulatory agencies for the collective farm markets are established by the local soviets working through the trading organizations. The directors appointed by the local soviets are in charge of regulating the collective farm markets. In rural areas where the collective farm markets are small, regulation is in the hands of inspectors appointed by the local soviets. The director collects fees and data on the volume of sales and takes measures to increase turnover of produce. He also provides services such as weighing machines, special garments, butchering of livestock, and so on at an extra cost to the seller.

The price structure of collective farm markets in general depends upon the supply and demand for a given commodity at any given time. However, prices for a given commodity sold by different organizations on the same market also fluctuate. The state and cooperative stores have the authority to establish retail prices on goods they sell at collective farm markets. At a collective farm market located in a region without rail or water transportation prices include transportation costs. Thus quite often the same commodity sold by similar state-operated establishments from different administrative areas trading on the same collective farm market have different prices.

## Public Catering

This is small business in the USSR. In 1940 about 19 million customers patronized Soviet public catering establishments, and by 1957 their number increased to 36 millions. It is expected that in 1960 about 58 million would consume 18 billion servings of food.[18]

Soviet catering is administered by cooperative associations which run this business through subordinate trusts and other similar organizations. On the average each trust administers about 30 to 50 dining rooms and restaurants. Rural catering is under the jurisdiction of the village cooperative associations and their role in public catering is relatively insignificant in comparison to the urban operations.

In 1956 over 84 per cent of the total Soviet public catering establishments were self-service or carry-out establishments. The carry-out enterprises are rapidly increasing in popularity, especially in the cities. The Soviets expect that by 1965 the number of dining rooms will be increased by over 50 per cent and the total volume of their business will double. Greater emphasis is placed on the expansion of dining rooms in industrial and mining enterprises, state-operated agricultural enterprises, and schools.

Prices on any dish may be changed at any time. The reasons for this flexibilty are many—for example, substitutions in the menu, changes in the retail price of the ingredients, and frequent revisions in the prices.

In 1958 state and cooperative catering establishments recorded sales amounting to 64.3 billion rubles, about nine per cent of the total retail turnover. This represents about 300 rubles per capita. Assuming that the average price of a meal is six or seven rubles, all the Russian can afford on the whole is to purchase 40 to 50 meals annually from the public eating places. Besides their generally low incomes, other reasons for not patronizing public catering establishments are the limited selection on the menu, the scarcity of the establishments, and the poor services.

## COMPETITION

The Soviet marketing system is vertically integrated with a rigid control of production and prices. Although the State acts as a monopolist to whom competition is of little significance, the competitive forces enter modestly into play, because the firm has opportunity to substitute expensive costs with the cheaper ones. A producer with an unusually favorable combination of factors of production may be able to reduce his costs to such a degree that he might even devote more effort to the quality of the goods and to timely delivery to customers.

In this case, then, he can create small-scale "buyer's" market for customers who would want to buy his products. However, not all buyers are free to choose their suppliers, and quite frequently they are tied to local or regional suppliers. Thus, if a producer is located in a region where his supplies have high costs, the buyer pays higher prices and also, in turn, charges high prices for his products. The extent to which the State interferes is sufficiently great to be felt through most of the marketing system, but the objective of securing a maximum net gain in no way differs from the objective of the individual producer or the State. The only difference is that the producer may maximize his gains on a short-run whereas the State's goal is the long-run and overall gain. Since the individual producer cannot keep his profits indefinitely, his incentives toward securing a gain are of no great significance to him. Moreover, the goal closely associated with his survival is to produce planned volumes of goods, which he does frequently by disregarding the high cost of production.

The average Soviet consumer is unaware of competition among producers even though he is educated to believe that he is the producer and the consumer at the same time. He is trained to believe that all scarce resources belong to him because there is no private ownrship of factors of production. As a participant in production of goods and services he is rewarded for his efforts in terms of wages and thus he becomes a consumer. He is led to believe that the reduction in the cost of production and distribution depends upon him since he is the owner of all scarce resources and as a consumer he wants goods and services at fair and reasonable prices. But since the State controls overall production at regulated prices the consumer finds himself at the receiving end and tries to allocate his wages to best advantage. The best he hopes for is better quality of goods since the durability of merchandise means that more of his limited income can be available for other goods.

In general, the State is trying to improve the quality of durable and consumer goods, and every article is inspected by an army of inspectors at the producer's plant and at the buyer's warehouse in accordance with standards established by the State or contractual specifications. But because great numbers of producers, inefficient as they may be, are in a race against time to fulfill their planned quota of production, quite frequently the quality of produced goods is below that of established standards. In the absence of competition among producers for the same market many of them keep on producing low-grade goods. For example, during nine months of 1955 retail establishments refused to accept goods produced by 752 industrial enterprises.[19] The greatest degree of poor workmanship is found in ready-made garments, footwear, and furniture. In general, about 15 to 20 per cent of all the footwear produced in the Soviet Union is of low quality. About 80 per cent of low quality footwear is due to poor materials used, the other 20 per cent is caused by faulty workmanship. In 1955, the Kursk Shoe Factory No. 1, produced some 4,000 pairs of shoes of which 31 per cent were rejected by the retailers and returned to the factory and another 34 per cent were of low grade. This is a total loss to the producer. The Tushinsk Hosiery Factory paid 124,000 rubles in fines for production of defective merchandise during a few months of 1955.

## CONSUMERS' CHOICE

The Soviet consumer is confronted with an array of market prices for all the things he can buy with his income. Since he cannot alter the prices the problem of choice becomes apparent. His choice, however, is limited not only by price structure but also by scarcity of goods in general and the lack of variety in particular.

Since March 1957 the Soviets of Ministers of the constituent republics were permitted to establish prices of certain goods produced in their respective areas. Since many constituent republics produce the same merchandise at different costs the price charged to the consumer also differs. For example, in Moscow in 1958 the "Three Stars" brand of cognac brandy was selling at seven different prices ranging from 35 to 47 rubles per bottle. Again, the price of a shovel in the Kara-Kalpak ASSR was established at 10.60 rubles whereas similar shovels imported from other republics were sold there at 2.70 rubles.[20]. But how would Soviet consumers benefit from the difference in prices in an economy which is short in all consumer goods? In the absence of strong competition among sellers and the lack of shopping time the best consumers can do is to buy needed goods at any price when they can find them.

Since market information in the Soviet Union is almost non-existent, the consumers tend to buy at any quoted price without waiting for a better deal in the face of shortages of goods, or else simply get along without them. To assume that the Soviet consumer does not choose his goods as consumers do in other societies would be wrong because they must balance their meager incomes against limited volumes of goods. It is the scarcity of goods on the market which confronts Soviet consumers who are at the mercy of clerks in the stores who frequently remain indifferent to their demands, and skimp on weighed goods.

## EFFICIENCY IN MARKETING

The Soviets have recognized the fact that efficiency in marketing is desirable from a social point of view only to the extent that it helps to move the largest physical volume of goods from producer to consumer with the least expenditure in time and money. In the absence of competition and in an economy of inadequate supplies of consumer goods this goal is difficult to achieve. Since the State controls production and distribution the only agency which can improve marketing efficiency is the State itself. The State issues various decrees, promotes slogans, and educates producers and retailers to effect improvement of efficient marketing, but this is a slow process and requires constant checking on the part of consumers.

Every retail establishment in the USSR has a complaints book in which dissatisfied consumers write their grievances about service or quality of merchandise sold in the establishment. More irate consumers take their complaints to the inspectors whose task is to improve retailing functions. This has been the practice since 1918, yet no considerable improvement has been registered.

It is possible that efficiency in Soviet marketing may be socially undesirable because of a shortage of facilities more urgently needed elsewhere. The basic problems in the USSR are not only the shortages of retail shops and the scarcity of goods, but the lack of competition leading toward improvement in efficiency. Then, too, practically all workers in the marketing are employed either by the State or by cooperative associations. Trained sales clerks are scarce, and this occupation is not considered as glamorous as that of construction workers on huge and well-publicized hydroelectric projects. Again, clerks know well enough that if an article is rejected by one consumer there will be others willing to buy it. Nevertheless, in an expanding economy such as exists in the Soviet Union, improvement in the quality of the goods and production of new goods sooner or later are bound to come. This takes time, but as more and better goods have appeared on the market consumers have quickly realized the value of trademarks and brands of individual producers.

However, it was not until 1956 that the Soviets intensified their efforts in an attempt to improve the quality controls for goods reaching retail counters. New standards were issued and many stores were forced to reduce prices on low-grade goods, sustaining great losses in the process. Retail stores now worry not only about the goods which do not sell well but also about the means of disposing of them, even at a loss; thus bargain counters become a part of the retail operation, especially for dresses, which can be sold at 20 to 60 per cent less than the original price. In 1956 alone reduction in the price of old goods held by cooperatives amounted to 700 million rubles.[21] In January 1958 retail prices on one kind of television set were reduced by 17 to 20 per cent. It is claimed that this reduction was made because of sluggish demand. By reducing prices on this item the State was able to increase sales of sets without reducing production .

Reduction in retail prices may be due to government action which, at one time or another, may reduce prices on a group of items. This means losses to retailers who purchased them at high prices prior to a government decree. On the other hand, if goods do not move the store manager must apply to higher authority for approval to reduce the price, and this may be denied. Since every store has its norm of turnover of goods, the manager must know what volume other stores are doing at what price, especially in large cities with many stores selling similar products. The selling norms are based upon the capability of the store itself for supplying a given number of consumers within the city and the number of stores planned to supply the entire population of the city.

When the planned turnover of goods is exceeded the manager receives bonuses, and it is in these instances that competition among stores comes into play. If a store manager provides better services to consumers, guarantees the quality of his goods, and displays them attractively, the consumers will tend to patronize his store. In this manner competition among retailers in large cities is gradually taking hold on a small scale.

But in general, the field of retailing in the USSR is neglected. In many small cities, stores are dirty, dimly lighted, with goods heaped in careless fashion on the counters. Salesmanship in most of the Soviet stores is not developed and salespeople are not aggressive since the USSR as a whole is a seller's market. Advertising, as it exists in the United States, is on a small scale—even in its infancy. Most advertising is done by customers themselves by word of mouth. Occasionally, radio stations will announce an opening of a new store, describing the type of merchandise to be sold there. At times an advertisement appears in a local newspaper concerning a large shipment of certain commodities, especially of perishable goods, and there are advertisements in buses advising commuters as to where to buy ready-made garments, shoes, and other items. The broad complexity of retailing and its problems relating to consumer's choice, competition among producers and retailers, advertising, quality controls, and so on cannot be successfully solved in the USSR until more and better goods and services can be available to the Soviet market.

### Chapter 13—Bibliography

[1] *Ekonomika Sotsialisticheskoy Promyshlennosti,* Moscow, 1957, p. 123.

[2] Lifits, M. M., *Optovaya Torgovlya v SSSR,* Moscow, 1956, p. 10.

[3] *Ekonomika Sovetskoy Torgovli,* Moscow, 1958, p. 48.

[4] *Izvestia,* June 27, 1958; and *Ezhegodinik Bolshoy Sovetskoy Entsiklopedii,* Moscow, 1957, p. 64.

[5] *Ekonomika Sovetskoy Torgovli,* op. cit., p. 36; *Narodnoye Khozaystvo SSSR v 1958 Godu,* Moscow, 1959, p. 707.

[6] *Sovetskaiya Torgovlya,* Moscow, 1956, pp. 137, 138, 145; *Ekonomika Sovetskoy Torgovli,* op. cit., p. 162; *Narodnoye Khozaystvo, op. cit.,* pp. 776-79.

[7] Embassy of the USSR, *Press Department,* No. 31, Washington, D. C., March 2, 1959.

[8] *Zasedaniya Verkhovnogo Soveta SSSR,* chetvertogo sozyva (devyataya sessiya), Moscow, 1958, p. 194; *Narodnoye Khozaystvo, op. cit.,* p. 717.

[9] *Sovetskaiya Torgovlya,* No. 4, 1958, p. 42.

[10] *Sovetskaiya Torgovlya,* op. cit., pp. 20, 21, 24, 25, 26; *Narodnoye Khozaystvo, op. cit.,* pp. 707, 713-15, 787.

[11] *Sovetskaiya Torgovlya,* No. 2, 1958, p. 3; and No. 4, 1958, p. 3; Embassy of the USSR, *Press Department,* No. 31, Washington, D. C., March 2, 1959; *Voprosy Ekonomiki,* No. 2, 1959, p. 14.

[12] *Ekonomika Sovetskoy Torgovli,* op. cit., p. 44.

[13] *Sovetskaiya Torgovlya,* No. 12, 1957, p. 7; and No. 4, 1958, p. 47.

[14] *Ogonek,* August 1959, p. 24.

[15] Lifits, M. M., *op. cit.,* p. 25; *Ekonomika Sovetskoy Torgovli,* op. cit., p. 144. op. cit., p. 144.

[16] *Ekonomika Sovetskoy Torgovli,* op. cit., p 71, 162.

[17] *Sovetskaiya Torgovliya,* No. 6, 1958, p. 15.

[18] *Sovetskaiya Torgovliya,* No. 12, 1957, p. 43.
[19] *Voprosy Ekonomiki,* No. 2, 1956, p. 70.
[20] *Sovetskaiya Torgovliya,* No. 4, 1958, pp. 15-16.
[21] *Voprosy Ekonomiki,* No. 5, 1957, p. 133.

# CHAPTER 14

# The Pricing Mechanism

~~~~~~~~~~~~~~~~~~~~~~~~~~~~~~~~~

## INTRODUCTION

Marx and Lenin did not lay down the basic theory for the pricing mechanism. Nevertheless, in the Soviet Union it is directly linked with the entire complex economic and political structures. Since the pricing policy is interwoven with other socio-economic objectives it is monopolistic. Moreover, this monopoly is not solely for the purpose of gaining larger profits as such, but it is used as one means of controlling wages, purchasing power, production, and the whole intricate system of monetary and fiscal policies.

With its economic and political characteristics the price policy of the Soviet Union is flexible, being keyed to the attainment of certain goals. Prices might be reduced when popular support for the government is desired. They might be increased when the volume of money at the disposal of the population is greater than the value of the goods available for them. But again, prices might be reduced because the production costs of capital goods and thus of consumer goods have declined, or because the volume of goods on the market increased and no additional taxation is deemed necessary. This may occur on either the short-or long-run, depending on the policy adopted to yield a given end.

From the economic viewpoint, the government prices the volume of goods available to the market at any given period of time to equal available spending money in the hands of consumers. Any disequilibrium of the two volumes, theoretically, is corrected by reducing prices, or by increasing incomes of the consumers, or by reducing the planned production of consumer goods, or any combination of these measures. A large reduction of planned production politically would be undesirable even under the monopolistic pricing system, yet on a small-scale it is possible.

The Soviet pricing system has many functions. It is used not only in the control of production of consumer goods and the purchasing power of the consumers but also in subsidizing industry. In many cases, prices on capital goods are below their cost of production and are subsidized by the State. This policy was adopted in the early days of the Soviet regime in order to obtain higher profits needed for industrial investment. Theoretically, an ideal state of affairs for the Soviets would be when the price of capital goods is equal to their cost of production. This goal has not been attained and cannot be reached as long as the State permits the existence of submarginal enterprises subsidized by the government. In general, the average prices of consumer goods in relation to their cost of production is two-thirds higher than the prices of capital goods in relation to their cost of production.

In the recent years Soviet economists have written many articles devoted to the Soviet pricing mechanism. Some writers have even advocated marketing conditions uncontrolled by the State where supply and demand would determine price levels of capital goods. All writers have been against subsidies and have recommended a closer price relationship between capital and consumer goods. These opinions expressed in the controlled press indicate that the whole pricing system of the Soviet Union is lacking theoretical interpretation.

In a politically incremental society as the USSR, the pricing mechanism historically experienced numerous adjustments in its simplification and economizing process (khozraschet) among enterprises. However, the pricing mechanism, no matter how effective or ineffective it may be, cannot describe the actual Soviet pricing policy alternatives because of the economic setting which may be called "system-mix." A pricing policy plays a very important part in the planned economy and it may be adjusted only when other tools in the overall planning mechanism are undergoing changes.

The government's price control, although monopolistic, does not constitute a complete monopoly, since the peasants are permitted to sell their produce on the collective farm markets where prices are not regulated directly by the State.

There is a paradox here. On one hand, where wholesale prices for all types of consumer goods are concerned there is a complete state monopoly, but in regard to foodstuffs, although the State controls the greatest part, some free play of supply and demand is allowed on the collective farm markets.

## PRICES AND PLANNING

In a free enterprise economy prices are sensitive regulators of supply and demand as the "true" measure of social evaluation of goods and services through competition. When competition prevails on the market, prices become the criterion of worth of all scarce things. Thus each unit of goods becomes a source of demand for other goods. The motivation of the individual entrepreneur in a free enterprise economy is to maximize his profit, but it does not follow that he is operating in the "profit system," for the market in the free economy is made up of profits and losses as it is in the USSR.

In the Soviet Union the problem of marketing allocations to conform with "free consumer choice" is not involved, though from time to time concessions are made in this direction. Because of the desire for expanded production in virtually all areas,, the problem of shifting resources has been related to how rapidly heavy industries could be expanded. This expansion has usually been at the expense of the consumption goods industries and has been accomplished by raising their prices to discourage consumption. Thus prices have been used less as a measure of the relative scarcity of goods than as instruments for controlling consumption.

In the USSR, prices as a measure of consumer's "choice" or of his decision-making in response to bids and offers on the market are of secondary importance. Basic decisions for economic plans have other considerations, such as the desire to attain certain targets in production of different capital goods. It is in this area that prices play an important role.

The director of a Soviet enterprise is expected to operate at the lowest possible cost to achieve maximum profit. His production and profits are planned for him. For attaining planned output and profit during any year, he receives premium payments for his efforts. Under this incentive system he tries to buy his supplies at the lowest possible price and sell his goods at the highest possible price. Although his costs might be influenced by supply and demand they are not reflected in the supply and demand conditions for the country. To satisfy his raw material demands the director might develop his own source or shift to substitutes in order to increase his profit.

Similarly, any changes in production plans by the State would have an impact on costs and prices to individual enterprise or for the industry. For example, at the end of World War II, the Soviets experienced a petroleum shortage. In a competitive economy, prices would have risen to the level where demand would be reduced to available supply; in the Soviet Union, there was no change in the price of petroleum but the government forced their enterprises to convert from petroleum to coal, even though coal prices were higher than those of petroleum. Production costs increased not only because of higher fuel price but also because of conversion. Consequently some prices were increased and subsidies were given to cover losses.

From the early days of industrialization, Soviet planners were confronted with problems related to the rapid development of the economy. To achieve their goals priority in investment was given to the heavy industries. Soviet leaders felt that investments should come from internal sources of each individual enterprise. It was expected that with increased labor productivity, modernized equipment, and state revenues there would be sufficient savings for continuously increased investments in heavy industry which eventually would produce consumer goods at lower prices. But the brutal collectivization of 1930 caused not only a decline in consumer goods and agricultural outputs but also increased inefficiency.

Although plans specified the output, costs, and profits, in a great many cases they were seldom attained, and the spread between the actual cost of production and planned prices on capital goods and raw material widened. To allow free play of supply and demand in the market was unthinkable for the planned economy. On the other side of the coin, in their efforts to stimulate industrial production the Soviets were forced to sell these goods below production costs.

As a result, the Soviet pricing mechanism accepted two principles: the planned cost of production and planned profit were established for every enterprise as a goal, aimed at reducing the cost of production; along with this principle, as a paradox, the State adopted a policy at which goods were sold to enterprises at prices below the cost of production. Thus emerged the concept that the cost of production (sebestoimost) of an individual enterprise or industry need not be equal to the price of a commodity produced by the whole society, and its price (stoimost) may be below the actual cost of production. The Soviets reasoned that since both profit- and loss-making enterprises exist in the economy, the overall cost-price relationships of all enterprises must be considered in order to determine the cost of any commodity produced by the whole society. Under these cost-price relationships coal, metal products, machinery, and so on were sold at prices below the actual cost of production; the difference was paid from budgetary appropriations for subsidies.

The presence of two values in the pricing mechanism is vaguely defended by the Soviets. Stalin claimed that the production of capital goods and raw materials cannot be evaluated solely in terms of the cost of production but in terms of economic necessity required for the planned development of the economy.[1] After his death this reasoning was criticized on the ground that in any large-scale investment the cost of production and the profitability of new technology only would determine the size of investment. Other writers justified the presence of the "social" value of a good as an important tool in production planning and in evaluation of the results of economic activity of the country. Nevertheless, most Soviet economists agree that this double value in pricing mechanism is imperfect.

Soviet economists agree that a free play in supply and demand of capital goods and raw materials cannot exist in the USSR because mines, factories, power plants and so on are owned and operated by the State and there are no free bids and offers for these goods on the state-controlled market. Goods are simply transferred from one state enterprise to another. Nevertheless, subsidies are strongly opposed. Prices used in planning for production of industrial goods, they maintain, must be based on planned prices which include the cost of production and profits so that control of cost-price relationships (khozraschet) can be enforced in submarginal enterprise.

## SUBSIDIES AND PRICES

Because of high production costs in heavy industry, budgetary subsidies were introduced in the early 1930's. It was done to stimulate industrial production at the expense of other economic sectors. As enterprises installed new technology some reduction in the cost of production and in the prices charged to buyers took place. But the same firms were at a disadvantage with other enterprises which installed their technology at a lower cost two or three years later. As a result, with increased industrial production the subsidy payments followed the trend at an alarming rate. And only in 1936 were the Soviets able to end the general budgetary subsidies. This led to price increases on many industrial goods, which in turn forced the adoption of selective subsidy practices. Under this new setting, profit-making enterprises under the jurisdiction of a given ministry were heavily taxed in order to subsidize submarginal enterprises. The so-called "price reform" of 1936 was nothing but a transfer of responsibility in subsidy payments from the State budget to the ministries on the assumption that they might be more effective in reducing losses of their own enterprises.

These practices existed until World War II, at which time the gulf between the cost of production and prices of industrial goods again widened. Contributing factors were increases in wages and a decline in labor productivity while prices on capital goods, mostly military hardware, were unchanged or only slightly increased. As a result, budgetary subsidies were reinstated. The amount of subsidies to be paid to all sectors in 1948 was planned at 45.2 billion rubles.[2] Even at inflated prices the subsidy was a staggering figure, representing about 12 per cent of all budgetary expenditures.

The impact of state subsidies weakened the role of money in the economy and caused a decline in purchasing power of the ruble. It retarded initiative to produce goods not supported by the State. Important recipients of subsidies were mostly heavy industries where shifting to production of more profitable goods does not exist at all, or only perhaps on a limited scale. The mining industries, for example, have no opportunities to produce other goods. There are different economic conditions even in the machine-building industry which require subsidies when new equipment or armaments are produced. But the main factor is the absence of competition among enterprises. Heavy industry was subsidized by the State for 20 years and coal, timber, and some other industries producing basic raw materials for more than 20 years.[3]

Between 1947 and 1949 several important factors developed within the Soviet pricing system. The monetary reform of 1947 increased the purchasing power of the ruble and the prices on a great number of consumer goods were reduced, while wholesale prices generally, remained unchanged. Increased subsidies for the producers were necessary to cover those expenditures to which they were committed prior to price reduction of consumer goods. Apparently this was achieved during 1948, and beginning with January 1, 1948, the budgetary subsidies were abolished.

As a result, in 1949 transportation rates and wholesale prices on a number of capital and consumer goods, raw materials, and other items were increased. On an average, heavy industry's wholesale prices increased by 56 per cent.[4] Assuming that this increase replaced the whole amount paid in subsidies, it would then be reasonable to say that over one-half of all expenditures in 1948 in heavy industry were subsidized. This indicates a very low productivity within the industry. True, the years 1948-49 fall in the period of postwar reconstruction and conversion from wartime to peacetime production; nevertheless it shows how unprofitable heavy industry was during this period.

The Soviets claim that these price increases were temporary while other economic measures were devised and implemented to offset the rise in the cost of production. In 1949 efforts were made to increase labor productivity and to reduce production costs. As a result, a reduction in many wholesale prices amounting to 13.6 per cent occurred in 1950. As efficiency improved there was another cut in wholesale prices in 1952. These two reductions amounted to 30 per cent of the 1949 wholesale prices in heavy industry. However, wholesale prices were still 26 per cent above the 1949 level. Then another reduction amounting to 19.6 per cent was announced on July 1, 1955.[5] Thus, the total wholesale price reductions during the 1950-55 period amounted to 49.6 per cent whereas the 1949 price increase was 56 per cent. Consequently, in 1955 the wholesale price level was still 6.4 per cent above the level of 1949. Perhaps the real reduction in wholesale prices of heavy industry in 1955 was less than 19.6 per cent because this percentage includes reduction not only in heavy industry but also in fuel, electric power, chemicals, construction materials, and transportation rates. However, although the budgetary subsidies were abolished in many sectors, the timber industry in 1957 was still subsidized by the government.

The 1946-55 period witnessed instability in labor productivity and production costs in different sectors of heavy industry. At the end of 1955 prices of timber, lumber, and coal were still considerably above prewar levels whereas prices of certain types of machinery and equipment were below. However, although state subsidies were abolished and attempts were made to put all industrial enterprises on a "pay-as-you-go" basis, the 1956 production plans still considered losses in the production costs. Out of 5,193 enterprises in the heavy and light industries 33.9 per cent were submarginal enterprises with planned losses which were covered from profits from other enterprises. In 1956 of all operating enterprises which anticipated losses, 56.7 per cent were coal producers, 69.6 per cent in the timber industry, 21.5 per cent in the automobile industry, 26.5 per cent in the construction-materials, 18.4 per cent in textiles, and 49 per cent in the fishing industry.[6] No wonder that Soviet economists are crying for abolishment of general subsidies and for the elimination of submarginal enterprises.

The State establishes prices on capital and consumer goods in accordance with specific long-term objectives. These objectives comprise a number of targets such as the development of new industry or new products, regional economic expansion, an increase in revenues, stabilization of monetary policy, or any other objective which must be considered in overall economic planning in distribution of scarce resources among different uses.

Long-term objectives, of course, might force the planners to establish new enterprises with high production costs. And it might not be possible to reduce their costs until better coordination with other economic sectors is achieved. Again, some enterprises might produce goods at a loss because of obsolete technology and high labor costs. As a result, subsidies are necessary to cover the losses because it is impossible to introduce new technology to all enterprises at the same time. It is claimed by the Soviets that since 1955 many enterprises producing capital goods have shown a profit of from 20 to 30 per cent, yet because of the need for revenues for economic expansion there were no price reductions on capital goods and raw materials. As long as the industrial build-up continues at its present rate the Soviet Union will continue to pay subsidies to submarginal firms. And in an economy of scarcity without competition the existence of submarginal firms has to be flexible. The coal industry today has the largest number of submarginal firms. But as their efficiency increases other industry will take the lead in cost reduction.

## WHOLESALE PRICES

The most important prices in production planning are the wholesale prices. Soviet wholesale prices are completely dominated and rigidly controlled, even where there is a flexibility in retail price determination. With this control, the State determines what goods are to be produced and in what quantities. Wholesale prices are "guaranteed" prices for the enterprises. They include the cost of production and profit. Profit is included in order to provide an opportunity for management to buy new technology and thus to lower the cost of production. There are a number of consumer goods, production costs of which are close to the prices charged to consumers with only small or no additions in turnover taxes. Among these goods are furniture, fuel, paper, textbooks, soap, children's footwear, and several others. But most consumer goods are still priced above the cost of production and reasonable profits and include heavy turnover taxes.

Wholesale prices are established on capital goods, raw materials, and most consumer goods. To these a planned profit ranging from three to five per cent is added.. The planned wholesale price for an enterprise is calculated on the basis of average costs of all enterprises producing a similar commodity. Thus, the planned costs established for the producer have no relation to his actual costs. But this average, among other things, provides a yardstick in the planned reduction in the price of a commodity. It also makes enterprises having high costs reduce them. In this sense the management of an enterprise is forced to maximize its profits so that government may collect them. The motivation in maximizing profit for personal gain for the Soviet plant director is limited, indeed.

The establishment of planned wholesale prices in the USSR is hampered by great variations in costs among different enterprises producing the same product. For example, in 1958 the cost of production of a metric ton of coal averaged 175.30 rubles in the Moscow region, 80.30 rubles in the Donbass, and 7.30 ruble in the Irsha-Borodinsk region of Eastern Siberia. Again, even the same commodity produced from different raw materials varies greatly in cost. A given unit of ammonia produced from natural gas costs 490 rubles and 980 rubles when it is derived from coke.[7] Even plants located in the same region have different costs of production. In 1958 for every ruble spent by enterprises of the Sverdlovsk Sovnarkhoz, output ranged from 67 kopeks to 2.23 rubles.

TABLE 1—*Value of Output per Ruble of Investment in Sverdlovsk Sovnarkhoz in 1958* [8]

| All plants in industry: | Range of output in rubles |
|---|---|
| Food processing | 0.830 - 0.99 |
| Machine-building | 0.756 - 1.01 |
| Non-ferrous metallurgy | 0.800 - 1.29 |
| Mining | 0.723 - 1.62 |
| Ferrous metallurgy | 0.845 - 1.31 |
| Timber, paper, cellulose | 0.757 - 1.87 |
| Building materials | 0.669 - 2.23 |

Table 1 shows that in 1958 the food processing industry in Sverdlovsk Sovnarkhoz had to be subsidized, although the rate of subsidy varied among the plants. The machine-building industry was also subsidized. In other industries profit-making enterprises were penalized and were obliged to cover the excessive production costs of submarginal establishments. The Sverdlovsk Sovnarkhoz is not an exception. The ferrous metallurgy in the Chelyabinsk Sovnarkhoz shows an ever greater range of losses. Even the huge producer of machinery, the Ural Plant, shows a profit of 30 to 40 per cent on some items, but it also shows ten to 20 per cent losses on other items. It is clear, although the planned cost of production is set by the government, that many enterprises ignore it or because of adverse economic conditions cannot comply with it. And since divergence from the planned cost of production is widespread among enterprises the government cannot apply drastic measures to curb it without creating disequilibrium in the economy.

Wholesale price-fixing is considered as one of the most important measures in stimulating maximum production at constantly decreasing costs. Any reduction in the planned cost of production tends to lower the actual cost of production which in turn increases profit. Moreover, some prices· may be adjusted upward to stimulate the growth of various sectors of the industry or even of an economic region. They also may be pulled downward so that enterprises will seek production of goods more profitable to them. Flexibility in the pricing mechanism is based on economic and political problems faced by the State at any given period. Since prices are used as an agent in the distribution of national income, one can appreciate the importance of price structure in the planned economy.

As has been mentioned, state-established wholesale prices on many capital goods and raw materials are below the cost of their production. In this way machinery, equipment, products of mining, electric power, and so on can be purchased by other enterprises with smaller cost outlays. Consequently, by subsidizing the production of basic industries, the Soviets are also subsidizing other sectors as well. As a result the consumer has to pay higher prices.

Theoretically, wholesale prices are set at the level which would guarantee the enterprise some profit. They are calculated with consideration for conditions to stimplate increased output of goods which the government deems necessary for the country and simultaneously to reduce the output of goods of lesser importance to the State. However, as has been shown, these theoretical concepts are goals rather than actual experience.

The Soviet Union has two wholesale prices: the wholesale price for the industry producing the same commodity and the wholesale price of the enterprise.

The wholesale price for the industry is the average price of all enterprises within a given industry. It includes average costs of production, profit, distribution, and turnover tax. They are rigidly controlled by the government. These prices are used for commodities for which the government does not fix retail prices and also on capital goods used in the production of other goods, the price of which includes the turnover tax.

However, it must be remembered that a large number of capital goods and raw materials do not carry turnover tax. Among industries whose prices exclude turnover tax are the metallurgical, machine-building, instrument, electronic, and many other branches of heavy industry. Products of raw textile materials, glass laboratory equipment, synthetic fabrics, and the like are also free from turnover tax. But prices of commodities which are used by collective farms and the general public include turnover taxes. Among these are petroleum products, electric power, building materials, lumber, and many others. By exempting certain sectors of heavy industry from turnover taxes, the light industry producing consumer goods is being penalized in terms of turnover taxes.

Wholesale prices for individual enterprises cover all expenditures related to production and profit. When the distribution function is undertaken by the producer the cost of distribution is also included. In general, these prices are uniform throughout the Soviet Union, as in the case of automobiles. Exceptions are found among certain commodities, mostly food items, for which differential wholesale prices are established by zones. Such prices are beyond the control of the enterprise and are influenced by such factors as the high cost of transportation or the low turnover of goods. As a rule, wholesale prices of an enterprise are used for both consmer durable and nondurable goods purchased by wholesale distributing organizations and supply establishments. The wholesale price of an enterprise does not include turnover tax, since it is collected by the distributing and supply organizations. Thus, although the wholesale price of an enterprise excludes turnover tax, it is collected by other organizations just the same.

The wholesale price of individual enterprise, on an average, consists of 92 to 95 per cent of the cost of production and five to eight per cent of the profit.[9] Usually planned profits for different commodities are established uniformly by the State. Profit above the planned amount is possible because planned wholesale prices and planned profits are established for a period of one year, during which time the enterprise has the opportunity to reduce its cost of production.

The wholesale price of any one commodity once established does not assure its buyer of price stability. This price may be increased or decreased at any time depending on the policy taken by the government. To increase production of a given commodity, the State can and does reduce prices of raw materials used by the industry and also increases the price to other users to cover the difference. The price of salt to fishing and chemical industries is considerably lower than to other consumers. Alcohol for the synthetic rubber industry and electric power for aluminum industries is cheaper than to others. Even a commodity produced by the same enterprise is often sold at different prices to different consumers. One eastern electric power system with an average price of 8.3 kopeks per kilowatt-hour for industrial users charged a preferential rate of 5.3 kopeks per kilowatt-hour to the zinc plant and 6.5 kopeks to the aluminum plant.[10]

This is not an exception, and many wholesale prices often deviate from the established and "rigidly" controlled wholesale price structure. During the meeting of the Plenum of the Central Committee of the USSR Communist Party in December 1958, the delegate from the Kaliningrad Oblast stated that his region and its neighbor, the Lithuanian SSR, have similar soil and growing conditions, yet they receive different prices for the same commodities. As typical examples, the state procurement price for red clover seed is 20 rubles per kilogram in Kaliningrad Oblast but 32 rubles in the Lithuanian SSR, while timothy seed is eight rubles in Kaliningrad and 15 rubles in Lithuania. Because of similar economic and geographic conditions, the delegate from the Kaliningrad requested treatment similar to that of Lithuania. Commenting on this, Khrushchev said: "The wisest of men would not explain why this was done." [11] It may be added that Khrushchev's remark is the best rationale of the pricing mechanism in the country he rules.

All wholesale prices on industrial goods of national importance are established by the USSR Council of Ministers. Prices on goods of lesser significance are set by the constituent republics and sovarkhozy. The sovnarkhoz producing one or more new commodities for another sovnarkhoz or ministry has the right, upon agreement with the purchaser, to establish temporary wholesale prices. These prices are based on costs for close substitutes produced by the maker in the past. In the absence of past price patterns, the price is calculated on the basis of the cost of production plus five per cent profit. These temporary prices are in effect until a large-scale production of goods is reached at which time permanent wholesale prices are determined.

The sovnarkhoz has the right to establish temporary wholesale prices for its own enterprises for a period of six months on all new consumer goods undertaken, provided that prices on these goods have not already been set by higher authorities. Likewise, the sovnarkhoz has the right to establish wholesale prices of all goods produced by joint efforts of several enterprises under its jurisdiction, if these prices were not previously established by higher authorities.

Goods produced by local industries and cooperatives, the prices of which have not been established by the State, are priced differently. Wholesale prices of raw materials or semi-finished commodities produced by newly organized local or cooperative enterprises are established by the Council of Ministers of each constituent republic. Wholesale prices on consumer goods and food items produced by them are determined by the oblast or city Executive Committees of the Soviet of Deputies. In every case these newly established prices are to be closely related to planned prices of similar goods and authorized by higher authorities.

The Soviet Union has a complex system of wholesale distributing and supplying organizations. The wholesale distributing organizations pay wholesale prices established for the producers. If this price is set by the USSR Council of Ministers it is for the commodity of highest quality. Since any array of the same commodity would include items of different qualities, the price of lower quality goods would carry a different discount (torgovaya skidka). For example, the price of footwear below the top quality would have a discount of five per cent and for the third quality from the top it would be 15 per cent. All undergrade goods have different discount rates, varying with the importance of the grade. Since wholesale prices for the enterprise are established on the basis of top quality, these discounts serve as a penalty for the enterprise for its poor workmanship and must be covered from its profit.

The wholesale distributing organizations cover their expenses by charging the buyer with all of their operations costs in connection with the transfer of goods, plus a small profit. For some goods these charges are expressed in terms of percentage to retail prices and for other goods in rubles per unit. For example, in dry goods this charge is only 0.7 per cent of the retail price, 1.7 per cent for footwear, 2.5 per cent for meat and meat products, 3.0 per cent for fish, 70 rubles per metric ton for salt, and 50 rubles per case for eggs.[12]

The agency which buys in wholesale lots has a choice of several f.o.b. prices. These are:

         a. f.o.b. plant (warehouse of the supplier)
         b. f.o.b. railroad station or pier point of shipment
         c. f.o.b. railroad station or pier point of destination
         d. f.o.b. warehouse of purchaser

Using this f.o.b. list price, the purchasing agency has, at least theoretically, the right to select the least expensive delivery. But with a scarcity of goods, many purchasers disregard the least-cost principle and buy goods from any seller who provides assurance of delivery. This, of course, reduces profit and in some instances retail prices may be increased.

## RETAIL PRICES

In the Soviet Union retail prices are planned and controlled by the State. Over 80 per cent of all cash income of the Soviet population is spent on goods purchased from retail channels. These expenditures are planned and constantly compared with the total cash income of the people. In this way supply and demand for consumer goods, people's purchasing power and their incomes are balanced. The retail price of an article includes the cost of production, profit to the producer, turnover tax, the cost of wholesale distribution, the cost of retail distribution, and profit to the retailer. The USSR Council of Ministers establishes retail prices on the most important necessities.

With the formation of the sovnarkhozy, the Council of Ministers of each constituent republic was empowered to establish retail prices on goods produced by state and cooperative enterprises located there. Constituent republics set retail prices on goods which represent from 45 to 50 per cent of the total turnover of goods in the state and cooperative stores. Prices established either by the USSR Council of Ministers or by the Councils of Ministers of constituent republics are average prices and for a specific period of time, usually a year, and subjected to changes when deemed necessary. But enterprises under the jurisdiction of local authorities often change their prices, disregarding the overall price level. However, the volume of goods produced by local industries is very small, and violation in their pricing structure is important politically rather than economically.

Although the State establishes and controls retail prices, there are commodities whose prices are uniform throughout the Soviet Union, while prices of others vary from region to region. For example, tea, tobacco, footwear, cameras, bicycles, and automobiles as well as many other goods are uniformly priced throughout the country. On the other hand, prices for bakery goods, meat, fish, sugar, salt, canned goods, furniture, lumber, window glass, and so on are different in each price zone.

Before World War II the whole country was divided into from four to eight price zones, depending on the commodity. At present there are three zones, except for lumber which has seven. Different price zones exist because of the cost of transportation from producing to consuming regions. The first price zone is considered the major producer and therefore its price is the lowest. For example, the difference in the price of sugar between the first and the fourth zones in 1940 was 40 per cent. In 1957, with the elimination of two zones, the difference narrowed to 24 per cent. This simply means that a consumer in Yakutsk must pay 24 per cent more for sugar than if he were in Kiev. Zone differences in the price of butter in 1940 amounted to 32 per cent and only seven per cent in 1957.[13]

## A. RETAIL PRICES IN STATE AND COOPERATIVE STORES

State and cooperative retail stores have two methods of calculating their prices to consumers. In the first instance there are goods for which the retail markup is established when the wholesale price is set by the USSR Council of Ministers. The rate of the markup varies from commodity to commodity. The markup is put not on the cost of goods to the retail establishment but on the planned price to the ultimate consumer. This group of commodities includes most consumer goods and food items; it represents about 80 per cent of the total retail trade by the state and cooperative stores.

TABLE 2—*Percentage of Markup to Retail Price in 1957* [14]

| Commodity | City | Village | Isolated settlement |
|---|---|---|---|
| Bakery products _____ | 6.5 | 6.5 | 6.5 |
| Sugar _____ | 5.0 | 5.7 | 6.7 |
| Meat and meat products _____ | 6.5 | 6.5 | 6.5 |
| Salt _____ | 20.0 | 26.0 | 26.0 |
| Cotton fabrics _____ | 3.0 | 5.5 | 7.7 |
| Footwear _____ | 4.6 | 6.0 | 7.7 |
| Knitted goods _____ | 5.2 | 8.2 | 9.7 |

Table 2 shows that, excluding bakery products and meats, rural consumers pay higher prices for other goods than the urban consumers. Consumers residing in isolated settlements pay still higher prices. Exceptionally distant regions such as Kamchatka have still higher markups. Consumers in Kamchatka pay a markup amounting to 19 per cent for sugar, 20 per cent for meats, 50 per cent for salt, 15 per cent for footwear and knitted goods, and 12 per cent for cotton fabrics. Their markup for bakery products, however, is the same as in Moscow since the government subsidizes the bakery industry.

In the second instance there are goods for which the retail selling expenses and profit are added to the wholesale price. This group of commodities is produced locally with a considerable variation in price levels among different regions. Prices on these goods are established by the Councils of Ministers of autonomous republics or by the Executive Committees of the Council of Deputies of the kray, oblast or city.

There are a number of cooperatives which take goods from collective farms and their members for sale on commission. Usually the retail establishment charges about one to two per cent of the selling price. This is similar to what is called a "spread" in the United States, allegedly sufficient to cover the cost of sale. Sales on commission ·represent a recent development, started in 1953. In 1954 about 2.2 billion rubles worth of farm commodities were sold on this basis and about nine billion rubles in 1958.[15]

## B. RETAIL PRICES IN COLLECTIVE FARM MARKETS

The Soviet Union has a "forward" pricing system which is intended to reduce the risk in price fluctuation of agricultural products. Prices offered by the State and the amount of agricultural commodities the State will buy from each collective farm are known in advance. This facilitates better marketing planning for the farms in respect to the State's needs and the volume to be sold on the collective farm market.

The term "collective farm market" is not entirely accurate, since others who are not members of collective farms use the same facilities. The independent peasant who has surpluses or is in need of cash may sell his goods there. The workers and employees who have harvested abundant crops beyond their needs from their small plots use these facilities. A man who is in need of immediate cash may take his extra pair of shoes or suit of clothes and sell them there. A woman who has embroidered a blouse may exchange it for any product she needs. In short, in any large city the collective farm market will have a variety of goods for sale or for barter. Of course the agricultural goods will predominate.

Since prices in collective farm markets are not directly regulated by the State they are more erratic than those in the state and cooperative stores. When a supply of agricultural goods is limited sellers ask high prices; when an abundant supply of goods exists in the state and cooperative stores prices are lowered. Under such conditions the bargaining ability of the seller and buyer may clash, which results in haggling over quality and price of the commodity.

Most of the sellers on collective farm markets are peasants and most of the buyers are the housewives who either cannot find the same goods in state and cooperative stores or have no time to shop there. But the state and cooperative enterprises may also purchase agricultural goods on collective farm markets. For example, if a restaurant runs short of potatoes or onions it may dispatch an employee to a collective farm market to buy enough to tide it over until the next delivery from the state warehouse comes in.

Since the prices on collective farm markets are uncontrolled and since the sellers themselves do not know the exact cost of the goods they sell, fluctuation in prices occurs within a single day. When peasants bring their small amounts of eggs, apples, tomatoes or any other commodity to the market in the morning the price they ask would be determined by the number of buyers pricing their products, by the weather, and the distance from the farm. If many buyers want a certain commodity early in the morning, sellers would raise the asking price immediately. When the demand for any commodity is low, prices are reduced. When it is raining and it is about time for the seller to start back to the farm market price becomes the buyer's price. Therefore, comparison of prices for a commodity with abundant supply on the same market will reveal a wide fluctuation within a short period of time. Because of this peculiarity the comparison of prices for similar goods found in state and cooperative stores and the collective farm market is not a precise measure of the difference between the two prices.

Nevertheless, as a rule, prices on the collective farm market at any time and in any place are higher than those for the state and cooperative stores. The amount of difference between the two prices varies from city to city and from region to region. According to one source prices on collective farm markets for eggs, tomatoes, mutton, and apples were twice the price of the same commodities in state-controlled markets in Tbilisi, Georgia, in 1956. Perhaps this is an exception, since Georgia is lagging behind in expansion of its state and cooperative retail outlets when compared with the USSR as a whole.

Table 3 shows that in 1950 the sales on collective farm markets throughout the country were 63 per cent above the 1940 level, whereas the average price increase was only four per cent. In 1950 the peasants sold four times more grain than in 1940 charging 28 per cent more in price. Vegetables, except potatoes, were scarce in 1950 and urban buyers paid 32 per cent more. Other items, excluding pork, were sold in larger quantities. But only prices of meat, potatoes, and milk were somewhat below that of the 1940 level.

In 1958 the overall price index on collective farm markets was reduced by six per cent below the 1940 level, whereas total sales increased by about 70 per cent. The greatest price reduction occurred in grain and potatoes, while prices of fruits and vegetables were still much above the prewar level. In general, fluctuations in collective farm market prices depend on the availability of goods in state retail outlets and the ability of the buyers to pay higher prices on collective farm markets. It is interesting to note that in their efforts to increase the cattle population after 1950 the peasants offered less beef and veal and their price increased. By the same token, as they increased pork supplies in 1958 the price became five per cent

TABLE 3—*Index of Volume of Sales and Prices of Foodstuffs on Collective Farm Markets: USSR* [16]
(*1940 = 100 percent*)

|  | 1950 | | 1955 | | 1958 | |
|---|---|---|---|---|---|---|
|  | Sales | Prices | Sales | Prices | Sales | Prices |
| All goods: _____ | 163 | 104 | 167 | 107 | 169 | 98 |
| Grain _____ | 406 | 128 | 288 | 114 | 320 | 89 |
| Potatoes _____ | 295 | 77 | 298 | 102 | 285 | 98 |
| Vegetables _____ | 105 | 132 | 130 | 123 | 127 | 129 |
| Fruit _____ | 141 | 113 | 175 | 136 | 179 | 137 |
| Meat and backfat: _____ | 114 | 93 | 112 | 111 | 124 | 99 |
| Beef and veal _____ | 152 | 100 | 89 | 122 | 83 | 101 |
| Pork _____ | 89 | 99 | 121 | 113 | 137 | 95 |
| Milk and milk products ____ | 116 | 92 | 137 | 109 | 99 | 93 |
| Eggs _____ | 114 | 104 | 261 | 98 | 259 | 102 |

lower than the 1940 level. The average 1958 prices of dairy items and eggs were approximately at the 1950 level.

## STATE PROCUREMENT PRICES

State procurement practices were described in Chapters 7, 8, and 9. In this section changes in price policies are examined.

To repeat, prior to 1958, prices paid by the State for agricultural commodities depended upon the method of purchase. There were two major price levels: the lowest price (zagotovka) was for that part of the gross agricultural output which producers were required to deliver to the State; a higher price (zakupka) was paid for the commodities purchased on contractual agreements. Still higher price (premium) was paid for the amount after all other obligations to the State were fulfilled. This created a wide discrepancy between prices received by the producers for the same commodities. And whatever incentives the State allowed in premium prices they were not adequately attractive to inspire the average member to intensify his efforts in production.

The gap between zagotovka and zakupka prices during the 1953-55 period was indeed great. During this period zakupka prices of grain were 12 to 15 times greater than zagotovka prices and in 1957 it narrowed to 3.2

times. Cattle zakupka prices were 13.6 times greater than zagotovka and reduced to 2.6 times in 1957. Only in 1958 these price discrepancies were abolished and new zakupka prices were set up for each of the major producing regions.

TABLE 4—*State Prices Paid for Required Delivery and for Contractual Basis in 1952* [17]

| | | Rubles per unit | |
| Commodity | Unit | Required delivery (zagotovka) | Procurement price (zakupka) |
|---|---|---|---|
| Potatoes _____metric ton | | 100-250 | — |
| Beef and lamb (average fat) _____kilogram | | 1.50 | 4.10 |
| Pork _____liveweight | | 3.20 | 7.00 |
| Chickens and chicks _____liveweight | | 5.00 | 8.50 |
| Turkeys _____liveweight | | 6.00 | 8.50 |
| Geese and ducks _____liveweight | | 4.00 | 8.50 |
| Rabbits _____liveweight | | 1.20 | — |
| Milk, basic fat content _____liter | | 0.55 | 1.20 |
| Butter _____kilogram | | 9.00 | — |
| Wool, high grade _____kilogram | | 28.20 | — |
| Wool, rough _____kilogram | | 9.53 | — |
| Eggs _____10 pieces | | — | 5.00 |

The spread from 100 to 250 rubles per metric ton of potatoes reflects regionalization and the variety of potatoes. It is interesting to note that for six commodities for which both prices are available procurement prices were 86.7 per cent higher than the prices paid for required deliveries.

In order to simplify our anaylsis in comparing the price the State paid in 1952 for a commodity and the price it received from the consumer, we shall deal with mutton and eggs. Assuming that 75 per cent of all mutton is obtained from required deliveries and the other 25 per cent from the procurement program, the average price paid was 2.15 rubles per kilogram liveweight. And assuming that on the average a sheep butchered produces only 41 per cent of its weight on the hoof, then a kilogram of mutton would cost the government about 8.20 rubles. In 1952 the price of mutton in the state stores was 13.65 rubles per kilogram, a profit of 4.75 rubles or over 50 per cent of the original cost. In the case of eggs, which need less handling and processing than mutton, the Soviets paid 5.00 rubles per ten eggs and sold them in Georgia, for instance, for an average price of 6.75 rubles, with a profit of 1.75 rubles, or 33 per cent of the original cost. This is an example, perhaps limited in scope, of the amount of turnover taxes the consumer had to pay.

To overcome apathy among peasants and to stimulate their interest in greater production the Soviets, beginning with 1953, increased both required delivery and procurement prices on a number of commodities. The greatest increase occurred in livestock products. For example, the price for required delivery of meat was increased by 5.5 times and procurement price by 30 per cent; the price of milk for required delivery increased 3.3 times and the procurement price by 73 per cent. However, the average price increase on vegetables for required delivery ranged between 25 and 40 per cent, but the increase in procurement prices averaged about 70 per cent.[18] These increases indicate which commodities were in short supply in the USSR. It may be added that there were no increases in prices on cotton at all.

It is interesting to note that in 1952 the difference between the price of meat which the State paid for required delivery and meat retail prices was 49 per cent, 55 per cent in milk, and 70 per cent in vegetables. By increasing prices to the peasants some of the retail prices were slightly adjusted upward. Nevertheless, the 1953 and consequent reforms in the price system have considerably improved the economic position of the collective farms and their members. As a result of these reforms the average annual cash income per collective farm increased from 441,000 rubles in 1952 to 1.1 million rubles in 1956, an increase of 2.7 times, and the total incomes for all collective farms in cash and in kind increased from 47.5 billion rubles in 1952 to 83.8 billion rubles in 1957.[19] This suggests that cash income advanced more rapidly than the income in kind.

Revamping of the state price policy was aimed at greater agricultural output rather than at betterment of the peasants' lot, but the goal was achieved through higher prices. Having achieved this target the Soviets in 1958 completely broke away from the old system by adopting one price for each commodity which, depending upon supply and demand, may be adjusted upward or downward. It is expected that the new price policies in the procurement program will stimulate agricultural output—the main target of this policy.

Even with recent price reform the peasants are still underpaid for their efforts. Moreover, both the prices and the norms are established by the State. Prices may again be reduced and norms may be increased at the will of Moscow's planners. There is a deep-rooted economic conflict between the peasants and the Soviet leadership. Existence of this conflict was denied by Khrushchev on his "Face The Nation" television appearance in June, 1957, but it is there just the same. On the one hand the peasants want more income for their efforts; on the other, the Communists could not permit peasants to have higher incomes while the production of consumer goods is still inadequate. With higher income on hand the peasants would have a greater advantage over factory workers and would outbid them for scarce goods and services on the market. This the Soviets cannot and will not tolerate for this means preferential treatment of the peasants over urban workers.

Since the wage of factory workers is completely controlled by the State the only other group which has the opportunity to increase earnings is the peasants. Certainly, if the government would considerably increase farm prices the peasants would increase their profits in an economy of scarcity and this would endanger the economic stability of the country. The Soviet leaders and the peasants know this, and both groups are well aware that the government would apply economic brakes should peasants' incomes increase to the point of causing a relaxation in breater output by them.

### RETAIL PRICE REDUCTIONS

One of the most interesting aspects in the Soviet price structure is the reduction of price levels. How do the Soviet planners know when and by how much a price of a given commodity may be reduced? Presumably decisions in retail price reductions are based on efficiency recorded for the past several years. For example, when there is a constant reduction in the cost of production of shoes for several years, it is reasonable to believe that there will be further reductions, and thus the Soviets reduce the price of shoes.

With the beginning of the war in 1941 production of a great many consumer goods ceased, and most of the state and cooperative stores were closed. In 1942 the state stores supplied only a fraction of what they had supplied in 1940. Meat and meat products were reduced to almost one-half, cotton fabrics were reduced to one-fifth, and leather footwear was reduced to one-third of the 1940 levels. The best supplied items were flour and cereals, but even there a 15 per cent reduction occurred, and the quality was much below that of 1940.[20] By April 1942 all urban residents were put on rationing. At the same time the government divided the whole country into from four to seven rationing zones, where different prices on food products were established. Even the sales from collective farms to individual consumers were controlled under this law.

In 1942 the index of prices in state stores increased by 20 per cent above the 1940 level, but the scarcity of goods in the stores forced civilian consumers to buy food at higher prices in collective farm markets. As a result, in 1942 the number of collective farm markets expanded by 30 per cent over 1941. Thus, the war caused adjustments in the policy toward private trading; instead of suppressing it as in the past the government actually encouraged it. The peasants reacted by increasing outputs of their private plots. Socialistic morality was pushed aside and the peasants again, as in the days of the NEP, became important producers. The shortage of food boosted its prices, which began to move upward in late 1941, accelerated their rise in 1942, and by 1943 the price index on field products like grain was 12.6 times over the 1940 level, and on livestock it was 13.2 times.[21]

The alarming increase in the price index disturbed Soviet leaders, and as soon as there were evidences of a successful counterattack by the Red Army in 1943 the government increased the output of consumer goods, and the turnover of sales in state and cooperative stores increased. In 1944 retail sales of meat were 41 per cent.above those of 1942, fish products 69 per cent, fats and oils 65 per cent, and cereals and macaroni 56 per cent.[22] In general, it is reasonable to say that runaway prices on collective farm markets were, if not reduced, at least checked in 1944, and by 1945 these prices began a downward trend. The whole span of 1942-44 was a confusing period, during which price control in food was a hodge-podge and food items became a currency medium for almost everything else. Defective and unpalatable food was often sold, jeopardizing the health of the population and creating still another problem for the government.

The first postwar official price reduction in state stores came with a decree of August 21, 1945. This decree reduced by 15 per cent the price of food in Moscow, Leningrad, and in other large cities of central and northern USSR, and in the southern regions by 14 per cent.[23] Many of these cities were besieged by the Germans and cut off from supply regions, and it was only by 1945 that transportation was established and food became available in greater volumes to these "hero-cities." The effect of this decree was reflected in some reduction of food prics on collective farm markets. But because of general confusion, both prices were reduced at different rates in different cities and regions.

To end such price disparities, to show its economic stability to the West, and to check inflation the government abolished the rationing system. The Soviets had planned to end rationing as early as 1946, but the drought in White Russia and the Ukraine delayed this program and resulted in further increases in overall food prices. To minimize this rise in prices the Soviets in September 1946 increased the monthly wage of many workers, ranging from 80 to 110 rubles. This measure, although one-sided, affected all prices as well as wages, and it boomeranged. The prices of rationed food products were raised on an average of 80 per cent over 1945, and the prices on unrationed goods were decreased by 30 to 35 per cent. As a result of these doubled price changes the official prices for unrationed food commodities became only three to eight times the rationed prices. This caused a sharp increase in prices on collective farm markets, increased speculation, and also forced the government to establish measures to combat such speculation. It proved to be both deflationary and inflationary, and both the peasants and the factory workers deeply resented it.

To overcome the resentment and to compensate for the increased cost of living the Soviets in September 1947 reduced prices of many food products in the state stores from 15 to 30 per cent.[24] Then in December 1947 a decree was published devaluating the ruble, decreasing prices, and at long last abolishing rationing. Under this decree retail prices in state stores were reduced by 12 per cent on bread and flour and by ten per cent on cereals and macaroni. The result of this decree was some reduction in prices on collective farm markets, especially in dairy products, vegetables, and meat. How much of this reduction was due to the decrease of prices in the state stores and how much to the devaluation of the ruble is a question for speculation. Perhaps the devaluation of the ruble had a greater impact in effecting lower prices on collective farm markets since most of the state stores had empty shelves anyway. Nevertheless, regardlesss of which measure was more responsible, both measures forced the prices on collective farm markets down 31 per cent in the first quarter of 1948 as compared with the same quarter of 1947.[25]

Another price reduction occurred in the second half of August 1948, but it was not uniformly applicable and varied widely from region to region and from commodity to commodity. During 1949, except for some price reductions in consumer goods, there was no major cut back in the price of the food sold on the collective farm markets. With wartime production reconverted to civilian goods and with a greater volume of goods supplied through the state and cooperative stores, the collective farm market prices were also reduced. Then in 1950 another major price reduction took place, affecting 234 items consisting of food and consumer goods, with price reductions ranging from 15 to 35 per cent.[26]

The years 1951 and 1952 were not eventful years as far as official price reductions were concerned, but because of increased output of food and consumer goods all prices were somewhat reduced. In April 1953 another official price reduction took place, and in April 1954 still another. Under these two price reductions buyers in state stores officially saved 46 million rubles and another seven million rubles in collective farm markets—a total of 53 million rubles. The 1954 reduction in prices in state stores alone amounted to 20 million rubles, and it was claimed that, in general, retail prices on consumer goods in 1954 were 26 per cent below the 1950 level.[27] Most price reductions reflected increasing efficiency in production, adjustments in the norms and prices in agriculture, and curtailment of overstaffed agencies.

Since 1954 price reductions have been granted to individual commodities rather than to a formal list of commodities. For example, beginning with January 1, 1955, prices paid by the State for required delivery of livestock and dairy products to the peasants were increased; in return, the peasants increased production of these products, forcing prices down.

Another official retail price reduction occurred on June 30, 1959, and averaged 16 per cent on consumer goods such as wines, nylon stockings, radios, cameras, bicycles, and toys.[28] A total savings on the purchase of these items would amount to about six billion rubles. However, in 1958 the retail price index was still 30 to 35 per cent above the prewar level, though th ecost of production as a whole was below the 1940 level and labor productivity almost doubled.[29] This disparity between retail prices and the cost of production suggests that in 1958 the Soviets were still investing heavily in basic industry, attempting to control inflation by keeping retail prices at a high level.

Independent construction of price indices for the Soviet Union is difficult because of State interference in the normal movement of prices. This interference is made up of many short-run price adjustments, subsidies, and non-economic considerations. The effect of these forces may be directed to a few commodities or even an entire industry, yet the impact made by such adjustment results in changes in all other relative costs and prices. Because of these considerations the price index in Table 5 is based upon official Soviet data to be used as a general guide to the retail price index for the state-controlled prices, excluding the prices found in collective farm markets.

Table 5 indicates that during and after the war the real problem was runaway food prices even though prices in the state retail stores were controlled by the government. Since consumer goods were better

Table 5—*Retail Price Index in the State-Controlled Stores* [30]
(*average annual 1940 = 100*)

| Year | All goods | Food | Consumer goods |
|------|-----------|------|----------------|
| 1940_____ | 100 | 100 | 100 |
| 1947_____ | 329 | 382 | 255 |
| 1948_____ | 273 | 313 | 219 |
| 1949_____ | 232 | 260 | 199 |
| 1950_____ | 186 | 203 | 165 |
| 1951_____ | 170 | 181 | 157 |
| 1952_____ | 161 | 166 | 156 |
| 1953_____ | 146 | 146 | 145 |
| 1954_____ | 138 | 141 | 134 |
| 1955_____ | 138 | 141 | 134 |
| 1956_____ | 138 | 143 | 133 |
| 1957_____ | 138 | 143 | 133 |
| 1958_____ | 141 | 149 | 133 |

controlled, their prices were more manageable than those of food. The divergence between the price indices for food and for consumer goods began to narrow in 1952 and 1953; in 1954 and through 1957 it widened again because of the decrease in prices of consumer goods. The official retail price index was stabilized in the 1954-57 period, but increased in 1958. The 1958 price reductions are mostly on individual commodities, prices of which are still high but lower than in the past. Excluding alcoholic beverages, the 1958 price index for "all goods" would have been 130 and for "food" only 126. This, of course, suggests the high prices of these beverages and the Russians' enormous capacity for them.

The list in Table 6 represents the bulk of consumers' demand, and except for bread made of refined flour and kerosene, all other commodities are priced higher in 1958 than in 1940. The range is from 184 per cent for sugar to 118 per cent for meat and poultry. Most vegetables, milk, and eggs are not included in the list. In 1940 Soviet consumers allocated 63 per cent of their purchasing power for the foodstuffs obtained from state-controlled stores and restaurants. In 1950 only 58 per cent was spent on foodstuffs and in 1958 it became 55 per cent. True, the Russians have increased consumption of consumer goods from 37 per cent of their total purchases in 1940 to 45 per cent in 1958. Yet the ratio between foodstuffs and non-food items indicates the presence of high prices and low incomes.

The 1959 retail prices were reduced on some of the consumer goods, and then in March 1960 another reduction took place. Like the 1959 cutback, the 1960 price reduction also occurred in consumer goods rather

TABLE 6—*Retail Price Index for Certain Commodities in the State-Controlled Stores* [31]
(*in percentage of average annual prices in 1940*)

| Commodity | 1940 | 1950 | 1951 | 1952 | 1953 | 1954 | 1955 | 1956 | 1958 |
|---|---|---|---|---|---|---|---|---|---|
| **Food Items:** | | | | | | | | | |
| Meat and poultry | 100 | 179 | 153 | 132 | 112 | 108 | 108 | 123 | 118 |
| Fish | 100 | 173 | 154 | 152 | 140 | 137 | 137 | 137 | 133 |
| Butter | 100 | 179 | 149 | 132 | 117 | 114 | 114 | 116 | 116 |
| Sugar | 100 | 231 | 227 | 209 | 189 | 184 | 184 | 184 | 184 |
| Bread, rough flour | 100 | 247 | 205 | 181 | 162 | 149 | 147 | 147 | 146 |
| Bread, refined flour | 100 | 164 | 135 | 117 | 104 | 97 | 96 | 96 | 95 |
| Bakery items | 100 | 232 | 223 | 202 | 182 | 177 | 177 | 178 | 178 |
| Cereals | 100 | 208 | 176 | 149 | 131 | 128 | 128 | 128 | 126 |
| Potatoes | | | | | | | | | |
| (Moscow only) | 100 | 100 | 100 | 100 | 50 | 67 | 111 | 111 | 111 |
| Cabbage | | | | | | | | | |
| (Moscow only) | 100 | 85 | 85 | 85 | 43 | 60 | 60 | 80 | 133 |
| **Consumer Goods:** | | | | | | | | | |
| Cotton fabrics | 100 | 249 | 243 | 243 | 214 | 182 | 176 | 176 | 176 |
| Wool fabrics | 100 | 190 | 185 | 184 | 176 | 174 | 173 | 173 | 173 |
| Silk fabrics | 100 | 186 | 184 | 184 | 176 | 171 | 170 | 169 | 168 |
| Ready-to-wear | | | | | | | | | |
| clothing | 100 | 185 | 182 | 182 | 174 | 168 | 167 | 167 | 167 |
| Knitted fabrics | 100 | 195 | 193 | 193 | 185 | 173 | 171 | 170 | 170 |
| Leather footwear | 100 | 201 | 198 | 198 | 181 | 166 | 163 | 163 | 163 |
| Tobacco products | 100 | 135 | 119 | 117 | 112 | 111 | 111 | 111 | 110 |
| Kerosene | 100 | 274 | 217 | 213 | 171 | 111 | 99 | 99 | 99 |
| Dry goods | 100 | 153 | 150 | 149 | 137 | 133 | 133 | 133 | 132 |
| Matches | 100 | 325 | 258 | 250 | 220 | 178 | 171 | 171 | 171 |

than in foodstuffs. For example, the prices of fur goods made of silver or white fox were cut by 20 per cent; silk and artificial silk by 15 per cent; certain makes of radios by 25 per cent; cameras up to 30 per cent; electric sewing machines by 20 per cent; motor scooters 18 per cent; accordions 20 per cent; and so on. All in all, the 1960 price reduction, at the existing wage levels, would increase the purchasing power of the Russians by some 2.5 billion rubles a year or about 12 rubles per capita, which could not possibly greatly increase the standard of living of the average Russian worker.

Moreover, since the 1960 price cuts were made on expensive items, this tended to benefit the high income groups rather than the masses. Nevertheless, the Soviets are claiming that in 1960 the Soviet consumer pays 43 rubles for goods for which he had to pay 100 rubles at the end of 1947, and the government has promised further price reductions before the end of the current Seven-Year Plan in 1965.[32]

The Soviet pricing mechanism is unique since it is based on factors other than supply and demand. Of course, the Soviets must feed their citizens and must provide them with consumer goods, but because their economy is a planned one many factors are taken into consideration before the price of any one item is reduced. Despite the complexity of the mechanism Russians still have opportunities for reduction in prices. The most important factor is the fact that the Russians started their economy with low mechanization. It is only during the last few years that considerable progress toward mechanization has been made, and as the cost of production is reduced price reductions will follow. Even with unchanged turnover taxes, increased output through improved mechanization and mass production will inevitably reduce the cost of production, which will increase industrial savings in addition to turnover taxes. The Soviets seem to be headed in this direction.

## Chapter 14—Bibliography

[1] *Materialy Vsesoyuznogo Soveshchaniya Zaveduyushchikh Kafedrami Obshchestvennykh Nauk*, Moscow, 1958, p. 225.

[2] Kismin, N. and Slavnyy, I., *Sovetskiye Finansy v Pyatoy Pyatiletke*, Moscow, 1956, p. 10.

[3] *Voprosy Ekonomiki*, No. 5, 1957, p. 61.

[4] Kismin and Slavnyy, *op. cit.*, p. 12.

[5] Shass, M. E., *Ekonomika Stroitel'noy Promyshlennosti SSSR*, Moscow, 1958, p. 389; *Voprosy Ekonomiki*, No. 8, 1955, p. 47.

[6] Bachurin, A., *Ekonomicheskoye Soderzhaniye Byudzheta pri Sotsialisme*, Moscow, 1957, p. 41.

[7] *Voprosy Ekonomiki*, No. 5, 1959, pp. 130-34.

[8] *Teoriya i Praktika Khozaystvennogo Rascheta*, Moscow, 1958, p. 117.

[9] Kantor, L. M., *Sebestoimost v Sotsialisticheskoy Promyshlennosti*, Moscow, 1958, p. 236.

[10] *Ibid.*, p. 257.

[11] *Plenum Tsetral'nogo Komiteta Kommunisticheskoy Parti Sovetskogo Soyuza*, December 15-19, 1958, Moscow, 1959, p. 203.

[12] *Ekonomika Sovetskoy Torgovli*, Moscow, 1958, p. 274.

[13] *Ibid.*, p. 260.

[14] *Ibid.*, p. 276.

[15] *Sovetskaya Torgovlya*, Moscow, 1956, p. 179; *Narodnoye Khozaystvo SSSR v 1958 Godu*, Moscow, 1959, p. 669.

16 *Narodnoye Khozaystvo,* op. cit., pp. 788-89.

17 Pavlov, I. V., *Kolkhoznyy Dvor i ego Pravovoye Polozheniye,* Moscow, 1954, pp. 41-42.

18 *Teoriya i Praktika Khozaystvennogo Rascheta,* op. cit., pp. 254-56.

19 *Pobedy Sotsialisticheskogo Sel'skogo Khozaystva,* Moscow, 1958, p. 405; Embassy of the USSR, *Press Department,* No. 47, Washington, D. C., March 18, 1959.

20 Voznesenskiy, N., *Voennaya Ekonomika SSSR v Period Otechestvennoy Voyny,* Moscow, 1948, p. 126.

21 *Ibid.,* p. 129.

22 *Sovetskaya Torgovlya za 30 Let,* Moscow, 1947, p. 124.

23 *Izvestia,* August 21, 1945.

24 *Izvestia,* September 13, 1947.

25 *Izvestii Akademii Nauk SSSR,* No. 1, 1949, p. 29.

26 *Izvestia,* March 1, 1950.

27 Aleksandrov, N. G., *Sovetskoye Trudovoye Pravo,* Moscow, 1954, p. 113; *Istoriya SSSR* (Epokha Sotsialisma 1917-1957), Moscow, 1958, p. 700.

28 *The Washington Post and Times Herald,* July 1, 1959.

29 *Teoriya i Praktika Khozaystvennogo Rascheta,* op. cit., p. 102.

30 *Narodnoye Khozaystvo SSSR v 1956 Godu,* Moscow, 1957, p. 232. Index numbers for 1947, 1958 and 1949 are estimated; *Narodnoye Khozaystvo SSSR v 1958 Godu,* op. cit., p. 770.

31 *Vestnik Statistiki,* No. 5, 1956, p. 83; *Narodnoye Khozaystvo SSSR v 1958 Godu,* op. cit., p. 770.

32 Embassy of the USSR, *Press Department,* No. 127, Washington, D. C., March 9, 1960.

# CHAPTER 15

# Education, Health and Welfare

## INTRODUCTION

Education, health, and welfare in the Soviet Union represent an integral part of the theoretical socio-economic belief that as indispensible public services they are to be completely dominated by the State. Moreover, it must be recognized that higher standards in education, health, and welfare are desirable for the State and the people alike, and since they cannot be static the Soviet government has accomplished a great deal in these areas since 1917.

In 1913 about 25 per cent of the Russian population was literate. Today illiteracy is claimed to be less than one per cent, and education is almost totally state-supported and state-oriented. The Soviet educational system is designed to provide the required number of workers of various skills needed by the economy and to build loyalty to the State.

An example of the role of the educational system in the planned economy may be seen in its sweeping reform inplemented in 1959 which replaced the seven-year schools in the rural areas and the ten-year schools in the cities by the eight-year school program throughout the country. Under the new program basic schooling combines academic and vocational training. Although the ten-year school system has not been completely discarded, nearly all students are required to work in factories, mines, construction sites, and on farms and spend less time in the classrooms. The Soviets are expecting to develop enthusiasm among youth for work while attending schools in order to produce a new crop of students "with a many-sided education, well-versed in the rudiments of science, and fit at the same time for systematic labor." The significance of the reform lies not so much in what it will do to the educational system as in what it will do to the academic goals of the students themselves. Unfortunately, it is too early to evaluate this aspect.

Students are expected to graduate from the eight-year schools at the age of 15 or 16. After this required schooling they are allowed to enroll in a tekhnikum for the next three years and graduate at 18 or 19. This is important because many industries, especially mining, are not permitted to hire workers under 18 years of age. The change from seven- to eight-year compulsory education added another year to the average age of the students, and this permits the Soviets to use them in factories and on collective farms.

The student successfully graduated from the eight-year school and from a tekhnikum may be admitted to an institution of higher learning. But his admittance is based not only upon his scholastic achievements but also upon recommendations of the Komsomol (Communist Youth League) and unions in industrial enterprises or from the collective farm. In short, only those with good grades and in good standing with the Komsomol and unions are selected for enrollment in colleges and universities.

Since the establishment of public health in the Soviet Union it has been based on a highly centralized preventive and therapeutic medicine to keep people well. Medical care is free and generally accessible to all citizens, and there are more hospital beds, more physicians, and better services. As a result, during the 1926-59 period, longevity increased by 23 years.

Closely associated with health is the welfare program, the principal aim of which is to provide financial assistance to those of retirement age, war veterans, maternity cases, the disabled, and orphaned children.

The impact of World War II increased welfare payments greatly, but it was only in 1956 that the government was able to increase assistance to compensate for the increased cost of living. Since the Soviet population is growing older rapidly the problems of health and welfare have become more important than they were in the past, and Khrushchev promised improvements in both during the current Seven-Year Plan. However dear to his heart the old folks may be his prime objective is the youth, who are needed in industry and whom he is attempting to regiment more than they were under Stalin.

## EDUCATION

The Soviet Union provides an education system for its children which reflects the socio-economic trends of the country. Education is controlled and dominated by the State. It does not reflect an intellectual vacuum, for no education which stimulates imagination can be static or fail to build the talents of the people involved. Although education serves the needs of the State and every citizen is expected to contribute his best efforts to the society, the system does utilize the imagination of its people, if only in a controlled way.

The Soviets feel that a child is born with undeveloped talents, that he cannot inherit them, and that consequently they must be developed through education. Since he is a member of Soviet society and has a definite responsibility for the welfare of his country he must develop his talents and increase his efficiency to enable him to respond to the demands made on him. In other words, the educational system of the Soviet Union is not designed to produce independent self-determination but is a part of the theoretical socio-economic belief in the unity of all citizens under the guidance of the Communist Party.

Without education no other socio-economic advances can be undertaken. Soviet education is therefore a means of effecting nationwide advancement, and its achievements in this field are astonishing indeed. During the 1914-15 school year, only 6.2 per cent of the total population was enrolled in the school system of Tsarist Russia. Including all types of schools, the 1958-59 total school enrollment was almost four times the figure for the 1914-15 period, whereas the total population increased by about 31 per cent. Moreover, Soviet education is not confined to the schools. Responsibility for the conduct and achievements of school children also rests with the parents. These two factors, parental instruction and the State, insure quality in the Soviet educational system which slowly but surely broadens the possibilities for economic advancement.

Education in the Soviet Union is largely state supported and includes stipends and tuition, as well as food, shelter, uniforms, and other benefits. Only the boarding schools, newly organized in 1956, require tuition, which is based on the parents' ability to pay. However, full state support is available to poor children admitted to these schools. Thus, the only tuition fees now required are for nurseries and kindergartens. These fees range from 30 to 150 rubles a month, depending on the income of the pupil's parents, the number of children in the family, the number of hours the child is in school, and the location of the school. In rural areas, these monthly fees are at least ten rubles less than in urban centers; fees are waived for children of pensioners, war invalids, unmarried mothers, and some other groups.

By supporting education the State maintains uniformity in instruction and guidance of the children, but even in a planned economy the system has shown an ability to adjust itself to meet changing conditions. With changing technology and political flexibility the Soviets must employ intellectual concepts in coping with new problems. Then, too, tuition-free education can be viewed as a means of developing higher economic standards of the Russian people. One might reason that these standards could have been achieved by the Russian people themselves had the government increased the average income of the workers. This might have been true if the Soviet Union had not faced the shortage of consumer goods and the increase of purchasing power of the people at the same time. What the Soviets did accomplish by providing free education was to increase the real wage of the families at the same time they improved the skills of workers.

In its short history the Soviet educational system has passed through a transformation from the system inherited from Tsarist days. The Tsarist educational system had to be destroyed before a new system could be established. The system which exists now is a product of socio-economic adjustments and experimentation. Since it is new and without tradition it needs discipline, stability, and most of all, the loyalty of new citizens. Now, however, ideological aspects of earlier Soviet educational processes are being challenged by technological advances. The Russians are meeting this challenge with less of the monolithic rigidity of the past and more flexibility which brings them closer to realities of the sputnik era. In 1959 the Soviet school system, including kindergartens through postgraduate levels, trained and drilled over 50 million persons, or 24 per cent of the total population. The qualitive value of these courses is uncertain, but what is certain is the fact that the Soviets are seriously attempting to educate and train their children and adults.

## Nurseries and Kindergartens

The Soviet Union is a nation where most women work in factories, farms, or offices. At the end of 1958, 25.1 million, or 46 per cent of the state-employed workers, were women. Millions of them are mothers with small children who must work to supplement their husbands' low incomes. Therefore, pre-school institutions which care for children are an integral part of the Soviet economy. Both nurseries and kindergartens are regarded as pre-school institutions, although the major function of nurseries is to render child-care only.

Nurseries and kindergartens may be established by a factory, cooperative enterprise, trade union, large apartment house, collective farm, or by any other group having a large number of women workers with children. Nurseries take care of children up to three years of age. Kindergartens provide care and training for children from three to seven years of age. Children in nurseries are kept during the day while their mothers are at work, but mothers may visit them during feeding time. Children in kindergartens may be kept nine to 12 hours and there are establishments where children may stay 24 hours a day. The cost of keeping a child in nursery school or in kindergarten to the parents is about 15 per cent of the total cost; the rest is covered by the State, enterprise, or establishment.

TABLE 1—*Pre-School Educational Systems of the Soviet Union* [1]
(in thousands)

|  | 1940 | 1950 | 1955 | 1958 |
|---|---|---|---|---|
| Nurseries |  |  |  |  |
| Total beds: _____ | 824.1 | 735.1 | 851.0 | 1,134.9 |
| Urban _____ | 523.8 | 470.1 | 567.6 | – |
| Rural _____ | 300.3 | 265.0 | 283.4 | – |
| Number of children _____ | 4,049.1 | 1,813.1 | 2,334.0 | 3,000.0 |
| Kindergartens |  |  |  |  |
| Number of establishments: ____ | 24.0 | 25.6 | 31.6 | 36.8 |
| Urban _____ | 14.4 | 17.0 | 21.0 | 24.3 |
| Rural _____ | 9.6 | 8.6 | 10.6 | 12.5 |
| Number of children: _____ | 1,171.5 | 1,168.8 | 1,730.9 | 2,357.7 |
| Urban _____ | 905.4 | 958.1 | 1,422.6 | 1,947.6 |
| Rural _____ | 266.1 | 210.7 | 308.3 | 410.1 |

Nurseries and kindergartens in urban centers are twice as numerous as in rural areas, as can be seen in Table 1, and they are better equipped. In rural areas they may be organized only for the duration of heavy field work. However, urban centers also may and often do organize kindergartens only for the summer. Again, whereas nurseries may provide similar care for all children, kindergartens are more specialized and can handle blind, deaf, mentally retarded, and physically deformed children.

It is expected that by 1965 Soviet nurseries will expand to take care of 4.2 million children.[2] The 1958 enrollment in kindergartens was twice as large as in 1940 and undoubtedly the 1958 figure will be surpassed by at least one million in 1965. The main emphasis is on the improvement of facilities by providing better playgrounds, more equipment, and methods for developing self-expression and acquiring the culture which fits the pattern of Soviet society.

## Primary-secondary Education

General primary-secondary education in the Soviet Union is coeducational. Prior to the 1959 change to the eight-year school program, general primary-secondary school systems consisted of several levels: (1) the four-year or primary schools for children between seven and 11 years of age; (2) the seven-year, or incomplete secondary schools for children between seven and 14 years of age; and (3) the "middle" ten-year, or complete secondary schools for children between seven and 17 years of age. However, Georgia, Estonia, Latvia, and Lithuania had 11-year "middle" schools with the extra year providing for study of Russian language and literature. In addition, during the 1956-57 school year 285 boarding schools were organized where 67,000 children were enrolled. By 1965 it is expected that 2.5 million students will be enrolled in these schools.

TABLE 2—*Primary-Secondary Education System* [3]

| Indices | 1940-41 | 1950-51 | 1955-56 | 1958-59 |
|---|---|---|---|---|
| Total number of schools (thousands) | 198.6 | 222.1 | 213.0 | 215.0 |
| Total enrollment (millions) | 35.5 | 34.7 | 30.1 | 31.5 |
| Urban Sector: | | | | |
| A. Total number of schools (thousands): | 21.5 | 24.3 | 26.0 | 26.6 |
| 4-year schools | 6.9 | 9.2 | 7.2 | – |
| 7-year schools | 4.8 | 7.2 | 6.3 | – |
| 10-year schools | 8.9 | 7.4 | 11.9 | – |
| Others | 0.9 | 0.5 | 0.6 | – |
| B. Total enrollment (millions): | 10.8 | 11.7 | 12.1 | 13.7 |
| 4-year schools | 1.4 | 1.6 | 0.8 | – |
| 7-year schools | 2.2 | 3.6 | 2.2 | – |
| 10-year schools | 7.1 | 6.4 | 9.0 | – |
| Others | 0.1 | 0.1 | 0.1 | – |
| Rural Sector: | | | | |
| A. Total number of schools (thousands): | 170.0 | 177.3 | 169.3 | 173.1 |
| 4-year schools | 119.0 | 117.3 | 101.6 | – |
| 7-year schools | 40.9 | 52.4 | 52.5 | – |
| 10-year schools | 9.9 | 7.5 | 14.9 | – |
| Others | 0.2 | 0.1 | 0.3 | – |
| B. Total enrollment (millions): | 24.0 | 21.6 | 16.1 | 15.9 |
| 4-year schools | 8.4 | 5.9 | 2.8 | – |
| 7-year schools | 10.3 | 11.9 | 7.2 | – |
| 10-year schools | 5.1 | 3.8 | 6.1 | – |
| Others | 0.2 | 0.02 | 0.02 | – |
| Number of schools for workers (thousands): | 7.1 | 20.5 | 17.7 | 15.3 |
| Enrollment in schools for workers (millions): | 0.7 | 1.4 | 1.9 | 1.9 |

Military academies are open only for boys who have already completed the four-year school, and offer cadets a seven-year educational and military program. Thus, although military academies are similar to general secondary schools, the cadets study eleven years before they can be admitted to officer training schools.

For rehabilitation of children with physical or mental defects or for those who need prolonged medical care, the Soviets established special schools leading to an educational level equivalent to that of the ten-year school.

Many Soviet educators admit that their rural education system is weak. As educational levels and prerequisites are raised in the urban centers, rural education becomes more and more important if the State is to be served equally well by both its urban and rural populations. Again, with emphasis on practical work in secondary schools prerequisites for the admission to higher educational institutions must be lowered, and new admission prerequisites are now being worked out. No doubt Khrushchev's idea of "learning while working" might speed up the training of scarce workers, but in the long run it also would lower the quality of academic training.

Between 1940 and 1956 the number of primary-secondary schools in the USSR, including the workers' schools, increased by about eight per cent, though the total enrollment declined by four million pupils. During the 1956-59 period, with 2,000 additional school units, the total enrollment increased by 1.4 million, suggesting that Soviet primary-secondary schools are small and overloaded with pupils. Even in 1955-56, because of shortages of school space, the Soviets used three shifts to accommodate students. The first shift accommodated 63 per cent of the total Soviet primary-secondary school enrollment, 36.5 per cent were in the second, and only 0.5 per cent attended the third shift. Use of multiple shifts varies from region to region.

Between 1940 and 1941 the average enrollment per school was 179 pupils; it was 156 in 1950-51 and only 146 during the 1958-59 school year. Urban schools are larger than rural schools, with an average of 502 pupils per urban school in 1940-41 as compared to 141 in rural areas. By 1958-59 the urban average became 515 but the rural 92. Comparing enrollment by grades, the four-year and the ten-year urban schools averaged twice as many pupils as the rural schools.

The decline in total enrollment in 1950-59, as compared with 1940-41 period, was the result of World War II and its aftermath—reduced birth and increased death rates, especially in areas occupied by the Germans and within areas of military operations. Children born during the war began to attend primary schools in 1949, yet the impact of the war was still felt in 1956, especially among rural populations. In comparison with 1940-41, the 1945-46 enrollment in all primary-secondary schools in rural areas was

5.6 million pupils fewer, and urban areas were 2.9 million short. The greatest drop in enrollment between the two periods amounted to 50 per cent and occurred in seven- and ten-year schools, with rural school enrollment showing the heaviest drop. The larger drop in rural schools may be attributed not only to the effects of World War II but also to the migration from villages to urban centers.

The prestige of teachers is high; their salaries are comparable with those of doctors and engineers, especially in the ten-grade urban schools. Only the best talent is employed in training future Soviet citizens, with only one out of six applicants for teaching positions accepted. Yet there seems to be no evidence of a shortage of teachers, and there is an abundance of staff assistance such as curriculum experts, physicians, nurses, and laboratory help. The educational process is continued after school hours and during the summer under trained personnel.

TABLE 3—*Subjects and Total Hours in the 1955-56 Curriculum* [4]

| Subject | Schools | | |
| --- | --- | --- | --- |
| | 4-Year | 7-Year | 10-Year |
| Russian language and literature | 1,584 | 759 | 445.5 |
| Arithmetic and mathematics | 792 | 594 | 594.0 |
| History | 66 | 198 | 396.0 |
| Geography | 66 | 231 | 181.5 |
| Biology | 66 | 231 | 99.0 |
| Drawing (technical) | 132 | 99 | 99.0 |
| Physics | – | 165 | 379.5 |
| Chemistry | – | 66 | 280.5 |
| Foreign language | – | 363 | 297.0 |
| Physical education | 264 | 198 | 198.0 |
| Singing | 132 | 66 | – |
| Practical work (factory and farm) | 132 | 198 | 198.0 |
| Constitution of the USSR | – | – | 33.0 |
| Astronomy | – | – | 33.0 |
| Psychology | – | – | 33.0 |
| TOTAL | 3,234 | 3,168 | 3,267.0 |

Soviet primary-secondary education, the backbone of the new order, is centralized and planned. Pupils are drilled in subjects valuable to Soviet society, and less attention is given to questions involving the application of knowledge to new situations. Pupils are regarded as the future builders of the country, ants in industrial and agricultural production lines, well disciplined and trained for the task assigned to them by the State. Individual expression and creativeness are permitted only if they benefit and enrich the Soviet society. Since children in primary-secondary schools are intended to be bees in a huge economic beehive, there is heavy emphasis placed on sciences. The curriculum in every school is standardized throughout the country and is taught in 58 native languages. This is particularly important in four-grade schools, where pupils of various ethnic groups are taught.

By the time the student graduates from a ten-year school his training in the humanities has absorbed about 47 per cent of his time; 42 per cent is devoted to sciences and related technical training; only 11 per cent is spent on physical education, drawing, and singing—the "snap" courses in the curriculum. Since girls are trained to be workers, not homemarkers, no home economics courses are offered. But, automobile drivers' training is part of the practical work course, even though one must still wait at least a year for a chance to purchase an automobile.

In addition to science, special attention is given to the study of foreign languages. About 45 per cent of the ten-year school students study English, 35 per cent German, and 20 per cent French. During the 1957-58 school year the Soviets launched an experimental venture in the field of foreign-language instruction. They organized 17 new schools, of which eight were "English" schools, seven "German", and two "French", with all class instruction carried on in the foreign language. In other schools instruction in literature, history, and geography was given in a foreign language at the fifth-grade level. At the beginning of the 1958-59 school year foreign language was taught in 78,000 schools to over 11 million pupils.

It is the aim of primary-secondary education in the USSR that every pupil have the opportunity to pass. To accomplish this, extra teaching services are provided, with free individual tutoring, incentives, and awards for good marks and fewer privileges to those who lag behind. Low marks received by pupils are deemed a reflection on the ability of the teacher rather than the pupil. Under these conditions "dropping out" should not be very extensive, yet there are many children who fail to pass, drop out, or do not attend school at all. It was reported that in 1955 about 3,000 children in Kalinin Oblast and another 2,000 in Leningrad did not attend schools. In Novosibrisk Oblast 2,700 children failed to attend schools, and of those who were enrolled 3,929 dropped out. In general, during the 1954-55 school year 84.9 per cent of all pupils enrolled in all Soviet primary-secondary schools passed their courses or were graduated. Only 6.7 per cent of all pupils in urban schools failed to pass their courses and were unable to advance to higher grades or to graduate; in rural schools this percentage was 8.1.

The drop-out rate of primary-secondary school pupils is relatively low despite the fact that pupils come from different cultural backgrounds. Only three per cent of the total first grade enrollment in 1954-55 dropped out at the end of the first year, and only 5.1 per cent at the end of the fourth-grade year. The highest academic mortality rate occurred in the five- to seven-grade schools, especially in the fifth grade. One of the reasons for the low drop out rate in the first four grades is the training in kindergartens where the children are taught discipline and how to get along with other children.

However, serious shortcomings are present in the schools, especially in their failure to provide a link between theoretical and practical work required in the curriculum for higher grades. In many areas industrial and farm enterprises are unable to provide practical work for pupils. Furthermore, school supplies such as textbooks, maps, instruments, and other equipment are scarce. These shortcomings, however, can be and are gradually being corrected. The important thing is that the Soviet Union is improving its primary-secondary school system and that the quality of training in many schools is much higher than in schools in many western countries.

## SPECIALIZED EDUCATION

Soviet specialized education consists of three distinctly separate educational levels. The first, or lower, level includes all trade schools where youngsters and adults are trained in skills. This level includes trade and railroad schools, factory schools (FZO), schools giving simplified courses related to agricultural mechanization and electrification, and technical and mining schools where handling of equipment is taught. All these schools are organized and run by the Main Administration for Labor Reserves. In addition, some factories and plants, primarily producing consumer goods, organize training programs offering courses to advance the skill of their own workers. The main objective of all these schools and training programs is to provide qualified workers for industry, transportation, and agriculture.

The second, or middle, educational level is more advanced both in prerequisites and requirements. These schools are considered semiprofessional. Their main objective is to provide auxiliary staffs for specialists graduated from higher educational institutions. As a rule, in middle educational schools to obtain çertificates as medical aides, primarily-second-ary teachers, nurses, laboratory technicians, and the like requires two to four years of general education and practical work.

The third, or higher, educational level is made up of all higher educational institutions such as universities and institutes where highly specialized per-sonnel are educated and trained.

## Lower Educational Level

The Soviets were forced to create the lower educational level when they launched their industrialization in 1930. To bridge the gap between the masses of unskilled workers and the increasing demand for skilled labor, the Soviets organized schools and courses where workers could be trained on the job to acquire technological knowledge quickly and could be in-doctrinated into communist discipline. Many changes have taken place since 1930; training programs have been modified and indoctrination into Marxism has become less important than in the past when workers were the "eyes and ears" of the new regime in the effort to combat sabotage.

Boys and girls with a four-year education may enroll in any school or course for on-the-job training or in railroad or factory (FZO) schools. The pupils are provided with free uniforms, board, and quarters. They are taught general educational subjects and practical work for four years, at the end of which their general education becomes comparable to a eight-year school education. Other schools and courses have shorter train-ing programs which vary with the specialty. To improve workers' efficiency, some loss in time and increased investments in training are necessary in order to equalize the efficiency of a worker and the machine. In 1929-30 it was the belief of Soviet economists that if a given illiterate unskilled worker could produce a certain amount of goods at 100 per cent, then the same worker with one year's schooling would produce 124 per cent; with a four-year education, his output would be increased to 142 per cent, and a worker with seven years education would produce 167 per cent. It was calculated for the 1929-30 period that every ruble spent on the education and training of workers increased the national income at a rate of six rubles per year.[5] As a result the Soviets have increased their educational and training programs at every level.

During World War II and the postwar reconstruction period the demand for skilled workers was high, especially in factories, mining, and railroads. Because of the shortage of youngsters in the national labor pool the number of trainees in these schools declined considerably after 1950. At the same time, new programs were launched to provide skilled workers to operate and to repair agricultural machinery and to train others in technical matters. But in 1957 these schools trained approximately as many workers as the average number trained during the 1946-50 period.

TABLE 4—*Number of Trained Workers in Schools Administered by the Main Administration for Labor Reserves* [6]

(in thousands)

| Schools | 1941-45 | 1946-50 | 1951-55 | 1956 | 1957 |
|---|---|---|---|---|---|
| Total: _____ | 2,475 | 3,392 | 2,364 | 665 | 696 |
| Factory (FZO), mining and construction | 1,790 | 2,368 | 990 | 202 | 204 |
| Mechanical, railroad and mining _____ | 685 | 1,024 | 719 | 118 | 93 |
| Mechanical agricultural _____ | – | – | 628 | 255 | 318 |
| Technical _____ | – | – | 27 | 90 | 81 |

The labor reserves schools presently offer more than 500 different courses. Some courses which were given in 1951-55 have been abandoned and new ones introduced to meet the demands of advanced technology. To keep up with new technological advances it is expected that during the 1959-65 period the labor reserves schools will receive more metal cutting and forging equipment.

## Middle Educational Level

The middle educational level fills the gap between general secondary education and higher educational institutions. It consists of technical schools (tekhnikum) and other specialized educational establishments training semiprofessional personnel. As a rule, four years of general education and practical work are required of most students. Tekhnikums and other specialized schools train "supporting" staffs in a variety of specialized fields. For example, they train physician aides; midwives; secondary school teachers; junior supervisors for industry, construction, transportation, and communication; assistants in economics and law; public health junior staffs; and specialists in physical education, sports, arts, and the moving picture industry. Persons from 15 to 30 years of age may enroll in any of these schools as full-time students. Those over 30 years of age may enroll as part-time students at night school or take correspondence courses in fields closely related to their employment. Upon graduation they are granted diplomas equivalent to ten- or 11-grade schools and higher. In highly specialized fields such as medicine, pharmacy, and teaching, only persons with a ten-grade education are accepted for the two to three years of training.

Apparently there is an increased number of students wishing to enter the middle specialized schools, and the Soviets have set certain restrictive entrance prerequisites. Beginning with the 1959 academic year each new student must submit with the application for acceptance his character recommendation from the local Party organization, trade union, Komsomol,

TABLE 5—*Educational Network of Tekhnikums and Specialized Schools* [7]
(*in thousands*)

|  | 1940-41 | 1950-51 | 1955-56 | 1957-58 | 1958 |
|---|---|---|---|---|---|
| Number of schools _____ | 3.8 | 3.4 | 3.7 | 3.5 | 3.3 |
| Total enrollment: _____ | 974.8 | 1,297.6 | 1,960.4 | 1,941.0 | 1,876.0 |
| Full-time _____ | 819.5 | 1,116.9 | 1,673.9 | 1,540.0 | 1,125.0 |
| Part-time and correspondence___ | 155.3 | 180.7 | 286.5 | 401.0 | 751.0 |
| Admissions: _____ | 282.9 | 426.3 | 587.5 | 580.7 | 584.1 |
| Full-time _____ | 331.2 | 365.1 | 478.7 | 361.0 | 363.7 |
| Graduates: _____ | 236.8 | 313.7 | 387.8 | 504.0 | 551.2 |
| Public health, physical education and sports _____ | 90.4 | 54.2 | 56.3 | 89.7 | 77.2 |
| Education _____ | 85.8 | 76.6 | 73.5 | 78.2 | 63.4 |
| Industry and construction ____ | 21.7 | 85.4 | 140.8 | 168.7 | 219.7 |
| Agriculture _____ | 21.5 | 48.6 | 57.8 | 82.8 | 96.3 |
| Transportation and communication _____ | 8.3 | 18.9 | 23.9 | 36.8 | 42.2 |
| Economics and law _____. | 7.2 | 24.9 | 30.9 | 41.4 | 45.2 |
| Arts and moving pictures ____ | 2.0 | 5.0 | 4.9 | 6.4 | 7.2 |
| Percentage of females to total enrollment: _____ | 55 | 54 | 55 | 48 | 47 |
| Public health, physical education and sports_____ | 83 | 85 | 89 | 86 | 84 |
| Education _____ | 63 | 81 | 85 | – | 76 |
| Economics and law _____ | 60 | 73 | 82 | – | – |
| Arts and moving pictures ____ | 41 | 44 | 51 | – | – |
| Agriculture _____ | 37 | 41 | 43 | 38 | 38 |
| All others _____ | 32 | 35 | 42 | – | – |

or any other public organization. Now all new students must pass the entrance examination. Part-time and correspondence students must have at least two years of practical work in their chosen field of specialization.

The honor students from eight-and ten-year schools and veterans of World War II are given preference in enrollment, provided they have passed the entrance examination.

In general, students enrolled in specialized schools are required to carry about 40 hours of instruction per week, although a heavier load is carried by many engineering and public health technicians. Hours of instruction range from 1,200 to over 1,500 hours per year and are supplemented by practical work in each field of specialization.

Between 1940 and 1958 the total enrollment in specialized schools more than doubled, but the number of graduates increased by about 64 per cent, suggesting that large numbers of students failed or dropped out. In the 1955-56 school year, for example, about 34 per cent of the students failed to graduate, and approximately seven per cent of the total graduating class received their diplomas through correspondence courses. Only about four per cent of the total graduating body attended evening classes. Thus, evening and correspondence students represent about 40 per cent of the total middle educational level.

The general educational and technical levels of these graduates varies from field to field and from region to region. Textbooks are in short supply and too wide in scope, and often the curriculum for a given specialty is modeled on that of the higher education institute even though tekhnikums have different functions. Nevertheless, the shortage of professional manpower enabled these specialists and technicians to advance to positions requiring a high level of professional training, particularly if they were members of the Communist Party. In many instances they were inefficient and demonstrated poor judgment and lack of initiative when moved up to positions of higher power. This may be considered as a temporary but inevitable ill in an economy where highly trained labor is scarce. But despite the criticism it should be recognized that the Soviets are gradually improving the skills and abilities of their technicians and they are not being used on many jobs or in places suited for graduates from universities. A veterinary specialist, for example, employed by the collective farm does not have the authority to write prescriptions, but he may well recognize the symptoms of a cow's illness and in many cases may treat it without calling on the professional veterinary many miles away. Thus, specialists and technicians have a definite place in the Soviet economy until better public services are organized and a greater number of college graduates are available.

## Higher Educational Level

The highest level of education is provided at institutions referred to as VUZ. These are universities and other specialized higher educational institutions such as academies, conservatories, and institutes. Acceptance by one of these institutions is a real accomplishment for any Russian boy or girl because selection of students is based on the premise that their talents and abilities are needed for the country. For this reason they are regarded as an indispensable part of the national resources and play a distinct role in the concept of socio-economic gains. They are not, however, philosophers seeking unknown values. Values and goals have already been defined and set forth by communist leaders, and students are challenged to build a new society within these sharply defined values. The official Soviet functions and goals in higher educational institutions are to provide qualified specialists for the economy and to train research workers and educators to fill the gap between advanced and scholarly knowledge and that of the masses. In other words, Soviet higher educational institutions are not intended to be isolated from the masses, but to be a part of the total economic and cultural structure of the country. The intellectual elite graduated from these institutions are not outside or above Soviet society, rather they are an integral part of the whole society.

Educational programs in higher educational institutions consist of four to six years of study beyond secondary education. A degree in social science requires four years of study, and such majors as medicine require six years. Anyone who is under 35 years of age with a secondary education and who has passed the State examination for the "certificate of maturity" may be eligible for admission to higher educational institutions. Students from among the top five per cent of the graduates from tekhnikums also may apply. Those over 35 may apply for admission to a part-time program at night or take correspondence courses. Those who have committed crimes against the State, however, are barred from enrollment. Each applicant must pass competitive entrance examinations in at least five fields. Only those who pass the examinations in Russian language and literature are permitted to take the others. Although anyone possessing a secondary education and a clean political and criminal record has the right to apply for admission, the entrance examination often proves to be a stumbling block. The entrance examinations are more difficult in highly skilled fields such as aviation, engineering, and physics than in geography. Nevertheless, majors in engineering are very common among Russian students for they combine liberal education with specialization. Since 1954 the Soviets have encouraged enrollment in engineering related to industry, construction, electric power, agricultural machinery, and other fields so that there would be one specialist from a higher education institution for each two to four specialists from the middle educational institutions.

In 1955, out of the total of some three million graduates from ten-year schools, only 299,000 were admitted to higher educational institutions. However, the total number admitted as full-time, part-time, and correspondence course students was 469,000. In 1958 a total of about 450,000 were admitted to freshmen standing. Thus, competition is very keen and only the best students are accepted. For the rest of those who want higher education or training the doors of the tekhnikums or other specialized schools are open. During the 1954-57 period, over 2.5 million graduates from secondary schools failed to meet the requirements for the higher educational institutions or did not wish to go there. Free tuition, stipends, various incentives, and greater future earning power make enrollment in higher educational institutions very attractive indeed. These incentives are used by the State to channel students into fields where trained manpower is most needed.

Upon admission the student must maintain at least satisfactory grades. This is important, for, once admitted to an institution, the student cannot transfer to another institution nor is he allowed to drop out and apply for admission to another institution. Moreover, better than average grades means greater stipends and other rewards. An exceptional student may receive three to four times as many benefits as an average one. This tends to push the average grades upward, and students with below-average ability must improve their work or drop out.

As a rule, the higher educational institutions are divided into schools. Some larger institutions may have as many as eight to ten schools. Each school devises a program for the student consisting of lectures, seminars, laboratory work, and term papers. In some institutions "creative" practical work of 12 to 13 weeks per year is required in addition to independent study at home.

Graduates of higher educational institutions are assigned to jobs at which they are to remain for three years. Graduates with honors or better than average grades get the best job assignments. After the three-year period they are free to look for jobs elsewhere. This three-year job assignment is considered as a part of practical education and looked upon by graduates as an inevitable repayment for their state-supported education. Only the most promising graduates are kept for research work or for postgraduate studies.

Students in part-time and correspondence courses in higher educational institutions have the same rights and privileges as full-time students. However, their academic status as such is considered to be below that of the full-time students, who enjoy closer relationships with the faculty members. The three-year job assignment required from full-time students is not required of part-time students since they are already employed. Stipends and awards are not available to part-time students.

Table 6—*Higher Educational Institutions* [8]
(in thousands)

|  | 1940-41 | 1950-51 | 1955-56 | 1958-59 |
|---|---|---|---|---|
| Number of Institutions | 817 | 880 | 765 | 766 |
| Total enrollment: | 811.7 | 1,247.4 | 1,867.0 | 2,179.0 |
| Full-time | 585.0 | 845.1 | 1,227.9 | 1,333.0 |
| Part-time and correspondence | 226.7 | 402.3 | 639.1 | 846.0 |
| Total admission: | 263.4 | 349.1 | 461.4 | 453.3 |
| Full-time | 161.5 | 237.5 | 285.6 | 256.1 |
| Part-time and correspondence | 101.9 | 111.6 | 175.8 | 197.2 |
| Graduates: | 126.1 | 176.9 | 245.8 | 290.7 |
| Full-time | 102.2 | 147.9 | 183.8 | 213.9 |
| Part-time and correspondence | 23.9 | 29.0 | 62.0 | 76.8 |
| Enrollment by field of study: |  |  |  |  |
| Education | 398.6 | 607.0 | 741.6 | – |
| Industry and construction | 168.4 | 272.8 | 550.6 | – |
| Public health, physical education | 109.8 | 111.5 | 158.8 | – |
| Agriculture | 52.1 | 104.1 | 195.9 | – |
| Economics and law | 36.3 | 89.2 | 106.7 | – |
| Transportation and communication | 36.2 | 47.9 | 99.0 | – |
| Arts and moving pictures | 10.3 | 14.9 | 14.4 | – |
| Percentage of female students (total): | 58 | 53 | 52 | 47 |
| Public health and physical education | 74 | 65 | 69 | 62 |
| Economics and law | 64 | 57 | 67 | – |
| Education | 66 | 72 | 72 | 65 |
| Agriculture | 46 | 39 | 39 | 31 |
| Arts and moving pictures | 45 | 43 | 42 | – |
| All others | 40 | 30 | 35 | 32 |

In 1956 the Soviet Union had over 30 evening and correspondence schools and 617 branches for part-time students enrolled in higher educational institutions. The largest correspondence school is the All-Union Correspondence Politechnical Institute, with ten departments where over 30,000 part-time students were enrolled in 1956. The largest centers for correspondence courses are concentrated in the Ural, Siberia, and the Kazakh SSR where new industrial expansion is currently underway. In general, enrollment of part-time students is growing rapidly, and during the 1959-65 period the Soviets anticipate an enrollment of four million persons in part-time and correspondence courses.

As enrollment in the higher educational institutions increases, the whole system feels the impact upon its training program. In a great many cases the number of faculty members within individual departments is based upon so-called "fixed staffs," and this number is determined by the number of students within the department. Those departments having limited scope in economic advantages, such as Latin, Tibetan, and so on, try to encourage students to enroll by liberalization of admission standards. Graduates of such disciplines, of course, have less opportunity to make economic adjustments in the industrial society than their friends majoring in engineering, economics, or education.

In 1958 there were 114 fewer higher educational institutions than there were in 1951, despite the fact that between 1950 and 1958 over 50 new institutions were established. During this period many institutions were merged with other systems. For example, 65 teachers' institutes were transferred to pedagogical institutes. Of the total number of higher educational institutions 40 are universities, but the majority are institutes, academies, and conservatories. In all, 225 urban centers have higher educational institutions of one sort or another.

Between 1940 and 1959 the total enrollment in higher educational institutions more than doubled, increasing from 800,000 to 2.2 million students; the total full-time enrollment, however, declined from 72 per cent of the total in 1940 to 61 per cent in 1959. This indicates a greater emphasis on the completion of education in spare time while working.

In comparison with the Soviet Union, the total enrollment in institutions of higher education in the United States in the 1956-57 school year was over 3.2 million students.[9] However, excluding junior colleges and technological and professional schools, which are equivalent to Soviet middle educational institutions, both countries have approximately the same number of students enrolled in higher educational institutions. In the USSR full-time students constitute about 60 per cent of the total enrollment; in the United States this percentage is about 80.

Enrollment in the field of education dominates in both the USSR and the United States. It is followed by engineering in the United States and by industry and construction in the USSR. The curricula in agriculture, public health, and physical education are emphasized more in the USSR than in the United States whereas the home economics and theology courses taken by over 50,000 students in the United States do not exist in the Soviet curriculum.

It is expected that during the 1959-65 period the Soviets will graduate 2.3 million college students, or an average of 330,000 annually. Despite much bureaucratic underbrush in higher educational institutions the Russians are developing a veritable passion for education. This in engendered by the rigorous selective process that demands more of students' efforts than is required in the United States. The fast-moving world of science requires increasing numbers of highly skilled technicians and engineers, and the Russians are training more of them than are trained in the United States. In 1956 the United States graduated 32,000 engineers and the Soviets graduated 71,000 engineers of all types, including 5,000 instrumentation and control engineers. Instrumentation is essential in controlling nuclear processes and guided rockets, and the USSR appears to be training all the instrument experts they need. In 1958 the Soviets graduated 94,000 engineers. The Soviets are graduating about 120,000 engineers and scientists every year whereas only about 70,000 graduate in the United States.

Soviet higher education, however, is not Eldorado, even for the elite selected by the State. Full-time enrollment in higher educational institutions during the 1951-52 year was 255,500 students; four years later only 183,000 graduated, approximately 72 per cent of the 1951-52 enrollees. Thus about 28 per cent of the preliminary enrollment for the country as a whole failed to graduate during the four-year period. In any school system withdrawals cannot be completely eliminated. By comparison, the 1950-54 study showed that drop-outs in the United States were 63 per cent, an alarming waste of competent manpower.[10] The higher drop-out rate of new students in the United States is a result of the freedom to transfer from one institution to another and the ease with which one can delay education after a brief unsuccessful period. In the USSR this drop-out rate is reduced by the highly selective process in admission and the supplementary help or instruction by the professional staff for those lagging in their studies.

The workload carried by Soviet students in the science courses is much heavier than in the United States. For example, the physics major at Kharkov State University totals 4,290 lecture hours, whereas at the Massachusetts Institute of Technology only 2,415 lecture hours are required. The Kharkov students spend 3,356 hours on physics, mathematics, and chemistry, almost twice the load offered in the United States.[11]

There are many reasons for withdrawal from higher educational institutions in the USSR. Scholastic standards are too high for many students. A Turkmen boy may be an excellent student at the secondary school, but upon arrival at the big urban centers such as Moscow he often is unable to cope with a different culture, the pace in studies, or he may wish to return home. Another reason is the availability of jobs with opportunities for advancement without a college degree. The older students taking part-time or correspondence courses are a more determined group and their drop-out rate is lower than among the younger group. But higher education is a paramount goal in the USSR. It is a passion among many young Russians who are convinced that hard work at school will win them their place on the earth and on the moon. There seems to be unbounded enthusiasm for the belief that only those with the best-trained abilities may lead the country in their economic advancement.

## Research

In 1959 the Soviets maintained 3,197 research institutions which, together with their branches and subsidiaries, employed 141,000 scientists and specialists of various disciplines and levels. In addition, the faculty members of higher educational institutions are required by law to spend about three hours a day on research. Often they are consulted by non-academic establishments; thus, faculty members are not isolated from the socio-economic activity of the country. All research is closely linked with the Academy of Sciences of the USSR and the Academies of Sciences of each constituent republic.

The most highly esteemed organization, the Academy of Sciences of the USSR, has eight departments, each of which is divided into specialized discipline such as mathematics, analytical chemistry, geography, history, and others. The Academy conducts research work in various laboratories, observatories, museums, and experimental stations. Only the outstanding scholars from the Soviet Union and abroad are elected to membership. In 1958 the Academy had 167 academicians and 361 member-correspondents. Similar organizational structures, but on a smaller scale, are found in the Academy of Medical Sciences of the USSR, the All-Union Lenin's Academy of Agricultural Sciences, the Academy of Arts of the USSR, and the Academy of Construction and Architecture of the USSR. Research is best organized in agriculture, and since this is a subject dear to Khrushchev's heart, appropriations are quite sufficient. It is claimed that the research by the Timiriazev's Academy of Agricultural Sciences was responsible for the abolishment of the MTS and for allowing collective farms to own farm machinery.

Between 1941 and 1959 the number of research establishments increased by 1,376. Main research establishments are the institutes. Other research establishments are experimental stations, laboratories, museums, libraries, commissions, committees, and the like.

Table 7—*Number of Research Establishments* [12]

| Establishment | 1941 | 1950 | 1956 | 1959 |
|---|---|---|---|---|
| Total number: _____ | 1,821 | 2,805 | 2,797 | 3,197 |
| Sciences—research and branches___ | 786 | 1,156 | 1,210 | 1,482 |
| Experimental stations _____ | 507 | 566 | 574 | 477 |
| Others _____ | 528 | 1,083 | 1,013 | 1,238 |

The most intensive research work is concentrated in industry and deals primarily with practical problems. In 1956 there were 295 research establishments working on problems concerning industry with staffs of over 35,400 research workers. There were 234 research establishments devoted to problems related to public health employing over 9,900 persons. Agricultural research work was conducted in 588 establishments employing some 9,500 workers. The Academy of Sciences of the USSR in 1956 had 102 research institutes where some 11,600 research workers sought solutions to a variety of problems. In 1959 the number of research institutes increased to 136 employing almost 19,000 scientists and their supporting staffs. The Academies of Sciences of the constituent republics had 262 research institutes with 7,500 people on the research staff in 1956. All research work conducted in the USSR must be "creative" and a distinct contribution to the economy and the State. Simple research projects are directed by a single scholar; more complex work is directed by a number of scholars.

Postgraduate students are the main source of potential scholars and research workers. In 1930, because of a scarcity of scholars, the Soviets allowed loyal citizens, without completed college work, to enroll in postgraduate studies after a year of preparatory work. This was the period during which the so-called "Red Universities" were organized to train loyal scientists from the working class. With the emergency now over, admission to the postgraduate level is permitted only for those who have acquired not less than two years of practical work in a selected field. Only those who are seeking entrance to postgraduate studies in theoretical disciplines, such as mathematics, may be admitted without practical work.

The highest academic degree that the postgraduate student may obtain is that of "Doctor of Sciences." This is a degree of honor usually held by all full professors. Below this degree is that of "Candidate of Sciences," which is equivalent to a Ph.D. degree. These degrees are the basic prerequisites for membership in the Academy of Sciences of the USSR.

The large postgraduate enrollment in 1955 was the result of a decree, promulgated in 1950, which made possible a procedure called "prikoman-dirovka" under which many persons who completed their class work for Candidate of Sciences degree but failed to write the required dissertation could receive a degree.

TABLE 8—*The Scientific Manpower of the USSR* [13]

|  | 1950 | 1955 | 1958 |
|---|---|---|---|
| Total number: | 162,508 | 223,893 | 284,038 |
| In higher educational institutions | 86,542 | 119,059 | 135,700 |
| In scientific establishments | 70,462 | 96,511 | 141,000 |
| In industry and state services | 5,504 | 8,323 | 7,338 |
| Doctor of Sciences | 8,277 | 9,460 | 10,282 |
| Candidates of Sciences | 45,530 | 77,961 | 89,960 |
| Postgraduate students enrollment: | 21,905 | 29,362 | 23,084 |
| In higher educational institutions | 12,487 | 16,774 | 12,328 |
| In scientific establishments | 9,418 | 12,588 | 10,756 |
| Postgraduates receiving higher degrees | 4,093 | 7,607 | 6,802 |

This procedure was especially attractive to educators who could fulfill all the requirements for the higher degree, including the dissertation, during a year's time. During 1949-56, there were 1,900 persons under this program. There are also part-time postgraduate students, "soiskateli" who already have a large amount of practical experience and who wish to obtain a Candidate of Sciences degree. The "Institute Soiskateley," or the institute for part-time postgraduate study, conducts these special programs.

During the 1946-55 period 5,588 degrees of Doctor of Sciences and 66,390 degrees of Candidate of Sciences were bestowed, or an annual average of about 7,200 persons for both degrees. Excluding law, dentistry, and medicine, the United States in 1956-57 granted about 8,800 Ph.D. degrees. The greatest number of Soviet degrees were granted in medicine, biology, engineering, history, chemistry, agriculture, physics, and mathematics. However, a great deal of criticism has been raised since 1956 that many new Candidate of Sciences and Doctors of Sciences were poorly prepared for independent research. In a great many cases the research presented was simply a historical summary rather than an original piece of research making a creative contribution to the given field of learning. Some of these young scientists might have been good research workers, but they were inadequate lecturers, or vice-versa. This and the fact that many dissertations for higher degrees dealt with the past rather than with present conditions are among the main objections.

## HEALTH

In the USSR, medicine is based on a preventive and therapeutic plan. In 1958 alone as many as 2.4 million people had disease-prevention medical examinations, making possible the early detection of disease—particularly important in cancer detection. Medical care is free and generally accessible to all citizens in the sense that patients are not required to pay for visits to clinics, visits by physicians and nurses, or treatments. The cost, however, is indirect, being included in the prices of consumer goods from which the State derives revenue. Medicine which patients need is free or sold at low cost. Those in the higher income groups can call on private practicioners whose services, especially in emergency cases, are expensive but quicker.

The majority of public health establishments are under the administration of the Ministry of Public Health. However, a number of health establishments are organized by other establishments and administration. In addition, the USSR Red Cross and the USSR Red Crescent (for the Moslem population), with a membership of about 21.4 million persons, are engaged in work related to public health. All major non-administrative problems dealing with public health are undertaken by the USSR Academy of Medical Sciences and by special scientific, research, and medical institutes.

Administration of health services in the USSR is on four levels. The USSR-Republic Ministry of Health is an integral part of the USSR-Republic Councils of Ministers. It is responsible for the planning and coordination of health programs and services for the entire Union, the establishment of standards, and approval of health budgets and health plans. Each constituent republic has a Republic Ministry of Health, concerned with the administration of health services in the republic. At the district level of each republic is a district health service, and at the local level is a local health service, which consists of a hospital, a sanitary and epidemiological station, and a health center.

A typical town of 80,000 inhabitants is usually divided into two districts, and each district into ten sections. Each section has 4,000 inhabitants and is served by six and one-half medical personnel—two internists, one surgeon, one pediatrician, one obstetrician-gynecologist, one dentist, and a half-time chest physician who serves two sections. They give home care, hospital care, and polyclinic or dispensary care. That is the basic medical care structure throughout the urban areas of the USSR. Besides a general hospital, there is a sanitary-epidemiological station staffed with eight physicians who are concerned with sanitary inspection and statistical activities.

In each district, supplementing the basic services of a city, are a children's and maternity hospital and specialized dispensaries, one concerned only with the supervision of people engaged in athletics. Each industrial establishment of any size has additional services, including a hospital. There are also day nurseries run by the health authorities where working mothers leave their children.

In rural areas, public health is administered by the Rural Councils of Workers' Deputies, which are responsible for medical aid, maternity centers,

TABLE 9—*Number of Public Health Establishments* [14]

| Type of Establishment | 1940 | 1950 | 1956 |
|---|---|---|---|
| Total ------------------------------------- | 13,472 | 17,359 | 24,105 |
| Urban, Total: ---------------------------- | 5,851 | 7,056 | 9,315 |
| Oblast hospitals ------------------------ | – | 133 | 158 |
| City hospitals ------------------------- | 4,352 | 2,429 | 3,496 |
| Special hospitals ---------------------- | – | 1,044 | 1,189 |
| Rayon hospitals ----------------------- | – | 1,429 | 1,454 |
| Permanent dispensaries ---------------- | 131 | 794 | 1,774 |
| Scientific—research institutes ---------- | 116 | 120 | 119 |
| Clinics of higher educational institutions | 41 | 26 | 18 |
| Maternity establishments -------------- | 961 | 731 | 722 |
| Leprosy and lupusy -------------------- | 26 | 23 | 21 |
| Psychoneurological establishments ------ | 207 | 179 | 255 |
| Others ------------------------------- | 17 | 148 | 109 |
| Rural, total: --------------------------- | 7,621 | 10,303 | 14,790 |
| Rayon hospitals ----------------------- | 2,104 | 2,556 | 2,325 |
| Local hospitals ----------------------- | 4,499 | 7,126 | 11,914 |
| Special hospitals ---------------------- | 77 | 161 | 183 |
| Permanent dispensaries ---------------- | – | 31 | 234 |
| Maternity establishments -------------- | 895 | 415 | 105 |
| Others ------------------------------- | 46 | 17 | 29 |

and nurseries. In addition, they undertake measures for preventing infectious diseases and for public health education. The recent trend in the USSR has been toward increasing the powers and duties of the local health bodies. The regional officers have become more independent of headquarters control. A rural district with three or four collective farms usually has a small hospital, including maternity and pediatric services, and a sanitary-epidemiological station. In addition, there may be two or three first-aid- stations.

During the 1940-50 period, the Soviet Union created 10,633 additional medical establishments, the rural areas receiving 67 per cent of the increase. This is misleading, however, for urban medical establishments are larger than those in the rural areas. Then, again, rural establishments do not have the facilities available in larger urban centers, and as a result serious medical cases are usually transferred to larger hospitals. Although the number of establishments in 1956 was 24,105, the number of out patient establishments was 33,854, evenly distributed among urban and rural areas. Since the urban population in 1956 was only 43.5 per cent of the total Soviet population, the use of out-patient service is more highly developed in urban centers than in rural clinics.

Between 1940 and 1956 the number of medical establishments increased by 79 per cent, but the total number of hospital beds increased by only 70 per cent, suggesting that during that period the Soviets built new medical establishments in addition to enlarging the existing floor space. In 1958 there were 25,975 medical establishments, an increase of some eight per cent over 1956, whereas the total number of beds increased by about 13 per cent. Apparently the 1956-58 building program of new medical units caught up with the expansion of hospital beds.

Table 10—*Number of Hospital Beds* [15]

| Type of Establishment | 1940 | 1950 | 1956 |
|---|---|---|---|
| Total  USSR: | 760,843 | 964,924 | 1,292,717 |
| Therapeutical | 88,681 | 160,648 | 254,982 |
| Surgery | 90,230 | 136,935 | 184,760 |
| Gynecology | 30,823 | 39,712 | 58,604 |
| Eye | 13,015 | 15,250 | 22,737 |
| Ear | 6,586 | 8,341 | 12,634 |
| Tuberculosis (adults and children) | 30,056 | 72,421 | 111,565 |
| Skin | 14,305 | 29,258 | 27,610 |
| Infection (adults and children) | 91,471 | 123,770 | 148,181 |
| Psychic | 92,479 | 80,864 | 113,777 |
| Maternity | 107,827 | 116,306 | 142,911 |
| Children, non-infectious | 49,682 | 74,247 | 107,013 |
| General purpose | 117,897 | 70,633 | 57,158 |
| Others | 27,791 | 33,538 | 30,785 |

To meet the 1959-65 plan for construction of new hospitals, polyclinics, and other medical establishments, one billion rubles has been allocated. It is planned to construct new hospital floor space for 19,000 to 20,000 beds and another 2,300 beds in rural tuberculosis sanitariums. But the emphasis under this plan is the expansion of obstetrical and gynecological services.

Between 1940 and 1956 the number of therapeutical and surgical beds more than doubled. The impact of World War II sharply increased the number of cases of tuberculosis, an important disease requiring more beds in 1956 than in 1940. Bone tuberculosis seemed to be more prevalent among children than among adults. Venereal diseases also increased during the war but were on the decline in 1956. Psychic disorders which showed an increase during the 1940-56 period were not, however, as serious a problem as tuberculosis. Maternity beds between 1940 and 1956 increased by 33 per cent while children's beds more than doubled. The increase in beds for children with non-infectious diseases did not mean, however, that more children were ill in 1956 than in 1940. It was rather that more attention was given to them in 1956 than in 1940 and that the Baltic republics were excluded from 1940 statistics.

Medical personnel in the USSR consists of two levels. The first level includes all who have graduated from medical school; the second is made up of supporting personnel such as medical aides, nurses, dental technicians, X-ray technicians, and the like who were trained in the middle schools.

TABLE 11—*Civilian Medical Personnel* [16]

|  | 1940 | 1950 | 1956 |
|---|---|---|---|
| Number of Medical Schools | 72 | 73 | 77 |
| Number of graduates (M.D.) | 16,373 | 18,345 | 17,967 |
| Number of middle medical schools | 990 | 562 | 603 |
| Number of graduates: | 84,054 | 49,504 | 73,057 |
| Medical aides (fel'dshers) | 20,515 | 14,320 | 25,317 |
| Midwives | 16,246 | 11,981 | 23,724 |
| Nurses | 39,843 | 13,942 | 15,891 |
| Dental technicians | 3,219 | 2,187 | 879 |
| Pharmacists | 3,771 | 3,791 | 4,617 |

During the 1940-56 period the number of graduating physicians grew by ten per cent; the total number of supporting medical staff personnel graduated from middle medical schools was reduced by some 13 per cent. At the same time the number of medical aides (fel'dshers) and midwives increased considerably. Nevertheless in 1940 for every physician there were five supporting members of medical personnel and in 1956 there were only four. The country's total number of physicians, excluding civilian dentists and military physicians and dentists, was 140,800 in 1940 and reached 361,600 in 1958. In 1940 there were seven physicians, excluding dentists and military doctors, per 10,000 persons and by 1958 the number was 17. In 1940 there were 40 hospital beds per 10,000 persons and in 1958 the number increased to 73.

In 1958 the Soviet government spent 41 billion rubles for public health and physical education. This is almost twice the amount that was spent in 1950. By 1965 the Soviets expect to increase the number of hospital beds and to open new medical establishments, especially in the eastern parts of the Soviet Union. There should be no doubt that the medical care provided for the Soviet population has improved, not only organizationally but also in its effectiveness, especially for out-patient assistance. This has been achieved by coordinating the medical services network, which includes the hospitals, and the out-patient establishments, by increasing medical budgets, and by adopting modern medical practices.

## Vital Statistics

Consideration of the past, present, and future total population is a vital part of the study of public health. Every major change in the population has considerable impact on the nature and emphasis of public health in the endeavor to eliminate or decrease the number of deaths in infancy and childhood. The age composition of the population thus reflects the results of this endeavor.

There are no data available on World War I, the Revolution, the Civil War, and World War II vital statistics. The available figures, however, show a decline in the death rate since 1950, and the net increase has somewhat stabilized at about 18 per cent per 1,000 persons. Applying this increase to a larger population means a larger number of infants and a larger annual increment to the population. In 1958 the net increase was greater than in any given previous year, even though the USSR experienced a rapid pace of industrialization, and despite the influx of women into gainful employment and the concentration of people in urban and urban fringe areas. Moreover, under these social pressures the public health services have substantially contributed to longevity. During the 1926-27 period in the European parts of the USSR life expectancy was 44 years; during 1955-56 it was 67 years, with 63 years for men and 69 for women. This increase in the average life expectancy resulted from a considerable reduction in the annual death rate. The reduction in the death rate may reflect an increase in the standard of living in terms of improvement in public health as well as increased supply of food and consumer goods.

Between 1940 and 1950 the birth rate in the USSR decreased by about 16 per cent and the death rate by 48 per cent. During this period the Soviet Union experienced a considerable decline in the young adult age group.

TABLE 12—*Birth and Death Rates and Net Population Increase* [17]
(per thousand of population)

| Year | Births | Deaths | Net increase | Number of children died before reaching one year of age per 1,000 |
|---|---|---|---|---|
| 1913_____ | 47.0 | 30.2 | 16.8 | 273 |
| 1926_____ | 44.0 | 20.3 | 23.7 | -- |
| 1940_____ | 31.7 | 18.1 | 13.2 | 184 |
| 1950_____ | 26.7 | 9.7 | 17.0 | 81 |
| 1951_____ | 27.0 | 9.7 | 17.3 | 84 |
| 1952_____ | 26.5 | 9.4 | 17.1 | 75 |
| 1953_____ | 25.1 | 9.1 | 16.0 | 68 |
| 1954_____ | 26.6 | 8.9 | 17.7 | 68 |
| 1955_____ | 25.7 | 8.2 | 17.5 | 60 |
| 1956_____ | 25.2 | 7.6 | 17.6 | 47 |
| 1957_____ | 25.4 | 7.8 | 17.6 | 45 |
| 1958_____ | 25.3 | 7.2 | 18.1 | 41 |
| 1959_____ | 25.0 | 7.6 | 17.4 | 41 |

Undernourishment during the war and the scarcity of food after the war resulted in an increase of diseases such as tuberculosis. It was a period of all-out sacrifices during which the old and the young with weak resistance to hardships were the victims. It is true that many of them would not have lived much longer even if there had been no war, but wartime shortages of food and medical care hastened their deaths. As a result the Soviet Union emerged from the war with people who had been tough and healthy enough to survive the war years despite undernourishment and long hours of work. The others had died permaturely. Beginning with 1950 the increasing availability of food, medical care, and leisure time for the sturdier and younger population resulted in a greater survival.

## SOCIAL INSURANCE

Before 1917 there was virtually no pension provision in Russia, except for a limited number of pensions paid to Tsarist officials and the court aristocracy. Only one-sixth of the workers were insured. The funds for this insurance came from joint contributions of workers and employers, with workers paying between one and three per cent of their earnings. Five days after the Revolution of 1917 the new government published a "Declaration of Social Insurance." Social security includes the system of pensions and is one of the important gains of the October Revolution.

The aged of the USSR receiving social benefits are not a homogeneous group. They are men and women of dissimilar cultural, economic, and physical fiber. Included are Russians, Ukrainians, Uzbeks, Tartars, and the rest of the Soviet nationalities, each with different personal needs, different traditional status among their families, and different requirement for housing or medical care and hospitalization. As in other countries, because of a longer life expectancy among women the problem of social welfare for aged women and for widows with a large number of children is gaining in importance in the Soviet Union. Soviet workers retire voluntarily for various reasons: ill-health, a large number of children to look after, or advanced age. Retired workers may still be productive, yet no real attention is given to prevention of retirement and to the rehabilitation of retired workers to new activities. This implies a shift towards younger workers. The difference between the retired industrial workers and the workers of the collective farms is unique. All aged persons formerly employed by the State receive support from the government and trade unions, but members of collective farms receive support from the State and also from the collective farms and none from the trade unions.

Social insurance in the USSR covers many aspects of social welfare. Its principal aim is to provide financial assistance and other social services to those who have reached the retirement age, for the temporarily or permanently disabled, pregnant women, children without parents, and veterans. Soviet social insurance is extended to workers and their families and includes free medical services, maintenance of nurseries, kindergartens, summer camps, and other measures dealing with welfare. When a worker becomes disabled his social insurance is paid to him from the first day of disability until he has recovered or is pensioned.

Expectant mothers receive 56 days off at full pay before and after childbirth, a total of 112 working days as compared to the 77 days granted prior to 1956. A portion of the social insurance appropriation is allocated to a network of rest homes and sanitariums where millions of workers receive medical care. In addition, other millions are rehabilitated in various establishments organized and operated by trade unions. In these institutions, maintenance is completely free or at a nominal cost to workers—up to 70 per cent of the cost is covered by social insurance.

The total cost of budgetary social payments in 1940 amounted to 9.4 billion rubles, approximately seven times greater than in 1930.[18] World War II increased these payments considerably. During the war subsidies and pensions were established for families of military personnel, invalids of World War II and their families, and for survivors of military personnel killed in action. The total sum allocated for subsidizing social payments during the war years amounted to 83.4 billion rubles, of which widows and destitute mothers received 2.1 billion rubles in 1945 against 1.2 billion rubles in 1940. Since the end of World War II the number of pensioners and the appropriations for their support has increased. Then in 1956 a more liberal welfare program was enacted under which higher pension payments were granted to aged and disabled persons who had worked in non-collective farm establishments, to families who had lost their wage-earners, and also to military personnel and their families. Moreover, many people who previously were outside the system were included. Under this law, aged workers receive as a rule from 50 to 100 per cent of their wage.

The 1956 welfare program increased the average pension rate by 81 per cent. It was a matter of necessity because pensions had been fixed in 1930 in absolute money terms and remained unchanged until then. The average pension for the aged and for the families of military personnel was doubled, and for disability the rate was increased by 1.5 times. However, families who had lost their wage earners received an increase of only 64 per cent. The 1956 social security law also established minimum and maximum pensions for each category of workers. In 1959 there were 18 million pensioners, of whom 8.7 million were veterans and their dependents, 7.2 million were aged and disabled persons, and 2.1 million were dependents without wage earners. In 1958 expenditures for pensions more than doubled. Payments to temporarily disabled workers alone amounted to 10.3 billion rubles or five times more than in 1940. Payments for maternity reached 4.4 billion rubles, eight times the amount paid in 1940. In 1958 there were about 3.4 million widows and mothers with several children receiving budgetary subsistence amounting to 5.3 billion rubles. Under the Soviet system any mother with three children and a fourth new-born baby receives a monthly stipend.

To pay for this extended welfare system, the state expenditures are growing rapidly. The 1958 budget allocated 87 billion rubles for this purpose and 94 billion rubles for 1959. Although the Soviets claim their welfare system is free, the truth is that the funds come from the workers themselves and from the taxes levied on the goods and services the workers buy.

## Bibliography—Chapter 15

[1] *Zdravookhraneniye v SSSR,* Moscow, 1956, pp. 126-28; *Kulturnoye Stroitelstvo SSSR,* Moscow, 1956, pp. 190-91; *Narodnoye Khozaystvo SSSR v 1958 Godu,* Moscow, 1959, pp. 821, 829.

[2] *Kontrolnye Tsifry Razvitiya Narodnogo Khozaystva SSSR na 1959-1965 Gody,* Moscow, 1958, p. 102.

[3] *Kulturnoye Stroitelstvo SSSR,* op. cit., pp. 76, 82-85; *Narodnoye Khozaystvo SSSR,* op. cit., pp. 807, 813, 814.

[4] *Education in the USSR,* U. S. Department of Health, Education and Welfare, Bulletin No. 14, 1957, Washington, D. C., pp. 68-70.

[5] *Voprosy Politicheskoy Ekonomii,* Leningrad, 1957, p. 46.

[6] *Ezhegodnik Bolshoy Sovetskoy Entsiklopedii,* Moscow, 1957, p. 94; *SSSR v Tsifrakh,* Moscow, 1958, p. 331.

[7] *Kulturnoye Stroitelstvo SSSR,* op. cit., 202-05, 238-39; *SSSR v Tsifrakh,* op. cit., p. 335; *Narodnoye Khozaystvo SSSR,* op. cit., pp. 830, 835, 836, 840.

[8] *Kulturnoye Stroitelsvo,* op. cit., pp. 202-07; *Narodnoye Khozaystvo,* op. cit., pp. 830, 835-37

[9] U. S. Department of Health, Education and Welfare, *Progress of Public Education in the United States of America, 1957-1958,* Washington, D. C., 1958, p. 10.

[10] U. S. Department of Health, Education and Welfare, *Retention and Withdrawal of College Students,* Washington, D. C., 1958, p. 152.

[11] Bockris, John O'M., *Current History,* July 1958, p. 25.

[12] *Kulturnoye Stroitelstvo,* op. cit., pp. 244-45; *Narodnoye Khozaystvo,* op. cit., p. 842.

[13] *Kulturnoye Stroitelstvo,* op. cit., pp. 252-58; *Narodnoye Khozaystvo,* op. cit., pp. 843-48.

[14] *Zdravookhraneniye v SSSR,* Moscow, 1957, p. 79.

[15] *Ibid.,* p. 84.

[16] *Ibid.,* pp. 151, 155, 161.

[17] *Ibid.,* p. 9; *SSSR v Tsifrakh,* op. cit., p. 432; *Narodnoye Khozaystov,* op. cit., p. 31.

[18] *Finansy i Sotsialisticheskoye Stroitelstvo,* Moscow, 1957, p. 216.

# CHAPTER 16

# Foreign Trade

~~~~~~~~~~~~~~~~~~~~~~~~~

## INTRODUCTION

From a theoretical viewpoint foreign trade is based on the advantageous economic positions of different geographical regions endowed with different factors of production. This is the principle of comparative advantage which assists in selection of the market where one country buys commodities or services of another produced at the lowest cost. There are no political considerations in the principle, since it is assumed that all countries have free access to any market where only the cost of production is the determining factor in buying and selling.

The classical concepts of international trading, however, are fused now with political policies. Although this process started even before the Great Depression, with the advent of Hitler it was intensified, and by the end of World War II, political and economic considerations had become increasingly important partners.

Soviet foreign trade policies have also undergone drastic revisions since the early days of the Bolshevik Revolution. There have been several phases in their development. The first phase may be placed roughly from the time of the creation of the Soviet State through the beginning of World War II. During this period the foreign trade policies of the Soviets were those of an isolationist state, but they were flexible enough to accept the economic advantages offered by foreign trade. The second phase took place during World War II, when wartime necessity forced the Soviets to relax restrictions on imports and on foreign aid. A third phase appeared with the formation of satellite states in 1944. The fourth phase began when Khrushchev assumed leadership in the Soviet Union in 1955. Each phase has a distinct role in the development of the Soviet foreign trade policies, embracing economic, political, and psychological elements, which are entwined in the present Soviet relations with other nations.

429

The present role of Soviet foreign trade is to serve as a tool for Soviet foreign policy, which is altered to fulfill the need of the political situation at any given time. True, Soviet foreign trade in relation to its Gross National Product (GNP) is small. The USSR's exports and imports represent less than two per cent of its GNP for each account. It is true that the Soviets are less oriented toward non-communist trade than to that of the communist bloc, which takes approximately three-fourths of the Soviet foreign trade. But it is also true that the Russians are placing increasing emphasis on machinery and equipment in their foreign trade. In 1950 the Soviet Union held eleventh place in the world's export of machinery and equipment; by 1957, it had moved up to fifth place. Consequently, competition for the world's market for these goods between USSR and non-communist countries is becoming keener and may eventually lead to adjustments in the foreign trade policies of non-communist countries.

## POLICIES

Soviet foreign trade became a State monopoly in April 1918. At the beginning of the Red regime functions of foreign trade were to assist the development of industrial production in the USSR and to protect the young and unstable State from anticipated economic warfare with the capitalist nations. At this early date Russians feared penetration of foreign capital which could undermine the Marxian reliance of self-sufficiency. The principle of self-sufficiency, to the Russians, was the stone from which world socialism was to be cut.

World War II jolted the value of self-sufficiency, a policy which was more a political than an economic consideration anyway. Since then self-sufficiency has not been considered as the ultimate goal, and with the beginning of trade expansion between the USSR and the satellite states, foreign trade and to some degree the principle of self-sufficiency had to be adjusted to face reality.

Khrushchev's pronouncements of "friendly competition" and "peaceful coexistence" have adjusted values of foreign trade still further. Now it is an accepted fact, by the Russians, that through implementation of foreign trade, countries of different socio-economic patterns may live peacefully side by side, trade with each other for mutual benefit, and pave the road to political understanding. These assertions, according to the Russians, were laid down by Lenin. But Lenin, preoccupied with the organization of a new society, was not in a position to dictate to the free world the conditions for peaceful coexistence nor for friendly competition. He was begging for it. He was striving for more time to lead Russia out of economic and political turmoil to safer ground. Khrushchev, on the other hand, has more reason to be confident than Lenin ever had. He challenges the West.

The question of peaceful coexistence and friendly competition in international trade is really a fascinating one. Does it mean that Khrushchev recognizes capitalism as a force which cannot be crushed by communism, as advocated by others before him? One may ask how friendly competition may be. Can competition be friendly at all? Can there be peaceful coexistence between two nations while they are trying to undersell each other? Generally speaking, the answers to these questions depend upon one's belief, and apparently the Russians have faith in peaceful coexistence and friendly competition. They are their popular slogans, but they are also working tools in international relations.

Concepts of peaceful coexistence and friendly competition cover more ground than expansion of foreign trade for mutual benefit. With the transfer of goods from the USSR to another country, economic, political, and cultural contacts are established. By this means the Russians are trying to exploit the ignorance, poverty, and pride of the "have not" countries and the world's forgotten countries, the economic potentials of which are still undeveloped. In general, during some 43 years of existence, the Soviets have drastically revised their practices in foreign trade. But let us trace them from the beginning.

### First Phase (1918-40)

The first phase of development of Soviet foreign trade is closely connected with internal economic expansion. This phase consists of several periods, each influencing the Soviets in shifting the emphasis to achieving the desired goal of the period.

The first period occurred during the Civil War of 1918-20. Because of the instability of the new Red regime, the confusion created by the Civil War, and distrust and fear of the Bolsheviks by the rest of the world, the Soviet turnover in foreign trade was very small indeed. In 1918 many goods were still coming into the country as a result of the agreements made by the Tsarist and Kerensky governments. When the country was divided into Red and White armed camps in 1919 the turnover in foreign trade consisted mainly of exports by the Red regime.

After the end of the Civil War the Bolshevik government was unable to obtain credit from abroad. The gold which was offered for the goods was either refused by the West or accepted at reduced prices. The Bolsheviks called this period the time of the "gold credit blockade."

Then the new regime was recognized as a sovereign state by Estonia, Latvia, and Lithuania, countries needing Russian trade. Other small nations followed in the establishment of diplomatic relations with Moscow, and then in March 1921, the London-Moscow trade agreement was signed. During the few years following the Soviets imported many raw materials and grain. Grain was urgently needed because of the widespread hunger of 1921-22 and again in 1924-25. Exported goods consisted mainly of timber, petroleum products, and other raw materials.

In general, during the 1918-28 period the emphasis was on imports to speed the economic recovery from World War I and the Civil War. Imports consisted chiefly of raw materials and semi-manufacturers such as hides, leather, raw cotton, wool, yarn, pulp and paper. In addition, considerable amounts of metals and industrial equipment were imported to restore industrial production. In their effort to speed up industrialization the Russians began to dump their products abroad for foreign currency with which they hoped to buy machinery, and Great Britain, as the main dumping market, ceased diplomatic relations with the Red regime in 1927.

During the early years of industrialization and collectivization (1926-34) foreign trade became a vital source for obtaining industrial equipment and machinery, the percentage of which rose from 28 per cent of the total import in 1929 to 52.5 per cent in 1932. Tractors were imported in increasing number during the 1929-31 period, but in 1932 the Soviet-made tractors appeared and import was completely halted. Even the import of raw materials for production of consumer goods was reduced. This was the beginning of the optimistic era connected with the reliance of self-sufficiency and faith in industrialization which was to make the Soviet Union economically and politically strong. Consequently, with the revival of domestic industrial and agricultural production, the Soviet imports in equipment and machinery were considerably reduced, and the percentage of imported machinery and equipment dropped to 27.3 per cent of the total 1937 imports. However, imports of commodities such as wool, rubber, coffee, and cocoa were increased. At the same time, the structure of exported goods also changed. Meat, eggs, bacon, vegetable oils, and the like were no longer exported. By 1938 the share of exported grain to the total export became 21.9 per cent. Instead, the Russians began to export railroad equipment, furs, ores, and machinery. Exports of petroleum products were also reduced due to the increased domestic demand.

It was during this period that the Soviets adopted a policy in which the role of foreign trade became a retaliatory instrument in international politics. For example, during the 1936-38 period, without serving public notice of its action, the USSR "punished" Italy for it participation in the Spanish Civil War by ending their mutual exchange of goods. Germany, a more important trade partner and at times a more generous creditor than Italy, was also subjected to restrictive treatment for the same offense but its "punishment" fell short of risking a complete break in trade between the two countries.

TABLE 1—*Soviet Foreign Trade: 1929-40* [1]
(*billions of rubles, March 1, 1950 prices*)

| Year | Exports | Imports | Total turnover |
|------|---------|---------|----------------|
| 1929 | 3.0 | 2.9 | 5.9 |
| 1930 | 3.4 | 3.5 | 6.9 |
| 1931 | 2.7 | 3.6 | 6.3 |
| 1932 | 1.9 | 2.3 | 4.2 |
| 1933 | 1.7 | 1.2 | 2.9 |
| 1934 | 1.5 | 0.8 | 2.3 |
| 1935 | 1.3 | 0.8 | 2.1 |
| 1936 | 1.1 | 1.1 | 2.2 |
| 1937 | 1.3 | 1.0 | 2.3 |
| 1938 | 1.0 | 1.1 | 2.1 |
| 1940 | 1.1 | 1.1 | 2.2 |

In 1929 the Soviets were still in the process of building up foreign currency with which to purchase goods abroad for their industrialization. Beginning with the Second Five-Year Plan (1932-37) there was a gradual reduction of international trading activities, and between 1938 and 1940 the Russians reached the balance of trade. The Soviets claimed that the USSR had finally achieved self-sufficiency in most goods which were so important for starting their industrialization drive in 1929. This balance of trade, however, was achieved as a result of the commercial agreement signed with Germany in 1939.

The first phase of foreign trade of the Soviet Union during the 1918-40 period is identified with the original policy of self-sufficiency. The main objective, of course, was to become independent of the international market and to protect the USSR from infiltration of non-communist capital. The Soviets denounced foreign trade as one of the evils of capitalist exploitation; yet they did not hesitate to use its channels in obtaining goods, services, and currencies which were scarce in the USSR at that time. Policies during this early period were flexible and operated on the short-run basis to suit the needs of the political leadership. But there were not trade agreements established solely for political reasons as there were in later priods.

## Second Phase (1941-45)

The second phase of Soviet foreign trade falls between the beginning of World War II and early 1945. This period coincides with the Lend-Lease program of the United States, which started on March 11, 1941, and ended on August 1, 1945.

The war and its aftermath marked the beginning of a new phase in Soviet foreign trade policy. While the war was still going on the Soviets decreased their exports to a minimum but boosted imports many times. In 1942 the Soviets imported 2.8 billion rubles worth of goods and 8.6 billion rubles in 1943, whereas annual exports during those two years averaged only 0.4 billion rubles. In 1945 the turnover reached 16.2 billion rubles of which over 90 per cent was imports.[2] Probably most, if not all, of the imports during the war were made up of Lend-Lease goods and of goods from similar wartime arrangements.

With the occupation of Eastern Europe a new phase in Soviet foreign trade policy came to life. Since the economies of the satellites were at a low ebb after the war, it was necessary to provide them with raw materials, machinery, and equipment to rehabilitate their productive forces. The principles of equality and mutual benefit advocated prior to the war were ignored and the satellites were forced to sign agreements disadvantageous to them with the all-powerful USSR. Poland was compelled to sign a trade agreement the terms of which were so unfavorable that on December 1, 1956, the Russians agreed to pay back 500 million dollars for all the coal, grain, and other products shipped to the USSR since August 1, 1945.[3] By the end of 1945 all the Eastern European communist countries were forced to tie their economics to the Soviet Union, and with the formation of the East German Republic in October 1949 there followed the established pattern of signing a trade agreement with the USSR. The remarkable thing about this period is the realization by the Russians that self-sufficiency was not necessarily the sole driving goal for their country alone. The satellites and the USSR had become a unified bloc with political and economic domination of the satellites by the Soviet Union.

## Third Phase (1946-54)

The most important change in Soviet foreign trade policy came in the third phase, which falls roughly between 1946 and 1954. During the earlier years of this period the Soviet Union was preoccupied with the tightening of economic and political controls in the satellites. They were tied to the USSR and to each other as well. Then about 1950 a new force affected Russian policies regarding the whole structure of international relations. In 1949, 15 non-communist nations which carry on some 60 per cent of their foreign trade outside the communist orbit began to control the shipment of strategic goods to the entire Soviet bloc. (The communist orbit includes all communist countries; the Soviet bloc only the USSR and satellites.) To overcome its impact the Soviets launched a systematic program of contacting nations having access to the free market for goods to supplement their domestic production. As a result, the principle of comparative advantage in foreign trade for the Soviet bloc and for the West alike was minimized. This partial Western embargo, perhaps unintentionally, forced the USSR and satellites to draw closer together economically, particularly with Red China where there is a complete embargo by the United States.

To find a gap in the embankment created by the West the Soviets adjusted their trading practices of the prewar years and began to purchase foodstuffs and consumer goods not previously sought in the world market. Simultaneously, more Soviet-made industrial goods and raw materials were offered to the free world. But these offers were not readily accepted by the West. In 1949 the Soviet Union traded with some 50 nations including the communist orbit countries. About two-thirds of the total trade turnover was taken by the satellites. By 1955 the number had increased to 58 nations. In 1959 the Soviet Union traded with about 65 nations, including the communist orbit, but had only 45 trade agreements and treaties. The orbit countries accounted for 74 per cent of the total Soviet trade turnover.

Simultaneously with increased offers of trade the Soviet bloc, in January 1949, organized the Eastern European Council for Mutual Economic Assistance (CEMA). Member nations included the USSR, Czechoslovakia, Bulgaria, Hungary, Poland, and Rumania. In February of that year Albania joined the organization, and in October 1950 the East German Republic signed the agreement.[4] In 1956 Red China had its observers at the meeting of CEMA; in 1957 and 1958 North Korea, Mongolia, and North Vietnam sent their representatives to CEMA.

The main purpose of CEMA was division of labor, coordination of members' economies, mutual economic assistance, equality among the partners, exchange in innovations and technology, and unrestricted movement of raw materials, food, machinery and equipment among member nations. It was a clever device. Since the Soviet trading practices were not respected and were often feared by non-communist countries, trade agreements with other CEMA member nations like Poland or Czechoslovakia were more acceptable to them. With this organization the Soviet block actually created a common pool of imported goods from which member nations supplied their own needs, or at least directed a larger share of their domestic output to other member nations. Moreover, this organization was not purely of economic value but also had political aspects by having the right to create economic blockades against other countries.

The past success of CEMA was overemphasized. The weakness of cost accounting in the Soviet bloc countries has created irrationality in their economic activities, and throughout the existence of CEMA during the past ten years too much time was spent in an attempt to coordinate production of basic industrial raw materials, machine building, and processing industries. Only in 1959 did Khrushchev realize the value of CEMA, and concrete plans were set to unify energy power networks for East Germany, Poland, Czechoslovakia, Hungary, western parts of the Ukraine, and Poland with the Kaliningrad network. This is to be accomplished between 1959 and 1964. Later on a similar unified power network is to be established for Rumania and Bulgaria. Although imperfect, CEMA is nevertheless functioning and integrates economically many aspects of the Soviet-satellites relations which ideologically and politically were divisive prior to 1959, as in the case of Hungary and Poland.

In an attempt to publicize their good intentions in regard to non-communist countries, the Soviets became increasingly interested in the Far and Near Eastern countries after the death of Stalin in 1953. They offered them favorable trade agreements, technical assistance, and outright grants either directly or through existing international organizations. For instance, in July 1953, the USSR joined the Technical Assistance Fund of the United Nations (UNTAA), contributing four million rubles as its first annual contribution. Then in February 1954 the Soviet government extended an offer of technical assistance to all nations which organized the Economic Commission for Asia and the Far East (ECAFE). Since the Soviet Union is politically and economically aggressive its membership in these international organizations served only as a wedge to widen the gap between non-communist countries.

The postwar period created notable changes in the prewar conviction. that foreign trade has only two functions—supplementing the domestic resources of the USSR and protecting its economy from infiltration by the capitalists. From the early formation of the satellite states Soviet trade with them was based on the planned economic development of each and every state concerned. Since every satellite country was consolidated in an overall planned production scheme within the Soviet bloc, that part of the policy which supposedly protected the USSR against capitalist infiltration became useless.

However, Stalin's policy toward the satellites was a "tough" one with complete socio-economic control in the sense that all major decisions undertaken by the satellities were either formulated in the Kremlin or at least approved there. To Stalin, those vassal states were incapable of shaping their own destinies and were not to be trusted in theoretical evaluation of their own development, even though they followed the communist line. Khruchchev's pronouncement of peaceful coexistence replaced to some degree the outdated concepts in foreign trade with the satellites. Since the satellites are not capitalist nations and since their economies are closely linked with the USSR and each other, the old theoretical interpretations of meaning of the value of foreign trade can no longer be used in dealing with them. The concept of peaceful coexistence replaced the tough policy of Stalin's era, creating a more lenient policy toward the satellites which changed their statue from vassal statehood to what may be called junior associates, strengthened by economic ties, political affiliations, trade agreements, numerous mutual benefit cooperations, and defense pacts.

## Fourth Phase (1955 on)

The fourth and present phase in Soviet foreign trade policy may be set at the beginning of 1955, when Khrushchev replaced Malenkov. This period also coincides with visits by Bulganin and Khrushchev to India, Burma, Afghanistan, and Great Britain; Mikoyan's visit to the United States, Cuba, and Mexico; and Khrushchev's appearance in the United States, Indonesia, France, and other countries.

As was pointed out, the Russians have finally recognized that international specialization and division of labor would benefit the Soviet Union and the old fear of capitalist infiltration had now become nothing but an illusion of the past. The experience in trading with the satellites must have been a good lesson for the Communists in how to deal with the free world. They mu: t have learned quickly how to deal with "have not" countries, promising economic advantages which lead, under proper conditions, to political if not ideological ties. Perhaps the aggregate gains from foreign trade with non-communist nations are small now, but they can grow larger, and increased foreign trade in small lots would affect a larger number of countries. This provides good propaganda material for nations which are still unwilling to look upon Khrushchev as a benefactor. The Soviets are rapidly learning the art of persuading underdeveloped nations to break away from the old colonial ties. To the Russians this is still a virgin and long-neglected area, and to the nations which have recently cast off the chains of colonialism, getting "equality," "friendship," and "mutual benefit" even from the Russians is a rare experience.

The Soviets are seemingly converted to the idea of respectability and they stress that trade agreements are "without strings attached" in regard to political loyalty or military alliance with the Soviet Union. Theirs is a business-like approach to a problem of common interests with full respect for native pride and self-determination. The Soviets propagandize the fact that they are becoming new suppliers of capital goods to exchange for goods produced by the native labor which are wanted only by a few of the Western powers. But above all, a new concept has developed which emphasizes the assumption that foreign trade between different socio-economic systems facilitates normalization of political questions leading to lasting peace in the world. At least this is the situation in the eyes and words of the Russians.

Thus, to the Soviets, foreign trade has become a mechanism through which peace in the world may be realized. This can be a powerful force. However, economic and political forces cannot be ignored in any realistic analysis of exchange of goods and services, and in spite of the Russians' highly publicized "objectivity," these forces are used to win friends and to punish nations which get out of line or have chosen a different path of self-determination.

For example, in 1949 the Soviets promised to supply Iran with 30,000 metric tons of sugar, but when the sugar arrived the Soviets held it off the Iranian market. This raised the prices on sugar on the local market, and later on the Soviets sold it at higher prices. Again, with the deepening of the ideological split between the Soviet bloc and Yugoslavia in 1956, the Soviets put pressure on Tito through the satellites by holding up delivery of promised raw materials to him. As a result, his plans for industrial expansion did not materialize and the country experienced considerable industrial unemployment. In 1957, to prove its sympathy with Egypt, the Soviet Union cancelled its ten-million dollar trade agreement with Israel for the purchase of Israeli oranges. Although the sum itself was not large it is difficult to dispose of a corresponding volume of oranges on short notice. The main export of Burma is rice. The Soviet trade agreement with Burma called for the purchase of 200,000 metric tons of rice in 1956. The USSR, Red China, Poland, Czechoslovakia, Rumania, Hungary, and East Germany collectively purchased about 30 per cent of the total Burmese rice crop.[5] In the absence of other markets Burma cannot jeopardize its economic stability under present conditions and thus must play ball with the Soviets.

Perhaps a few words should be said about the Soviet perference for dealing with foreign manufacturers. Generally speaking, the Soviets would perfer to make trade agreements with individual producers rather than with their governments. Most Soviet trade agreements with individual producers are short-term, with provisions for expanding volumes. Expecting that his products will be purchased in increasing volume, an individual producer often expands his output. Then the Soviets inform him that his government obstructs the normal trade transactions with him. To avoid losses the manufacturer appeals to the government and, at times, the USSR may get concessions which were unavailable before. Therefore, by dealing directly with many individual producers whose interests lie in keeping their facilities running at full capacity, the Russians benefit from indirect pressure placed on the governments.

## AGENCIES

The USSR Ministry of Foreign Trade is responsible for trade operations within the communist orbit and with all free countries. The Ministry is divided into specialized divisions, each assigned to deal with a specific problem, such as regional foreign trade, commodity divisions, foreign exchange, legal problems, and other administrative tasks arising from the decisions taken by the government. The Ministry is a non-policy-making body and has limited powers, since the volume and the types of goods to be imported and exported are determined by the Soviet planning apparatus, which, in the main, includes normal flow of imported and exported goods in the national plans.

Moreover, political short-run decisions on the spot may also bypass the normal channels in international relations. As an example, while visiting in India, Bulganin and Khrushchev promised agricultural machinery to the Indians, and within ten weeks of the promise, 66 tractors, 60 harvesters, 60 tractor ploughs, 50 cultivators, 81 seed drills, and other farm machinery began to arrive in India. Considering the distances between the two countries, this was unusually prompt delivery.[6] It is doubtful that the Ministry anticipated such a shipment to India and held it ready for delivery at short notice. Similarly, it is also doubtful that Bulganin and Khrushchev knew exactly what the Indians would want prior to their arrival in India. It is obvious that higher political personages may bypass the usual governmental channels and interrupt the normal operations of the Ministry.

However, inasmuch as the USSR Ministry of Foreign Trade is entrusted with the operations of foreign trade, it maintains an extensive network of agencies. As a rule, depending on the volume of trade, the Soviets may maintain an officially accredited trade delegation in each country with which trading is in effect or be represented by specialized trade agencies. In addition, many small-scale transactions are carried out by members of the regular diplomatic missions, acting as commercial counselors or attaches. In the United States, the Soviets were permitted to organize a trading agency (Amtorg Trading Corporation), which was incorporated under the laws of New York State in May 1924, about ten years prior to recognition of the Soviet Government. This agency is still in operation.

## TRADE AGREEMENTS

There are two types of trade agreements. The first is signed by officially accredited representatives of both governments. Under this type, each government is responsible for the fulfillment of all obligations specified in the agreement. Any supplementary adjustments in the agreement are ratified by both governments. All agreements are bilateral and may be extended indefinitely after expiration of the terms of the current agreement by mutual consent.

For example, trade agreements with the satellite countries are bilateral and made for periods which coincide with the respective national plans— one year or longer. At times, due to forces not anticipated in the past, supplementary amendments are added to include any emergency that might arise. Prices which are linked to the world market are determined by both governments and in the main hold firm for the duration of the agreement. Since rubles are used in trading among bloc countries, prices for the same commodities among different member countries are without wide fluctuations. However, rubles cannot be transferred from one satellite to another. If, for example, Poland runs up a ruble balance due to an export surplus with the Soviet Union, it cannot transfer the rubles to another satellite country in payment of Polish debts. In this way no country is able to accumulate rubles with which it could buy Soviet goods which are not planned for foreign trade. Under certain conditions, payments to the Iron Curtain countries are made in foreign currency or in gold for the purpose of expanding their trading on the international market.

Since dollar and sterling funds are scarce, a non-communist country trading with the Soviet Union may agree on payments in other currency. This may be illustrated by an agreement between the USSR and Iceland signed in 1953 and renewed in 1956. Under the renewed agreement all payments were to be made in Iceland's kronur through the USSR Gosbank and the National Bank of Iceland. But the agreement with Indonesia, signed in 1956, specified that payments were to be made in British sterling. Therefore, in an attempt to win friendship from the non-communist nations, the Soviets do not insist on restricting them to the ruble, as they do with the satellite nations.

The second type of trade agreement is made between state trading agencies, either in the Soviet Union or abroad. Depending on the volume of trade and the type of goods involved, the USSR may be represented by one or more agencies. Great Britain, Sweden, and Belgium, for instance, each have only one agency, Red China has five, Poland and Finland each have four, India and Denmark have three agencies each, Norway and Italy have two, and so on.

Officially these agencies are called All-Union Combines. Each combine has a charter with clearly defined purpose, functions, and the right to sign agreements in the field for which it was set up. Each combine has its own legal staff, establishes its own monetary funds, and has offices at home and abroad. One notable peculiarity is that although they act within the framework of the Soviet national plans, the government is not responsible for any obligations made by them to foreign traders, nor are they answerable to the government since they are organized and supported by individual industries. This is, of course, a technicality to protect the Soviet government from involvement in any legal action considered by the foreign courts.

In 1956 there were reportedly 24 All-Union Combines. Some of them are highly specialized agencies dealing with one commodity or closely related commodities or services, while others handle a variety of commodities. The scope of activities of some of these agencies is beyond the simple import-export operation. In general, the All-Union Combines provide all the services for domestic and foreign trade organizations, including technical assistance and training facilities when requested by foreign traders. Problems of transportation, freight forwarding, storage. chartering of ships, travel to and from the USSR, printing of books in foreign languages, and selection of firms are solved by combines specializing in such matters. Upon instructions from home offices in Moscow, they purchase commodities which are not included in any agreements or in the plan. Such items include recent foreign innovations and new products.

Beginning with 1954, in line with the policy of friendly competition and peaceful coexistence, there has been a notable revival of old, expired foreign trade agreements and signing of new ones. The number of bilateral trade agreements between the West and the USSR has increased considerably. They make good publicity, but their significance is exaggerated, since a trade agreement in itself provides no assurance of actual transfer of goods. Moreover, when a trade agreement is put into effect, a certain amount of time usually elapses before goods can be assembled for transfer to new ownership. While the bulk of foreign trade is still with the bloc countries and with Western Europe, there has been an increasing number of agreements with Asian and African countries.

It is difficult to determine the value of some agreements with Far and Near Eastern countries, but by these agreements the Soviets attracted attention, which is part of the Communists' campaign to extend their influence there and to create disturbance among the Western powers. The persistence of Soviet efforts in these areas may be illustrated by an incident which occurred in Lebanon. In 1956 the Soviet economic mission spent two months there for the purpose of expanding trading activities between the two countries. The mission offered help to Lebanon in development of industry. Upon return to Moscow the head of the mission was interviewed in regard to the success of his trip. Among other things, he stated that the contact with local business circles and with the workers was very limited, and he was shocked at the degree of ignorance of the Lebanese people in regard to the Soviet Union and its relations with other countries. On the other hand, where political leadership of a country is sympathetic toward the Soviets or at least is anticolonial, the reception of the Soviet trade offers has been more appreciative, as in India, Egypt, and Afghanistan.

As was previously stated, the Soviet foreign trade agreements are bilateral. It is maintained by the Soviets that all nations are sovereign states. It is only reasonable, according to the Soviets, that two sovereign states should deal with each other on an equal basis, striving for mutual benefit, which will lead to understanding among various socio-economic societies and will ultimately establish peace on earth. This is a noble goal for any time and place. However, there are several important "ifs" in it.

Two nations may be sovereign states, yet one may be large, powerful, and wealthy, whereas the other may be small and poor. The wealthy nation may have trade agreements and political affiliations with a number of nations while the small and poor nation, specializing in production of homogeneous products, may not have the same opportunity. Therefore, the economic and political pressures on small and poor nations may come from different sources. Moreover, the marginal productivity of capital invested in foreign trade by wealthier nations may not be of the same value to the poorer nation, which may be forced to put all its eggs in one basket and thus become open to economic and political pressures .

Since the concept of self-sufficiency was changed in scope, a new purpose for the building up of Soviet might had to be found. The Kremlin cannot remain inactive in economic or political affairs at home or abroad. Like the economy of the United States, the Soviet economy cannot be dormant. Both countries must produce more goods and services, provide employment for their increasing populations, and expand their philosophies. Acceptance or rejection of these philosophies is becoming increasingly important. Now that the satellite countries are closely tied to the USSR, self-sufficiency for the Soviet Union, like isolationism in the United States, has become outdated, and new areas of activities must be found to proclaim the glory of socialism.

Trading with the satellites, after many trials and errors, has become standardized. In a sense the trade between Eastern European satellites and the USSR may be considered as interregional trade similar to the trade that existed between the United States and the Philippines before the Philippines became an independent republic. The satellite countries enter into multilateral agreements among themselves, but there is no crisscross of shipment of the same goods. However, the Soviet Union, receiving petroleum from Rumania, may direct it to one of the satellite countries by virtue of the fact that it came from the Soviet reserves. Red China and North Korea have trade agreements with the Soviet Union and individual satellite countries, but these are on the basis of bilateral agreements where prices, tariff duties, payments, and other aspects of transfer of goods are defined in each agreement.

Most of the Soviet trade agreements with countries outside the bloc are bilateral and annual agreements. Moreover, since the adoption of "trade not-aid" policy in dealing with underdeveloped countries and since expanding the types of goods offered and purchased, the Soviets have increased their attention to the non-communist countries during the past few years. The Soviet Union concluded eight bilateral annual agreements with non-communist countries in 1952 and 35 in 1959.[7]

One of the reasons for annual agreements is that the Soviet Union is trying to create a feeling of security among samller nations which still fear committing themselves in any direction. Also, the questions of costs and prices, tariff duties, and the like, as well as the volume and selection of commodities can be more easily adjusted after one year than after a longer period of time. Perhaps another reason for short-term agreements, especially in dealing with underdeveloped countries, is to provide a training period in which to plan production in these countries after the Soviet model. It also allows the Soviets to discontinue trading with those countries which attempt to disagree with the interests of the Soviet Union.

One may ask why the underdeveloped countries, especially those which have just recently shaken off colonialism, will trade with the Soviet Union in the face of possible spread of communism there. Most of the underdeveloped countries are facing the same problem in the effort to build up their economic stability. The problem of communism is secondary. And since very few of the underdeveloped countries have great accumulations of capital in private ownership, the immediate danger of confiscation of privately owned investments is not as vital a matter to them as it is in the West.

## BALANCE OF TRADE

During the postwar period the Soviets, in the main, instituted a kind of a rough regional balance in foreign trade, especially with the bloc countries. In a planned economy like the Soviet Union an equilibrium in demand for goods and services is controlled by the State. Under normal conditions the Soviets would try to get the necessary volume of imported goods to match the domestic demand for them and would try to export the quantity of goods which would not jeopardize their own domestic needs.

With the establishment of the Western embargo, Soviet trade with communist countries increased from some 50 per cent of the total in 1946 to

81 per cent in 1950. Then in 1954 the Soviet bloc launched its own drive in trade agreements with non-communist countries, and the share of the total Soviet trade turnover with communist countries declined to 73 per

TABLE 2—*Soviet Foreign Trade Turnover* [8]
(*in rubles*)

| Turnover | 1950 | 1955 | 1956 | 1957 | 1958 |
|---|---|---|---|---|---|
| Total (billions): | 13.0 | 26.1 | 29.1 | 33.3 | 34.6 |
| Non-communist countries | 2.5 | 5.4 | 7.0 | 8.8 | 9.1 |
| Communist countries: | 10.5 | 20.7 | 22.1 | 24.5 | 25.5 |
| Albania (millions) | 62 | 83 | 105 | 187 | 233 |
| Bulgaria | 667 | 995 | 1,012 | 1,482 | 1,614 |
| Czechoslovakia | 1,688 | 2,970 | 3,081 | 3,747 | 3,835 |
| East Germany | 1,383 | 3,940 | 4,791 | 6,506 | 6,464 |
| Hungary | 841 | 1,047 | 991 | 1,426 | 1,450 |
| Mongolia | 278 | – | 631 | 471 | 448 |
| North Korea | – | – | 420 | 490 | 420 |
| North Vietnam | – | – | 15 | 52 | 72 |
| Poland | 1,806 | 2,874 | 2,562 | 2,747 | 2,568 |
| Red China | 2,330 | – | 5,989 | 5,129 | 6,061 |
| Rumania | 1,013 | 1,910 | 1,787 | 1,763 | 1,940 |
| Yugoslavia | – | 136 | 475 | 520 | 408 |

cent in 1958. During the 1950-58 period trade with communist countries increased 2.4 times whereas with non-communist countries it increased 3.6 times.

Between 1950 and 1958 the total Soviet foreign trade turnover increased 2.7 times. The turnover includes imports, exports, and reexports. It also includes goods purchased by the Soviets abroad and transported directly to other countries, bypassing the Soviet Union's ports. But goods delivered as free aid to other countries, goods assigned to the United Nations for technical assistance, and goods shown at international fairs in the Soviet Union or by the Soviets in other countries are not included in the foreign trade turnover. For these reasons, it is difficult to estimate the exact volume of imports and exports originated by and for the Soviets without reexports and other middleman's activities. Nevertheless the bulk of imported goods stay in the Soviet Union.

The increased amount of trade with non-communist countries is not very great in itself, and apart from a few areas of special interest to the USSR the trade agreements were made throughout the scattered non-communist areas. But it indicates the intense interest of the Soviet Union in under-developed areas. Undoubtedly this interest will grow with time, and a larger share of the Soviet foreign trade will be devoted to these non-communist countries. A trade agreement with any small underdeveloped country, no matter how modest it may appear, will create strong public relations. A cement plant, petroleum storage facilities, or even a mechanized bakery, not to mention a steel mill, become the symbol of Russian good will.

Table 3 includes a few selected non-communist countries of Europe, Asia, Africa, and America which are important to the Soviet Union for economic or political reasons.

TABLE 3—*Soviet Trade Turnover with*
*Selected Non-communist Countries: 1956-59* [9]
(*in millions of rubles*)

| Country | 1956 | | 1957 | | 1958 | |
|---|---|---|---|---|---|---|
| | Export | Import | Export | Import | Export | Import |
| Finland | 459.1 | 584.8 | 601.8 | 660.8 | 468.6 | 548.8 |
| Great Britain | 592.6 | 297.6 | 704.5 | 448.4 | 582.2 | 291.5 |
| France | 278.5 | 202.3 | 268.0 | 190.1 | 348.4 | 322.3 |
| West Germany | 167.2 | 272.5 | 286.8 | 247.4 | 262.5 | 288.3 |
| Egypt | 153.7 | 201.4 | 328.8 | 443.7 | 350.5 | 428.5 |
| Malay Federation | 1.3 | 335.9 | 2.4 | 195.2 | 0.2 | 471.8 |
| Belgium | 116.9 | 128.2 | 112.7 | 122.7 | 92.1 | 64.8 |
| Sweden | 138.6 | 104.1 | 125.7 | 100.8 | 120.8 | 112.3 |
| Italy | 135.7 | 103.9 | 116.6 | 181.5 | 154.2 | 141.1 |
| India | 161.6 | 73.2 | 338.6 | 167.8 | 520.0 | 203.7 |
| Iran | 76.7 | 60.6 | 126.6 | 74.1 | 109.9 | 105.7 |
| Afghanistan | 73.0 | 60.5 | 72.5 | 82.7 | 92.5 | 50.4 |
| Argentina | 76.5 | 51.8 | 18.7 | 83.3 | 68.7 | 64.2 |
| United States | 108.7 | 19.2 | 63.7 | 40.6 | 104.2 | 19.0 |
| Burma | 17.1 | 49.1 | 25.9 | 36.2 | 10.3 | — |
| Uruguay | 11.4 | 49.2 | 0.5 | 72.5 | 22.1 | 99.2 |
| Japan | 11.9 | 3.1 | 33.7 | 34.7 | 79.7 | 71.2 |

As can be seen from Table 3, during the 1956-58 period there was a considerable increase in trade between the Soviet Union and India, Egypt, the Malay Federation, West Germany, Uruguay, France, Iran, and Japan.

At the same time Finland, Great Britain, Belguim, the United States, and Burma have reduced their trade with the USSR. Some of these increases such as with Egypt and India more than doubled while other countries show only moderate increases. Only Burma drastically reduced its trade with the Soviets.

The 1959 Soviet foreign trade turnover reached 42 billion rubles, of which 20.3 billion rubles were imports and 21.7 billion rubles were exports. In that year the Soviets imported more machinery and equipment, especially equipment for the chemical industry, sugar, milk products, cement, paper and pulp industries, railroad stocks, and ships than in 1958. Approximately 27 per cent of the total Soviet imports represented machinery and equipment, of which about 80 per cent came from the bloc countries. Approximately 21 per cent of the total Soviet exports likewise was made up of machinery and equipment. The Soviets claim that although the USSR has only recently become a large exporter of machinery and equipment, by 1960 foreign countries, mostly bloc countries, purchased more than 300,000 Soviet automobiles and 65,000 tractors. In 1959 communist countries took roughly 75 per cent of the total Soviet exports and imports.

## Trade With Non-communist Countries

Soviet trade with non-communist countries in 1958 underwent a considerable change, especially in regard to the types of exported and imported goods. The Soviets substantially increased machinery and equipment exports from 4.2 per cent of its total in 1956 to 14.6 per cent in 1958. A large part of it went to underdeveloped countries. It is interesting to note that in 1958 the volume of Soviet exports of machinery to non-communist countries almost equaled the volume of imports from them. In 1958 the USSR imported from them a larger volume of crude rubber, nonferrous metals, raw materials for the textile industry, and chemical and construction equipment. At the same time imports of ships, marine equipment, and machinery for the food and light industries were reduced.

In 1958 trading with some of the non-communist countries was less favorable than in previous years. Many countries introduced more restrictions on imports and foreign exchange. The Egyptian part of the UAR, India, Burma, Indonesia, and some Latin American countries adopted stricter licensing policies. The UAR and Mexico raised their tariffs. As a result of such restrictions trade with Burma in 1958 was only 16 per cent that of 1957.

In 1958 Finland, Great Britain, and West Germany were the major trading partners among the industrial countries of Europe. A drop in Soviet-

Finnish trade in 1958 was due to a decline in Finnish industrial output. Following the signing of an agreement in March 1959 Soviet-Finnish trade for 1959 was expected to be increased by some 15 per cent; the actual increase was about ten per cent. But there was a substantial increase in the turnover of trade with Italy, France, and other countries.

Great Britain is of particular interest to the Soviet Union. During their visit to London in April 1956 Bulganin and Khrushchev offered 2.8 billion dollars in purchases to the British. Negotiations were slow in starting, but in April 1957 a trade mission representing five British firms returned from Moscow with an order from the Soviet Union worth "many millions of pounds." It was a package deal for a period of more than 20 years. While the Soviet offer involved an obvious political attempt to divide the West, the British treated it seriously. Since the Russian orders promised to become a more steady transaction than the erratic buying of the past, many British firms became more interested in the Soviet offers. As a result of this optimistic trade outlook the 1957 turnover increased. However, the Soviet-British trade turnover in 1958 declined, due largely to a drop in the prices of certain goods, but in 1959 it increased by 152.3 million rubles.

In February 1957 the Soviets signed a long-term agreement with France for mutual deliveries of goods during the 1957-59 period. In accordance with this agreement France was to fulfill a number of large Soviet orders for machinery and equipment and supply the USSR with raw materials. The Soviet Union, on its part, was to export to France anthracite, oil and oil products, manganese and chromium ores, timber, cotton, and other commodities. Soviet-French trade during the past five years increased almost fourfold, and another trade agreement for 1960-62 was signed in November 1958 which is expected to increase the 1957-59 level by about 20 per cent. The 1959 turnover of trade was 82.3 million rubles more than in 1958.

West Germany imports Soviet timber, oil products, non ferrous metals, raw cotton, grain, manganese ore, asbestos, and apatite concentrates. The Soviets import West German equipment for chemical, building, and printing industries. The 1959 turnover of trade with West Germany was 289.2 million rubles above the 1958 level, and in 1960 a new trade agreement was signed by the two countries for still larger trade.

The UAR occupies second place, after Finland, in the Soviet Union's trade. Principal items of Soviet export to the UAR are oil and oil products, wheat, timber, plywood, pulp, machinery and equipment, rolled iron and steel, tin, and aluminum. Major Russian imports from the UAR are raw cotton and rice. The 1960 Soviet exports of machinery and equipment for the construction of the Aswan High Dam will undoubtedly increase trade between the two countries.

United States trade with the Soviet Union has been drastically curtailed since 1950 on the assumption that this could significantly slow the Soviet economic expansion. Great Britain needs expanding markets elsewhere and can use Soviet foodstuffs and mineral products, but the United States is less dependent on foreign markets and has little use for most Russian exports, with the exception of furs and certain metals and ores. Although in 1958 the American-Soviet trade turnover was about the 1957 level, the 1959 turnover was only slightly above the 1958 value.

American-Soviet trade in the last decade has been erratic. United States exports to the USSR at any one time may bulk several hundred thousand dollars and in the next period within the same year it may be only a few tens of thousands of dollars. This erratic trade is due mainly to restrictions on exports of strategic goods to the Soviet bloc countries. For example, during the first three months of 1959 American businessmen applied for export licenses to the Soviet bloc countries amounting to 21.8 million dollars. Of this amount, 15.2 million dollars worth of goods, almost 70 per cent, was rejected by the Department of Commerce. Licenses were denied for 14.7 million dollars worth of polyethylene, carbon-welded line pipe and stainless steel sheets and plates wanted by the Soviet Union. In the second quarter of 1959 license rejections totaled over 60 per cent.[10] These rejections were exceptionally high in comparison with previous periods. This indicates that American businessmen are willing to sell even strategic goods to the Soviet Union. Curiously enough, during the July to September quarter of 1958 export licenses for 33,000 tons of automotive steel valued at some 5.6 million dollars were granted whereas in the first quarter of 1959 similarly strategic goods were prohibited. However, it should be pointed out that the 1958 deal was mainly a barter transaction for Soviet chromium ore.

Relaxation in American-Soviet trade hinges upon settlement of Russia's Lend-Lease account with the United States, talks on which were broken off in 1951. With Khrushchev's visit to the United States, there was a hope that these talks would be resumed, but shortly after negotiations were started they were broken off because the Russians attempted to tie their request for a new loan to the old settlement. It was hoped, however, that with the settlement of the Lend-Lease account the United States might reconsider present restrictions in trade with the Soviets and perhaps most-favored-nation treatment which was abrogated during the Korean War might be granted. As it now stands, the United States considers the USSR indebtedness to be 800 million dollars while the Soviet Union maintains it owes the United States only three million dollars.

The 1951 law forbids importation of Soviet ermine, fox, minks, and crabmeat. Crabmeat was barred in 1951 because the Soviet Union used Japanese prisoners of war in processing it, and the law was still on the books in 1960. But even with relaxation in trade restrictions, any dramatic trade expansion between the two countries is not expected because the Russians do not have the goods needed by the Americans. Nevertheless the Soviets can increase their exports of furs, manganese ore, chrome ore, platinum, cellulose, and crabmeat. On the other hand, Russians want to buy American textile equipment, synthetic yarn-making and other machinery, plastics, pipe, artifical leather, hides, steel sheets, and electronic equipment.

## Trade With Communist Countries

Soviet trade with communist countries is planned, and the types of exported and imported goods are taken into account for anticipated expansion of industrial output. Consequently, trade among bloc countries is less erratic than with non-communist countries.

It is interesting to note that between 1946 and 1950 the trade turnover collectively of Bulgaria, Czechoslovakia, Hungary, Poland and Rumania with the Soviet Union increased more than fourfold. However, with the organization of CEMA, the rate of increase in trade with the USSR slowed down but the trade among satellites considerably increased. This shift was due to expansion of Soviet trade with Red China and East Germany rather than of free choice of the satellites.

In 1958, as in 1956 and 1946, the Soviet Union imported more from communist countries than it exported to them. But in 1950, 1955, and 1957 the Soviets exported more than they imported. Aside from these three years the Soviet turnover with communist countries was closely balanced.

Of the 12 communist countries, East Germany is the principal trader with the Soviet Union, taking 19 per cent of the total Soviet turnover. Next in importance are Red China, Czecholsovakia, Poland and Rumania. Other countries are of lesser significance. Unlike 1956 and 1957, in 1958 the Soviets increased their imports, mainly because of larger imports of machinery and equipment, food, and especially manufactured goods. In the same year the USSR also slightly increased its exports, notably of machinery, rolled iron and steel, iron ore, crude oil and oil products, to communist countries. Significantly enough, the 1958 Soviet exports to communist

TABLE 4—*Soviet Trade with Communist Countries* [11]
*(in millions of rubles)*

| Country | 1 9 5 6 | | 1 9 5 7 | | 1 9 5 8 | |
|---|---|---|---|---|---|---|
| | Export | Import | Export | Import | Export | Import |
| Albania _____ | 72.9 | 32.6 | 130.6 | 56.4 | 177.2 | 56.2 |
| Bulgaria _____ | 433.6 | 578.7 | 690.1 | 792.4 | 802.3 | 812.2 |
| Czechoslovika _____ | 1,494.8 | 1,585,8 | 2,205.2 | 1,542.3 | 1,787.0 | 2,048.4 |
| East Germany _____ | 2,285.4 | 2,505.3 | 3,448.2 | 3,057.4 | 3,199.0 | 3,263.7 |
| Hungary _____ | 507.4 | 483.3 | 998.9 | 426.9 | 802.2 | 647.7 |
| Mongolia _____ | 413.6 | 217.2 | 270.7 | 200.5 | 259.4 | 188.7 |
| North Korea _____ | 215.3 | 204.8 | 239.9 | 250.2 | 232.2 | 188.2 |
| North Vietnam _____ | 9.5 | 5.4 | 38.9 | 12.8 | 32.6 | 39.7 |
| Poland _____ | 1,429.0 | 1,133.0 | 1,723.4 | 1,023.6 | 1,507.2 | 1,060.6 |
| Red China _____ | 2,932.1 | 3,056.9 | 2,176.4 | 2,952.5 | 2,536.0 | 3,525.0 |
| Rumania _____ | 848.1 | 941.4 | 1,003.0 | 760.2 | 1,005.6 | 934.0 |
| Yugoslavia _____ | 276.2 | 198.7 | 292.4 | 227.3 | 204.3 | 203.5 |

countries in mineral commodities represented 35 per cent of the total value while imports of them was 25 per cent. The rest of the export-import transactions were made up of machinery, food, and consumer goods.

The Soviet Union is the main supplier of the minerals for East Germany while the Soviets import a large volume of machinery, especially metal-cutting lathes, forge and press equipment, machinery for the food and chemical industries, rolling stock and ships. Trade turnover between the two countries expanded rapidly. In 1958 East Germany's share in the total Soviet imports of machinery amounted to about 40 per cent.

Soviet trade with Red China is increasing rapidly. In 1954 the turnover was doubled in comparison with 1950. More than 50 per cent of Red China's foreign trade during the 1952-58 period was with the USSR while about 18 per cent of Soviet foreign trade today is with Red China. That country is a large purchaser of Soviet machinery and equipment such as metal-cutting lathes, drilling machines, tractors, and trucks, amounting to 40 per cent of the total Soviet exports of machinery and equipment. In addition, Red China imports a considerable volume of industrial raw materials. Red China's exports to the USSR consist mainly of agricultural goods, especially meat, meat products, rice, fresh fruits, and certain consumer goods. Soviet imports of unprocessed agricultural commodities from Red China represent 40 per cent of the total Soviet imports of such goods. Red China's share of the total Soviet imports of food products is about 50 per cent and of consumer goods 40 per cent. The 1959 trade turnover agreement accounted for some 7.2 billion rubles and consisted of the same goods as in 1958.

Soviet-Czechoslovak trade turnover is the largest within the bloc. Even in 1950 the Czech exports and imports to the USSR represented about 52 per cent of the country's total trading volume. This percentage was only 30 in 1956. The Soviets export to Czechoslovakia goods needed for industrial expansion, and in return the Czechs export to the USSR chemical industry and sugar-refinery equipment as well as other complex equipment and machinery.

By 1960 the Soviet trade turnover with Poland declined, mainly because of reduced sales of Soviet grain to the Poles. Apparently this decline was anticipated. In 1950 almost 60 per cent of the total Polish trade turnover was assigned to the Russians but only 31 per cent in 1956.

In 1950 over 83 per cent of the total foreign trade turnover of Rumania was with the Soviet Union but only 48 per cent in 1956 and a still smaller share in 1957. But in 1958 Rumanian turnover was somewhat increased. In that year Rumanian main imports were Soviet equipment for complete factories, rolled iron and steel, iron ore, ferro-alloys and many other industrial goods. The Soviets import large quantities of Rumanian petroleum products, pipe, cement, corn, and wine.

About 88 per cent of the total Bulgarian foreign trade turnover in 1950 was with the Soviet Union, but with the expansion of Soviet trade with Red China and East Germany the share of Soviet trade turnover for Bulgaria was reduced to 40 per cent in 1956. Bulgaria imports Soviet machinery and equipment, oil products, rolled iron and steel, and raw cotton. The main Soviet imports from Bulagria consist of electrical engineering equipment, ships, and fresh fruits, and vegetables.

Because of the Hungarian uprising Hungary's total trade turnover with the USSR declined from 61 per cent in 1950 to 30 per cent in 1956. A trade revival came in 1957 and 1958. Though 1958 Soviet exports of food to Hungary were reduced from the 1956 and 1957 level, exports of passenger cars, oil, and iron ore were increased. Soviet imports from Hungary in 1958 were 50 per cent above the 1957 level. The main imported Soviet commodities are machinery and equipment, medical equipment, trucks and passenger cars, and consumer goods.

Since Mongolia is surrounded by the USSR and Red China it has no direct trade with other countries. Even if Mongolia wanted to trade with other countries its exports and imports would have to come through the Soviet Union or Red China. Consequently, almost all of its trade is assigned to its two powerful neighbors. In 1957 about 79 per cent of the total Mongolian imports and 83 per cent of exports went to the USSR. The main Mongolian export items are wool, furs, hides, and butter. It imports Soviet machinery, equipment, and consumer goods. Imported Soviet machinery and equipment represent 40 per cent of the total Mongolian imports.

The Soviet-North Korean trade turnover in 1958 was below that of 1957 and approximately of the same volume as in 1956. In 1958 North Korea reduced its imports from the Soviet Union. But at the same time the Soviets increased its exports to North Korea of electric locomotives and trucks. In March 1959 both countries signed an agreement for Soviet technical aid to North Korea in the construction and expansion of a number of industrial enterprises. This would increase the volume of trade between the two countries in the coming years.

In 1950 Albania's total foreign trade was conducted with the Soviet Union but in 1956 it was reduced to 40 per cent when Albania started trade with other satellites. The Soviet-Albanian trade turnovers during the last eight years, though of little importance to the USSR, are of considerable significance to small Albania. In 1958 this increase amounted to almost 25 per cent. Albania imports Soviet machinery and equipment for its new oil industry and for ships. The main Soviet imports from Albania are tobacco, bituminous coal, and raw oil products.

Soviet trade with North Vietnam started in 1956 on a modest scale, but as a member of the communist orbit it had to be tied up with the USSR. In 1958 North Vietnam exported to the USSR oil seeds, coffee, tea, rice, fruits, and other agricultural commodities and imported machinery and equipment, pipe, fertilizer, yarn, textiles, and some other consumer goods. For all practical purposes, ties between the two countries are of political rather than economic significance.

Soviet trade with Yugoslavia is decidedly political, and the Soviets are using trade agreements with Yugoslavia as an economic whip to punish Yugoslavia for its political independence from Moscow. In 1956 both countries signed economic agreements under which the Soviet Union promised loans during the 1957-64 period for the construction of an aluminum plant and for other industrial expansion. In 1958, however, Tito was still defying Moscow's attempts to influence his political independence, and the Soviet Union altered its obligations set forth in the 1956 agreement.

Promised loans to Yugoslavia were deferred to some unspecified later date on the basis that the Soviet Union needed increasing investments in its own expanding chemical industry. It was not however, a complete break with Tito. The Soviets still wanted to fulfill the 1956 obligations, not in terms of loans to be repaid at some future time but in terms of current world prices or in terms of goods currently produced by Yugoslavia.

As a result of this "punitive" action industrial production in Yugoslavia took a turn for the worse, labor productivity declined, and prices increased. The depressed economy of Yugoslavia could not stand the burden of paying the Soviets either in terms of world prices or in goods out of its current production. Consequently, trade between the two countries is at a standstill.

## TYPES OF GOODS EXPORTED AND IMPORTED

There seems to be no clear-cut policy concerning goods exchanged between the USSR and other countries. In dealing with the bloc countries the most significant commodities exported consist of machinery required in mining, metallurgy, and oil-well drilling, pneumatic hammers, machine tools, chemical equipment, transportation facilities, and the like. The Soviet imports from the bloc are nonferrous and ferrous metals, agricultural products, chemicals, and consumer goods. Since the domestic markets of the Soviet Union are undersupplied and since commitments to other nations are diversified, the Soviets import any item which can be sold on the domestic market or used in domestic production or by any other country trading with the Soviet Union.

Table 5 shows the share of each broad commodity in the total export or import account. The monetary values of exports and imports have increased tremendously between 1950 and 1958. Consequently, a decline in the percentage of any one account does not mean a reduction in export or import, rather the table gives a bird's-eye view of the composition of export or import within a single year.

The most interesting years are between 1950 and 1958 when inflationary pressures were more or less corrected and prices were stabilized. Between these years the monetary value of exports more than doubled while imports tripled. Table 5 indicates that Soviet exports are made up of four major accounts: (a) fuel, raw materials, and stocks, (b) machinery and equipment, (c) grain, and (d) consumer goods. The imports consist of three main accounts only, since the USSR does not import grain. The most important account is still fuel, raw materials, and stocks followed by machinery and equipment, and consumer goods.

TABLE 5—*Structure of Exports and Imports of the USSR* [12]
*(in per cent to total)*

| | Exports | | | | Imports | | | |
|---|---|---|---|---|---|---|---|---|
| | 1938 | 1950 | 1956 | 1958 | 1938 | 1950 | 1956 | 1958 |
| Total: _____ | 100.0 | 100.0 | 100.0 | 100.0 | 100.0 | 100.0 | 100.0 | 100.0 |
| Machinery and | | | | | | | | |
| equipment _____ | 5.0 | 11.8 | 17.3 | 18.5 | 34.5 | 21.5 | 24.8 | 24.5 |
| Fuel, raw materials, stocks: | 57.7 | 64.4 | 69.5 | 65.9 | 60.7 | 63.3 | 55.7 | 51.6 |
| Coal _____ | 1.0 | 0.6 | 2.8 | 3.7 | – | 6.0 | 2.9 | 1.4 |
| Petroleum products | 7.8 | 2.4 | 7.9 | 10.0 | 1.2 | 5.2 | 3.8 | 3.1 |
| Ferrous and non- | | | | | | | | |
| ferrous metals_____ | 1.6 | 8.5 | 15.0 | 16.1 | 25.9 | 7.2 | 8.0 | 7.3 |
| Timber and lumber | 20.1 | 2.4 | 3.3 | 4.6 | – | – | – | – |
| Cotton, unginned __ | 1.9 | 9.7 | 7.6 | 5.6 | 1.8 | 2.8 | 1.5 | 3.1 |
| Flax, fiber _____ | 1.7 | 0.2 | 0.3 | 0.2 | – | – | – | – |
| Furs _____ | 9.4 | 2.3 | 1.1 | 0.8 | – | – | – | – |
| Ores and concentrates | 2.3 | – | 3.6 | 4.4 | 2.6 | 5.8 | 10.4 | 9.3 |
| Rubber _____ | – | – | – | – | 3.5 | 3.1 | 3.0 | 3.5 |
| Raw textiles | | | | | | | | |
| (except cotton) __ | – | – | – | – | 7.9 | 5.0 | 4.5 | 4.0 |
| Oil seeds | | | | | | | | |
| (soybeans, etc.) __ | – | – | – | – | 0.1 | 3.7 | 2.8 | 1.5 |
| Grain _____ | 21.3 | 12.1 | 6.3 | 8.3 | – | – | – | – |
| Consumer goods: _____ | 16.0 | 11.7 | 6.9 | 7.3 | 4.8 | 15.2 | 19.5 | 23.9 |
| Meat, dairy, eggs __ | 0.3 | 3.5 | 1.3 | 1.0 | 0.3 | 2.3 | 3.2 | 2.6 |
| Sugar _____ | 2.5 | 0.9 | 0.6 | 0.6 | – | 3.1 | 0.7 | 0.8 |
| Fabrics _____ | 4.8 | 2.0 | 0.9 | 1.3 | 0.4 | 3.9 | 3.8 | 3.0 |
| Fruits and vegetables | – | – | – | – | 1.9 | 0.5 | 1.5 | 2.4 |

During this period Soviet exports of machinery and equipment increased from 850 million rubles to 3.2 billion rubles whereas imports went up from 1.2 billion rubles to 4.3 billion rubles. The value of Russian imports of machinery and equipment exceeds exports. In the case of consumer goods the 1950 exports and imports were practically balanced, with exports amounting to 840 million rubles against 885 million rubles in imports. But in 1958 the USSR exported 1.2 billion rubles worth of consumer goods and imported 4.2 billion rubles, almost fourfold the value of exports.

Although Table 5 does not include Soviet exports of all ores and chemicals, the Russians export a large volume of them. About 3.2 million metric tons of iron ore was exported in 1950, 11.9 million metric tons in 1958, and 13.4 million tons in 1959. In 1950 the Russians exported almost 300 million metric tons of manganese ore but 980 million metric tons in 1959. Export of other ores and concentrates was likewise increased.

As to grain exports the Soviets have considerably increased sales from 2.9 million metric tons in 1950 to seven million metric tons in 1959. Along with grain the Russians increased exports in crabmeat and sugar but reduced butter sales. On the import side the Soviets take a larger volume of fruits, raw sugar, cereals, vegetable oils, fishery products, processed meat, tea, coffee, and tobacco.

The types of commodities exported and imported by the Soviets in 1958 have changed considerably since 1938, and even since 1950. In 1958 the communist orbit countries had altered their demands considerably from those made in 1950. Their economies had completely recovered from the devastation of World War II. The trend seems to be for orbit countries to import larger quantities of Soviet raw materials and machinery and to supply the Soviet Union with a greater volume of consumer goods. This does not mean to imply that the USSR is incapable of producing the goods received from them. It means that they are short of many raw materials but have the manpower and capacity to produce consumer goods in greater volume than capital goods. These imports, of course, increase the Soviet per capita consumption.

Generally, Soviet trade with non-communist countries has undergone a considerable alteration during the past few years, not only in the types of goods accepted by the Soviet Union but also in a more direct and efficient attitude on the part of Soviet officials. There is less haggling, less emphasis on the political affiliations, and greater stress on a business-like approach in the concluding of agreements to the satisfaction of both countries. The Russians, being good Marxists, know that materialistic interests between two countries will eventually lead to political questions, and since the Soviets are in a relatively favorable bargaining position they can bide their time. But at present their slogan seems to be "let's do it now on an equal basis and for mutual benefit."

As a result of this policy more and more orders are placed with non-communist countries for highly specialized industrial machinery such as chemical-processing equipment. This is evidenced by the willingness on the part of non-communist countries to lower the barriers to trade, and at the present negotiations in Paris, of the cooperating countries of NATO, to reduce the list of controlled commodities exported to the Soviets. This suggests that trading with the whole Soviet bloc may be increased in the future.

## Bibliography—Chapter 16

[1] *Bolshaya Sovetskaya Entsiklopediya*, No. 8, 2d Edition, Moscow, 1951, p. 288 for 1929-38 period; *Basic Data on the Economy of the USSR*, U. S. Department of Commerce, Bureau of Foreign Commerce, Washington, D. C., February 1956, p. 34.

[2] *Basic Data on the Economy of the USSR*, op. cit., p. 34; *Narodnoye Khozaystvo SSSR v 1958 Godu*, Moscow, 1959, p. 798.

[3] *Pravda*, December 2, 1956.

[4] *Bolshaya Sovetskaya Entsiklopediya*, op. cit., p. 290.

[5] *Moscow Radio Broadcast*, April 4, 1956.

[6] *The Washington Post and Times Herald*, April 29, 1956.

[7] Embassy of the USSR, *Press Department*, No. 342, October 21, 1959.

[8] *Ekonomicheskoye Sotrudnichestvo i Vzaimopomoshch Mezhdu Sovetskim Soyuzom i Evropeyskimi Stranami Narodnykh Demokratii*, Moscow, 1958, p. 144; Embassy of the USSR, *Press Department*, No. 342, 1943 and 252, October 21-22 and September 1959; *Vneshnaya Torgovlya SSSR za 1957 God*, Moscow, 1958, p. 9; *Sovetskaya Torgovlya*, October 16, 1958.

[9] *Vneshnaya Torgovlya SSSR za 1957 God*, op. cit., pp. 7-10; *Vneshnaya Torgovlya SSSR za 1958 God*, Moscow, 1959, pp. 7-10.

[10] *The New York Times*, August 16, 1959.

[11] *Vneshnaya Torgovliya SSSR za 1957 God*, op. cit., pp. 7-9.

[12] *Narodnoye Khozayastvo*, op. cit., pp. 798-804; *Norodnoye Khozaystvo SSSR v 1959 Godu*, Moscow, 1960, p. 722.

# CHAPTER 17

## Foreign Investments

### INTRODUCTION

As a debtor nation, precommunist Russia depended upon credit from industrial European countries. When the Bolsheviks refused to honor debts incurred by the Tsarist and Kerensky governments, these credit channels were closed. The lack of foreign credit at the time when the Soviets started the rehabilitation of their devastated economy was a strong motive in 1923 for formulation of the policy to "keep foreign investments out of Russia." Despite this policy the Soviets were forced to seek foreign credit to be used in payment for capital goods and raw materials purchased abroad. During the 1921-25 period the Soviets signed trade agreements with Great Britain and Germany, but only during the 1926-34 period was short-term credit finally granted to them. By 1931 Soviet Russia again became a debtor nation to the extent of 1.4 billion rubles.

As domestic industrial output of the Soviet Union increased dependence upon imports was reduced and exports increased. At the same time production of gold was expanded. Consequently, by 1933 Soviet foreign indebtedness was reduced to 450 million rubles. Confident of the stability of their government, the Soviets in that year asked Western countries for long-term credit. Czechoslovakia, the first country to take the risk, provided long-term credit to the USSR in 1935; Great Britain followed in 1936, Germany in 1939, and Sweden in 1940. Meantime, all short-term debts were paid off in 1936 and the Soviets claimed a foreign balance of payments. Nevertheless, during the 1918-40 period the Soviet Union, in general, was a debtor nation despite its credit worth eight million dollars granted to Turkey in 1934 and smaller amounts to Mongolia. Credit to the Turks was decidedly a political venture attempting to win the "Young Turks" and their leader Kemal Ataturk to the Soviet side.

458

With the beginning of World War II the Soviet Union again became a heavy debtor. During the war most of the credits came from the United States in the form of Lend-Lease, long-term assistance and from short-term loans amounting to 50 million dollars. Great Britain and Canada also provided the USSR with long-term credits. In 1945 the United States granted another credit of 244 million dollars to be used for payment of the Lend-Lease program. However, only a part of this sum was actually used by the Russians. Another postwar credit amounting to 772 million rubles was granted to the USSR by Sweden in 1946 but only half of this sum was spent.

Within a few years after the end of World War II the Soviet Union ceased to be a debtor nation. This sudden and perhaps unexpected change was achieved through military occupation of Eastern European countries. The satellites needed credit in order to restore and stabilize their economies. Since some of the industries located in the satellite countries required less capital and human resources to restore their normal production than similar industries located in the Soviet Union, it was more profitable for the Russians to invest in satellite countries than at home.

Soviet investments in non-communist countries started in 1953. The prime objective is economic and political penetration in the less developed countries, particularly those with a colonial past. While many of these countries are opposed to communism they are often impressed by Soviet industrial growth, technical achievements, and the types of assistance offered to them by the Soviets, who encourage this response by various slogans such as "equality" and "mutual benefit." These slogans are closely linked with ideas which show new political and economic horizons. The Russians well know from their own experiences that new ideas can be treated like future events; that ideas eventually lead to consequences profitable to the Soviets.

Soviet investments in non-communist countries are made by the State or its agencies for specific purposes. Before World War II such small-scale investments were made in foreign publishing enterprises, theaters, and in similar activities which attempted to facilitate the spread of the communist cause in many lands. Large-scale foreign investments were organized and implemented after World War II and took various forms, such as cash credits for the purpose of buying goods from the USSR, shipments of capital and consumer goods to countries which previously had no desire to deal with the Soviets, lending services and technical assistance to smaller nations, and providing outright gifts. In addition, a number of trading organizations sponsored by local Communists were established in Belgium, France, and Italy, serving as middlemen between the Soviet Union and foreign markets.

Like the United States after World War I, the Soviet Union emerged at the end of World War II as a great power and required new standards in international relations. Just as the United States was forced to abandon its isolationism, the Soviets were impelled to adjust their policies of self-sufficiency and to enter the field of foreign investments. Both nations were pushed into a new economic and political sphere of influence by circumstances beyond their control.

The 30-year period from the beginning of World War I to the end of World War II was a remarkable one. It was during this short span of time that many colonial societies became sovereign states and several sovereign states (the Baltic countries) became vassals of a larger state. It was the period of disillusionment for many nations who weighed the wisdom and goodness of the old values by which relations between "have" and "have not" countries were conducted. Old colonial ties were broken, political and economic loyalties were shaken, and new national meanings and values were sought by many societies. Many turned toward the USSR simply because there was no other way to turn at the time when the West was ineffective in providing·the needed leadership.

Soviet investments in underdeveloped areas are concentrated on projects of particular interest to the natives. Moreover, they are long-term investments, which do not involve a large and an immediate export commitment and can be spread over a longer period of time, thereby reducing the immediate burden on Soviet industrial capacity. By providing favorable credits to underdeveloped countries, the Soviets are attempting to bring these countries under their influence. It is true that economic assistance as a tool in directing of the political and economic lives of free countries is much slower than military occupation; nevertheless, it is less expensive and in the long run more certain.

## TYPES OF INVESTMENTS

Soviet foreign investments are of two types: first and most important are investments in communist countries; second is the assistance granted to non-communist countries.

The early pattern of Soviet total economic exploitation of the communist countries was alleviated by 1956, as indicated by the 1957 Soviet cancellation of debts amounting to six billion rubles, or some 21 per cent of the total credits granted to communist countries.[1] In addition, there were many other forms, of concessions, adjustments, and postponements in payments. The early Soviet economic assistance to communist countries was for the purpose of boosting their industrial production. It was erratic and involved little drain on the Soviet economy. Since 1956, however, the Soviets have attempted to establish economic cohesion among the USSR and Eastern European satellites, and this new objective constitutes a significant burden on Soviet resources.

In the case of Soviet investments in underdeveloped countries, Russian assistance represents about 28 per cent of the total grants to communist countries throughout the postwar period.[2] Such assistance is given for a number of purposes, mainly for industrial expansion, technical and military assistance, and educational programs. Since most underdeveloped countries do not have the resources to support rapid growth of their own economies, they welcome favorable assistance from the USSR. In their new nationalistic pride, they also feel that they are capable of controlling the internal threat of communism; many of them may overestimate their strength in this area.

## Soviet Assistance to Communist Countries

Beginning with 1945 the Soviet Union initiated assistance programs to Eastern European satellite countries. Poland was the first to receive credit. The Soviets grant four types of credits: long-term; intermediate; short-term; and foreign currency or gold.

Long-term credits are the most important and are usually for from ten to 15 years in duration, carrying an average annual interest rate of two per cent. Only Red China was able to obtain Soviet credit in 1950 at the rate of one per cent. As a rule, long-term credits are used for payments on imported Soviet machinery, equipment and technical assistance. In the main, long-term credits are repaid in goods. Only in a few exceptional cases are payments made either in gold or in freely convertible currency.

Intermediate credits have become prominent since 1947. They are granted when payments for current deliveries of goods cannot be covered by short-term credits. For example, because of unstable economic conditions in Hungary the Soviets granted this country intermediate credits in 1956 and again in 1957. To stabilize declining economic conditions in Poland in

1957, the Soviets granted such credit at two per cent annual interest, to be repaid in Polish goods during the 1958-60 period.

Short-term credits were more important prior to 1947. They are used to cover current deliveries of industrial raw materials, foodstuffs, and consumer goods. As a rule these credits are repaid within a year. Frequently short-term credits are needed to cover temporarily increased value of delivered goods from the USSR. This may happen when the Soviets deliver more expensive goods than anticipated. It is claimed by the Soviets that such adjustments in the value of delivered goods are spelled out in agreements, in which case the difference in value between exports and imports is covered by short-term credits.

Credits in convertible currency or in gold are granted to communist countries in order that they may settle their accounts with non-communist countries or to stabilize their shaky currencies. Only a few such credits have been granted.

Between 1945 and 1957 the Soviet Union claims to have given to communist countries over 28 billion rubles (seven billion American dollars) of which 21 billion rubles were long-term and intermediate credits.[3] The other seven billion rubles, or 25 per cent of the total, were short-term credits or credits in convertible currency or in gold. About 21 per cent of the total credits went to Poland and Red China (15 and six per cent, respectively).[4]

At the end of World War II, the Russians found themselves in a precarious position. Their own economy was facing inflation and scarcities of foodstuffs and consumer goods. During three years of war the circulation of money increased by 2.4 times, whereas production of consumer goods in 1945 was 59 per cent of the 1940 level.[5] Harassed by scarcities at home the Soviet government acted ruthlessly indeed.

In every country where Soviet troops were stationed, stripping of industrial facilities and equipment was well organized. Immediately upon entering the country special detachments of troops and civilians dismounted equipment; stocks of raw materials, semi-finished and finished goods were removed under the guise of "German assets" and "war booty." In some instances dismounted equipment and machinery were shipped as far as the Urals, and upon realizing that they could not be used there or elsewhere the Russians shipped them back to the original location. Removal of industrial facilities from already devastated economies further intensified the seriousness of the economic conditions in these stripped countries. In

Manchuria the Soviets removed about 858 million dollars worth of equipment. Even when the Austrian treaty was signed in May 1955 it was discovered that the Russians held about 300 more Austrian factories and other properties than were specified in the treaty and which the Austrian government expected to receive intact.[6] Other countries, too, experienced similar treatment.

In the occupied countries the Soviets used several methods of obtaining economic and political advantages. This was due to the difference in damage inflicted on each country during the war. In Poland and Hungary destruction of property was the greatest, whereas Czechoslovakia, Bulgaria, Rumania, and Albania generally escaped mass destruction. Poland was dealt the heaviest blow. In 1945 its agricultural output was only 38 per cent of the prewar level. Conditions in Poland were so bad that the UNRRA had spent 500 million dollars for the rehabilitation of the Polish economy by the end of 1947.

Perhaps the earliest Soviet investments, best known to the West, were the "joint" corporations formed with the satellites and in China. In the satellite countries, especially in Bulgaria, Hungary, Rumania, and the Soviet zone of Austria, a large share of the investments in the form of joint corporations and companies was obtained from German war assets. The total volume of such assets acquired by the USSR is not known, but it is estimated that in 1948 the German assets in Hungary alone were about 100 million dollars.[7]

During the 1945-47 period Hungary was forced to establish joint enterprises, such as the Soviet-Hungarian Civil Air Transportation Company, and joint companies in navigation and in the production of aluminum, crude oil, and other commodities. The Soviet Union gained substantially from these enterprises, which along with goods delivered by Hungary as reparations accelerated the recovery of the Russian economy.

In Rumania joint Soviet-Rumanian companies penetrated most of the economically important sectors, especially oil production and transportation. The Soviet-Rumanian oil-producing corporation Sokronpetrol was formed from confiscated assets. Similar examples of such joint investments were those built on Japanese war assets taken by the Soviets in Manchuria and North Korea. The top executive personnel of these enterprises were Russians, while local people held the lesser posts.

The magnitude of the jointly controlled and operated enterprises in European satellite countries is unknown. Nevertheless, it is reasonable to assume that from the viewpoint of the individual satellite country their contribution to Russian industrial recovery was significant. By 1957 the Soviet economy had fully recovered, and the socio-economic relations between the USSR and other communist countries underwent a drastic revision. As a result, Soviet ownership of these companies was returned to the satellites.

The role of Red China in the overall industrial expansion is extremely important. The success or failure of the industrialization of China's mainland is the determining factor in future political and economic trends, not only in Asia but in the Near East and Africa as well.

With the defeat of the Japanese in 1945 the Red Chinese government and the USSR agreed upon formation of several jointly controlled enterprises. Soviet investments came mainly from the confiscated Japanese assets. Holdings of shares in these companies were equally divided between the two countries, giving equal rights in ownership and operation. The list of joint companies included industrial plants, rail and air transportation, and banking facilities. Darien was established as a free port and Port Arthur was used jointly as a naval base, but upon turning over Port Arthur to the Chinese the Soviets received payments for defense work there.

The 1956-57 period was marked by heavy economic assistance to communist countries from the USSR. Hungarian uprisings and socio-economic adjustments in Poland and East Germany required large Soviet credits in addition to other grants. Only Czechoslovakia, North Vietnam, and Red China managed without Soviet assistance. This period was also marked by the loosening of the Soviet economic holds upon the Eastern European communist countries. This change came as a result of heavy financial obligations on the part of some of the countries to the USSR at the time when Khrushchev was talking about better living under communism. To relieve the economic pressure the Soviets cancelled old debts for Albania, Hungary, Poland, and Rumania. At the same time payment on old credits granted to Hungary, Poland, and Rumania were postponed for a period ranging from four to five years. Similarly, various other grants amounting to **over 2.8 billion rubles were provided** to East Germany, Hungary, Mongolia, North Korea, North Vietnam, and Poland.[8]

Data in Table 1 must be considered as an approximation rather than a precise evaluation because the Soviet Union provides assistance through other channels, not included in official statistics. Nevertheless, despite shortcomings in these statistics it is clear that during the 1956-57 period Hungary, Poland, and East Germany were major recipients of Soviet credits—over 60 per cent of the total.

TABLE 1—*Soviet Economic Assistance to Communist Countries: 1956-57* [9]
(in millions of rubles)

| Country | Credits | Credits Convertible currency or gold | Cancelled debts |
|---|---|---|---|
| Albania _____ | 191 | – | 422 |
| Bulgaria _____ | 570 | – | – |
| Czechoslovakia _____ | – | – | – |
| East Germany _____ | 1,120 | 720 | – |
| Hungary _____ | 1,340 | 490 | 680 |
| Mongolia _____ | 200 | – | – |
| North Korea _____ | 170 | – | – |
| North Vietnam _____ | – | – | – |
| Poland _____ | 1,200 | 147 | 2,100 |
| Red China _____ | – | – | – |
| Rumania _____ | 414 | – | 1,075 |
| Yugoslavia _____ | 776 | 440 | – |
| TOTAL _____ | 5,981 | 1,797 | 4,277 |

The currency credits include convertible foreign currencies and gold. The Soviets granted such credits to Poland in 1947 amounting to 147 million rubles, to Czechoslovakia in 1948, and to East Germany in 1953. The last two credits, of unspecified amounts, are probably less than those to Poland. The 1956-57 currency credits make up 30 per cent of the total credits. Increased emphasis on such credits is closely associated with expanding international trading contacts among Eastern European communist countries and the West.

Cancelled debts, according to the Soviets, amounted to six billion rubles during the 1945-57 period. However, the 1956-57 cancellation represents over 70 per cent of the total. Moreover, this account includes cancellation of credits and other accounts not related to credits indebtedness.

The 1956-57 cancellation of Albanian debts was as a result of increased trade with other European communist countries which needed a rapid turnover of their investments. If Albania had to pay all its debts to the Soviet Union and to other communist countries simultaneously, it would have to depend upon new credits, would increase its indebtedness with other countries, and the USSR would have to provide additional credits to Albania. On the other hand, by cancelling Albania's debts the Soviets gain in propaganda as an "unselfish" and "generous" giant, always ready to help out a smaller country.

Cancellation of Hungarian credits took the form of the transfer of joint Soviet-Hungarian investments, mostly German assets, to Hungary. This account represented 50 per cent of the total Hungarian cancellation. The other half of the cancellation was on Russian-credits.

The largest recipient of cancellations was Poland. At the end of the war the Poles were forced to sign an agreement with the Soviet Union for the delivery of 12 million metric tons of coal per year to the Soviets at low rates for as long as Germany was occupied by the Russians. The so-called Polish debt cancellation was actually the accumulated difference between the low price on coal which the Soviets paid and the agreed higher price to recover the losses inflicted by the USSR during the 1946-53 period.

As in the case of Hungary, Rumanian debts were cancelled mainly through the transfer of Soviet investments in joint Soviet-Rumanian enterprises. In addition, some of the payments which were due during the 1957-59 period also were cancelled.

True, the sum of cancelled debts is large, especially during the 1956-57 period, but they did not drain Soviet resources. Moreover, there is no assurance that these debts will not be reinstated by the Soviet Union. It can be assumed that these accounts will never appear in the press but they may take different types of accounts payable to the USSR. Besides, these cancellations can be used by the Soviets to obtain other political or economic gains.

## Soviet Assistance to Underdeveloped Countries

Soviet economic assistance to highly developed countries is non-existent. However, the Soviets provided credits to so-called intermediate countries. For example, Argentina obtained credit from the USSR in 1953 to be used in payments for Soviet goods. Finland in 1954 and 1955 received Soviet credit amounting to 320 million rubles from which she could draw in gold, dollars, or any other currency during the period of three years. Credit was to be repaid in ten years at two per cent annual interest. These credits are politically inspired. The bulk of Soviet economic assistance is flowing to underdeveloped countries. In general, more economically advanced non-communist countries have trade agreements and scientific and cultural exchange programs with the USSR.

Soviet assistance to underdeveloped countries consists of interest-bearing credits, technical and educational assistance, grants, and gifts. These represent a definite pattern in investments and in activities. Most important is the credit granted to another government to be used for the purchase of Russian goods and for technical assistance. Another type of credit, provided to foreign business firms or organizations, usually consists of short-term credit for the payment of imported Soviet consumer goods.

Soviet credits are attractive since they are granted at low interest rates, usually at 2.5 per cent annually. These rates as a rule are higher than to communist countries by one-half of one per cent. In addition, prices which the Soviets use in their relations with non-communist countries are based mostly on the average world market prices. But certain Soviet prices have been much higher, and at times the USSR quoted still higher prices to discourage foreign demand for specific goods which are still in short supply in the Soviet Union.

As a rule, Soviet long-term credits provide for annual negotiations in the future as far as types of goods, prices, and volume of goods to be delivered in payment. This, of course, leaves a wide margin for later Soviet bargaining, which may become a source of friction as with Yugoslavia, or of politically motivated generosity as with Indonesia. These are short-run protective measures which can be effectively used by the Soviets.

This pattern of Soviet investment is significant, for it reveals Russian interests, which lead to conclusions that the Soviet Union, at least at present, does not fear competition from countries which they help to industrialize. There are indications that such a policy has four main objectives: (1) it attempts to increase industrialization of the country for the purpose of producing more goods for the local population, thereby increasing the level of living; (2) it is directed toward more self-sufficiency in goods which were previously imported from the West; (3) it provides raw materials for the Soviet economy; and (4) it creates good will and friendship toward the Soviet Union.

Since present concentrations of Soviet investments are found in transportation, electric power development, storage facilities, plants, and factories, the immediate impact of such investments may not affect the trade relations with the Western exporting countries. But at the same time it is reasonable to assume that with better transportaion, for example, more raw materials may be produced and transported to plants and factories which may be built in the near future, producing greater volumes of goods for domestic and foreign markets. It can also be assumed that increases in production of goods which are now being imported from the West may result in keener competition among exporting Western nations, creating disagreements even among the nations of similar political loyalties. This is most certainly a political objective of the USSR.

The postwar development in international relations caused a radical change from the prewar self-sufficiency doctrine. The new phase of Soviet foreign relations is based on the principle of closer bonds linking the Soviet Union with the broad masses of disillusioned peoples throughout the world. Propaganda methods of the past were never very successful. Military occupation of sovereign countries also became outmoded. One of the newest and still unexplored methods of the USSR is the far-flung program of economic assistance to underdeveloped countries. It is a new twist in the original faith of the communist doctrine that distribution of wealth could be achieved through increased production of goods and services by the people in each country and at the same time would destroy economic dependence on the Western market. In other words, traditional anticipation of internal revolution by the masses is losing ground. But the Russians still hope to contribute, in their own way perhaps, to build a better life for underprivileged people. Since internal revolutionary forces cannot be used for this purpose, another avenue for the Russians, at least theoretically, is to provide help to the peoples in terms of economic assistance.

Soviet foreign assistance is selective and heavily concentrated in a few underdeveloped countries which are important to the Soviet Union as friendly or potentially friendly nations who may influence world opinion in favor of the USSR. The largest recipients of Soviet assistance are the UAR, India, Iraq, Indonesia, and Afghanistan. Afghanistan, like Finland, is too close to the USSR to reject Soviet assistance. The earlier Soviet tactics of economic assistance differ from the current approach, as shown in the contrast between the tactics used in Iran in 1946 and in India in 1954.

While the Soviet troops were still in Iran at the end of World War II, the Soviet government put strong pressure on the Iranian government for the formation of a joint stock Soviet-Iranian oil company to be operated near the Caspian Sea. This was a move to prevent other countries, especially Great Britain and the United States, from obtaining oil concessions there. A tentative agreement was proposed in April 1946, with 51 per cent of the company's stock to be owned by the Soviet Union and 49 per cent by the Iranian government for a period of 25 years. The Iranian government appealed to the United Nations for protection from the Soviet pressures, and this created unfavorable world opinion toward the USSR. In defense against further Soviet menacing tactics, in October 1947 the Iranian government enacted a law that prohibited the granting of oil concessions under any circumstances to any country, and the Soviets failed to obtain oil concessions there. Apparently the Soviets are satisfied with this arrangement and no longer exert pressure for Iranian oil.

After a lull of about seven years the USSR and Afghanistan in August and September of 1954 signed agreements for industrial credits. The Soviet Union was to expand petroleum storage facilities previously built by the Soviets, and another credit of 14 million rubles was granted for the construction of two grain elevators, a mechanized flour mill, and a bakery to be completed in 1956. The annual interest rate for these intermediate credits was set at three per cent. Then in October 1956 a long-term credit amounting to 400 million rubles was given to Afghanistan, a 30-year credit at two per cent interest payable after eight years of utilization of the credit. Payments are to be made in Afghan commodities.[10] This credit covers the cost of construction of 14 projects and technical assistance associated with these projects. Among other things, the Soviets pledged to construct two hydroelectric power plants, three automobile repair shops, and several highway and irrigation projects. It was also reported that in October 1958 another credit of an unspecified amount was granted to Afghanistan for the purpose of purchasing Soviet-made equipment for complete factories.

Trade relations between India and the USSR were established in December 1953. At that date it was a modest trade agreement, but important agreements involving large investments came in 1955 and 1956. On February 2, 1955, India and the Soviet Union signed an agreement under which the Soviets were to build a modern metallurgical plant at Bhilai. All instruments, equipment, machinery, and tools were to be Russian-made, and installations were to be under the supervision of Russian technical personnel. The total cost of the project was estimated at one billion rupees (840 million rubles). The project was to be completed by December 31, 1959. Payments to the Soviet Union on this loan are to be made in 12 annual installments. The annual rate of interest on the amount outstanding each year is to be 2.5 per cent. Payments are to be made in rupees and put into a special account opened for this purpose in the Reserve Bank of

India. The amounts thus credited to this account may be used by the Russians for the purchase of goods in India, or, if desired, may be converted into pounds sterling. Prices for exported and imported goods were negotiated on the presentation of the final report on the progress of the project.

Then on May 21, 1956, another agreement was signed in Delhi for the purchase from the Soviet Union of oil drilling equipment worth 7.4 million rupees. Under the agreement Soviet specialists were to install this equipment without charge. They were to supervise the installation of the equipment and to train Indian operators to use it. In addition, the Soviet Machine Exporting Agency was to supply seismological equipment for oil survey and equipment for the drilling of blasting bores. In November 1957 another credit amounting to 500 million rubles was made for the purpose of buying Soviet goods. In the same year the Soviet Union made the Indian government an offer to supply equipment and technical assistance to modernize the operations of the Panna diamond mine, India's only active diamond mine. Soviet experts estimate this mine's reserves at 33 million carats and anticipate that with modernization the daily output may be increased to 1,900 carats, whereas in 1954 this mine produced only 1,950 carats.[11]

Soviet-Indian economic relations were further cemented by Khruschev's visit to India early in 1960. It was promised that a number of new enterprises will be built in India by Russian engineers, technicians, and workers. At the same time, in addition to previous credits, the Soviet Union granted India a new credit of 1.5 billion rubles.[12] The Russians emphasized that such friendly relations are economically desirable not only for the peoples of the two countries but also as an important contribution to the strengthening of the principles of peaceful coexistence, of which Khrushchev is the greatest advocate.

Still another type of Soviet investment may be mentioned. In September 1956 the Soviet Union and Indonesia signed an agreement by which a loan of 400 million rubles worth of goods, machinery, and industrial equipment was granted to Indonesia. The Indonesian Parliament finally ratified this agreement in February 1958. Indonesia is to repay the Soviet Union in 12 annual installments, beginning after the first three years of effective use of Russian-made equipment. As with India, this, too, is a long-term credit carrying 2.5 per cent interest but to be paid by Indonesia in American dollars or British pound sterling. At the same time it was reported that the Soviet trading organization negotiated short-term credit with private Indonesian firms at no interest on credits which are to be used for the purchase of capital goods from the USSR. In 1957 and 1958 two **credits, of unspecified amounts, were granted** at two per cent annual interest for the purchase of 4,000 Soviet motor vehicles, repair shops, and spare parts.

Then in 1960 the USSR granted another loan of 250 million dollars to the Indonesian government for the construction of steel foundries, steel works, chemical and other plants, textile mills, and other industrial establishments. The Russians agreed to deliver a nuclear reactor for scientific research and to train local specialists. At the same time Khrushchev, who was in Indonesia, promised to build a hospital in Jakarta with 200 beds and an attached polyclinic as a gift to the Republic of Indonesia. Khrushchev also presented two libraries to Indonesian universities and a technological institute to train the natives in shipbuilding and oceanography.

It is obvious even from these few examples of Soviet foreign investments that their success is based on a few simple factors. In the first place, the Soviets' charges for interest are below those of the Western countries not only in the rate itself but also in terms of currency. For example, the interest rate on Soviet long-term credit is 2.5 per cent in terms of rubles or in the local currency which easily may be converted into prices of importing or exporting commodities. The Western countries charge about five per cent. In long-term credit the Soviets allow time for the construction and actual operation of facilities before the interest rate is required. In the second place, Russians take the locally produced goods which, at times, many of the Western nations refuse to accept in payments. In the third place, the Soviets grant credit for any enterprise without fear of potential competition. The leaders of underdeveloped countries, therefore, do see advantages in Soviet aid.

However, much of the Soviet exported equipment, machinery, and instruments are actually produced not in the Soviet Union but in satellite countries, and are ordered or obtained from them by the Soviets through trade agreements and re-exported to non-communist countries. Again, some of the communist-made equipment is as good as can be found on the Western market, and in many cases skepticism as to its quality is unfounded.

According to Table 2 the large credit recipients—the UAR and India —received more than 42 per cent of the total credits granted by the Soviet Union. Recently, Ethiopia was granted a 400 million ruble credit and the

Republic of Guinea 140 million rubles. But the precise amount of money involved in foreign commitments by the Russians is not revealed. It has been estimated that Russia's foreign credits to non-communist countries

TABLE 2—*Estimated Soviet Credits to Selected Underdeveloped Countries: 1956-1957* [13]

| Country | Million rubles |
|---|---|
| Afghanistan | 400 |
| Burma | 160 |
| Egypt | 700 |
| India | 840 |
| Indonesia | 400 |
| Iraq | 550 |
| Syria | 672 |
| Turkey | 40 |
| Others | 1,238 |
| TOTAL | 5,200 |

between 1956 and 1957 total approximately 5.2 billion rubles or about 1.3 billion dollars.[14] Therefore, in 1957 the total Soviet commitment to communist and non-communist countries may be estimated at 33.2 billion rubles, or 8.4 billion dollars.

The importance which the Soviet Union places on international relations is rapidly increasing. This may be seen in the fact that in July 1957 Mikhail Pervukhin, a member of the Presidium of the Communist Party, was transferred from the post of Minister of Medium-Machine Building and appointed Chairman of a new State Committee for Foreign Economic Relations. This committee was reorganized from the old one which was previously entrusted with economic relations with the countries of the communist orbit only. Presumably the new committee is to deal with economic relations with all countries, and it is reasonable to believe that the USSR Ministry of Foreign Trade was also reorganized, since the present Soviet emphasis is not only on foreign trade but also on foreign investments.

If these changes mean expansion in economic assistance, then perhaps the USSR would have to allocate a greater volume of its resources for that purpose. However, no country has unlimited capabilities for economic assistance and the Soviet Union already has difficulties in supplying the

Seven-Year Plan with resources. These internal shortages were admitted by Khrushchev during his visit to the United States, and whatever economic assistance the underdeveloped countries receive from now on would come increasingly from other communist countries rather than from the USSR. Reduction of the military expenditures, by the way, is used by the Russians as a source of greater assistance to underdeveloped countries.

The question of Soviet investment in underdeveloped countries was emphasized by Khrushchev on his visits to the United States, Asia, and France. According to Khrushchev, the Soviet Union will continue to invest in this sphere independently of other members of the United Nations as long as agreement on disarmament is not reached. This policy was applied in the Congo. He also stressed the fact that the USSR's policy is to assist underdeveloped countries in creating their own industry. This, of course, means a larger industrial labor force and unionization of the natives from which a potential revolutionary movement, encouraged by the Russians, may be created to speed up the process of socialization of politically weak nations.

All in all, Khrushchev is satisfied with Soviet investment in underdeveloped countries. In 1960 the Soviet Union will invest in 22 countries where 383 various industrial enterprises will be constructed or under construction. He also hopes that the successful fulfillment of the current Seven-Year Plan and the cuts in military appropriations will enable the USSR to invest even more in Afro-Asian countries. In the UAR alone, the Soviets render assistance in the construction and expansion of nearly 100 projects ranging from the Aswan Dam to the installation of an atomic reactor.

Another phenomenon related to foreign relations is the number of Soviet citizens traveling abroad and the number of foreign businessmen now visiting the Soviet Union. It is reported that in 1956 a total of 487,000 visitors from 84 nations including communist countries visited the USSR; 319,000 were persons on business. About 548,000 Soviet citizens, including 416,000 officials making business trips, visited 61 countries. In contrast, about 2,500 Americans visited the USSR in 1956 while only 350 Russians went to the United States. The Soviet Intourist Bureau estimated that in 1957 about 500,000 foreign citizens came to the Soviet Union, and of this number more than 300,000 were on business. Foreign visitors on business to the Soviet Union include government officials who must go to Moscow to clarify certain aspects of their economic dealings with the Soviets and private businessmen coming to seek new business with Moscow or to iron out misunderstandings which the Soviet local trade representatives are unable to solve. In 1958 over 50,000 foreign tourists from the free world visited the USSR against 30,000 in 1957, and tourism to the Soviet Union continues to expand.

## TECHNICAL ASSISTANCE AND AID

Foreign investments include not only credit in currency and goods but also factors directly or indirectly associated with promotion of foreign investments. Since such activities represent costs and are devised to create certain impressions upon potential consumers, they are included in foreign investments. Some expenditures of this nature may be redeemed, but the bulk of them can be associated with creation of good will and advertising.

One of these is technical assistance. In most of the Soviet agreements a clause for technical assistance and cultural exchange is included and covers a variety of purposes. The Soviet technicians install machinery and equipment and train natives to operate it. In the case of India's steel mill, the Russians are to provide technicians for three years after the mill reaches its full capacity. Since the full capacity of this mill was reached at the end of 1959, the Soviet technicians will remain there until 1962.

Soviet technical personnel are present in Afghanistan, Iran, Burma, and in other underdeveloped countries. They make surveys in the field, estimate the demand for materials and equipment, calculate availability of raw materials, and draw plans for construction of enterprises. Most of their activities are devoted to major economic problems dealing with natural resources and potential use of them. Thus, Soviet technicians—less than 3,000 of them—are mapping out the local resources, and data based on their findings are available to the Soviets.

In addition to direct technical assistance the Soviets train thousands of foreign students and workers in the Soviet Union in specific fields ranging from the use of tractors on farms to the operation of complex equipment in steel mills. Besides this, individual Soviet plants and factories invite foreign workers for short visits to see their plants; they also send their own workers to foreign factories to see how they are run and to advise in increasing efficiency. The number of Soviet students going abroad for completion of their studies in modest, but emphasis on the exchange of students and scientific personnel is being intensified even with the United States.

The Soviet foreign-aid program consists of well-publicized construction or "gifts" of hospitals, recreation installations, and educational facilities. In Cambodia the construction of a 500-bed hospital supplied with Soviet medical equipment was started in 1958. Libya, too, accepted the Soviet offer to construct, equip, and staff two hospitals. In Burma the Soviets are building a 200-bed hospital, and in Nepal they· are constructing a 50-bed hospital. Other countries also have received Soviet medical supplies, vaccine, drugs, X-ray units, and free medical training for the natives. These gifts and aid are humanitarian, but they are also a part of Soviet tactics which effectively entrench the Russians wherever they have established permanent residence.

Since 1953 the Soviets have expanded their advertising campaign abroad. Advantages of advertising were realized as an important implement in mass communication. A large share of such advertising is conducted by the Soviet trade agencies which use billboards, brochures, and local newspapers to announce the openings of showrooms where Soviet-made goods may be seen by businessmen, industrialists, and engineers. The largest share of advertising is done in the form of brochures, which include information such as the Soviet annual output of coal, oil, and the like along with announcements of displays.

Even prior to 1953 the Soviet Union began to participate in international fairs, both in the bloc and in non-communist countries. In 1954 the Soviet Union exhibited its products in 11 non-communist countries, of which eight were in Western Europe and only three were in underdeveloped countries. In 1955 the Soviets exhibited their wares in 16 international fairs, including nine in Western Europe and five in underdeveloped countries. Even Argentina and Ecuador had Soviet fair exhibits. The 1956 participation in international fairs was even more extensive and the exhibits were larger, better planned, and more impressive than in previous years. In 1959 Soviet exhibits were held in the United States and Mexico. Most of the Soviet exhibits are made up of large items, impressive in size but poorly adapted to local conditions. For example, in 1955 the Soviets exhibited their large grain combines in India, where grain plots are too small for effective use of large-scale machinery. Nevertheless, the Russians learn quickly from their Western competitors, and greater numbers of Soviet-made consumer goods are being exhibited. Many of the exhibited items are not for sale and prices are not quoted; they are shown to impress the masses rather than to encourage individual transactions.

## Bibliography—Chapter 17

[1] *Ekonomicheskoye Sotrudnichestvo i Vzaimopomoshch Mezhdu Sovetskim Soyuzom i Evropeyskimi Stranami Narodnykh Demokratii* (hereinafter referred to as *Ekonomicheskoye Sotrudnichestvo*), Moscow, 1958, p. 55.

[2] *Ibid.; The Sino-Soviet Economic Offensive in the Less Developed Countries,* U. S. Department of State, Government Printing Office, Washington, D. C., 1958, p. 23.

[3] *Gosudarstvennyy Bank SSSR,* Moscow, 1957, p. 209; Atlas, Z. V., *Denezhnoye Obrashcheniye i Kredit SSSR,* Moscow, 1957, p. 432.

[4] *Ekonomicheskoye Sotrudnichestvo,* op. cit., pp. 55, 57; Atlas, *op. cit.,* p. 432.

[5] Lifits, M. L., *Sovetskaya Torgovlya i ee Rol' v Ekonomicheskoy Zhizni Strany,* Moscow, 1950, p. 40; *Narodnoye Khozaystvo SSSR,* Moscow, 1956, p. 47.

[6] *Soviet Political Agreements and Results,* Committee on the Judiciary, U. S. Senate. 84th Congress, 2d Session, Washington, D. C., 1956, pp. ix, 20.

[7] *Soviet Bloc Economic Activities in the Free World,* Mutual Defense Assistance Control Act of 1951, 6th report to Congress, 2d half of 1954, Washington, D. C., June 30, 1955, p. 4.

[8] *The Sino-Soviet Economic Offensive, op. cit., p.* 16.

[9] *Ibid.; Economicheskoye Sotrudnichestvo,* op. cit., pp. 55-8; Atlas, *op. cit.,* pp. 432-33; *Finansy i Sotsialisticheskoye Stroitel'stvo,* Moscow, 1957, pp. 329-31.

[10] Leontiev, L. A., *Osnovnaya Ekonomicheskaya Zadacha SSSR,* Moscow, 1956, p. 179; *The Washington Post and Times Herald,* October 18, 1956.

[11] *Jewelers' Circular Keystone,* April 29, 1956.

[12] Embassy of the USSR, *Press Department,* No. 121, Washington, D. C., March 8, 1960.

[13] *Vneshnaya Torgovlya SSSR so Stranami Azii, Afriki i Latinskoy Ameriki,* Moscow, 1958, pp. 16, 30, 49, 106-09; *The Washington Post and Times Herald,* August 27, 1957; *The Baltimore Sun,* April 26, 1959; *The Sino-Soviet Economic Offensive,* op. cit., pp. 26-7.

[14] *The Sino-Soviet Economic Offensive,* op. cit., p. 21.

## CHAPTER 18

# Standard of Living

~~~~~~~~~~~~~~~~~~~~~~~~~~~~~

## INTRODUCTION

Communist Russia organized its economy on the principle of public ownership of factors of production and on "administered" distribution of goods, services, and incomes. In other words, theoretically, the society as a whole, represented by its leadership, determines priority in production, the volume to be produced, and what each citizen should contribute to the society. The products derived are the property of the society, to be divided in accordance with socially determined rules. Since the Communist Party represents the society, production and distribution are thus administered by a small group of people who are responsible for the welfare of the country and improvement in the standard of living of the Russian people.

The Soviets are boastfully proud of their spectacular development in industrial production. They point out that the illiterate peasant of 1917, who was ignorant of technology, now produces complex modern equipment, airplanes, sputniks, and hydrogen bombs. No matter how much one might distrust Soviet statistics the growth of industrial output is indeed impressive. Continuous growth of industrial output reflects several factors. In the first place, the USSR is still a relatively young country industrially, so that any increase in relation to past output seems to be large. In the second place, the utilization of manpower is not as efficient as in the United States, and can be improved. In the third place, a relatively rapid rate of industrial growth is maintained by holding down personal consumption, by low incomes in industry and agriculture, and by greater diversion of investments into production of capital goods.

Although the Soviet consumer is restricted in freedom of choice, social welfare does exist in the USSR, and administered by the few for the many.

Soviet concentration on production of non-consumer goods seems to be of a long-range nature, but it is not necessarily a permanent phenomenon. Lenin insisted that only an increased volume of capital goods can serve as the material basis for socialism. Later, Stalin emphasized the fact that a decline in the rate of expansion in capital goods would be suicidal. Stalin declared in 1950 that a completely communist state could exist only when production of consumer goods in the Soviet Union reached three times the 1940 level. Thus, to Lenin and Stalin, expansion of capital goods was the only correct policy through which production of consumer goods would be increased. This policy was formulated in the early part of the Soviet regime; it has been accepted by Khrushchev and will continue in the future until Soviet leaders are satisfied with the achievement of their goals.

According to Soviet statistics, Stalin's dream of consumer goods attaining three times the 1940 level is to be reached in 1965. Yet, to Khrushchev, increasing the availability of consumer goods will not insure a completely communist state. To reach such a goal not only involves availability of consumer goods but also requires reshaping the existing institutions to fit the pattern of a pure communist society. Actually, the Russians have increased output of consumer goods and improved their standard of living without moving any closer to a completely communist state than they were in Stalin's era. What is more important is the response of the Russian people to a slight improvement of their standard of living. They compare their level of existence today with that of last month or last year but never with that of the United States or Great Britain.

## FAMILY EARNINGS

How do conditions of administered distribution affect a family's standard of living? The Soviet distribution system has moved from the early policy "to each according to his needs" to the present policy—"to each according to his ability." The early policy is always in the background, representing a pure communist state, implying that in the distant future goods will be distributed almost freely to all. The present distribution system is more realistic and based on the principle that different people, unequal in their abilities and requirements, are remunerated according to his efforts in social production. This is the stage which the Soviets have reached now.

Since a planned economy requires tight control over wages, prices, taxes, and consumption, the average worker is subjected to many economic forces controlled by the State. Under these conditions the State may decide to increase the purchasing power of the people by increasing the wage level and keeping prices and taxes unchanged, or by reducing prices and holding the wage level stable, or by reducing taxes while other factors remain equal. The government also might use a combination of several forces of varying degree at the same time. Since 1953 the Soviets have employed flexible monetary and fiscal policies in increasing the purchasing power of the people. The average wage has been increased, taxes have been reduced, and prices paid by the State for agricultural commodities have been increased. Other social measures have also been undertaken which resulted in the increase of purchasing power of the population. This trend started before World War II; it was interrupted by the war, to be resumed after the end of the war but at a much slower rate than before it.

The Soviets began to consider increasing wages and production of consumer goods during the Second Five-Year Plan. These increases were planned in close relationship with industrial expansion. During World War II the whole complex relationship of controlled wage-price-tax-consumption levels was distorted and was, in the main, ignored. As a result, strong inflationary forces developed which were checked only in 1947. After the end of the war, and particularly after the recovery of the economy in 1950, the Soviet leaders and their press began to emphasize real income, which is quite different from cash income. Cash income represents a money wage, whereas real income, in general, includes all state and social payments to employed and unemployed workers and their families. Therefore, the Soviets' real income relates to the society as a whole, whereas the cash income applies to that sector of the population which actively participates in the economic activity of the country.

## Cash Income

The average industrial worker in the Soviet Union receives his cash income from many sources, according to his skill, overtime work, seniority, geographic location of employment, and the like. From these sources the average annual cash income for the country is derived.

In 1955, as in 1958, the most important sources of cash income for industrial workers were piecework and progressive rates, which together represented 65 per cent of the total income. Hourly rates accounted for another 16 per cent. These three sources, plus premium payments, represented about 85 per cent of the average worker's cash income.

TABLE 1—*Sources of Cash Income for Industrial Workers for the Economy as a Whole in 1955* [1]

| Source | Per cent |
|---|---|
| Total: | 100.0 |
| Stable piecework rate | 59.5 |
| Hourly rates | 15.6 |
| Payments for vacation | 6.3 |
| Progressive rates for piecework | 5.5 |
| Premiums | 4.1 |
| Seniority payments | 3.7 |
| Extra payments for adverse working conditions | 0.4 |
| Overtime payments | 0.2 |
| Payments for stoppages and delays | 0.2 |
| Other | 4.5 |

The average annual cash income of state employees in 1940 was 4,054 rubles, and in 1956 it reached 8,500 rubles, or more than double, but between 1954 and 1956 the increase was about four per cent.[2] Between 1956 and 1958 this income remained practically unchanged. But workers in the lower income brackets received much less than that average. To assist the lower income groups the Soviets in 1956 increased their annual cash income. By this act the Soviets somewhat increased the purchasing power of the low income groups, and at the same time reduced bidding power of higher income groups.

One may wonder how workers receiving low incomes fared when the average income for the country was three times what they received. There is a simple explanation. Most Russian families have more than one wage earner. In 1956 the average size of a Soviet family was about three persons. The average urban family consisted of 2.3 persons, and the average collective farm family 4.1 persons. In that year 45 per cent of all state-employed workers were women. Moreover, between 1940 and 1956 the proportion of dependents per family was reduced from 52.9 per cent to 46.2 per cent. Thus, in general, family income is derived from more than one provider. On the other hand, there are workers receiving more than the average monthly income. This group includes physicians, dentists, lawyers, professors, writers, artists, and others who have private practices or are self-employed. The Soviet tax form covers different annual incomes ranging from 1,800 rubles to 70,001-and-over rubles. Anyone receiving 1,800 rubles annually from sources other than state employment pays 2.5 per cent in income tax. If one is fortunate enough to make 70,001 rubles or over from private sources, he is taxed 31,714 rubles plus 69 per cent for the amount over 70,000 rubles. A man earning 70,000 rubles gross annually would net about 38,290 rubles after taxes, which is 4.5 times above the average gross earnings of industrial workers.

Undoubtedly, the income range, from a minimum of 270 rubles to a maximum of about 6,000 rubles a month, includes a far greater number of wage earners in the lower range than the higher. But there should be no doubt that the Soviet wage range is not wide. The messenger, janitor, watchman and domestic are in the low wage bracket. An elevator operator receives 540 rubles a month, and a salesgirl in a large department store receives a straight 900 to 1,000 rubles a month. But many top executives receive as much as 6,000 rubles a month. These represent the Soviet elite—business and intellectual leaders, including managers of large-scale enterprises and men and women of the arts and sciences. In 1956 the USSR counted about 206,000 enterprises employing high-salaried personnel; 240,000 scientists working in research, education, and state enterprises; over 329,000 physicians; not to mention countless high-ranking personnel in the Armed Forces, many of whom receive a monthly income of 6,000 rubles or more.

In the middle-income range, wage control has been difficult to achieve for many reasons. First, the Soviet Union has many industries which are inadequately mechanized where the average income is far below that of highly mechanized industries. Again, the penalities for paying wages above those specified in government plans are less severe than those for below-plan production. This encourages management to hoard high-priced labor. To provide incentives for highly skilled workers, scientists, and administrators, higher incomes must be offered.

Let us assume that a worker in Moscow receives an average gross cash income of 8,500 rubles a year, or about 708 rubles a month, to support his wife and one child. From this he must pay income tax, rent, household expenses, and make other expenditures. His first 370 rubles of monthly income, or 4,400 rubles annually, is tax exempt. The rates of taxation range from 0.15 to 13 per cent. A maximum of 13 per cent is taken in taxes from the amount received over 12,000 rubles annually and does not apply to incomes in the middle bracket. If a worker has more than three dependents his income tax is reduced by 30 per cent, but since the worker under our consideration has only two dependents his taxable income amounts to 4,100 rubles, on which he pays 5.2 per cent—about 213 rubles a year.[3]

His rent is low. It is calculated in terms of occupied square meters including kitchen and bathroom. Each square meter of occupied space costs the worker 1.32 rubles per month. In 1957 the city of Moscow constructed new housing for 71,800 families averaging 11.6 square meters per family.[4] This is equivalent to about 125 square feet, or roughly a small one-bedroom apartment. For such an apartment the worker pays 15.30 rubles a month, including steam heat and janitor service. This represents about two per cent of his gross monthly income. His gas costs him about ten rubles a month, telephone 29 rubles; if he has a television set he pays a monthly tax of ten rubles, and another three rubles tax on his radio. In all, his income tax, rent, and utility expenditures amount to approximately 85 rubles per month, or 12 per cent of his gross monthly income.

The other 623 rubles of his monthly income are allocated for food, entertainment, contributions to various causes, trade union fees, transportation, vacations, consumer goods, and other expenditures. Education for the worker's children is free, as is his medical care; medicine is inexpensive. His expenditure for state bonds in 1956 amounted to 59 rubles, or 8.4 per cent of his gross income, but this compulsory purchase of bonds was abolished in 1958. His non-food and non-consumer goods expenditures amount to roughly 100 rubles per month, plus the 85 rubles for income tax, housing, and utilities—a total of 185 to 200 rubles. Thus, out of his gross cash monthly income of 708 rubles the worker has about 500 rubles for food, consumer goods, and services.

At the beginning of 1956 the population of Moscow was 4,847,000. During the entire year of 1955 the state and cooperative retail stores, restaurants, tea house, and other state retail establishments in Moscow sold 44.7 billion rubles worth of food and non-food commodities.[5] The average monthly per capita sale of food and consumer goods amounted to 768 rubles, of which 54 per cent (415 rubles) was spent on food and 46 per cent (353 rubles) on non-food commodities. It is obvious that a worker with two dependents cannot support his family on his 708 rubles alone when his basic expenditures must be upwards of 2,300 rubles, of which food for three persons would amount to 1,245 rubles. To supplement his earnings his wife must be fully employed, and even if she receives as much as he does their combined total gross income of 1,416 rubles will not be sufficient to cover the average monthly expenditures for food and non-food items in Moscow.

In general, the average industrial worker in Moscow purchases less goods and services than he would like to have. One may wonder why the average per capita consumption of food and non-food commodities is higher than the average monthly income of the industrial worker. This is because of the large number of highly paid workers and employees—especially in Moscow, the administrative center of the USSR—who have greater purchasing power than the average industrial workers. On January 1, 1941, the Soviet Union was employing 2.4 million persons with higher or middle education and on December 1, 1957, this number had increased to 6.8 million persons— an increase of 2.8 times.[6] Out of 50.5 million workers employed by the State in 1956, 9.3 million were receiving incomes below the average, and 6.2 million made more than the average, leaving 35 million in the average income group. Thus, the high-paid group of 6.2 million workers could overbid the lower income groups in their demand for scarce consumer goods and foodstuffs. If one allows for the large number of government officials and for the presence of foreign diplomats, visitors, and peasants from near-by collective farms who purchase goods from Moscow, the high purchasing power of millions of workers throughout the Soviet Union is still impressive.

## Real Income

As was stated before, real income in the Soviet Union is calculated on the basis of cash income received by all employed persons plus state assistance. The sum of these two sources, then, is compared with costs of goods and services to determine the real income. This income, however, excludes income derived from private occupations of handicraft workers, professional

TABLE 2—*Total Sum of Assistance Paid by the State* [7]
(*in billions of rubles*)

| Year | Total amount | Pensions and social insurance |
|------|--------------|-------------------------------|
| 1940 | 42 | 7 |
| 1950 | 122 | 35 |
| 1953 | 135 | 38 |
| 1955 | 155 | 44 |
| 1956 | 169 | 52 |
| 1957 | 192 | 78 |
| 1958 | 215 | 83 |
| 1959 | 230 | – |
| 1965 (Plan) | 345 | – |

services, domestic servants, and the like. Figures in Table 2 include all sources and are somewhat higher than budgetary accounts.

The sum total of assistance between 1940 and 1958 increased fivefold. But between 1950 and 1959 this increase was about 90 per cent. The largest increase took place between 1956 and 1958, mainly because of increases in pension allotments and the abolishment of educational fees. The 1950-58 average annual increase in assistance was 11.6 billion rubles, whereas the planned increase during the 1959-65 period amounts to 18.6 billion rubles. These payments cover social insurance, grants, pensions, stipends, free education, medical services, paid holidays, and other items from the state budget and the funds of enterprises.

The largest increase occurred in pensions and in social insurance. These payments amounted to 8.2 billion rubles in 1940 and to 81.7 billion rubles in 1958, an increase of almost ten times. Pensions and social insurance payments represented 19 per cent of all state assistance in 1940, whereas in 1958 it was over 38 per cent. In 1950 about 3.1 million widows and mothers with three or more children received assistance from the State. Their number in 1958 increased to 3.4 million and they received 5.3 billion rubles.[8] In 1958 there were 18 million pensioners of whom eight million were aged and retired persons. Of the total number of pensioners, 2.2 million were persons who lost their providers and were dependent on the State and 7.7 million were veterans of World War I, the Civil War, and World War II and their dependents receiving aid. In 1957, as a result of increased wage payments to the low income groups, increased pension payments, and termination of state loans, the purchasing power of the people was increased by 41 billion rubles. In 1958 this figure was estimated at 60 billion rubles.[9]

TABLE 3—*Official Increase in Real Income of State-employed Workers* [10]

| Year | Index |
|---|---|
| 1940 | 100 |
| 1950 | 136 |
| 1951 | 157 |
| 1952 | 164 |
| 1954 | 173 |
| 1955 | 175 |
| 1956 | 183 |
| 1957 | 190 |
| 1958 | 194 |
| 1965 (Plan) | 234 |

Between 1940 and 1950 the real income of Soviet workers increased by 36 per cent, and by 1958 it advanced to 94 per cent. Between 1950 and 1958 the increase in real income was about 43 per cent, or about five per cent annually. However, the 1940-56 increase in real income of all state-employed persons was 82 per cent. The increase for factory workers alone was 95 per cent.[11] Thus, industrial workers advanced their real income at a more rapid rate than other workers. The overall increase in real income during the 1959-65 period is planned at 40 per cent. This increase is to be in terms of rises in wages and social benefit payments and through a decline in taxes and retail prices. It is interesting to note that prior to the current Seven-Year Plan the rise in real income index by 1960 was expected to be 227 whereas a less optimistic 1965 plan calls for an index of 234.

In the Soviet Union the increase in real income materializes in two powerful forces. One is the increase in cash income and in subsidies and allowances. The second is a reduction in prices paid by the consumers for goods and services they purchase. Both forces are used simultaneously or at different times when required. At times when it is economically or socially impossible to reduce retail prices, as it was during World War II, the Soviets increase cash payments, and bread allowances, or take similar direct measures. The upswing in retail prices started with the Second Five-Year Plan. However, to minimize increases in prices and to provide an incentive at the same time, wage rates have advanced much faster than the prevailing retail prices.

As was noted before, during World War II, inflationary pressures were high and prices were increased to several times their prewar level, while the general wage level remained below the price level. Only since 1947 have the Soviets been able to start a chain of price reductions. Yet postwar inflation is still present.

Of the many economic groups, members of collective farms are the least fortunate. Since their incomes are derived from many sources, including work on collective farms, their small-scale agricultural enterprises, work outside the collective farms, and the like, the Soviets have looked upon the collective farmers as a self-supporting sector. Only when it becomes absolutely necessary and when the State would benefit more than the peasants, is assistance given to them. The greatest attention to the economic problems of the peasants came after 1950 when incentives were provided to increase the peasants' cash and real incomes.

The gross cash income of collective farms increased by 3.8 times between 1950 and 1958. As a result of increased prices paid by the State, expansion in sales of farm produce on collective farm markets, a reduction in taxation, and other benefits, the peasants at last started to breathe easier and improved their standards of living considerably.

The figures below represent all incomes earned on all collective farms from the sale of agricultural commodities and services. In 1950 gross cash income per collective household was 1,668 rubles and 3,818 rubles in 1955. In 1956 another 20 billion rubles was poured into peasants' cash income through increase in prices paid by the State, so that gross cash income per

TABLE 4—*Gross Cash Income of Collective Farms* [18]
(*in billions of rubles*)

| Year | Rubles |
|------|--------|
| 1950 | 34.2 |
| 1952 | 42.8 |
| 1953 | 49.6 |
| 1954 | 63.3 |
| 1955 | 75.6 |
| 1957 | 94.0 |
| 1958 | 130.0 |

household reached 4,804 rubles. In 1958 this income reached almost 7,000 rubles, still 1,500 rubles below the industrial income. Taxes and other state payments were deducted, but these deducions were less than the increase in income. To this the peasants added incomes derived from their private small-scale agricultural enterprises and from work outside the collective farms.

The actual improvement in real income of members of collective farms started in 1951, and the Soviets claimed that in comparison with that year, the real income of the peasants increased to an index of 150 in 1955 and to 170 in 1956.[13] The Soviets declare that in 1956 alone the cash income and income in kind of collective farm members increased by 12 per cent. Nevertheless, the real income index of these workers in 1956 was 170 compared to 182 for all state workers and 195 for the industrial workers. Therefore, despite improvements in the real and cash income of the members of collective farms, it is still below that of other sectors. The 1959-65 plan anticipates another 40 per cent increase in real income of collective peasants. Despite this increase the real incomes of industrial workers would still be above those of peasants, and the peasants would continue to be secondary citizens.

## CONSUMPTION PER CAPITA

Consumption of goods per capita in the USSR cannot be precisely determined since official data on consumption are given for state and cooperative retail outlets and exclude entirely goods produced and consumed at home. It is difficult to calculate how much fruit, vegetables, fish, poultry, dairy products, and wild game are consumed by those who have small-scale private plots of land or who fish and hunt. Nevertheless, since state and cooperative stores supply the greatest number of consumers, especially the urban population, these data are useful in determining trends in the welfare of the people.

TABLE 5—*Per Capita Consumption of Foodstuffs and Consumer Goods by State-employed Workers and Peasants* [14]

(*1940 = 100*)

| Commodity | Workers | | | Peasants | | |
|---|---|---|---|---|---|---|
|  | 1952 | 1956 | 1958 | 1952 | 1956 | 1958 |
| Bread _____ | 90 | 81 | 76 | 95 | 100 | 98 |
| Potatoes _____ | 175 | 161 | 156 | 164 | 140 | 125 |
| Vegetables _____ | 93 | 126 | 135 | 88 | 124 | 127 |
| Meats _____ | 132 | 188 | 213 | 83 | 163 | 187 |
| Fish _____ | 149 | 169 | 180 | 138 | 244 | 296 |
| Milk and milk products _____ | 144 | 214 | 250 | 105 | 148 | 164 |
| Eggs _____ | 112 | 176 | 222 | 112 | 210 | 262 |
| Sugar _____ | 179 | 200 | 215 | 199 | 438 | 576 |
| Bakery products _____ | 133 | 155 | 161 | 138 | 252 | 304 |
| Textile fabrics _____ | 172 | 175 | 183 | 126 | 211 | 204 |
| Footwear _____ | 133 | 146 | 158 | 112 | 174 | 188 |
| Ready-made clothing _____ | 198 | 245 | 285 | 74 | 221 | 258 |
| Furniture, household goods _____ | 207 | 328 | 445 | 104 | 295 | 346 |
| Books, radios, musical instruments, watches, etc. ____ | 432 | 891 | 1,219 | 203 | 892 | 1,050 |

Table 5 shows the trend rather than actual consumption per capita. It also shows a shift away from collective farm markets toward state and cooperative stores. Nevertheless, in comparison with 1940, consumption of foodstuffs and consumer goods in 1958 was considerably increased. The increased consumption of foodstuffs is more notable. As bread has become less important in the diet other foods have replaced it in volume of consumption. There was a slight increase in consumption of factory-made bread for the peasants in 1956 as compared with 1940 but a decline in the consumption of potatoes. The peasants generally have improved their diet. The greatest increase occurred in the consumption of sugar for the peasants and milk for the non-farm workers.

Between 1940 and 1958 the per capita consumption of consumer goods for both workers and peasants also improved considerably. Increases can be noted particularly in textiles, ready-to-wear garments, household goods, and recreation items. The rate of increase was higher for the peasants, and as their incomes increased they demanded more and better goods. Table 5 also suggests that in 1940 the purchasing power of the peasants was far below that of industrial workers.

Since state and cooperative stores supply most urban and rural consumers, their total retail turnover of goods can be used as an indicator in the consumption of any one item among consumer goods. Per capita purchase of all goods was about 800 rubles in 1940 and 3,243 rubles in 1958. It should be noted that the official average annual price level for all goods in 1958 was 41 per cent above the 1940 level, making the 1958 purchasing power of the ruble 59 per cent of the prewar level. Yet the purchasing power of the ruble in 1958 was 2.3 times above the 1947 level. This suggests that between 1947 and 1958 there was a considerable increase in the purchasing power of the ruble, but it was still much below the 1940 period.

Table 5 shows remarkable advances in per capita consumption of material goods in the Soviet Union. This reflects a worldwide phenomenon. Other countries with less dynamic advances in industrial growth have recorded equal, if not superior, achievements in personal consumption as compared with the Soviet Union. The real goal in economic growth in any country is to raise the standard of living of the people and to make them as free as possible from fear of material need. Allowing for the fact that in the Soviet Union the postwar retail prices were higher than they were in 1940, the favorable relationship between prices, wages, and availability of consumer goods leads to the conclusion that, despite the gaps created by maladjustment in income distribution, the Russian people have advanced their standard of living in general. The average Russian citizen of 1958 dressed better, ate more and better food, and his health was better than his counterpart in 1940. But one must remember that if the Russian's standard of living has undergone such a rapid advance it is primarily because he had so little before.

In 1940 the most essential food items—bread, meats, flour, cereals and macaroni, fats and oils, milk and milk products, and vegetables—accounted for about 51 per cent of the total expenditures on foodstuffs. In 1955 they were approximately 42 per cent and in 1958 almost 44 per cent.

In 1958 the Russians spent 3.8 times more money on foodstuffs than in 1940. Though prices increased during this period, money incomes advanced at a faster rate than prices. As the income increased the Russians began to buy more beverages, particularly alcoholic beverages. In 1940 this item took about 14 per cent of the total cost for all foodstuffs, and by 1958 it increased to 26 per cent. The greatest increases in expenditures between 1940 and 1958 were for alcoholic beverages and sugar. Purchases of non-food items also were greater in 1958, especially in ready-made garments and headwear, footwear, radio sets, and furniture.

TABLE 6—*Annual Per Capita Consumption of Goods from State Retail and Cooperative Stores in Rubles* [15]
(*in prices of each year*)

| Commodity | 1940 | 1955 | 1958 |
|---|---|---|---|
| Total: | 800 | 2,213 | 3,243 |
| Foodstuffs: | 461 | 1,095 | 1,771 |
| Bread | 142 | 185 | 207 |
| Vodka, wines, beer, soft drinks | 67 | 276 | 460 |
| Meat and meat products | 37 | 82 | 172 |
| Bakery products | 30 | 86 | 126 |
| Flour, cereals, and macaroni | 25 | 89 | 130 |
| Fats and oils | 24 | 86 | 126 |
| Sugar | 24 | 97 | 146 |
| Fish and fish products | 14 | 42 | 58 |
| Milk and milk products | 9 | 23 | 78 |
| Vegetables | 9 | 17 | 45 |
| Fruits | 8 | 21 | 45 |
| Others | 72 | 81 | 178 |
| Non-food: | 339 | 1,118 | 1,472 |
| Ready-made clothihng and headwear | 60 | 217 | 396 |
| Footwear | 33 | 121 | 159 |
| Tobacco products | 27 | 46 | 65 |
| Soap | 20 | 32 | 39 |
| Furniture | 10 | 34 | 52 |
| Books, printed materials | 9 | 25 | 32 |
| Radio sets | 1 | 14 | 23 |
| Others | 179 | 629 | 706 |

It is to be noticed that the per capita sale of consumer goods and foodstuffs from state and cooperative stores by 1965 is planned to be 4,790 rubles, an increase of 48 per cent over that in 1958. Khrushchev has promised some reduction in prices, but they are not to be as dramatic as they were during the 1947-55 period.

In general, the Russians had more money to spend in 1958 than in 1940. A single industrial worker with his average gross annual income of 8,500 rubles could easily have purchased the amount of goods given in Table 6, plus some of the scarcer items such as meat, fresh fruits, and vegetables on the collective farm market. Still, not all persons buy similar goods at the same time. The members of collective farms, for example, buy mostly non-food items from the state and cooperative stores. Most of their food-stuffs are obtained from collective farms or from their own kitchen gardens.

In 1940 Soviet citizens spent about 58 per cent of their total expenditures in state and cooperative stores on food items and in 1958 about 55 per cent. Since food prices affect the low income group more acutely and since con-sumers have some degree of choice between various grades of foodstuffs at different prices either in the state-controlled stores or in the collective farm markets, the importance of food prices is more significant than the prices of non-food items.

In 1956 the Soviets made a study of food expenditures of a family con-sisting of seven persons residing in Gorky, an industrial city close to Moscow and located in the same price belt as Moscow. The family consisted of the father, mother, four girls, and one boy. All children were contributing to the family total income either by working part-time or by receiving stipends and grants for attending school. The gross family income from all direct and indirect sources in 1956 amounted to 41,530 rubles, of which 52.5 per cent covered household expenditures for rent, heat, electricity, water, taxes, transportation, amusement, and books, and included 12,000 rubles for clothing, footwear, and other non-food items.[16] No doubt this family was selected for its high total income since even the children were contributors.

According to Table 7, bread, vegetables, and milk were the main food items purchased. Monthly consumption of bread was equivalent to 37.8 pounds per person per month or more than a pound of bread per day. Consumption of vegetables (of which potatoes were the main item) was about one pound per person per day and milk consumption was about 0.86 pints per person per day. Combined per person consumption of meat and fish was about one-fourth pound per day and about one egg per week per person. However, this family includes young members, who naturally love sweets, and consumed over 5.5 pounds of sugar per person per month, and over three pounds of butter.

In general, the family, much better off than the average, consumed greater shares of cheap foodstuffs such as bread, cereals, macaroni, vegetables, and milk than expensive items. Consumption of meat and fish per capita was sufficient for minimum health requirements. Culinary ingenuity of Russian housewives makes possible fullest utilization of meat and fish, but in terms of T-bone steaks the Soviet per capita meat con-sumption is insufficient, as is the consumption of eggs. It must be added that alcoholic and non-alcoholic beverages are excluded from this family's table, and the sale of these items from state retail stores represented about 25 per cent of the total purchases of foodstuffs. It is interesting to note that because of higher prices on collective farm markets the family paid 3,500 more rubles for food than it would have paid in state stores, provided that these items could be found there.

TABLE 7—*Average Prices of Most Popular Grades of Foodstuffs in State Stores and on Collective Farm Markets in Gorki in 1956* [17]

| Item | For Family of Seven Per Month | | | Per Capita | |
| | Quantity (kilograms or liters) | Price per kilogram or liter in rubles | Total rubles | Monthly quantity (kilograms or liters) | Total rubles |
|---|---|---|---|---|---|
| Bread, rye | 50 | 1.24 | 62.00 | 7.1 | 8.86 |
| Bread, white | 70 | 1.90 | 133.00 | 10.0 | 19.00 |
| Meat | 30 | 12.00 | 360.00 | 4.3 | 51.43 |
| Cereals, (rice, millet) | 12 | 5.30 | 63.60 | 1.7 | 9.09 |
| Macaroni, etc. | 6 | 4.00 | 24.00 | 0.8 | 3.43 |
| Butter | 10 | 27.00 | 270.00 | 1.4 | 38.57 |
| Vegetable oil | 3 | 16.00 | 48.00 | 0.4 | 6.86 |
| Milk | 90 | 1.80 | 162.00 | 12.9 | 23.14 |
| Cream and curds | 3 | 12.00 | 36.00 | 0.4 | 5.14 |
| Eggs (pieces) | 30 | 8.00 | 24.00 | 4.3 | 3.43 |
| Fish, fresh | 8 | 8.00 | 64.00 | 1.1 | 9.14 |
| Potatoes | 70 | 1.00 | 70.00 | 10.0 | 10.00 |
| Other vegetables | 30 | 1.00 | 30.00 | 4.3 | 4.29 |
| Sugar | 18 | 10.70 | 192.60 | 2.6 | 27.51 |
| Tea | 0.2 | 68.00 | 13.60 | 0.03 | 1.94 |
| Spices | – | – | 10.00 | – | 1.43 |
| Fruit, cakes, sweets | – | – | 82.20 | – | 11.74 |
| TOTAL | | | 1,645.00 | | 235.00 |

Next to food, clothing expenditures are the most important. Workmanship and style in clothing were considerably improved in 1956 and there was a wider choice of materials. Despite this notable improvement it is still an expensive undertaking to purchase clothing and requires considerable savings and careful consideration of what garments are essential. Russians, especially the urban folks, may buy ready-made garments in the state stores or buy material and hire a tailor, who charges about 300 rubles to make a suit and about 500 rubles to make an overcoat. If one has the time, skill, and facilities, one may make a suit, overcoat, or dress at home.

Many state enterprises have tailor shops for their own employees where garments are made at much lower cost than on the free market.

Since most of the wage earners in the USSR, or in any other country for that matter, do not purchase suits, overcoats, or shoes every month, and since some items of clothing are replaced at intervals of two years or more, the monthly outlay for clothing purchases is meaningless. Such purchases depend on need, price, cash on hand, and "degree of substitution." The last is an important factor since the Soviets reject the idea that "clothes make the man."

Table 8—*Prices of Consumer Goods
in Urban Centers in 1956-57* [18]

| Item | Rubles |
|------|--------|
| Man's winter overcoat | 2,000.00 |
| Woman's winter overcoat | 1,500.00 |
| Man's woolen winter suit | 1,800.00 |
| Man's spring overcoat | 1,200.00 |
| Man's semi-woolen summer suit | 800.00 |
| Man's raincoat | 500.00 |
| Man's shoes | 400.00 |
| Woman's shoes | 125.00 |
| Man's felt hat | 150.00 |
| Man's shirt | 75.00 |
| Necktie | 15.00 |
| Man's socks | 2.50 |
| Man's haircut | 1.50 |
| Pay phone call | .15 |
| Refrigerator | 150.00-500.00 |
| Television set with 7-inch screen | 300.00 |
| Television set with 17-inch screen | 550.00 |
| Small wringer-type washing machine | 200.00 |
| Pobeda automobile, 4-cylinder sedan | 30,000.00 |
| Volga 21 G, similar to a 1958 Studebaker | 40,000.00 |
| Marriage license | 15.00 |

At the above prices the average Soviet industrial worker can buy each year one winter suit, one pair of shoes, and four shirts for himself, and he could manage to purchase only a winter overcoat and a pair of shoes for his wife. The next year, he could buy more shoes, shirts, and other items, but must keep his and his wife's winter coats for several years. Of course, the number of articles a family can purchase depends upon the wife's imagination in producing her own and her children's clothing from "hand-me-down" items, and many garments are used for many more years than in the United States.

## HOUSING

Soviet housing space, which has always been inadequate, is insufficient to satisfy the growing demand or to relieve overcrowding. The Soviets are boasting that by 1965 the housing shortage will be greatly relieved, if not ended. To achieve this goal the budgetary appropriations have been increased considerably. The state loans for the improvement of existing housing and the construction of individual dwellings are also increased, especially those in the larger cities and fast-growing industrial centers.

The Soviets inherited inadequate housing facilities from the days of the Tsar. During World War I, the Revolution, and the Civil War, many houses were destroyed, and private and public construction of housing was reduced to a minimum. Only after the Civil War did the Soviets begin to rehabilitate old and build new floor space. During the period 1918-41, about 166 million new square meters were occupied. This represents somewhat less than the total floor space existing in urban centers before the Revolution of 1917. Moreover, this expansion was still not enough to provide any relief for the increased urban population.

World War II inflicted tremendous destruction on housing facilities. The Soviets reported that over 1,710 towns and cities and over 70,000 villages were burned, destroyed, or damaged. Over six million dwellings providing shelter to 25 million persons were burned or destroyed.[19] Assuming that these statistics are accurate, the amount of damaged shelter area almost equalled all the dwelling area constructed by the Soviets during the 1918-41 period. As a result, the USSR at the end of World War II found itself with approximately the same floor space as it had in 1917, whereas the total population had increased by 30 per cent.

After World War II an intensive drive to speed up rehabilitation of old housing and construction of new was launched. State housing programs, cooperatives, and private housing construction were encouraged by the government with greater appropriations to public agencies and easy long-term credit to cooperative and private home building.

During the 1946-56 period construction of new urban housing amounted to 219.5 million square meters, of which about 80 per cent were replacement of destroyed, damaged, or obsolete dwellings. Actually, new additions of floor space, aside from replacements, were not more than 45 mil-

TABLE 9—*New Construction of Urban Floor Space* [20]
(*in millions of square meters*)

| Year | Total | State and cooperatives | Private |
|------|-------|------------------------|---------|
| 1946 _____ | 17.4 | 12.6 | 4.8 |
| 1947 _____ | 18.2 | 11.8 | 6.4 |
| 1948 _____ | 21.1 | 14.7 | 6.4 |
| 1949 _____ | 21.9 | 15.5 | 6.4 |
| 1950 _____ | 24.2 | 17.8 | 6.4 |
| 1951 _____ | 27.6 | 20.3 | 7.3 |
| 1952 _____ | 27.4 | 20.0 | 7.4 |
| 1953 _____ | 30.8 | 23.2 | 7.6 |
| 1954 _____ | 32.5 | 24.4 | 8.1 |
| 1955 _____ | 33.4 | 25.0 | 8.4 |
| 1956 _____ | 41.0 | 29.5 | 11.5 |
| 1957 _____ | 52.0 | 38.5 | 13.5 |
| 1958 _____ | 71.2 | 46.7 | 24.5 |
| 1959 _____ | 80.0 | – | – |

lion square meters. The state and cooperative urban housing construction represented about 70 per cent of the total; the other 30 per cent was constructed by private owners.

TABLE 10—*Total Urban Floor Space at Years' End* [21]
(*in millions of square meters*)

|  | 1940 | 1950 | 1955 | 1956 | 1958 |
|--|------|------|------|------|------|
| Total: _____ | 421 | 513 | 640 | 673 | 781 |
| State and cooperatives_____ | 267 | 340 | 432 | 454 | 524 |
| Private ownership _____ | 154 | 173 | 208 | 219 | 257 |

In 1940 state and cooperative housing authorities possessed 63.4 per cent of all urban floor space and 67.1 per cent in 1958. Consequently, although private urban housing construction between 1940 and 1958 increased by about 54 per cent its share of the total floor space was less in 1958 than in 1940. The State and cooperatives held equal shares of the total urban floor space. The destruction of private housing during World War II was responsible for this decline.

In comparison with 1940, the 1958 floor space in urban centers was increased by 85 per cent. In 1940 an average per capita occupancy of floor space was about seven square meters or about 75 square feet. Based on 1956 per capita floor occupancy, about 2.8 million private citizens (or approximately 700,000 families) lived in their own dwellings. Since the minimum norm of occupied floor space is estimated by the State at nine square meters, or about 97 square feet, the 1958 average per capita floor occupancy was below the established standards. A family of three is entitled to a minimum of 27 square meters, plus an additional 4.55 square meters for the family in common, or a total of 31.55 square meters (326 square feet).[22] Only a few are lucky enough to occupy even the minimum floor space established by the government. Some members of the elite Soviet society with high incomes live in larger apartments, but the great bulk of low and middle income groups are occupying much less than the minimum nine square meters to which each person is entitled.

To relieve this chronic shortage of urban floor space, the Soviets in 1957 launched a long-range housing program to liquidate the housing shortage during the following ten to 12 years. This goal, however, was set aside with the introduction of the 1959-65 Plan, which calls for the construction of additional space amounting to 650 to 660 million square meters, or about 15 million apartments. This means that the annual average additional space is to be about 93 million square meters. Yet in 1959, the first year of the enthusiastic plan, only about 80 million square meters were constructed, or about 2.2 million apartments. Apparently the Russians are experiencing considerable difficulties in fulfilling their optimistic housing goal. Though it is true that the number of apartments constructed in 1959 was achieved as planned, they are smaller in space than the planned construction calls for.

The accelerated plan envisages mass production of prefabricated houses, the use of cement blocks, and simplified design. Even if the Russians could add more urban floor space, as they plan for 1965 a housing scarcity would still exist in spite of their claims to the contrary. Actually, the urban housing shortage at the present accelerated tempo cannot possibly subside any earlier than 1972, nor can the minimum of nine square meters of floor space per person be provided. Liquidation of housing shortages is more difficult for the Soviets than was the liquidation of kulaks in 1930.

In 1956 only two of the 31 large urban centers provided the minimum floor area per capita. These cities were Riga and Tallinn, the capitals of Latvia and Estonia. It is ironic that only these two cities not even in Russia, have more than the minimum floor space per capita; however, urban populations in these cities since the war have declined, while postwar expansion of housing has been rapid. The most critical shortage in urban housing is in Central Asia, followed by large Siberian cities such as Novosibirsk and Omsk. Recently developed industrial centers are even more deficient in housing than the older urban centers. In 1956 housing in the suburbs was even less adequate than in the cities, and for this reason current emphasis is on expanding suburban housing.

In an effort to provide minimum living facilities for the working people the Soviets tightened up their housing regulations as of February 1957, when eviction of an unemployed worker from his apartment actually became possible. Prior to 1953 a worker living in a housing project provided by his enterprise was subject to eviction if he resigned or was fired, but because of the shortage of housing elsewhere, this law was difficult to enforce. The new law is more widely enforced and counteracts the effect of the law which permits workers to resign from their jobs on two weeks' notice. Since housing is so scarce throughout the country, workers must think twice before resigning from their jobs, especially if they have satisfactory housing at their places of employment.

Rural residents have faced the same problem of postwar reconstruction as have urban residents, since about 70,000 villages were destroyed or damaged during World War II. To relieve rural housing shortages the government has encouraged construction of new peasant housing and rehabilitation of destroyed or damaged property by augmenting the savings of the peasants with easy, long-term credit. During the period 1946-57 rural residents built, reconstructed, or rehabilitated about 6.4 million dwellings.[23] This was done by the members of collective farms, village intelligentsia, and all others who reside in the rural areas. It is reasonable to assume that by 1957 rural residents were not only able to replace their war losses but to add new houses or to move into better ones. The 1959-65 Plan calls for the construction of about seven million additional rural homes. Although the rural housing program, like the urban, was accelerated, the initial goal was not met. Only 850,000 additional rural homes were built in 1959 instead of the average annual planned number of one million units.

In connection with rural housing expansion it must be remembered that with the merging of small collective farms into larger units, housing programs in the countryside have not been concerned so much with finding new houses for the existing population as with relocating the peasants in new sites by pooling isolated peasant households into larger communities.

Inadequacy in housing in the Soviet Union is felt mainly in the urban areas. As a result, the government restricts migration of industrial enterprises to large industrial centers where housing for the already existing population is scarce. Few of the newly constructed apartment houses in cities are taller than four or five stories. The opinion among housing authorities was recently divided in regard to the value of tall buildings in the USSR. Many Soviet architects believed that tall buildings are not economical and since the value of real estate, in the speculative sense, does not exist in the USSR, they favored horizontal rather than vertical expansion.

## LEISURE TIME

Soviet statistics show that on the average each worker is expected to work 286 days a year. The other 80 days are spent resting, celebrating official holidays, on vacation, on sick leave, or in some other way. The worker has 52 days off (Sundays) plus six state holidays. The average vacation ranges from 11.5 to 14.0 days. Sick leave averages seven days, to which a statistical average 0.2 day is added for pregnancy and childbirth. Required state duties such as serving on a jury take an average of 0.3 day; daily stoppage of work amounts to 0.1 day annually; and all other causes take an additional 0.1 day per year.[24] Of course, an individual's absence from work depends upon his age, sex, other sources of income, and many other things associated with his well-being.

On an average, the worker works eight hours a day five days a week but only six hours on the day before his day off, a total of 46 hours per week. However, during the current Seven-Year Plan, measures are being undertaken to reduce working hours to seven a day for a six-day week; for underground work a six-hour working day is being initiated. It was planned that by 1962 the average weekly working time would be 40 hours and by 1965 it would be reduced to 30 to 35 hours with no reduction in wages. Then in September 1959 a new policy was put into effect to make the transfer to a six- or seven-hour working day, in the main, in 1960.

The reduction in working hours per day must not be interpreted as a recognition of the need for leisure time in the USSR. This reduction resulted mainly from increased labor efficiency, shortages in scarce resources, and the inability of industrial and administrative organizations to absorb all those who are willing to work longer hours. In general, the problem of free time in the Soviet Union cannot be considered an important factor when compared to low income and the inadequate supply of consumer goods. Nevertheless, increased labor productivity using available resources creates conditions under which the Soviets have begun to consider leisure as "growing pains" associated with economic expansion.

What the Soviets are attempting to do now is to provide more leisure not for younger people recently joining the labor force, but for those who have already served the country for the last 15 to 20 years. The retirement age for male workers is 60 years with no less than 25 years of service. Female workers can retire at the age of 55 years with 20 years of service. Male workers employed underground or on difficult or dangerous jobs may retire at the age of 50 or after 20 years of continuous service, and female workers working under similar conditions may retire at 45 or after 15 years of continuous service. However, as the number of these older workers grows and the length of life in the USSR increases as well, the problem of leisure will become more and more important.

The average worker's day off may or may not fall on Sunday. If personal chores are not completed in the evening the worker must do them on his day off. He might have to go to the store where a considerable amount of time is spent in waiting in lines. Waiting is a regular part of marketing at the dry cleaners, barber shop, grocery shops, public bath house, and elsewhere. No matter what alternatives are taken to enjoy the day off, a part of it must be spent waiting in line. Even if the worker decides to "forget it all" and leave the city for the country, the inevitable waiting for the bus or train consumes precious time. Only when the worker has a high enough income or his household is being run efficiently by others may he or she have a full day of enjoyment.

Those who are retired, of course, stay at home and try to work part-time, if possible; many are confined to homes for the aged. Only about six per cent of the state-employed workers are lucky enough to be sent by their trade unions to sanitoria, holiday homes, or resort areas for their vacations. In 1956, 3.2 million workers had such vacations, but only 30 per cent of this number were sent to sanatoria, and ten per cent of all workers assigned to holiday homes were paying a nominal cost of not over 30 per cent of the total cost for their vacation. The remaining vacationists paid the full cost themselves. Of course, people in the higher income brackets pay their own way without trade union grants, but the great majority of workers, especially those in the lower and middle income groups, entertain themselves as best as they can at home.

But how can one enjoy his leisure at home with several people in the room and during the winter months? Table 6 shows that in 1958 state retail stores sold 460 rubles worth of alcoholic and soft beverages per capita, roughly 26 per cent of the total volume of footstuffs purchased. Even at high prices the Russians satisfy their great thirst for alcoholic beverages. In addition, the peasants and others make their own wines and other alcoholic beverages so that the actual per capita consumption of alcoholic beverages is considerably higher than the figure listed in Table 6. Alcohol serves as an escape from the dreary everyday realities for the great mass of people in the lower and middle income brackets. The Soviet intelligentsia, having higher incomes, spend their leisure at summer resorts, museums, theaters, camps, and on tours to Red China and Eastern Europe; a few extremely privileged might even go to Western Europe. For the most part, however, free time is too short and too expensive to break the monotony of the fast pace of the Russian's daily existence.

## RECREATION FACILITIES

The average Soviet worker may spend his day off at home performing household chores, reading, listening to radio broadcasts, or even watching television. Because of cramped living quarters and the high cost of entertaining his friends at his home, he most likely joins others like himself at his club or spends an evening at the motion picture theater, museum, public park, theater, or even in the library.

Every large industrial enterprise or organization has a club for its workers and employees. Clubs may be expensively furnished and decorated as is the Officers' Club in Moscow, or they may be small huts as in the Arctic Circle. These clubs provide cultural services for the masses such as lectures, plays by amateur theater groups, dances, moving pictures, and concerts, but they also have pool rooms, rooms for card playing, and of course, lending libraries, reading rooms, and sports equipment, as well as space for physical education. In 1956, these clubs numbered 242,600 with a membership of 3.4 million persons. Next in importance are the clubs organized by collective farms. These are more like guilds, being restricted to the members of a particular collective farm. Large and wealthy collective farms may have elaborate club houses with large halls for lectures, entertainment, and moving pictures. The club house will have a small library and radio receiver and might even have a television set. In many cases non-alcoholic beverages and food may be obtained. It is the place where young blades and their girls gather for entertainment, gossip, and bits of culture. In addition, there are the clubs organized by professional men and women which provide the same facilities as other clubs, but on a more dignified level.

The average worker living in a large city has a wider range of recreational facilities at his disposal, especially in the summer. Large industrial or administrative centers usually have annual exhibits and fairs which can be enjoyed at nominal cost. There are many outdoor events such as soccer games, wrestling matches, horse races, and the like. However, workers living in isolated industrial areas or in rural districts have fewer attractions. For these workers, local recreation facilities such as clubs, moving picture theaters, and street dancing are the main events.

TABLE 11—*Recreation Facilities in the USSR* [25]

| Facility | Unit | 1940 | 1950 | 1957 | 1958 |
|---|---|---|---|---|---|
| Total number of clubs: _____ | Thousand | 111.4 | 128.6 | 127.0 | 128.5 |
| Urban areas _____ | " | 9.4 | 9.2 | 11.8 | 12.9 |
| Rural areas _____ | " | 102.0 | 119.4 | 115.2 | 115.6 |
| Total moving picture units:_____ | " | 29.3 | 37.0 | 69.7 | 77.9 |
| Urban areas _____ | " | 11.7 | 9.2 | 14.8 | 16.3 |
| Rural areas _____ | " | 17.6 | 27.8 | 54.9 | 61.6 |
| Sound-producing units _____ | " | 19.5 | 36.9 | 69.7 | 77.9 |
| Annual attendance _____ | Million | 88.3 | 1,144.0 | 3,100.0 | 3,390.0 |
| Public Libraries: _____ | Thousand | 86.3 | 110.4 | 144.0 | 137.6 |
| Urban _____ | " | 17.0 | 16.3 | 28.0 | 29.0 |
| Rural _____ | " | 69.3 | 94.1 | 116.0 | 108.6 |
| Book titles printed _____ | " | 46.0 | 43.0 | 59.0 | 63.6 |
| Theaters _____ | Number | 908 | 569 | 512 | 528 |
| Theater attendance _____ | Million | – | 68.0 | 79.0 | 83.0 |
| Museums _____ | Number | 991 | 937 | 840 | 870 |
| Museum attendance _____ | Million | – | 27.0 | 35.0 | 39.0 |

There are more clubs, moving picture theaters, and libraries in rural areas, however small they may be, than in urban centers. Moreover, these facilities are used for political purposes as well. Since direct communication in rural areas is inadequate, mass propaganda methods for influencing rural residents can be easily applied through use of radio, motion pictures, and library displays.

In rural areas community life is centered around the club. Participation in a club's activities is open to all and in this sense the club is a community affair. But the urban residents as individuals are lost in the mass. There is less community pride among urban residents. There is less personal participation, and the increasing use of radio and television creates an even deeper cleavage and contributes to the decline of community life in the large cities. Radio and television, as in the United States, are gradually changing the habits of many Russians who are seemingly more attached to their homes than ever in the past.

Considering the standard of living the Russians had in 1940, their current level of living is much better. They are better fed, dressed, and entertained; they have better social security than in prewar days; and Khrushchev has promised to abolish their taxes entirely by 1965. What is more important is the Russians' belief in a still better life in the future.

## Bibliography—Chapter 18

1 *Ekonomika Sotsialisticheskoy Promyshlennosti*, Moscow, 1957, p. 485.

2 Lifits, M., *Sovetskaya Torgavlya i ee Rol v Ekonomicheskoy Zhizni Strany*, Moscow, 1951, p. 34; Bachurin, A., *Ekonomicheskoye Soderzhaniye Budzheta pri Sotsialisme*, Moscow, 1957, p. 133.

3 Mar'yakhin, G., and Burmistrov, D., *Nalogi s Naseleniya*, Moscow, 1957, pp. 70-86.

4 *Izvestia*, March 15, 1958.

5 *Sovetskaya Torgovliya*, Moscow, 1956, p. 222.

6 *SSSR v Tsifrakh*, Moscow, 1958, p. 316.

7 *Narodnoye Khozaystvo SSSR v 1956 Godu*, Moscow, 1957, p. 44; *Dostizheniye Sovetskoy Vlasti za 40 Let*, Moscow, 1957, p. 326; *Sovetskaya Sotsialisticheskaya Ekonomika: 1917-1957*, Moscow, 1957, p. 193; *SSSR v Tsifrakh*, op. cit., p. 414; *Kontrol'nye Tsifry Razvitiya Narodnogo Khozaystva SSSR na 1959-1965 Gody*, Moscow, 1958, pp. 15, 95; *Zasedaniya Verkhovnogo Sovieta SSSR*, Moscow, 1959, p. 28.

8 *Narodnoye Khozaystvo SSSR v 1958 Godu*, Moscow, 1959, p. 894.

9 *Izvestiya*, March 11, 1958.

10 *Narodnoye Khozaystvo SSSR v 1956 Godu*, op. cit., p. 43; *Sovetskaya Sotsialisticheskaya Ekonomika: 1917-1957*, op. cit., pp. 201, 596; *Voprosy Ekonomiki*, No. 12, 1953; *Pravda*, April 26, 1955; *Izvestiya*, March 11 and 12, 1958.

11 *Narodnoye Khozaystvo SSSR v 1956 Godu*, op. cit., p. 43; *Sovetskaya Sotsialistcheskaya Ekonomika: 1917-1957*, op. cit., p. 201.

12 Birman, A. M., *Finansy Otrosley Narodnogo Khozaystva SSSR*, II, Moscow, 1957, p. 119; USSR Embassy, *Press Department* No. 37, Washington, D. C., March 6, 1959.

13 *Sovetskaya Sotsialisticheskaya Ekonomika: 1917-1957*, op. cit., pp. 597, 600.

14 *Narodnoye Khozaystvo SSSR v 1956 Godu*, op. cit., pp. 219-20; *Narodnoye Khozaystvo SSSR v 1958 Godu*, op. cit., pp. 796-97.

15 *Sovetskaya Torgovliya*, Moscow, 1956, pp. 48-50; *Vestnik Statistiki*, No. 9, 1959, pp. 82-83. Calculated from turnover of trade in rubles and total population for 1940 and estimated April 1956 and the 1959 census population figures.

16 Tatarskaya, N. and Guryanov, A., *A Soviet Family Budget*, Moscow, 1957, p. 15.

17 *Ibid.*, p. 30. A kilogram is equivalent to 2.2 pounds; a liter is about two pints.

18 *The Sun*, Baltimore, May 18, 1958; *The Washington Post and Times Herald*, March 4 and June 10, 1956; *The Evening Sun*, Baltimore, April 18, 1958.

19 *Sovetskaya Sotsialisticheskaya Ekonomika: 1917-1957*, op. cit., p. 613.

20 *Narodnoye Khozaystvo SSSR v 1958 Godu*, op. cit., p. 636; *Intelligence Report No. 8102*, Department of State, Washington, D. C., September 1, 1959, p. 2; Embassy of the USSR, *Press Department*, No. 85, Washington, D. C., February 12, 1960.

[21] *Narodnoye Khozaystvo SSSR v 1958 Godu,* op. cit., p. 641.

[22] Birman, A. M., *op. cit.,* p. 285.

[23] *SSSR v Tsifrakh,* op. cit., p. 446.

[24] *Ekonomika Sotsialisticheskoy Promyshlennosti,* Moscow, 1957, p. 467.

[25] *Kulturnoye Stroitelstvo SSSR,* Moscow, 1956, pp. 273, 300, 261, 293, 286, 289; *Dostizheniye Sovetskoy Vlasti za 40 Let,* op. cit., pp. 288, 289, 290, 291, 292, 293; *Narodnoye Khozaystvo SSSR v 1956 Godu,* op. cit., pp. 264, 266; *SSSR v Tsifrakh,* op. cit., pp. 367-72; *Narodnoye Khozaystvo SSSR v 1958 Godu,* op. cit., pp. 851, 858, 863, 865, 867.

## CHAPTER 19

# Economic Potential

## INTRODUCTION

The term "economic potential" refers to productive forces associated with growth or decline of economic activity. Specifically the term means ability to produce more and perhaps better goods and services from the existing factors of production or from their expansion. Needless to say, growth of industrial output is possible only if there exist an abundance of natural resources, skilled workers, and increasing investments in technology. These are the three economic factors: land, labor, and capital. In addition, we must not forget the ideological preconception of the Communists that rapid economic growth is essential in order to win the competition with Western countries.

The history of economic growth in the Soviet Union is a radical one indeed. While industrial growth in other societies had its historical sequence, the Soviets bypassed the Renaissance, Reformation, and Industrial Revolution and within a brief period of 43 years leaped forward, surpassing the growth of more industrially mature countries. It is true that this was achieved by the imposition of ruthless controls upon the economy and the people, but at the same time there were large-scale and daring actions which would be unthinkable in more orthodox societies.

As is shown in Chapter 1, the Soviet Union has ample natural resources. Thus, at the beginning of their industrial "leap forward" in 1928, the Soviet leaders were not as concerned with the availability of land as with labor and capital. Approximately at that time they formulated the policy of self-sufficiency in order to build up military power to safeguard the national security.

To achieve this goal the Soviet leaders forced millions of peasants into industry where they were trained in new skills and in modern technology.

As their productivity increased the Gross National Production (GNP) rose. With the increased GNP the Soviets channelled a high proportion of it into new capital investment, especially to heavy industry, electric power, metallurgy, and transportation. Expanded capital goods in urbanized regions and a greater concentration of the industrial labor force created a general centralization of population in the European regions while the huge eastern parts still remained unexploited.

It is precisely because of this historical development that the economic growth of the USSR during the 1959-65 Plan and all future planned expansions will be more dependent upon natural resources in the eastern parts of the country. The development of these resources involves relocation of producers' goods and population from the West to the East. By this transfer the Russians expect to assure their favorable economic potential for many decades to come.

The economic potential of the Soviet Union has become a political issue. From the economic viewpoint rapid industrial growth means that the Russian people must sacrifice their current leisure and consumption in order to produce more capital goods which at some future time will compensate for the past losses in leisure and consumption plus a dividend for the waiting. This is the general theory. However, once the economy has reached the expected high productivity level, continuous growth would cause a more rapid obsolescence of capital goods and of the skill of workers. It simply means that at a high productivity level a greater volume of capital gains will be used for the replacement of old technology. It also means that such replacements will create demands for more highly skilled workers, necessitating the relocation of less skilled workers to less profitable occupations. These conditions, however, do not represent problems now, but eventually the Soviets will have to cope with them.

The fact that Soviet GNP in recent years has grown considerably more rapidly than in the United States, cannot be dismissed casually. By projecting the industrial growth of the two countries the Soviet industrial output would equal that of the United States by 1988 or 1990, but confident Khrushchev intends to surpass the United States economically by 1970. It is doubtful that he will still be the human dynamo behind the race for economic supremacy in 1970, but driving forces toward this goal are already firmly secured by him and will be strengthened while he is alive. It would be difficult, if not impossible, without serious economic, political, or military maladjustments, to deviate from these targets. Khrushchev, the Party, and the Russian people are committed to this goal.

## DIVERSIFIED PRODUCTION

The industrial growth in the Soviet Union is planned so as to achieve a proportional expansion in all economic sectors. But this does not mean a permanency, and the growth of any one sector can be spurred by the planners, thereby neglecting other sectors. Time after time the Soviet leaders have allocated more resources to lagging industries whose products were needed by others. Moreover, by merciless enforcement of planned targets the Soviets have succeeded in increasing the industrial production and capacity in many industries and created industries which did not exist in 1917 or 1928. In general, the country now enjoys self-sufficiency in a wide range of natural resources and manufactured goods in which they were deficient in the past. True, the production of many capital and consumer goods is still small in comparison with Western countries, but this is not because the Russians are unable to produce them; they choose to produce other goods instead.

The huge resources of a host of metals and minerals plus the climatic heterogeneity facilitate diversified production. The Soviet Union claims the leading place in the world in its resources of manganese, iron ore, coal, copper, zinc, tin, nickel, aluminum, tungsten, mercury, mica, potassium, sulphur, phospate, timber, and peat. Although some resources are less concentrated than others and many are located at considerable distances from the consuming centers, nevertheless their abundance encourages diversified production and potential self-sufficiency.

The concept of diversified production is generally used in the context of a single country, but in the case of the Soviet Union it has a much broader meaning. In considering the diversified production of the Soviet Union the bloc countries must be included, at least for the present, because of the existence of the "division of labor" among the USSR and Eastern European bloc countries. The bloc's division of labor emphasizes specialization in production of some 600 industrial items needed by the whole block. As was noted, it stresses exchange of technological achievements, and specialization is intended for the purpose of stimulating a rapid economic growth in all communist countries.

How successful this type of division of labor will be is still difficult to estimate, but it must be included when one speaks of diversified production in the Soviet Union. Certainly it is reasonable to believe that the bloc's coordination in production, no matter how weak it was in 1960, might lead to a more permanent structure in the future. In that case the whole concept of diversified production within any bloc country will take on a different meaning, and self-sufficiency will also take a different form.

The Societ Union has the resources and capability to produce most of the goods the country needs, but because of the bloc's division of labor its potential diversification, especially in certain types of equipment and consumer goods, might be curtailed simply because of their availability in other bloc countries where production costs are lower. This is a long-run approach. In the short run, diversification in the USSR will be expanded considerably. The anticipated high industrial growth rate during the current Seven-Year Plan is based on heavy investments in the construction of plants and equipment. Eventually the added capacity will start to manufacture a greater volume of consumer goods now scare on the market, plus new goods. As the rate of production in consumer goods is increased the growth in producer goods will cease to be as spectacular as it is now. Along with a greater volume of consumer goods and a higher standard of living, still more diversification will be called for. From this will stem new or expanded activities such as in electrical appliances, toys for a larger baby crop, amusements, barbershops, and a host of other industries and services. In a nutshell, diversification depends upon investment in plants and equipment which the Russians are rapidly increasing, thereby providing potential opportunity for even greater diversification.

## EXPANSION TO THE EAST

The Soviet East includes the Urals, Western Siberia, Eastern Siberia, the Far East, the Kazakh SSR and Central Asia (the Uzbek, Kirghiz, Tadzhik, and Turkmen constituent republics). Although the economic expansion to the East can be traced to the Tsars, it is the current Seven-Year Plan that really puts the East on the industrial map of the USSR.

As show in Chapter 1, the East occupies about 6.9 million square miles, or 80 per cent of the total Soviet territory. The population of the East had increased from 46.9 million in 1939 to 63.1 million in 1959, some 35 per cent, with its 1959 population representing only about 30 per cent of that of the total USSR. The Soviet East, about twice as large as the continental United States but with a population equal to that of Brazil, is obviously underpopulated, especially the Kazakh SSR, Turkmen SSR, and the whole of Siberia and the Far East.

While the industrial development of the East has always been favored by Soviet leaders, exploitation of the rich resources was hampered by deficiencies in manpower and in large-scale investments. Past drives to populate and develop the East were not as intensive and as thoroughly planned as under the current Seven-Year Plan. In a sense the Russians had similar problems in the development of the East as Canada and Australia had in their quick exploitation of resources with a minimum outlay of labor and investments.

Nevertheless the Soviet East continued to grow. Even under the adverse economic conditions of the 1940-56 period it achieved a remarkable economic growth. For example, whereas the RSFSR during this period increased its gross industrial output by 3.5 times, Eastern Siberia expanded 3.7 times and Western Siberia 6.3 times. All this was accomplished through fuller utilization of available resources and manpower, increased migration of the workers from the West, and improved technology.[1] The potential industrial growth of Siberia alone at the end of 1965 is expected to be one-third of the total Soviet industrial output against one-fourth recorded in 1959.[2]

Favorable economic and political considerations for the development of rich but underpopulated regions are many. From the political viewpoint the Soviets want to develop these regions in order to relieve the population pressure on the older regions which have already been intensively exploited for many decades. The economic reasons are obvious. The Soviets are attempting to produce more consumer goods and services for their increasing population and to improve the standard of living of the country with a minimum of investments. But no resources, however rich, can be converted into consumer goods without additional manpower. In this respect the government encourages the migration of experienced workers but in the main relies on adventurous youths who are willing to go to the wilderness of the East and become pioneers and frontiersmen, as the Party calls them.

True, the Soviets can recruit in a short period of time a large number of youths willing to go to distant places. This is just the beginning of the investments there. Certainly many of the recruits have to be trained to new tasks and must learn to live under hardship conditions. But even ignoring the self-interests of migrated workers, profit maximization by the State might be undermined simply because there might not be sufficient investment in human capital and funds for plant and equipment. This could occur even though exploitation of eastern resources with a well-trained and stabilized labor force and adequate technology might show much lower costs than in older regions. No doubt Soviet planners do recognize all the intricate problems associated with the migration of workers to sparsely populated regions, but no matter how good the planning of large-scale migration and industrial growth in the East may be, forces unforeseen by the planners at the beginning will interfere with expected goals. Major troubles in the expected industrial growth of the East will be caused by the human element and by inadequacy of investments.

In the process of rapid development of the East, the Soviets are faced with many obstacles. Cultural traits of the people as an obstacle to industrialization in the East are of minor importance, but there are other problems which must be overcome. Migrated people might not be enthusiastic about working hard under adverse conditions and without sufficient mechanization. Because of a conflict of interests of the workers and the State, a return migration of workers might be too costly in terms of numbers as well as money. To reduce this labor mobility the government must provide incentives greater than in the European part. They must build adequate housing for a large influx of workers of different cultural backgrounds who might find it difficult to acclimate in new environments. In addition, the Soviets must provide schools for the migrated children, entertainment, and goods and services. There are thousands of problems associated with a sudden mass influx of workers in regions without established communities. Many of these problems must be solved quickly to prevent irritation and discontent among the workers.

Another aspect of rapid development of the East is capital mobility. It may be true that geological resources are there, but the precise knowledge of an area to be developed might be lacking. Perhaps exploitation would require new technology, new techniques which could not be applied without preliminary research. This mobility of capital from known to unknown applications creates a host of new problems: in what should investments be made? how much should be invested? where should mines or factories or new settlements be built? In short, the mobility of manpower and capital in the economic expansion is not assured in the East as in the older regions. Of course, it is possible that the Russians, because of the planned type of expansion, have been able to eliminate some of the major obstacles and hope to solve others as they arise.

During the current Seven-Year Plan the Soviets are investing in the East from 800 to 850 billion rubles, about 40 per cent of the total planned investment for the USSR. The magnitude of this investment may be seen from the fact that the current investment is 25 or 30 per cent greater than during the previous seven years for the whole Soviet Union.[3] The most important investments are earmarked for the creation of a new metallurgical base. There is to be a rapid development of fuel, power, chemicals, and machine-building industries. Plans are made for a more rational distribution of means of production throughout the East, to improve and to expand the transportation network, and to bring the industrial potential of the East into closer coordination with the European part. The biggest share of the total sum is assigned for Siberia and the Kazakh SSR, especially for the development of the oil and allied industries. In general, overall investments during the 1959-65 period are expected to be between three and four times greater in these regions than in the European part.

About 76 per cent of the total investment is committed to the Eastern RSFSR—the Urals, Western Siberia, Eastern Siberia, and the Far East. Western Siberia and the Urals are given the largest part of this total, followed by the Kazakh SSR. The magnitude of the 1959-65 average annual investment in the Urals, all of Siberia, the Far East, and the Kazakh SSR may be seen from the fact that the planned 1958 investment in these regions was 47 billion rubles, more than the total investment allocated between 1938 and the beginning of World War II.[4] During the 1959-65 period the planned average annual investment in these regions is to be more than twice the 1958 amount, ranging between 104.3 and 111.3 billion rubles. Even assuming that the 1959-65 costs will be considerably higher than they were during the 1938-41 period, these figures still indicate a significant boost in investment, a large part of which is devoted to producer goods.

In general, it is expected that by 1965 all eastern regions of the USSR will be able to produce 88 per cent of the total Soviet copper, up to 71 per cent of aluminum, 50 per cent of the coal, 49 per cent of rolled metals, 48 per cent of the steel, 46 per cent of the coking coal and the same percentage of electric power, 45 per cent of wood-mill products, 44 per cent of pig iron, and 30 per cent of petroleum. Coal is to be the backbone of the industrial development of the East. By 1965 Western and Eastern Siberia and the Far East are expected to produce from 42 to 45 per cent of the total Soviet coal. By including coal production from the Kazakh SSR, these regions collectively will be responsible for about 60 per cent of the total country's coal increase anticipated for the 1959-65 period.[5]

One important factor in the development of eastern regions is that the 1959-65 investments are not concentrated in any one region as they are in European parts. Because of the huge territory and abundance of raw materials in many regions, the current investments are made with the view of maximizing gains from these investments in the shortest possible time.

Rich coal deposits in Siberia, exploitation of which is to be mostly by the open-cast method, will provide cheap fuel for many thermoelectric power plants to be constructed by 1965. In addition, the huge Bratsk and Irkutsk hydroelectric sites will create the powerful, low-cost energy base needed for the development of the eastern metallurgical industry and in the processing of raw materials. With greatly increased electrical power the exploitation of iron ore, aluminum, copper, nickel, and other minerals and metals is expected to be accelerated to support other industries.

Along with industrial expansion, numerous workers' settlements are to be established. In Western and Eastern Siberia over 70 new mines are to be opened between 1959 and 1965. This necessitates the establishment of communities providing at least minimal services. Undoubtedly this phase of "growing pains" will cause many bottlenecks throughout the whole scheme of expansion plans. Already the abundance of resources and limited investments in Siberia have created new problems for the decision-makers as to where to establish a new industry or expand production. This may be illustrated by a competition between Krasnoyarsk Kray in Eastern Siberia and Kemerovo Oblast in Western Siberia. Both regions have similar resources, and the problem of establishing new mines and factories is not based solely on the availability of raw materials. Resources in the Kemerovo region are located in already populated areas, thereby requiring less investments for new settlements. The region has an adequate transportation and communication network. On the other hand, Krasnoyarsk Kray is less populated than Kemerovo region but has richer resources, with an abundance of valuable minerals and metals, rare metals, and huge timber reserves. All in all, Krasnoyarsk Kray has a greater industrial potential than Kemerovo Oblast. This problem was not solved in 1959 and required a more intensive study of the potentialities of the two regions.

The past industrial drives in Siberia were based on the ability of European regions to provide the East with plant and equipment necessary for the expansion. During the 1959-65 period Siberia is expected to produce a considerable part of these requirements by its own efforts. This does not imply that Siberia is to be self-sufficient; it simply means that Siberia has the ability to produce many capital goods in greater volume than in the past. Along with this, Siberian labor is now better trained in mass production techniques than in the past. It is because of expansion in plant and equipment, plus the increase in labor productivity, that Siberia is expected to increase its industrial production from 16 per cent of the total RSFSR output in 1958 to 25 per cent by 1965.[6]

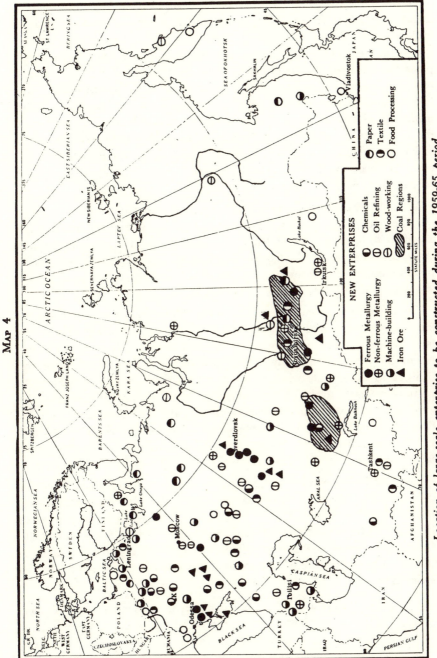

Map 4

Location of large-scale enterprise to be constructed during the 1959-65 period.

To be more specific, the Soviets have decided to establish a third metallurgical base in the East, producing annually between 15 and 20 million metric tons of pig iron. This base is to be supported by resources located in the Kuzbass and Karaganda. While this base is being developed, plans for a fourth metallurgical base are being worked out. The fourth base is to be located in Eastern Siberia and is to be supported by resources in Southern Yakutia and Irkutsk Oblast. The main objective of the third metallurgical base is to satisfy the industrial demands of Western Siberia, the Kazakh SSR, and Central Asia; the fourth base is to serve the needs of Eastern Siberia and the Far East. It is claimed by the Soviets that surveyed resources of the whole East indicate a potential output of pig iron ranging from 60 to 70 million metric tons annually.[7]

As to the development of oil and natural gas industries, the oil fields in the "Second Baku" are to improve their efficiency and the natural gas output is to be greatly expanded in the Uzbek SSR in order to facilitate a rapid development of the chemical industry, especially in Central Asia. In addition, greater efforts are to be devoted to exploitation of timber resources in Omsk, Novosibirsk, Krasnoyarsk, and Irkutsk regions.

The complexity of eastern industrial growth is mainly centered around construction of new and increase in old capacities. The Kuzbass Metallurgical Combine, for example, during the 1959-65 period is to increase its steel output by 48 per cent. The Magnitorgorsk Metallurgical Plant in the Urals is to expand its production of rolled metals from 5.2 million to 8.5 million metric tons. The new large-scale metallurgical plants are to be constructed at Stalinsk in Western Siberia and at Tayshet in Eastern Siberia. The Magnitka Metallurgical Combine will be at Ermakovsk in the Kazakh SSR. It is claimed that the last metallurgical combine was already in partial operation in 1959 and will reach full capacity by 1964.[8]

Any considerable increase in metallurgy requires an additional output of coal, especially coking coal. To satisfy all the demands for coal, Siberia, the Far East, and the Kazakh SSR by 1965 are expected to produce from 230 to 235 million metric tons of coal annually, of which the Kazakh SSR is to produce between 48 and 49 million metric tons.[9] It is obvious that the eastern parts of the RSFSR are to be the major producers of coal in the Soviet East.

Natural gas is new in the East but it has been discovered in the Tumen Oblast, Yakutia, and Central Asia. Only the resources in Central Asia are being exploited. The rich Bukhara-Khiva natural gas reserves in the Uzbek SSR are estimated at 1.3 trillion cubic meters, which is equivalent to two billion metric tons of coal. They are considered to be the largest deposit in the USSR. By 1965 the production of natural gas by the Uzbek SSR is expected to amount to 18 billion cubic meters, large enough to supply all of Central Asia, the Kazakh SSR, and the southern parts of the Urals. By the end of 1965 Uzbek gas is to be piped from Bukhara to Chelyabinsk, about 1,300 miles, and from Gazlit to Sverdlovsk, about 1,400 miles. Actual piping of gas to the Urals, however, is not expected before 1963. The natural gas industry is of tremendous significance to the Uzbek SSR. For example, in 1958 natural gas accounted for 3.3 per cent of all fuel consumption; by 1965 it is expected to be 60 per cent.

As shown in Chapter 1, the energy resources of the East are to be greatly expanded through additional capacities of thermoelectric and hydroelectric facilities. By the end of 1965, at least five large-scale hydroelectric power plants providing sufficient energy for the development of eastern industries will be partially or fully operative. One interesting point is that hydroelectric power resources are concentrated in Siberia, whereas the thermolectric resources are fund largely in the Kazakh SSR and Central Asia. The reason is obvious: the presence of great rivers in Siberia.

The eastern non-ferrous resources are more dispersed than the ferrous deposits. The potential key locations of non-ferrous metallurgy in the Kazakh SSR, Central Asia, the Urals, and Eastern Siberia are to be considerably developed. It is expected that before the end of 1965 a large-scale aluminum industry utilizing local raw materials and cheap energy is to be established in Krasnoyarsk Kray and in Irkutsk Oblast. The copper industry of the Kazakh SSR, Central Asia, and Eastern Siberia is expected to enlarge it capacity, and the production of other non-ferrous metals such as nickel, lead, and gold are destined for expansion. It must be remembered that a large part of the anticipated expansion in production of many non-ferrous metals is to be achieved through the introduction of modern technology in processing of ores containing more than one product.

## REGIONAL INDUSTRIAL SELF-SUFFICIENCY

Regional industrial self-sufficiency does not imply an absolute independence in all types of goods and services. However, an abundance of basic raw materials, technology, and manpower with required skills are the most important factors in self-sufficiency for a region.

Generally, the European part of the Soviet Union is more self-sufficient than the Eastern part. European resources are better balanced in terms of concentration, manpower, transportation, communication, technology, and location in relation to consuming markets. The Eastern part, although rich in resources, lacks many economic factors indispensable for rapid economic development. True, it would be easy for the Soviets to increase the Eastern population by forceful means as has been done in the past, but the problem would still be to provide jobs and housing for migrants once they are there. Thus, voluntary migration to the East and its industrial expansion are inseparable problems and must be solved simultaneously. Since it is much easier to train masses of unskilled workers in mining and construction than in production of capital and consumers' goods, the logical thing for the Russians to do first was to establish mining and metallurgy in the East as the foundation of modern industry.

In the past, Soviet leaders felt that rapid economic development in Siberia and the Far East was bound to be costly. This attitude can be found in the resistance of the so-called "anti-Party" group to Khrushchev's agricultural expansion to the East. But Khrushchev puts his faith in the superiority of natural resources of the East and in the enthusiasm of the people to support him there.

In the pre-Khrushchev era the Russians felt that the huge eastern territory with its sparse population could not be economically developed. The 1939-59 population growth was rapid. A large part of this increase occurred in the regions where the economic expansion is currently planned. In addition to an abundance of resources and the increased population, modern technology has increased labor productivity in these regions. Consequently, these three basic considerations—ample resources, increase in the manpower and its skill, and modern technology— are behind the potential expansion of the most profitable eastern areas rather than all the regions simultaneously.

Severe climatic conditions in northern Siberia and the Far East make life and work difficult. These regions require a special approach in their development. But the climate is better in the southern regions, and most of the urbanization and industrialization are centered there. Primarily there is an abundance of resources in coal, iron ore, energy power, timber, and non-ferrous metals in the south. Considering its resources on a per capita basis, the eastern part of the RSFSR is more than self-sufficient in most basic industrial minerals and metals.

Between 1959 and 1965 Western and Eastern Siberia are expected to produce over one-fourth of the total Soviet coal output—about one billion metric tons at a cost ranging from 40 to 45 billion rubles less than if this volume were produced in the European part. During the same period the production of electric power for the country as a whole is to be doubled, whereas in Siberia it is expected to be quadrupled.[10] The Seven-Year Plan, as developed for Siberia, foresees expansion in mining, metallurgy, oil refineries, lumber mills, and chemical works, conversion of the Trans-Siberian Railroad to electric traction, and many other activities. The only items so far lacking are crude oil, natural gas, potassium salts, and phosphorites. However, the Russians are optimistically convinced that even these scarce resources will be discovered in Siberia. Thus, Siberia as a whole has a great potentiality in economic self-sufficiency, even though its current capacities are small.

Another important factor in the long-run self-sufficiency of Siberia and the Far East is its economic position as related to China, Mongolia, and the Korean People's Democratic Republic. Already there are joint research projects on the Russo-Chinese frontiers, cooperation in the construction and operation of industrial enterprises, and exchange of goods and services between the USSR and its eastern neighbors. Plans are under consideration for construction of bridges across the Amur River to provide overland transportation between the Russian Far East and China. It is also planned to build hydroelectric power plants on the Amur River and the Black Dragon River, the power of which would be used for the economic development of these regions.

With the potential increase of energy resources in Siberia, the planned capacity seems to be much above the normal requirement of the whole region. The question might then be raised: why do the Soviets want such a rapid and great increase in energy capacity? The newly established aluminum industry and increasing energy demands for the production of other light metal industries will consume about 20 per cent of the total output of energy by 1965.[11] Most of this energy for aluminum will come from hydroelectric power plants. But what the Soviets are planning to do with the excess energy is a question. The Uzbek SSR also has an excessive energy output, a considerable part being utilized in nuclear research. Considering their experience in the Uzbek SSR, it is quite possible that the Russians are moving their nuclear research, which requires a large amount of cheap energy, to Siberia.

By 1965 the Kazakh SSR expects to increase it non-ferrous and ferrous metallurgy, machine-building, energy power, chemical and petroleum industries. However, this republic, as in the case of Siberia, lacks consumer goods, housing, and all other factors needed to establish permanent urbanization, even though it now produces more than enough grain and livestock products. What is lacking is transportation, communication, and electric power, for which there seems to be no large investment in these areas.

In Central Asia, the Uzbek SSR by 1965 will still remain the leader in cotton growing. In industrial development the emphasis is on newly developed natural gas resources in Bukhara. In general, the Uzbek SSR in 1965, as in the past, will still be deficient in consumer goods and food-stuffs. Other Central Asian republics, where the main emphasis is on agriculture rather than on industry, are assigned the task of expanding industrial capacity. Since the Kazakh SSR and Central Asia are deficient in timber, they would import it from Siberia and export surplus agricultural products such as grain, cotton, livestock in addition to non-ferrous products, coal, natural gas, and a few other industrial goods. The greatest industrial expansion is to be in Western Siberia, Eastern Siberia, the Kazakh SSR, and the Urals, where self-sufficiency in natural resources is more than assured.

## NEW INDUSTRIAL BASES

During the 1959-65 period, which is already projected to 1970-73, the European industrial bases are expected to increase their production through larger investments in technology. The East, however, is earmarked for expansion of capacity, mainly through development of new industrial complexes specializing in production of a few goods.

During the current seven-year period the total Soviet industrial investment will be from 1,940 to 1,970 billion rubles. Of this, from 1,485 to 1,510 billions rubles are allocated for the construction of plant and equipment, from 455 to 460 billion rubles for the construction of public and private housing.[12] The total average annual investment is to be between 277 and 287 billion rubles. However, in 1959 the total investment amounted to 230 billion rubles; in 1960, 255 billion rubles.[13] Apparently the 1959-65 planned investments are not to be at any uniform rates and it is quite possible that the Soviets are already having difficulties in investing the planned sums. On the other hand, investments in some industries are being made at higher rates than in others. For example, in 1960 the chemical industry was expected to invest 30 per cent more than in 1959; the iron and steel industry's outlay in 1960 was to be 20 per cent greater; 15 per cent more investments are earmarked for the extraction of gas and oil. Only housing in 1960 was within the 1959-65 average annual investment of 64 billion rubles.

Of the 144 major projects to be constructed during the 1959-65 period, 54 per cent—78 of them—are to be located in the East. Excluding the energy power plants, 61 enterprises, or 56 per cent of the total undertakings, are to be located in the East. As can be seen from the table below, the greatest expansion in the East is in ferrous, non-ferrous, oil refining, woodworking and thermoelectric plants while the West is to have an expansion in machine-building, chemicals, paper, textiles, and food-processing enterprises.

TABLE 1—*Number of Large-Scale Enterprises Planned for Construction During the 1959-65 Period* [14]

| Type of enterprises | Total number of enterprises | Urals | Western Siberia | Eastern Siberia | Far East | Kazakh SSR | Central Asia |
|---|---|---|---|---|---|---|---|
| Ferrous | 12 | 4 | 1 | 1 | – | 3 | – |
| Non-ferrous | 10 | – | – | 3 | – | 4 | – |
| Machine-building | 19 | 1 | – | – | 1 | 4 | – |
| Chemicals | 19 | 3 | 1 | – | – | 1 | 1 |
| Oil Refinery | 13 | 2 | 1 | 1 | – | 1 | 1 |
| Woodworking | 6 | – | 1 | 2 | 1 | – | – |
| Paper | 9 | – | – | 1 | 2 | – | – |
| Textile | 8 | – | 2 | 1 | – | – | 1 |
| Food Processing | 12 | – | – | 1 | 2 | 1 | 1 |
| Thermoelectric | 24 | 1 | 3 | 3 | – | 2 | 5 |
| Hydroelectric | 10 | – | – | 2 | – | – | – |
| Atomic power | 2 | 1 | – | – | – | – | – |

During this period the Urals and the Kazakh SSR will lead in the construction of ferrous metallurgical undertakings. In non-ferrous metallurgy the Kazakh SSR ranks first, followed by Eastern Siberia. In the machine-building industry the Kazakh SSR is to have four new plants of various capacities, but chemicals and oil refining go to the Urals.

The chemical industry in the Soviet Union may well be called the "baby industry" because of its recent establishment. In the current Seven-Year Plan the total investment in this industry is to be from 100 to 105 billion rubles, over fivefold the amount invested during the previous seven-year period. Approximately half of the current investment is earmarked for the construction of new plant and equipment. All in all, 140 large and small new chemical enterprises are planned for construction, and over 130 existing plants are to be enlarged or reconstructed.[15] The Plan emphasizes a rapid rise in the output of plastic and synthetic products, with the major producers to be located in Stavropol, Krasnoyarsk, Western Ukraine, Second Baku, and the Uzbek SSR.

The first Siberian large-scale oil refinery was built in Omsk in 1950, and crude oil was shipped there from the Second Baku in tank cars. Now, however, oil is piped to Omsk some 930 miles away from the oil fields. The Omsk refinery is still not fully utilized, and only 12 different products were produced there in 1959. It is expected that by 1965 this plant, destined to become one of the largest refineries in the USSR, will be operating at full capacity, producing up to 60 different products.[16] A refinery is planned for construction in Angarsk, near Irkutsk; another small refinery at Khabarovsk in the Far East has been in operation for a number of years. The Omsk and Angarsk refineries are to be supplied with crude oil from Second Baku. The Khabarovsk plant uses oil produced at Okha, on Sakhalin Island.

The woodworking, paper, textile, and food-processing enterprises are of less significance in the Urals than they are in Siberia and the Far East. The most important regions in these activities are Western and Eastern Siberia. Although the Far East is to increase its output of wood, paper, and processed food at the end of 1965, these increases, in comparison with regions having larger populations, will be much smaller, except of course in fishery products, where the Far East is the USSR's leading region.

## SHORTCOMINGS

Past Soviet industrial growth is largely attributable to discoveries of new and richer resources and adaptation of new technology in use in more advanced countries. These factors alone, under any economic system, are bound to produce unusually high gains in industrial production. Moreover, since 1955 the Soviets have made a number of socio-economic adjustments which, in general, increased the efficiency of the whole economic system. But the main factors in the rapid industrial growth depend almost entirely on the quality and quantity of plant, equipment, and personnel. This also implies that the Soviet Union, as any country for that matter, cannot maintain its past high industrial growth rate indefinitely; the law of diminishing returns rules out the idea that high investment rates will always result in high growth rates.

For many reasons the growth rate may abate when the economy becomes complex. Resources may be exhausted, deterioration of plant and equipment without timely replacement may cause the decline, or any changes in socio-economic factors individually or collectively might be powerful enough to create conditions which would adversely affect the growth rate. Soviet planners, and Western students of the USSR as well, anticipate the impact on the past growth rate and predict that future growth rates will be smaller. Western specialists in Soviet economics expect the average annual rate during the 60's to be about six per cent, somewhat under the rate achieved during the 50's. The Soviets themselves expect their growth rate during the 1959-65 period to be only 8.6 per cent as compared with 15.9 per cent recorded for the 1947-57 period.[17] This is a reduction of some 46 per cent. Moreover, the planned 1960 industrial growth rate is expected to reach only eight per cent. Apparently the enthusiastic planners of the current Plan are incapable of overcoming the obstacles encountered even at the beginning of the Plan. What is more important is that the anticipated 1960 growth rate in producers' goods is expected to be 8.8 per cent, against the planned average annual rate of 9.3 per cent; the 1960 rate for consumers' goods is to be 6.4 per cent instead of 7.3 per cent as predicted in the Plan. Unless the Russians can make some drastic revisions in their investments and timing, it is highly unlikely that they can obtain the original planned growth rate. It is probable that the rate will be considerably below the original rate throughout the whole 1959-65 period.

It is true that during the 1947-57 period the official growth rate was high, but economic conditions during this period, especially the first half, were quite different from the 1959-65 conditions. It is also true that immediately after the end of the war investments were earmarked mostly for the reconstruction and rehabilitation of existing plant and equipment, gains from which were at much higher rates than if these investments were applied to the construction of new plant and equipment as they are now.

## Cost of Production

Since about 40 per cent of the total gross investment in the current Seven-Year Plan is committed to backward regions of the East, a large share of it would be devoted just to maintain past growth rates. Any increase in the past growth rate would tend to increase the current costs. Exploitation of natural resources and production of many basic materials in eastern regions is less costly than in the European part, but these are statistical costs based on assumptions that a given technology and manpower of a given skill are to be used in the exploitation of the resources. Other factors may significantly affect the rate and the cost of production.

To increase output at the rapid rate required would entail additional labor, which in turn would mean urbanization of now isolated regions. It means a considerable increase in the standard of living for workers in the East. Should their wants not be fully satisfied their demands for consumer goods and services will stay ahead of the expansion of output of their mines, steel mills, lumber camps, and so on. Should this be the case, and there are indications that it might be, then a rapid labor turnover and a lack of enthusiasm among workers would reduce productivity and increase the cost of production. Since the Russians are anxious to industrialize eastern regions, these problems will inevitably crop up and will accelerate the rise in the cost of production. In the past the Soviets attempted to correct these conditions with higher premium payments to workers; these cannot be ruled out now.

## Technology

Economic growth stems primarily from investments in more and better technology or "know-how." In general terms, technology and automation are applicable to large-scale enterprises such as oil refineries and steel mills where production of goods is automatically controlled from beginning to end or where a part of the production process is controlled. It is through increased investments in technology, controlled by the monopolistic State, that the Russians are expecting to increase labor productivity. Moreover, potential technological growth in the USSR is voluminous because of the present low level in technology and because of the emphasis on capital goods to which automation processes are more adaptable than in the production of consumer goods.

The Russians are enthusiastic about advances in technology and science. They see a real benefit in adopting scientific production techniques, without fear that it might create unemployment, which allegedly is absent in the USSR. They claimed that if the 1955 technology in the USSR had been on the save level as it was in 1940, it would have required an additional 15 million workers to produce the 1955 gross industrial output.[18] Also, scientific discoveries and practices are being adopted on a large scale. It is claimed that the use of aluminum and plastics in the production of cable during the 1959-65 period will save over 10 billion rubles in the cost of production and will supplant the need for 400,000 metric tons of copper and an equivalent tonnage of lead. A rapid conversion from coal to natural gas and oil during the same period will save another 125 billion rubles.[19] These economic considerations influence the current expansion in production of natural gas, plastics, and aluminum.

Although new technology is profitable and being used intensively in certain economic sectors, it cannot be as advanced in the Soviet Union as it is in countries with competitive markets where research and development in industrial innovations tend to reduce the cost of production and increase profits for competitors of similar goods on the same market. Another drawback lies in the planning system itself. Only large-scale technological adaptations approved by the government are permitted. Since large-scale technological changes often require temporary reduction in production for the factory, such changes usually are possible only when a new factory is constructed or when existing facilities are being expanded.

It is for these reasons that adaptation of new technology or techniques in many industrial sectors is at a slow pace. Even in sectors where technology and automation are relatively advanced, there still are many tasks performed manually. This is especially noted in supporting occupations in coal, timber, steel mills, and machine-building industries. Partial automation is more extensively used in chemical, oil, timber, consumer goods, and food-processing industries. But even these achievements are far behind the development of many Western countries. Nevertheless, complete automation does exist in fields such as the bottling of milk, assembly lines in production of passenger cars and trucks, and in other products, especially when they are produced by a large-scale enterprise.

Emphasis on modern technology during the 1959-65 period is enthusiastically advocated by the Russians, but this is centered around a few basic industries, including matallurgy, oil, chemical, coal, machine-building, and some other major industries. Another important fact is that since Russian equipment is generally of a low quality and handled by poorly trained workers, its replacement is at a high rate. Consequently, even though the production of modern technological means might be rapid, its actual benefit will be reduced by a high replacement rate.

## Labor Force

The size, skill, mobility, and standard of living of the labor force in any society tend to indicate how rapidly economic growth can be paced. The past industrial growth of the Soviet Union could not have been achieved merely by increasing the number of workers, and the 1959-65 production targets require all-out exploitation of land, labor, and capital. The planned average annual industrial growth rate of 8.6 per cent cannot be matched to the average annual increase in population of 1.5 per cent, and the size of labor force cannot be drastically increased in a short period of time. For example, during the 1950-58 period the gross industrial output was increased by 148 per cent against an increase of 40 per cent in the total number of state-employed workers and employees. It is expected that by 1965 the gross industrial output, as compared with 1950, will be 3.5 times larger, while the state-employed labor force by 70 per cent.[20] Thus, the expected industrial growth rate will outstrip the labor force increase by many times.

Even if the Soviets wanted to increase industrial output by enlarging the labor force they cannot simply transfer farm labor to industry. Such transfers would be insufficient numerically and the labor productivity too low to have a real impact on industrial growth.

For substantial gains in industrial growth rates, the Russians must increase the level of education of their people, which would increase productivity and technology. The first phase of this program is already in effect. However, recent adjustments in the educational system are devised to produce skilled workers for factories rather than inventors or designers of plant and equipment. This would present new problems. Assuming that a large number of workers have become highly skilled and assuming that as a result there have been greater technological advances, there would then be slower net gains in the quality of labor. This disparity would occur upon attainment of higher level of skill and would in turn be followed by a rapid obsolescence of existing skills because of a more rapid development of technology requiring new skills.

A larger, more highly skilled labor force with an increasing amount of technology will increase industrial growth rates. Official Soviet figures show that during the 1951-55 period the industrial labor force was increased by 3.3 million workers or 23.4 per cent. During the same period the official average annual industrial growth rate was 13.2 per cent and the average annual labor productivity was 7.6 per cent. Thus, an increase of one per cent in labor productivity resulted in more than one per cent in output. The Soviets claimed that during this period 32 per cent of the total increase in the gross industrial output was due enlargement of the labor force; increased labor productivity accounted for the other 68 per cent.[21]

During the 1959-65 period the Soviets are planning to increase their industrial labor force at a rate twice as high as in the 1950-58 period. Though there will be a larger total population and fewer men in military services the expected growth rate for the industrial labor force is still overly optimistic. Moreover, much of this labor growth has to come from the least educated and least industrially skilled population of the East, where mobility would be high and productivity low. Nevertheless, the Soviets estimated that the additional labor would be responsible for not less than 25 per cent of the total increase in the industrial output; the other 75 per cent would come from increased labor productivity. Consequently, by comparing the 1951-55 period with that of 1959-65, it is clear that greater gains in technology are anticipated in the later period. This may be seen from the official Soviet figures estimating the 1959-65 average annual industrial growth rate of 135 billion rubles against 90 billion rubles recorded for the previous seven years.[22] But industrial labor productivity in the Soviet Union in 1958 was between 40 to 50 per cent of that in the United States; in agriculture it was about 33 per cent.[23] Consequently, a slight increase in labor productivity in the USSR results in higher economic growth rates.

Perhaps the greatest obstacle in the potential industrial expansion during the current Seven-Year Plan will be the labor force, especially in the East.

TABLE 2—*Average Annual Number of*
*State-employed Persons in the East* [24]
(*in millions*)

| Region | 1955 | 1958 | Percent increase 1955 to 1958 |
|---|---|---|---|
| Urals _____ | 4.6 | 5.1 | 11 |
| Western Siberia _____ | 3.1 | 3.6 | 16 |
| Eastern Siberia _____ | 1.8 | 2.0 | 11 |
| Far East _____ | 1.3 | 1.4 | 8 |
| Kazakh SSR _____ | 2.0 | 2.6 | 30 |
| Central Asia _____ | 1.2 | 2.4 | 100 |
| Total _____ | 14.0 | 17.1 | 22 |

During the 1955-58 period the number of state-employed persons in the USSR increased by about 13 per cent. The increase in eastern regions was 22 per cent, indicating that eastern state employment expanded at a much higher rate than for the country as a whole. If during this period eastern regions increased their state employment by 3.1 millions or roughly one million workers annually, it would be reasonable to assume that to maintain the industrial growth rate during the current Seven-Year Plan at the 1955-58 rate the East would need an additional seven million workers. This increase alone would represent about 58 per cent of the total increase in the industrial labor force planned for the 1959-65 period.

A second assumption can also be made: since over 40 per cent of the total investments during the present Plan are earmarked for the East, it may be assumed that additional labor requirements may also be roughly 40 per cent, or a total of about 4.8 million. Based on these two assumptions a roughly estimated increase in state employment in the East might be placed at between five and seven million workers, about one-half of the total planned increase for the country. A figure of six million is reasonable because a large part of the current investments in the East are allocated for mining and construction activities, requiring a large number of unskilled or semi-skilled workers.

From where can these workers and their families be recruited? If half of them had only one dependent, then the total number of persons depending on earnings from eastern industrial expansion would become nine million instead of six million. Certainly the six million peasants now living in the East cannot be recruited for industrial jobs. In fact, the peasants must be encouraged to stay on the farms to produce more foodstuffs to satisfy the increasing demands of an enlarged industrial labor force. There should be no doubt that the industrial labor force in the East must be increased considerably, but the establishment of the well-propagandized third metallurgical base would require tens of thousands of new workers. The construction of power plants, non-ferrous metallurgical, chemical, and many other enterprises requires not only unskilled and semi-skilled but highly trained personnel, many of whom would come to the East with their families. Perhaps some of the highly skilled workers would be transferred from the West for temporary duty but they, too, must be provided with housing, consumer goods, and services which are scarce in the East. Obviously these scarcities will not encourage enthusiasm on the part of the workers; it would rather increase their job mobility.

The problem of providing additional unskilled or even semi-skilled workers for the East is much simpler than that related to technical personnel who must be recruited largely in the West. Anticipating this problem the Siberian and the Far Eastern Institutes of Economics have already made a study of the local population—occupations, education, age, sex, marriage, mobility, and so on—in order to determine how many of them can be recruited for industrial jobs.

Since the eastern regions, especially Siberia and the Far East, have a large number of natives living in isolated settlements, occupied in hunting and fishing, the government is contemplating transferring many of them to the industrial sector. Again, because of the dispersed population and the absence of opportunities for industrial employment, many eastern housewives stay home. These are the two largest potential sources of additional unskilled and semi-skilled workers, and the Soviets hope to encourage their participation in the industrial development of the East. It is significant that during the 1959-65 period an increased number of nurseries and kindergartens are planned to free women for industrial employment. Whether the women will respond to it wholly is doubtful since their men will be getting higher incomes and the women will not need to participate to maintain the standard of living already established.

It is also no coincidence that the government announced the reduction in working hours. Expansion in the number of nurseries and kindergartens and reduction in working time serve as incentives to encourage direct participation of all able-bodied persons. On the other hand, joining the industrial labor force means a sacrifice in leisure time to many of these persons. Leisure time is not necessarily idleness. A Soviet housewife stays home, takes care of her children, cooks meals, and so on, but since her efforts are not sold on the market and cannot be included in the gross national product her staying home becomes leisure, in economic terms.

The 1959-65 targets call for strenuous efforts by all Russians to increase their standard of living sometime in the future. Certainly, the current industrial goals are aimed at greater sacrific of leisure, of consumption, or a combination of both for a great many people. From the theoretical viewpoint the net gain will become obvious at some future date when people will be able to enjoy all the leisure and all the consumption which they sacrifice now in order to achieve the industrial growth rate. But the masses do not think in terms of the future. They want to increase their standard of living now. Sacrifices which the government has imposed upon people are already backfiring. In October 1959 young people who were recruited in the Ukraine and White Russia to work in Karaganda revolted against the conditions under which they were required to work and live. It has been reported that it was a bloody revolt and some 100 workers were killed and 1,000 wounded.[25] The use of force indicates a gap between the interests of the people and those of the State. Such differences in interest, if expanded to other regions, would adversely affect the expected growth rates or would force them to be extended beyond 1965.

## Consumer Goods

Soviet leaders believe that current sacrifices in consumption and in leisure eventually will produce a higher standard of living for the Russian people. They believe that by 1965 plants and equipment which are being constructed now will enable them to produce more goods and services. As industrial output increases the labor force also follows the upswing, which spells out higher income and more diversified goods. This would lead to the gradual transfer of labor and resources from industries with a high rate of productivity, such as mining and capital goods, to industries with lower productivity, such as services. In countries where the State does not interefere with such processes the conversion from one type of investment to another may be rapid, but in the Soviet Union, where the State controls the economy, this conversion can easily be retarded by the State itself.

In 1940 the production of capital goods represented 61 per cent of the total industrial output and consumer goods 39 per cent. In 1958 this ratio was changed to 72 per cent and 28 per cent, respectively. The planned 1965 ratio for capital goods to consumer goods is about 75 per cent to 25 per cent. Moreover, in comparison with 1958, the 1965 increase in output of capital goods is estimated at 85 to 88 per cent but in consumer goods only 62 to 65 per cent.[26] Nevertheless, at the end of 1965 Soviet planners expect more consumer goods and enough capital goods for replacement and for future expansion.

These are the plans and hopes of Soviet leaders. They assume that they can control investments and the people's demands for consumer goods. Their control over investments is unquestionable; but the control of consumers' demands is not automatic, as it is with investments. The bloody revolt of young workers in Karaganda against involuntary sacrifices demanded by the State revealed that workers no longer can be treated as elements requiring the minimum in investment for the maintenance of their standard of living. If Soviet planners have failed to recognize and to consider the wishes of the workers for more of the comforts of life and if this wish is ignored for the sake of a greater growth rate, then it is reasonable to assume that similar revolts may occur more frequently, especially at the end of the current industrial drive when tempers of the masses could become more unruly. Consequently, it seems reasonable to assume that the long-run industrial growth in the Soviet Union would, to a large degree, depend upon greater diversion of investments from capital to consumer goods.

## Bibliography—Chapter 19

[1] *Voprosy Ekonomiki*, No. 8, 1959, p. 27.

[2] *Planovoye Khozaystvo*, No. 12, 1959, p. 67.

[3] Efimov, A. N., *Perspektivy Razvitiya Promyshlennosti SSSR*, Moscow, 1959, p. 82.

[4] Vedishchev, A. I., *Chto i Gde Budet Postroeno v 1959-1965 Godakh*, Moscow, 1959, p. 38.

[5] Efimov, *op. cit.*, p. 82.

[6] *Ogonek*, No. 3, January, 1958, p. 8.

[7] *Voprosy Ekonomiki*, No. 5, 1959, p. 129.

[8] *Ibid.*

[9] Vedishchev, *op. cit.*, p. 43.

[10] *Planovoye Khozaystvo*, No. 12, 1959, p. 69.

[11] *Ibid.*

[12] *Voprosy Ekonomiki*, No. 8, 1959, pp. 121-123.

[13] *USSR*, No. 12, (39), 1959, p. 19.

[14] *Atlas SSSR*, Moscow, 1959, p. 49.

[15] Vedishchev, *op. cit.*, pp. 24-27.

[16] *Sovetskiy Soyuz*, No. 1, (107), 1959, p. 15.

[17] Tikhonov, I. A., *Osnovnaya Ekonomicheskaya Zadacha SSSR*, Moscow, 1959, pp. 178-81; Central Intelligence Agency, *Soviet Manpower 1960-1970*, Washington, D. C., May 1960, p. 15.

[18] Tikhonov, *op. cit.*, p. 230.

[19] *Voprosy Ekonomiki*, No. 8, 1959, p. 124.

[20] *Narodnoye Khozaystvo SSSR v 1958 Godu*, Moscow, pp. 55, 61, 156; *Kontrol'nye Tsifry Razvitiya Narodnogo Khozaystva SSSR na 1959-1965 Gody*, Moscow, 1958, p. 93.

[21] *Narodnoye Khozaystvo SSSR*, *op. cit.*, *p.* 661; Tikhonov, *op. cit.*, pp. 226, 275.

[22] Efimov, *op. cit.*, p. 13.

[23] *Tikhonov*, *op. cit.*, p. 227.

[24] *Narodnoye Khozaystvo SSSR*, *op. cit.*, p. 661; *Narodnoye Khozaystvo RSFSR v 1958 Godu*, Moscow, 1959, p .370.

[25] *The Washington Post and Times Herald*, April 17, 1960.

[26] Efimov, *op. cit.*, p. 23.

## CHAPTER 20

# Challenge to the West

~~~~~~~~~~~~~~~~~~~~~~~~~~~~~~~~~~~~~~~~~~

## INTRODUCTION

The United States and the Soviet Union, the two colossuses, are engaged in a gigantic struggle for scientific, military, political, economic, and ideological supremacy of the world. In this struggle every phase of the socio-economic structure of the West is openly and aggressively challenged by the Soviet Union in its determination to convert the world to the Soviet image. Clearly the sweeping nature of this challenge will not depend on victory in any single phase of the struggle. Many phases of this struggle are not of the West's own choosing; likewise they cannot be determined solely by the USSR because in the race for supremacy new forces will emerge which might change the whole nature of the contest. Perhaps the most important phase of this contest is the economic challenge to the West and specifically the United States. In November 1957 Khrushchev said:[1]

"We declare war upon you—excuse me for using such an expression—in the peaceful field of trade. We declare war. We will win over the United States. The threat to the United States is not the ICBM, but in the field of peaceful production. We are relentless in this and will prove the superiority of our system."

Certainly this cannot be an idle boast on the part of Khrushchev. Should he fail, it would be a joyful victory for the West and a devastating blow for the Communists. But it cannot be mere propaganda, and many Western students of Soviet affairs have already realized the danger of Soviet industrial growth during the last few years. Many fear that the Soviet challenge to outstrip the industrial output of the United States will be a blow to belief in the superiority of American productivity and standard of living.

As proclaimed by Khrushchev, the challenge in multidimensional, threatening dislocation of all overlapping aspects in the socio-economic

528

framework. But it is the economic contest in foreign markets that is considered to be the most vital to Western superiority. The West knows the Soviet military and political tactics, and necessary measures have been taken to weaken them; but the economic aspect in the conflict is new and has caught the West unprepared. Certainly, prior to 1955 Soviet maneuvering in international matters was mostly military; between 1955 and 1957 it became more political, and now it is economic.

The prime tactic now is rapid industrial growth, and by its success the Soviet Union is expecting to impose socio-economic changes advantageous to the USSR in underdeveloped and uncommitted countries of the world. The Russians believe that their spectacular industrial progress would make their socio-economic pattern irresistable for many underdeveloped countries. By adopting partial Soviet-type societies, these countries would become prospective areas for communist infiltration. In this lies the danger to the stability and superiority of Western institutions.

## "NEW LOOK" POLICY

There are many reasons for Khrushchev's relaxation of the "tough" policy maintained by Stalin toward the West. Some have been analyzed in past chapters. In this chapter the "New Look" policy is scrutinized in terms of peaceful coexistence, as proclaimed by Khrushchev in February 1956, and its impact on the West, specifically on the leading nation—the United States.

As was explained before, the concept of peaceful coexistence was developed by Lenin for the purpose of winning time during which the young country could stabilize and expand its economy. Peace was important to Lenin and to the Communists from both the humanitarian and economic viewpoints. But economic reasons were predominant, for it was believed that with a rapidly expanding economy and a rising standard of living and without war the Soviet Union could influence other countries to become communist states.

Khrushchev revived, overhauled, and expanded this policy, which has become the major Soviet goal in world politics. He maintains that peaceful coexistence of countries with different social systems is a necessity since the West and the East possess nuclear weapons which would inflict fatal consequences upon mankind if brought into action. He describes peaceful coexistence as the condition needed for relaxation of tensions created by the philosophy of the "position of strength" maintained during the Cold War, as a force stemming from the assumption of mutual concessions in the interests of peace. He states that this term implies elements of mutual interest among different countries, since otherwise normal conditions cannot be maintained.

Specifically, Khrushchev emphasizes the fact that coexistence is the recognition of the right of every country to settle independently all its political and social problems, recognition of the existence of different social systems, respect for sovereignty, adherence to the principle of non-interference in internal affairs, and settlement of all international questions by negotiation. These are the central points behind Khrushchev's peaceful coexistence theory and his "reasonable foundation" for it. And as he construes the noble but broad conditions for coexistence, he rattles his sword and tells the world that mutual concessions for the sake of peaceful coexistence must not be confused with concessions in matters of idealogy or communism.[2] Therefore, the policy serves as a tool devised for the protection of all gains the Communists hold now and which cannot be upset by the West or by its assistance to peoples dissatisfied with the communist rule, as was the case with Hungary.

Since the revival of this policy Khrushchev has not altered its original title. It is always "peaceful coexistence," or "coexistence" or "peace." Moreover, he never uses the word "peace" with modifiers such as "just," "lasting," "with honor," "with safety," "under the rule of law," as it is used in the West. The Russians have no objections to these modifiers but since Lenin failed to use them, the Communists are reluctant to employ them, and instead stick to broad phrasiology.

Both antagonists want "peace" because any prolonged war would be too expensive, and Khrushchev advocates general and complete disarmament within a short period of about four years, assuming that any country relieved of its weapons would automatically abolish the threat of war. He tells his listeners that maintenance of large armed forces is not only costly but it denies their employment for economic expansion. He points out that because of the formation of NATO and the beginning of the Cold War, the Russians had to enlarge their armed forces from 2.9 millions in 1948 to 5.8 millions by 1955; only with the relaxation of the Cold War did the Russians reduce this number to 3.6 millions in 1958 and in 1960 promised another reduction of 1.2 millions to a total strength of 2.4 millions.[3]

However, in all his discussions on the subject of peace Khrushchev does not refer to the fact that partial or total disarmament would not destroy the threat of war; it would simply leave every country temporarily without weapons in the event of war, and no signed treaty is sure security against violations. He purposely ignores the fact that the monolithic structure of the Soviets and their ethical inconsistency could swiftly increase the armed forces and nuclear armament at a time advantageous to them, while non-communist societies have a tendency to be slow in altering their economies from peace to war preparedness. As long as there are men who are able to assemble the hydrogen bomb, peace is not assured. He describes the intentions of the Soviet Union and of the whole Soviet bloc as peaceful and claims that universal disarmament is needed since peace no longer can be guaranteed through the efforts of two or three countries. Although possessing nuclear weapons, Khrushchev assures the West that they will not be used against anyone; yet during the last four years Soviet spokesman have threatened some 20 countries with nuclear devastation in reprisal for endangering Soviet security and interests.

The establishment and maintenance of some kind of stability by peaceful coexistence leading to complete disarmament would depend upon the good intentions of the West and the Communists alike. Prior to 1939 Hitler also emphasized his good intentions—until it was too late to stop him without war. Likewise, the Soviet postwar pressure upon Europe forced the West to distrust the good intentions of the USSR and to check any further advances by unified forces of NATO and similar organizations elsewhere. This mutual distrust resulted in the formation of two hostile camps, each seeking a breathing spell in order to find a solution.

As the cost of maintaining military competition became too high for the Russians, Khrushchev began more and more to emphasize coexistence, peace, and disarmament. And while he advocated peace to the West the current Seven-Year Plan was put into operation. Through it, Soviet leaders expect to create a powerful industrial base to assure the USSR of economic victory over the capitalist countries. The basic goal thus is to gain maximum time for increasing industrial production in order to win the competition with the West.[4] The Russians claim that their ideology will win in the economic contest over the West, particularly over United States. If the Russians are so sure of the superiority of their system, then why this hurry to beat the West in the shortest possible time? It is reasonable to assume that this rush offers a valuable clue to the Soviet's own fears. Apparently Soviet leaders believe that the West is ready to accept the principle of united action against the USSR. Perhaps because of this fear the Russians are trying to divide the West by driving a wedge between Western countries. Since it is important to Khrushchev that the West be a house divided against itself, it must be just as important to the West not only to proclaim alliance, mutual security, and common solidarity, but also to find some way for greater economic cooperation, perhaps even on a scale similar to that of the Soviet bloc.

Khrushchev's peaceful coexistence is the core of the "New Look" policy. The Communists had to formulate some kind of new policy to replace the obsolete policy of military aggression. The policy had to be labeled peaceful and of mutual benefit if it was to be attractive to newly independent but underdeveloped countries in Asia, the Far and Near East, and Africa. The Soviet Union itself needs peace to speed up its industrial expansion, to stimulate the efforts of the Russian people for the successful completion of current targets, and to demonstrate to all Communists and non-Communists alike that the Soviet system is better than capitalism. In essence, Khrushchev is trying to replace the current "balance of terror" with traditional concept of the balance of power.

Khrushchev challenges the capitalist countries to develop their science and culture to their fullest potential for the benefit of all mankind, to lower the cost of production in order to bring about a higher standard of living, and to maintain peace in the world. The challenge extends not only to the United States but to countries such as Greece and Monaco as well. It is easy to challenge Greece or Turkey to economic competition, but Khrushchev admits that it would require another ten or 12 years of all-out effort before such competition can take place with the United States. He discounts the purpose, vitality, and intellectual powers of capitalism in matters of self-preservation, and he cannot visualize what steps capitalism may take to protect its basic institutions. He assumes that capitalism has no philosophy as the Communists have found in Marx, and this is his error.

## SPHERE OF INFLUENCE

Soviet leaders believe that the establishment of a world-wide capitalist system is now impossible because it would require military action to force communist countries to join capitalism. They also believe that this act alone would develop a crisis in capitalism which would lead to its destruction and to the supremacy of communism as a world-wide system. According to the Russians, this is the main cause for the general crisis of capitalism and they feel that the balance of power between the two systems is now constantly changing to the detriment of capitalism and to the advantage of communism.

The Russians point out that in 1940 the USSR was the only communist country in the world, with less than 17 per cent of the world's territory, nine per cent of the world's population and about ten per cent of the industrial output of the world. Now, they say, the Communist orbit occupies 25 per cent of the territory of the globe, has about one-third of its total population and accounts for one-third of the total world's industrial output.[5] According to Soviet Academician Stanislav Strumilin, between 1937 and 1957 the industrial output of what he calls capitalist countries doubled whereas in the Communist orbit it increased by 8.7 times.[6] He claims that industrial growth between 1940 and 1958 almost doubled in the United States but was 4.3 times in the Soviet Union. These high growth rates in the USSR, Strumilin claims, were possible because of the superior communist system.

Communists are convinced of the weakness of capitalism because it had the opportunity to destroy communism when it existed in one country only. Now the Communist orbit includes 12 countries. It formed its own world market (CEMA) and the destruction of or even ideological changes in the orbit are beyond the power of capitalism. Thus, as they see it, humanity has entered a new stage of world power, divided into the capitalist and the communist blocs.

The formation of two great rival blocs of world powers was caused by the military, political, and economic postwar aggressiveness of the Soviet Union. The West was forced to seek collective security on the assumption that a group of countries can successfully defend each other against Soviet aggression. As a result the West organized military alliances in different parts of the world—NATO in Europe, CENTO (formerly the Baghdad Pact) in the Middle East, and SEATO in East Asia. The Soviet bloc likewise set up its own mutual defense alliance—the Warsaw Pact.

The main objective of the Western Alliance is defense, whereas the Communists are united in major military, political, economic, and philosophical questions. The Communists know where they are going, while the destination of the West is less definite. Even though the Communist orbit has its ideological difference, such differences are of greater proportions in the Western camp. The lack of unity among Western countries resulted in an attack by France, Great Britain, and Israel on Egypt in 1956, Turkey's saber-rattling at Syria in 1957, revolution in Iraq in 1958, and troubles in Lebanon, to name a few conflicts. In the weakness of Western unity lies communist strength. Having similar indeological and international aspirations, the Communist countries can act in unity and simultaneously.

Their dedication to principles of communism is responsible for clearer political unity. By pooling their resources for collective action they have committed themselves to the alliance for as long as the alliance exists. And, like it or not, they are represented by the Soviet Union as their leader, as the United States is the leader of the West.

Since the world is divided into two ideological spheres, Khrushchev feels that it is only logical that he be the spokesman for his sphere. Khrushchev, like Stalin, is for a two-power world. To him the settlement of international conflicts and the maintenance of international order and peace can be effected by the decisive voices of the United States and the Soviet Union. Khrushchev wants such division of power. This division might also be attractive to some Western leaders, but it cannot be publicly admitted because of the equality principle to which the West is committed in the United Nations, NATO, and in other pacts. Nevertheless, whether admitted or not, the fact is that the world is divided into two spheres of influence where major political and economic issues, if not now solved, are at least discussed by the leaders of the two spheres. Thus, the balance of power is used by the Soviets as a tool through which international stability can be maintained.

The existence of the spheres of influence is perhaps less risky for world peace than the existence of only two great countries, each having overwhelming destructive and economic powers. It would be extremely dangerous for the world if either country starts minor hostilities, which would be difficult to keep from spreading into general conflict. That is why Khruschev wants the world's division into two spheres with participation of smaller countries to control their behavior. By gaining such division he expects to increase his political and economic powers in relation to the powers of smaller non-communist countries. The Soviet goal to communize the world is the same now as it was in 1917; only the tactics are changed.

Since the Soviet bloc operates with a plan and systematically develops its economies presumably for the mutual benefit of its members, the members of the Western bloc must realize that competition, the heart of the capitalist system, requires some changes. In the past, competition was an important force among individual countries. Now competition involves blocs of countries. The United States is challenged to compete with the Soviet Union on an international level, and if the United States is to compete successfully it must devise a better means of controlling its own sphere of influence. It also must be recognized that pushing communism to uncommitted areas is a complex problem involving not only unorthodox methods, but numerous stages, timing, coordination of Russian economic expansion with that of other communist countries, and the external interests of non-communist countries. Realization and acceptance of this principle by the West would facilitate unity of action in the free world.

## INDUSTRIAL GROWTH

The Soviet industrial growth pattern is of considerable interest because of disagreement among Western students of Soviet affairs on the past and present rates. Even the rates estimated by different students for the same period are different. Computed industrial indices by Nutter, Seton, Shimkin-Leedy, and Kaplan-Moorsteen for the 1950-55 period show a variation in the average annual rate from 7.7 to 10.8 per cent whereas the official Soviet rate is 12.8 per cent, against 5.3 per cent for the United States. As if these rates are not confusing enough, Governor Nelson A. Rockefeller added to the bewilderment in the guessing game by estimating the Soviet post-war economic growth during the 1950-57 period at "about" six per cent.[7]

As was stated in previous chapters, variations in estimated Soviet industrial growth rates are due to selection of certain series in the estimates. In general, Soviet statistics are not standardized, and as a result the estimated growth rates would inevitably be biased. But even when the figures are standardized the comparison between the United States and the USSR may also be biased. For example, the national product in the United States is calculated from market transactions whereas in the Soviet Union it is calculated at the producers' value. Another troublesome deficiency in measuring industrial growth for the USSR is the exclusion of improvement in the quality and variety of goods and services. This omission is of significant magnitude in the current series. True, in the past the Soviets expanded their industrial output without similar expansion in quality and variety of goods and services, but it is reasonable to assume that in 1955 or in 1957 there was greater variety and better workmanship in Soviet-produced goods and services than in 1950.

The official Soviet industrial target for 1965 is 80 per cent over and above the base year of 1958. By 1965 the Soviets expect to reach the United States' 1958 production level in staple farm products. To reach the level of per capita production in industrial goods another five years is officially required. The Soviet Union hopes that by 1975 the Russians will be able to surpass the industrial production of the United States in both absolute and per capita output. The boast to surpass the United States is meaningless because it does not specify the goods and services and leaves the door open for imagination. Certainly the Soviet Union can easily surpass the United States' production in goods that are not used in America, such as felt footwear, or even in the ICBM—which surely would not increase the standard of living of the Russians.

But while the current Seven-Year Plan is being carried out and Western students continue to debate about industrial growth, the Russians are developing a 20-year plan to be submitted to the XXII-nd Communist Party Congress to be held in 1961. If the length· of time required to devise the new Plan can be used to evaluate its significance, it apparently will be sweeping, with major changes in existing targets. Based on past experience, it is certain that the present goals will be revised with the approval of the 20-year Plan since there is no need for new goals now before the expiration of the current Plan. Perhaps more consideration would be given to consumer goods as reflected by the greater demand of the masses for a better standard of living. Already the 1960 planned targets for consumer goods have been allocated an additional 25 to 30 billion rubles above the original volume.[8] This also indicates that Soviet planned targets are flexible and resources are moved from one use to another as conditions change. Prediction of these changes is quite difficult.

The Central Intelligence Agency (CIA) has estimated the Soviet gross national product (GNP) for 1960 and projected it to 1970.[9] According to this study, during the 1959-65 period the Soviet GNP will be increased by roughly 60 per cent, and between 1960 and 1970 the average annual growth rate is estimated at six per cent. Based on this rate the Soviet 1970 GNP, in 1958 American dollars, would be roughly 420 billion dollars, close to the GNP of the United States of about 442 billion dollars recorded for 1958. Governor Rockefeller, using the American growth rate at four per cent, has estimated the 1960 GNP at 510 billion dollars, which he projected to 755 billion dollars for 1970, or about 48 per cent above the 1960 estimate. In comparison with the American increase, the Soviet GNP during the 1960-70 period is expected to rise by almost 80 per cent. According to these estimates the 1960 Soviet GNP is to be about 44 per cent ·of the United States and in 1970 it would be some 54 per cent. The accuracy of these comparisons is difficult to evaluate because of expected changes in Soviet investments and unforeseen diversions in the United States. Nevertheless, comparisons reveal that the Soviet Union is expected to maintain a higher economic growth rate than the United States, and it will be harder to reject Soviet claims of superiority of their system, especially in the underdeveloped areas, which themselves seek a type of social system which would lead to rapid economic growth.

According to the CIA study, the 1970 Soviet standard of living is expected to be 40 per cent higher than it was in 1960. Indeed this is a tremendous rise considering the increase in total population of only about 10.7 per cent. Yet even with this rapid increase in the standard of living the 1970 level would be at about 60 to 65 per cent of the 1958 level in the United States. Should the West welcome or be alarmed at such a rapid rise in the Russian standard of living? Does this represent a challenge for the West and particularly for the United States? Can the American people increase their standard of living during the next decade by 40 per cent? What changes in Western motivations would this cause, and would Soviet motivations be reoriented in other directions?

These questions are difficult to answer because of vast differences in methods and priorities in evaluation of standards of living. It would be inadequate to compare the standard of living in the United States with that of the USSR in terms of steel production or in terms of passenger automobiles. The Russians use less steel in housing than in the United States, and they are planning to increase the use of passenger cars by establishing rental services in large urban centers. Food, clothing, and shelter have different meaning to different people, too. And in general the Western students of the Soviet Union disagree in their evaluation of Soviet society and the adjustments in idealogical, political, social, and international matters caused by an improved standard of living. Because of this disagreement the West fails to develop a theoretical solution to world problems initiated by the Soviet Union.

One school of thought holds that rapid industrialization and urbanization creates militant motivation in a society. It tends to encourage the development of the classless society advocated by Communists as the optimum goal of the Marxian doctrine which must be spread to other peoples by every means. Acceptance of this viewpoint means inevitability of war with the Soviet Union.

Another school points out that an improved standard of living and increased leisure tend to encourage elevation of educational standards. With an improved standard of living and better education, the people would demand a greater degree of individual freedom which, through intellectual curiosity, would stimulate the feeling of international brotherhood and reduce the aggressiveness of the Soviet Union. It is not expected that the Russians will learn to sing "Yankee Doodle," but it is hoped that with a broader cultural level the Russians will see that the United States does not exploit its workers and that workers are not starving and not interested in revolution, as the Russians are taught to believe.

Still another school feels that the USSR cannot forever continue producing capital goods at a greater volume than consumer goods. Eventually emphasis has to be placed on consumer goods and services. Concessions to the consumer in the original announcement of the Seven-Year Plan are small, but these concessions have been increased in 1960 and perhaps will be increased still more in later years. This school believes that with abundance of all types of goods and services, with a chicken in every pot and hi-fi sets in every home, the socio-economic conditions will be so altered that the Soviet Union would become harmless to the West. If and when this level is reached the Russians would become as complacent, consumption-oriented, peace-directed, and undisciplined as most Americans are now. Acceptance of this reasoning means waiting for deterioration of communist society through wealth.

However, despite disagreement in evaluation of the rise of industrial output in the USSR, all schools agree that it will create disturbance in the socio-economic structure and therefore represents a challenge to the West. To meet this challenge, it is argued, the United States must increase its growth rate if its industrial leadership is to be maintained. On the other hand, the United States Chamber of Commerce, although it admits that "the growth bandwagon is a crowded one," is skeptical about the value of rates as a weapon in meeting the Russian challenge. It is pointed out that if a given rate is accepted as desirable it might become a national goal and in time might be implemented by a "plan," leading toward acceptance of national planning.[10]

History tells us that in the past many wealthy societies disappeared when they ceased to be dynamic. But the changes were not basic economic transformations; they were mostly changes in leadership. In the case of the Soviet Union we have different economic motivation, and the country can be wealthy and still maintain its Messianic complex to convert other countries to its system. Consequently, the USSR with its rapidly rising standard of living and its stable social institutions is more of a menace to the West than if the country were poor and weak. Yet such reasoning is dangerous because it stems from the assumption that capitalism is unable and unwilling to adjust its basic economic philosophy in order to keep its economic growth ahead of the communist system.

It is true that adjustment in the basic principles of capitalism in itself endanger the status quo, but it is not necessarily a harakiri for the system. It might require greater emphasis in welfare measures, control over the economy, and general limitation of the individual freedom enjoyed by the people for the last 100 or so years. In short, it is not the Soviet growth rate the West should fear but a mode of distribution of resources which are arbitrarily allocated every time the Soviets create a crisis of their choosing. However, without strong and wise leadership and general public support, any basic changes in the existing method of distribution of resources would be difficult to undertake.

Whatever happens in the Soviet Union during the next 20 years will have a direct impact on disciplined thinking of the West and especially that of the United States. This does not imply that the West must immediately adjust its socio-economic institutions recklessly. Capitalism still has time for serious thinking, time to devise new goals aimed not only at the survival of its basic philosophy but oriented to successful competition with communism. Even though the Soviet Union has already started the battle for greater production it will be another 20 or 30 years before a new Russian generation, brought up in an economy of abundance, will assume control of Soviet society. The West still has time to counterattack the Soviet challenge, provided that some kind of long-term goals can be devised by which to operate. To deal successfully with the Russian challenge perhaps it would be necessary to adjust existing price and profit structures and to revamp the concept of entrepreneurship.

## AVAILABILITY OF TECHNICAL PERSONNEL

The world is now in the midst of a new and unprecedented scientific revolution which undoubtedly will bring about profound changes in socio-economic values. The rapid Soviet drive for education was achieved during the last ten years and still greater progress is expected during the next decade. However, despite its general educational advancement, the higher educational attainment in the Soviet Union is not so outstanding. According to the 1959 population census only 2.6 per cent of all persons in the age group of 15 and over completed colleges and universities. Another 5.3 per cent received degrees from specialized schools (tekhnikums). Only 7.8 per cent were graduated from high schools and 23.8 per cent from elementary schools. The bulk of this age group, representing 60.5 per cent, failed to complete elementary seven-year schools.

Soviet technical personnel, of course, come from the higher educational institutions including tekhnikums. In 1959 colleges and universities graduated 330,000 persons, and 530,000 persons received degrees from tekhni-kums, a total of 860,000 graduates. Looking ahead to the end of 1965 the Soviets expect to graduate a total of 2.3 million specialists, or 600,000 more than were graduated during the past seven years.[11] The bulk of this in-crease would come from tekhnikum graduates while universities continue to graduate about the same number as in 1958.

Since the current industrial expansion in the Soviet Union will demand more specialists of all skills, sharing them on an increased scale with un-derdeveloped countries is not expected to take place. The best the Rus-sians can do during the next decade is to allocate about the same number as they did in 1958 or perhaps only slightly above that number.

In 1960 the Soviet Union was assisting 22 countries for which the Rus-sians provided machinery, equipment and technical personnel. In addi-tion, the Soviets provide materials and technical assistance in the construc-tion and maintenance of educational, medical, and cultural institutions in many countries. Assuming that the Soviet Union has provided 100 special-ists to each of the 22 countries, excluding the usual diplomatic staffs, then their total number may be estimated at about 2,200—or at most 2,500 persons—not an alarmingly large number. Perhaps the shortage of these specialists at home may also be the reason why the Soviets do not insist on a larger number. However small the number of Soviet technical person-nel may be, other communist countries have their specialists, at times working side by side with the Russians.

In most cases the use of Soviet technical personnel is included in eco-nomic agreements with the recipient country, but in some cases they come with Soviet grants, mostly for medical and educational services. In general, the Soviet specialists abroad have a considerable background in cultural, historical, and economic trends of the country to which they are assigned as well as in their own fields of specialization. Many of them are carefully prepared for career work in underdeveloped countries. Since their standard of living at home is not as high as that of similar specialists from the United States, their adaptation to working and living conditions does not present hardships and is often of psychological and political ben-efit to the Russians. Even though the Russians may be unable to increase future technical assistance to underdeveloped countries, they have already succeeded in laying a favorable cornerstone in this area for expansion of other programs such as student and cultural exchange programs. In 1960 the "Friendship University" was opened in Moscow for students from Asia, Africa, and Latin America. Accepted students receive free transportation to and from the USSR, free education and maintenance, and may study any field they desire. Eventually the enrollment at the university is expecting to reach 4,000 to 5,000 students.

## INFILTRATION OF FOREIGN MARKETS

The Soviet Union trades with well-developed and underdeveloped countries, but its assistance program is concentrated primarily in the underdeveloped areas. Both activities are used for the same purpose—the establishment of political and economic ties. The Soviet Union claims that it renders help to underdeveloped countries without any political, economic, or military strings attached. This is done, according to the Soviets, from a sincere and disinterested desire to help underdeveloped countries and to do away with backwardness and poverty. "We stand for aid to underdeveloped countries," said Khrushchev, "which would not make them dependent on rich and economically highly-developed countries."[12]

As a rule the Soviet Union grants to underdeveloped countries long-term credits at lower interest rates than they can get from the West. While credits from the West may be limited to four or six years, the Soviets grant for 10 or 12 years during which time they are in position to develop and to solidify their position in other directions profitable to them. Thus the non-existent "strings" of which Khrushchev speaks are there just the same.

Moreover, the Soviet Union accepts payments for credits in the traditional export commodities of recipient countries. On the short run this tends to stimulate the growth of export resources, insuring a stable market for their goods and providing an opportunity for greater output, which is expected to be absorbed by the USSR and other communist countries. But there is no assurance that once expanded output is reached its volume would be taken by the communist countries. At the same time this would put the Soviet Union in an advantageous bargaining position in negotiations for increased purchases, provided that some political, economic, or military concessions are made to the USSR or other communist countries. Again, "strings" are there, even though they may not be evident at the beginning.

It is easy to visualize that once an underdeveloped country, with Soviet assistance, had increased its production it might cease to be dependent upon the West and would be forced to shift its alliance to the Soviet Union because of increasing assistance. Therefore the "no strings attached" is nothing but a misleading slogan and the string might well become a rope around the neck which can be tightened when the Soviets want certain concessions, as in the case of Finland.

An example of Soviet persistence in the field of assistance to underdeveloped areas may be seen in India. India is important because it makes up more than 40 per cent of the uncommitted world and is now the symbol of potential power in Asia. The Indo-Soviet relationship is closely watched by other uncommitted countries modeling themselves after India's social and economic patterns. The Bhilai iron and steel plant in India was built with Russian assistance—more than 400 Soviet enterprises produced machinery and equipment, and hundreds of Indians were trained to operate the furnaces and other installations. The project was successful. Now the Soviet government is assisting India in building other enterprises which upon completion will relieve India of the need to import many goods. Since past economic relations between India and the USSR were good, the Indian government asked and received from the USSR another credit of 1.5 billion rubles for the development of its Third Five-Year Plan. Such relationships assure the Soviet Union of India's economic development and provide a hope for India becoming increasingly independent of the West while she becomes more dependent on the Soviets.

The underdeveloped areas are short of capital for investment in their economies. They are lacking in management and technological competence. They are attempting to raise their educational levels, and in some countries education takes as much as 40 per cent of the government budget, leaving other sectors of investment with meager resources. Underdeveloped areas need all types of material, educational, and financial help. They need "intra-structure" investments—investments in railroads, harbors, hydroelectric projects, and the like—which are beyond the means of internal private enterprise but are vital to the development of their economies. These are long-term investments, profits from which may be realized only after many years.

The West, particularly the United States, knows this, but present long-term public assistance from the United States is not sufficient, not certain, and cannot go on indefinitely. It would be desirable that Western private enterprise supplant public assistance if the West is planning to build the kind of society which would be best for the West and for underdeveloped areas themselves. This is a real challenge to Western private enterprise: the areas are vast, they are of critical importance to the world, and they are reaching a decisive stage in their development. Many Western business leaders do recognize that the Soviet challenge to private enterprise calls for a drastic revision in profit-making decisions. If, however, private enterprise fails to provide such initiative and if public assistance declines these areas will be forced to turn increasingly to the Communist orbit for help. The communist countries realize the vital importance of these areas to the social and economic stability of the world; by expanding their influence they would emphasize the hesitancy of capitalism.

Western failure to assist underdeveloped areas could produce tragic results should the West let 800 million people and all their resources ally with the Communist orbit. The Communists would then control about two-thirds of the world's population, educated, trained and self-directed in anti-capitalist ways. Should this be allowed to happen, no single Western country or group of countries would be able to stand up to the communist political and economic powers.

It is true that West Germany, France, Italy, and Great Britain are beginning to grasp the communist challenge and increasingly move their investments and skill to these areas. Unfortunately only a few American firms are, thus far, committed to such expansion. The main problem of course is that long-term investments in these areas do not provide quick turnover of capital with handsome profits nor can the capital, once invested, be pulled out on short notice. Without a doubt, private enterprise would face hardships and frustrations, but if supported by the government the overall gains for capitalism would be immeasurable. These underdeveloped areas are ripe for Western public and private assistance. More and more underdeveloped countries are becoming independent, and their needs are so great and evergrowing that public assistance from the West alone is not sufficient and must be supplemented by private sources. The job is simply too big for the government of the United States; it is just as big for the Soviet Union alone, without other communist countries.

Moreover, it would be an error for the West, and particularly the United States, to permit economic infiltration by Red China to areas where the Soviet Union and Red China have interests on the assumption that this would create a wedge between the two. Their basic ideology and goals are the same—to destroy capitalism. There is no security for capitalism in allowing the Arab countries, for example, to join the Communists. The West might then spend a large sum to fortify Israel with an illusory hope that a strong Israel would check the spread of communism and would "contain" communism in this part of the world.

## CULTURAL COOPERATION

Cultural cooperation of the Soviet Union extends to exchanges in science, arts, and education between the Soviet Union and other countries. The closest cooperation in all fields, of course, is among communist countries. In general, the artistic accomplishments of the Soviet Union, no matter how enchanting they may be, have less impact on the culture of many underdeveloped countries than their scientific and educational cooperation. It is true that the arts bring the image of other cultures and peoples together and they can be and are used for propaganda purposes, but it is science and, most of all, the educational programs which have the lasting effect.

The Soviet Union is very much interested in providing educational facilities to underdeveloped countries. They not only train engineers, physicians, chemists, and other specialists, but they also indoctrinate them in Marxism-Leninism as a matter of educational programming. Many students from underdeveloped areas are taken by the Russians into their circles in order that they may absorb the idea of "coexistence" directly from the people. The cultures of Asia and Africa are of course diverse, with Hindus, Mohammedans, Buddhists, and Christians. Yet the objective of all cultures is the same—to improve the standard of living of their people within the social framework of their societies. Moreover, as the Asian and African as well as other students learn to live on an equal basis in the USSR, they are persuaded to realize that they have to live under "coexistence" with many different peoples and cultures which are much closer to all Asians and Africans than the Western culture. With its historic Asiatic characteristics and with strong propaganda against colonialism, the Soviet Union is probably better understood by the students from many underdeveloped countries than the United States. The Russians know all this and use their past backwardness to attract Asians and Africans to their educational and cultural programs.

The most important part of cultural cooperation, of course, is the education and training programs offered to underdeveloped countries. In 1959 the Soviet Union offered college and university scholarships to 47 countries including the communist countries. A considerable number of offers were unfilled because of the unwillingness of foreign students to attend Russian universities; still, many preferred to go to other communist countries. All in all, during the 1958-59 period the Soviets trained about 700 students from non-communist areas, of whom almost 80 per cent were from the UAR. Only 22 American students studied in the

USSR, and 17 Soviet students were enrolled in American universities. In 1959 their number increased to 27 students from each country.

In contrast with Soviet educational exchange programs, the United States in the 1958-59 school year trained 47,200 foreign students, plus about 8,400 foreign resident physicians and interns in hospitals. About 55 per cent of all foreign students in the United States came from the Far East and Latin America and nearly 300 students from the communist countries, about a third of them from Yugoslavia.[13] It is quite clear that the United States allocates a greater share of its educational resources to foreign students than the USSR does. Even the scholarships offered by Soviet bloc countries comprise a total of only 1,100 students against 2,300 students receiving total and 1,000 receiving partial support from the government of the United States.

The Soviet Union has two student exchange programs. One is through direct negotiations between the Soviet Union and individual countries. The other is through Soviet contributions to the technical assistance fund of the United Nations. Later contributions, thus far, total over 32 million rubles for the training of 450 students from Asia, Africa, and Latin America in the USSR and for the maintenance of 90 Soviet specialists and laboratory equipment in these areas.[14] In comparison with the United States, the Soviet contribution to the educational program is meager indeed.

The Soviet Union offers scholarships in a variety of fields ranging from nuclear physics to ballet dancing. Professional training such as medicine or engineering takes from three to four years but other programs may last only three months and are usually associated with specific problems of learning Soviet techniques.

As a rule, the country receiving Soviet assistance sends a number of students and specialists to the USSR in order that they may become familiar with Soviet equipment and techniques. Since the Bhilai Iron and Steel Plant in India has Russian-made equipment, India had to send to the USSR some 300 technicians for additional training, while 250 Soviet technicians worked in India. Since the United Arab Republic is developing its huge hydroelectric resources, power from which will be used in atomic and chemical enterprises, the UAR had to send some 300 Egyptian students to the Soviet Union for study. True, the language barrier hinders the movement of students and technicians from underdeveloped countries to the Soviet Union, but steps are taken to alleviate this trouble by providing an intensive Russian-language course in the first year; in some majors such as medicine a greater proficiency in Russian has been demanded of incoming students.

In general, with Khrushchev's pronouncement of peaceful coexistence, Russian educational exchange programs have improved the Soviet position in many underdeveloped countries. It was further improved with offers of a training program in atomic energy for peaceful purposes. This and other programs are designed to support the Soviets' claim to world leadership in technology and science. In sharing their scientific progress with the underdeveloped areas, the Soviets have increased their prestige in many areas originally dependent upon Western science. This is the case with India and Indonesia, not to mention the UAR. As a rule, the students from underdeveloped countries go to the Soviet Union while Soviet technicians go to underdeveloped countries. Traffic of foreign technicians to the Soviet Union is negligible.

## FLEXIBILITY OF FOREIGN POLICIES

For 43 years the West expected disorders within the Soviet Union, revolts, and an eventual return to a social order acceptable to the West. Now the West is surprised that instead of withering the Soviet economic position has become stronger, with an impressive economy challenging the leadership of the Western world.

There are many reasons for the rapid rise of the USSR to economic and political power in the world. The Russian ability to control the relationship between modern scientific achievements and society may be considered as an important contributing factor in their progress. Rapid scientific discoveries without corresponding adjustments in the social structure of the society bring about disparities in values and cause social and economic disequilibrium. For example, instituting automation on a large scale within a short period of time would generate a crisis in social adjustments. In the past, science, in general, was controlled by economic, political, and social decision-making processes and the fusion between science and society was slow but painless. Now it is science which triggers the socio-economic motivation of the society. And the Russians with their faith in science were able to discipline science to their motivations without developing a crisis in the already rigidly-controlled social structure. In fact it is science and its adaptation to practical purposes that has helped Soviet society become so advanced.

Soviet scientific transformation is responsible for changes in the cherished material and ideological values inherited from Marx and Lenin. In his speech in Rumania in June 1960, Khrushchev declared that Lenin's prophecy of many decades ago on the inevitability of imperialist wars leading towards the destruction of capitalism and the triumph of socialism throughout the world is not realistic now. He said that the forces of socialism are increasingly growing in power now and there is no longer a need to wait for wars among capitalist countries to destroy them. He further emphasized that it is no longer necessary to depend on physical warfare to extend the communist ideology globally. He told the West that the challenge from the Communists is not from military but from economic and ideological forces which are now sufficiently flexible to fit any new conditions that might arise in the world. Consequently, present Russian foreign policy is not a product of past theoretical pronouncements.

This is not a radical departure from broad principles of Marx and Lenin but a realistic adjustment of their philosophy to existing conditions that science has brought to mankind. Ideologically the Communists continue to follow the basic goal of world domination but with streamlined dogma. It is no longer claimed that the highly industrialized capitalist countries have priority for revolution. The underdeveloped areas of Asia and Africa which are attempting to develop their economies without the historical development of capitalism, according to Russians, are opening the door to a new era in social values and expect to become a lever to push the world into socialism. Khrushchev believes in the new role of recently lethargic colonial countries; publicly he emphasizes that he helps them because of the "natural sympathy" and "brotherly obligation" of his country, which itself was underdeveloped and depressed by capitalism. The Russians describe their assistance as "unselfish"; they portray the West as an exploiter and monopolist which looks upon underdeveloped countries only as potential millions of consumers from whom to reap profits.

No longer do the Communists insist on immediate establishment of their type of society in other areas. They realize that what the recently independent countries are interested in is not ideology but science and technology which can be adopted by any society. Many of these countries do accept the official Soviet claims of their superiority in science, technology, and industrial production. Meanwhile, no recognition is given to the West for its achievements, which are taken for granted; no romanticism is seen as it is in the achievements of the Soviet Union.

Another factor in making Soviet foreign policy flexible is the Russian ability to blend two different ideas into one to promote still another. The Russians say that their assistance to underdeveloped areas is not for any profit but for "humanitarian" reasons—to raise the standard of living and to establish "human solidarity" under the banner of peaceful coexistence of all poor and wealthy countries on the basis of mutual advantages. With these slogans the Russians could propose a merger, say, of all Arab countries or all Central American Republics into one larger country in the name of mutual advantages and human solidarity. It would be just fine for the Russians if in this process physical resistance would develop to accelerate the demise of the capitalist system in these areas. True, the Russians do not propose such a merger yet; but they will encourage it. In the meantime, Soviet coexistence and assistance are going concerns to many people in the underdeveloped areas since they are not involved in a direct ideological conflict between the great powers of the world.

This conflict is real, and it is not an accident that many Russian goods can be purchased in other countries at much lower prices than in the USSR. For instance, the "USSR Statistical Handbook for 1958," used in compiling this book, cost 14.7 rubles, or at the official rate of exchange about 3.5 dollars, in Moscow but only two dollars in Washington, D. C. In India a pocket edition of the works of Dickens and other Western classical authors and volumes of Marx and Engels printed in Moscow can be purchased for one rupee (20 cents). The lowest priced book the West offers in India costs two rupees. It is the same with many other goods which are in ample supply in the USSR. Moreover, the Soviets reduce prices on necessities which the low-income groups need and are willing to buy—items such as tobacco products or bicycles rather than luxuries.

Flexibility in Soviet foreign policy may also be traced to the purpose behind assistance to underdeveloped areas. As the cost of production through such assistance declines for any particular goods, the Russians are willing to buy them at reasonable prices. Western markets, however, respond differently. When the cost of production falls below the so-called fair market price established by the West for the supplying country, a high dumping duty is often put on the imported goods. And when this happens Soviet propaganda cries out that the West is not really interested in economic development of underdeveloped areas. Some Western countries maintain high protective duties against low-priced textiles and other primary goods. Many underdeveloped countries are best suited for the expansion of production in primary goods and it is no wonder India's textile men question the sincerity of the West in wishing to see India expand its economy for its own sake. In short, to compete successfully with the Soviet Union the West must not only provide assistance to underdeveloped areas but must stabilize economic conditions there through revision of its own policies, if these areas are not to be sucked into the Soviet sphere of influence.

The test, then, is whether the West and especially the United States can become an "arsenal of ideas" in order to combat Soviet infiltration into underdeveloped areas. To be successful the West has to reevaluate its existing social and economic values. The present economic aims of the West do not justify private investments in underdeveloped areas on the scale and scope which are available at home or were available under colonialism. It is doubtful that the West can voluntarily mobilize the private resources necessary to outmatch the Soviet centralized policy. Therefore both private and public resources must be pooled for this purpose, even though some cherished economic and social beliefs may have to be abandoned and new ones devised.

Acceptance of new values would inevitably bring more centralized power in political and economic controls. It means public sacrifice on one hand and bold actions on the other. It calls for national stamina, for a new search for peace without appeasement, for settlement of present differences, and for preventing future causes of differences which might be more complex and costly than the present sacrifices.

The Russians' goal is to undermine the prestige of the West in underdeveloped areas. They are determined to shake or even to replace Western leadership in Asia, Africa, and Latin America. However, Soviet vitality lies not in the people but in their leaders, whose dictatorial decision-making power is much quicker than that of the West. In the USSR a few leaders can change foreign policy, undertake development of any industry, or adjust monetary-fiscal policies with a minimum of public participation; they can simultaneously unify opinion of their people by propaganda.

While the Soviets have pronounced their intention to destroy capitalism, the West talks about freedom's survival through moral, spiritual, political, economic, and military strength as if the mere acceptance of these principles by underdeveloped countries would rally them solidly behind the West and would put an end to all troubles for all time. But when greater material sacrifices are asked for the purpose of unifying the front against the spread of communism, the West is not as keen on adjusting its economic motivations and insists that any additional increase in resources for that purpose must come through a rapid growth of labor productivity but without inflation, without increasing government controls, through the elimination of "featherbedding" of all types, and through reorientation of the farm program. In short, the West lacks political and economic unanimity, and there is no clearcut policy on how to rebuke the Communists or who is to do it. Even though the West realizes its predicament and is aware of the danger in the challenge from the USSR, it would require a specific long-term policy to avert a long and costly undertaking.

The West may be indecisive but it is certainly not weak, it is capable of acting vigorously and with purpose in times of actual challenge. For example, when the Russians in 1948 cut off overland access to Berlin and for ten months probed Western unity and its intellectual flexibility and determination they miscalculated Western intentions and underestimated its endurance and willingness to invest in a costly airlift rather than to push through on land with armed convoys. The Soviets blundered in Berlin and have learned that the West can act in time of emergency with firmness; but the Soviet drive into the underdeveloped areas does not present an immediate jeopardy to peace as was the case in Berlin or Korea, and the Western society is hesitant to alter its relaxed way of living.

Khrushchev (how wrong he is!) is convinced that the United States wishes continuation of the Cold War because this policy is already in operation and can be kept going by the United States for several decades during which time many different things might happen. If this policy is to continue at length, many of the old and seemingly unsolved problems might disappear and new issues will crop up. Dealing with isolated problems is much easier than coping with a host of different issues simultaneously. This would be advantageous to the West and not to the Soviet Union.

In general, overall Soviet foreign policy is as strong as that of the United States. The Soviets are dedicated to the destruction of capitalism, and the United States is devoted to its preservation. Because of Soviet aggressiveness its foreign policy is more flexible and more opportunistic than that of the United States. If and when the United States formulates and implements an equally flexible policy the USSR will be on the defensive. Perhaps all the West needs is a more dynamic leadership to guide the destiny of capitalism to still greater achievements than those recorded in the past. And Khrushchev has said that if capitalism can prove that its system is better than that of communism, then he would be the first to discard his beliefs and become a capitalist. Communism is not homogeneous, monopolistic, or inflexible; it undergoes evolutionary changes. Neither is capitalism immune to changes, for evolution is part of life and progress.

## Bibliography—Chapter 20

[1] Committee for Economic Development, *The New Role of the Soviets in the World Economy,* May, 1958, Foreward.

[2] Khrushchev, N. S., Speech at the 3d session of the USSR Supreme Soviet, Moscow, October 31, 1959.

[3] *Soviet Affairs Notes,* No. 241, Department of State, Washington, D. C., May 18, 1960, p. 41.

[4] Sorokin, G. M., *Semiletniy Plan-Novyy Etap Stroitel'stva Kommunisma v SSSR,* Moscow, 1959, p. 35.

[5] Department of State, *op. cit.,* p. 74.

[6] *Sovetskiy Soyuz,* No. 1, (107), 1959, p. 18.

[7] *The American Economic Review,* June 1960, p. 301; *Accelerated Economic Growth, A Key to the American Future,* State of New York, June 1960, p. 11; Volodarskiy, L. M., *Reshayushiy Shag v Osuschestvlenni Osnovnoy Ekonomicheskoy Zadachi SSSR,* Moscow, 1959, p. 13.

[8] The USSR Embassy, *Press Department,* No. 298, Washington, D. C., June 24, 1960.

[9] *Soviet Manpower 1960-70,* Central Intelligence Agency, Washington, D. C., May 1960, pp. 1, 15; *The New York Times,* June 23, 1960.

[10] *The Promise of Economic Growth: Prospects, Costs, Conditions,* Chamber of Commerce of the United States, Washington, D. C., 1960, p. 4.

[11] The USSR Embassy, *op. cit.,* No. 297, September 22, 1959, and No. 105, February 25, 1960.

[12] *Ibid.,* No. 196, April 22, 1960.

[13] Department of State, Intelligence Report, No. 7880, *Soviet Bloc Student Exchanges, 1958-59,* Washington, D. C., November 21, 1958, p. 1; U. S. Office of Education, *School Life,* Washington, D. C., March, 1960, p. 4.

[14] The USSR Embassy, *op. cit.,* No. 268, June 3, 1960.

# Index